the Instant Pot® Bible

MORE THAN 350 RECIPES AND STRATEGIES

THE ONLY BOOK YOU NEED

FOR EVERY MODEL OF INSTANT POT®

Bruce Weinstein and Mark Scarbrough

HODDER &
STOUGHTON

First published in Great Britain in 2019 by Hodder & Stoughton
An Hachette UK company

First published in the United States of America by Little, Brown
and Company, a division of Hachette Book Group, Inc.

1

A CIP catalogue record for this title is available from the British
Library

Trade paperback ISBN 978 1 529 36205 3
eBook ISBN 978 1 529 36206 0

Printed and bound in Great Britain by Clays Ltd, Elcograf S.p.A.

Hodder & Stoughton policy is to use papers that are natural,
renewable and recyclable products and made from wood grown
in sustainable forests. The logging and manufacturing processes
are expected to conform to the environmental regulations of the
country of origin.

Hodder & Stoughton Ltd
Carmelite House
50 Victoria Embankment
London EC4Y 0DZ

www.hodder.co.uk

Contents

Chapter 4: Pasta Casseroles 152

Chapter 5: All Things Pulled 192

Chapter 6: All Things Curried 224

Chapter 7: All Things Steamed and Cooked with the Sous Vide Method 256

Chapter 8: Shorter Braises and Stews (Fewer than Twenty Minutes Under Pressure) 288

Chapter 12: Puddings and Desserts 452

Introduction

WELCOME TO THE INSTANT POT REVOLUTION.

This extraordinary multi-purpose countertop cooker has changed the way millions of us cook, opening up new opportunities in our kitchens and saving us countless hours of time along the way.

The Instant Pot® Bible is the first cookbook written *for all models,* even the Instant Pot® Max, which features both a new, powerful **MAX** cooking function and the ability to cook sous vide. But you don't need a **MAX** for this book. You can have a Lux. A Duo. A Smart BT. An Ultra. A 3-litre Mini. Or a 7.5-litre of any sort. These recipes are fully forwards-and-backwards compatible no matter which Instant Pot you have. What's more, over one-quarter of the recipes can use either the **PRESSURE COOK** or the **SLOW COOK** function, depending on your timing needs. Everybody uses their pot to cook fast. Some of us still like a slow cooker. Now we can choose. (And yes, this is the first Instant Pot book with sous vide recipes. Those are *only* for the Max machine. But the other 342 were crafted for every model, every make.)

That's a lot of good news, so permit us to be blunt. This cookbook is not an owner's manual. Because each model varies slightly from another, we won't tell you how to turn yours on, how to get the **SAUTÉ** function to the right heat or how to open the pressure valve. Some models have preset buttons (**MEAT/STEW**, **SOUP/BROTH**, etc); others don't. Some models require you to press **START**; others automatically switch the machine on after you've keyed in your cook time. You can find this sort of information in your owner's manual (or online, if yours has gone missing). We've accounted for the variables that matter once you start cooking, but we count on you to have a basic understanding of your model.

Then what is this book? The cover says it's a collection of 350 recipes. But it has many more. Countless, probably, given that we provide 25 flexible 'road map' recipes. Not standard recipes at all, these are detailed layouts for chilli and risotto, winter vegetable soup and rotisserie-style chicken. Each is a culinary outline that teaches you the basics and allows you to customise a dish with countless proteins, vegetables, herbs and flavourful liquids. Consider these road maps to be embellished master recipes with the ratios set and the variables laid out so you can prepare whatever you and yours prefer. (Desserts are a matter of greater precision, of course.)

In the more traditional recipes, we sometimes use the headnotes to explain how to make other, similar recipes in the pot. In the end, we hope you'll treat almost every recipe as a road map. Cook with a pen in hand so you can alter the recipe on the page. Or if you're scrolling on an e-reader, make notes in the recipe with the call-out function. And post your versions in the various Instant Pot Facebook or Instagram groups. We'd be more than flattered if you took our ideas and made them your own. Creativity is the best part of our job. We have a feeling it may be the same for you – at least, at times other than 5:45pm, when the kids are starving and the situation is rapidly moving from 'severe' to 'critical'.

But even with all those road maps and inventive recipes, there are a few dishes this book doesn't address. Most are utter basics. There's no plain rice recipe, for example. Nor ones for kefir or plain beans. These recipes are found in the booklet that accompanies each model. Some are even part of the owner's manual. And some, like those for yoghurt, are too complicated to be written for all models, given the differences amongst the pots.

Instead, we offer a veritable bible of advice on mastering the art of using your machine. There are over 20 recipes for everything that can be pulled (chicken, pork, you name it). There are braises galore. There's a breakfast chapter, a sides chapter and a puddings and desserts chapter. But most of this cookbook isn't laid out in a traditional manner. Instead, the main courses are divided into chapters like Pasta Casseroles, All Things Curried, Shorter Braises and Longer Braises. If you look in one place and don't find a meat cut, a favourite vegetarian main course or a cooking technique you prefer, flip elsewhere or look in the index. For example, there are recipes for chicken thighs in the Soups, Pasta Casseroles, All Things Pulled, All Things Curried, All Things Steamed, Shorter Braises, Longer Braises and even Rice and Grains chapters. As on any grand tour, your first stop probably isn't your last.

And there are lots of stops on the tour because this book is *big*. Try the Chicken Noodle Paprikash (page 172). Or the Eggnog Cheesecake (page 471). Or any one of the ten mouthwatering ragùs (starting on page 141). There's something in here for nearly every taste and occasion. And if you're curious about our favourite? Well, let's just say we made the Bundt Banana Bread (page 40) about half a dozen times *after* we got it right in testing because, well, banana bread is so great with a morning cup of coffee. Or at night in front of the TV while we binge-watched yet another Scandinavian box set.

We live in rural New England and wrote this book during a long, hard winter. If the recipes in these pages helped us get through one of those, you'll be fine no matter where you are.

An Owner's Manual for this Cookbook

You need the manual for your Instant Pot, and you need one for this book. Ours is a little simpler. Keep the following seven points in mind:

1. Read the chapter openers.
We know: this is bog standard cookery book advice. But in those openers, we've included important information that you'll need again and again, especially under the FAQs. Five minutes reading these will pay off as you'll understand how the recipes work.

2. Avoid the presets.
Many machines come with programmed, default features. Let's take timing as an example. When you press **SAUTÉ** and the heat level (say, **LOW** or **LESS**), or when you press the **MEAT/STEW** button (available in some but not all models), you get 10 minutes, maybe 15 on the timer. You can then manually adjust this timing up or down. Some models will return to the timing you last selected the next time you press **SAUTÉ** or **MEAT/STEW**. Others return to the default. Just skip it all. We give you the timings (and more). Manually adjust the variables each time and you'll never go wrong.

3. Pay attention to the size of the pot in the main recipe.
We have written all the recipes with the **5.5-litre cooker** as the standard. However, more than three-quarters can also be made, *as stated,* in a **7.5-litre cooker**. In these recipes, there will be a note in the *Beyond* section on how to alter the recipe for a **3-litre cooker**. (Although a few times we note that the recipe unfortunately cannot be done in the smaller pot.) A few recipes were written for a **3- or 5.5-litre cooker**. Again, there will be notes in the *Beyond* section on how to scale up the ingredients so the recipe can work in a **7.5-litre cooker**. And some recipes can *only* be made as written in a **5.5-litre cooker**. The *Beyond* section will again explain the necessary alterations for both the **3- and 7.5-litre cookers**. Finally, a handful of recipes can be made in any size cooker.

4. Notice the two types of charts in the recipes.
One chart is for basic cooking techniques like browning a chicken breast or reducing a sauce (the same kinds of things you could also do on the hob). This chart is often the first and/or right before the last step of a recipe (see opposite page).

Read the chart left to right to figure out how to get the pot to the place it needs to be. The exact name for the heat level is different between the models – thus, '**MEDIUM, NORMAL** or **CUSTOM 150°**'. That last 'custom' marker is for the Max machine, which has a **HIGH** and a **LOW** for the **SAUTÉ** function, then adjustable temperatures in-between. The Ultra also has an adjustable sautéing temperature, plus a more traditional **MEDIUM** setting.

Pay careful attention to the heat level indicated for the **SAUTÉ** function. Although the vast majority of recipes in this book use **MEDIUM, NORMAL** or **CUSTOM 150°**, some use **LOW** or **LESS**; others, **HIGH** or **MORE**.

Notice, too, that when sautéing, we always round the time *up* to the nearest 5-minute mark. So a recipe may tell you to cook the onions for 2 minutes and the chart will say to set the time for 5 minutes, or the recipe will say to brown the roast for a total of 12 minutes and the chart will say 15 minutes. We built in a little extra time because we don't want the heating element to turn off on you – just in case your onion is juicier than ours, or your joint takes a little longer to brown. As a result, you will often finish sautéing with a couple of minutes on the timer to spare. Go right ahead and turn off the **SAUTÉ** function when you're ready to carry on with the recipe.

Here's one more thing. In all models, **MAX** or any other, the **SAUTÉ** function doesn't remain on for longer than 30 minutes. You may need to restart it to continue with a recipe that involves multiple browning and sautéing steps. Such recipes are quite rare, but see the Bistro-Style Braised Short Ribs with Mushrooms on page 354 as an example. Here, we've given the timing as 35 minutes in the first chart, even though we well know that the setting is impossible, given the machine's limit. We wrote the recipe that way to avoid a second chart, to be honest. We trust you'll know how to turn it back on when the machine switches off. And let's face it: most of us start sautéing before the machine actually beeps to tell us it's warmed up to the desired temperature. So the 30-minute cut-off in even the most complicated recipe may never worry those of us who lack saintly patience.

The other chart is for using the pot as a pressure cooker or a slow cooker (see page 14).

A Max machine *can* (but doesn't have to) cook at 15 psi (that is, pounds per square inch), the same pressure as almost all countertop pressure cookers. The chart's top instructional row (under the headers) is for a Max machine *at its MAX setting*. This model also automatically opens or closes the valve, so you don't have to fiddle with it after you latch on the lid and set the cooking function. That's why there are dashes in the third box of that instructional row.

The second row, the one with the **HIGH** pressure setting, is the row you'll use if you have a Luxe, Duo, Smart, Ultra or Mini. (You can also use it for a Max – see below.) All Instant Pot models except the Max cook at 12.6 psi (slightly higher than most other electric pressure cookers). For this row of the chart, you can either use the **MANUAL** or **PRESSURE COOK** setting or you can press (as here) the **MEAT/STEW** button (or other buttons like **SOUP** or **GRAINS** as the recipe indicates).

The Chart for Basic Cooking Techniques

Press	Setting	Time	Press
SAUTÉ	MEDIUM, NORMAL or CUSTOM 150°C	5 minutes	START

Set the machine	Level	The valve must be	Time	Press
PRESSURE COOK	MAX	——	3 minutes with the KEEP WARM setting off	START
MEAT/STEW, PRESSURE COOK or MANUAL	HIGH	Closed	4 minutes with the KEEP WARM setting off	START
SLOW COOK	HIGH	Opened	3 hours with the KEEP WARM setting off (or on for 2 hours)	START

We call out all the options in all the charts. But you must *always* override the presets to set the specific time noted in the chart.

We should also note that the Max machine *can* cook on the older **HIGH** setting. Max users can also use the chart's line for the **HIGH** setting, if they prefer a slightly longer cooking time and a slightly lower pressure setting.

Some charts are missing the last row, the **SLOW COOK** instructions. This is because these recipes cannot be completed using this function without major modifications to the ingredient list (in most cases: less liquid and oil, more spices and vegetables).

A few are even missing the first instructional row, the one with the Max instructions. It's not that these recipes can't be done in a Max machine. It's that they can't be done on the **MAX** pressure setting without, say, a cheesecake buckling into waves or more delicate ingredients dissolving into the sauce. These few recipes can only be done on **HIGH**, even in a Max machine.

5. Pay attention to the design and function changes in the Max machine.
For one thing, this pot's missing the old buttons for, say, **MEAT/STEW** or **BEAN/CHILLI**. The Max machine is oriented towards cooking technique, not the type of dish cooked. While this change doesn't affect these recipes, don't get tripped up looking for the old functions, especially if you're

used to another model or if you see those button indicators in the second instructional row of the chart.

The Max machine is not necessarily the first electric pressure cooker to cook at as high a pressure as a countertop cooker. Some others hit that pressure mark and immediately fall off it. The Max is the first electric pressure cooker to *keep the pressure that high for the duration of the cooking*. Because of that and the Max model's design changes, you'll need to follow its specific instructions and set the pot manually every time for all of these recipes.

One feature added to the Max is the **SOUS VIDE** function. We'll have much more to say about this feature in its chapter (page 256). For now, let's just say that this function is a game-changer for a home cook who wants to try out this cheffy technique.

One feature missing from the Max machine is the **GRAIN** button. On former models, this button was something of a wonder to us. It brought the water in the pot up to a certain temperature and held it there so the raw grains got a warm, 45-minute soak before the machine then flipped to pressure cooking for the stated time. Frankly, the **GRAIN** button resulted in the most perfect wheat berries and rye berries we've ever had. But we've found a way round the loss in the Max machine, as you'll see in the recipe for wheat berries on page 395.

The Max machine also offers a **NUTRIBOOST** feature, which lets out steam in tiny bursts. This means that every time the pressure valve opens, even for a second, the liquid in the pot goes from being super-heated but essentially placid to almost apoplectic. When the valve closes again, the liquids calm back down until the next shock. Call it 'intermittent fury'. It's great for bone broth and more assertively flavoured stocks, none of which will be clear (as they would be if the valve remained closed, followed by a natural release). These stocks would not be favoured by a cordon bleu chef who wants to be able to read a menu through them, but they are indeed bolder and more complex, better not only for sipping but even for cooking. We advocate using this feature only where we feel it's appropriate. For example, we don't feel the **NUTRIBOOST** function is right for broth-rich dishes like Beef Barley Soup (page 84). The grains become soft enough to dissolve, and the soup is just too mucky.

6. Follow the release method for each recipe.
As you may know, cooking under pressure is as much about releasing said pressure as it is about building it. That pressure is made only one way: by steam. Liquids produce steam as they boil. That steam fills up the air space above the ingredients in the pot and eventually packs the space so tight that no more steam can be released from the liquids. The bubbling slows down and the pressure begins to build, ultimately bringing the liquids to a state in which they can't boil. (When a bubble pops, where would the gas go?) The result is that the boiling point of water in the pot rises from 100°C to around 112°C (the exact temperature depends on the model and the pressure it reaches). In addition, the *volume* of almost everything in the pot expands, wine to lamb shanks, carrots to cheesecakes.

Eventually, all that pressure has to go somewhere. There are two ways to get rid of it:
- the quick-release method
- the natural release method (worded in these recipes as 'let the pressure return to normal naturally, about X minutes'.)

For the **quick-release method,** the pressure valve on the lid must be opened to let go of the steam. Doing so requires different moves for different models. In some, you must turn the valve one way or another. For the Ultra, you must push a steam release button next to the valve. For the Max, you must press the indicator on the touchpad without fooling around with the valve. In all cases, steam will shoot out of the small hole in the valve.

Learning to release the pressure quickly is a key part of learning to cook in the pot. Don't ever release the steam under a cabinet overhang. Keep the geyser away from cabinet facings. And never consider the released steam an easy way to get a facial. Instead, put pets and small children out of the room until you get the hang of the method your machine requires. Don't be afraid; there are countless videos online to help you. We've even got two popular classes on *craftsy.com* that can get you more comfortable with the whole notion of pressure cooking.

By contrast, the **natural-release method** is easier. Basically, turn the cooker off (or let it lapse into stand-by mode) and wait. Over time, what's inside the pot will cool down enough that the steam in the pot's air space will condense. (Remember secondary-school physics?) At this point, the locking mechanism – a pin or cylinder in the lid called the 'float valve' – will drop down (or, in fact, *release*). You can now unlatch the lid and open the pot. A natural release can take anywhere from 15 minutes to 1 hour, depending on the amount of liquid and the mass of the ingredients in the pot.

Do not vary the release from the one stated in the recipe, even if you skipped lunch earlier in the day and want that beef stew *right now*. The recipes were written to take into account the stated method. Even though the machine is off and nothing appears to be happening, a natural release is not dead time. Those cubes of beef continue to cook as the pressure falls.

We didn't simply just write all the recipes with the **quick-release method** because of what happens inside the pot when you release the pressure in one fell swoop. As we've indicated, things in the pot are pretty calm when the pressure's on. You'll hear almost nothing. But the second that valve opens, the liquids leap to a furious boil. That sudden switch can help stop delicate ingredients getting overcooked, and it can offer faster soups and stews when it's warranted. But it can also turn braised vegetables to mush, cause potatoes or roots to cloud a sauce and render more delicate cuts of meat a little too soft.

No, a quick release will not *ruin* a pork chop. But in testing the difference time and again, we found a quick release can make some cuts of meat a little too squishy for our taste. And they're not necessarily the ones we expected when we started writing about pressure cooking. Leaner cuts – like boneless skinless chicken breasts – are often able to withstand a quick release better than fattier ones like pork shoulder. (Our tests were conducted with cuts of meat in water in the pot. There are other factors that come into play in actual recipes – fat, starches and even liquid-mass ratios – so we sometimes call for a quick release even with a fatty cut.)

Hey, we get it. The **natural-release method** makes pressure-cooker recipes look like bald-faced lies. 'Twenty minutes under pressure yet the dish took an hour to make,' someone inevitably says. We didn't want to mislead you, so we always indicate about how long the natural release takes. Some writers shy away from these things. They want you to believe that a soup takes 10 minutes when in fact it takes 15 minutes to brown the meat and sweat the onions, another 10 minutes for the machine to come up to pressure, and then another 10 minutes for it to cook under pressure, and a further 20 minutes for it to come back to normal pressure naturally. If you glance through a full recipe on any page of this book, you'll have a pretty good notion of the *real* timing.

7. Check out the *Beyond* for each recipe.
We started writing this book with an oath that we wouldn't call for any ingredient we couldn't find in our rural supermarket. It's nicely stocked but it isn't a gigantic suburban superstore. That's why we substituted a mixture of balsamic vinegar and Worcestershire sauce for Chinese black vinegar in a couple of recipes. True, the real-deal vinegar is available online with a click but otherwise only with a long drive for us. Yes, we can travel over an hour to some big gourmet supermarkets, even a decent Asian one and a great kosher one. But there was no Chinese black vinegar down the road. We should also admit up front that we made an exception for Sichuan peppercorns. There'll be more about them when we get to the two appropriate recipes.

Even though we (mostly) held to our oath, we often wanted to tell you how to nudge a recipe towards authenticity or how to make X, Y and Z substitutions to our ingredient list that would make the dish, well, 'cheffier' – and thus began the *Beyonds*. Over time, these grew to include serving suggestions and even garnishes. As we've indicated before, this section is also where you'll find any modifications needed to make a recipe work in a **3- or 7.5-litre pot.**

The Recipe Tags

We've tagged the recipes in this book to help you make better decisions about what to make for dinner. Not every recipe has every tag. Most have three or four. Here's what they mean:

FOR MAX MACHINES ONLY. Sous vide recipes are the only ones so marked.

SUPER FAST. These recipes are either 1) shockingly speedy, ready in just a few minutes, like the kid-friendly Buttery Pasta (page 155); or 2) absurdly quick given all that's going on in the pot – like a barbecue-sauce-based casserole with dried pasta that comes together in mere minutes (page 166).

SUPER EASY. In general, these recipes are what we call 'dump and stir'. You toss everything in the pot, stir things up and cook under pressure (or slow cook at will). Most require no browning. If you buy prechopped onion and a jar of prechopped garlic, most require little to no work at the chopping board. In a few cases, we've marked a recipe as super easy even if it requires you to sweat some onions, boil down a sauce or use frozen gnocchi to make a kicked-up casserole with a two-step pressure process.

FEWER THAN 10 INGREDIENTS. In other words, nine at most. Or to put it another way, about one-third of the book's recipes. We don't play that funky game in which water, salt and pepper don't count. They count. However, some of the road map recipes are tagged this way; when they claim you could use two or three items from a list, you can sometimes get away with using only one.

FAST/SLOW. These recipes can be made either under pressure or with the **SLOW COOK** function.

Perhaps unbeknownst to you, there have been big changes in the heat levels for slow cooking amongst the Instant Pot models. One pot's low is *not* another's low. To keep things simple, all the **SLOW COOK** recipes have been written using the slow-cooker **HIGH** setting. Therefore, they cook more quickly. There are almost no 8-hour braises here. But you can use the **KEEP WARM** function to hold the dish until you're ready to eat it. By the way, some recipes tagged *fast/slow* have the slow cooking instructions in the *Beyond* section attached to that recipe instead of in the chart in the recipe steps.

QUICK RELEASE. You must manually release the pressure at the end of cooking by opening the pressure valve, by pushing the button next to the valve (for the Ultra model) or by pressing the appropriate function on the touchpad (for the Max model).

MODIFIED QUICK RELEASE. Here, use the quick-release method to drop the pressure (and drop the temperature in the pot) but do not open the lid. Instead, leave it alone for a stated number of minutes with the valve open and the **KEEP WARM** setting off. This method is particularly useful for plumping up grains and rice.

NATURAL RELEASE. After cooking, turn the pot off and let its pressure 'return to normal naturally, about X minutes'. Take special note here. Some pots default to the **KEEP WARM** function. For a natural release, you must set the pot so it *does not*.

MODIFIED NATURAL RELEASE. In this case, turn the machine off and let its pressure come down naturally for a stated number of minutes, for example, 'let the pressure **return to normal** for 10 minutes'. After that, use the **quick-release method** to get rid of any residual pressure, either by opening the valve or pressing the quick-release function on the touchpad. This method is particularly useful for getting a little moisture back into a cut of lean meat.

QUICK RELEASE TWICE. NATURAL RELEASE TWICE. QUICK RELEASE, THEN NATURAL RELEASE. QUICK RELEASE, THEN MODIFIED NATURAL RELEASE. NATURAL RELEASE, THEN MODIFIED QUICK RELEASE. There are even more permutations. These are all the markers to indicate two-step recipes. Each one details what happens at the end of the first step, then what happens at the end of the second. These seem complicated now, but don't worry. Each recipe tells you exactly what to do.

VEGETARIAN. There's no meat or seafood in the dish. There are, however, animal products like milk, honey or eggs.

CAN BE VEGETARIAN. In this case, a simple swop will morph the recipe into a vegetarian one, for example, vegetable stock for chicken stock in an otherwise meatless recipe. And remember that most Worcestershire sauce contains anchovies. Use vegetarian (or vegan) Worcestershire sauce, if it matters to you.

VEGAN. In this case, there are no animal products at all: no meat, honey, eggs, nada.

CAN BE VEGAN. Again, simple modifications can turn the recipe vegan: a swopped-out stock, or vegan Worcestershire sauce, or maybe oil for the butter.

GLUTEN-FREE. There's no wheat gluten in the recipe. However, your kitchen, chopping board, measuring spoons and pot may have been contaminated. If you're cooking for someone who needs to eat gluten-free, you may need to take further precautions. For ingredients, we follow the Celiac Disease Foundation's requirements and rules. Some people have more drastic requirements or disagree with the organisation. For reference, celiac.org is where we set the bar. You can also check out www.coeliac.org.uk.

CAN BE GLUTEN-FREE. In this case, you need to substitute gluten-free versions of some ingredients without making any other alterations. We *do not* list the specific ingredients that need to be switched out. Those to watch out for include, but are not limited to, Worcestershire sauce, soy sauce, sausage meat (which can have wheat derivatives as filler or preservatives), some dried spice blends and some condiments (particularly fat-free versions that may use wheat or a wheat derivative as a thickener). Use certified gluten-free versions of these products (and more), even including rolled oats, pinhead oats or coarse oatmeal. (Naturally gluten-free oats can be processed in facilities that also process wheat, the dust of which can get onto the oats.) Watch out for hoisin sauce, a Chinese condiment. (We show how to make a gluten-free version in the *Beyond* section of the Vegetable Lo Mein recipe on page 184.) Pay attention to baking powder and always read the label because some manufacturers mix cornflour into it to preserve freshness (that is, to trap ambient humidity) while others may use wheat gluten. Finally, as to breadcrumbs, use Italian-seasoned gluten-free breadcrumbs or plain gluten-free panko breadcrumbs, both of which are increasingly available in stores and online.

FREEZES WELL. We tested these recipes with stacks of 1-litre, plastic, resealable containers on the countertop. We put leftovers in the freezer. Those we enjoyed another day are so marked.

A Few Notes about Basic Ingredients

We give either the supermarket equivalent or the weight of common ingredients, particularly fresh produce that is prepped in a standard way.

We assume you may well buy prechopped onion, peppers and carrots, and possibly cubed and deseeded squash. We also assume you may have jars of prechopped garlic and root ginger in the fridge. Feel free to use these ingredients. When using frozen chopped onions and peppers from the freezer, you'll have to cook them an extra minute or two.

Long-time cookery book readers will note that some ingredient volume equivalents seem a tad off. We say, for example, '1 medium garlic clove, peeled and finely chopped (1 teaspoon)'. A medium garlic clove finely chopped bulks up to more than 1 teaspoon. *However, we have given the volume amount for the convenience product.* This is because *jarred* prechopped garlic has (ahem) stewed in its own juices and is therefore more pungent than the freshly chopped stuff. Even prechopped onions and peppers have a more assertive flavour if they've been sitting on the shelves at the shop.

On another note, the two of us *under-salt* food. It's not that we don't love salt. (One of us adds more to every tortilla chip.) It's just that we'd rather add sea salt at the table.

In fact, we prefer *reduced-sodium* versions of common packaged ingredients in the Instant Pot. For our taste, a dish turns too salty if it includes standard tins of tomatoes or beans or ready-made stock. We also tested every recipe that calls for soy sauce with the reduced-sodium version. But tastes vary. And this is not a health or diet book. So we have not specifically called for reduced-sodium ingredients unless we felt doing so was important to the dish's success.

Finally, we need to make a comment about butter, which in this book is salted. But we just wittered on about reduced-sodium ingredients. To compensate, we've reduced the added salt in recipes to take salted butter into account. If you use unsalted butter, increase the salt in a recipe by at least half, if not double.

All the Special Equipment You'll Need

Although there are now dozens, if not hundreds, of speciality cooking gadgets for the Instant Pot, not everyone wants to cough up so much money on gear. So beyond wooden spoons, rubber spatulas, digital scales, and the like, we call for eight speciality items:

1. A 2-litre, high-sided, round soufflé dish.
That is, a round baking dish with sides 10cm high that's also 20cm in diameter (outside edge to outside edge). It must be heat- and pressure-safe. Most are, but check with various manufacturers to be sure. Ours is made of thick porcelain. Not every piece of porcelain can withstand the cooker.

For the **3-litre cooker**, we often recommend halving the recipe and substituting a **1-litre soufflé dish** with sides 8cm high and 15cm in diameter.

2. An 18cm Bundt ring cake tin.
No matter the flutings and designs, the diameter is sacrosanct. Most fit snugly in a **3-litre cooker.** In this case, don't worry about the **Max Fill** line. The water level needed to make the steam is well below that mark, even if the Bundt tin sits above it.

Getting an 18cm Bundt tin out of a **3-litre cooker** (or really any cooker) can be a pain. We stick the handle of a wooden spoon into the hole in the tin's centre post, then use the spoon to lever the tin up a bit before grasping its edge with oven gloves. But always remember that the tin is super hot.

3. An 18cm round springform tin.

This tin has a detachable side wall over an 18cm bottom. Its sides should be 8cm tall. Because of the way the latch sticks out from the side of the pan, this gadget will not work in a **3-litre cooker**. You can substitute an 18cm cheesecake tin (without a lip) in some cases but you may not be able to unmould the fare inside. We've heard there will soon be new Instant Pot springform tins without the latch, specifically designed for the Mini. These were not yet available as we finished writing this book.

4. A heat- and pressure-safe trivet.

We're talking about the one that comes with the machine. If you've misplaced your trivet, order another. If you don't have one and want to use whatever you've got, it must not have rubber feet and must be built to withstand the pressure's onslaught. Some pottery or ceramic types will not.

You can often turn a couple of small Pyrex custard cups or ramekins upside down and use them as a base for a springform tin in a **5.5- or 7.5-litre cooker**. To do so, put them in the cooker *before* you add the water or other liquid for steaming. But the best advice is to use the trivet that comes with the pot. It has collapsible side handles, which are indispensable (as you'll see) in the sous vide recipes.

5. A heat- and pressure-safe collapsible steaming basket.

This is not the machine's trivet. This is an old-school, metal basket that opens out like daisy petals. Some new-fangled ones are made of silicone. These do not open out. Keep in mind the diameter of your pot. A giant silicone basket, made for a lidded casserole, won't work.

You'll need this gadget in rare instances to hold a lot of stuff so it doesn't sit in the water. The basket's feet should *not* be rubberised or plastic-coated. (Silicone is definitely okay.) The basket should have relatively tall legs. Always use the amount of water (or other steaming liquid) indicated in the recipe, even if it touches some of the food in the basket (thus the need for tall legs). The steam's the thing.

6. Heat- and pressure-safe 250ml ramekins.

We used these in some desserts, particularly the puddings. We tested the recipes in Pyrex custard cups, the sort our grandmothers had. You can get fancier ones, but (again) they must be able to withstand the heat and pressure.

7. A fine-mesh sieve.

Small ingredients like wheat berries or rice grains can slip through the holes of a standard colander. A fine-mesh sieve can catch them. The best is a *chinois* (see page 48). We also always give you instructions on how to line a standard colander with muslin or (sometimes) kitchen paper.

8. An aluminium foil sling.

Here's the one piece of equipment you must make. A sling is necessary as everything in the cooker is crazy hot, especially if you've quickly released the pressure and opened the lid straight away. It's tricky reaching in without touching the metal insert. Yes, the machine's trivet has collapsible handles. We still ended up with blisters on our knuckles. A sling gives you an easy way to raise and lower things into the pot (or even on to that trivet, provided its collapsible sides are up).

To make this sling, stack *two* 60cm pieces of aluminium foil on top of each other. Fold them together in half lengthways (so that the thing is now a four-ply strip of foil). Put this sling on the countertop as close to the cooker as possible, then set the baking dish or tin in the centre of the sling. Fold its two ends over several times to create secure handles. Lift the whole contraption by these handles and put it in the cooker. Crimp the ends down so the lid will latch tightly but also so you can grab them later to lift the baking dish or tin out of the cooker.

And finally, while we never call for them, at the end of recipe-testing we discovered clamps with silicone-coated handles, designed for grabbing the edge of the Instant Pot's insert and lifting it out. We also discovered hand-length silicone gloves, perfect for grabbing the edge of the insert. If we'd had either of these while testing, our knuckles would have thanked us time and again.

A Dozen Up-Front FAQs

1. Why doesn't food squish flat when it cooks under pressure?

The pressure isn't coming straight down onto the food. The pressure comes from all directions at once. Think of a chicken breast. Think of a zillion arrows pointing at every spot on the breast, even every molecule. Then think of a zillion more arrows *inside* the breast, pushing out towards the surface. That's pretty much how the pressure works. The chicken breast can't go flat. It's being pushed (quite literally) in every direction. That said, softer items – like cheesecake batters – can expand because the liquid inside is blowing up with the pressure. Batters billow, which is why they require extra care.

2. My pot has an elevation setting. Should I use it?

Sure. And you're talking about the Max pot. This elevation setting is specifically designed for the tinning function. For all other models, don't worry about your specific elevation. A couple of years ago, we taped our pressure cooker classes for *craftsy.com* in the mile-high city of Denver, one class at a studio in a suburb with an elevation of nearly 2000m. We never tinned anything but we

also never had a single problem. Here's why. Although the pressure in the room was altered because of our higher elevation, the pressure in the pot was not. It's a sealed environment. It comes to **HIGH** (or **LOW** or **MAX**) internally. We even included quite a few baking recipes in those classes and did not make a single change to any cake, cheesecake, pie or pudding.

3. What's with the weird verbiage in the road map recipes?

As we said, these recipes can be endlessly customised. The ingredient lists include culinary terms like 'creamy liquid' or 'flavour enhancer'. These items are then immediately explained with a list of possible options and even ways to combine those options. We've set the ratios and left you to fill in the blanks, all while giving you plenty of options for those blanks. But in so doing, we had to use some terminology that smacks of chef school.

4. What's 0 minutes at pressure?

It's a way to make sure that delicate items like prawns or orzo don't get overcooked. Every model lets you choose '0 minutes' as an option. The pot comes up to **MAX** or **HIGH** pressure and immediately stops cooking.

By the way, we should note a slightly different technique for some pasta dishes. We set the time for 1 minute, then release the pressure, not when the machine actually hits high pressure, but *the moment the lid's float valve jumps up and clicks closed* (that is, before the pot is actually all the way up to pressure). You'll also know the float valve (or pin) has closed because no more steam can escape from it (or from the pot at all). You'll hear it click and see it happen. For this rather odd technique, use the **quick-release method** to get rid of the pot's pressure right when the float valve closes, so delicate items don't stick, burn or turn gummy.

5. You say to 'turn the machine off' when it undergoes a natural release. Do I have to?

No. If the **KEEP WARM** setting has been turned off, the pot has turned off at the end of cooking (or actually, has moved to stand-by mode). That said, we're both a tad neurotic. OCD, really. One of us even unplugs the machine from the wall. (The writer, not the chef.) We turn the pot off just so nothing *can* happen. See? Neurotic.

6. What's with the lean minced beef, pork and turkey?

Because of the way the lid fits tightly on the pot (even in the **SLOW COOK** mode with the valve open), there's almost no reduction amongst the liquids, even those trapped in interstitial fat. We find that standard mince results in dishes too oily for our taste. We prefer 90 per cent (or more) lean minced beef, white-meat turkey mince and lean pork mince. Your taste may differ.

7. What's with scraping up *'every speck of browned stuff'* off the pot's bottom?

Many models of the Instant Pot have a safety feature that turns the pot off if things stick to the bottom of the insert and begin to burn. To avoid that, we've come up with ways to avoid the sticking problem altogether in pasta casseroles and some rice dishes. Even so, when proper browning happens, all sorts of natural sugars get stuck on the pot's bottom (aka the 'browned stuff'). In a traditional braise, you would most likely deglaze the saucepan (starting the process of getting the browned bits unstuck from the bottom), then the remainder would eventually dissolve into the sauce over the next hour or so. In a pressure cooker, not enough time elapses. Some of the browned stuff hangs around and acts like glue on the pot's bottom. Ingredients fall down there or float by and get caught. They adhere and burn; the pot turns off.

In some recipes, you don't need to scrape up every speck. For instance, when you deglaze the pot with, say, wine or stock, we simply indicate that you should scrape it up without being assiduous. But for many pasta casseroles and grain dishes, you must get obsessive. In those, the direction *every speck of browned stuff* is in italics so you won't miss it. Listen, you want the caramelised stuff in the sauce anyway.

8. I tried to lock the lid onto my pot and it wouldn't do it. What's going on?

Most likely, you've been cooking on the **SAUTÉ** function for a while. The pot is hot. There's steam inside the insert. Liquids may be boiling. The lid resists a firm lock because the pressure's already too high in the air space above the food. To remedy this problem, turn the **SAUTÉ** function off and wait a bit. Or if you've opened the pot after the first stage of a two-step cooking process, let the machine cool down a little. Or – and this is the only case where such advice is *ever* applicable – use a skewer to press down the float valve (or the pin lock) so that it can't get in the way of locking the lid onto the pot. If none of these options work, you may need to contact Instant Pot for a repair.

9. My Max machine asks me how I want to release the pressure right up front. Should I do that?

You can but you don't need to. The machine will default to a natural-release setting. Here's what we do. We let it default to the natural-release function. When the machine beeps to indicate the timing is done, we press the quick-release function on the touchpad and let the pot rip. Of course, you can also set the pot to rip at the right moment when you start the pressure-cooking process. It's really a matter of taste. (And we're a bit fogeyish.) Just don't confuse the quick-release function with the one that has the Max machine make microbursts of pressure throughout the cooking, the **NUTRIBOOST** function.

10. The valve on my Max machine can't be manually closed. What do I do?

Nothing. The Max machine has been designed so that the valve opens or closes automatically, based on the function you request. This increased automation is why the requisite block in our charts for the valve's function has been left blank for the **MAX** setting on the Max machine. Remember, too, that you can also cook on **HIGH** in the Max machine and even use the **SLOW COOK** function. In all cases, setting the valve is irrelevant.

11. You call for a lot of dried herbs and spices. Seriously? I'm not running a spice shop.

First off, many pressure cooker recipes yield better results with dried herbs, not fresh. The latter can end up squishy if they're not very finely chopped or if the braise is not well-stocked (in which case the herbs are more noticeable). What's more, the flavours of dried herbs and spices are often earthier and soften considerably under pressure, rendering them a great choice in many recipes since the pot tends to foreground sweet flavours in a dish.

In the end, you can't create wonderful food in the pot without layering the flavours. The pressure also kills a lot of the hot stuff in chillies. It can even mute some of the subtle notes in vegetables and herbs. To compensate, we need to up the spice game so the food isn't dull.

Here's an idea. Do you know other people in your neighbourhood with multi-cookers? Run a spice co-operative. You take care of dried herbs, Henry does dried spices and Jane takes care of speciality blends. Now you don't have to run a spice shop. You just have to have a few more house keys on your key ring.

12. Wait! What about when I...? Did you really mean to...? What if I can't eat...?

We can't predict every question, so look us up. We're happy to help. Bruce is on Facebook as Bruce Weinstein, on Twitter @bruceweinstein, and on Instagram as @bruceaweinstein. Mark is on all those platforms under Mark Scarbrough or @markscarbrough. Or go to our website: bruceandmark.com. Or listen to our podcast: Cooking with Bruce and Mark. We'd be honoured to answer your questions wherever you find us.

In Conclusion...

Well, really, that's it. The rest we'll leave to the chapter openers and the recipes. You didn't buy an Instant Pot to read a book. You bought it to get busy. And to get a meal on the table. And then to get on with your morning, your day, your evening. You bought the pot to save time, right? So get cooking.

1

Breakfast and Brunch

Although this is the first chapter of recipes, it's probably not the first place you'll turn to. It shouldn't be the last either. True, weekday mornings are hectic. There are just a few recipes here to fit that schedule: the porridges, maybe the soft-boiled eggs. But when the weekend comes, consider your pot the best tool for getting a morning meal on the table.

Throughout, pay attention to the temperature of the eggs before they're cooked. The recipes for straight-on egg dishes – say, the ones for a frittata or for coddled eggs – were formulated for eggs right out of a 5°C refrigerator. But the recipes for the breakfast bread puddings and banana bread were tested with *room-temperature* eggs, so they quickly cohere into a custard or form a good crumb with the flour and leavening.

The quickest way to get eggs to room temperature is to fill a large bowl with warm (not hot) water, then submerge them in their shells in this water and let them sit for 5–10 minutes. Or you can go old-school and stumble into the kitchen to put them out on the countertop for 25–30 minutes, then go take a shower. To us, doing so seems unthinkable moments just after an alarm (or a visiting baby) goes off.

And one more thing: we've been asked in countless cooking classes how to cook faster. Intriguingly, the question seems to come up most frequently when we're talking about breakfast or brunch. Time's precious in the morning, so we always give the same answer. We don't have a TV or a streaming device in the kitchen. And we can't see one from the kitchen. Keeping distractions to a minimum makes cooking faster and more efficient. And that's the whole reason you bought an Instant Pot, right?

FAQs

1. Can I use rolled oats instead of pinhead oats?
No, both standard and instant rolled oats will foam too much. And since both are par-cooked, they'll turn to mush under pressure.

Listen, pinhead oats (also called steel-cut oats or coarse oatmeal) are a pressure-cooker dream: a whole grain, the germ and bran intact, not compromised by all the processing rolled oats endure. And pinhead oats are ready in a multi-cooker in about the same amount of time as regular oats require on the hob. Satisfying pinhead oats are one of the biggest reasons to own an Instant Pot.

But with this warning: pinhead oats go rancid fairly quickly. If you open the bag and detect a funky odour like wet, dirty socks filled with coriander (ugh!), you'll know something's wrong. If you just bought that bag, take it back and get a refund. If you've had the oats for a while, there's nothing to do but bin them. We store ours in a tightly sealed container in the pantry for about 3 months or in the freezer for up to a year. Pinhead oats can be used in the pot straight from the freezer.

2. What's with all the cream or milk added at the end? Can't I add it up front?

If online recipes are to be believed, many people do. These cooks must open the pot after cooking and stir like mad to get a smoother texture in the dish before they take a photo. They have to, because cream or milk breaks under pressure, unless it's put in a baking dish (to lift it off the hot bottom surface) or mixed into a batter of some sort. We add it at the end to avoid the gross gunk. All that said, evaporated milk does *not* break. We can add it directly to cereals before they undergo the pressure.

3. Must I use large eggs?

Yes. They're especially important for eggs cooked in their shells or (relatively) on their own – as in, for example, hard-boiled eggs and coddled eggs. Only large eggs will come out right using the indicated timing. And for baking recipes, the calibration must be even more precise.

4. And while we're at it, how do you store coffee beans?

Now *that's* the eternal question. So let us ask you this. Ever walked into a coffee shop? Or noticed the coffee at the supermarket? Where are those beans? Out on the shelves (or maybe in the bulk bins). They're *not* stored in a refrigerator and *never* in a freezer. Cold temperatures can switch off certain flavour molecules that will never get turned on again, no matter how fancy your coffeemaker is. And the ambient moisture in a humid refrigerator – or the condensation on the beans when they pop out of the freezer and on to the work surface – can break down more flavour chemicals, rendering the coffee flat and dull. Keep coffee beans or even ground coffee in a cool, dark cabinet or pantry. A 340g bag doesn't last two weeks in our house. Of course, we write books. Coffee comes with the territory. But we have a feeling yours won't last much longer if you enjoy a cup (or four) every morning.

SUPER EASY / FEWER THAN 10 INGREDIENTS / FAST/SLOW / NATURAL RELEASE / VEGETARIAN / CAN BE VEGAN / CAN BE GLUTEN-FREE

BREAKFAST AND BRUNCH | **27**

Road Map: Basic Porridge

4 servings

Nothing could be easier than pinhead oats from a multi-cooker. They're done in minutes, ready by the time you're on to your second cup of coffee (second one, because the natural release takes a little time). Don't be tempted to give it a quick release. The pot will sputter and spatter your cabinets. Worse yet, the oats won't be done because you'll have cut the cooking time short.

Unfortunately, oat milk will not work as the liquid in this recipe; it will break and turn stringy. But fat like butter or oil is necessary to help break up the foam the pinhead oats inevitably produce. And we've left the sweetener out of this basic recipe; add whatever you like at the table.

1. Mix all the ingredients in a **3, 5.5- or 7.5-litre cooker**. Lock the lid onto the pot.

2.

Set the machine	Level	The valve must be	Time	Press
PRESSURE COOK	MAX	—	3 minutes with the KEEP WARM setting off	START
PRESSURE COOK or MANUAL	HIGH	Closed	4 minutes with the KEEP WARM setting off	START

3. When the machine has finished cooking, turn it off and let its pressure **return to normal naturally**, about 15 minutes. Unlatch the lid and open the cooker. Stir well before serving.

650ml liquid
Choose one or two from water, unsweetened cloudy apple juice, rice milk, cashew milk, soya milk and/or almond milk – or a 50/50 combo of water and tinned evaporated milk.

160g pinhead oats

1 tablespoon fat
Choose butter, coconut oil or vegetable, corn, rapeseed, safflower, grapeseed or any nut oil.

½ teaspoon table salt (optional)

Beyond

- You can (but don't need to) double this recipe if you have a 7.5-litre cooker.
- Add your preferred sweetener to each bowlful: white granulated sugar, brown sugar, honey, maple syrup, agave syrup, date syrup, palm sugar or coconut sugar.
- To add dried fruit – raisins, currants, blueberries, raspberries, chopped pitted dates or prunes, or chopped stemmed figs, nectarines or peaches – stir it into the porridge after the pressure has been released. Set the lid askew for 2–3 minutes to warm and plump the dried fruit before serving.
- To use the SLOW COOK setting, increase the liquid to 950ml and cook on HIGH with the pressure valve open for 4 hours, with the KEEP WARM setting off (or on for 2 hours).

40g butter

160g pinhead oats

650ml water

¼ teaspoon table salt

Buttery Toasted Porridge

4 servings

Toasting raw oats in butter gives them a nutty flavour that is more complex than basic porridge. Again, there's no sweetener in the pot to keep the recipe basic. Add whatever you like to each serving.

Because pinhead oats can sit on the shelf and are not sold quickly in this go-go world, they have varying amounts of remaining, residual moisture. If your oats are dried out, if they do not easily absorb liquid as they cook and end up soupy in the finished dish, set the lid askew over the pot for 5 minutes after opening. Once softened from the pressure, they will absorb liquid as they sit.

1.

Press	Setting	Time	Press
SAUTÉ	MEDIUM, NORMAL OR CUSTOM 150°C	5 minutes	START

2. Melt the butter in a 3- or 5.5-litre cooker. Add the oats and stir until they smell toasty, about 3 minutes. Turn off the SAUTÉ function; stir in the water and salt. Lock the lid onto the pot.

3.

Set the machine	Level	The valve must be	Time	Press
PRESSURE COOK	MAX	—	3 minutes with the KEEP WARM setting off	START
PRESSURE COOK or MANUAL	HIGH	Closed	4 minutes with the KEEP WARM setting off	START

4. When the machine has finished cooking, turn it off and let its pressure **return to normal naturally** for 10 minutes. Then use the **quick-release method** to remove any residual pressure. Unlatch the lid and open the pot. Stir well before serving.

Beyond

- For a 7.5-litre cooker, you must increase all the ingredients by 50 per cent. Or you can double them in either a 5.5-litre or 7.5-litre cooker.

- For an even nuttier porridge, substitute a *toasted* or *roasted* nut oil of any sort (hazelnut, pecan, pistachio, walnut) for the butter.

- Letting the pot come back to normal pressure naturally for 10 minutes results in porridge that's still a tad chewy. If you want super creamy porridge, let it return to natural pressure for 20 minutes before releasing the remainder of the pressure with the quick-release method.

- To use the SLOW COOK mode, increase the water to 950ml and cook on SLOW COOK on HIGH for 4 hours, with the KEEP WARM setting off (or on for 2 hours).

Cinnamon Apple Porridge

4 servings

Like a bakery breakfast bun in porridge form (huh?), this is warm, comforting and sweet. Adding the sugar up front gives the cereal a creamier finish. You can, of course, skip the sugar for a less-sweet breakfast. Or use an artificial sweetener (½ teaspoon liquid stevia works particularly well).

The dried apples should be finely chopped, the better to get one or two pieces per spoonful. To chop them without a hassle, spray your knife with nonstick spray, or simply wet the knife repeatedly as you chop the dried fruit. There's more liquid in this recipe than in the previous ones because the dried fruit also absorbs it under pressure.

600ml water

125ml whole or low-fat evaporated milk (do not use fat-free)

160g pinhead oats

40g chopped dried apples

2 tablespoons light or dark brown sugar (optional)

30g butter

½ teaspoon ground cinnamon

½ teaspoon table salt (optional)

2 tablespoons single or double cream

1. Mix the water, milk, oats, apples, brown sugar (if using), butter, cinnamon and salt (if using) in a 3-, 5.5- or 7.5-litre cooker. Lock the lid onto the pot.

2.

Set the machine	Level	The valve must be	Time	Press
PRESSURE COOK	MAX	—	3 minutes with the KEEP WARM setting off	START
PRESSURE COOK or MANUAL	HIGH	Closed	4 minutes with the KEEP WARM setting off	START

3. When the machine has finished cooking, turn it off and let its pressure **return to normal naturally** for 15 minutes. Then use the **quick-release method** to get rid of any residual pressure in the pot. Unlatch the lid and open the cooker. Stir in the cream before serving.

Beyond

- You can double this recipe in a 5.5-litre cooker. You can double or even triple it in a 7.5-litre cooker.

- If you have leftovers, pack them into a 20cm square cake tin or a small loaf tin lined with clingfilm. Cover and refrigerate for up to 2 days. When ready, take the 'cake' or 'loaf' out of the tin and cut it into squares or slices. Fry these in butter in a nonstick frying pan set over a medium heat until brown and a little crunchy, turning several times. Serve with plenty of butter and maple syrup.

40g butter

55g dark brown sugar

2 very ripe bananas, peeled and thinly sliced

650ml water

160g pinhead oats

2 teaspoons vanilla extract

½ teaspoon ground cinnamon

¼ teaspoon table salt

60ml single or double cream

Caramel Banana Porridge

4 servings

By creating a caramel-like sauce as the base for this hot breakfast cereal, we turn it into a replica of Bananas Foster, the classic New Orleans dessert (even though, incidentally, the recipe was first published in *The New York Times*). The release here is just a straight-on natural one because there's more sugar than in other porridge recipes in this book. We need the sugar to make the caramel, of course. But hot sugar syrup is particularly dangerous if it sputters from the vent.

1.

Press	Setting	Time	Press
SAUTÉ	MEDIUM, NORMAL OR CUSTOM 150°C	5 minutes	START

2. Melt the butter in a **3- or 5.5-litre cooker.** Add the brown sugar and stir until the sugar has dissolved and the mixture is bubbling. Stir in the bananas to coat them in the sugar syrup. Turn off the **SAUTÉ** function. Stir in the water, oats, vanilla, cinnamon and salt. Lock the lid onto the pot.

3.

Set the machine	Level	The valve must be	Time	Press
PRESSURE COOK	MAX	—	3 minutes with the KEEP WARM setting off	START
PRESSURE COOK or MANUAL	HIGH	Closed	4 minutes with the KEEP WARM setting off	START

4. When the machine has finished cooking, turn it off and let its pressure **return to normal naturally**, about 20 minutes. Unlatch the lid and open the cooker. Stir in the cream before serving.

Beyond

- For a 7.5-litre cooker, you must use 55g butter and increase the remaining ingredients by 50 per cent.

- For brunch, add up to ½ teaspoon rum extract with the vanilla.

Tropical Oat Porridge

4–6 servings

We make this dairy-free porridge super creamy by overcooking the barley and the oats until they break down into a soft, warm cereal. Use only pearl barley, the sort without the hull or germ. It will almost disappear in the porridge.

1. Mix the water, barley, oats, coconut, brown sugar, lime juice and salt in a **3-, 5.5- or 7.5-litre cooker**. Lock the lid onto the pot.

2.

Set the machine	Level	The valve must be	Time	Press
PRESSURE COOK	MAX	—	12 minutes with the KEEP WARM setting off	START
PRESSURE COOK or MANUAL	HIGH	Closed	15 minutes with the KEEP WARM setting off	START

3. When the machine has finished cooking, turn it off and let its pressure **return to normal naturally**, about 20 minutes. Unlatch the lid and open the cooker. Stir in the coconut milk or coconut cream before serving.

700ml water

100g pearl barley

80g pinhead oats

30g unsweetened grated coconut

55g light brown sugar

1 tablespoon fresh lime juice

¼ teaspoon table salt

60ml coconut milk or coconut cream

Beyond

- You can double this recipe in a 7.5-litre cooker.

- Garnish the servings with either chopped, peeled and cored fresh pineapple or chopped dried pineapple with some toasted flaked almonds.

1 litre water

70g bulgur wheat, preferably medium or coarse grind

85g raw buckwheat groats

80g raisins or dried cranberries, chopped

50g white granulated sugar

1 teaspoon vanilla extract

½ teaspoon ground cinnamon

¼ teaspoon table salt

125ml single or double cream

Buckwheat and Bulgur Porridge

6 servings

In this oat-free hot cereal, bulgur offers both wheaty flavour and creamy texture, while buckwheat contributes a stickiness reminiscent of traditional porridge. Use only raw buckwheat groats, not toasted groats (often called 'kasha'). Adding the cream at the end and bringing the porridge to a momentary bubble avoids the irritatingly raw taste of double cream.

1. Mix the water, bulgur, buckwheat, raisins, sugar, vanilla, cinnamon and salt in 3-, 5.5- or 7.5-litre cooker. Lock the lid onto the pot.

2.

Set the machine	Level	The valve must be	Time	Press
PRESSURE COOK	MAX	—	12 minutes with the KEEP WARM setting off	START
PRESSURE COOK or MANUAL	HIGH	Closed	16 minutes with the KEEP WARM setting off	START

3. When the machine has finished cooking, turn it off and let the pressure **return to normal naturally**, about 15 minutes. Unlatch the lid and open the cooker.

4.

Press	Setting	Time	Press
SAUTÉ	MEDIUM, NORMAL OR CUSTOM 150°C	5 minutes	START

5. Stir often as the porridge comes to a bubble. Stir in the cream and continue stirring over the heat for 1 minute. Turn off the **SAUTÉ** function and remove the *hot* insert from the machine to stop the cooking. Serve warm.

Beyond

- You can double this recipe in a 7.5-litre cooker.
- Swop the raisins for dried blueberries (which you needn't chop).
- For a bolder flavour, substitute dark brown sugar or even date sugar for the white granulated sugar.

Cream of Rice Porridge

6 servings

By overcooking rice, we can get the grains to break down into
something like the type of cream of rice cereal you can buy in
a box, but with a much better flavour (and less watery texture).
Although you can use more expensive basmati or jasmine rice for
this porridge, it works just as well with any brand of long-grain
white rice. Do not use parboiled or instant rice.

1.5 litres water

185g long-grain white rice

40g butter or 45ml
neutral-flavoured oil like
vegetable oil

½ teaspoon table salt

1. Mix all the ingredients in a **5.5- or 7.5-litre cooker**.
Lock the lid onto the pot.

2.

Set the machine	Level	The valve must be	Time	Press
PRESSURE COOK	MAX	——	35 minutes with the KEEP WARM setting off	START
PRESSURE COOK or MANUAL	HIGH	Closed	45 minutes with the KEEP WARM setting off	START

3. When the machine has finished cooking, turn it off and let its
pressure **return to normal naturally**, about 35 minutes. Unlatch
the lid and open the cooker. Stir well before serving.

Beyond

- You must halve the recipe for a 3-litre cooker.

- The cereal is not sweet. Add your preferred sweetener to each serving to taste. See Road Map: Basic Porridge (page 27) for a fairly complete list.

- The hot cereal takes well to dried fruit such as raisins or dried blueberries. Stir these into individual servings with the sweetener.

- For a creamier cereal, use only 950ml water and add one 410g tin regular, low-fat or fat-free evaporated milk.

250ml water

1–12 large eggs, cold

Easy in-the-Shell Eggs

Makes up to 12 eggs

Here's the best way to make a variety of in-shell cooked eggs in the Instant Pot. But keep a few things in mind. First, the pressure is LOW, not HIGH (and certainly not MAX). Second, because of the way the pressure builds, the best results are to be had with *cold large eggs*, straight from the fridge. And finally, there's a range of timings given. You'll have perfect soft-boiled eggs in 3 minutes, the yolks not set and the whites barely set. (For a firmer set to those soft-boiled eggs, use the quick-release method but leave the lid on the pot after the pressure has escaped for 1 minute.) For soft-set eggs with a jammy yolk like you might find in a bowl of Ramen Broth (page 104), give them 6 minutes. And hard-boiled eggs take 12 minutes.

By the way, the secret to a crunchy piece of toast is putting sliced bread straight from the freezer into the toaster.

1. Place a heat- and pressure-safe trivet inside a **5.5-litre cooker**. Or set a heat- and pressure-safe vegetable steamer in the pot. Pour in the water. Pile as many eggs as you like onto the trivet or steamer. Lock the lid onto the pot.

2.

Set the machine	Level	The valve must be	Time	Press
PRESSURE COOK or MANUAL	LOW	Closed	3 minutes for soft-boiled eggs, 6 minutes for soft-set eggs or 12 minutes for hard-boiled eggs with the KEEP WARM setting off	START

3. Use the **quick-release method** to bring the pot's pressure back to normal. Unlatch the lid and open the cooker. Transfer the eggs to a bowl or wire rack. Peel as soon as you can handle them.

Beyond

- For a 3-litre cooker, you must use 250ml water as stated, although you'll only be able to fit four or five eggs on the trivet.

- For a 7.5-litre cooker, you must use 350ml water.

- Warm eggs peel more easily than cold. However, to save the eggs in their shells for a later use, transfer them from the pot to a bowl of cold water with an ice cube or two in it.

- An easy way to get the eggs out of the cooker without touching the hot metal inside is to use a large balloon whisk. Gently press it down over one egg, capture the egg inside and lift it out of the pot. (Or just use kitchen tongs with silicone tips.)

- The filling for our best devilled eggs is made by mixing 6 large hard-boiled yolks with 3 tablespoons mayonnaise, 2 tablespoons yellow mustard, 1 teaspoon dried dill and ½ teaspoon table salt. Grind lots of black pepper over each filled egg half.

Coddled Eggs

1–6 servings

This recipe is the closest we can come to poached eggs in the cooker without simply using the SAUTÉ function to boil water and poach the eggs (at which point, seriously, there's no reason not to use a saucepan on the hob). The little bit of cream in each ramekin stops the whites becoming tough.

Use only LOW pressure. The 2 minutes we suggest will result in soft-set eggs, the whites set but a little jiggly around the yolks. For a firmer set, give the eggs 3 minutes under LOW pressure, then continue on as directed.

1. Place a heat- and pressure-safe trivet in a **5.5-litre cooker**. Pour in the water. Butter or oil the inside of one to six heat- and pressure-safe 250ml ramekins. Crack an egg into each, spoon 1 teaspoon cream on top and season with salt and pepper to taste.

2. Place – or even stack – the ramekins on the trivet, making sure that no one ramekin completely covers another (that is, balancing a second layer as necessary on the rims of at least two ramekins in the row below). Lock the lid onto the pot.

3.

Set the machine	Level	The valve must be	Time	Press
PRESSURE COOK or MANUAL	LOW	Closed	2 minutes with the KEEP WARM setting off	START

4. Use the **quick-release method** to bring the pot's pressure back to normal. Unlatch the lid and open the cooker. Transfer the *hot* ramekins to heat-safe serving plates and dig in.

250ml water

Butter or vegetable, corn, rapeseed or olive oil for greasing the ramekins

1–6 large eggs

1–6 teaspoons double cream

Table salt and ground black pepper for garnishing

Beyond

- For a 3-litre cooker, you must use 250ml water as directed although you'll only be able to fit four ramekins.

- For a 7.5-litre cooker, you must use 350ml water, no matter how many eggs you make.

- Add finely chopped herbs to each ramekin before you add the egg. Try chives or oregano leaves or thyme leaves. For heat, add a pinch of crushed chilli flakes.

350ml water

Fat for greasing the baking dish

Choose a solid fat like butter or coconut oil; or an oil like vegetable or a nut oil of any sort.

9 large eggs

90ml creamy liquid

Choose whole milk, semi-skimmed, single cream, double cream, hemp milk, soya milk, coconut milk, cashew milk or any nut milk.

½ teaspoon table salt

Up to 1 teaspoon ground black pepper

200g filling

Choose one or several from chopped baby spinach; chopped, jarred roasted red pepper; cooked onions, shallots or spring onions (in butter or oil of any sort); cored, deseeded and finely chopped pepper; cooked sliced mushrooms; cooked diced and peeled potatoes; grated semi-firm or hard cheese like Swiss, Cheddar, mozzarella, pecorino or Parmigiano-Reggiano; sliced sun-dried tomatoes; and/or thawed, frozen broccoli or cauliflower florets.

Beyond

- For a 3-litre cooker, you must use 6 large eggs, 60ml creamy liquid, ¼ teaspoon table salt, ¼ teaspoon ground black pepper and 180g filling. Put the egg mixture in a buttered or greased 1-litre, high-sided, round soufflé dish and add 250ml water to the pot.

- Add fresh or dried herbs at will, up to 3 tablespoons fresh herbs or 1 tablespoon dried (or even a bottled dried herb blend). Add fresh herbs to the baking dish, then gently pour the egg mixture on top. Whisk dried herbs right into the egg mixture.

- For a spicy frittata, serve Sriracha, Tabasco or another hot pepper sauce at the table. Bottled hot sauce can curdle the dairy if you add it before cooking.

Road Map: Instant Pot Frittata

4–6 servings

Okay, fair enough, this isn't a true frittata. It's more like an egg casserole – and a fine brunch main course, no matter what you call it. Use this road map to create your own signature version. Go ahead, make notes right on this page so you remember what you did or what you want to do next time. But take note: Fat-free, skimmed or semi-skimmed milk and rice milk are all too thin for a good result. And oat milk will break under pressure.

Step 5 offers directions for inverting the frittata onto a plate. You can skip the step and cut wedges right in the baking dish. They'll be uneven, maybe a little torn, but you also won't have to do a complicated kitchen dance with a hot dish early in the morning.

1. Pour the water into a **5.5- or 7.5-litre cooker**. Set a heat- and pressure-safe trivet in the pot. Butter or grease the inside of a 2-litre, high-sided, round soufflé dish. Make an aluminium foil sling (see page 20) and set the baking dish in the middle of it.

2. Whisk the eggs, creamy liquid, salt and pepper in a large bowl until smooth and uniform, about 2 minutes. Stir in the filling mixture. Pour and scrape every drop of this mixture into the prepared baking dish. Cover it tightly with foil, then use the sling to pick it up and lower it onto the trivet. Fold down the sling's ends so they fit in the cooker. Lock the lid onto the pot.

3.

Set the machine	Level	The valve must be	Time	Press
PRESSURE COOK or MANUAL	LOW	Closed	25 minutes with the KEEP WARM setting off	START

4. Use the **quick-release method** to bring the pot's pressure back to normal. Unlatch the lid and open the cooker. Use the sling to transfer the baking dish to a wire rack. Uncover the baking dish and leave the frittata to cool for 5 minutes.

5. Run a palette knife around the interior perimeter of the baking dish. Set a large plate or a serving platter over the top, then invert the *hot* baking dish and plate so that the frittata comes free. Cut into quarters or smaller wedges to serve.

No-Crust Ham and Spinach Quiche

4 servings

A traditional quiche is none too satisfying from the pot. The crust gets gummy and even bubbles up. We know. We've seen a zillion internet recipes, too. They've never worked for us.

But a crustless quiche does. We use a springform tin (rather than a 2-litre dish) so we can get even slices when unmoulded. The spinach mixture gets packed into the tin, sitting at the seam to help seal it. That said, the tin's seam must be tight. Test your 18cm round springform tin by filling it with water to see if it leaks.

1. Generously coat or butter the inside of an 18cm round springform tin. Pour the water into a **5.5- or 7.5-litre cooker.** Set a heat- and pressure-safe trivet inside the pot. Make an aluminium foil sling (see page 20) and set the springform tin in the middle of it.

2. Mix the spinach, ham, oregano, pepper and salt (if using) in a medium bowl and smooth it into an even layer in the tin. (Do not clean the bowl.) Sprinkle the cheese evenly over this mixture.

3. Whisk the eggs, milk and flour in that same bowl until smooth, about 2 minutes. Gently pour this mixture over the ingredients in the tin (so as not to dislodge them). Cover the tin tightly with foil. Use the sling to pick it up and lower it onto the trivet in the pot. Fold the ends of the sling down to fit in the cooker. Lock the lid onto the pot.

4.

Set the machine	Level	The valve must be	Time	Press
PRESSURE COOK or MANUAL	LOW	Closed	25 minutes with the KEEP WARM setting off	START

5. Use the **quick-release method** to bring the pot's pressure back to normal. Unlatch the lid and open the cooker. Use the sling to transfer the *hot* baking dish to a wire rack. Uncover and leave to cool for 10 minutes. Run a palette knife around the inside perimeter of the tin (or use a nonstick-safe knife for a nonstick tin). Unlatch the sides and remove the ring. Slice the quiche into quarters to serve.

Cooking spray or butter for greasing the baking dish

350ml water

280g frozen chopped spinach, thawed and squeezed dry by the handful

110g smoked ham, any coatings removed, the meat diced

½ teaspoon dried oregano

½ teaspoon ground black pepper

¼ teaspoon table salt (optional)

85g grated Swiss cheese

4 large eggs

125ml whole milk

2 tablespoons plain flour (for a gluten-free alternative, see the Beyond section)

Beyond

- Because of the way the latch is designed on the springform tin, this recipe cannot currently be made in a 3-litre cooker.

- For a richer quiche, substitute single or even double cream for the milk.

- The flour is necessary to get the right set. However, if you need the recipe to be gluten-free, use a gluten-free baking mix for a similar consistency. Make sure the ham doesn't have any wheat by-products injected into it or coated on it.

40g butter

1 medium onion, chopped (160g prechopped)

1 medium green pepper, stemmed, cored and chopped (175g prechopped)

1 medium red pepper, stemmed, cored and chopped (175g prechopped)

450g smoked ham (not thinly shaved), any coating removed, the meat diced

2 medium garlic cloves, peeled and finely chopped (or 2 teaspoons prechopped)

1 teaspoon dried sage

1 teaspoon dried thyme

½ teaspoon celery seeds (optional)

¼ teaspoon table salt

¼ teaspoon ground black pepper

450g potatoes, diced (no need to peel)

350ml chicken stock

Breakfast Hash

4–6 servings

Not a side dish at all, this is a well-stocked breakfast main course. Make sure the potatoes are diced into evenly sized 1cm pieces so they cook in the stated time. Skip processed sandwich meat and look for whole, roasted smoked ham at the deli counter. Have the butcher cut it into 1cm slices to make the dicing easier.

1.

Press	Setting	Time	Press
SAUTÉ	MEDIUM, NORMAL OR CUSTOM 150°C	5 minutes	START

2. Melt the butter in a **5.5-litre cooker**. Add the onion and both peppers. Cook, stirring occasionally, until softened, about 4 minutes. Add the ham, garlic, sage, thyme, celery seeds (if using), salt and pepper. Cook, stirring often, until fragrant, about 1 minute.

3. Turn off the **SAUTÉ** function. Stir in the potatoes and stock, scraping up any browned bits on the pot's bottom. Lock the lid onto the cooker.

4.

Set the machine	Level	The valve must be	Time	Press
PRESSURE COOK	MAX	—	10 minutes with the KEEP WARM setting off	START
PRESSURE COOK or MANUAL	HIGH	Closed	12 minutes with the KEEP WARM setting off	START

5. Use the **quick-release method** to bring the pot's pressure back to normal. Unlatch the lid and open the cooker. Stir well.

6.

Press	Setting	Time	Press
SAUTÉ	HIGH or MORE	10 minutes	START

7. Bring the mixture to a simmer, stirring often. Continue without stirring until the liquid boils off and the hash touching the hot surface starts to brown, 3–4 minutes. Turn off the **SAUTÉ** function and remove the *hot* insert from the machine to stop the cooking. Some of the potatoes may have fused to the surface. Use a palette knife to dislodge them. The point is to have some browned bits and some softer bits throughout the hash.

Beyond

- For a 3-litre cooker, you must use 250ml stock and halve the remaining ingredients.
- For a 7.5-litre cooker, you must increase all the ingredients by 50 per cent.
- Substitute corned beef for the ham – or get fancy and substitute shredded, skinless boneless duck confit.

Pull-Apart Cinnamon Bread

6 servings

Baking monkey bread is a holiday tradition in the USA, but here's a quicker, easier version that might put this breakfast speciality on the menu all year-round. It's made with tinned quick-bread biscuit dough and lots of butter, a real treat. Use only home-style (sometimes called 'Southern-style') biscuits, not 'flaky' biscuits, as they need to cook up flat and dense, rather than light and layered.

1. Pour the water into a **5.5- or 7.5-litre cooker**. Place a heat- and pressure-safe trivet inside the pot. Generously butter the inside of an 18cm round springform tin. Make an aluminium foil sling (see page 20) and set the prepared baking dish in the middle of it.

2. Mix the white sugar, brown sugar, cinnamon and salt (if using) in a large, microwave-safe bowl. Cut the raw quick-bread biscuit dough into quarters, then add them to this bowl and toss well to coat. Lightly pack the quick-bread biscuits into the springform tin. (Much of the sugar mixture will stay behind in the bowl.)

3. Add the butter to the sugar mixture. Microwave on high in 15-seconds bursts, stirring after each, until the butter melts and the mixture bubbles. Pour and scrape this mixture over the dough in the tin. Use the sling to pick the tin up and lower it onto the trivet in the pot. Lay a piece of aluminium foil or baking parchment over the top of the tin without crimping or sealing it to the tin. Fold down the ends of the sling so they fit inside the machine. Lock the lid onto the cooker.

4.

Set the machine for	Level	The valve must be	Time	Press
PRESSURE COOK	MAX	——	15 minutes with the KEEP WARM setting off	START
MEAT/STEW, PRESSURE COOK or MANUAL	HIGH	Closed	20 minutes with the KEEP WARM setting off	START

5. When the machine has finished cooking, turn it off and let its pressure **return to normal naturally** for 10 minutes. Then use the **quick-release method** to get rid of any residual pressure in the pot. Unlatch the lid and open the cooker. Use the sling to transfer the *hot* tin to a wire rack. Uncover and leave to cool for 10 minutes, then run a palette knife around the inside perimeter of the tin (or a nonstick-safe knife if the tin has a nonstick finish). Unlatch the sides and remove the ring. Serve by pulling apart the warm bread.

350ml water

65g white granulated sugar

70g light brown sugar

1½ teaspoons ground cinnamon

¼ teaspoon table salt (optional)

460g pack regular or buttermilk home-style quick-bread biscuit dough (enough for 8 quick-bread biscuits)

55g butter, plus extra for greasing the tin

Beyond

- For a 3-litre cooker, you must halve all the ingredients and make the pull-apart bread in a buttered 1-litre, high-sided, round soufflé dish. It won't unmould well, but you can pick it apart right in the baking dish.

- Sprinkle up to 3 tablespoons chopped raisins or dried cranberries amongst the quick-bread biscuits before adding the melted butter mixture.

- Or sprinkle 60g plain chocolate chips amongst the quick-bread biscuit pieces as you layer them in the tin.

- For a bigger kick, add up to ¼ teaspoon grated nutmeg and/or ¼ teaspoon ground allspice with the cinnamon.

350ml water

Nonstick baking spray

100g white granulated sugar

2 large eggs

40g butter, at room
temperature

2 very ripe medium
bananas, peeled

125ml low-fat or fat-free
plain yoghurt

2 tablespoons fresh
lemon juice

1 teaspoon vanilla extract

180g plain flour

1½ teaspoons bicarbonate
of soda

¼ teaspoon table salt

50g walnut halves

Beyond

- This recipe works in a 3-litre cooker as written; an 18cm Bundt tin will just fit. Make sure the kitchen paper doesn't catch on the rim of the lid. The amount of batter will rise up and almost touch the top of the cooker. It can get a little wet around the edges, but we didn't mind this in testing. For pitch-perfect aesthetics, when you fill the Bundt tin, leave a 1cm space between the top of the batter and the top of the pan. (Discard that little bit of leftover batter.)

- Substitute any nut you like – pecans, almonds, skinned hazelnuts.

- Scrape the batter from the food processor into a bowl, then fold in up to 80g raisins, dried cranberries or plain chocolate chips before getting the batter into the tin.

- A baking spray is easiest for getting the fat-and-flour mixture into every crevasse of a Bundt tin. But feel free to go old-school, using butter and plain flour to coat the inside of the tin.

Bundt Banana Bread

8 servings

There's no worry about *this* banana bread drying out at the edges, given the pot's steamy environment. Here are the two secrets to success: First, make sure that tin is sprayed well, very nicely coated. If you think you've sprayed it enough, spray it a little more. The cake can stick like mad in the corners and indentations of the Bundt tin. And second, make sure the bananas are truly ripe, beyond the point you'd slice them on to cereal.

1. Pour the water into a **3-, 5.5- or 7.5-litre cooker**. Set a heat- and pressure-safe trivet into the pot. Generously spray the inside of an 18cm Bundt tin with baking spray, making sure it gets into all the crevices. Make an aluminium foil sling (see page 20) and set the tin in the middle of it.

2. Put the sugar, eggs, butter and bananas in a food processor. Cover and process until smooth, stopping the machine once to scrape down the canister. Add the yoghurt, lemon juice and vanilla. Cover and process until smooth. Stop the machine and scrape down the inside.

3. Add the flour, bicarbonate of soda and salt. Cover and pulse until a uniform batter forms. Add the nuts and pulse to chop a bit and blend them in.

4. Pour, dollop and scrape the batter into the prepared tin. Use a rubber spatula to smooth the top of the batter. Use the sling to pick up the tin and set it on the trivet in the pot. Fold down the ends of the sling so they fit into the pot without touching the batter. Lay a large piece of kitchen paper over the top of the cake to cover it without touching the batter below. Lock the lid onto the cooker.

5.

Set the machine	Level	The valve must be	Time	Press
PRESSURE COOK	MAX	——	18 minutes with the KEEP WARM setting off	START
PRESSURE COOK or MANUAL	HIGH	Closed	25 minutes with the KEEP WARM setting off	START

6. When the machine has finished cooking, turn it off and let the pressure **return to normal naturally**, about 25 minutes. Unlatch the lid and open the cooker. Remove the kitchen paper, then use the sling to lift the Bundt tin out of the cooker and onto a wire cooling rack. Leave to cool for 5 minutes, then invert the tin onto a plate and shake gently to release the cake. Slip it back onto the wire rack and continue cooling for at least 20 minutes before slicing into wedges.

Peanut Butter Bread Pudding

4–6 servings

Here's a bread pudding for breakfast, a treat that cries out for crunchy bacon on the side. Use only natural-style peanut butter, without any added fat. If you use salt-free peanut butter, whisk in ½ teaspoon table salt with the peanut butter.

The best bread for this recipe (and for all subsequent bread puddings in this book) is packaged, sliced, 'hearty' or 'country-classic' white bread, rather than a loaf you might buy in the bakery. The recipe calls for about half of a standard loaf.

And one more thing: mound the bread cubes into the baking dish without pressing down. Otherwise, the liquids they've soaked up will come out and sear against the pan.

1. Pour the water into a **5.5- or 7.5-litre cooker**. Set a heat- and pressure-safe trivet in the pot.

2. Generously butter the inside of a 2-litre, high-sided, round soufflé dish. Make an aluminium foil sling (see page 20) and set the baking dish in the centre of it.

3. Whisk the eggs, milk, cream, peanut butter, maple syrup, brown sugar and vanilla in a large bowl until the peanut butter dissolves and the mixture is uniform, about 2 minutes. Add the bread cubes and toss well to soak up the egg mixture.

4. Pile the bread cubes into the prepared baking dish in a fairly even layer, pouring any additional liquid in the bowl over them. Cover the baking dish tightly with foil, then use the sling to pick up and lower the baking dish onto the trivet. Fold down the ends of the sling so they fit in the pot. Lock the lid onto the cooker.

5.

Set the machine	Level	The valve must be	Time	Press
PRESSURE COOK	MAX	——	10 minutes with the KEEP WARM setting off	START
PRESSURE COOK or MANUAL	HIGH	Closed	12 minutes with the KEEP WARM setting off	START

6. Use the **quick-release method** to bring the pot's pressure back to normal. Unlatch the lid and open the cooker. Use the sling to transfer the *hot* baking dish to a wire rack. Uncover and leave to cool for 5 minutes before serving by the big spoonful.

350ml water

Butter for greasing the baking dish

2 large eggs, at room temperature

180ml whole or low-fat milk

125ml single or double cream

125g creamy natural-style peanut butter

60ml maple syrup

2 tablespoons light brown sugar

2 teaspoons vanilla extract

225g white bread, preferably country-style bread, cut into 2.5cm squares (do not remove the crusts)

Beyond

- For a 3-litre cooker, you must halve all the ingredients and use a 1-litre, high-sided, round soufflé dish.

- Sprinkle up to 3 tablespoons chopped raisins amongst the bread cubes as you layer them into the baking dish.

- For peanut butter and jam bread pudding, omit the brown sugar and smear a light coating of your favourite fruit jam (not jelly or preserves) over the bread slices before you cut them into squares. Stir these gently in the liquid to keep the jam on the bread (as well as you can).

350ml water

Cooking spray or butter for
greasing the baking dish

4 large eggs, at room
temperature

500ml whole milk

2 tablespoons light
brown sugar

½ teaspoon vanilla extract

¼ teaspoon table salt

3 large cinnamon-raisin
bagels, halved as if to toast
them, then the halves cut
into 2.5cm pieces

Cinnamon-Raisin Bagel Bread Pudding

4–6 servings

Finally, here's a use for cinnamon-raisin bagels! (We have a long-running fight about their legitimacy. The Christian on our team thinks they aren't and the Jewish guy thinks they are. We live strange lives.) This bread pudding is chewy and dense. It's made with bagels, after all. They'll need to soak in the egg mixture for 10 minutes because they're so thick.

1. Pour the water into a **5.5- or 7.5-litre cooker**. Set a heat- and pressure-safe trivet in the pot.

2. Generously coat or butter the inside of a 2-litre, high-sided, round soufflé dish. Make an aluminium foil sling (see page 20) and set the baking dish in the centre of it.

3. Whisk the eggs, milk, brown sugar, vanilla and salt in a large bowl until uniform, about 1 minute. Add the bagel pieces, toss well and set aside for 10 minutes to soak up more of the egg mixture.

4. Stir the bagel mixture again, then pile the pieces into the prepared baking dish, pouring any additional liquid over them. (Do not press down to compact them but try to make as even a layer as possible.) Cover the baking dish tightly with foil, then use the sling to pick up and lower the baking dish onto the trivet. Fold down the ends of the sling so they fit in the pot. Lock the lid onto the cooker..

5.

Set the machine	Level	The valve must be	Time	Press
PRESSURE COOK	MAX	—	10 minutes with the KEEP WARM setting off	START
PRESSURE COOK or MANUAL	HIGH	Closed	12 minutes with the KEEP WARM setting off	START

6. When the machine has finished cooking, turn it off and let its pressure **return to normal naturally** for 10 minutes. Then use the **quick-release method** to get rid of any residual pressure in the pot. Unlatch the lid and open the cooker. Use the sling to transfer the *hot* baking dish to a wire rack. Uncover and leave to cool for 10 minutes before serving by the big spoonful.

Beyond

- For a 3-litre cooker, you must use 250ml water, halve all the remaining ingredients and use a 1-litre, high-sided, round soufflé dish.

- Use any flavoured, sweet bagel – blueberry, chocolate chip – for this recipe.

- For a savoury-sweet mix, fry up to 4 thin rashers streaky bacon until crunchy, then cool and chop into small bits to stir into the egg mixture with the bagel pieces.

Savoury Sausage Bread Pudding

4 servings

This bread pudding has no added sugar, so it's a savoury meal for a weekend morning. With cheese and sausage in the mixture there's plenty of fat, so feel free to use milk of any sort, even fat-free. (For a discussion about the right sort of bread, see the headnote for Peanut Butter Bread Pudding on page 41.)

15g butter, plus extra for greasing the baking dish

340g smoked sausage (such as kielbasa), diced

350ml water

3 large eggs, at room temperature

350ml whole, low-fat or fat-free milk

225g white bread, preferably country-style bread, cut into 2.5cm squares (do not remove the crusts)

25g finely grated Parmigiano-Reggiano

1 teaspoon dried thyme

½ teaspoon ground black pepper

1.

Press	Setting	Time	Press
SAUTÉ	MEDIUM, NORMAL OR CUSTOM 150°C	5 minutes	START

2. Melt the butter in a **5.5- or 7.5-litre cooker**, then add the sausage. Cook, stirring often, until lightly browned, about 3 minutes. Turn off the **SAUTÉ** function. Scrape the contents of the *hot* insert into a large bowl. Set aside to cool for 15 minutes. Wipe out the insert and return it to the machine.

3. Pour the water into the cooker. Set a heat- and pressure-safe trivet in the pot. Generously butter the inside of a 2-litre, high-sided, round soufflé dish. Make an aluminium foil sling (see page 20) and set the baking dish in the centre of it.

4. Whisk the eggs and milk in a second large bowl until uniform, about 2 minutes. Add the cooled sausage, the bread cubes, cheese, thyme and pepper. Stir well until the bread is thoroughly coated in the egg mixture.

5. Pile the bread cubes into an even layer in the prepared baking dish, pouring any additional liquid over them (without pressing down on the bread). Cover the baking dish tightly with foil, then use the sling to pick up and lower the baking dish onto the trivet. Fold down the ends of the sling so they fit in the pot. Lock the lid onto the cooker.

6.

Set the machine	Level	The valve must be	Time	Press
PRESSURE COOK	MAX	——	12 minutes with the KEEP WARM setting off	START
PRESSURE COOK or MANUAL	HIGH	Closed	16 minutes with the KEEP WARM setting off	START

7. When the machine has finished cooking, turn it off and let its pressure **return to normal naturally** for 10 minutes. Then use the **quick-release method** to get rid of any residual pressure in the pot. Unlatch the lid and open the cooker. Use the sling to transfer the *hot* baking dish to a wire rack. Uncover and leave to cool for 10 minutes before serving by the big spoonful.

Beyond

- For a 3-litre cooker, you must use 250ml water, halve all the remaining ingredients and use a 1-litre, high-sided, round soufflé dish.

- There's no salt because of the butter, sausage and cheese. Add some at will, probably at the table.

- Instead of the sausage, substitute 340g bulk breakfast sausage or mild or hot Italian sausage meat (that is, any casings removed).

- Drizzle maple syrup over the servings.

1.5kg tart apples, such as Granny Smith, peeled, cored and chopped

250ml unsweetened apple juice

Up to 55g light brown sugar (optional)

1 tablespoon fresh lemon juice

½ teaspoon ground cinnamon

¼ teaspoon grated nutmeg

¼ teaspoon table salt

Spiced Applesauce

8 servings

Nothing beats *fresh*, warm applesauce, especially on a cold autumn morning. It's so easy to make that you may never go back to the ready-made stuff. But here's a warning. Pre-sliced apples won't work because they've softened and even dried out in storage. Their flavour may also have been compromised. Sorry about that. But if you're not going to open a jar, real applesauce is worth a little effort, no?

1. Stir all the ingredients in a **5.5-litre cooker** until the brown sugar dissolves. Lock the lid onto the pot.

2.

Set the machine	Level	The valve must be	Time	Press
PRESSURE COOK	MAX	—	4 minutes with the KEEP WARM setting off	START
PRESSURE COOK or MANUAL	HIGH	Closed	6 minutes with the KEEP WARM setting off	START
SLOW COOK	HIGH	Opened	3 hours with the KEEP WARM setting off (or on for no more than 2 hours)	START

3. If you've used a pressure setting, when the machine has finished cooking, turn it off and let its pressure **return to normal naturally**, about 25 minutes.

4. Unlatch the lid and open the cooker. Use a potato masher to pulverise the apples into sauce right in the cooker. Serve warm or pack into two litre-sized containers, seal and store in the fridge for up to 4 days, or in the freezer for up to 3 months.

Beyond

- For a 3-litre cooker, you must use 180ml unsweetened apple juice and halve the other ingredients.
- For a 7.5-litre cooker, increase all the ingredients by 50 per cent.
- Add 125g fresh raspberries or 200g fresh, pitted, sweet cherries to the mix.
- Serve with heaping spoonfuls of plain Greek yoghurt.

Dried Fruit Compote

4–6 servings

You can use any dried fruit for this compote, although we suggest using larger pieces rather than raisins or dried cranberries, which become a bit too soft during cooking. Notice that the mixture is only cooked under LOW pressure. Doing so preserves the texture of the fruit (but won't save the raisins, if you use them).

1. Mix all the ingredients in a **3-, 5.5- or 7.5-litre cooker** until the brown sugar dissolves. Lock the lid onto the pot.

2.

Set the machine	Level	The valve must be	Time	Press
PRESSURE COOK or MANUAL	LOW	Closed	4 minutes with the KEEP WARM setting off	START
SLOW COOK	HIGH	Opened	2 hours with the KEEP WARM setting off (or on for no more than 2 hours)	START

3. If you've used the pressure setting, when the machine has finished cooking, turn it off and let its pressure **return to normal naturally**, about 15 minutes.

4. Unlatch the lid and open the cooker. Find and discard the cinnamon stick. Stir well before serving. If desired, store in a sealed container or covered bowl in the fridge for up to 3 days. (The compote will then taste better after it's been warmed in the microwave.)

450g mixed dried fruit, such as pitted prunes, apricots, quartered pear halves and/ or quartered nectarines or peaches

250ml water

250ml unsweetened apple juice

115g light brown sugar

1 tablespoon fresh lemon juice

¼ teaspoon table salt

One 10cm cinnamon stick

Beyond

- Instead of using vanilla extract, halve a vanilla pod lengthways and add it to the pot with the other ingredients.

- For a more sophisticated take, substitute red wine for the water.

- For more punch, substitute a star anise pod for the cinnamon stick.

- Serve the warm compote over plain Greek yoghurt for breakfast, or over dollops of ricotta or scoops of vanilla ice cream for dessert.

2

Soups, Stocks and Infusions

If you're an Instant Pot novice, start here. A soup is the easiest way to introduce yourself to what the cooker can do. The large amount of liquid ensures there'll be plenty of steam; there are mostly no worries about delicate calibrations, so dinner is easy to accomplish; and you're relatively free to play around with ingredients.

Since this chapter also includes homemade stocks (even Ramen Broth!), we'd be remiss if we didn't talk a bit about stock and broth in general. We assume that you won't first make homemade stock for most of these recipes. You'll use ready-made, right? So here's another question. Have you ever tasted the stuff? We're amazed that so many people cook with this pantry staple yet have little understanding of what it tastes like.

If you want to take your cooking to the next level – and why not, since the Instant Pot makes it so easy? – invest a few pounds and buy five or six brands of, say, chicken stock. Put a little of each in separate cups, and barely warm them in the microwave before doing a side-by-side taste test. You'll discover one is too onion-y; another, too salty. One tastes like chicken; another, like a barnyard. One will be rich; another, watery. And since you're going all out, taste them side-by-side at room temperature, too. You'll soon know which suits your taste and which makes the best food for you and yours.

And since we're on this jag, let's add that you should do the same taste-testing with vegetable stocks, which have an even wider range of acceptable (and unacceptable) flavours. You might be surprised that a less expensive brand tastes better. Price is not a guarantee of quality. It may be a function of a celebrity's face.

And one last note on the matter of patience: even in the Instant Pot, soup takes time – not as much as it takes on the hob, but enough that dinner isn't a 5-minute job. It also shouldn't be a 5-minute stint at the table. Pour a glass of wine or iced tea. Settle in. Soup's on.

FAQs

1. Must I soak the dried beans?
For most of these recipes, yes. Soaked beans cook more quickly, whether under pressure or in the **SLOW COOK** mode. But more importantly, they cook more evenly and don't become as mushy since they're under pressure for less time.

That said, if soaked beans have not almost doubled in size from their dried state and if almost all of their wrinkles are not smoothed out, they may never get tender, no matter how long they endure the pot's pressure. Why? See the next answer.

2. What if the dried beans don't get tender in the time stated?
Here's some bad news. Dried beans do not move off store shelves quickly in our *I-want-it-now* world. The poor legumes hang out day after day, losing so much moisture through natural evaporation that they may not be tender in a recipe's stated time. You'll be able to tell if they're old by how they plump up after they have been left to soak.

If, however, the dried beans did plump up, yet you find they're still too tough for your taste when you open the pot, do not add any vinegar or salt as the recipe may require at this stage. Instead, lock the lid back onto the pot and give them another 4 minutes at **MAX** or 5 minutes at **HIGH**, followed again by which ever method of pressure release the recipe requires.

3. Can you oversoak beans?
Yes, dried beans can get waterlogged, particularly dried beans that are relatively 'fresh'. Reckon on 12 hours as the longest soak.

We may have just cramped your style. Most people want to do the soak overnight, even though they could just put the beans in water in the morning before they head off to the day. However, if you're an overnight fanatic, soak away, drain them in the morning, pour them into a large bowl, set a piece of clingfilm right against their surface to protect them from moisture loss, and set them in the fridge for up to 12 hours.

4. Why do some beef stews call for beef *or* chicken stock?
Decent chicken stock is relatively easy to find; acceptable beef stock, next to impossible. In most cases, packaged beef stock tastes like a bouillon cube soaked in murky water. Chicken stock usually has more oomph. (Beef trimmings, the sort to make stock, usually go to the dog-food industry, while chicken trimmings, not so much.) If you can find decent beef stock – or make your own (page 103) – you'll be well on your way to a better soup.

5. Why should I bother making my own stock?
There's nothing like homemade stock, not only on its own but as part of a recipe: an intense, deep and satisfying base for a stew or braise. Make stock and squirrel it away in the freezer, especially since the prep is so easy in an Instant Pot. Even if you substitute 250ml of homemade stock and use ready-made for the remainder of the amount called for, the results will be dramatically better.

6. And what's a *chinois*?
A racist, culinary nightmare. Also, it's the term for a conical sieve with a very fine mesh, so called in French (*shee-NWAH*) because it's said to look like a Chinese guy's hat. (See?) The gadget's also called a 'china cap' or a 'bouillon strainer' (probably in a bid for a more PC kitchen). A good *chinois* costs about 20 pounds. It's the best tool for straining out fine, particulate matter from any soup or stock. A decent substitute is a standard colander lined with a double thickness of muslin. But given that muslin can cost up to ten pounds a package, it's probably more economical to invest in the *chinois*.

Pesto Minestrone Soup

6 servings

This summer delight is a version of minestrone with the flavours of pesto, with lots of basil, some nuts, and even cheese stirred in at the end. We didn't sauté the onions and other vegetables first because we wanted a cleaner, brighter flavour. The soup's actually a bit sour, best on a warm evening (with a G&T – trust us). Calm it down with lots of crunchy bread to mop up every drop.

1. Mix the stock, beans, tomatoes, onion, carrots, celery, courgette, basil, walnuts, garlic, salt and crushed chilli flakes in a **5.5- or 7.5-litre cooker**. Stir in the pasta and lock the lid onto the pot.

2.

Set the machine	Level	The valve must be	Time	Press
PRESSURE COOK	MAX	—	6 minutes with the KEEP WARM setting off	START
SOUP/ BROTH, PRESSURE COOK or MANUAL	HIGH	Closed	8 minutes with the KEEP WARM setting off	START
SLOW COOK	HIGH	Opened	3 hours with the KEEP WARM setting off (or on KEEP WARM for no more than 2 hours)	START

3. If you've used a pressure-cooking setting, use the **quick-release method** to bring the pot's pressure back to normal.

4. Unlatch the lid and open the pot. Stir in the cheese, set the lid askew over the pot and set aside for about 5 minutes to blend the flavours.

1.75 litres vegetable stock

One 400g tin white beans, drained and rinsed

800g chopped fresh tomatoes

1 medium onion, chopped (160g prechopped)

260g chopped carrots

2 medium celery stalks, chopped

1 medium courgette, halved lengthways and thinly sliced into half-moons

30g fresh basil leaves, chopped

60g roughly chopped walnuts

Up to 3 medium garlic cloves, peeled and chopped (1 tablespoon prechopped)

1 teaspoon table salt

Up to ½ teaspoon crushed chilli flakes

55g regular, whole-wheat, or gluten-free elbow macaroni

55g finely grated Parmigiano-Reggiano

Beyond

- You must halve the recipe for a 3-litre cooker.
- Make the soup less sour by adding up to 1 tablespoon white granulated sugar with the vegetables.
- Substitute 40g pine nuts for the walnuts.
- Substitute 175g spiralised courgettes for the courgette slices.
- Finish the bowls with a drizzle of fine, aromatic olive oil.

2 tablespoons liquid fat
Choose from olive oil, any vegetable or grain oil, or almond oil.

155g chopped or thinly sliced (and trimmed as necessary) allium aromatics
Choose one or two from onions (of any sort), spring onions, shallots and/or leeks (white and pale green parts only, well washed).

175g chopped (and deseeded and/or trimmed as necessary) sturdier aromatics
Choose one or two from peppers of any colour, celery, fennel and/ or radishes.

1.5 litres vegetable stock

900g fresh tomatoes, stemmed and chopped
Use any variety, even cherry tomatoes – or a mixture of tomatoes – so long as they smell fresh and sweet.

15g chopped fresh herbs.
Choose one or even several from basil, dill, marjoram, oregano, parsley, rosemary, sage, savory, tarragon and/or thyme.

600g chopped (and trimmed as necessary) quick-cooking summer vegetables
Choose a big selection from corn kernels, green beans, runner beans, mange tout, sugar snap peas, beans, squash and/or courgettes.

1 teaspoon table salt

Road Map: Summer Vegetable Soup

6 servings

When farmers' markets are bursting with tomatoes and summer vegetables, here's a way to make a soup that fits the season. This recipe's a two-stepper, even if it's summer and you'd rather be outside. During the first cooking under pressure, the tomatoes break down into the broth as the herbs infuse it. Then the vegetables get added for a second, super quick blitz under pressure so they don't turn mushy. During this second round of pressure, do not use the MAX setting (if it's available with your model). Bring the pot to HIGH pressure, then immediately release the pressure to keep the summery vegetables crisp and flavourful.

The real key to success is to chop everything to the same size. All the aromatics and tomatoes should be in 1cm pieces and all the summer vegetables in about 2cm pieces.

Two particularly appealing herb combos are basil, tarragon and thyme, and dill, parsley and oregano.

1.

Press	Setting	Time	Press
SAUTÉ	MEDIUM, NORMAL or CUSTOM 150°C	10 minutes	START

2. Warm the oil in a **5.5- or 7.5-litre cooker** for a minute or two, then add both the allium and the sturdier aromatics. Cook, stirring often, until the allium aromatics begin to soften, 3–5 minutes. Stir in the stock, tomatoes and fresh herbs. Turn off the **SAUTÉ** function and lock the lid onto the pot.

3.

Set the machine	Level	The valve must be	Time	Press
PRESSURE COOK	MAX	——	10 minutes with the KEEP WARM setting off	START
SOUP/ BROTH, PRESSURE COOK or MANUAL	HIGH	Closed	14 minutes with the KEEP WARM setting off	START

4. When the machine has finished cooking, turn it off and let the pressure **return to normal naturally,** about 30 minutes. Unlatch the lid and open the pot. Stir in the quick-cooking summer vegetables. Lock the lid onto the pot.

5.

Set the machine	Level	The valve must be	Time	Press
PRESSURE COOK or MANUAL	HIGH	Closed	0 minutes with the KEEP WARM setting off	START

6. Use the **quick-release method** to bring the pot's pressure back to normal. Unlatch the lid and open the pot. Stir in the salt before serving.

Beyond

- You must halve the recipe for a 3-litre cooker.
- The best garnish on each serving is a highly flavourful olive oil.
- If you don't care about a vegan soup, use butter as the fat (and reduce the salt to ½ teaspoon).
- And grate lots of Parmigiano-Reggiano or pecorino over each bowlful.
- Or go all out and ladle the soup over big, crunchy croutons (see the *Beyond* section of the Beef Stew road map on page 345).

2 litres vegetable stock

800g chopped (peeled and/or deseeded as necessary) root vegetables

Choose one or several from butternut squash, carrots, celeriac, parsnips, potatoes of any variety, pumpkin, swede, winter squash of any variety and/or yellow beetroot.

155g chopped (and trimmed as necessary) allium aromatics

Choose one or a combo from onions (of any sort), shallots and/or leeks (white and pale green parts only, well washed).

60ml soy sauce, preferably reduced-sodium

30g small dried mushrooms, crumbled

Choose any sort from porcini, shiitake, chanterelle, morels or even a ready-made blend – but avoid large, dried mushrooms (like wood ear mushrooms), often found at Asian markets.

1½ tablespoons dried herbs

Choose dried basil, coriander, oregano, rosemary and/or thyme, or a ready-made herb blend like an Italian blend or herbes de Provence.

Up to 3 medium garlic cloves, peeled and chopped (1 tablespoon prechopped)

50g chopped stemmed greens

Choose one or several from kale, spring greens, escarole, mustard greens and/or turnip greens.

Road Map: Winter Vegetable Soup

6–8 servings

This road map is designed to create a root vegetable soup with leafy greens in the mixture. There are no tomatoes, of course. (Who's ever heard of a good tomato in December? And be quiet, if you live in Southern California.) Make sure you chop the root vegetables into 2.5cm pieces.

If you buy them prechopped from the produce section, you'll probably need to chop them more to get the right size. (Unless you have a vegetable concierge at your supermarket. Again, you Southern Californians need to be quiet.)

We listed some more common leafy greens. Use what you find, from dandelion greens to Chinese flowering broccoli. If you want to go all out, stop by an Asian supermarket some time to see the incredible range of leafy greens available. However, skip over chard, beetroot greens and any baby greens for this soup. They turn too squishy.

1. Mix the stock, root vegetables, allium aromatics, soy sauce, dried mushrooms, herbs and garlic in a **5.5- or 7.5-litre cooker.** Lock the lid onto the pot.

2.

Set the machine	Level	The valve must be	Time	Press
PRESSURE COOK	MAX	——	10 minutes with the KEEP WARM setting off	START
SOUP/BROTH, PRESSURE COOK or MANUAL	HIGH	Closed	12 minutes with the KEEP WARM setting off	START

3. Use the **quick-release method** to bring the pot's pressure back to normal. Unlatch the lid and open the pot.

4. Stir in the stemmed greens. Lock the lid back onto the pot.

5.

Set the machine	Level	The valve must be	Time	Press
PRESSURE COOK or MANUAL	HIGH	Closed	0 minutes with the KEEP WARM setting off	START

6. Use the **quick-release method** to bring the the pressure back to normal. Unlatch the lid and open the pot.
Stir well before serving.

Beyond

- You must halve the recipe for a 3-litre cooker.
- For a simpler soup without the greens, simply omit steps 4, 5 and 6.
- Unfortunately, red beetroot turns the soup a lurid colour. Maybe you don't mind. Our linens did.
- For heat, add up to 1½ teaspoons crushed chilli flakes with the dried herbs.
- The second cooking is designed to keep some chew in the greens. If you like softer greens, use a natural release in step 6.
- If you don't care about this soup being vegan, toss an 8cm piece of Parmesan rind into the pot with the root vegetables and place a poached egg in each serving.

30g butter

2 thick-cut rashers of streaky bacon, chopped

1 medium onion, chopped (160g prechopped)

1 medium potato (about 175g), peeled and cut into 2.5cm pieces

3 medium tart green apples, such as Granny Smith, peeled, cored and cut into 2.5cm pieces

½ teaspoon caraway seeds

½ teaspoon dried thyme

Up to ½ teaspoon table salt

½ teaspoon ground black pepper

1 litre vegetable stock

125ml double cream

2 teaspoons cornflour

Potato, Bacon and Apple Chowder

6 *servings*

Yep, we put apples in chowder. They add an essential sweetness that pairs well with bacon in this easy soup, a welcome lunch or dinner in cooler weather. The potatoes are not cooked until they can be puréed, but rather just until tender.

Do not use flavoured bacon here, or even pepper bacon. The soup needs a cleaner flavour profile to let the potatoes shine through.

1.

Press	Setting	Time	Press
SAUTÉ	MEDIUM, NORMAL or CUSTOM 150°C	10 minutes	START

2. Melt the butter in a **5.5- or 7.5-litre cooker**. Add the bacon pieces and cook, stirring often, until well browned, about 3 minutes. Add the onion and continue cooking, stirring more often, until the onion begins to soften, about 3 minutes.

3. Stir in the potato, apples, caraway seeds, thyme, salt and pepper. Pour in the stock and scrape up *every speck of browned stuff* on the pot's bottom. Turn off the **SAUTÉ** function and lock the lid onto the pot.

4.

Set the machine	Level	The valve must be	Time	Press
PRESSURE COOK	MAX	——	5 minutes with the KEEP WARM setting off	START
SOUP/BROTH, PRESSURE COOK or MANUAL	HIGH	Closed	7 minutes with the KEEP WARM setting off	START
SLOW COOK	HIGH	Opened	3 hours with the KEEP WARM setting off (or on for no more than 2 hours)	START

5. If you've used a pressure-cooking setting, use the **quick-release method** to bring the pot's pressure back to normal.

6. Unlatch the lid and open the pot. Whisk the cream and cornflour in a small bowl until smooth.

7.

Press	Setting	Time	Press
SAUTÉ	MEDIUM, NORMAL or CUSTOM 150°C	5 minutes	START

8. Bring the soup to a low simmer, stirring constantly. Add the cream slurry and continue cooking, stirring constantly, until thickened, about 1 minute. Turn off the **SAUTÉ** function and immediately remove the *hot* insert from the pot to stop any cooking. Serve warm.

Beyond

- You must halve the recipe for a 3-litre cooker.
- Add up to 2 thinly sliced celery stalks with the onion.
- And/or add up to 2 medium garlic cloves, peeled and chopped (2 teaspoons prechopped), with the onion.
- Stir up to 200g corn kernels (thawed if frozen) into the soup with the cream slurry.
- Use chicken stock for a much richer soup.

1.5 litres chicken or vegetable stock

1.3kg baking potatoes, peeled and chopped

1 small onion, chopped (80g prechopped)

40g butter, cut into 3 pieces

½ teaspoon table salt

½ teaspoon ground black pepper

125ml regular or low-fat soured cream

115g regular or low-fat cream cheese, cut into small bits

At least 2 tablespoons whole or low-fat milk, plus more as needed

Grated Cheddar cheese for garnishing

Finely chopped spring onions, preferably just the green part, for garnishing

Loaded Baking Potato Soup

6 servings

For this baking-potato-in-a-bowl, you must only use baking potatoes. Only these have the right amount of starch to make a soup that tastes like the classic steakhouse side. And you must chop those potatoes. Yes, it's a pain. Here's how to work efficiently. Peel them, then slice them into discs 1cm in thickness. Cut these into 1cm strips, gather them together, and cut these strips into 1cm pieces.

Because potatoes endure long transport and often sit on the store's shelf a good while, there's no real way to judge how much internal moisture each holds. We give the amount of milk as a mere suggestion. In the end, you'll need to add enough to get the consistency you like – much looser than mashed potatoes, of course, but maybe not as loose as a more traditional soup.

1. Mix the stock, potatoes, onion, butter, salt and pepper in a **5.5- or 7.5-litre cooker**. Lock the lid onto the pot.

2.

Set the machine	Level	The valve must be	Time	Press
PRESSURE COOK	MAX	—	10 minutes with the KEEP WARM setting off	START
SOUP/ BROTH, PRESSURE COOK or MANUAL	HIGH	Closed	13 minutes with the KEEP WARM setting off	START

3. Use the **quick-release method** to bring the pot's pressure back to normal. Unlatch the lid and open the pot. Use a potato masher or the back of a wooden spoon to mash the potatoes into a coarse purée. (Do not use a hand blender or even a regular blender to purée the soup as both will cool it down too quickly.) Without delay, whisk in the soured cream and cream cheese until smooth.

4. Add 2 tablespoons milk and whisk for a creamy consistency, adding more milk as needed to get your preferred texture. Serve in bowls, garnished with the Cheddar and spring onions.

Beyond

• You must halve the recipe for a 3-litre cooker.

• To take the soup to another level, also garnish the servings with crumbled, crisp-fried streaky bacon.

• Or offer unexpected garnishes like pickled jalapeño rings, sliced avocado and/or jarred pickled cocktail onions.

• If you're feeling luxurious, substitute single or double cream for the milk.

Kale-Is-the-New-Black Soup

6 servings

No doubt, kale's hip. Better, it's easy in this recipe, since you can use bagged, chopped kale. (Don't use baby kale, which will overcook.)

Of course, you can also use fresh whole leaves, particularly the more tender ones you can find at a farmers' market. Try red Russian, Toscano, scarlet or red Ursa varieties.

The best way to wash whole kale leaves is to fill a clean kitchen sink with cool water, add stemmed leaves and agitate the water a little. Let the leaves rest in the water for 5 minutes as the grit floats down, then skim them off the top of the water before pulling the plug to drain away the water and grit.

For this recipe, brown the onions and cook the vegetables a little longer than you might usually, mostly to give these ingredients a deep, complex flavour to pair with the earthy, slightly bitter kale, which is itself cooked for a fairly long time to soften it considerably. A garnish of soy sauce brings everything into a more savoury balance.

2 tablespoons olive oil

1 medium onion, chopped (160g prechopped)

1 small fennel bulb, trimmed and chopped

2 medium garlic cloves, peeled and chopped (2 teaspoons prechopped)

130g chopped stemmed kale

1.5 litres vegetable stock

One 400g tin chopped tomatoes

2 medium potatoes (about 140g each), diced

2 tablespoons fresh rosemary leaves, chopped

2 tablespoons fresh sage leaves, chopped

Soy sauce for garnishing

1.

Press	Setting	Time	Press
SAUTÉ	MEDIUM, NORMAL or CUSTOM 150°C	15 minutes	START

2. Warm the oil in a **5.5- or 7.5-litre cooker** for a minute or two. Add the onion and fennel. Cook, stirring often, until the onion starts to get a little brown and even sweet, about 10 minutes. Stir in the garlic for a few seconds.

3. Add the kale. Stir well and continue cooking, stirring occasionally, until the greens wilt, about 3 minutes. Pour in the stock and scrape up the browned bits on the bottom of the pot. Turn off the **SAUTÉ** function and stir in the tomatoes, potatoes, rosemary and sage. Lock the lid onto the pot.

4.

Set the machine	Level	The valve must be	Time	Press
PRESSURE COOK	MAX	—	10 minutes with the KEEP WARM setting off	START
SOUP/ BROTH, PRESSURE COOK or MANUAL	HIGH	Closed	14 minutes with the KEEP WARM setting off	START

5. Use the **quick-release method** to bring the pot's pressure back to normal. Unlatch the lid and open the pot. Stir well, then ladle into bowls, garnishing each with a little soy sauce.

Beyond

- You must halve the recipe for a 3-litre cooker.

- For heat, add up to 1 teaspoon crushed chilli flakes with the herbs.

- For a brighter flavour, add up to 2 teaspoons finely grated lemon zest with the herbs.

- If you don't need the soup to be vegan, use chicken stock for a bolder flavour and feel free to add up to 225g very thin slices of smoked kielbasa, bratwurst or chorizo with the kale.

1 large fennel bulb
(about 900g), trimmed
and chopped

1 litre vegetable stock

Two 400g tins
chopped tomatoes

1 medium onion, chopped
(160g prechopped)

75g sultanas

45ml white wine vinegar

2 tablespoons light
brown sugar

1 teaspoon dried dill

1 teaspoon caraway seeds

½ teaspoon celery seeds

½ teaspoon table salt

Not-Your-Jewish-Grandmother's Sweet-and-Sour Soup

6 servings

Back in the day (and on Delancey Street), a soup made with cabbage, tomatoes and sultanas was a standby, making an appearance at many a Shabbos dinner. We've updated the classic by substituting fennel for the cabbage. Cabbage can be, well, bland, but fennel gives the soup an aromatic hit, sort of like a big dose of celery with many herbaceous notes.

As you can imagine, the flavours are bright, even a little acidic, best on a summer evening when fennel is fresh at the farmers' market. (And best with a pale ale or a Hefeweizen.)

1. Mix all the ingredients in a **5.5- or 7.5-litre cooker**. Lock the lid onto the pot.

2.

Set the machine	Level	The valve must be	Time	Press
PRESSURE COOK	MAX	—	15 minutes with the KEEP WARM setting off	START
SOUP/ BROTH, PRESSURE COOK or MANUAL	HIGH	Closed	20 minutes with the KEEP WARM setting off	START

3. Use the **quick-release method** to bring the pot's pressure back to normal. Unlatch the lid and open the pot. Set aside for 5 minutes to cool a bit, then stir well before serving.

Beyond

- You must halve the recipe for a 3-litre cooker.
- Garnish the servings with a drizzle of aromatic olive oil.
- And/or garnish with finely grated Parmigiano-Reggiano or pecorino.
- To make a more traditional cabbage soup, substitute 300g cored and chopped cabbage for the fennel.
- Soups like this one often included beef, particularly flanken (beef short ribs cut across the bones or 'Korean-style'). To do that here, put up to 450g beef flanken and the stock in the pot and cook at MAX for 37 minutes or HIGH at 45 minutes, followed by a natural release. Open the pot, then continue with the recipe as written from step 1 (having already used the stated amount of stock).

The New Standard Cabbage Soup

6 servings

Here's our dressed-up version of the old-world cabbage soup that was transformed with fennel in the previous recipe. We've again modernised it, this time with apple, orange zest and cinnamon, all to get more flavour in every bowl, a noble goal.

Unfortunately, you can't use bagged shredded cabbage here. The strands are so thin, they'll turn into baby food under pressure. Halve a fresh cabbage, core it, then cut each half into slices 1cm in thickness, which you can then cut crossways into strips 1cm thick.

1.

Press	Setting	Time	Press
SAUTÉ	MEDIUM, NORMAL or CUSTOM 150°C	10 minutes	START

2. Warm the oil in a **5.5- or 7.5-litre cooker** for a minute or two. Add the bacon and cook, stirring occasionally, until lightly browned, about 4 minutes. Add the onion and carrot; continue cooking, stirring more often, until the onion begins to soften, about 3 minutes.

3. Stir in the cabbage and cook, stirring all the while, until it begins to wilt, about 2 minutes. Pour in the stock and scrape up any browned bits on the bottom of the pot. Turn off the **SAUTÉ** function. Stir in the apple, vinegar, brown sugar, orange zest, nutmeg, black pepper, bay leaves and cinnamon stick until the sugar dissolves. Lock the lid onto the pot.

4.

Set the machine	Level	The valve must be	Time	Press
PRESSURE COOK	MAX	——	20 minutes with the KEEP WARM setting off	START
SOUP/ BROTH, PRESSURE COOK or MANUAL	HIGH	Closed	28 minutes with the KEEP WARM setting off	START
SLOW COOK	HIGH	Opened	4 hours with the KEEP WARM setting off (or on for no more than 3 hours)	START

5. If you've used a pressure-cooking setting, use the **quick-release method** to bring the pot's pressure back to normal.

6. Unlatch the lid and open the pot. Find and discard the bay leaves and cinnamon stick. Stir the soup well before serving.

1 tablespoon vegetable, corn or rapeseed oil

175g thin-cut rashers of pork, turkey or beef bacon, chopped

1 medium red onion, chopped (160g prechopped)

130g chopped carrots

1 medium green or red cabbage (about 700g), cored and thinly sliced into strips

1½ litres chicken stock

1 medium tart green apple, such as Granny Smith, peeled, cored and chopped

60ml apple cider vinegar

2 tablespoons dark brown sugar

1 tablespoon finely grated orange zest

½ teaspoon grated nutmeg

½ teaspoon ground black pepper

2 bay leaves

One 10cm cinnamon stick

Beyond

- You must halve the recipe for a 3-litre cooker.

- For a richer soup, substitute up to 30g butter for the oil.

- Dollop the servings with soured cream, or soured cream mixed with snipped chives.

1 litre water

800g plum or Roma tomatoes

1 medium onion, chopped (160g prechopped)

90g dried wheat berries, preferably soft white wheat berries

80g sun-dried tomatoes packed in oil, chopped

2 tablespoons packed oregano leaves, finely chopped

1 tablespoon packed rosemary leaves, finely chopped

2 medium garlic cloves, peeled and finely chopped (2 teaspoons prechopped)

Up to 1 teaspoon table salt

½ teaspoon fennel seeds

½ teaspoon ground black pepper

Tomato and Wheat Berry Soup

4–6 servings

Whole grains are terrific in soups, although some people remain afraid of wheat berries in a pressure cooker. Perhaps they once used a **quick-release method** at the end of cooking and splattered their kitchen cabinets with wheaty gunk. Those people also forgot the basic safety mechanism for cooking whole grains under pressure: add a little fat. Here, the oil from the sun-dried tomatoes helps keep the wheat berries from foaming by breaking the surface tension in the liquid so bubbles cannot easily form. Ta da: a rich, summery-yet-whole-grain soup.

1. Mix all the ingredients in a 5.5- or 7.5-litre cooker. Lock the lid onto the pot.

2.

Set the machine	Level	The valve must be	Time	Press
PRESSURE COOK	MAX	—	35 minutes with the KEEP WARM setting off	START
HIGH PRESSURE or MANUAL	HIGH	Closed	45 minutes with the KEEP WARM setting off	START

3. When the machine has finished cooking, turn it off and let its pressure **return to normal naturally**, about 25 minutes. Unlatch the lid and open the pot. Stir well before serving.

Beyond

- You must halve the recipe for a 3-litre cooker.

- For a richer (not vegan) soup, slice some chorizo into discs 1cm thick and stir them into the soup with the other ingredients.

- Or throw the small rind from a chunk of Parmigiano-Reggiano into the pot with the other ingredients. Or just grate lots of Parmigiano-Reggiano over each serving.

- For a gluten-free version, use certified gluten-free oat groats for the wheat berries. Increase the time under MAX to 43 minutes or HIGH pressure to 55 minutes.

Road Map: Creamy Vegetable Soup

4–6 servings

Here's culinary magic we can't conjure in a saucepan. By adding bicarbonate of soda, we actually change the pH of butter so that the milk solids don't burn while they're under pressure. We can then *poach* vegetables in butter, a trick we can never perform on the hob but only in a pressure cooker. The result is an intensely creamy soup without a smidgen of cream. Make several batches during a weekend cooking spree and get them into the freezer in individual servings. You'll have a fabulous dinner anytime you want to stream half a season of something.

1.

Press	Setting	Time	Press
SAUTÉ	MEDIUM, NORMAL or CUSTOM 150°C	5 minutes	START

2. Melt the butter in a **3- or 5.5-litre cooker.** Add the chopped vegetable and stir until fully coated in the butter. Turn off the **SAUTÉ** function. Add the salt, dried spice(s) and bicarbonate of soda. Stir well, pour the water over everything, and lock the lid onto the pot.

3.

Set the machine	Level	The valve must be	Time	Press
PRESSURE COOK	MAX	—	10 minutes with the KEEP WARM setting off	START
SOUP/ BROTH, PRESSURE COOK or MANUAL	HIGH	Closed	12 minutes with the KEEP WARM setting off	START

4. Use the **quick-release method** to bring the pot's pressure back to normal. Unlatch the lid and open the cooker. Pour in the liquid, then use a hand blender right in the pot to purée the soup until smooth. Serve warm.

100g butter, cut into chunks

500–600g chopped vegetable

Choose from 4cm cauliflower florets, 4cm broccoli florets and stems, 2.5cm peeled sweet potato cubes, 2.5cm peeled celeriac cubes, 2.5cm peeled turnip cubes, 2.5cm peeled swede cubes, or 2.5cm peeled and deseeded winter or butternut squash cubes.

½ teaspoon table salt

½ teaspoon dried spice or spice blend

Choose one from grated nutmeg, ground caraway, ground cardamom, ground cinnamon, ground cumin, sage, thyme, garam masala, curry powder or other spice blends.

¼ teaspoon bicarbonate of soda

60ml water

600ml liquid

Choose chicken, beef or vegetable stock, or a combo of 500ml stock and 100ml dry white wine.

Beyond

- For a 7.5-litre cooker, you must increase all the ingredients by 50 per cent.

- For an even creamier texture, add up to 125ml double cream before you purée the soup. Simmer for 1 minute with the SAUTÉ function on LOW or LESS if you don't like the taste of raw cream.

- If you don't have a hand blender, pour the soup in batches into a blender, cover, remove the centre knob of the lid, lay a clean tea towel over the opening and blend until smooth, eventually getting all the batches into a large bowl and stirring them together.

- For a cleaner flavour, omit the dried spice or spice blend.

450g dried medium-sized beans

Choose one or two from Anazasi, appaloosa, azuki, bolita, calypso, cannellini, cranberry, haricot, butter, mortgage runner, pinto, rattlesnake, red, red kidney, scarlet runner, Steuben yellow, Tolosana and/or trout beans.

2 tablespoons fat

Choose from vegetable oil, corn oil, rapeseed oil, safflower oil, olive oil, grapeseed oil, walnut oil, pecan oil, butter, coconut oil, rendered bacon fat, schmaltz or lard.

300g chopped aromatic vegetables

Choose two to make up the total volume from onions (of any sort), shallots, leeks (white and pale green parts only, well washed), spring onions, stemmed, deseeded and cored peppers of any variety, celery, carrots and/or trimmed fennel.

Up to 2 tablespoons dried herbs or spices

Choose two or three to make up the total volume from ground allspice, ground cinnamon, ground cumin, coriander seeds, dried basil, dried marjoram, dried oregano, dried rosemary, dried sage, dried savory and/or dried thyme.

2 litres stock

Use any sort.

2 tablespoons acid

Choose from lemon juice, lime juice or vinegar of any sort.

½ teaspoon table salt

Road Map: Bean Soup

6–8 servings

There are a few things a pressure cooker seems to be made for. Pinhead oatmeal? Sure thing. Beef short ribs? You bet. And bean soup. There's nothing like it. The tender beans release enough starch to enrich the mix, making pure comfort food.

Although this road map lets you concoct your own version, we find the best herb/spice combinations involve more dried, leafy herbs and fewer dried spices, for example, 1 tablespoon dried sage, 2 teaspoons dried thyme and 1 teaspoon ground cinnamon; or 2 teaspoons dried oregano, 2 teaspoons dried rosemary, 1 teaspoon ground allspice and 1 teaspoon coriander seeds. Really, the only way to tell which blend you like is to do exactly what we do when we're recipe-testing: hold the bottles together under your nose and gently inhale.

1. Place the dried beans in a large bowl, fill it with cool water and leave to soak overnight, for at least 8 hours or up to 12 hours.

2.

Press	Setting	Time	Press
SAUTÉ	MEDIUM, NORMAL or CUSTOM 150°C	10 minutes	START

3. Warm the oil or melt the solid fat in a **5.5- or 7.5-litre cooker**. Add the aromatic vegetables and cook, stirring often, until they begin to soften, about 4 minutes. Add the dried herbs or spices; cook until aromatic, stirring all the while, just a few seconds.

4. Pour in the stock and scrape up any browned bits on the pot's bottom. Turn off the **SAUTÉ** function. Drain the beans in a colander set in the sink, then stir them into the pot. Lock the lid onto the cooker.

5.

Set the machine	Level	The valve must be	Time	Press
PRESSURE COOK	MAX	——	15 minutes with the KEEP WARM setting off	START
SOUP/ BROTH, PRESSURE COOK or MANUAL	HIGH	Closed	20 minutes with the KEEP WARM setting off	START
SLOW COOK	HIGH	Opened	4 hours with the KEEP WARM setting off (or on for no more than 2 hours)	START

6. If you've used a pressure setting, when the machine has finished cooking, turn it off and let its pressure **return to normal naturally**, about 40 minutes. Unlatch the lid and open the cooker. Stir in the acid and salt before serving.

Beyond

- You must halve the recipe for a 3-litre cooker.

- There are no black turtle beans in this road map. They cook a bit differently. Use the method given here but use the quick-release method to return the machine's pressure to normal after cooking.

- If you'd like to skip the experiment with the herbs and spices, simply use a bottled spice blend.

- For more oomph, add up to 2 bay leaves with the herbs and spices. Or 1 star anise pod. And/or up to 1 teaspoon crushed chilli flakes.

- For a meaty bean soup, complete the recipe through adding the stock to the pot in step 4. At this point, add your choice of 1 lamb shank, trimmed; 1 veal shank; 1 beef shin; up to 350g beef flanken; 1 fresh or smoked pork hock; *or* 2 turkey wings (smoked or not), cut into their individual segments. (Remember that smoked meats can be very salty.) Lock the lid onto the pot and put it under MAX pressure for 30 minutes or HIGH pressure for 40 minutes, followed by a quick release. Now add the soaked beans and carry on with the recipe as stated (leaving the meat in the pot). At the end of all the cooking, take the meat out of the pot, shred the meat off the bone and stir the shredded meat back into the soup.

450g dried black turtle beans

1½ tablespoons vegetable, corn or rapeseed oil

2 medium green peppers, stemmed, cored and chopped (350g prechopped)

1 large onion, chopped (240g prechopped)

280g smoked kielbasa, cut into 2.5cm pieces

2 medium garlic cloves, peeled and finely chopped (2 teaspoons prechopped)

2 teaspoons ground cumin

2 teaspoons dried oregano

2 teaspoons dried thyme

1 teaspoon ground allspice

½ teaspoon ground black pepper

1.5 litres chicken stock

2 tablespoons fresh lime juice

Black Turtle Bean and Kielbasa Soup

6–8 servings

Black turtle beans need special attention, so we crafted this recipe to highlight their decidedly sweet flavour, pairing them with lots of vegetables, smoked sausage and spices. The soup will be fairly thin when it's finished. If you want to thicken it, scoop out 170g cooked beans with some of the liquid and purée in a small blender or food processor until smooth, then stir it back into the pot.

1. Pour the beans into a large bowl, fill it with cool water and leave to soak at room temperature overnight, for at least 8 hours or up to 12 hours. Drain the beans in a large colander set in the sink.

2.

Press	Setting	Time	Press
SAUTÉ	MEDIUM, NORMAL or CUSTOM 150°C	10 minutes	START

3. Warm the oil in a **5.5- or 7.5-litre cooker** for a minute or two. Add the chopped peppers and onion; cook, stirring often, until the onion begins to soften, about 4 minutes. Add the sausage and cook, stirring once in a while, just until lightly browned, about 3 minutes.

4. Stir in the garlic, cumin, oregano, thyme, allspice and pepper until aromatic, just a few seconds. Pour in the stock and scrape up any browned bits on the pot's bottom. Turn off the **SAUTÉ** function, stir in the drained beans and lock the lid onto the pot.

5.

Set the machine	Level	The valve must be	Time	Press
PRESSURE COOK	MAX	—	15 minutes with the KEEP WARM setting off	START
SOUP/ BROTH, PRESSURE COOK or MANUAL	HIGH	Closed	20 minutes with the KEEP WARM setting off	START
SLOW COOK	HIGH	Opened	4 hours with the KEEP WARM setting off (or on for no more than 2 hours)	START

6. If you've used a pressure setting, when the machine has finished cooking, use the **quick-release method** to return its pressure to normal.

7. Unlatch the lid and open the pot. Stir in the lime juice and serve hot.

Beyond

- You must halve the recipe for a 3-litre cooker.
- Substitute chorizo for the smoked sausage. Also add 1 tablespoon mild smoked paprika with the other spices.
- Garnish with soured cream or chopped avocado, as well as finely chopped red onion and coriander leaves. Even top with grated Cheddar cheese.

Southern Black-Eye Bean Soup

6–8 servings

Black-eye beans don't need to be soaked before going under pressure. (When soaked, they turn too mealy.) Without that additional effort, we felt free to craft a slightly more complicated recipe. First, we make a rich base by cooking a ham hock for a good while, mostly to get all its flavour into the broth. Then we put the remaining ingredients in the pot for a second, quicker cooking.

By the way, you can complete the recipe through step 3 in advance. Pour the cooked broth and hock into a large bowl, cover and refrigerate for up to 2 days. There's no need to return them to room temperature before proceeding with the remainder of the recipe.

1. Pour the stock into a **5.5- or 7.5-litre cooker.** Add the hock and lock the lid onto the pot.

2.

Set the machine	Level	The valve must be	Time	Press
PRESSURE COOK	MAX	——	45 minutes with the KEEP WARM setting off	START
SOUP/ BROTH, PRESSURE COOK or MANUAL	HIGH	Closed	1 hour with the KEEP WARM setting off	START

3. Use the **quick-release method** to bring the pot's pressure back to normal. Unlatch the lid and open the pot. Stir in the black-eye beans, onion, celery, green pepper, rosemary, sage, thyme, pepper and bay leaves. Lock the lid back onto the pot.

4.

Set the machine	Level	The valve must be	Time	Press
PRESSURE COOK	MAX	——	18 minutes with the KEEP WARM setting off	START
SOUP/ BROTH, PRESSURE COOK or MANUAL	HIGH	Closed	25 minutes with the KEEP WARM setting off	START

5. Again use the **quick-release method** to bring the pot's pressure back to normal. Unlatch the lid and open the pot. Find and discard the bay leaves. Transfer the hock to a chopping board and set the lid askew over the pot. Cool the hock for a few minutes, then shred the meat from the bones. Stir the meat and the vinegar into the soup to serve.

1.75 litres chicken stock

1 smoked ham hock (about 350g)

450g dried black-eye beans

1 medium onion, chopped (160g prechopped)

4 medium celery stalks, thinly sliced

1 medium green pepper, stemmed, cored and chopped (175g prechopped)

1 teaspoon dried rosemary

1 teaspoon dried sage

1 teaspoon dried thyme

½ teaspoon ground black pepper

2 bay leaves

2 tablespoons apple cider vinegar

Beyond

- Because of the size of the hock, this recipe doesn't work well in a 3-litre cooker.

- The hock provides plenty of salt to the dish. Offer more at the table, preferably sea salt flakes.

- Hocks come with the skin attached. We like to chop it up after cooking and add it back into the soup with the meat. If doing so disgusts you (seriously?), discard the skin before chopping the meat.

- Add up to 130g chopped carrots with the other vegetables.

- Omit the rosemary and substitute a star anise pod for the bay leaves.

450g dried pinto beans

1.5 litres vegetable stock

1 large red onion, chopped
(240g prechopped)

2 large carrots,
very thinly sliced

1 small, thin-skinned orange,
preferably a Valencia
orange, chopped (rind
intact) and pips removed

3 tablespoons packed fresh
oregano leaves

2 tablespoons sultanas

1 teaspoon ground cumin

1 teaspoon table salt

½ teaspoon ground cinnamon

½ teaspoon ground
black pepper

Pinto Bean and (a Whole!) Orange Soup

6–8 servings

Indeed, this soup includes a *whole* orange. Chopped up, too. It's another trick you can't accomplish on the hob. The rind softens under pressure without becoming bitter. In fact, it will almost melt and give the soup a spark of bright flavour. We'll admit that this recipe was a bit of a revelation when we were testing for this book: savoury/sweet, mellow and absurdly good with a drizzle of balsamic vinegar and lots of ground black pepper over each bowlful.

1. Pour the beans into a large bowl, fill it with cool water and leave to soak at room temperature overnight, for at least 8 hours or up to 12 hours.

2. Drain the beans in a large colander set in the sink; pour them into a **5.5- or 7.5-litre cooker**. Stir in the stock, onion, carrots, orange, oregano, sultanas, cumin, salt, cinnamon and black pepper. Lock the lid onto the pot.

3.

Set the machine	Level	The valve must be	Time	Press
PRESSURE COOK	MAX	——	18 minutes with the KEEP WARM setting off	START
SOUP/ BROTH, PRESSURE COOK or MANUAL	HIGH	Closed	20 minutes with the KEEP WARM setting off	START

4. Use the **quick-release method** to bring the pot's pressure back to normal. Unlatch the lid and open the pot. Serve hot.

Beyond

- You must halve the recipe for a 3-litre cooker.

- For a sweet-and-sour soup, open the pot after cooking and stir in 2 tablespoons apple cider vinegar and 2 tablespoons orange marmalade until it melts.

- Garnish the servings with soured cream and finely snipped chives, maybe even dusted with a little more ground cinnamon.

Pinto Bean and (Heaps of!) Bacon Soup

6–8 servings

When it comes to bacon, why go halfway? Sure, you could cut back on the bacon here, to 175g or so. But honestly, the flavour will be tamed by either the pressure or the slow cook. You might as well follow us up and over the top of this bacon mountain. That said, for a (slightly) healthier soup, spoon out all but 2 tablespoons rendered fat before adding the vegetables.

1. Pour the beans into a large bowl, fill it with cool water and leave to soak at room temperature to soak overnight, for at least 8 hours or up to 12 hours.

2.

Press	Setting	Time	Press
SAUTÉ	CUSTOM 150°C	15 minutes	START

3. Melt the butter in a **5.5- or 7.5-litre cooker**. Add the bacon and cook, stirring often, until browned but not crisp, about 5 minutes. Add the chopped peppers, onion and garlic. Continue cooking, stirring often, until the onion begins to soften, about 4 minutes. Stir in the sage, thyme and pepper until aromatic, just a few seconds.

4. Pour in the wine and scrape up *every speck of browned stuff* on the pot's bottom. Turn off the **SAUTÉ** function and pour in the stock. Stir well and lock the lid onto the cooker.

5.

Set the machine	Level	The valve must be	Time	Press
PRESSURE COOK	MAX	——	15 minutes with the KEEP WARM setting off	START
SOUP/ BROTH, PRESSURE COOK or MANUAL	HIGH	Closed	20 minutes with the KEEP WARM setting off	START
SLOW COOK	HIGH	Opened	4 hours with the KEEP WARM setting off (or on for no more than 2 hours)	START

6. If you've used a pressure setting, when the machine has finished cooking, turn it off and let the pressure **return to normal naturally**, about 35 minutes.

7. Unlatch the lid and open the pot. Stir the soup well before serving.

450g dried pinto beans

15g butter

280g thin slices of pork or turkey bacon, chopped

2 medium yellow peppers, stemmed, cored and chopped (350g prechopped)

1 large onion, chopped (240g prechopped)

2 medium garlic cloves, peeled and finely chopped (2 teaspoons prechopped)

2 teaspoons dried sage

1½ teaspoons dried thyme

½ teaspoon ground black pepper

250ml dry white wine, such as Chardonnay

1.25 litres chicken or vegetable stock

Beyond

- You must halve the recipe for a 3-litre cooker.
- To omit the wine, substitute 160ml unsweetened apple juice and increase the stock to 1.5 litres.
- Add ½ teaspoon ground allspice with the sage and thyme.
- Add up to 2 teaspoons crushed chilli flakes with the herbs.
- For a more well-stocked stew, stir up to 60g baby rocket into the pot after cooking under pressure. Set aside with the lid askew over the pot for 5 minutes to wilt the greens.

450g dried butter beans

2 tablespoons olive oil

450g spicy pork or turkey Italian sausage, cut into 2.5cm pieces

2 medium onions, chopped (320g prechopped)

1.5 litres chicken stock

4 fresh oregano sprigs

350g chopped kale leaves

1 tablespoon fresh lemon juice

Butter Bean, Kale and Sausage Soup

6–8 servings

Butter beans' mild, slightly sweet, but still decidedly neutral taste makes them a flavour sponge. In this recipe, we've paired them with spicy Italian sausage to make a well-stocked soup reminiscent of a Sicilian braise.

1. Pour the beans into a large bowl, fill the bowl with cool water, and leave to soak overnight, for at least 8 hours or up to 12 hours.

2.

Press	Setting	Time	Press
SAUTÉ	MEDIUM, NORMAL or CUSTOM 150°C	10 minutes	START

3. Warm the oil in a **5.5- or 7.5-litre cooker** for a minute or two. Add the sausage pieces and brown *well*, stirring occasionally, about 6 minutes. Transfer the pieces to a nearby bowl.

4. Add the onion and cook, stirring often, until softened, about 3 minutes. Pour in the stock and scrape up *every speck of browned stuff* on the pot's bottom. Turn off the **SAUTÉ** function. Drain the beans and add them to the pot along with all the sausage in the bowl and the oregano sprigs. Lock the lid onto the pot.

5.

Set the machine	Level	The valve must be	Time	Press
PRESSURE COOK	MAX	——	12 minutes with the KEEP WARM setting off	START
SOUP/ BROTH, PRESSURE COOK or MANUAL	HIGH	Closed	15 minutes with the KEEP WARM setting off	START

6. Use the **quick-release method** to bring the machine's pressure back to normal. Unlatch the lid and open the pot. Discard the oregano sprigs, then stir in the kale. Lock the lid back onto the pot.

7.

Set the machine	Level	The valve must be	Time	Press
PRESSURE COOK	MAX	——	4 minutes with the KEEP WARM setting off	START
SOUP/ BROTH, PRESSURE COOK OR MANUAL	HIGH	Closed	5 minutes with the KEEP WARM setting off	START

8. When the machine has finished cooking, turn it off and let the pressure **return to normal naturally**, about 35 minutes. Unlatch the lid and open the pot. Stir in the lemon juice before serving.

Beyond

- Because kale is so bulky, this soup does not work well in a 3-litre cooker.
- Add 1 teaspoon ground allspice or ¼ teaspoon ground cloves with the oregano sprigs.
- Add up to 1 tablespoon peeled and finely chopped garlic just before you pour in the stock.
- For a more luxurious soup, omit the lemon juice and stir in up to 125ml single or double cream in its place.
- Garnish the bowls with a finely grated hard cheese, such as pecorino, aged Asiago, a well-aged Gouda or even a hard goat's cheese.

Lentil Soup with Carrots and Cinnamon

6 servings

Brown lentils break down under pressure, adding a creamy smoothness to this warming soup as well as an earthy savouriness, which is balanced by the honey. To make sure the soup doesn't get too sweet, we decided not to cook the onions as a first step, thereby leaving their sugars undeveloped and offering the broth a more aromatic finish.

During your prep, truly *chop* the carrots. Don't just slice them into discs. Slice them lengthways into strips 1cm in thickness, then slice these into 1cm pieces.

And use only brown lentils – not red, pink or green.

1.5 litres vegetable stock

280g brown lentils

260g chopped carrots

1 medium onion, chopped (160g prechopped)

2 tablespoons honey or agave nectar

2 medium garlic cloves, peeled and finely chopped (2 teaspoons prechopped)

½ teaspoon table salt

½ teaspoon ground black pepper

One 10cm cinnamon stick

1. Stir all the ingredients in a **5.5- or 7.5-litre cooker**. Lock the lid onto the pot.

2.

Set the machine	Level	The valve must be	Time	Press
PRESSURE COOK	MAX	——	15 minutes with the KEEP WARM setting off	START
SOUP/ BROTH, PRESSURE COOK or MANUAL	HIGH	Closed	20 minutes with the KEEP WARM setting off	START
SLOW COOK	HIGH	Opened	3 hours with the KEEP WARM setting off (or on for no more than 1 hour)	START

3. If you've used a pressure setting, when the machine has finished cooking, use the **quick-release method** to bring the pot's pressure back to normal.

4. Unlatch the lid and open the pot. Find and discard the cinnamon stick, then stir the soup well before serving.

Beyond

- You must halve the recipe for a 3-litre cooker.

- For a sweeter soup, substitute 300g peeled and diced sweet potato or peeled, deseeded and diced butternut squash for the carrots.

- With cinnamon and lentils, this soup leans Middle Eastern in flavour. Add 1 teaspoon ground coriander and ½ teaspoon ground cardamom too and/or drizzle pomegranate molasses over the bowls and serve with pitta bread crisps.

2 litres chicken stock

350g plain ham, chopped

400g dried green split peas

1 small onion, chopped
(80g prechopped)

1 teaspoon dried thyme

1 teaspoon finely grated
lemon zest

½ teaspoon celery seeds

½ teaspoon ground
black pepper

2 bay leaves

Absurdly Easy Split Pea Soup

6 servings

Of course, you could spend all day braising a ham hock or a ham
bone to create split pea soup. But you bought an Instant Pot
because you wanted dinner faster, right? This recipe takes the easy
route and uses ham to make a wintry favourite in no time.

Most split-pea recipes for the pressure cooker have the peas
go under pressure for a relatively long time, followed by a quick
release. We opt for a shorter time under pressure, followed by a
natural release, to avoid split-pea gunk spewing out of the valve.
Also, when the pressure is released quickly, the soup jumps to an
instant vigorous boil, causing the split peas to become more like
porridge. Frankly, we prefer soup, not paste.

1. Mix all the ingredients in a **5.5- or 7.5-litre cooker**. Lock the lid
onto the pot.

2.

Set the machine	Level	The valve must be	Time	Press
PRESSURE COOK	MAX	——	6 minutes with the KEEP WARM setting off	START
SOUP/BROTH, PRESSURE COOK or MANUAL	HIGH	Closed	8 minutes with the KEEP WARM setting off	START

3. When the machine has finished cooking, turn it off and let its
pressure **return to normal naturally**, about 15 minutes. Unlatch
the lid and open the pot. Find and discard the bay leaves. Stir
well before serving.

Beyond

- You must halve the recipe for
a 3-litre cooker.

- If the soup is too thin (yes,
some people like wallpaper
paste), set the machine to the
SAUTÉ function at its MEDIUM,
NORMAL or CUSTOM 150°C
(for the Max machine) setting
after opening the pot.
Simmer, stirring almost
constantly, until the soup
reaches your desired
consistency, 5–10 minutes.

- If you can find roasted,
on-the-bone ham at your
supermarket's deli counter,
buy 350g chunk and chop it
up for the soup.

- Add up to 130g finely
chopped carrots and 130g
finely chopped peeled turnip
with the other ingredients.

Yellow Split Pea Soup with Kimchi

6 servings

Kimchi is basically Korean sauerkraut: fermented cabbage packed
with chillies. It adds a salty, savoury base to this soup, which is
thickened with yellow split peas (*not* chana dal, see page 229).
If you can't find yellow split peas at your supermarket (we, in fact,
did), they're available via a quick online search. Sounds weird, right?
Try it! The soup's a sweet-salty-spicy mash-up.

     As to the kimchi, some brands are fiery; others, not so much.
You may even find radish kimchi or chunkier, 'country style' kimchi
at Asian supermarkets.

1. Stir all the ingredients in a **5.5- or 7.5-litre cooker.** Lock the lid
onto the pot.

2.

Set the machine	Level	The valve must be	Time	Press
PRESSURE COOK	MAX	——	7 minutes with the KEEP WARM setting off	START
SOUP/ BROTH, PRESSURE COOK or MANUAL	HIGH	Closed	10 minutes with the KEEP WARM setting off	START

3. When the machine has finished cooking, turn it off and let
the pressure **return to normal naturally**, about 20 minutes.
Unlatch the lid and open the pot. Stir well before serving.

2 litres vegetable stock

400g yellow split peas

225g kimchi, chopped

1 medium leek, white and
   green part only, well
   washed and thinly sliced

3 medium garlic cloves,
   peeled and finely chopped
   (1 tablespoon prechopped)

½ teaspoon ground
   dried turmeric

½ teaspoon ground
   black pepper

Beyond

- You must halve the recipe for
a 3-litre cooker.

- For a less assertive flavour in
the soup, substitute drained
sauerkraut for the kimchi.

- If you don't mind a khaki
colour, substitute green split
peas for the yellow.

- This recipe's probably not a
full meal. Consider serving it
with skewers off the grill.
Brush chicken breast or sirloin
steak skewers with this
marinade: 125ml soy sauce,
2 tablespoons dark brown
sugar, 1 tablespoon toasted
sesame oil and 2 teaspoons
ground black pepper. Grill
quickly over high heat,
mopping with additional
marinade as the meat cooks.

55g butter

500g trimmed
cauliflower florets

1 teaspoon table salt

½ teaspoon ground
dried ginger

¼ teaspoon bicarbonate
of soda

750ml vegetable stock

55g Cheddar cheese,
grated

60ml double cream

Cauliflower and Cheddar Soup

4–6 servings

Using a modified version of the baking-soda-and-butter poaching
technique, we used to make an absurdly creamy vegetable soup
(see page 61). This recipe turns a mundane cauliflower soup into
a cheese fest. Cheddar works best, partly to keep the overall look of
the soup pale, but also to offer a mellow flavour. At the end, you
must remove the insert from the pot to wait for the flavours to meld.
Otherwise, the cheese will break into an oily mess and any milk
solids will stick to the still-hot bottom of the pot.

1.

Press	Setting	Time	Press
SAUTÉ	MEDIUM, NORMAL or CUSTOM 150°C	5 minutes	START

2. Melt the butter in a **3-, 5.5-, or 7.5-litre cooker**. Add the
cauliflower and stir well until the florets are coated in butter.
Stir in the salt, dried ginger and bicarbonate of soda. Turn off
the **SAUTÉ** function, then pour in the stock and stir well. Lock
the lid onto the pot.

3.

Set the machine	Level	The valve must be	Time	Press
PRESSURE COOK	MAX	—	10 minutes with the KEEP WARM setting off	START
SOUP/ BROTH, PRESSURE COOK or MANUAL	HIGH	Closed	12 minutes with the KEEP WARM setting off	START

4. Use the **quick-release method** to bring the pot's pressure
back to normal. Unlatch the lid and open the pot. Use a hand
blender to purée the soup right in the cooker. Or transfer about
half the contents of the cooker to a large blender, cover but
remove the centre knob in the blender's lid, cover with a tea
towel and blend until smooth. Then transfer this purée to
a large bowl and purée the rest of the soup before returning
it all to the pot.

5.

Press	Setting	Time	Press
SAUTÉ	LOW or LESS	5 minutes	START

6. Add the cheese and cream. Stir until quite steamy *but not yet
boiling*, less than 1 minute. Turn off the **SAUTÉ** function, remove
the *hot* insert from the machine, set the lid askew over it, and
set aside for 5 minutes to blend the flavours.

Beyond

- For a more assertive taste,
  substitute an aged, semi-firm
  goat's cheese for the Cheddar.

- For a cheese beer soup, use
  only 500ml stock and add
  250ml blond beer, lager, IPA
  or pilsner.

- Make a broccoli Cheddar soup
  by substituting chopped
  broccoli florets and stems for
  the cauliflower. (The stems
  should be in pieces no more
  than 5cm long.) Warning: the
  soup will be a rather garish
  green but still delicious.

- Garnish the bowls with
  caraway or fennel seeds.

Lemony Chicken Rice Soup

6 servings

Consider this our simplified version of *avgolemono,* a Greek (or probably Arabic) chicken soup made with rice and thickened with eggs. The broth is fairly sour, a good contrast to the sweet, white rice. In effect, we overcook that rice so that it thickens the soup.

Do not 'cook' the soup after you whisk the egg mixture into it. Otherwise, the eggs will fail to emulsify into a thickener and simply scramble. Make sure they are *thoroughly* whisked with the lemon juice, then temper them by whisking in some of the hot soup before this combined mixture goes into the pot. All the while, don't let the whisk leave your hand.

And one more thing: there's no chicken in this recipe, other than the stock itself. Use the best stock you can find. Or use homemade (page 102).

1. Mix the stock, rice, dill, oregano, lemon zest and salt in a 3-, 5.5-, or 7.5-litre cooker. Lock the lid onto the pot.

2.

Set the machine	Level	The valve must be	Time	Press
PRESSURE COOK	MAX	—	18 minutes with the KEEP WARM setting off	START
SOUP/ BROTH, PRESSURE COOK or MANUAL	HIGH	Closed	23 minutes with the KEEP WARM setting off	START

3. Use the **quick-release method** to bring the pot's pressure back to normal. Unlatch the lid and open the pot. Whisk the eggs and lemon juice in a large bowl until smooth. Whisk about 250ml of the hot soup into the egg mixture. Then whisk this combined mixture into the pot with the soup until smooth. Serve warm.

1.5 litres chicken stock

135g long-grain white rice, such as white basmati

1 tablespoon finely chopped fresh dill fronds

1 tablespoon finely chopped fresh oregano leaves

1 tablespoon finely chopped lemon zest

1 teaspoon table salt

4 large eggs, at room temperature

80ml fresh lemon juice

Beyond

- Garnish the servings with finely snipped chives or the sliced green part of a spring onion.

- Morph this into a Caribbean soup (sort of) by substituting lime zest for the lemon zest and 60ml fresh lime juice for the lemon juice. It'll also need a little heat, so add up to 2 teaspoons crushed chilli flakes with the herbs.

- If desired, top servings with cooked, peeled, and deveined prawns or shelled crabmeat.

2 tablespoons olive oil

One 450g bone-in skinless
chicken breast

Two 225g bone-in skinless
chicken thighs

½ teaspoon table salt, plus
more if necessary

½ teaspoon ground
black pepper

1.5 litres chicken stock

1 medium red onion, peeled
and halved

4 medium carrots, peeled and
cut in half widthways

2 garlic cloves, peeled

3 fresh thyme sprigs

2 fresh sage sprigs

115g dried egg pasta

1 tablespoon finely chopped
fresh dill fronds

Chicken Soup

6 servings

Okay, all you chicken soup fanatics, forgive us. Our version is not
pure yellow. We lobby for browning the chicken before cooking it
in the stock with the vegetables and herbs (which we then discard
since they've leached their flavour into the broth). The result is
cloudy, even brown. But the flavour is fabulous: rich, decadent and
decidedly, well, chicken-y.

    If you insist on old-school aesthetics, skip browning the
chicken (omit the olive oil, too) and cook them in the stock with
the vegetables and aromatics before carrying on as written.
But honestly, why would anyone skimp on flavour for colour?

1.

Press	Setting	Time	Press
SAUTÉ	MEDIUM, NORMAL or CUSTOM 150°C	15 minutes	START

2. Warm the oil in a 5.5- or 7.5-litre cooker for a minute or two.
Meanwhile, season the chicken pieces with ½ teaspoon salt and
the pepper. Set the breast in the cooker and brown *well*, turning
a couple of times, about 6 minutes. Transfer the breast to a
nearby plate and add the thighs. Brown them, too, turning
them a couple of times, about 5 minutes. Transfer them to that
plate as well.

3. Pour in the stock, turn off the **SAUTÉ** function and scrape
up *every speck of browned stuff* on the pot's bottom. Return the
chicken to the pot; add the onion, carrots, garlic, thyme and
sage. Lock the lid onto the cooker.

4.

Set the machine	Level	The valve must be	Time	Press
PRESSURE COOK	MAX	—	15 minutes with the KEEP WARM setting off	START
SOUP/ BROTH, PRESSURE COOK or MANUAL	HIGH	Closed	18 minutes with the KEEP WARM setting off	START

5. Use the **quick-release method** to bring the pot's pressure back to normal. Unlatch the lid and open the pot. Transfer the chicken to a chopping board. Scoop out and discard all the vegetables and herbs. Stir the pasta and dill into the broth. Lock the lid onto the pot again.

6.

Set the machine	Level	The valve must be	Time	Press
PRESSURE COOK	MAX	—	3 minutes with the KEEP WARM setting off	START
SOUP/ BROTH, PRESSURE COOK or MANUAL	HIGH	Closed	4 minutes with the KEEP WARM setting off	START

7. Meanwhile, remove and discard any bones and tough cartilage from the meat. Chop the meat into small, spoon-sized bits.

8. When the machine has finished cooking, use the **quick-release method** to bring its pressure again back to normal. Unlatch the lid and open the pot. Stir in the chicken meat and check for salt before serving.

Beyond

- For a 3-litre cooker, you must omit the chicken breast and just use the two chicken thighs. Halve the remaining ingredients and cut the carrots into smaller pieces to fit in the pot.

- Substitute any herb sprigs you like: tarragon, rosemary, oregano, savory. And swop the dill for just about any finely chopped, leafy, green herb.

- For turkey noodle soup, substitute two 450g turkey thighs for the chicken breast and thighs; cook for 25 minutes at MAX or 30 minutes at HIGH, followed by a quick release.

- For more flavour, add up to 4 allspice berries with the herb sprigs during the first cooking (remove and discard the allspice as well).

- For a more peppery accent, skip sprinkling the chicken pieces with ground pepper and add up to 10 black peppercorns with the herbs during the first cooking (discard these peppercorns, too).

- For a discussion of the best kind of gluten-free pasta to use in a soup like this, see page 154.

Two 450g bone-in skinless chicken breasts

1 medium onion, peeled and halved

Up to three 8cm pieces fresh root ginger, peeled and thinly sliced

1 medium head of garlic, any papery outer bits removed, sliced in half through the root end

1 tablespoon black peppercorns

1 teaspoon table salt

2 litres water

450g courgettes, spiralised

Gingery Chicken Soup with Courgette Noodles

6 servings

If you've got a winter cold, you *need* this soup, a combination of root ginger and garlic without any pasta in the mixture, just spiralised courgettes. The spiciness of the soup is determined by the amount of root ginger.

Here, the chicken is overcooked the first time under pressure to get its bony flavour into the broth and turn the meat luxuriously soft. The second cooking is fast, just until the machine comes to full pressure. Don't overcook those vegetable noodles! They should provide a textural contrast to the chicken.

1. Place the chicken, onion, root ginger, garlic, peppercorns and salt in a **5.5- or 7.5-litre cooker**. Add the water and lock the lid onto the cooker.

2.

Set the machine	Level	The valve must be	Time	Press
PRESSURE COOK	MAX	——	20 minutes with the KEEP WARM setting off	START
SOUP/ BROTH, PRESSURE COOK or MANUAL	HIGH	Closed	30 minutes with the KEEP WARM setting off	START

3. When the machine has finished cooking, turn it off and let its pressure **return to normal naturally**, about 35 minutes. Unlatch the lid and open the pot. Transfer the chicken breasts to a large chopping board. Fish out and discard all the other vegetables and aromatics in the pot.

4. Leave the chicken to cool for a couple of minutes, then remove and discard any bones and tough cartilage. Chop the meat into small bits and stir these along with the courgette noodles into the pot. Lock the lid back onto the cooker.

5.

Set the machine	Level	The valve must be	Time	Press
PRESSURE COOK or MANUAL	HIGH	Closed	0 minutes with the KEEP WARM setting off	START

6. Use the **quick-release method** to bring the pot's pressure back to normal. Unlatch the lid and open the pot. Stir well before serving.

Beyond

- You must halve the recipe for a 3-litre cooker.

- Spiralised courgettes are now available in some supermarkets.

- Substitute any other spiralised vegetable you might like: butternut squash, yellow summer squash or whatever your market has in stock. If you use roots or winter squash, keep the timing as stated but don't open the pot for 5 minutes after you've released the pressure the second time to soften the 'noodles' completely.

- Adding white wine will create a sweeter soup. Add no more than 250ml with the water.

- For a more savoury soup, omit the salt and garnish each bowlful with soy sauce.

Streamlined Pho

6 servings

This recipe puts a simplified version of this classic Vietnamese soup within reach of a weeknight dinner. (By the way, the name's pronounced something like 'fun' without the 'n'.) Make the stock up to 4 days in advance and store it, covered, in the fridge. Or, store it in a sealed container in the freezer for up to 3 months. In either case, bring it to a simmer in the Instant Pot with the SAUTÉ function at HIGH or MORE before turning off that function, then add the remaining ingredients and continue with the recipe (that is, adding the beef, noodles and fish sauce).

Straining the stock can be a challenge. Use a long-handled sieve to pull out the ingredients. Or pour the entire contents of the *hot* insert through a fine-mesh sieve such as a *chinois* or through a colander lined with a double thickness of muslin, into a big bowl. (You may have to work in batches.) Or do as any grandmother would do and fish things out one by one with a slotted spoon.

2 litres water

1.3kg beef or pork soup bones

1 large onion, peeled
and halved

15g chopped peeled fresh
root ginger

2 teaspoons table salt

1 teaspoon whole cloves

One 10cm cinnamon stick

2 star anise pods

700g beef sirloin, sliced
against the grain into
stir-fry thin strips; or 700g
beef cut up for stir-fry

2 tablespoons fish sauce
(nam pla)

350g dried rice stick noodles
or rice noodles for pad Thai

1. Put the water, bones, onion, root ginger, salt, cloves, cinnamon stick and star anise in a **5.5- or 7.5-litre cooker.** Lock the lid onto the pot.

2.

Set the machine	Level	The valve must be	Time	Press
PRESSURE COOK	MAX	——	30 minutes with the KEEP WARM setting off	START
SOUP/BROTH, PRESSURE COOK or MANUAL	HIGH	Closed	40 minutes with the KEEP WARM setting off	START

3. When the machine has finished cooking, turn it off and let its pressure **return to normal naturally**, about 40 minutes. Unlatch the lid and open the pot. Strain out all the ingredients, leaving the aromatic broth behind. Stir in the beef and fish sauce. Add the rice noodles, breaking them as necessary so they fit. Lock the lid back onto the pot.

4.

Set the machine	Level	The valve must be	Time	Press
PRESSURE COOK	MAX	——	3 minutes with the KEEP WARM setting off	START
MEAT/ STEW, PRESSURE COOK or MANUAL	HIGH	Closed	4 minutes with the KEEP WARM setting off	START

5. Use the **quick-release method** to bring the pot's pressure back to normal. Unlatch the lid and open the pot. Serve hot.

Beyond

- Because of the size of the bones, this soup is not easily made in a 3-litre cooker.

- Make the broth in step 2 with the SLOW COOK setting. Cook with the pressure valve open on HIGH for 7 hours (the soup can then stay on the KEEP WARM setting for up to 4 hours).

- Garnish this streamlined pho with coriander leaves, finely chopped spring onions, thinly sliced green chillies, bean sprouts, basil leaves (particularly Thai basil leaves) and/or lime wedges.

1.2 litres chicken stock

450g boneless skinless chicken breasts, diced

One 280g tin Rotel tomatoes with green chillies

One 125g can hot or mild diced green chillies

225g white button mushrooms, thinly sliced

1 tablespoon standard chilli powder

1 teaspoon ground cumin

1 teaspoon onion powder

1 teaspoon garlic powder

¼ teaspoon table salt

125ml double cream

1½ tablespoons cornflour

225g grated mild or mature Cheddar

King Ranch Chicken Soup

6 servings

If you grew up in Texas, you already know about King Ranch chicken, a layered casserole with tomatoes, chillies and chicken, something like a Texas version of lasagne with tortillas standing in for the pasta.

You can't use tortillas in this soup (they'll fall to the bottom of the pot and scorch) but you can offer them alongside this admittedly whimsical concoction, made to taste like that Lone Star family favourite, now served in bowls, not on plates.

1. Mix the stock, chicken, tomatoes with chillies, green chillies, mushrooms, chilli powder, cumin, onion powder, garlic powder and salt in a **5.5- or 7.5-litre cooker**. Lock the lid onto the pot.

2.

Set the machine	Level	The valve must be	Time	Press
PRESSURE COOK	MAX	—	10 minutes with the KEEP WARM setting off	START
SOUP/ BROTH, PRESSURE COOK or MANUAL	HIGH	Closed	13 minutes with the KEEP WARM setting off	START

3. Use the **quick-release method** to bring the pot's pressure back to normal. Unlatch the lid and open the pot.

4.

Press	Setting	Time	Press
SAUTÉ	MEDIUM, NORMAL or CUSTOM 150°C	5 minutes	START

5. Bring the soup to a bubble. Whisk the cream and cornflour in a small bowl until smooth, then whisk this slurry into the soup. Continue cooking, whisking constantly, until thickened, about 1 minute. Turn off the **SAUTÉ** function and remove the *hot* insert from the pot to stop the cooking. Stir in the cheese, set the lid askew over the insert and set aside for 5 minutes to melt the cheese. Stir well before serving.

Beyond

- You must halve the recipe for a 3-litre cooker.
- Substitute any semi-firm cheese you wish, even a Tex-Mex blend of grated cheeses (so long as there are no spices mixed into the cheese).
- Serve with lots of pickled jalapeño rings and diced avocado.
- Crumble tortilla chips over each bowlful.

Buffalo Chicken Soup

6 servings

Who doesn't like buffalo chicken wings? Who hasn't always wanted them as soup? Okay, no one. Still, we took those flavours and morphed them into a satisfying meal, best on a winter evening. The pressure will take a lot of the sting out of the hot sauce. Pass more at the table for those (like us) who enjoy the burn.

1.

Press	Setting	Time	Press
SAUTÉ	MEDIUM, NORMAL or CUSTOM 150°C	10 minutes	START

2. Melt the butter in a **5.5- or 7.5-litre cooker**. Add the onion and celery. Cook, stirring often, until the onion begins to soften, about 4 minutes. Add the chicken and stir well until the pieces are coated in the butter. Turn off the **SAUTÉ** function.

3. Stir in the hot sauce, Worcestershire sauce, thyme and garlic powder until everything is uniform and well coated. Pour in the stock and stir well. Lock the lid onto the pot.

4.

Set the machine	Level	The valve must be	Time	Press
PRESSURE COOK	MAX	—	5 minutes with the KEEP WARM setting off	START
SOUP/ BROTH, PRESSURE COOK or MANUAL	HIGH	Closed	7 minutes with the KEEP WARM setting off	START

5. Use the **quick-release method** to bring the pot's pressure back to normal. Unlatch the lid and open the pot. Place the cream, cream cheese and 500ml of the broth from the pot in a food processor; cover and process until smooth and uniform. Whisk this mixture into the hot soup in the pot and serve at once, crumbling blue cheese over each bowl.

55g butter, cut into chunks

1 medium onion, chopped (160g prechopped)

4 medium celery stalks, thinly sliced

900g boneless skinless chicken breasts, diced

90ml hot red pepper sauce

2 teaspoons Worcestershire sauce

1 teaspoon dried thyme

1 teaspoon garlic powder

1.5 litres chicken stock

125ml double cream

115g regular or low-fat cream cheese

Crumbled blue cheese for garnishing

Beyond

- You must halve the recipe for a 3-litre cooker.

- Because the cream cheese cannot be reheated (or it will break), the soup does not freeze well. That said, you could make the recipe through opening the pot in step 5, then cool and freeze the soup in a covered container for up to 4 months. Thaw and reheat on the stove, then remove it from the heat, prepare the cream cheese mixture as directed and whisk it into the hot soup.

- For a sweeter finish, substitute a spicy barbecue sauce or Thai sweet chilli sauce for the hot red pepper sauce.

800g boneless skinless chicken breasts cut for stir-fry (unseasoned, discard any flavour packets); or boneless skinless chicken breasts, cut into 1cm strips

1.5 litres chicken stock

1 large onion, chopped (240g prechopped)

200g frozen or fresh corn kernels (no need to thaw)

Up to 6 medium garlic cloves, peeled and finely chopped (2 tablespoons prechopped)

Up to 2 medium fresh jalapeño chillies, stemmed, deseeded and chopped

2 tablespoons finely chopped fresh oregano leaves

½ teaspoon table salt

4 medium Hass avocados, peeled, pitted and diced

60ml fresh lime juice

Mexican-Style Chicken Soup

6 servings

The Yucatán was once the only place you could find versions of this tasty chicken-lime soup. It's since flashed across Mexico to become a favourite in every province. We don't add the lime juice until the very end in order to retain its tart bite (something the pressure would temper). There's a range for the amounts of garlic and jalapeño to use, so you can tweak the soup to suit your taste.

If you like it fiery, don't seed the chillies. Simply stem them and slice them into thin rings. If you dice the avocados as the soup cooks, stir the pieces with the lime juice in a medium bowl to stop them turning brown.

1. Stir the chicken, stock, onion, corn, garlic, jalapeño, oregano and salt in a **5.5- or 7.5-litre cooker**. Lock the lid onto the pot.

2.

Set the machine	Level	The valve must be	Time	Press
PRESSURE COOK	MAX	—	5 minutes with the KEEP WARM setting off	START
SOUP/ BROTH, PRESSURE COOK or MANUAL	HIGH	Closed	7 minutes with the KEEP WARM setting off	START

3. Use the **quick-release method** to bring the pot's pressure back to normal. Unlatch the lid and open the cooker. Stir in the avocado and lime juice before serving.

Beyond

- You must halve the recipe for a 3-litre cooker.
- Stir peeled, deveined and chopped prawns into the hot soup with the avocado and lime juice, then set the lid over the pot and set aside for 5 minutes to cook the prawns.
- For a more Caribbean feel, use 1 litre chicken stock and 500ml fish stock (see page 105). And really kick it up by substituting 1 fresh habanero chilli, stemmed and chopped, for the jalapeños.

Turkey Rice Soup

4–6 servings

It doesn't get much simpler than using turkey breast steaks for pressure-cooker soup. Since these steaks lack any bones to put flavour into the broth, make sure you use a highly flavoured chicken stock. Some larger supermarkets even sell turkey stock these days. Use that!

The steaks should be chopped into pieces *no larger* than 2.5cm square. You can even cut them into smaller bits, down to 1cm each, the better to get more than one in each bite.

1. Stir the turkey, stock, onion, pepper, garlic, rice, thyme, zest, pepper and salt in a **5.5- or 7.5-litre cooker**. Lock the lid onto the pot.

2.

Set the machine	Level	The valve must be	Time	Press
PRESSURE COOK	MAX	—	12 minutes with the KEEP WARM setting off	START
SOUP/ BROTH, PRESSURE COOK or MANUAL	HIGH	Closed	15 minutes with the KEEP WARM setting off	START

3. Use the **quick-release method** to bring the pot's pressure back to normal. Unlatch the lid and open the pot. Stir in the lemon juice before serving.

450g turkey breast steaks, cut into 2.5cm pieces

1.5 litres chicken stock

1 medium red onion, chopped (160g prechopped)

1 small green pepper or medium Cubanelle pepper, stemmed, cored and chopped (90g prechopped)

2 medium garlic cloves, peeled and finely chopped (2 teaspoons prechopped)

140g long-grain white rice, preferably white basmati

2 tablespoons fresh thyme leaves

2 teaspoons finely grated lemon zest

1 teaspoon ground black pepper

½ teaspoon table salt

1 tablespoon fresh lemon juice

Beyond

- You must halve the recipe for a 3-litre cooker.
- For a heftier soup, add 40g chopped carrots and/or 2 medium celery stalks, thinly sliced, with the onion.
- Substitute finely chopped oregano or parsley leaves for the thyme. Or substitute 1 tablespoon curry powder for the thyme.
- Add up to ½ teaspoon crushed chilli flakes with the garlic.

700g turkey breast steaks, cut into 2.5cm pieces

1.5 litres chicken stock

175g Brussels sprouts, trimmed and shaved

One 225g jar peeled chestnuts, drained (if necessary), each chestnut halved

1 medium onion, chopped (160g prechopped)

2 medium celery stalks, thinly sliced

55g fresh or frozen cranberries, chopped (no need to thaw)

1 tablespoon fresh thyme leaves

1 tablespoon finely chopped fresh sage leaves

¼ teaspoon table salt

125ml light, dry white wine, such as Pinot Grigio

1½ tablespoons cornflour

420g seasoned bread cube stuffing mix

Thanksgiving in a Bowl

6 servings

Why wait until November to make a meal that tastes like the holiday? This soup's got all the fixings, right down to the ready-made seasoned bread cubes placed in the serving bowls to make a version of bread soup. The overall texture is more like a rich gravy that's been thinned out a bit. In other words, it's pretty substantial. To make prep easier, look for shredded Brussels sprouts in the produce section of most supermarkets.

1. Mix the turkey, stock, Brussels sprouts, chestnuts, onion, celery, cranberries, thyme, sage and salt in a 5.5- or 7.5-litre cooker. Lock the lid onto the pot.

2.

Set the machine	Level	The valve must be	Time	Press
PRESSURE COOK	MAX	——	10 minutes with the KEEP WARM setting off	START
SOUP/ BROTH, PRESSURE COOK or MANUAL	HIGH	Closed	13 minutes with the KEEP WARM setting off	START

3. Use the **quick-release method** to bring the pot's pressure back to normal. Unlatch the lid and open the pot.

4.

Press	Setting	Time	Press
SAUTÉ	MEDIUM, NORMAL or CUSTOM 150°C	5 minutes	START

5. Bring the soup to a bubble. Whisk the wine and cornflour in a small bowl until smooth. Whisk this slurry into the soup and cook, whisking constantly, until thickened, 1–2 minutes. Turn off the **SAUTÉ** function and remove the insert from the pot to stop the cooking. To serve, place 70g of the seasoned bread cubes in each of the serving bowls, then ladle the soup on top.

Beyond

- You must halve the recipe for a 3-litre cooker.
- Skip the bread cubes and serve the soup over No-Drain Potato Mash (page 424) for a hearty meal in a bowl.
- To make this soup more like an Italian bread soup, after you thicken the soup, remove the insert from the pot and stir in the seasoned bread cubes, then set the lid askew over the pot for 5 minutes to let the bread absorb some of the broth.

Turkey Meatball Soup with White Beans and Kale

4–6 servings

We used an Italian flavour profile for this well-stocked soup, which is almost a stew because it's so loaded. If you want a thinner, more traditional soup, increase the stock to 1.5 litres.

White bean and kale soups are often made with sausage. We used turkey because it has a milder, sweeter finish, then threw in a little salami for just a touch of porky goodness.

The meatballs are fairly simple with just a few flavourings from the breadcrumbs. They're also quite tender once they've gone under pressure. Even with those breadcrumbs in the mix, the soup needs hunks of crunchy bread for every bowlful.

1. Mix the turkey mince, breadcrumbs and egg white in a large bowl until uniform. Use clean, dry hands to form the mixture into 16 balls, each made from about 2 tablespoons of the turkey mince mélange.

2.

Press	Setting	Time	Press
SAUTÉ	MEDIUM, NORMAL or CUSTOM 150°C	10 minutes	START

3. Warm the oil in a **5.5- or 7.5-litre cooker** for a minute or two. Add the onion, salami and garlic; cook, stirring often, until the onion begins to soften, about 4 minutes. Stir in the kale; continue cooking, stirring more frequently, until the greens wilt, about 3 minutes.

4. Stir in the stock, turn off the **SAUTÉ** function and scrape up the browned bits on the pot's bottom. Stir in the beans, oregano and thyme. Add the meatballs and lock the lid onto the pot.

5.

Set the machine	Level	The valve must be	Time	Press
PRESSURE COOK	MAX	——	15 minutes with the KEEP WARM setting off	START
SOUP/ BROTH, PRESSURE COOK, or MANUAL	HIGH	Closed	19 minutes with the KEEP WARM setting off	START

6. Use the **quick-release method** to bring the pot's pressure back to normal. Unlatch the lid and open the pot. Stir gently (to preserve the meatballs) before serving.

450g lean turkey mince

20g Italian-seasoned dried breadcrumbs

1 large egg white

2 tablespoons olive oil

1 medium onion, chopped (160g prechopped)

55g salami, chopped

2 medium garlic cloves, peeled and finely chopped (2 teaspoons prechopped)

225g chopped stemmed kale (do not use baby kale)

1.25 litres chicken stock

One 400g tin white beans, preferably cannellini beans, drained and rinsed

1 teaspoon dried oregano

1 teaspoon dried thyme

Beyond

- You must halve the recipe for a 3-litre cooker.

- If you want to take things to another level, brown the meatballs with a little olive oil in the pot on its SAUTÉ function set for MEDIUM, NORMAL or CUSTOM 150°C (for the Max machine). They're fairly fragile, so turn them gently with a thin spatula. Or brown them in olive oil in a frying pan on the hob or in a roasting tin in a 200°C oven for about 10 minutes.

- Substitute chopped pancetta for the salami.

- Top each bowl with lots of finely grated Parmigiano-Reggiano or even grated semi-firm mozzarella.

1 tablespoon vegetable, corn or rapeseed oil

3 bone-in beef short ribs (about 700g)

130g frozen baby onions (do not thaw)

2 medium celery stalks, thinly sliced

Up to 6 medium garlic cloves, peeled and finely chopped (2 tablespoons prechopped)

1.5 litres beef or chicken stock

220g pearl barley

1 tablespoon fresh thyme leaves

½ teaspoon ground allspice

½ teaspoon table salt

½ teaspoon ground black pepper

1 tablespoon balsamic vinegar

Beef Barley Soup

6 servings

Rather than just dumping ingredients into the cooker for this classic soup, the best way to make it is to take advantage of the one of the machine's best features, its SAUTÉ function, to brown the beef short ribs and add a complex, savoury flavour to the broth. Work to get the meat deeply coloured, even along the sides. The pressure will then force both that flavour and the savoury notes from the bones into the broth.

One warning: the browned bits on the bottom of the pot act like glue to the pearl barley, which can stick and burn. Make sure you scrape up every speck to prevent the pot shutting off because of scorched grains.

1.

Press	Setting	Time	Press
SAUTÉ	MEDIUM, NORMAL or CUSTOM 150°C	15 minutes	START

2. Warm the oil in a **5.5- or 7.5-litre cooker** for a minute or two, then add the short ribs and brown *well* on all sides, turning several times, about 10 minutes. Transfer the short ribs to a bowl.

3. Add the baby onions and celery to the pot. Cook, stirring often, until the onions begin to brown a bit, about 4 minutes. Stir in the garlic until fragrant, just a few seconds. Pour in the stock, turn off the **SAUTÉ** function and scrape up *every single browned speck* on the pot's bottom.

4. Stir in the barley, thyme, allspice, salt and pepper. Return the beef short ribs to the pot, as well as any liquid in their bowl. Lock the lid onto the cooker.

5.

Set the machine	Level	The valve must be	Time	Press
PRESSURE COOK	MAX	——	35 minutes with the KEEP WARM setting off	START
SOUP/ BROTH, PRESSURE COOK or MANUAL	HIGH	Closed	45 minutes with the KEEP WARM setting off	START
SLOW COOK	HIGH	Opened	5 hours with the KEEP WARM setting off (or on for no more than 2 hours)	START

6. If you've used a pressure setting, when the machine has finished cooking, turn it off and let its pressure **return to normal naturally**, about 40 minutes.

7. Unlatch the lid and open the pot. Transfer the short ribs to a large chopping board; leave to cool for 5 minutes.

8. Meanwhile, use a large spoon to skim any excess surface fat from the soup in the pot. Remove and discard the bones; chop the meat into small bits. Stir the meat as well as the balsamic vinegar into the soup, then serve warm.

Beyond

- For a 3-litre cooker, you must use one large 350g beef short rib and halve the remaining ingredients.

- For a heartier soup, add 1 medium carrot, thinly sliced, and/or 2 medium turnips, peeled and diced, with the baby onions and celery.

- For a sweeter yet more complex soup, reduce the stock to 1.2 litres and use 250ml light red wine, such as Pinot Noir, to deglaze the pot after all that browning.

- Garnish the bowls with snipped chives or finely chopped fresh dill fronds.

175g thin rashers of streaky bacon, chopped

1 large onion, chopped (240g prechopped)

1 medium green pepper, stemmed, cored and chopped (175g prechopped)

3 medium garlic cloves, peeled and finely chopped (1 tablespoon prechopped)

2 tablespoons dill pickle relish

1 tablespoon Dijon mustard

1 teaspoon dried thyme

1 teaspoon dried oregano

½ teaspoon ground black pepper

1.5 litres beef or chicken stock

550g lean beef mince

125ml single cream

2 tablespoons plain flour

225g mild Cheddar, grated

Beyond

- You must halve the recipe for a 3-litre cooker.
- Swop the Cheddar for Gouda, Gruyère, or even 115g crumbled blue cheese.
- Add up to 2 tablespoons hot red pepper sauce, with the relish.
- If you miss the buns for your cheeseburger, cut two or three hamburger buns in half, then cut these into quarters. Toast them on a baking sheet in a 180°C oven until lightly browned, then serve them in the bowls as croutons.

Bacon Cheeseburger Soup

4–6 servings

This family-friendly soup takes all the flavours of a cheeseburger (even the dill pickle relish) and turns them into a bowl of comfort. You don't have to settle for standard dill pickle relish. We've found savoury relish from India at our local supermarket, which would work here. You could even substitute any hot, vinegary relish (rather than the sweeter ones that have lately become popular).

1.

Press	Setting	Time	Press
SAUTÉ	MEDIUM, NORMAL or CUSTOM 150°C	10 minutes	START

2. Add the bacon, onion and green pepper to a 5.5- or 7.5-litre cooker. Cook, stirring occasionally, until the bacon begins to brown, about 5 minutes. Stir in the garlic, dill pickle relish, mustard, thyme, oregano and pepper; cook until aromatic, just a few seconds.

3. Pour in the stock and scrape up any browned bits on the pot's bottom. Turn off the SAUTÉ function, then crumble in the beef mince, leaving it in pieces about the size of small marbles. Lock the lid onto the pot.

4.

Set the machine	Level	The valve must be	Time	Press
PRESSURE COOK	MAX	—	5 minutes with the KEEP WARM setting off	START
SOUP/ BROTH, PRESSURE COOK or MANUAL	HIGH	Closed	7 minutes with the KEEP WARM setting off	START

5. Use the **quick-release method** to bring the pot's pressure back to normal. Unlatch the lid and open the cooker.

6.

Press	Setting	Time	Press
SAUTÉ	MEDIUM, NORMAL or CUSTOM 150°C	5 minutes	START

7. Bring the soup back to a simmer. Whisk the cream and flour in a small bowl until smooth and uniform. Whisk this slurry into the soup and continue cooking, whisking almost constantly, until slightly thickened, 1–2 minutes. Turn off the SAUTÉ function and remove the *hot* insert from the pot. Stir in the cheese and set the lid askew over the insert for 5 minutes to melt the cheese. Stir again before serving.

German-Style Steak and Pickle Soup

6 servings

In essence, this soup mimics the flavours of German *rouladen* – that is, thin beef strips wrapped around dill pickles and served in a rich gravy. We deconstructed all that, then added cloudy apple juice so that the soup takes on a sweet-and-sour quality. The horseradish will mellow quite a bit, offering an aromatic, almost sweet flavour, creating the background for the other ingredients and enriching the broth to make the soup satisfying on a cold night.

1. Run your hand along the steak to determine the grain of the meat. Slice the meat into strips 5mm thick against the grain, then cut these strips widthways into 2.5cm pieces. Put them and the remaining ingredients in a **5.5- or 7.5-litre cooker.** Lock the lid onto the pot.

2.

Set the machine	Level	The valve must be	Time	Press
PRESSURE COOK	MAX	——	18 minutes with the KEEP WARM setting off	START
SOUP/ BROTH, PRESSURE COOK or MANUAL	HIGH	Closed	22 minutes with the KEEP WARM setting off	START
SLOW COOK	HIGH	Opened	3 hours with the KEEP WARM setting off (or on for no more than 3 hours)	START

3. If you've used a pressure setting, when the machine has finished cooking, turn it off and let its pressure **return to normal naturally** for 10 minutes. Then use the **quick-release method** to get rid of any residual pressure in the pot.

4. Unlatch the lid and open the cooker. Stir the soup well before serving.

- 800g beef flank steak, such as bavette
- 1.25 litres beef or chicken stock
- 250ml unsweetened cloudy apple juice
- 3 large dill pickles, quartered lengthways and sliced into 1cm pieces
- 2 tablespoons ready-made white horseradish
- 1 teaspoon dried thyme
- ¼ teaspoon celery seeds
- ¼ teaspoon ground cloves
- ¼ teaspoon ground black pepper

Beyond

- You must halve the recipe for a 3-litre cooker.
- Serve over cooked white long-grain rice.
- Or skip the rice and toast slices of rye bread 10–15cm from a heated grill until a little crunchy, 1–2 minutes. Top each slice with a slice of Swiss cheese and grill until melted and gooey, about 1 minute. Ladle the soup into bowls and float one piece of cheese toast on each serving.

450g boneless beef chuck, cut into 2.5cm pieces

1.5 litres beef or chicken stock

60ml soy sauce

1 medium red onion, chopped (160g prechopped)

130g thinly sliced carrots

2 tablespoons finely chopped peeled fresh root ginger

1 teaspoon five-spice powder

450g pak choi, cored and thinly sliced

Beef Stir-Fry Soup

6 servings

This Asian-inspired soup is actually fairly light, despite the beef chuck. The flavours are brightened considerably by the five-spice powder, an aromatic contrast to the mildly bitter pak choi (which is merely warmed in the soup at the end).

When buying a large head of pak choi, look for stems that are white, not rust-coloured, and leaves that are dark green without any noticeable wilt. The heads are notoriously gritty, especially in the white stems near the core. Separate the leaves and rinse well before slicing them into thin strips.

1. Mix the beef, stock, soy sauce, onion, carrots, root ginger and five-spice powder in a **5.5- or 7.5-litre cooker**. Lock the lid onto the pot.

2.

Set the machine	Level	The valve must be	Time	Press
PRESSURE COOK	MAX	——	20 minutes with the KEEP WARM setting off	START
SOUP/ BROTH, PRESSURE COOK or MANUAL	HIGH	Closed	25 minutes with the KEEP WARM setting off	START
SLOW COOK	HIGH	Opened	4 hours with the KEEP WARM setting off (or on for no more than 3 hours)	START

3. If you've used a pressure setting, when the machine has finished cooking, turn it off and let its pressure **return to normal naturally**, about 30 minutes.

4. Unlatch the lid and open the pot. Stir in the pak choi. Set the lid askew over the top of the pot and set aside for 5 minutes to partially wilt the vegetable. Stir well before serving.

Beyond

- You must halve the recipe for a 3-litre cooker.

- Add up to 300g drained and rinsed tinned sliced water chestnuts or bamboo shoots with the pak choi.

- For a hotter soup, add 2 or 3 small dried red chillies with the beef.

- Ladle the soup into bowls over cooked long-grain white rice.

- Five-spice powder is a traditional Chinese blend of spices, available in almost every spice rack. To make your own, toast 2 tablespoons Sichuan peppercorns (or black peppercorns for a less piquant taste), 2 tablespoons fennel seeds, 10 whole cloves, 5 star anise pods, and a 5cm cinnamon stick broken into several pieces in a dry frying pan over a medium heat, stirring constantly until aromatic and lightly browned, about 4 minutes. Leave to cool to room temperature, then transfer to a spice grinder and grind until powdery. Push through a fine-mesh sieve or strainer to get rid of any hard bits. Seal in a jar and store in a cool, dark place up to 6 months.

Beef and Roots Soup

6 servings

This is our version of the retro beef soup usually made with oatmeal as its thickener, an Old World bowl of comfort that's right for a meal after working around the house (or the farm, given how filling it is).

Unfortunately, rolled oats can stick and burn in a multi-cooker, so we've substituted brown rice and overcooked the grains so that they thicken the broth. Get *every speck of browned stuff* off the pot's bottom so no gluey bits can latch onto the rice grains and cause them to burn.

30g butter

1 medium onion, chopped (160g prechopped)

700g beef silverside, cut into 2.5cm pieces

2 medium garlic cloves, peeled and finely chopped (2 teaspoons prechopped)

1.5 litres beef or chicken stock

65g long-grain brown rice

250g peeled and diced swede

130g thinly sliced carrots

2 teaspoons dried oregano

2 teaspoons dried thyme

¼ teaspoon table salt

Ground black pepper for garnishing

1.

Press	Setting	Time	Press
SAUTÉ	MEDIUM, NORMAL or CUSTOM 150°C	15 minutes	START

2. Melt the butter in a **5.5- or 7.5-litre cooker**. Add the onion and cook, stirring, until softened, about 4 minutes. Add the beef and garlic; continue cooking, stirring once in a while, until all the pieces of beef are browned, about 4 minutes.

3. Pour in the stock and scrape up *every speck of browned stuff* on the pot's bottom. Turn off the **SAUTÉ** function. Stir in the rice, then lock the lid onto the pot.

4.

Set the machine	Level	The valve must be	Time	Press
PRESSURE COOK	MAX	—	22 minutes with the KEEP WARM setting off	START
SOUP/BROTH, PRESSURE COOK or MANUAL	HIGH	Closed	30 minutes with the KEEP WARM setting off	START

5. Use the **quick-release method** to bring the pot's pressure back to normal. Unlatch the lid and open the cooker. Stir in the swede, carrots, oregano, thyme and salt. Lock the lid back onto the pot.

6.

Set the machine	Level	The valve must be	Time	Press
PRESSURE COOK	MAX	—	4 minutes with the KEEP WARM setting off	START
SOUP/BROTH, PRESSURE COOK or MANUAL	HIGH	Closed	6 minutes with the KEEP WARM setting off	START

7. When the machine has finished cooking, turn it off and let its pressure **return to normal naturally**, about 30 minutes. Unlatch the lid and open the cooker. Stir well before serving. Garnish the bowls with lots of ground black pepper.

Beyond

- You must halve the recipe for a 3-litre cooker.
- Brighten the flavours by stirring up to 2 tablespoons red wine vinegar into the soup before serving.
- Substitute an equivalent weight amount of diced peeled turnips or diced peeled celeriac for the swede. Or go for a mix of all these vegetables.
- Substitute dried marjoram for the oregano – or use 2 teaspoons of both.
- Skew the flavours sweeter by adding up to 2 tablespoons chopped raisins with the carrots and swede.
- For an even heartier soup, stir in up to 250ml double cream after it has finished cooking the second time. Set the lid over the pot and set aside for 5 minutes to take the edge off the cream's 'raw' taste. (Don't add cream if you've also added vinegar.)

30g butter

1 large beef shin
(about 675g)

200g thinly sliced carrots

3 medium celery stalks,
thinly sliced

1 medium onion, chopped
(160g prechopped)

1.5 litres beef or chicken stock

1 teaspoon dried thyme

1 teaspoon ground coriander

½ teaspoon ground cinnamon

¼ teaspoon table salt

100g long-grain brown rice

70g Puy lentils

Shin of Beef, Rice and Lentil Soup

6 servings

You may have to ask your butcher for a shin of beef. It's probably in the back, left over after preparing the popular cuts. This recipe is more like a lentil and rice soup, packed with a big beefy hit from the shin.

1.

Press	Setting	Time	Press
SAUTÉ	MEDIUM, NORMAL or CUSTOM 150°C	15 minutes	START

2. Melt the butter in a **5.5- or 7.5-litre cooker**. Add the beef shin and brown *well* on both sides, turning a couple of times, about 8 minutes. Transfer to a nearby bowl.

3. Add the carrots, celery and onion to the pot. Cook, stirring, until the onion begins to soften, about 4 minutes. Pour in the stock, turn off the **SAUTÉ** function and scrape up the browned bits on the pot's bottom. Stir in the thyme, coriander, cinnamon and salt. Return the shin and any juices in the bowl to the pot. Lock the lid onto the cooker.

4.

Set the machine	Level	The valve must be	Time	Press
PRESSURE COOK	MAX	——	35 minutes with the KEEP WARM setting off	START
SOUP/BROTH, PRESSURE COOK or MANUAL	HIGH	Closed	45 minutes with the KEEP WARM setting off	START

5. Use the **quick-release method** to bring the pot's pressure back to normal. Unlatch the lid and open the pot. Stir in the rice and lentils. Lock the lid back onto the pot.

6.

Set the machine	Level	The valve must be	Time	Press
PRESSURE COOK	MAX	——	24 minutes with the KEEP WARM setting off	START
SOUP/ BROTH, PRESSURE COOK or MANUAL	HIGH	Closed	30 minutes with the KEEP WARM setting off	START

7. Again, use the **quick-release method** to bring the pot's pressure back to normal. Unlatch the lid and open the cooker. Transfer the shin to a chopping board. Remove the meat from the bone and discard the bone; chop the meat into spoon-sized bits. Stir these back into the soup before serving.

Beyond

- For a 3-litre cooker, you must halve all the ingredients. (You're going to have to track down a 350g beef shin.)
- For a sweeter soup, substitute 140g chopped, peeled and deseeded butternut squash for the carrots.
- For a brighter flavour, stir up to 2 tablespoons white balsamic vinegar into the finished soup.

Ham and Potato Soup

6 *servings*

Using cooked ham, we can make a fairly fast soup. We're not talking about the shaved or sliced processed ham for sandwiches. Look for a big ham joint, preferably on the bone. Ask for several thick slices, each maybe 1cm thick, that you can chop up. And truly *dice* the potatoes, into about 5mm cubes, so they'll cook quickly with the ham. The starch they give off will begin to thicken the broth as they cook, but the milk-and-flour slurry will finish the job and give the soup a creamy, rich texture.

1. Stir the stock, potatoes, ham, celery, onion, butter, sage and pepper in a **5.5- or 7.5-litre cooker**. Lock the lid onto the pot.

2.

Set the machine	Level	The valve must be	Time	Press
PRESSURE COOK	MAX	—	5 minutes with the KEEP WARM setting off	START
SOUP/ BROTH, PRESSURE COOK or MANUAL	HIGH	Closed	8 minutes with the KEEP WARM setting off	START

3. Use the **quick-release method** to bring the pot's pressure back to normal. Unlatch the lid and open the pot. Stir well.

4.

Press	Setting	Time	Press
SAUTÉ	MEDIUM, NORMAL or CUSTOM 150°C	5 minutes	START

5. Bring the soup to a simmer, stirring occasionally. Whisk the milk and flour in a medium bowl until smooth. Whisk this slurry into the bubbling soup. Continue cooking, whisking constantly, until thickened, 1–2 minutes. Turn off the **SAUTÉ** function and remove the *hot* insert from the pot to stop the cooking. Whisk a few more times to stop the bubbling, then serve hot.

2 litres chicken stock

700g potatoes, peeled and diced

700g ham, any coating or fat removed, the meat diced

2 medium celery stalks, thinly sliced

1 small onion, chopped (80g prechopped)

30g butter, cut into small bits

1 teaspoon dried sage

½ teaspoon ground black pepper

250ml whole or low-fat milk

30g plain flour

Beyond

- You must halve the recipe for a 3-litre cooker.

- Morph this soup into a stew by decreasing the stock to 1 litre. Keep the slurry thickener at the end at the stated amounts. The soup will have a chowder-like texture.

- Serve pretzel rolls smeared with mustard with this soup. Or for crunch, break up pretzels right into the bowls.

- Garnish the bowls with chopped fresh herbs: parsley, thyme, oregano or savory.

30g butter

900g smoked kielbasa, cut into 2.5cm sections

1 medium onion, chopped (160g prechopped)

1 teaspoon dried sage

1 teaspoon dried thyme

½ teaspoon grated nutmeg

¼ teaspoon table salt

1 litre chicken stock

One 350ml bottle lager, preferably a pilsner

125ml single cream

2 tablespoons plain flour

175g mature Cheddar, grated

Sausage, Beer and Cheddar Soup

6 servings

The success of this favourite soup depends on the quality of the kielbasa. If you want to take things to another level, buy the sausage from a delicatessen or a speciality meat market. Or, see what stockists you can discover online.

1.

Press	Setting	Time	Press
SAUTÉ	MEDIUM, NORMAL or CUSTOM 150°C	10 minutes	START

2. Melt the butter in a 3-, 5.5- or 7.5-litre cooker. Add the sausage pieces and cook, stirring occasionally, until lightly browned, about 4 minutes. Add the onion and continue cooking, stirring more often, until the onion begins to soften, about 3 minutes.

3. Stir in the sage, thyme, nutmeg and salt until fragrant, just a few seconds. Pour in the stock and scrape up the browned bits on the pot's bottom. Turn off the **SAUTÉ** function and pour in the lager. Stir a few times to reduce the foam, then lock the lid onto the pot.

4.

Set the machine	Level	The valve must be	Time	Press
PRESSURE COOK	MAX	——	5 minutes with the KEEP WARM setting off	START
SOUP/ BROTH, PRESSURE COOK or MANUAL	HIGH	Closed	7 minutes with the KEEP WARM setting off	START

5. Use the **quick-release method** to bring the pot's pressure back to normal. Unlatch the lid and open the cooker. Stir well.

6.

Press	Setting	Time	Press
SAUTÉ	MEDIUM, NORMAL or CUSTOM 150°C	5 minutes	START

7. Bring the soup to a simmer, stirring occasionally. Whisk the cream and flour in a small bowl until smooth and uniform. Whisk this slurry into the simmering soup and continue cooking, whisking constantly, until slightly thickened, 1–2 minutes. Turn off the **SAUTÉ** function and stir in the cheese. Remove the *hot* insert from the pot, set the lid askew over the insert and set aside for 5 minutes to melt the cheese and blend the flavours.

Beyond

- For a richer soup, use 2 medium onions, chopped (320g prechopped).
- For a thicker soup, reduce the stock to 700ml.
- For a darker and sweeter soup, use beef stock and a dark beer, preferably a brown ale.
- For a 'brothier' soup, skip the single-cream slurry but also consider stirring in 115g cooked and drained pasta before serving.

Italian-Style Sausage and White Bean Soup

6 servings

Despite its immigrant heritage, this soup has become an American standard. And no wonder: the flavours are mellow and satisfying enough to make a filling meal with little effort. But since the standard recipe is so prevalent, we couldn't resist jazzing up our version with a bit with orange zest, and saffron (if you like). Even so, the success of the soup will turn on the quality of the sausage. If you buy large, house-made Italian sausages from a butcher or high-end supermarket, cut them into pieces 1cm thick.

1.

Press	Setting	Time	Press
SAUTÉ	MEDIUM, NORMAL or CUSTOM 150°C	10 minutes	START

2. Warm the oil in a **5.5- or 7.5-litre cooker** for a minute or two, then add the sausage pieces. Cook, stirring once in a while, until lightly browned, about 5 minutes. Add the carrots and onion; continue cooking, stirring more frequently, until the onion begins to soften, about 3 minutes.

3. Stir in the garlic, zest, oregano, saffron (if using) and salt until aromatic, just a few seconds. Pour in the stock and scrape up most of the browned bits on the pot's bottom. Turn off the **SAUTÉ** function and stir in the tomatoes, white beans and dried chillies (if using). Lock the lid onto the cooker.

4.

Set the machine	Level	The valve must be	Time	Press
PRESSURE COOK	MAX	—	5 minutes with the KEEP WARM setting off	START
SOUP/ BROTH, PRESSURE COOK or MANUAL	HIGH	Closed	7 minutes with the KEEP WARM setting off	START
SLOW COOK	HIGH	Opened	4 hours with the KEEP WARM setting off (or on for no more than 2 hours)	START

5. If you've used a pressure setting, when the machine has finished cooking, use the **quick-release method** to bring the pot's pressure back to normal.

6. Unlatch the lid and open the cooker. If you've included the dried chillies, find and discard them. Stir well before serving.

2 tablespoons olive oil

450g sweet Italian sausage, cut into 2.5cm pieces

260g chopped carrots

1 medium onion, chopped (160g prechopped)

2 medium garlic cloves, peeled and finely chopped (2 teaspoons prechopped)

2 teaspoons finely grated orange zest

2 teaspoons dried oregano

Up to ½ teaspoon saffron threads (optional)

½ teaspoon table salt

1.5 litres chicken stock

360g chopped fresh tomatoes

One 400g tin white beans, drained and rinsed

Up to 2 dried red chillies (optional)

Beyond

- You must halve the recipe for a 3-litre cooker.

- For a spicy soup, use hot Italian sausage.

- Grate lots of Parmigiano-Reggiano over each serving, or dollop the servings with pesto.

- If desired, add up to 40g chopped kale after the soup has cooked. Set the lid askew over the pot for 5 minutes to wilt the kale.

- For a Spanish-inspired soup, substitute chorizo for the Italian sausage. The chorizo will need to be cut into pieces 1cm in thickness. Also substitute one 400g tin of chickpeas, drained and rinsed, for the white beans; and one medium fennel bulb, trimmed and chopped, for the carrots.

450g boneless leg of lamb, any large pieces of fat removed, the meat cut into 2.5cm pieces

2 medium garlic cloves, peeled and finely chopped (2 teaspoons prechopped)

1 teaspoon dried oregano

1 teaspoon dried thyme

½ teaspoon ground turmeric

¼ teaspoon grated nutmeg

½ teaspoon table salt

2 tablespoons olive oil

1 medium red onion, chopped (160g prechopped)

2 litres chicken stock

450g parsnips, peeled and cut into 2.5cm pieces

450 baby potatoes, none larger than a golf ball, each quartered

10g fresh coriander leaves, finely chopped

Not-Your-Irish-Grandmother's Lamb and Potato Soup

6 servings

Here's the one and only lamb *soup* in this book. (There are plenty of lamb recipes in other chapters.) Frankly, we find lamb too strong for most soups that cook under pressure (or even in a slow cooker). The meat needs an oven reduction to mellow its flavours. However, by coating pieces of lamb in what's basically a barbecue rub, we gain some balance, getting bold flavours into the broth to match the meat.

Whenever you cut long, slender roots like parsnips and carrots, the dimensions stated for their size (here, 2.5cm pieces) are always given for the fatter ends. As the root tapers, the slices should be cut a little longer for more even cooking.

1. Mix the lamb, garlic, oregano, thyme, turmeric, nutmeg and salt in a large bowl until the meat is evenly and thoroughly coated. Set aside at room temperature for 10 minutes.

2.

Press	Setting	Time	Press
SAUTÉ	MEDIUM, NORMAL or CUSTOM 150°C	10 minutes	START

3. Warm the oil in a **5.5- or 7.5-litre cooker** for a minute or two. Add the onion and cook, stirring often, until it just begins to soften, about 4 minutes. Add the lamb and every speck of its rub. Cook, stirring frequently, until the lamb loses its raw, pink colour, about 3 minutes. Pour in the stock, turn off the **SAUTÉ** function and scrape up any browned bits on the pot's bottom. Lock the lid onto the pot.

4.

Set the machine	Level	The valve must be	Time	Press
PRESSURE COOK	MAX	⎯⎯	12 minutes with the KEEP WARM setting off	START
SOUP/ BROTH, PRESSURE COOK or MANUAL	HIGH	Closed	15 minutes with the KEEP WARM setting off	START

5. Use the **quick-release method** to bring the pot's pressure back to normal. Unlatch the lid and open the cooker. Stir in the parsnips and potatoes. Lock the lid back onto the pot.

6.

Set the machine	Level	The valve must be	Time	Press
PRESSURE COOK	MAX	⎯⎯	5 minutes with the KEEP WARM setting off	START
SOUP/ BROTH, PRESSURE COOK or MANUAL	HIGH	Closed	7 minutes with the KEEP WARM setting off	START

7. Again, use the **quick-release method** to bring the pot's pressure back to normal. Unlatch the lid and open the pot. Stir in the coriander leaves, then set the lid askew over the pot for 5 minutes to blend the flavours. Stir well before serving.

Beyond

- You must halve the recipe for a 3-litre cooker.

- The soup could stand some heat. Add up to 3 dried red chillies before the first cooking under pressure (remove these from the soup before serving). Or add up to 2 teaspoons crushed chilli flakes to the spice rub that goes on the lamb pieces.

- Don't like parsnips? Substitute 450g carrots. Or even 450g peeled and deseeded butternut squash, cut into 2.5cm cubes.

1.5 litres vegetable or chicken stock

115g brown or white rice stick noodles, or rice noodles for pad Thai

100g shiitake mushroom caps, thinly sliced

2 tablespoons soy sauce, preferably reduced-sodium

1 tablespoon finely chopped peeled fresh root ginger

450g shell-on prawns, peeled and deveined

225g small pak choi, washed well for grit and roughly chopped

Prawn and Rice Noodle Soup

4 servings

This simple soup is designed for a quick weekend lunch. It's straightforward, nothing heroic: a bowl of clean flavours with an umami richness from soy sauce.

1. Mix the stock, noodles, mushrooms, soy sauce and root ginger in a **5.5- or 7.5-litre cooker**. Lock the lid onto the pot.

2.

Set the machine	Level	The valve must be	Time	Press
PRESSURE COOK	MAX	—	3 minutes with the KEEP WARM setting off	START
SOUP/BROTH, PRESSURE COOK or MANUAL	HIGH	Closed	4 minutes with the KEEP WARM setting off	START

3. Use the **quick-release method** to bring the pot's pressure back to normal. Unlatch the lid and open the cooker.

4.

Press	Setting	Time	Press
SAUTÉ	LOW or LESS	5 minutes	START

5. Bring the soup to a simmer. Stir the prawns and pak choi into the soup. Cook, stirring occasionally, until the prawns are pink and firm, about 2 minutes. Turn off the **SAUTÉ** function and serve warm.

Beyond

- The recipe doesn't work well in a 3-litre cooker because the noodles have to be broken down into such small shards that they become rather irritating in the final dish.

- The noodles will most likely have to be broken into smaller pieces to fit in a 5.5-litre cooker (depending on the brand of noodle you use). They may fit whole in a 7.5-litre cooker.

- To go above and beyond, substitute white miso paste for the soy sauce.

- The pak choi will still be crunchy. If you like it softer, add it with the other ingredients to undergo the pressure cooking in step 2.

- If you can't find pak choi, substitute 225g cored and chopped Chinese cabbage.

Spicy Prawn and Rice Soup

6 servings

This spicy, coconut-milk soup is super thick, thanks to the rice, which absorbs much of the liquid as it cooks and creates something like a cross between a stew and a soup. If you have leftovers, thin out the soup with additional stock when reheating because the rice will continue to absorb more liquid in the refrigerator.

1. Mix the stock, tomatoes, coconut milk, onion, pepper, celery, rice, chillies and oregano in a **5.5- or 7.5-litre cooker**. Lock the lid onto the pot.

2.

Set the machine	Level	The valve must be	Time	Press
PRESSURE COOK	MAX	—	7 minutes with the KEEP WARM setting off	START
SOUP/ BROTH, PRESSURE COOK or MANUAL	HIGH	Closed	10 minutes with the KEEP WARM setting off	START

3. Use the **quick-release method** to return the pot's pressure to normal. Unlatch the lid and open the cooker.

4.

Press	Setting	Time	Press
SAUTÉ	LOW or LESS	10 minutes	START

5. Stir the prawns, parsley and lemon juice into the soup. Continue cooking, stirring frequently, until the prawns are pink and firm, about 2 minutes. Turn off the **SAUTÉ** function and serve warm.

1 litre chicken stock

Two 400g tins chopped tomatoes

250ml regular or low-fat coconut milk

1 medium onion, chopped (160g prechopped)

1 medium green pepper, stemmed, cored and chopped (175g prechopped)

2 medium celery stalks, thinly sliced

100g long-grain white rice, preferably jasmine or basmati

Up to 2 small jalapeño chillies, stemmed, deseeded and finely chopped

2 tablespoons packed fresh oregano leaves, finely chopped

680g shell-on medium prawns, peeled and deveined

10g loosely packed fresh parsley leaves, chopped

2 teaspoons fresh lemon juice

Beyond

- You must halve the recipe for a 3-litre cooker.

- For much more flavour (and if you don't mind getting your fingers dirty at the table), devein the prawns but leave them in their shells.

- For more heat, don't deseed the chillies.

- For a sweeter soup, use 700ml stock and 250ml dry white wine, such as Chardonnay.

450g shell-on prawns

1.5 litres chicken stock

260g thinly sliced carrots

3 medium celery stalks, thinly sliced

1 medium onion, chopped (160g prechopped)

2 small potatoes (about 85g each), chopped

100g fresh or frozen corn kernels (no need to thaw)

2 medium garlic cloves, peeled and finely chopped (2 teaspoons prechopped)

2 tablespoons tomato purée

1 tablespoon fresh thyme leaves

¼ teaspoon table salt

225g pasteurised claw or 'special' crabmeat, picked over for shell and cartilage

225g scallops, quartered

225g thin skinless white fish fillets, such as haddock, cut into 2.5cm pieces

125ml double cream

All-Out Fish Chowder

6 servings

This one's the real deal. You'll start by making prawn stock with the prawn shells. Then you'll add lots of vegetables and cook them under pressure before adding a vast array of fish and some cream right at the end. The technique's complicated. The results are fresh and light – not pasty and thick – and best with a glass of white wine (rather than beer). By the way, there's no call for expensive lump (or even jumbo lump) crabmeat for this recipe. 'Special' crabmeat is meat from the body, just not the large pieces.

1. Peel and devein the prawns (discard the veins). Put the shells in a 5.5- or 7.5-litre cooker. (Put the peeled prawns on a plate, cover with clingfilm and set in the fridge.) Pour the stock into the cooker, stir well and lock the lid onto the pot.

2.

Set the machine	Level	The valve must be	Time	Press
PRESSURE COOK	MAX	—	3 minutes with the KEEP WARM setting off	START
SOUP/ BROTH, PRESSURE COOK or MANUAL	HIGH	Closed	5 minutes with the KEEP WARM setting off	START

3. Use the **quick-release method** to bring the pot's pressure back to normal. Unlatch the lid and open the cooker. Use a slotted spoon to fish out and discard all the prawn shells, as well as any extraneous bits. Stir in the carrots, celery, onion, potatoes, corn, garlic, tomato purée, thyme and salt until the tomato purée dissolves. Lock the lid back onto the pot.

4.

Set the machine	Level	The valve must be	Time	Press
PRESSURE COOK	MAX	——	3 minutes with the KEEP WARM setting off	START
SOUP/ BROTH, PRESSURE COOK or MANUAL	HIGH	Closed	4 minutes with the KEEP WARM setting off	START

5. Again, use the **quick-release method** to bring the pot's pressure back to normal. Unlatch the lid and open the cooker.

6.

Press	Setting	Time	Press
SAUTÉ	MEDIUM, NORMAL or CUSTOM 150°C	5 minutes	START

7. Bring the soup to a simmer, stirring occasionally. Stir in the peeled prawns, crabmeat, scallops and fish. Continue cooking just until the prawns are barely pink, 2–3 minutes. Turn off the SAUTÉ function, stir in the cream and set the lid over the pot for 5 minutes to blend the flavours.

Beyond

- You must halve the recipe for a 3-litre cooker.
- For a looser soup, use 2 litres stock.
- If you want a thicker chowder, use 3 or 4 small potatoes. In addition, whisk the cream with 1½ tablespoons cornflour until smooth and stir this slurry into the soup after the prawns are *fully* pink and firm. Continue cooking until thickened, all the while whisking gently (to keep the fish intact), about 1 more minute.

1.5 litres chicken stock

1 medium leek (about 125g), white and pale green parts only, halved lengthways, washed well and thinly sliced

1 very small butternut squash, diced, peeled and deseeded

Up to 2 fresh medium jalapeño chillies, stemmed and thinly sliced

2 medium garlic cloves, peeled and slivered

10g coriander leaves, chopped

½ teaspoon ground allspice

½ teaspoon ground cinnamon

½ teaspoon table salt

900g skinned sea bass, cut into 2.5cm pieces

Fiery Jamaican-Style Fish Soup

4–6 servings

This recipe's a riff on a traditional Caribbean soup, sometimes made with chicken, sometimes (as here) with fish; sometimes puréed, sometimes (as here) left chunky. The only pain is dicing the butternut squash. If you buy it ready peeled, deseeded and chunked, you'll still need to cut it down into 1cm pieces at home.

You can make the recipe ahead, through the end of step 3. Cool the soup (without the fish), then store it in a sealed container in the fridge for up to 3 days, or in the freezer for up to 3 months. Bring the soup back to a simmer in a saucepan on the hob (or in the Instant Pot with the SAUTÉ function set at MEDIUM, NORMAL or CUSTOM 150°C) before proceeding to cook the fish.

1. Mix the stock, leek, butternut squash, chillies, garlic, coriander, allspice, cinnamon and salt in a **5.5- or 7.5-litre cooker**. Lock the lid onto the pot.

2.

Set the machine	Level	The valve must be	Time	Press
PRESSURE COOK	MAX	—	5 minutes with the KEEP WARM setting off	START
SOUP/ BROTH, PRESSURE COOK or MANUAL	HIGH	Closed	7 minutes with the KEEP WARM setting off	START

3. Use the **quick-release method** to bring the pot's pressure back to normal. Unlatch the lid and open the pot. Stir well.

4.

Press	Setting	Time	Press
SAUTÉ	MEDIUM, NORMAL or CUSTOM 150°C	10 minutes	START

5. Bring the soup to a simmer. Add the fish and cook, stirring occasionally but gently, until cooked through, 4–5 minutes. Turn off the **SAUTÉ** function and remove the *hot* insert from the pot to stop the fish overcooking.

Beyond

- You must halve the recipe for a 3-litre cooker.
- For a more authentic Jamaican flavour, substitute peeled, deseeded and diced fresh pumpkin for the butternut squash.
- For greater intensity, use fish stock (see page 105) instead of chicken stock.
- For an even hotter soup, substitute one or even two stemmed, deseeded and chopped habanero chillies for the jalapeños.
- Garnish the bowls with toasted unsweetened coconut.

Vegetable Stock

Makes about 2.5 litres

Here's our first recipe for homemade stock, the answer to all the insipid, watery vegetable stocks on the market. Note that the Max machines instructions here call for both the pressure-cooking function to be set for SOUP/BROTH and for the NUTRIBOOST function to be turned on. Doing so will get the absolutely best flavour into the stock.

1. Put the onions, potato, carrots, celery, mushrooms, parsley, thyme and peppercorns in a **5.5- or 7.5-litre cooker**. Pour in the soy sauce, then add as much of the water as possible without going over the **Max Fill** line. Stir well and lock the lid onto the pot.

2.

Set the machine	Level	The valve must be	Time	Press
SOUP/BROTH and NUTRI-BOOST	MAX	——	50 minutes with the KEEP WARM setting off	START
SOUP/BROTH, PRESSURE COOK or MANU-AL	HIGH	Closed	1 hour with the KEEP WARM setting off	START
SLOW COOK	HIGH	Opened	4½ hours with the KEEP WARM setting off (or on for no more than 4 hours)	START

3. If you've used a pressure setting, when the machine has finished cooking, turn it off and let its pressure **return to normal naturally**, about 40 minutes.

4. Unlatch the lid and open the cooker. Strain the contents of the insert through a fine-mesh sieve like a *chinois* (or through a colander lined with a double thickness of muslin) and into a large bowl. Leave to cool for 30 minutes, then store in covered containers in the fridge for up to 4 days, or sealed in 250ml resealable containers in the freezer for up to 6 months.

2 large onions,
   peeled and quartered

1 large potato (about 250g),
   washed and quartered

4 medium carrots,
   cut into quarters

4 medium celery stalks,
   including any leaves,
   cut into 5cm pieces

225g chestnut mushrooms,
   washed and halved

1 small bunch parsley,
   rinsed to remove grit

4 large thyme sprigs

1 teaspoon black peppercorns

60ml soy sauce, preferably
   reduced-sodium

At most 2.5 litres water

Beyond

- You must halve the recipe for a 3-litre cooker.

- This stock is a rich brown colour, mostly because of the mushrooms and the soy sauce.

- If you're the type of person who freezes vegetable trimmings in the hopes of one day making stock, now's your chance. All the vegetables in the ingredient list come out to about 700–800g of chopped vegetables and/or trimmings. Feel free to substitute your stash.

- Add other vegetables at will. Use skinned, peeled and chopped butternut squash instead of the carrots (the stock will be cloudier). Or substitute chopped trimmed fennel or even cubed peeled celeriac for the celery. Add 1 or 2 cubed, peeled medium turnips for a slightly bitter flavour in the stock, or up to 130g cubed, peeled swede for a sweeter flavour.

1.25kg chicken wings,
  necks and/or backs

2 medium carrots, cut
  into 5cm pieces

2 medium parsnips, cut
  into 5cm pieces

3 medium celery stalks
  including any leaves,
  cut into 5cm pieces

1 large onion, peeled
  and quartered

2 large garlic cloves, peeled

15g fresh dill fronds (optional)

2 teaspoons sea salt flakes

2 teaspoons black
  peppercorns

At most 2.5 litres water

Chicken Stock

Makes 2.8 litres

We have a friend who reads almost any recipe for a savoury dish
and says, 'Well, it'll all be about the stock.' Nothing could be truer.
Making your own chicken stock on a weekend afternoon will be
a sure-fire guarantee that your cooking is going to rise to another
level in the days (and months) ahead. Even if you reduce the
purchased stock you use by 250ml and add in 250ml of the
homemade stuff, that recipe will come out better.

The dill here is optional, if traditional for so-called 'Jewish
penicillin'. If you're making this stock to use in other recipes, leave
it out. If you're making this stock because someone you know is
poorly and needs a healthy pick-me-up, or if you're going to use
it to make a simple chicken noodle soup on your own with cooked
spaghetti and chicken meat just stirred into it later, or even matzo
ball soup at Passover, keep the dill in the mixture.

1. Put the chicken, carrots, parsnips, celery, onion, garlic cloves,
dill (if using), salt and peppercorns in a **5.5- or 7.5-litre cooker**.
Add as much of the water as possible without going over the
Max Fill line. Lock the lid onto the pot.

2.

Set the machine	Level	The valve must be	Time	Press
SOUP/ BROTH and NUTRIBOOST	MAX	——	1 hour with the KEEP WARM setting off	START
SOUP/ BROTH, PRESSURE COOK or MANUAL	HIGH	Closed	1½ hours with the KEEP WARM setting off	START
SLOW COOK	HIGH	Opened	5 hours with the KEEP WARM setting off (or on for no more than 4 hours)	START

3. If you've used a pressure setting, when the machine has
finished cooking, turn it off and let the pressure **return to
normal naturally**, about 45 minutes.

4. Strain the contents of the insert through a fine-mesh sieve
like a *chinois* (or through a colander lined with a double thickness
of muslin) and into a large bowl. Leave to cool for 20 minutes,
then store in covered containers in the fridge for up to 3 days,
or in 250ml resealable containers in the freezer for up to
3 months.

Beyond

- You must halve the recipe for
  a 3-litre cooker.

- For an old-world stock full of
  collagen and with an earthier,
  far-less-sweet flavour, add 1
  or 2 well-cleaned chicken
  feet.

- For a more intense flavour,
  add several chicken hearts
  and/or gizzards (but no liver).

- And for an absurdly complex
  flavour (but not a yellow
  stock, rather a brown one),
  first roast the chicken pieces
  in a large roasting tin in
  a heated 230°C oven for
  30 minutes before making
  the stock.

Beef Stock (aka Bone Broth)

Makes 2.8 litres

Those of us who've been making beef broth for years know its pleasures, no matter its name. But the surprise in our version may well be the vinegar. Beef is so naturally sweet that we feel that a little acid balances the flavour.

One warning: don't use marrow bones. They'll cloud the results and lend a funky flavour. Of course, you can save the bones from rib roasts and such for making stock, but make sure you've scraped off any seasonings or rubs.

And yes, this recipe takes more time than any other in this book. It's probably the definition of slow food. The point is to get all that collagen melted into the broth, enriching it considerably.

1. Position the rack in the centre of the oven; set the oven to 180°C. Arrange the beef bones on a large lipped baking tin and roast until lightly browned, about 30 minutes.

2. Transfer the bones and any juices to a **5.5- or 7.5-litre cooker.** (Add in any brown bits from the tin if you want a really rich – but not clear – stock.) Add the leek, carrots, garlic cloves, vinegar, thyme sprigs, peppercorns, salt and bay leaves. Pour in as much as of the water as possible without going over the **Max Fill** line. Lock the lid onto the pot.

1.3kg beef bones with some meat attached, preferably beef neck bones, oxtails or short ribs with most of the meat removed, or a combination

1 large leek, trimmed of only the roots, the bulb end halved lengthways, well washed, and the bulb and leaves thinly sliced

3 medium carrots, cut into 5cm pieces

4 large garlic cloves, peeled

2 tablespoons apple cider vinegar

4 large fresh thyme sprigs

1 tablespoon black peppercorns

2 teaspoons sea salt flakes

2 bay leaves

At most 2.5 litres water

3.

Set the machine	Level	The valve must be	Time	Press
SOUP/BROTH and NUTRIBOOST	MAX	——	2 hours with the KEEP WARM setting off	START
SOUP/BROTH, PRESSURE COOK or MANUAL	HIGH	Closed	2½ hours with the KEEP WARM setting off	START
SLOW COOK	HIGH	Opened	6 hours with the KEEP WARM setting off (or on for no more than 4 hours)	START

4. If you've used a pressure setting, when the machine has finished cooking, turn it off and let its pressure **return to normal naturally**, about 1 hour.

5. Strain the contents of the insert through a fine-mesh sieve like a *chinois* (or through a colander lined with a double thickness of muslin) and into a large bowl. Leave to cool for 30 minutes, then skim the fat off the surface of the stock. Store in covered containers in the fridge for up to 3 days, or in 250ml resealable containers in the freezer for up to 3 months.

Beyond

- You must halve the recipe for a 3-litre cooker.

- For a more aromatic broth, better for sipping than for recipes, add 1 star anise pod, 6–8 allspice berries and/or one 10cm cinnamon stick to the mix.

- For clearer stock, use a fat separator to skim the results. (Given the size of most home fat separators, you'll have to work in batches.)

**700g chicken wings,
necks or backs**

One 450g smoked ham hock

**One 175g piece salt pork
or pancetta, cut into chunks**

**One 15cm piece fresh root
ginger, peeled and thinly
sliced**

**6 medium spring onions,
trimmed and cut into
5cm sections**

**60ml soy sauce, preferably
reduced-sodium**

60ml mirin

At most 2.5 litres water

Ramen Broth

Makes 2.8 litres

Making the broth (well, really, the stock) for ramen can be a
three-day affair by the time you cook all the individual parts –
layering the flavours during a long, slow simmer in the oven, and
then later on the hob, and then later back in the oven. But our
Instant Pot recipe will let you make a knock-out ramen dinner for
friends on the weekend. Or keep some in the freezer for when
you're craving a bowl of comfort. See the *Beyond* section for ideas
about turning the broth into dinner. If you prefer a clear ramen
broth, set the Max machine just to PRESSURE COOK at MAX without the
NUTRIBOOST feature.

1. Put the chicken, ham hock, salt pork, root ginger, spring
onions, soy sauce and mirin in a **5.5- or 7.5-litre cooker.** Pour
in as much of the water as possible without going over the
Max Fill line. Lock the lid onto the pot.

2.

Set the machine	Level	The valve must be	Time	Press
PRESSURE COOK, or SOUP/ BROTH *and* NUTRIBOOST	MAX	—	2 hours with the KEEP WARM setting off	START
SOUP/BROTH, PRESSURE COOK or MAN-UAL	HIGH	Closed	2½ hours with the KEEP WARM setting off	START
SLOW COOK	HIGH	Opened	6 hours with the KEEP WARM setting off (or on for no more than 4 hours)	START

3. If you've used a pressure setting, when the machine has
finished cooking, turn it off and let its pressure **return to normal
naturally,** about 50 minutes.

4. Strain the contents of the insert through a fine-mesh sieve
like a *chinois* (or through a colander lined with a double
thickness of muslin) and into a large bowl. Leave to cool for
30 minutes, then skim the fat from the surface of the stock.
Store in covered containers in the fridge for up to 3 days, or in
250ml resealable containers in the freezer for up to 3 months.

Beyond

- This stock is not easily halved
for a 3-litre cooker because of
the ham hock. It's almost
impossible to find one small
enough. That said, if you can
find a very small 225g hock,
halve everything else and
have at it!

- Serve the warm ramen broth
over bowls of cooked and
drained ramen, udon or soba
noodles, along with chopped
greens (such as pak choi or
kale), and bean sprouts.

- Take it to the next level by
adding more to the bowls:
halved soft-cooked eggs (see
page 34), slow-roasted pork
belly and/or small bits of nori
(dried seaweed sheets).

Fish Stock

Makes 2.8 litres

If you want to get serious about making stock and wanted to know the one stock to make, we would say, 'This one.' Odd, no? But there are pretty decent versions of vegetable and chicken stock on the market. Fish stock is another matter. And there's no substitute for a fine fish stock in just about any fish soup, stew or braise. Some people try to jury-rig a fish stock by adding bottled clam juice to ready-made chicken or vegetable stock. It's a pale imitation. If you really want to become a pro, make your own fish stock and mix it in about 50/50 proportions with ready-made chicken or vegetable stock for any fish recipe in this book. Where do you get fish heads and such? Walk in to a fishmonger's. Ask and you might receive.

1. Put the fish parts, carrots, celery, onion, peppercorns, salt and parsley sprigs in a **5.5- or 7.5-litre cooker**. Pour in as much water as possible without going over the **Max Fill** line. Lock the lid onto the pot.

1.25kg fish heads, tails, fins, skin and bones, preferably with a little meat still adhering to them

4 medium carrots, cut into 5cm pieces

4 medium celery stalks including any leaves, cut into 5cm pieces

1 medium onion, peeled and halved

1 tablespoon black peppercorns

1 teaspoon sea salt flakes

10 fresh parsley sprigs

2 bay leaves

At most 2.5 litres water

2.

Set the machine	Level	The valve must be	Time	Press
SOUP/BROTH and NUTRI-BOOST	MAX	—	35 minutes with the KEEP WARM setting off	START
SOUP/BROTH, PRESSURE COOK or MANUAL	HIGH	Closed	45 minutes with the KEEP WARM setting off	START
SLOW COOK	HIGH	Opened	4 hours with the KEEP WARM setting off (or on for no more than 2 hours)	START

3. If you've used a pressure setting, when the machine has finished cooking, turn it off and let its pressure **return to normal naturally**, about 40 minutes.

4. Unlatch the lid and open the cooker. Strain the contents of the insert through a fine-mesh sieve like a *chinois* (or through a colander lined with a double thickness of muslin) and into a large bowl. Leave to cool for 30 minutes, then skim any impurities off the surface of the stock. Store in covered containers in the fridge for up to 2 days, or in 250ml resealable containers in the freezer for up to 4 months.

Beyond

- You must halve the recipe for a 3-litre cooker.

- To make shellfish stock (for étouffée, gumbo and other Louisiana favourites), substitute 1.25kg prawn, lobster and/or crab shells for the fish parts.

1 litre chicken stock

250ml regular or low-fat
coconut milk

50g chopped fresh turmeric
(no need to peel)

2 medium garlic cloves,
peeled and smashed

½ teaspoon table salt

Turmeric Broth

Makes 1.25 litres

This one's a hybrid, a broth mixed with a stock, or a stock made
from a broth. It's really a sipping drink, maybe for sick-room care or
on a day off when you need a little me-time. That said, you can also
use the broth in any of the Asian- or Caribbean-inspired recipes in
this book, provided they also have coconut milk in the mixture.

Fresh turmeric has become so popular that it even shows up
in our rural supermarket. Look for compact, plump pieces with tight
skins, free of too many black spots and certainly with no squishy
bits. We suggest storing the broth in 125ml servings in the freezer,
so you can serve up a little dose when you need it.

1. Put all the ingredients in a **3-, 5.5- or 7.5-litre cooker**. Lock the
lid onto the pot.

2.

Set the machine	Level	The valve must be	Time	Press
PRESSURE COOK	MAX	——	3 minutes with the KEEP WARM setting off	START
PRESSURE COOK or MANUAL	HIGH	Closed	5 minutes with the KEEP WARM setting off	START

3. Use the **quick-release method** to bring the pot's pressure
back to normal. Unlatch the lid and open the cooker. Strain its
contents through a fine-mesh sieve like a *chinois* (or through
a colander lined with a double thickness of muslin) and into a
large bowl or a heat-safe pitcher. Serve warm, or store, covered,
in the fridge for up to 1 week, or in the freezer for up to 6 months.

Beyond

• Add up to 25g chopped, fresh
root ginger for a spicier broth.

Ginger Tea

Makes 2 litres

If you've got a sore throat, here's your recipe. Or if you've got
someone you care about who needs a little boost, here's the stuff.
No doubt, it's spicy. It'll wake up those taste buds because the
pressure cooker forces so much of the root ginger into the tea to
make a warm and healing drink.

2 litres water

**50g grated fresh root ginger
(no need to peel)**

90g honey

60ml fresh lemon juice

**4 chamomile tea bags, any
labels removed**

One 10cm cinnamon stick

1. Mix all the ingredients in a **5.5- or 7.5-litre cooker**. Lock the lid
onto the pot.

2.

Set the machine	Level	The valve must be	Time	Press
PRESSURE COOK	MAX	——	2 minutes with the KEEP WARM setting off	START
PRESSURE COOK or MANUAL	HIGH	Closed	4 minutes with the KEEP WARM setting off	START

3. Use the **quick-release method** to bring the pot's pressure
back to normal. Unlatch the lid and open the cooker. Strain
its contents through a fine-mesh sieve like a *chinois* (or through
a colander lined with a double thickness of muslin) and into a
bowl or a heat-safe jug. Serve warm or cold. Store, covered, in
the fridge for up to 1 week, or in the freezer for up to 6 months.

Beyond

- You must halve the recipe for a 3-litre cooker.

- For more sweet-and-sour flavour, add up to 3 thin lemon slices with the other ingredients.

- For a less assertive flavour, substitute agave nectar for the honey.

1.25 litres almond milk

5 black tea bags,
any labels removed

10 green or white cardamom
pods, crushed

10 whole cloves, crushed

1½ teaspoons fennel seeds

One 10cm cinnamon stick

¼ teaspoon table salt

Almond Milk Chai

Makes 1.25 litres

Admittedly, this isn't standard chai made with whole milk.
Unfortunately, milk can break under pressure without special safety
precautions. So we've used almond milk and morphed the classic
into a vegan drink. It's mildly sweet (thanks to that almond milk)
and quite aromatic.

1. Mix all the ingredients in a 3-, 5.5- or 7.5-litre cooker. Lock the
lid onto the pot.

2.

Set the machine	Level	The valve must be	Time	Press
PRESSURE COOK	MAX	——	2 minutes with the KEEP WARM setting off	START
PRESSURE COOK or MANUAL	HIGH	Closed	3 minutes with the KEEP WARM setting off	START

3. Use the **quick-release method** to bring the pot's pressure
back to normal. Unlatch the lid and open the cooker. Strain its
contents through a fine-mesh sieve like a *chinois* (or through
a colander lined with a double thickness of muslin) and into
a bowl or heat-safe jug. Serve hot or cold.

Beyond

- Sweeten the chai with a little brown sugar (if serving hot) or agave nectar (if serving cold).
- If you don't care about this being vegan, consider using honey as the sweetener.

Five Infused Waters

Makes about 1 litre each

The Instant Pot is the perfect tool to infuse fruit flavours into water, making a concentrate for cocktails, summer quenchers or just a good swig after a long day gardening. So here are five versions to set you up for summer. All offer powerful, assertive flavours. Serve over lots of ice, preferably crushed ice for more melt. Or dilute in a ratio of 3 parts sparkling water to 1 part infused water for a jug of drinks.

We made terrific Palomas as a celebration at the end of this book's photo shoot. For one tall drink, take half a lime and cut it all into small bits, then muddle these with 2 teaspoons white granulated sugar in a cocktail shaker. Add 185ml Grapefruit Tarragon Water, 80ml tequila and ice cubes. Seal and shake well, then strain over fresh ice into a 450ml glass before topping up with sparkling water.

1. Place the ingredients for any infused water in a **3-, 5.5- or 7.5-litre cooker**. Lock the lid onto the pot.

2.

Set the machine	Level	The valve must be	Time	Press
PRESSURE COOK or MANUAL	HIGH	Closed	5 minutes with the KEEP WARM setting off	START

3. When the machine has finished cooking, turn it off and let its pressure **return to normal naturally**, 15–25 minutes (depending on the overall volume). Unlatch the lid and open the cooker. Strain its contents through a fine-mesh sieve like a *chinois* (or a colander lined with a double thickness of muslin) and into a bowl. Store in a covered container in the fridge for up to 1 week, or in individual 125ml resealable containers in the freezer for up to 6 months.

Lime Blackberry Water
1 litre water

250g fresh blackberries

Juice of 1 medium lime

Grapefruit Tarragon Water
1 litre water
1 medium grapefruit, preferably a ruby red grapefruit, quartered

1 sprig fresh tarragon

Orange Mango Water
1 litre water

1 medium orange, preferably a blood orange, quartered

1 medium mango, peeled and chopped (include the stone and any fruit adhering to it)

Strawberry Lemon Water
1 litre water

500g strawberries, hulled

1 medium lemon, scrubbed to remove any waxy coating, then halved

Orange Cinnamon Water
1 litre water

2 medium oranges, quartered

One 5cm cinnamon stick

Beyond

- Strain the infused water, then freeze undiluted in ice-cube trays to create fruit-laced cocktails this summer on the deck.

3

Chillies, Sloppy Joes, Pasta Sauces and Ragùs

Our hunch is that these recipes represent some of the main reasons you bought a multi-cooker: hearty chillies and deeply flavoured pasta sauces, all cooked under pressure in a fraction of the time they might take on the hob. Even so, about half of these recipes can also be made with the SLOW COOK function. You may not want to walk in the door and throw dinner together in seconds. You might want to put the ingredients in the pot earlier in the day and let them cook while you're off taking care of your life.

Please permit us to sound nanny-ish and remind you that it's never a good idea to leave a slow cooker unattended. And the cooker should certainly not be left to its own devices if you've got a lively cat or a nosy dog, not to mention curious children.

Okay, back to the recipes. Many are full meals; some are not. The pasta sauces and ragùs, for example, will at least need cooked pasta to make them dinner, if not a side salad, too. In those recipes, the serving-size notation near the recipe title gives you a notion of how much pasta would work with the amount of sauce made, rather than a strictly defined number of portions. Some people chow down; others barely touch the stuff. We thought it best to explain how much cooked pasta a particular sauce will coat.

In some cases, the batch will be larger than you may want in a single sitting. Rather than halving the recipe (which usually proves impossible or even disastrous in a **5.5- or 7.5-litre cooker** with only half the liquid to make the necessary steam for pressure cooking), save the rest in the freezer for another day when you're too tired to pull out even the Instant Pot. Or just go on a weekend cooking spree, stocking litres of tasty sauce in the freezer. You'll thank yourself some evening when you're too tired to cook.

FAQs

1. You want me to use dried chillies to make chilli? Seriously?

Most of these recipes don't call for dried chillies. But two do, including one of the big ones in this chapter: the road map for Chilli con Carne (page 116). We wanted to include a couple of honest-to-Texas chilli recipes. So, yes, we call for dried chillies, which, mind you, show up even in our rural New England shop.

That said, they don't show up in abundance in our supermarket. So we always call for a variety of dried chillies in case the selection at yours is just as limited. Of course, you don't have to pick just one type if you can find more. New Mexico reds (familiar from Southwestern *ristras*) are sweet and moderately spicy; anchos are dried poblanos, a little citrusy and (as a rule) not as hot. Mulatos have an almost chocolate flavour; pasillas, a brighter bite, lemony at its base. Chipotles are smoked and dried jalapeños, usually fiery (one or two chipotles will suffice amongst other chillies in any of these recipes). And there are many more chilli varieties available in Latin American, Spanish and Mexican supermarkets. Experiment to create your own blend.

The rule for buying dried chillies is the same as the one for buying any dried fruit. They should be supple, not desiccated. They should show no traces of mould or wet decay. They should be intact or at least in large pieces, not chipped up, and certainly not powdery. And they should smell sweet, if also hot.

2. Why do these recipes call for so much chilli powder?

Both the **PRESSURE COOK** and **SLOW COOK** functions destroy many of the flavour compounds found in chillies, even capsaicin, the stuff that brings on the burn. We need to use more chilli powder than we might on the hob to preserve the characteristic flavour.

Buy chilli powder in bulk, rather than in small jars. Look for large containers at most supermarkets or search online spice stockists.

3. Why do you call for two kinds of chilli powder?

Since we wanted a more complex flavour in some recipes and a more straightforward one in others, we used two types.

The first, *standard chilli powder,* is actually a blend of ground dried chillies plus dried oregano, ground cumin, sometimes salt, and maybe a few other spices.

The second type, *pure chilli powder,* is not a blend but (most often) one variety of chilli that has been dried and ground, with no cumin and other spices. (Some bottlings are a blend of dried

chillies, not one varietal.) We use a pure chilli powder when we want a cleaner flavour profile, even when we go ahead and add, say, additional ground cumin to the mix.

We never specify *which* pure chilli powder, leaving that decision to you and your supermarket's inventory. As a rule, pure ancho chilli powder is sweeter and milder; chipotle chilli powder is fiery and smoky. You can even find many more varieties of pure chilli powder at gourmet delis and from online spice sellers.

And one more thing: when we call for *standard chilli powder,* we often add more ground cumin. In our minds, there's never enough. Ground cumin may be even more essential to the flavour of an American chilli than ground dried chillies.

4. What are tinned chipotles in adobo sauce?

They're smoked and dried jalapeños that have been put in a rich, vinegar-and-spice-laced sauce. It's a concoction originally from the Philippines but now popular in Latin American and Caribbean cooking. We have looked for – and found – small tins of chillies in adobo sauce at supermarkets across North America.

One warning. When the recipe calls for '1 tinned chilli in adobo sauce, stemmed and deseeded', it doesn't mean that you should use one *entire tin of* chillies in adobo sauce. (One of us is side-eyeing his sister.) Use only one or maybe two chillies *out of the tin,* then cover the opened tin and store it in the fridge for up to 3 months or in the freezer for perhaps a year, even longer.

5. What's the difference between a pasta sauce and a ragù?

Basically, a pasta sauce is thinner than a ragù. A pasta sauce has a fresher flavour, less 'cooked'. And a sauce is usually not as well stocked as a ragù. That said, a thousand Italian grandmothers are lining up right now to smack us for this sort of over-simplification. If you, too, think we're being sloppy, get in the queue.

6. What's the best way to serve the pasta sauces and ragùs?

The easiest way to make dinner out of any of the pasta sauces and many of the ragùs is to prepare and drain the pasta while the sauce is cooking. After the sauce has finished, stir the pasta right into the Instant Pot and toss with the sauce until well coated. Set aside for 2 minutes with the lid askew so the pasta can absorb more of the sauce. Throughout, we've also given more serving suggestions beyond simple pasta.

7. I want to use fresh pasta. What do I do?

To use fresh pasta (gluten-free or regular), the general rule is that *450g of dried pasta when cooked and drained is about the same as 680g of fresh pasta when cooked and drained.* Such thinking is not always accurate (based on the shape and thickness of the pasta), but it's close enough for weeknight purposes.

And there's another rule that dried pasta goes better with chunky, hearty sauces while fresh works best with sauces that include cream. We're not sure we buy it. Bolognese is a delight with fresh pasta. And a creamy tomato sauce works well with dried pasta as well as fresh.

8. Do I have to crush the tinned tomatoes by hand? Haven't you heard of tinned chopped tomatoes?

Yes, we have. And we sometimes call for them. But the pressure cooker is an unforgiving environment. We find that tinned chopped tomatoes break down into tomato juice. For better texture, we advocate that you clean and dry your hands, then crush tinned whole tomatoes one by one over (and into) the pot. You'll end up with a less watery, more textural sauce – and thank us later, despite the mess.

2 tablespoons fat

Choose one or a 50/50 combo from butter, rendered bacon fat, lard, schmaltz, duck fat, olive oil, vegetable oil, corn oil, rapeseed oil, safflower oil, pecan oil and/or walnut oil.

160g chopped allium aromatics

Choose one or combine any two from onions (of any sort), shallots and/or well-cleaned, thinly sliced leeks (the white and pale green parts only).

175 chopped, deseeded and cored pepper

Choose green, red or yellow peppers, or even Cubanelle peppers.

Up to 2 medium garlic cloves, peeled and finely chopped (2 teaspoons prechopped)

35g standard chilli powder

Choose from mild, dark, smoked, roasted or hot.

1 tablespoon ground cumin

1 tablespoon dried oregano

½ teaspoon table salt

Two 400g tins chopped tomatoes

250ml clear liquid

Choose one or a 50/50 combo from broth of any sort, beer of any sort, and/or unsweetened cloudy apple juice.

One 400g tin beans, drained and rinsed

Choose from red kidney, black, white, pinto, haricot or even chickpeas.

675g lean minced meat

Choose one or a 50/50 combo from minced beef, pork, lamb, turkey, veal and/or goat.

60g tomato purée

Road Map: All-American Chilli

6 servings

In this road map recipe, you choose the fat, the liquid, the beans and even the type of mince to customise American chilli to your taste. And don't stand on ceremony. Mix beef and pork mince, or veal and turkey mince. (And if you can find goat mince, good grief you live near a good supermarket!) In the end, the point is to make the chilli you and yours would like for dinner. Have a blast. Make notes in the recipe margins. Create a signature recipe. It'll taste better because it's 100 per cent yours. But one warning: Tinned beans, after pressure cooking, do not stand up very well to freezing. Plan on eating it up!

1.

Press	Setting	Time	Press
SAUTÉ	MEDIUM, NORMAL or CUSTOM 150°C	10 minutes	START

2. Melt any solid fat or warm any liquid oil in a **5.5- or 7.5-litre cooker.** Add the allium aromatics, chopped pepper and garlic. Cook, stirring often, until the vegetables soften, about 4 minutes.

3. Stir in the chilli powder, cumin, oregano and salt until aromatic, just a few seconds. Then stir in the tomatoes, liquid and beans. Crumble in the mince and stir until well combined, not until the meat begins to brown. Turn off the **SAUTÉ** function and lock the lid onto the pot.

4.

Set the machine	Level	The valve must be	Time	Press
PRESSURE COOK	MAX	——	6 minutes with the KEEP WARM setting off	START
BEAN/CHILLI, PRESSURE COOK or MANUAL	HIGH	Closed	8 minutes with the KEEP WARM setting off	START
SLOW COOK	HIGH	Opened	3 hours with the KEEP WARM setting off (or on for no more than 2 hours)	START

5. If you've used a pressure setting, when the machine has finished cooking, use the **quick-release method** to bring the pot's pressure back to normal.

6. When ready, unlatch the lid and open the cooker.

7.

Press	Setting	Time	Press
SAUTÉ	MEDIUM, NORMAL or CUSTOM 150°C	5 minutes	START

8. Bring the chilli to a full bubble. Stir in the tomato purée until uniform throughout. Cook, stirring almost constantly, until slightly thickened, about 2 minutes. Turn off the **SAUTÉ** function, set the lid askew over the pot, and let the chilli rest for 10 minutes to blend the flavours.

Beyond

- You must halve the recipe for a 3-litre cooker.

- For a bulkier chilli, add 70g chopped celery and/or 70g chopped carrots with the allium aromatics and chopped peppers.

- There's not much heat (unless you used hot chilli powder). For more spice, add one stemmed, deseeded, and diced tinned chipotle in adobo sauce with the allium aromatics and chopped pepper.

- For more umami flavour, omit the salt and add up to 2 tablespoons soy sauce.

- Serve topped with soured cream and grated cheese.

- Top with finely chopped, deseeded and stemmed fresh jalapeños for their citrusy bite.

- Use this chilli to make a chilli casserole by layering it between corn tortillas and grated cheese in a 23cm square or 23 x 33cm baking dish. Bake covered in a 180°C oven for 20 minutes, then uncovered until bubbling and gooey, about 10 more minutes.

**12 dried red or black chillies,
stemmed and deseeded**

> **Choose one or a combo** from New
> Mexico reds, pasillas, mulatos
> and/or anchos.

8g fresh oregano leaves

**Up to 4 medium garlic cloves,
peeled**

2 teaspoons cumin seeds

½ teaspoon ground cinnamon

½ teaspoon table salt

2 tablespoons solid fat

> **Choose** from butter, rendered
> bacon fat, lard, duck fat or
> schmaltz.

**2 medium onions, chopped
(320g prechopped)**

**3 medium peppers, cored,
deseeded and chopped (500g
prechopped)**

> **Choose** from green, red, orange
> and/or yellow peppers.

**1.3kg boneless, long-cooking
red or white meat, diced**

> **Choose** from stewing beef, pork
> shoulder or skinless chicken
> thighs.

350ml liquid

> **Choose** from stock of any sort,
> or a 50/50 combo of stock and
> a dark beer, such as a stout or
> a porter.

Road Map: Chilli con Carne

6 servings

Here's the real deal: no beans, no tomatoes, just 'chillies with meat'
(as its name in Spanish indicates). We've tested this recipe using just
New Mexico reds (slightly sweeter and a little hot), a mixture of New
Mexico reds and anchos (a little more complex and certainly less
sweet), a combination of mulatos and pasillas (a bit like a mole
version of chilli) and a mixture of whatever chillies we had in the
house and could pick up at the shop (a little confusing, but darn
tasty). We find that a two-chilli mix is best. Crack the dried chillies
open and remove all the seeds and as much of their spongy
membranes as possible before soaking.

One important note: whichever meat you choose must
be diced to cook in the stated time, the pieces no more than
1cm in size.

1. Bring a large saucepan of water to the boil over a high heat.
Turn off the heat, add the chillies, cover the pan and leave for
20 minutes to soften. Or do this whole operation in the Instant
Pot starting with the **SAUTÉ** function set to **HIGH** or **MORE** until
the water boils.

2. Set a colander over a bowl in the sink. Drain the chillies into
the colander, catching the soaking liquid below. Put the chillies
in a large blender. Add the oregano, garlic, cumin seeds, cinnamon
and salt. Cover and blend, adding at least 1 tablespoon of the
soaking liquid a little at a time through the hole in the lid to
create a coarse purée. Stop the machine at least once to scrape
down the inside. Depending on the moisture content of the
chillies, you may end up adding up to 60ml of the soaking
liquid. Discard any remaining soaking liquid.

3.

Press	Setting	Time	Press
SAUTÉ	MEDIUM, NORMAL or CUSTOM 150°C	10 minutes	START

4. Melt the fat in a **5.5-litre cooker**. Add the onion and peppers. Cook, stirring often, until softened, about 5 minutes. Scrape every drop of the chilli paste into the pot. Cook for 1 minute, stirring almost constantly to coat the vegetables.

5. Add the meat and stir to coat in the chilli paste. Turn off the SAUTÉ function. Add the liquid and stir until uniform. Lock the lid onto the pot.

6.

Set the machine	Level	The valve must be	Time	Press
PRESSURE COOK	MAX	——	10 minutes with the KEEP WARM setting off	START
BEAN/CHILLI, PRESSURE COOK or MANUAL	HIGH	Closed	13 minutes with the KEEP WARM setting off	START
SLOW COOK	HIGH	Opened	4 hours with the KEEP WARM setting off (or on for no more than 2 hours)	START

7. If you've used a pressure setting, when the machine has finished cooking, use the **quick-release method** to bring the pot's pressure back to normal.

8. When ready, unlatch the lid and open the cooker. Stir well before serving.

Beyond

- For a 3-litre cooker, you must halve all the ingredients.

- For a 7.5-litre cooker, you must keep the ingredients as they are but increase the liquid to 350ml or simply double the recipe.

- Top the chilli with soured cream, dill pickle relish and pickled jalapeño rings.

- For a sweeter but more complex finish, use bourbon, brandy or even whisky – no more than 45ml – filling up the remainder of the liquid volume with stock.

- This is also the chilli to use for an enchilada casserole. Fill tortillas with grated cheese, roll them up, and lay them in a 23 x 33cm baking tin. Top with Chilli con Carne, then add more grated cheese on top. Cover and bake in a 180°C oven for 15 minutes, then uncover and continue baking until bubbling and hot, about another 10 minutes.

2 tablespoons olive,
vegetable, corn
or rapeseed oil

2 medium green peppers,
stemmed, cored and
chopped (350g prechopped)

1 medium onion, chopped
(60g prechopped)

2 medium garlic cloves,
peeled and finely chopped
(2 teaspoons prechopped)

900g plum or Roma
tomatoes, chopped

25g standard chilli powder

1 tablespoon dried oregano

2 teaspoons ground cumin

1 teaspoon ground coriander

1 teaspoon table salt

One 400g tin red kidney
beans, drained and rinsed

180ml chicken stock

900g lean beef mince

60g tomato purée

Firehouse Chilli

6 *servings*

Here's a chilli made with *fresh* tomatoes, not tinned. We modelled
it on the hearty, comfort-food chillies often made in fire stations
across the USA. As such, it's a little more savoury than some other
offerings, if also admittedly a little more work.

1.

Press	Setting	Time	Press
SAUTÉ	MEDIUM, NORMAL or CUSTOM 150°C	10 minutes	START

2. Pour the oil into a **5.5-litre cooker** to warm for a minute or
two. Then add the peppers, onion and garlic. Cook, stirring often,
until the onion softens, about 5 minutes. Stir in the tomatoes
and continue cooking, stirring several times, until they begin
to soften, about 2 minutes.

3. Stir in the chilli powder, oregano, cumin, coriander and salt
until fragrant, just a few seconds. Add the beans and stock, then
crumble in the beef mince and stir well. Turn off the **SAUTÉ**
function and lock the lid onto the pot.

4.

Set the machine	Level	The valve must be	Time	Press
PRESSURE COOK	MAX	——	6 minutes with the KEEP WARM setting off	START
BEAN/CHILLI, PRESSURE COOK or MANUAL	HIGH	Closed	8 minutes with the KEEP WARM setting off	START
SLOW COOK	HIGH	Opened	3 hours with the KEEP WARM setting off (or on for no more than 2 hours)	START

5. If you've used a pressure setting, when the machine has
finished cooking, use the **quick-release method** to bring the
pot's pressure back to normal.

6. Unlatch the lid and open the cooker.

7.

Press	Setting	Time	Press
SAUTÉ	MEDIUM, NORMAL Or CUSTOM 150°C	5 minutes	START

8. Stir in the tomato purée. Bring to a full simmer, stirring all the
while. Stir for 2–3 minutes at a full simmer until a little bit
thickened and almost irresistible. Turn off the **SAUTÉ** function
and remove the hot insert from the cooker to stop the cooking.

Beyond

- For a 3-litre cooker, you must
use 125ml stock and halve the
remaining ingredients.

- For a 7.5-litre cooker, you must
keep the ingredients as they
are but increase the stock to
300ml or simply increase all
the ingredients by
50 per cent.

- Serve with dollops of soured
cream or plain Greek yoghurt.

- And/or serve with spoonfuls
of dill pickle relish, or even
ready-made India relish (a
more savoury version of dill
pickle relish), as well as
bottled hot red pepper sauce.

- Use a 50/50 mix of lean beef
mince and lean pork mince.

Turkey Chilli Verde

6 servings

Good chilli verde uses lots of tomatillos. They're a member of the gooseberry family, sort of like small, hard, green tomatoes. They have a tart but savoury bite, not citrusy, more earthy-sour.

Fresh ones have a papery husk, which must be removed. They can also be sticky at their skins. Give them a quick rinse before chopping.

1.

Press	Setting	Time	Press
SAUTÉ	MEDIUM, NORMAL or CUSTOM 150°C	15 minutes	START

2. Warm the oil in a **5.5- or 7.5-litre cooker** for a minute or two. Add the peppers, onion, jalapeño and garlic. Cook, stirring often, until the onion begins to soften, about 5 minutes.

3. Crumble in the turkey mince. Cook, stirring once in a while and breaking up any large chunks, until the turkey begins to brown, about 4 minutes. Stir in the tomatillos, stock, coriander, oregano and salt. Turn off the **SAUTÉ** function and lock the lid onto the pot.

4.

Set the machine	Level	The valve must be	Time	Press
PRESSURE COOK	MAX	——	5 minutes with the KEEP WARM setting off	START
BEAN/CHILLI, PRESSURE COOK or MANUAL	HIGH	Closed	8 minutes with the KEEP WARM setting off	START
SLOW COOK	HIGH	Opened	3 hours with the KEEP WARM setting off (or on for no more than 1 hour)	START

5. If you've used a pressure setting, use the **quick-release method** to bring the pot's pressure back to normal.

6. Unlatch the lid and open the cooker.

7.

Press	Setting	Time	Press
SAUTÉ	MEDIUM, NORMAL Or CUSTOM 150°C	5 minutes	START

8. Bring the chilli to a full simmer. Stir in the cornmeal. Cook, stirring, until slightly thickened, about 4 minutes. Turn off the **SAUTÉ** function, set the lid loosely over the pot, and set aside to continue to thicken without any heat for 5 minutes.

2 tablespoons olive oil

2 medium green peppers, stemmed, deseeded and chopped (350g prechopped)

1 medium onion, chopped (160g prechopped)

Up to 2 fresh medium jalapeño chillies, stemmed, deseeded and chopped

2 medium garlic cloves, peeled and finely chopped (2 teaspoons prechopped)

900g turkey mince

450g fresh tomatillos, husked if necessary and chopped

250ml chicken stock

20g fresh coriander leaves, chopped

2½ teaspoons dried oregano

1 teaspoon table salt

2 tablespoons yellow cornmeal

Beyond

- You must halve the recipe for a 3-litre cooker.

- In a pinch, substitute *one and a half* 800g tins of whole tomatillos, which you must drain and chop.

- Serve with lime wedges to squeeze over the bowls. And have warmed corn tortillas at the ready.

- It's hard to imagine turkey chilli verde without soured cream.

- For a brunch, prepare the turkey chilli verde as directed, then pour it into a 23 x 33cm baking dish. Use a large spoon to make up to 8 wells in the chilli, then crack a large egg into each. Cover with a light layer of grated Gouda. Bake in a 180°C oven for 8–15 minutes, depending on how soft you like your egg yolks.

2 tablespoons vegetable, corn or rapeseed oil

1 medium onion, chopped (160g prechopped)

450g lean beef mince

1 medium garlic clove, peeled and finely chopped (1 teaspoon prechopped)

2 tablespoons standard chilli powder

1½ tablespoons unsweetened cocoa powder

1 teaspoon ground allspice

1 teaspoon ground cumin

1 teaspoon ground cinnamon

½ teaspoon table salt

500ml chicken stock

One 400g tin chopped tomatoes

1 tablespoon Worcestershire sauce

1 tablespoon red wine vinegar

225g dried spaghetti

Cincinnati Chilli

6 servings

Cincinnati chilli is usually served *over* pasta. We decided to make it easier by cooking the pasta right in the pot *with* the chilli. So shouldn't this recipe be in the chapter for pasta casseroles? Well, no – because the flavours are so decidedly 'chilli'. The spaghetti picks them up as it cooks under pressure, turning the recipe into a one-pot wonder.

The cocoa powder may be a bit of a surprise, but trust us. Its slightly bitter notes enhance the dish's overall umami goodness. (You don't have to tell picky eaters about the cocoa powder.) Use regular dried spaghetti – not wide pappardelle or thick bucatini.

1.

Press	Setting	Time	Press
SAUTÉ	MEDIUM, NORMAL or CUSTOM 150°C	10 minutes	START

2. Warm the oil in **5.5- or 7.5-litre cooker** for a minute or two. Add the onion and cook, stirring often, until softened, about 4 minutes. Crumble in the beef mince and cook, stirring often, until it loses its raw, red colour, about 3 minutes.

3. Stir in the garlic, chilli powder, cocoa powder, allspice, cumin, cinnamon and salt until fragrant, less than 1 minute. Stir in the stock, chopped tomatoes, Worcestershire sauce and vinegar.

4. Turn off the **SAUTÉ** function. Break the dried spaghetti in half and use a wooden spoon to push it into the liquid without its coming in contact with the bottom of the pot. Lock the lid onto the cooker.

5.

Set the machine	Level	The valve must be	Time	Press
PRESSURE COOK	MAX	——	5 minutes with the KEEP WARM setting off	START
BEAN/CHILLI, PRESSURE COOK or MANUAL	HIGH	Closed	7 minutes with the KEEP WARM setting off	START

6. Use the **quick-release method** to bring the pot's pressure back to normal. Unlatch the lid and open the cooker. Stir well before serving.

Beyond

- For a 3-litre cooker, you must halve the ingredients and break the uncooked spaghetti into thirds.

- For gluten-free pasta, we found the best success with spaghetti made from a mixture of rice and corn.

- Feel free to substitute lean pork mince for the beef mince.

- Top servings with grated Gouda or Cheddar, particularly a mature one.

White Bean and Pumpkin Chilli

8 servings

This tomato-free chilli has become an American favourite in the past few years, with versions served at lots of fast-casual restaurants. It's usually got quite a bit of sugar in the mixture. For us, the tinned pumpkin is sweet enough to do the trick. The number of servings is a little higher because the chilli is so rich and filling. If you've got hearty eaters (or teenagers), it may only serve six.

1. Soak the beans in a big bowl of water for at least 8 hours or up to 12 hours. Drain in a colander set in the sink.

2.

Press	Setting	Time	Press
SAUTÉ	MEDIUM, NORMAL or CUSTOM 150°C	10 minutes	START

3. Warm the oil in a **5.5- or 7.5-litre cooker** for a minute or two, then add the onion. Cook, stirring often, until softened, about 3 minutes. Stir in the red pepper and garlic; cook for a few seconds.

4. Crumble in the beef mince. Cook, stirring often, until lightly browned, about 4 minutes. Stir in the chilli powder, marjoram or oregano, cinnamon, ginger and cloves. Cook a few seconds, then pour in the stock and pumpkin. Turn off the **SAUTÉ** function. Add the beans and stir well until uniform. Lock the lid onto the pot.

5.

Set the machine	Level	The valve must be	Time	Press
PRESSURE COOK	MAX	—	18 minutes with the KEEP WARM setting off	START
BEAN/CHILLI, PRESSURE COOK or MANUAL	HIGH	Closed	25 minutes with the KEEP WARM setting off	START

6. Once the machine has finished cooking, turn it off and let the pressure **return to normal naturally**, about 20 minutes. Unlatch the lid and open the cooker. Stir well before serving.

400g dried haricot or cannellini beans

2 tablespoons olive oil

1 medium onion, chopped (160g prechopped)

1 jarred roasted red pepper, chopped

2 medium garlic cloves, peeled and finely chopped (2 teaspoons prechopped)

350g lean beef mince

3 tablespoons standard chilli powder

1½ tablespoons dried marjoram or oregano

1 teaspoon ground cinnamon

1 teaspoon ground ginger

½ teaspoon ground cloves

1 litre chicken stock

One 400g tin solid pack pumpkin (do not use pumpkin pie filling)

Beyond

- You must halve the recipe for a 3-litre cooker.
- Feel free to substitute lean pork or lamb mince for the beef mince.
- You can substitute 2 teaspoons pumpkin pie spice blend for the cinnamon, ginger and cloves. Make sure the blend includes no sugar or artificial sweetener.
- Stir in up to 250ml single or double cream after cooking for a looser, creamier consistency.
- The chilli's a little soupier than some others, mostly so there's enough liquid that the beans can cook properly. If it's too wet for your taste, use the SAUTÉ function at MEDIUM, NORMAL or CUSTOM 150°C after cooking under pressure to boil it down for a couple of minutes, stirring quite often.

8 dried chillies, preferably New Mexico red, pasilla, ancho and/or mulato, stemmed and deseeded

½ small red onion, roughly chopped (80g prechopped)

1 tinned chipotle in adobo sauce, stemmed and seeded

2 medium garlic cloves, peeled

1½ tablespoons red wine vinegar

1½ tablespoons honey

1 tablespoon adobo sauce from the tin

1 tablespoon cumin seeds

1 tablespoon dried oregano

1 teaspoon table salt

2 tablespoons olive oil

900g beef brisket, diced into 1cm cubes

350ml beer, preferably an amber ale or a pilsner (gluten-free, if necessary)

450g peeled butternut squash cubes, about 1cm pieces

Brisket and Butternut Squash Chilli

4 servings

To be flat honest, this chilli was our favourite. (It was also the favourite of our neighbours who ate the results from testing the recipes in this book.) Sort of like our road map for Chilli con Carne (page 116), this one's a more luxurious take on real-deal chilli: savoury fare made from dried chillies, which become the basis for an aromatic paste, without a tomato or a bean in sight. And using brisket ups the beef quotient exponentially! If you buy peeled, deseeded and cut-up butternut squash in the produce section, you'll have to cut the chunks into smaller bits.

Note that this recipe is a hybrid of sorts. The first part can be cooked either under pressure or in the slow cooker, but the second cooking is *only* done under pressure, thereby making this a potential weekday dish. Make the chilli paste the night before and store the blender canister in the fridge. Slow-cook the chilli during the day, then add the butternut squash and finish the whole thing off under pressure just before dinner.

1. Bring a large saucepan of water to the boil over a high heat. Turn off the heat, add the chillies, cover the pan and leave to soak for 20 minutes. Or do this whole operation in the Instant Pot, starting with the **SAUTÉ** function set to **HIGH** or **MORE** until the water boils.

2. Drain the chillies in a colander set in the sink and pile them into a large blender. Add the onion, chipotle, garlic, vinegar, honey, adobo sauce, cumin, oregano and salt. Cover and blend into a coarse paste, stopping the machine at least once to scrape down the inside.

3.

Press	Setting	Time	Press
SAUTÉ	MEDIUM, NORMAL or CUSTOM 150°C	5 minutes	START

4. Warm the oil in a **5.5-litre cooker** for a couple of minutes, then add every speck of the chilli paste from the blender. Cook for 2 minutes, stirring often, to toast the paste. Add the beef and stir well to get every little bit coated in the paste. Pour in the beer and stir well. Turn off the **SAUTÉ** function and lock the lid onto the pot.

5.

Press the button for	Level	The valve must be	Time	Press
PRESSURE COOK	MAX	——	25 minutes with the KEEP WARM setting off	START
BEAN/ CHILLI, PRESSURE COOK or MANUAL	HIGH	Closed	32 minutes with the KEEP WARM setting off	START
SLOW COOK	HIGH	Opened	4 hours with the KEEP WARM setting off (or on for no more than 3 hours)	START

6. If you've used a pressure setting, when the machine has finished cooking, use the **quick-release method** to bring the pot's pressure back to normal.

7. Unlatch the lid and open the cooker. Stir in the butternut squash cubes. Lock the lid back onto the pot.

8.

Press the button for	Level	The valve must be	Set the time for	Press
PRESSURE COOK	MAX	——	3 minutes with the KEEP WARM setting off	START
BEAN/CHILI, PRESSURE COOK, or MANUAL	HIGH	Closed	4 minutes with the KEEP WARM setting off	START

9. Use the **quick-release method** to bring the pot's pressure back to normal. Unlatch the lid and open the cooker. Stir well before serving.

Beyond

- For a 3-litre cooker, you must use 250ml beer and halve the remaining ingredients.

- For a 7.5-litre cooker, you must add 250ml beef stock with the beer.

- Our favourite dried chilli combo was four New Mexico reds and four pasillas. A couple of dried chipotles would add a smoky flavour (and a lot more heat).

- We poured Alabama white barbecue sauce over our bowlfuls: mix 500g regular or low-fat mayonnaise, 1 tablespoon ground black pepper and 1 teaspoon white granulated sugar in a medium bowl. Whisk in 60ml white vinegar, then continue adding more vinegar, maybe up to 60ml more, until the mixture is the consistency of a sauce, not a spread.

Two 400g tins chopped
tomatoes, preferably
fire-roasted

350ml Guinness

2 tablespoons pure
chilli powder

2 tablespoons mild
smoked paprika

1 teaspoon ground cumin

1 teaspoon dried oregano

1 medium onion, chopped
(160g prechopped)

900g low-sodium raw corned
beef, rinsed and any spice
packets removed, the meat
diced

Two 400g tins kidney or pinto
beans, drained and rinsed

Beyond

- You must halve the recipe for
a 3-litre cooker.

- To make a corned beef and
cabbage chilli, omit the beans
and stir a 450g bag of slaw
mix into the stew in step
3 before the second round
of cooking.

- The chilli is a bit loose, a bit
soupy. We preferred that
texture with the corned beef.
You can boil it down further
by setting the machine to its
SAUTÉ function at MEDIUM,
NORMAL Or CUSTOM 150°C
after step 5 and simmering it,
uncovered, for a couple of
minutes.

- To do without the alcohol,
substitute 350ml beef stock,
60ml unsweetened cloudy
apple juice, and 2 teaspoons
apple cider vinegar for the
beer.

- To cook this dish on the SLOW
COOK mode, put all the
ingredients in the pot up
front, lock on the lid, keep the
pressure valve open and press
the SLOW COOK function for
4 hours on HIGH with the
KEEP WARM function set for
up to 2 hours.

Corned Beef Chilli with Guinness

6 servings

Corned beef is terrific for chilli! (The cut is just brisket, after all.)
It adds a briny savouriness, sort of like a New York deli version of
Midwestern comfort food, laced with stout and beans: a rib-sticker
if there ever was one. We stock up on corned beef after Saint
Patrick's Day when it's on sale. Put a couple in the freezer for
a winter night when you're ready for this hearty stew.

1. Mix the tomatoes, Guinness, chilli powder, smoked paprika,
cumin, oregano, onion and corned beef in a **5.5- or 7.5-litre
cooker** until uniform. Lock the lid onto the pot.

2.

Set the machine	Level	The valve must be	Time	Press
PRESSURE COOK	MAX	—	22 minutes with the KEEP WARM setting off	START
BEAN/CHILLI, PRESSURE COOK or MANUAL	HIGH	Closed	30 minutes with the KEEP WARM setting off	START

3. Use the **quick-release method** to bring the pot's pressure
back to normal. Unlatch the lid and open the pot. Stir in the
beans. Lock the lid back onto the pot.

4.

Press	Level	The valve must be	Time	Press
PRESSURE COOK	MAX	—	3 minutes with the KEEP WARM setting off	START
BEAN/CHILLI, PRESSURE COOK or MANUAL	HIGH	Closed	4 minutes with the KEEP WARM setting off	START

5. Use the **quick-release method** to bring the pot's pressure
back to normal. Unlatch the lid, open the pot and stir well
before serving.

Bacon and Black Turtle Bean Chilli

4 servings

Bacon? Chilli? Together at last! Use thick-cut streaky bacon so the chilli has chunks of porky goodness in every spoonful. Also keep this in mind: Leaner bacon (of any sort) is a better choice. If the bacon's too fatty, it can leave an unappealing grease slick in the serving bowls.

1.

Press	Setting	Time	Press
SAUTÉ	MEDIUM, NORMAL Or CUSTOM 150°C	15 minutes	START

2. Melt the butter in a **5.5- or 7.5-litre cooker**. Add the bacon and onion. Cook, stirring often, until the bacon begins to brown well, about 8 minutes. Stir in the beer. Scrape up *every speck of browned stuff* on the pot's bottom.

3. Turn off the **SAUTÉ** function. Stir in the tomatoes, beans, chilli powder, cumin, garlic and tinned chipotles. Lock the lid onto the pot.

4.

Set the machine	Level	The valve must be	Time	Press
PRESSURE COOK	MAX	—	8 minutes with the KEEP WARM setting off	START
BEAN/CHILLI, PRESSURE COOK or MANUAL	HIGH	Closed	10 minutes with the KEEP WARM setting off	START
SLOW COOK	HIGH	Opened	4 hours with the KEEP WARM setting off (or on for no more than 2 hours)	START

5. If you've used a pressure setting, when the machine has finished cooking, use the **quick-release method** to bring the pot's pressure back to normal.

6. Unlatch the lid and open the cooker. Stir well before serving.

15g butter

450g thick-cut streaky bacon, chopped

1 medium onion, chopped (160g prechopped)

180ml amber beer or chicken stock

Two 400g tins chopped tomatoes

One 400g tin black turtle beans, drained and rinsed

2½ tablespoons pure chilli powder

2 teaspoons ground cumin

2 medium garlic cloves, peeled and finely chopped (2 teaspoons prechopped)

Up to 2 tinned chipotles in adobo sauce, stemmed, deseeded and chopped

Beyond

- You must halve the recipe for a 3-litre cooker.
- This chilli *needs* crunchy bread. Warm a baguette in the oven until the bread gets a crackly crust, so crackly it's almost a crouton.
- For a richer chilli, whisk up to 250g plain Greek yoghurt into the chilli after cooking. Do not let it come back to a simmer or the yoghurt will break.
- For a more sophisticated take, add ½ teaspoon ground cardamom, ½ teaspoon ground cinnamon and/or ¼ teaspoon grated nutmeg with the cumin.

450g boneless skinless chicken breasts, cut into strips 1cm in width

Two 400g tins white beans, drained and rinsed

350ml chicken stock

1 medium onion, chopped (160g prechopped)

Two 125g tins mild or hot chopped green chillies

2 medium garlic cloves, peeled and finely chopped (2 teaspoons prechopped)

2 teaspoons dried oregano

2 teaspoons ground cumin

60ml double cream

2 tablespoons yellow cornmeal

250g grated Cheddar or Gouda

White Chilli

4 servings

In the mood for a little decadence? Add cream to your chilli! Here's a version of so-called 'white' chilli: sweet-and-sour (from tinned green chillies), comforting and hearty. However, it doesn't freeze well. The cream tends to break and the cornmeal settles to the bottom of the batch. Plan on eating it up when it's ready. By the way, there's no salt because the tinned green chillies are notoriously sodium-rich. Pass salt at the table, if you wish.

1. Mix the chicken, beans, stock, onion, chillies, garlic, oregano and cumin in a **5.5- or 7.5-litre cooker**. Lock the lid onto the pot.

2.

Set the machine	Level	The valve must be	Time	Press
PRESSURE COOK	MAX	——	5 minutes with the KEEP WARM setting off	START
BEAN/CHILLI, PRESSURE COOK or MANUAL	HIGH	Closed	7 minutes with the KEEP WARM setting off	START

3. Use the **quick-release method** to bring the pot's pressure back to normal. Unlatch the lid and open the cooker.

4.

Press	Setting	Time	Press
SAUTÉ	MEDIUM, NORMAL Or CUSTOM 150°C	5 minutes	START

5. Bring the chilli to a simmer. Stir in the cream and cornmeal. Cook, stirring constantly, until the chilli thickens somewhat, about 3 minutes. Turn off the **SAUTÉ** function and remove the *hot* insert from the machine. Sprinkle the cheese over the chilli. Set the lid askew over the insert for 5 minutes to melt the cheese.

Beyond

- You must halve the recipe for a 3-litre cooker.
- We prefer the texture of the chicken strips. However, you can substitute 450g turkey mince (minced chicken gets depressingly squishy). Crumble the ground meat into marble-size bits in the pot.
- Add a heavy grind of black pepper (and even some crushed chilli flakes) over the melted cheese before serving.

Road Map: Bean Chilli

6 servings

Nothing makes great bean chilli like dried beans. But not every dried bean is created equal. Listen, the world's a mess. Hectic, too. Dried beans sit on the store's shelf for, um, forever. They can dry out so much that no matter how long you cook them, they never get tender.

Don't let any of that deter you from making your own brand of bean chilli. Instead, look for plump beans (even in their dried state) in the package. They shouldn't be chipped up at the bottom of the bag. Once soaked, they should have definitely gotten fatter, doubled (or maybe even more) in size. For more information about dried beans, see pages 47–48.

The herbs and spices you choose are what will make this your signature recipe. We have a preference for oregano, thyme and cinnamon with a pinch of ground cloves. You might prefer all oregano, or a mix of sage and thyme with just a pinch of nutmeg.

If you open the pot and they're still too tough for your taste, lock the lid back in place and give them another 5–10 minutes at HIGH pressure, followed by the **quick-release method**.

1. Soak the dried beans in a big bowl of water for at least 8 hours or up to 12 hours, until nicely plumped. Drain in a colander set in the sink, then pour the beans into a 5.5- or 7.5-litre cooker.

2. Stir in the stock, tomatoes, aromatics, root vegetables, quick-cooking vegetables, chilli powder, fresh herbs and/or dried spices, enricher and salt (if using). Lock the lid onto the pot.

3.

Set the machine	Level	The valve must be	Time	Press
PRESSURE COOK	MAX	—	18 minutes with the KEEP WARM setting off	START
BEAN/CHILLI, PRESSURE COOK or MANUAL	HIGH	Closed	25 minutes with the KEEP WARM setting off	START

4. Once the machine has finished cooking, turn it off and let the pressure **return to normal naturally**, about 20 minutes. Unlock and open the lid. Stir well before serving.

400g medium-sized dried beans
> **Choose one or a combo** from black turtle beans, haricot, cannellini, kidney, pinto or azuki.

700ml vegetable stock

One 400g tin chopped tomatoes

250g chopped aromatics
> **Choose one or any combo** from onions (of any sort), shallots, stemmed and deseeded, peppers of any sort, celery, trimmed fennel and/or jarred roasted red peppers.

250g diced root vegetables
> **Choose** from carrots, parsnips, sweet potatoes, winter squash (such as butternut squash), yellow beetroot, turnips or celeriac.

150g quick-cooking vegetables
> **Choose one or a 50/50 combo** from diced courgette, diced summer squash, trimmed and chopped green beans, chopped or small broccoli florets, chopped or small cauliflower florets and/or corn kernels.

3 tablespoons pure chilli powder
> **Choose** from ancho, New Mexico red, New Mexico hatch, chipotle or a pure chilli blend.

2 tablespoons fresh green herbs (leaves picked) or dried spices
> **Choose a blend** from oregano, marjoram, sage, thyme, cumin, cinnamon, cloves and/or nutmeg.

1 tablespoon flavour enricher
> **Choose** from Dijon mustard, ketchup, sweet chilli sauce, Worcestershire sauce or chutney.

½ teaspoon table salt (optional)

Beyond

- You must halve the recipe for a 3-litre cooker.
- Keep it vegan by garnishing the bowls with fresh, finely chopped, deseeded jalapeños, finely chopped spring onions and even a vegan barbecue sauce.

1 litre vegetable stock

Two 400g tins chopped tomatoes

One 400g tin haricot or cannellini beans, drained and rinsed

One 400g tin kidney or pinto beans, drained and rinsed

One 400g tin black turtle beans, drained and rinsed

350ml beer, preferably a pale ale (and gluten-free, if necessary)

1 medium onion, chopped (160g prechopped)

100g chana dal (that is, split and processed chickpeas)

80g buckwheat groats

70g Puy lentils

35g standard chilli powder

1 tablespoon ground cumin

1 tablespoon dried oregano

½ teaspoon ground cloves

½ teaspoon mustard powder

½ teaspoon table salt

The Ultimate Vegan Chilli

8 servings

You won't believe the texture of this chilli! Even if you're a committed carnivore, you'll swear there's meat in the bowl, thanks to the mix of chana dal, buckwheat groats and lentils. They provide an unbelievably savoury foundation for a chilli that's then stocked with beans. Admittedly, there are some funky ingredients in the list. Stock up because you're going to want to make this chilli more than once. After all, there's nothing to it except stirring everything in the pot, then getting the pressure going. (For a discussion about why buckwheat is gluten-free, see page 407.)

1. Mix all the ingredients in a **5.5- or 7.5-litre cooker**. Lock the lid onto the pot.

2.

Set the machine	Level	The valve must be	Time	Press
PRESSURE COOK	MAX	——	20 minutes with the KEEP WARM setting off	START
BEAN/CHILLI, PRESSURE COOK or MANUAL	HIGH	Closed	27 minutes with the KEEP WARM setting off	START
SLOW COOK	HIGH	Opened	4 hours with the KEEP WARM setting off (or on for no more than 2 hours)	START

3. If you've used a pressure setting, when the machine has finished cooking, use the **quick-release method** to bring the pot's pressure back to normal.

4. Unlock and open the lid. Stir well before serving.

Beyond

- You must halve the recipe for a 3-litre cooker.
- If you don't want the alcohol, substitute 350ml unsweetened cloudy apple juice for the beer.
- There's no reason to stand on ceremony with the beans. You can use any combination – or just, for example, all kidney beans. (Or whatever's on sale.) Use medium-sized beans, nothing big like butter beans or too small like haricot beans.

Quinoa Chilli

4 servings

Quinoa makes a thick, almost porridge-like chilli, which is why the beans help give this version a little tooth, a better texture against the silkiness. Quinoa has a naturally occurring enzyme (a saponin) that protects the grains from, well, predators (aka us). Not only does the enzyme taste bitter, but it can foam in the pressure cooker and cause the pot to malfunction. Rinse the grains well in a fine-mesh sieve such as a *chinois* or in a colander lined with a double thickness of kitchen paper. We do this even if the package says they've already been rinsed.

1. Stir all the ingredients in a **5.5-litre cooker**. Lock the lid onto the pot.

2.

Set the machine	Level	The valve must be	Time	Press
PRESSURE COOK	MAX	——	6 minutes with the KEEP WARM setting off	START
BEAN/ CHILLI, PRESSURE COOK or MANUAL	HIGH	Closed	8 minutes with the KEEP WARM setting off	START
SLOW COOK	HIGH	Opened	3 hours with the KEEP WARM setting off (or on for no more than 1 hour)	START

3. If you've used a pressure setting, when the machine has finished cooking, use the **quick-release method** to bring the pot's pressure back to normal.

4. Unlock and remove the lid. Stir well before serving.

500ml vegetable stock

200g red or white quinoa, well rinsed

One 400g tin red kidney beans, drained and rinsed

One 400g tin chopped tomatoes

One 125g tin mild or hot green chillies

2 jarred roasted red peppers, chopped

1 small courgette (about 175g), chopped

2 medium garlic cloves, peeled and finely chopped (2 teaspoons prechopped)

1 tablespoon pure chilli powder

2 teaspoons ground cumin

2 teaspoons dried oregano

Beyond

- For a 7.5-litre cooker, you must increase all the ingredients by 50 per cent.

- Because of the quinoa's need to dance in lots of liquid, we do not recommend making this chilli in a 3-litre cooker.

- Add up to 80g chopped onion and/or 70g chopped celery for a vegetable-heavy chilli.

- This chilli would be a savoury topping for chilli dogs (whether you use vegan hot dogs or the more standard-issue ones).

2 tablespoons vegetable, corn or rapeseed oil

1 large onion, chopped (160g prechopped)

1 medium red pepper, stemmed, cored and chopped (175g prechopped)

2 celery stalks, thinly sliced

2 medium garlic cloves, peeled and finely chopped (2 teaspoons prechopped)

800g lean beef mince

250ml beef or chicken stock

125ml ketchup

1 tablespoon yellow mustard (don't you dare use Dijon)

1 tablespoon treacle

1 tablespoon standard chilli powder

2 teaspoons apple cider vinegar

½ teaspoon table salt

6–8 regular burger buns

Beyond

- This chilli may be gluten-free depending on the buns, of course, but more importantly, the ketchup. Some are made with vinegars crafted from wheat. Look for brands that distil their vinegar from corn, as these are considered gluten-free.

- Sloppy joes are notoriously messy, maybe even a knife-and-fork affair. We tend to serve them to kids in hot-dog buns.

- If you don't mind alcohol, substitute a pale ale or amber beer for the stock.

- Even though there's mustard in the mix, we still like to smear more on the buns before we add the sloppy joe mixture. Dill pickle slices are pretty tasty, too.

Classic Sloppy Joes

Makes 6–8 sandwiches

This recipe will give you the classic sloppy joe, an American favourite since the 1960s. Traditionally, the beef mince mixture is thickened with tomato purée. We felt it muddied the flavours and wanted a more characteristic, sweet/sour palette from the pot. So we advocate for using ketchup and boiling down the mixture after cooking. The flavours stay brighter. And you can control how sloppy you want your joes. We prefer a 20-napkin event.

1.

Press	Setting	Time	Press
SAUTÉ	MEDIUM, NORMAL Or CUSTOM 150°C	10 minutes	START

2. Warm the oil in a 3-, 5.5- or 7.5-litre cooker for a minute or two, then add the onion, pepper, celery and garlic. Cook, stirring often, until the onion begins to soften, about 4 minutes.

3. Crumble in the beef mince. Continue cooking, stirring fairly often and breaking up any clumps of mince, until the meat begins to brown, about 5 minutes. Turn off the **SAUTÉ** function. Stir in the stock, ketchup, mustard, treacle, chilli powder, vinegar and salt until uniform. Lock the lid onto the pot.

4.

Set the machine	Level	The valve must be	Time	Press
PRESSURE COOK	MAX	——	4 minutes with the KEEP WARM setting off	START
BEAN/CHILLI, PRESSURE COOK or MANUAL	HIGH	Closed	5 minutes with the KEEP WARM setting off	START

5. Use the **quick-release method** to bring the pot's pressure back to normal. Unlatch the lid and open the cooker.

6.

Press	Setting	Time	Press
SAUTÉ	LOW or LESS	10 minutes	START

7. Bring the mixture to a low simmer. Cook, stirring fairly often, until thickened and not as soupy, about 7 minutes. Turn off the **SAUTÉ** function, set the lid askew over the pot, and set aside for 5–10 minutes to blend the flavours. Spoon the mixture into the burger buns.

Loaded Whole-Grain Sloppy Joes

Makes 6–8 sandwiches

Okay, these are not for school dinners. They're stocked with wheat berries and oats for a satisfying meal. There's no need to boil this mixture down since the oats will thicken it to hold together more easily than the filling for Classic Sloppy Joes (opposite). Plus, you can have old-school comfort food *and* eat healthy. Take your victories where you can.

1. Mix the water, wheat berries and oil in a **5.5-litre cooker**. Lock the lid onto the pot.

2.

Set the machine	Level	The valve must be	Time	Press
PRESSURE COOK	MAX	—	30 minutes with the KEEP WARM setting off	START
PRESSURE COOK or MANUAL	HIGH	Closed	40 minutes with the KEEP WARM setting off	START

3. Use the **quick-release method** to bring the pot's pressure back to normal. Unlatch the lid and open the cooker. Drain the wheat berries from the *hot* insert into a colander set in the sink. Rinse out the insert, return it to the cooker and put the wheat berries back in the insert.

4. Stir in the tomatoes, chillies, onion, oats, treacle, mustard, Worcestershire sauce, vinegar, paprika, cloves, garlic powder and salt. Crumble in the beef mince and stir until uniform, breaking up any large clumps. Lock the lid onto the pot.

5.

Set the machine	Level	The valve must be	Time	Press
PRESSURE COOK	MAX	—	5 minutes with the KEEP WARM setting off	START
PRESSURE COOK or MANUAL	HIGH	Closed	7 minutes with the KEEP WARM setting off	START

6. Use the **quick-release method** to return the pot's pressure to normal. Unlatch the lid and open the cooker. Stir well before serving in burger buns.

700ml water

90g dried wheat berries, preferably soft white wheat berries

1 tablespoon vegetable, corn or rapeseed oil

Two 400g tins chopped tomatoes

One 125g tin mild or hot chopped green chillies

1 small onion, chopped (80g prechopped)

50g rolled oats (do not use quick-cooking oats, pinhead oats or coarse oatmeal)

90g treacle

2 tablespoons Dijon mustard

2 tablespoons Worcestershire sauce

2 tablespoons red wine vinegar

2 tablespoons mild paprika

½ teaspoon ground cloves

½ teaspoon garlic powder

¼ teaspoon table salt

675g lean beef mince

6–8 burger buns

Beyond

- You must halve the recipe for a 3-litre cooker.

- For a 7.5-litre cooker, you must use the ingredients as stated but add 125ml stock (or water) with the mince.

- Garlic powder gives the dish a more assertive garlic flavour than finely chopped cloves. But if desired, substitute up to 2 teaspoons peeled and finely chopped garlic.

1 tablespoon olive oil

1 medium onion, chopped
(160g prechopped)

1 medium red pepper,
stemmed, cored and
chopped (175g prechopped)

700ml vegetable stock

280g Puy lentils

One 400g tin chopped
tomatoes

2 tablespoons soy sauce

1 tablespoon Dijon mustard

1 tablespoon dark
brown sugar

1 teaspoon ground
black pepper

6 burger buns

Vegan Sloppy Joes

Makes 6 sandwiches

Earthy lentils mixed with soy sauce and mustard make a pretty fine
sloppy joe filling, provided you mash some of the cooked lentils
into a purée to thicken the mixture. We've added some brown
sugar because lentils are so savoury. You could halve the amount
of sugar, but don't omit it. Only use green lentils; the brown ones
are too mushy for a successful sandwich filling.

1.

Press	Setting	Time	Press
SAUTÉ	MEDIUM, NORMAL or CUSTOM 150°C	5 minutes	START

2. Warm the oil in a **5.5- or 7.5-litre cooker** for a minute or two.
Add the onion and pepper. Cook, stirring often, until the onion
begins to soften, about 4 minutes. Turn off the **SAUTÉ** function.
Stir in the stock, lentils, tomatoes, soy sauce, mustard, brown
sugar and pepper. Lock the lid onto the pot.

3.

Set the machine	Level	The valve must be	Time	Press
PRESSURE COOK	MAX	——	18 minutes with the KEEP WARM setting off	START
BEAN/CHILLI, PRESSURE COOK or MANUAL	HIGH	Closed	24 minutes with the KEEP WARM setting off	START

4. When the pot is done cooking, turn it off and let its pressure
return to normal naturally, about 25 minutes. Unlatch the lid and
open the cooker. Use a potato masher or the back of a wooden
spoon to mash some of the lentils into a purée, stirring them
into the sauce to thicken it. Serve in burger buns.

Beyond

- You must halve the recipe for
a 3-litre cooker.

- For condiments in the buns,
slice a red onion and an
orange (peel and all) into very
thin discs (less than 5mm
thick, and remove the pips
from the orange). Coat these
in olive oil and grill them until
soft or even charred.

- Skip the buns and serve the
lentil filling alongside
scrambled eggs and grilled
sausages for breakfast.

Buttery Marinara Sauce

Makes enough for 700g dried pasta

Here's a decadent marinara in the style of a recipe from the great and now-sadly-gone Italian cookbook author, Marcella Hazan. The whole thing's about as satisfying as any sauce we can imagine. We even thinned it out with extra stock and cream one day and ate it for lunch as tomato soup with crunchy toast. Pure heaven.

1. Stir all the ingredients in a **5.5-litre cooker**. Lock the lid onto the pot.

2.

Set the machine	Level	The valve must be	Time	Press
PRESSURE COOK	MAX	—	4 minutes with the KEEP WARM setting off	START
PRESSURE COOK or MANUAL	HIGH	Closed	5 minutes with the KEEP WARM setting off	START

3. Use the **quick-release method** to return the pot's pressure to normal. Unlatch the lid and open the cooker. Fish out and discard the onion halves (or pieces, if they've come apart). Either use a hand blender in the pot to purée the mixture into a sauce; or pour the mixture into a large blender, cover and blend until smooth.

Four 400g tins chopped tomatoes

2 medium onions, peeled and halved

Up to 4 medium garlic cloves, peeled and finely chopped (4 teaspoons prechopped)

115g butter, cut into chunks

1 teaspoon dried oregano

½ teaspoon ground black pepper

¼ teaspoon table salt

Beyond

- You must halve the recipe for a 3-litre cooker.
- For a 7.5-litre cooker, you must increase all the ingredients by 50 per cent.
- To make this sauce even more savoury, add up to 2 finely chopped, tinned anchovy fillets and/or up to ½ teaspoon crushed chilli flakes with the other ingredients. (Omit the salt if adding anchovy fillets.)

Four 400g tins whole tomatoes, drained

125ml regular or low-fat evaporated milk

½ small onion, chopped (80g prechopped)

15g fresh basil leaves, roughly chopped

1 tablespoon fresh rosemary leaves, chopped (optional)

½ teaspoon table salt

60ml double cream

2 tablespoons tomato purée

Creamy Tomato and Basil Pasta Sauce

Makes enough for 900g dried pasta

This super rich pasta sauce is best in small doses with thick pasta like bucatini, rather than spaghetti. We've also made pasta casseroles with the sauce, and have even used it as the tomato sauce in a meat-free lasagne.

1. Wash and dry your hands. Crush the tinned tomatoes one by one into a **5.5-litre cooker**. Add the evaporated milk, onion, basil, rosemary (if using) and salt. Stir well and lock the lid onto the pot.

2.

Set the machine	Level	The valve must be	Time	Press
PRESSURE COOK	MAX	——	4 minutes with the KEEP WARM setting off	START
PRESSURE COOK or MANUAL	HIGH	Closed	5 minutes with the KEEP WARM setting off	START

3. Use the **quick-release method** to bring the pot's pressure back to normal. Unlatch the lid and open the cooker. Stir in the cream and tomato purée. Either use a hand blender to purée the sauce right in the pot, or pour the contents of the pot into a large blender, cover and blend until smooth, scraping down the canister's inside at least once.

Beyond

- For a 3-litre cooker, you must use the full amount of evaporated milk but halve the remaining ingredients.

- For a 7.5-litre cooker, you must add 125ml vegetable or chicken stock with the evaporated milk.

- Add up to 1 teaspoon finely chopped garlic with the basil.

- Grate nutmeg over the servings.

- Warm about 1cm of olive oil in a large frying pan set over a medium-high heat until wavy. Fry whole basil leaves in the oil until blistered, about 1 minute, turning once. Use these to garnish the pasta.

- For a vodka sauce, substitute vodka for the evaporated milk.

Arrabbiata Sauce

Makes enough for 450g dried pasta

This version of the super spicy sauce is fairly traditional in that it includes no onion, the better to let the heat blaze through. If you're worried, remember that pressure cookers eat up capsaicin, the burning chemical in chillies. Still, your first time you might want to use only one chilli and cut down on the crushed chilli flakes (to, say, ½ teaspoon), just to make sure you like the fire as much as you think you do. However, crushed chilli flakes are not all created equal. Some are tame, almost dull; others, hellacious. Sample one of yours to know what you've got.

1.

Press	Setting	Time	Press
SAUTÉ	LOW or LESS	10 minutes	START

2. Warm the oil in a **3- or 5.5-litre cooker** for a minute or two. Add the chillies and crushed chilli flakes. Cook, stirring occasionally, until the oil turns orange and becomes spicy-fragrant, about 4 minutes. Add the garlic and anchovy. Cook, stirring almost constantly, until the anchovy bits almost dissolve, about 3 minutes. Pour in the vermouth and scrape up any browned bits on the bottom of the pot. Turn off the **SAUTÉ** function.

3. Clean and dry your hands. Pick up the whole tomatoes one by one from the tin and crush them over the pot, letting the bits and pieces fall inside. When you've crushed all the tomatoes, pour in any remaining juice from the can. Lock the lid onto the pot.

4.

Set the machine	Level	The valve must be	Time	Press
PRESSURE COOK	MAX	—	3 minutes with the KEEP WARM setting off	START
SOUP/BROTH, PRESSURE COOK or MANUAL	HIGH	Closed	5 minutes with the KEEP WARM setting off	START

5. Use the **quick-release method** to bring the pot's pressure back to normal. Unlatch the lid and open the cooker. Stir well before serving.

60ml olive oil

2 medium fresh Anaheim or jalapeño chillies, stemmed and thinly sliced

Up to 1 teaspoon crushed chilli flakes

6 medium garlic cloves, peeled and finely chopped (2 tablespoons prechopped)

2 tinned anchovy fillets, finely chopped

125ml red (or sweet) vermouth

Two 400g tins whole tomatoes

Beyond

- For a 7.5-litre cooker, you must add 60ml vegetable stock (or water) with the vermouth.

- Toss this pasta sauce with cooked and drained penne or ziti.

- Try a little balsamic vinegar as the condiment over the servings of pasta.

- Also, consider sprinkling each serving with finely chopped fresh flat-leaf parsley leaves.

1.5kg cherry tomatoes, halved (use every drop of juice)

1 medium leek (about 125g), white and pale green part only, halved, washed well and thinly sliced

60ml vegetable stock

60ml dry white wine or dry vermouth

3 tablespoons olive oil

2 tablespoons fresh rosemary leaves, finely chopped

2 tablespoons fresh thyme leaves, finely chopped

1 teaspoon white granulated sugar

1 teaspoon table salt

Cherry Tomato and Herb Pasta Sauce

Makes enough for 900g dried pasta

Light, sweet and herbaceous – what more can we say about this simple sauce made from cherry tomatoes? Use the freshest you can find and none larger than a golf ball. Only true cherry tomatoes will work here, not grape or other tiny tomatoes. They're not juicy enough. If you find terrific ripe cherry tomatoes at a farmers' market, make a couple of batches of the sauce for the freezer.

1. Mix all the ingredients in a **5.5- or 7.5-litre cooker**. Lock the lid onto the pot.

2.

Set the machine	Level	The valve must be	Time	Press
PRESSURE COOK	MAX	——	4 minutes with the KEEP WARM setting off	START
PRESSURE COOK or MANUAL	HIGH	Closed	5 minutes with the KEEP WARM setting off	START

3. When the machine has finished cooking, turn it off and let the pot's pressure **return to normal naturally**, about 10 minutes. Unlatch the lid and open the cooker. Use a potato masher to crush the sauce into a loose purée, or use the back of a wooden spoon to press the sauce against the sides of the pot.

4.

Press	Setting	Time	Press
SAUTÉ	MEDIUM, NORMAL Or CUSTOM 150°C	5 minutes	START

5. Bring the sauce to a simmer, stirring occasionally. Cook, stirring once in a while, until thickened somewhat, not pasty, just less soupy, about 3 minutes. Turn off the **SAUTÉ** function and stir well before serving.

Beyond

- For a 3-litre cooker, you must use the full amount of stock and halve the remaining ingredients.

- For a more robust flavour, add up to 2 teaspoons finely chopped garlic with the leek.

- If you don't have a leek to hand, substitute 2 chopped medium shallots.

- Stir chopped ham and broccoli florets into the hot sauce to make a heartier meal.

Aubergine and Caper Pasta Sauce

Makes enough for 800g dried pasta

This recipe makes a lot of sauce. And with pasta, it's more of a meal than a first course or a side dish, given how stocked the sauce is. We used jarred marinara because we wanted that smooth texture without having to create a marinara, purée it and then carry on with the aubergine recipe. That said, you can always make your own Buttery Marinara Sauce (page 133) and use it here.

1.

Press	Setting	Time	Press
SAUTÉ	MEDIUM, NORMAL or CUSTOM 150°C	10 minutes	START

2. Melt the butter in a **3- or 5.5-litre pot**, then add the onion. Cook, stirring often, until softened, about 3 minutes. Add the garlic and cook for a few seconds, until fragrant.

3. Add the aubergine, pepper and capers. Stir for 1 minute. Turn off the **SAUTÉ** function. Pour in the marinara sauce, stock and parsley and stir until uniform. Lock the lid on the pot.

4.

Set the machine	Level	The valve must be	Time	Press
PRESSURE COOK	MAX	———	6 minutes with the KEEP WARM setting off	START
PRESSURE COOK or MANUAL	HIGH	Closed	8 minutes with the KEEP WARM setting off	START
SLOW COOK	HIGH	Opened	2 hours with the KEEP WARM setting off (or on for no more than 1 hour)	START

5. If you've used a pressure setting, when the machine has finished cooking, use the **quick-release method** to bring the pot's pressure back to normal.

6. Unlatch the lid and open the cooker. Stir well before serving.

30g butter

1 medium onion, chopped (160g prechopped)

2 medium garlic cloves, peeled and finely chopped (2 teaspoons prechopped)

One 450g aubergine, diced

1 medium yellow or green pepper, stemmed, cored and chopped (175g prechopped)

1 tablespoon drained and rinsed capers, chopped

One 680g jar plain marinara (tomato) sauce

125ml vegetable stock

5g fresh flat-leaf parsley leaves

Beyond

- For a 7.5-litre cooker, you must increase the stock to 180ml (use the remaining ingredients as stated).

- Top the sauced pasta with lots of finely grated Parmigiano-Reggiano or crumbled feta.

30g butter

1 medium onion, chopped (160g prechopped)

2 medium celery stalks, thinly sliced

60g thinly sliced carrots

2 medium garlic cloves, peeled and finely chopped (2 teaspoons prechopped)

550g lean beef mince

125ml tinned regular or low-fat evaporated milk

Two 400g tins whole tomatoes

2 tablespoons Italian seasoning blend, preferably salt-free

½ teaspoon grated nutmeg

¼ teaspoon table salt

¼ teaspoon ground black pepper

One 175g tin tomato purée

Classic Bolognese Sauce

Makes enough for 900g dried pasta

Sometimes, nothing will do except the classic. Here's a sauce from the Instant Pot that preserves the traditional creamy/chunky texture so prized in a fine Bolognese, thanks mostly to the magic of evaporated milk (which won't break under pressure).

It's really more of a ragù, so this one's a main course (with pasta, of course, or maybe Polenta, page 443). While the recipe does require a bit of work, it doesn't force you into a half-day simmer on the hob, the way a more traditional recipe would. You'll still end up with a traditional meat sauce, the centre of a great meal.

1.

Press	Setting	Time	Press
SAUTÉ	MEDIUM, NORMAL or CUSTOM 150°C	15 minutes	START

2. Melt the butter in a **5.5- or 7.5-litre cooker**. Add the onion, celery, carrot slices and garlic. Cook, stirring often, until the onion begins to soften, about 5 minutes. Crumble in the beef mince and cook, breaking up any clumps, just until the meat loses all its pink, raw colour, about 3 minutes.

3. Pour in the evaporated milk and scrape up any browned bits on the bottom of the pot. Cook, stirring quite a bit, until the milk comes to a full simmer, then continue cooking until the milk has reduced to about half its original volume, about 3 minutes.

4. Wash and dry your hands. Crush the whole tomatoes one by one into the pot, then pour any remaining juice from the tins into the pot. Stir well, then turn off the **SAUTÉ** function. Stir in the seasoning blend, nutmeg, salt and pepper. Lock the lid onto the pot.

5.

Set the machine	Level	The valve must be	Time	Press
PRESSURE COOK	MAX	—	8 minutes with the KEEP WARM setting off	START
MEAT/ STEW, PRESSURE COOK or MANUAL	HIGH	Closed	10 minutes with the KEEP WARM setting off	START

6. Use the **quick-release method** to bring the pot's pressure back to normal. Unlatch the lid and open the cooker.

7.

Press	Setting	Time	Press
SAUTÉ	MEDIUM, NORMAL Or CUSTOM 150°C	5 minutes	START

8. Stir in the tomato purée and bring the sauce to a full simmer. Cook, stirring often, until somewhat thickened, about 3 minutes. Turn off the **SAUTÉ** function and set the lid askew over the pot. Set aside for 10 minutes to blend the flavours.

Beyond

- You must halve the recipe for a 3-litre cooker.
- Toss the sauce with wide pasta like pappardelle.
- Use a 50/50 combo of butter and olive oil for a silkier finish.
- Feel free to use 350g lean beef mince and 200g lean pork mince.
- Make sure you've plenty of Parmigiano-Reggiano to hand for grating (or better, shaving) over each serving.
- We tried various dairy substitutes, none with good results (some broke; some were too sweet). The best substitute was 125ml chicken stock and 2 tablespoons rolled oats. The sauce is stickier but has a creamy feel, sort of like the original.

1 tablespoon olive oil

1 medium onion, chopped (160g prechopped)

450g lean pork mince

450g sweet Italian sausage, casings removed

125ml chicken stock or dry white wine

Two 400g tins chopped tomatoes

10g fresh basil leaves, finely chopped

2 tablespoons fresh oregano leaves, finely chopped

2 tablespoons fresh rosemary leaves, finely chopped

½ teaspoon table salt

Pork and Basil Meat Sauce

Makes enough for 900g dried pasta

This is a fairly traditional sauce, without the fuss of a Bolognese (see pages 138–139). We pack extra flavour into the sauce by using sausage meat, already seasoned with fennel seeds and other aromatics. It can be a mess to take the casings off sausages, but you can often find bulk seasoned Italian sausage meat in the butcher case of larger supermarkets. The sausage meat may have been salted in advance. Check the label and if so, omit any salt here. (And some sausage meat, particularly when in casings, can have wheat fillers or thickeners. If this is a concern, check the label.)

The easiest way to chop all those herbs is to gather all three together on a chopping board (with or without the salt), then rock a chef's knife through them, repeatedly moving the blade on an axis around the herbs and gathering them together several times to start again.

1.

Press	Setting	Time	Press
SAUTÉ	MEDIUM, NORMAL or CUSTOM 150°C	10 minutes	START

2. Warm the oil in a **5.5-litre cooker** for a minute or two. Add the onion and cook, stirring often, until softened, about 4 minutes. Crumble in both the pork mince and sausage meat. Cook, stirring often to break up any large clumps, until the meat is lightly browned, about 4 minutes.

3. Pour in the stock or wine and scrape up any browned bits on the pot's bottom. Turn off the **SAUTÉ** function. Stir in the tomatoes, basil, oregano, rosemary and salt. Lock the lid onto the pot.

4.

Set the machine	Level	The valve must be	Time	Press
PRESSURE COOK	MAX	——	8 minutes with the KEEP WARM setting off	START
MEAT/ STEW, PRESSURE COOK or MANUAL	HIGH	Closed	10 minutes with the KEEP WARM setting off	START

5. Use the **quick-release method** to bring the pot's pressure back to normal. Unlatch the lid and open the cooker. Stir well before serving.

Beyond

- For a 3-litre cooker, you must use 80ml wine or vermouth and halve the remaining ingredients.

- For a 7.5-litre cooker, you must add 60ml chicken stock (or water) with the wine.

- For a richer finish, substitute butter for the olive oil. (Reduce or omit the salt if your butter is salted.)

- To go all out, grate aged Asiago or an aged goat cheese over the servings.

- To skip any dairy, garnish servings with a little syrupy balsamic vinegar, and maybe finely grated orange zest.

- Substitute 1 tablespoon fresh thyme leaves for the rosemary.

Mushroom Ragù

Makes enough for 450g dried pasta

To put it bluntly, mushrooms grow in stuff you wouldn't want to eat. Don't believe the myth about not washing them. By all means, clean them with water before using them in this chunky but delicate pasta sauce. And there's no reason to use only chestnut mushrooms. Consider stemmed, sliced shiitakes; sliced white button mushrooms, or even a range of more exotic mushrooms like porcini, hen of the wood or oyster mushrooms. But skip portobello caps. The black gills turn the sauce a dark, unappetising colour.

1.

Press	Setting	Time	Press
SAUTÉ	MEDIUM, NORMAL Or CUSTOM 150°C	10 minutes	START

2. Melt the butter in a 3-, 5.5- or 7.5-litre cooker, then add the shallots and carrot. Cook, stirring often, until the shallots begin to soften, about 3 minutes. Add the mushrooms and continue cooking, stirring occasionally, until they begin to soften, about 4 minutes.

3. Stir in the garlic and turn off the **SAUTÉ** function. Continue stirring in the residual heat for 1 minute to concentrate the liquid the mushrooms have begun to give off. Stir in the tomatoes, stock, basil, sage, crushed chilli flakes, nutmeg and salt. Lock the lid onto the pot.

4.

Set the machine	Level	The valve must be	Time	Press
PRESSURE COOK	MAX	—	8 minutes with the KEEP WARM setting off	START
PRESSURE COOK or MANUAL	HIGH	Closed	10 minutes with the KEEP WARM setting off	START

5. Use the **quick-release method** to bring the pot's pressure back to normal. Unlatch the lid and open the cooker.

6.

Press	Setting	Time	Press
SAUTÉ	HIGH or MORE	10 minutes	START

7. Bring the sauce to a full simmer. Cook, stirring almost constantly, until thickened like a ragù, about 5 minutes. Turn off the **SAUTÉ** function and remove the *hot* insert from the machine to stop the cooking.

30g butter

2 medium shallots, chopped

65g chopped carrots

675g small or medium chestnut mushrooms

Up to 4 medium garlic cloves, peeled and finely chopped (4 teaspoons prechopped)

Two 400g tins chopped tomatoes

60ml vegetable stock

10g fresh basil leaves, finely chopped

1 teaspoon dried sage

¼ teaspoon crushed chilli flakes

¼ teaspoon grated nutmeg

¼ teaspoon table salt

Beyond

- There are three other ways to thicken the ragù in the last step: 1) stir in 60g tomato purée after pressure cooking and simmer for 1 minute, stirring often; 2) put about 350ml of the ragù in a blender, cover, blend until smooth, then stir this mixture back into the mushroom ragù without simmering it; 3) use a hand blender right in the pot for 4 or 5 quick bursts to purée some of the mixture, then stir well before serving.

- For a richer ragù, increase the butter to 55g.

- Top the servings with finely grated Parmigiano-Reggiano, a smattering of finely grated lemon zest and lots of freshly ground black pepper.

40g butter

4 medium onions, halved, then thinly sliced into half-moons

350ml beef stock

60ml balsamic vinegar

2 tablespoons loosely packed fresh rosemary leaves, finely chopped

¼ teaspoon table salt

¼ teaspoon ground black pepper

1kg lean beef mince

60g tomato purée

Venetian-Style Sweet-and-Sour Ragù

Makes enough for 900g dried pasta

The key to this classic sauce is to let the onions cook and cook (and cook some more) until they're super soft and sweet, all *without* letting them brown too much. Which means you'll need to stir quite a bit – particularly as they start to break down – since they lose much of their natural moisture while you're trying to concentrate their natural sugars. If you have an Ultra or a Max machine, you can drop the SAUTÉ level even lower (to, say, 109°C) and keep the onions even more mellow. After all that work, they'll pair perfectly with the balsamic vinegar. There's no need for an expensive bottle, just a tasty, sweet/sour vinegar you'd use to make a salad dressing.

1.

Press	Setting	Time	Press
SAUTÉ	LOW or LESS	30 minutes	START

2. Melt the butter in a **5.5- or 7.5-litre cooker**, then add the onions. Cook, stirring once in a while at first, then more and more, until the onions are golden, very soft and sweet, about 25 minutes.

3. Stir in the stock, vinegar, rosemary, salt and pepper. Scrape up any browned bits on the bottom of the pot. Crumble in the beef mince. Turn off the **SAUTÉ** function but stir the beef over the residual heat for 1 minute. Lock the lid onto the pot.

4.

Set the machine	Level	The valve must be	Time	Press
PRESSURE COOK	MAX	—	6 minutes with the KEEP WARM setting off	START
MEAT/ STEW, PRESSURE COOK or MANUAL	HIGH	Closed	8 minutes with the KEEP WARM setting off	START

5. Use the **quick-release method** to bring the pot's pressure back to normal. Unlatch the lid and open the cooker.

6.

Press	Setting	Time	Press
SAUTÉ	MEDIUM, NORMAL Or CUSTOM 150°C	5 minutes	START

7. Stir in the tomato purée until uniform as the sauce comes back to a simmer. Cook, stirring often, until slightly thickened, about 2 minutes. Turn off the **SAUTÉ** function and remove the *hot* insert from the machine to stop the cooking.

Beyond

• You must halve the recipe for a 3-litre cooker.

• To make this sauce using the SLOW COOK setting, complete the recipe as written through step 3 without turning off the SAUTÉ function. Crumble in the beef mince, cook until lightly browned, then stir in the tomato purée until uniform. Turn off the SAUTÉ function. Lock the lid onto the pot but leave the valve open. Use the SLOW COOK function on HIGH to cook for 3 hours. The sauce can be kept on the KEEP WARM setting for up to 2 hours after cooking.

Picadillo-Style Ragù

Makes enough for 900g dried pasta

Picadillo (*peek-ah-DEE-yoh*) is a traditional, sweet-and-savoury minced beef 'sauce', popular across the Caribbean and in Latin America. We morphed it into a ragù by making it a little wetter, the better to toss with cooked pasta (and the better to work in an Instant Pot without scorching). This is pretty fine deck food with a beer in the summer, considering you don't have to heat up the kitchen when the pot does its work. If it's really hot out, skip the pasta and scoop the sauce (via a slotted spoon) into lettuce cups.

1.

Press	Setting	Time	Press
SAUTÉ	MEDIUM, NORMAL Or CUSTOM 150°C	10 minutes	START

2. Warm the oil in a **3-, 5.5- or 7.5-litre cooker** for a minute or two, then add the onion. Cook, stirring often, until softened, about 4 minutes. Stir in the garlic, cumin, coriander seeds, bay leaves and cinnamon stick. Cook for a few seconds until aromatic, stirring a few times.

3. Crumble in the beef mince. Cook, breaking up any large clumps, just until it loses its raw, pink colour, about 4 minutes. Turn off the **SAUTÉ** function. Stir in the stock, raisins, olives, capers and oregano, making sure you get any browned bits off the bottom of the pot. Lock the lid onto the pot.

4.

Set the machine	Level	The valve must be	Time	Press
PRESSURE COOK	MAX	——	6 minutes with the KEEP WARM setting off	START
MEAT/STEW, PRESSURE COOK or MANUAL	HIGH	Closed	8 minutes with the KEEP WARM setting off	START

5. Use the **quick-release method** to bring the pot's pressure back to normal. Unlatch the lid and open the cooker.

6.

Press	Setting	Time	Press
SAUTÉ	MEDIUM, NORMAL or CUSTOM 150°C	5 minutes	START

7. Stir in the tomato purée and coriander as the mixture comes back to a boil. Cook, stirring often, until somewhat thickened if still a little soupy, about 3 minutes. Turn off the **SAUTÉ** function and remove the *hot* insert from the machine to stop the cooking. Find and discard the bay leaves and cinnamon stick and serve.

2 tablespoons olive oil

1 large onion, chopped (240g prechopped)

2 medium garlic cloves, peeled and finely chopped (2 teaspoons prechopped)

1½ teaspoons cumin seeds

1 teaspoon coriander seeds

2 bay leaves

One 10cm cinnamon stick

900g lean beef mince

250ml beef stock

60g raisins

110g sliced pitted green olives

1 tablespoon drained and rinsed capers, chopped

1 tablespoon fresh oregano leaves, finely chopped

One 175g tin tomato purée

20g coriander leaves, chopped

Beyond

- For a lighter ragù, substitute turkey mince for the beef and chicken stock for the beef stock.

- Although this dish can be tossed with pasta, we also like it over a bed of cooked long-grain white basmati rice.

- Garnish the servings with more sliced olives and even finely chopped celery leaves.

- There's no salt in the mixture because of the olives and capers. Offer some at the table.

- There's also no heat. Serve it with a hot red pepper sauce, such as Sriracha.

2 tablespoons olive oil

1 large onion, chopped (240g prechopped)

700ml vegetable stock

One 400g tin chopped tomatoes

90g brown lentils

70g Puy lentils

2 medium garlic cloves, peeled and finely chopped (2 teaspoons prechopped)

1 tablespoon dried basil

1 teaspoon dried oregano

½ teaspoon ground allspice

½ teaspoon table salt

¼ teaspoon crushed chilli flakes

3 tablespoons tomato purée

Lentil Ragù

Makes enough for 680g dried pasta

Lentils make an exceptionally earthy ragù, a hearty meal that's best on a winter evening. There are two kinds of lentils here: brown and green. The brown will melt under pressure, thickening the sauce, while the green will stay firmer to give the ragù a more, well, ragù-ish texture. All lentils can have small stones hidden in their packages. Before using, spread the lentils on a big chopping board and pick through them to discard the stones and avoid expensive dental bills.

1.

Press	Setting	Time	Press
SAUTÉ	MEDIUM, NORMAL or CUSTOM 150°C	10 minutes	START

2. Warm the oil in a **3-, 5.5- or 7.5-litre cooker** for a minute or two, then add the onion. Cook, stirring occasionally, until softened, about 5 minutes. Turn off the **SAUTÉ** function. Stir in the stock, tomatoes, brown lentils, green lentils, garlic, basil, oregano, allspice, salt and crushed chilli flakes. Lock the lid onto the pot.

3.

Set the machine	Level	The valve must be	Time	Press
PRESSURE COOK	MAX	—	10 minutes with the KEEP WARM setting off	START
CHILLI/ BEANS, PRESSURE COOK or MANUAL	HIGH	Closed	12 minutes with the KEEP WARM setting off	START

4. When the pot has finished cooking, turn it off and let the pressure **return to normal naturally**, about 25 minutes. Unlatch the lid and open the cooker.

5.

Press	Setting	Time	Press
SAUTÉ	MEDIUM, NORMAL or CUSTOM 150°C	10 minutes	START

6. Bring the sauce to a simmer, stirring constantly. Stir in the tomato purée until uniform, then continue cooking, stirring almost the whole time, until thickened, about 2 minutes. Turn off the **SAUTÉ** function and remove the *hot* insert from the machine to stop the cooking.

Beyond

- To make this ragù with the SLOW COOK function, complete the recipe through step 2, stirring in the tomato purée before locking the lid on the pot. Leave the pressure valve open and use the SLOW COOK function to cook on HIGH for 3 hours with the KEEP WARM setting off (or on for up to 1 hour).

- If you're not interested in making a vegan ragù, substitute up to 40g butter for the olive oil.

- Garnish the servings with pomegranate molasses and maybe with a light dusting of za'atar, the Middle Eastern spice blend.

Pork Ragù

Makes enough for 900g dried pasta

This ragù uses pork shoulder, which can be notoriously fatty. We're all for those rich bits when the cut is roasted. However, whether you make this ragù under pressure or use the SLOW COOK function, look for the leanest piece of pork shoulder you can find to stop the sauce being too oily.

We find that all our ragùs made with whole cuts of meat are better with dried pasta (rather than fresh). This ragù should go with substantial pasta, perhaps bucatini, pappardelle or mafaldine.

1. Mix the pork, tomatoes, stock, onion, celery, oregano, rosemary, salt and pepper in a **5.5- or 7.5-litre cooker**. Lock the lid onto the pot.

2.

Set the machine	Level	The valve must be	Time	Press
PRESSURE COOK	MAX	—	35 minutes with the KEEP WARM setting off	START
MEAT/ STEW, PRESSURE COOK or MANUAL	HIGH	Closed	45 minutes with the KEEP WARM setting off	START
SLOW COOK	HIGH	Opened	4 hours with the KEEP WARM setting off (or on for no more than 2 hours)	START

3. If you've used a pressure setting, when the machine has finished cooking, turn it off and let its pressure **return to normal naturally**, about 25 minutes.

4. Unlatch the lid and open the cooker. Use a large spoon to skim any excess surface fat from the top of the sauce. Break up the pork pieces into smaller bits and shreds, stirring these into the sauce.

5.

Press	Setting	Time	Press
SAUTÉ	MEDIUM, NORMAL or CUSTOM 150°C	10 minutes	START

6. Bring the sauce to a simmer. Stir in the cream, then cook, stirring often, until somewhat thickened, about 4 minutes. Turn off the **SAUTÉ** function, remove the *hot* insert from the machine, and stir in the parsley just before serving.

900g boneless pork shoulder, cut into 5cm pieces and any large chunks of fat removed

900g plum or Roma tomatoes, chopped

250ml chicken stock

1 small onion, chopped (80g prechopped)

2 medium celery stalks, thinly sliced

2 tablespoons fresh oregano leaves, finely chopped

2 tablespoons fresh rosemary leaves, finely chopped

½ teaspoon table salt

½ teaspoon ground black pepper

60ml double cream

5g flat-leaf parsley leaves, chopped

Beyond

- You must halve the recipe for a 3-litre cooker.

- If you don't want to add cream, substitute 3 tablespoons tomato purée to thicken the sauce.

- For a much more savoury stew, substitute goat's milk for the cream. To serve, set a small mound of soft goat's cheese in the bowls, top with hot, cooked and drained bucatini or mafaldine, then ladle the sauce over the pasta.

2 tablespoons olive oil

900g piece boneless beef
chuck, trimmed of any
large chunks of fat and
cut in half

Two 400g tins whole
tomatoes

65g frozen baby onions
(do not thaw)

180ml light dry red wine,
such as Pinot Noir

1 tablespoon drained and
rinsed capers, chopped

1 medium garlic clove,
peeled and finely chopped
(1 teaspoon prechopped)

1 tablespoon dried rosemary

2 teaspoons dried oregano

1 bay leaf

½ teaspoon table salt

½ teaspoon ground
black pepper

Italian Pot Roast Ragù

Makes enough for 900g dried pasta

This recipe's a hybrid of sorts. Stew + Ragù = voilà! You'll want to
deeply brown the pieces of beef chuck. Seriously. Don't grey them.
They should have dark spots across their surface, not just golden
patches. Be patient and let all those natural sugars become more
intensely flavoured.

To balance all that browned goodness, we call for dried herbs,
rather than fresh, because the dried ones have a slightly earthier
flavour, less bright and so more balanced in the ragù.

1.

Press	Setting	Time	Press
SAUTÉ	MEDIUM, NORMAL or CUSTOM 150°C	20 minutes	START

2. Warm the oil in a **5.5- or 7.5-litre cooker** for a minute or two.
Add the beef in two batches and brown, turning a couple of
times. Make sure the first piece is *well* browned before transferring
it to a bowl and adding the second one. At the end, both pieces
of beef should be in the bowl.

3. Wash and dry your hands. One by one, squeeze the whole
tomatoes over the pot, then add any remaining juice from the
tins. Add the baby onions and stir well to scrape up *all* the
browned bits on the bottom of the pot. Cook for 2 minutes,
stirring often, just until the onions begin to brown lightly.
Turn off the **SAUTÉ** function.

4. Stir in the wine, capers, garlic, rosemary, oregano, bay leaf,
salt and pepper. Return the beef pieces and any juice in the
bowl to the cooker. Lock the lid onto the pot.

5.

Set the machine	Level	The valve must be	Time	Press
PRESSURE COOK	MAX	——	44 minutes with the KEEP WARM setting off	START
PRESSURE COOK or MANUAL	HIGH	Closed	55 minutes with the KEEP WARM setting off	START
SLOW COOK	HIGH	Opened	5 hours with the KEEP WARM setting off or on for no more than 2 hours)	START

6. If you've used a pressure setting, when the machine has finished cooking, turn it off and let its pressure **return to normal naturally**, about 30 minutes.

7. Unlatch the lid and open the cooker. Use a large spoon to skim off any excess surface fat. Find and discard the bay leaf, then use two forks to shred the meat.

8.

Press	Setting	Time	Press
SAUTÉ	HIGH or MORE	10 minutes	START

9. Bring the sauce to a full simmer. Cook, stirring occasionally, until reduced to a fairly wet ragù, about 5 minutes. Turn off the **SAUTÉ** function and set the lid askew over the pot for 5 minutes to blend the flavours.

Beyond

- You must halve the recipe for a 3-litre cooker.

- Stir up to 30g butter into the ragù just before serving.

- This ragù takes well to pasta shapes like rigatoni or fusilli. Or serve it as a stew over large spoonfuls of ricotta.

- Garnish with finely chopped fresh flat-leaf parsley leaves.

Two 400g tins chopped tomatoes

125ml red wine

4 medium shallots, peeled and thinly sliced into rings

2 medium garlic cloves, peeled and finely chopped (2 teaspoons prechopped)

2 tablespoons fresh rosemary leaves, finely chopped

1 teaspoon white granulated sugar

Up to 1 teaspoon table salt

½ teaspoon ground cinnamon

2 bay leaves

2 bone-in skinless turkey thighs (about 550g each)

30g butter

Turkey Ragù

Makes enough for 680g dried pasta

Because we wanted to keep this ragù fairly thick, rather than soupy, we used turkey thighs, sometimes hard to track down but always available around the winter festive season. The easiest way to skin a turkey thigh is to grasp one corner of the skin with kitchen paper and pull the skin diagonally across and off the meat. Also remove any large globs of fat underneath before adding the thighs to the cooker.

1. Stir the tomatoes, wine, shallots, garlic, rosemary, sugar, salt, cinnamon and bay leaves in a **5.5- or 7.5-litre cooker**. Nestle the turkey thighs into this mixture. Lock the lid onto the pot.

2.

Set the machine	Level	The valve must be	Time	Press
PRESSURE COOK	MAX	—	40 minutes with the KEEP WARM setting off	START
PRESSURE COOK or MANUAL	HIGH	Closed	50 minutes with the KEEP WARM setting off	START
SLOW COOK	HIGH	Opened	5 hours with the KEEP WARM setting off (or on for no more than 2 hours)	START

3. If you've used a pressure setting, when the machine has finished cooking, use the **quick-release method** to return the pot's pressure to normal.

4. Unlatch the lid and open the cooker. Use kitchen tongs to transfer the turkey thighs to a chopping board. Cool for a few minutes. Meanwhile, find, remove and discard the bay leaves in the sauce.

5.

Press	Setting	Time	Press
SAUTÉ	MEDIUM, NORMAL or CUSTOM 150°C	5 minutes	START

6. Shred the meat off the bones. (Discard the bones and any cartilage.) Stir the meat into the sauce and add the butter. Cook at a full simmer, stirring frequently, until reduced to about the consistency of a fairly wet ragù, about 3 minutes. Turn off the **SAUTÉ** function and set the lid askew over the pot for 5 minutes to blend the flavours.

Beyond

- You must halve the recipe for a 3-litre cooker.
- For a richer ragù, substitute evaporated milk for the red wine.
- For a dish worthy of a dinner party, substitute 4 skinned duck leg quarters (225–350g each) for the turkey thighs. Make sure to garnish these servings with thyme leaves or finely chopped flat-leaf parsley leaves.

Creamy Beef Short Rib Ragù

Makes enough for 900g dried pasta

Imagine old-school Swiss steak shredded up and served over pasta. Okay, that doesn't make any sense. But this ragù has a mid-century-modern, comfort-food feel, a rich mix of flavours in a creamy tomato sauce, as if Dinner Lady Doris had been a really good cook. By the way, the secret to that old-school flavour in mid-century recipes is the combination of thyme and allspice.

1.

Press	Setting	Time	Press
SAUTÉ	MEDIUM, NORMAL or CUSTOM 150°C	20 minutes	START

2. Warm the oil in a **3-, 5.5- or 7.5-litre cooker** for a minute or two. Season the short rib pieces with the salt and pepper. Brown them in three batches, turning them occasionally until they are *well* browned, then transfer to a nearby bowl and brown more. At the end, all the short ribs should be in the bowl.

3. Pour the wine into the cooker and scrape up *every speck of browned stuff* on the pot's bottom. Stir in the tomatoes and garlic. Cook, stirring often, until very aromatic, about 1 minute. Turn off the **SAUTÉ** function. Stir in the evaporated milk, thyme and allspice. Return the short ribs and any liquid in the bowl to the cooker. Lock the lid onto the pot.

4.

Set the machine	Level	The valve must be	Time	Press
PRESSURE COOK	MAX	——	40 minutes with the KEEP WARM setting off	START
MEAT/STEW or PRESSURE COOK	HIGH	Closed	50 minutes with the KEEP WARM setting off	START

5. When the cooker has finished, turn it off and let the pressure **come back to normal** for 10 minutes. Then use the **quick-release method** to get rid of any residual pressure. Unlatch the lid and open the cooker. Use a large spoon to skim off any excess surface fat. Shred the short ribs in the pot with two forks, then stir in the cream.

6.

Press	Setting	Time	Press
SAUTÉ	MEDIUM, NORMAL or CUSTOM 150°C	10 minutes	START

7. Bring the ragù to a simmer, then cook, stirring often, until reduced to a fairly thick pasta sauce, about 5 minutes. Turn off the **SAUTÉ** function and set the lid askew over the pot for 5 minutes to blend the flavours.

2 tablespoons olive oil

900g boneless beef short ribs

½ teaspoon table salt

½ teaspoon ground black pepper

150ml bold dry red wine, such as a Zinfandel

One 400g tin chopped tomatoes

Up to 6 medium garlic cloves, peeled and finely chopped (2 tablespoons prechopped)

125ml regular or low-fat evaporated milk

1½ tablespoons fresh thyme leaves

½ teaspoon ground allspice

60ml double cream

Beyond

- If you don't want to use wine, use an equivalent amount of beef stock plus 1 teaspoon dark brown sugar.
- Consider serving this ragù over Polenta (page 443).
- The ragù is so creamy it doesn't need cheese as a garnish. Instead, use chopped fresh parsley leaves and/or a smattering of dried cherries.

125ml beef stock

80ml reduced-sodium soy sauce

55g dark brown sugar

3 medium garlic cloves, peeled and thinly sliced

2 teaspoons toasted sesame oil

1 teaspoon ground ginger

1 tablespoon ground black pepper

1 medium red onion, halved and sliced into thin half-moons

1.25kg piece boneless beef chuck, cut into 3 pieces and any large bits of fat removed

2 tablespoons cornflour

2 teaspoons water

Korean Beef Ragù

Makes enough for 900g dried pasta

Here's a pure flight of fancy, a fusion of an Italian ragù with a Korean stew. It's a sweet, sticky, almost unreal concoction, best on a winter night with a glass of beer. Use only reduced-sodium soy sauce: the pot doesn't allow any evaporation and concentration of flavours, so the regular stuff will end up making the ragù too salty.

1. Stir the stock, soy sauce, brown sugar, garlic, sesame oil, ginger and black pepper in a 3-, 5.5- or 7.5-litre cooker until the brown sugar dissolves. Stir in the onion, then nestle the pieces of beef into the sauce. They won't all be submerged, but get them all coated. Lock the lid onto the pot.

2.

Set the machine	Level	The valve must be	Time	Press
PRESSURE COOK	MAX	—	45 minutes with the KEEP WARM setting off	START
MEAT/STEW, PRESSURE COOK or MANUAL	HIGH	Closed	55 minutes with the KEEP WARM setting off	START
SLOW COOK	HIGH	Opened	5 hours with the KEEP WARM setting off (or on for no more than 2 hours)	START

3. If you've used a pressure setting, when the machine has finished cooking, turn it off and let its pressure **return to normal naturally**, about 30 minutes.

4. Unlatch the lid and open the cooker. Use a large spoon to skim off any excess surface fat from the sauce. Shred the meat in the pot with two forks.

5.

Press	Setting	Time	Press
SAUTÉ	MEDIUM, NORMAL Or CUSTOM 150°C	5 minutes	START

6. Bring the sauce to a full simmer, stirring often. Whisk the cornflour and water in a small bowl until smooth, then stir this slurry into the sauce. Continue cooking, stirring all the while, until the sauce is slightly thickened, about 1 minute. Immediately turn off the **SAUTÉ** function and remove the *hot* insert from the machine to stop the cooking. Set the lid askew over the insert for a couple of minutes to thicken further.

Beyond

- For an even more astounding set of flavours, add up to 2 tablespoons gochujang (a Korean chilli paste) with the ingredients in step 1.

- Serve the ragù with cooked and drained egg pasta, rice noodles or long-grain, white rice.

- No cheese, please! Garnish the servings with more toasted sesame oil.

Lamb Ragù

Makes enough for 900g dried pasta

Our final ragù is a Greek-inspired concoction that's fairly rich. Since the tomato purée is so necessary to this dish, it's a good time to remember that one tomato purée is *not* like another. Some taste nothing but sweet; others, more like tomatoes. Spend a fiver on several brands and do a taste test. You'll know exactly which one matches your taste.

3 tablespoons olive oil

1 large onion, chopped (240g prechopped)

260g chopped carrots

4 medium garlic cloves, peeled and finely chopped (4 teaspoons prechopped)

675g boned leg of lamb, cut into 5cm pieces

250ml chicken stock

2 tablespoons fresh rosemary leaves, chopped

2 tablespoons fresh sage leaves, chopped

½ teaspoon table salt

½ teaspoon ground black pepper

One 175g tin tomato purée

1.

Press	Setting	Time	Press
SAUTÉ	MEDIUM, NORMAL or CUSTOM 150°C	10 minutes	START

2. Warm the oil in a 3-, 5.5- or 7.5-litre cooker for a minute or two. Add the onion and carrots. Cook, stirring often, until the onion begins to soften, about 5 minutes. Stir in the garlic and cook for a few seconds.

3. Add the lamb pieces; stir over the heat for 1 minute, just until the lamb is thoroughly mixed into the vegetables. Turn off the SAUTÉ function. Stir in the stock, rosemary, sage, salt and pepper. Lock the lid onto the pot.

4.

Set the machine	Level	The valve must be	Time	Press
PRESSURE COOK	MAX	—	23 minutes with the KEEP WARM setting off	START
MEAT/STEW, PRESSURE COOK or MANUAL	HIGH	Closed	30 minutes with the KEEP WARM setting off	START

5. When the pot has finished cooking, turn it off and allow its pressure to **return to normal naturally**, about 30 minutes. Unlatch the lid and open the cooker. Use two forks to break up the meat into smaller pieces. Stir in the tomato purée until uniform.

6.

Press	Setting	Time	Press
SAUTÉ	MEDIUM, NORMAL or CUSTOM 150°C	10 minutes	START

7. Bring the sauce to a simmer, stirring constantly. Cook, stirring occasionally, until thickened, about 5 minutes. Turn off the SAUTÉ function and set the lid askew over the pot for 5 minutes to blend the flavours.

Beyond

- For more complex flavours, use 125ml stock and 125ml dry white wine.

- To give it a more Greek feel, omit the salt and add up to 40g sliced pitted black olives. Also, substitute oregano for the sage.

- Try this with boneless goat's leg meat sometime!

- Beyond pastas like farfalle or ziti, serve this ragù over cooked orzo or even giant couscous.

- Crumble feta over the servings. And drizzle them with a fine, aromatic olive oil.

4

Pasta
Casseroles

Here comes serious comfort food: macaroni cheese; tuna noodle casserole; sausage gravy over pasta; cheeseburger casserole and even some new favourites like dan dan noodles. True, not every recipe yields a casserole. Some are pasta in sauce or, as in the case of the first recipe, just in butter (heaven!). Most use standard dried pasta. A couple turn frozen gnocchi, a supermarket staple, into rich casseroles. And a few use rice noodles or giant couscous, a toasted pasta.

In no case will you make the pasta or noodles separately. Every recipe happens fully in the Instant Pot, starting with dried pasta (or frozen gnocchi, as the case might be). The creamy sauces are particularly astounding, although you *must* use tinned evaporated milk, not regular milk (which can curdle under pressure without its being in a baking vessel of some sort or mixed into a batter). We'll let you know when low-fat evaporated milk can work. Fat-free never led to good results.

Dried pasta is a kitchen cupboard must-have. The quality of the results will be directly related to the quality of the pasta. Cheaper isn't worse; more expensive, better. That said, it's sometimes worth it to spend a little extra for better dried pasta. Stock up when you see sales.

There are no *fast/slow* recipes in this chapter. The texture of pasta is too compromised over many hours in a slow cooker. We know there are plenty of internet recipes for the stuff. But we find slow-cooker pasta becomes unappealingly gummy without major modifications to the recipe. Due to those changes, we can't use the same ingredient list for both the fast and slow settings. So we've opted out of the **SLOW COOK** function in this chapter. We hope you'll forgive us, given that there's so much comfort to go round.

FAQs

1. Why do you use ready-made marinara (tomato) sauce from a jar in some recipes?
Mostly, for convenience but with this caveat: there's a *wide* variety of marinara sauce on the supermarket shelf. Read the labels carefully to find a brand that includes nothing more than what you'd put in that sauce if you were making it from scratch. Don't use chunky bottled sauces or ones with cream or milk in them, but feel free to substitute jarred arrabbiata sauce for the marinara in almost all cases.

Of course, you can use homemade Buttery Marinara Sauce (page 133) in every recipe that calls for marinara. And just to be shameless in self-promotion, we do have an absolutely fabulous, five-minute marinara sauce (made on the hob) in another of our books, *The Kitchen Shortcut Bible*.

2. What's 'unseasoned rice vinegar'?
Technically, it's just 'rice wine vinegar', although few manufacturers label it so. Rice vinegar comes in two forms: seasoned and so-called 'unseasoned'. The seasoned has added sugar and maybe a few aromatics. The unseasoned is a mild vinegar that is not sweet. It is *the only kind* called for in this book.

As a maddening bit of labelling confusion, seasoned rice vinegar is sometimes, but not always, so labelled; and 'unseasoned', the sort you want, is rarely labelled 'unseasoned'. Bottom line: Read the label and make sure there's no sugar or other sweetener in the bottle.

3. Can I substitute gluten-free pasta and noodles?

Yes, in almost all cases. We had better success with gluten-free pasta made from a combination of grains, rather than just one. We had the best success with dried pasta made with corn and rice. When it comes to the pasta casseroles that round out this chapter, multi-grain, gluten-free, no-boil lasagne sheets are available at large supermarkets or online suppliers.

4. Do I have to make adjustments for cooking gluten-free pasta?

Yes, especially if you use the multi-grain varieties we recommend. In all cases, increase the time under pressure by 1 minute (whether for the **MAX** or the **HIGH** setting). That said, tastes vary. Some people like chewier pasta. If you're in that lot, consider trying one of the recipes as written with gluten-free pasta and see if you prefer that texture to a softer feel.

6. What about rice noodles?

We call for two kinds: 1) rice stick noodles (also called 'rice noodles for pad Thai' or even 'stir-fry rice noodles' on some packets) and 2) rice vermicelli (sort of like a rice version of angel-hair pasta). Use the one specifically called for in the recipe, but feel free to substitute brown rice noodles *of the same variety* in any of these dishes with no other change in the recipe. But never substitute rice noodles for gluten-free noodles in any recipe in this chapter. The timing and the liquid ratios will be off.

Buttery Pasta

6 servings

Simple and satisfying, this pasta dish takes no time in an Instant Pot, a boon when you've got hungry kids in the house. One warning: you must stir constantly at the last step to make sure the delicate pasta does not stick.

Even without kids, make a pot when you're feeling under the weather. There's nothing like old-fashioned comfort food to perk you up. This pasta would also be welcome (and a little retro) alongside anything off the grill. You might want to fancy them up. See the suggestions in the *Beyond* section.

55g butter

700ml vegetable or chicken stock

350g dried egg pasta

¼ teaspoon table salt

1.

Press	Setting	Time	Press
SAUTÉ	MEDIUM, NORMAL or CUSTOM 150°C	5 minutes	START

2. Melt the butter in a **5.5- or 7.5-litre cooker.** Stir in the stock. Add the pasta and salt. Turn off the **SAUTÉ** function and lock the lid onto the pot.

Set the machine	Level	The valve must be	Time	Press
PRESSURE COOK	MAX	—	3 minutes with the KEEP WARM setting off	START
PRESSURE COOK or MANUAL	HIGH	Closed	4 minutes with the KEEP WARM setting off	START

3. Use the **quick-release method** to bring the pot's pressure back to normal. Unlatch the lid and open the pot.

4.

Press	Setting	Time	Press
SAUTÉ	MEDIUM, NORMAL or CUSTOM 150°C	5 minutes	START

5. Stir constantly until any excess moisture evaporates and only buttered pasta remains, about 2 minutes. Turn off the **SAUTÉ** function, remove the *hot* insert from the machine to stop the cooking, stir well, and serve warm.

Beyond

- **You must halve the recipe for a 3-litre cooker.**

- **After cooking, season the pasta to taste with ground black pepper, poppy seeds, caraway seeds and/or crushed chilli flakes.**

- **And/or stir up to 50g finely grated Parmigiano-Reggiano, pecorino, or an aged Asiago into the pasta.**

450g dried pasta
Choose from cellentani, medium shells, large elbows, fusilli or penne.

700ml water

250ml regular or low-fat evaporated milk

30g butter, cut into little bits

1 teaspoon onion powder

1 teaspoon mustard powder

¼ teaspoon table salt

250ml double cream

350g grated cheese
Choose one or a 50/50 combo from Swiss, Cheddar, mozzarella, provolone, Gruyère, semi-firm Gouda, Havarti, fontina, Parmigiano-Reggiano and/or Jarlsberg.

Beyond

- You must halve the recipe for a 3-litre cooker.

- Substitute a flavoured cheese like pepper or horseradish Cheddar. Or use a bagged, grated cheese blend with spices (Italian, Mexican) for a bolder dish.

- There's no chance of a crunchy topping in the pot. Get one by spooning the finished casserole into a 23 x 33cm baking dish; grill about 10cm from the heating element until well browned and super crunchy, 3–4 minutes.

- Or toast fresh breadcrumbs in a frying pan with a little olive oil or butter until lightly browned, stirring often, then sprinkle these over each serving. If desired, add dried herbs (parsley, thyme and/or oregano) to those breadcrumbs before toasting.

- Or just crunch handfuls of thick, ridge cut crisps over each serving.

Road Map: Macaroni Cheese

6 servings

Here's the best way to create your own version of the ultimate comfort food. Because the pasta cooks right in the evaporated milk, it becomes astoundingly luxurious, even better than a lot of oven versions. Note that you *cannot* use small pasta (like small elbows); they'll sink to the bottom of the pot and burn. And you can't use any thick-walled pasta like ziti or rigatoni because these won't cook in the time stated with the given liquid level. As a general rule, cooking dried pasta under pressure is mostly a matter of using a liquid level appropriate to the *thickness* of the pasta, rather than its length or shape.

1. Mix the pasta, water, evaporated milk, butter, onion powder, mustard powder and salt in a **5.5- or 7.5-litre cooker.** Lock the lid onto the pot.

2.

Set the machine	Level	The valve must be	Time	Press
PRESSURE COOK	MAX	—	4 minutes with the KEEP WARM setting off	START
PRESSURE COOK or MANUAL	HIGH	Closed	5 minutes with the KEEP WARM setting off	START

3. Use the **quick-release method** to bring the pot's pressure back to normal. Unlatch the lid and open the pot.

4.

Press	Setting	Time	Press
SAUTÉ	MEDIUM, NORMAL or CUSTOM 150°C	5 minutes	START

5. Stir in the cream and grated cheese until uniform. Continue stirring constantly over the heat until the cheese melts and coats the pasta, 1 or 2 minutes. Turn off the **SAUTÉ** function, remove the *hot* insert from the machine and set the lid askew over the insert. Set aside for 5 minutes so the pasta can absorb most of the remaining liquid.

Creamy Tomato Macaroni Cheese

6 servings

Consider this recipe a cross between macaroni cheese and old-school tomato soup, a double dose of old-fashioned comfort. While testing recipes, we delivered a litre of this to a picky schoolboy down our country road. He scarfed it.

For us adults, the dish's sweet-tart bite calls out for something crunchy. If you're not in the mood to pair this with a baguette, stir thinly sliced carrots into the pot with the cheese to add texture.

1. Mix the pasta, stock, tomato passata, evaporated milk, thyme, nutmeg, salt and pepper in a **5.5- or 7.5-litre cooker** until uniform. Lock the lid onto the pot.

2.

Set the machine	Level	The valve must be	Time	Press
PRESSURE COOK	MAX	——	5 minutes with the KEEP WARM setting off	START
PRESSURE COOK or MANUAL	HIGH	Closed	7 minutes with the KEEP WARM setting off	START

3. Use the **quick-release method** to bring the pot's pressure back to normal. Unlatch the lid and open the pot. Add the cheese and cream; stir until the cheese melts. Set the lid askew over the pot and set aside for 5 minutes to mellow the flavours.

450g dried ziti

700ml vegetable or chicken stock

500g tomato passata

250ml regular or low-fat evaporated milk

1 teaspoon dried thyme

½ teaspoon grated nutmeg

½ teaspoon table salt

½ teaspoon ground black pepper

225g grated Cheddar or Swiss cheese

125ml double cream

Beyond

- You must halve the recipe for a 3-litre cooker.

- For a more aromatic dish, add dried herbs to the mixture, up to 1 tablespoon total volume, choosing between thyme, oregano, parsley, basil and/or marjoram.

- For a more autumnal feel, substitute ground allspice for the nutmeg.

- For heat, add up to 1 teaspoon crushed chilli flakes with the nutmeg.

- For more richness, consider adding up to 30g butter with the grated cheese.

30g butter

450g mild breakfast sausage meat (any casings removed)

1 teaspoon dried sage

350g dried egg pasta

700ml chicken stock

180ml double cream

Sausage Gravy and Pasta

6 servings

Nope, the title's not missing a comma between 'sausage' and 'gravy'. This dish is Southern sausage gravy with pasta. We considered putting the recipe in the breakfast chapter. Then we ate half a pot for lunch one day. So, voilà.

1.

Press	Setting	Time	Press
SAUTÉ	MEDIUM, NORMAL or CUSTOM 150°C	5 minutes	START

2. Melt the butter in a **5.5- or 7.5-litre cooker**. Crumble in the sausage meat; add the sage. Cook, stirring occasionally, until the meat loses its raw, pink colour, about 3 minutes.

3. Mix in the pasta and stock. Stir well, although some of the pasta will stick up above the liquid. Turn off the **SAUTÉ** function and lock the lid onto the pot.

4.

Set the machine	Level	The valve must be	Time	Press
PRESSURE COOK	MAX	—	3 minutes with the KEEP WARM setting off	START
PRESSURE COOK or MANUAL	HIGH	Closed	4 minutes with the KEEP WARM setting off	START

5. Use the **quick-release method** to bring the pot's pressure back to normal. Unlatch the lid and open the pot.

6.

Press	Setting	Time	Press
SAUTÉ	MEDIUM, NORMAL or CUSTOM 150°C	5 minutes	START

7. Stir in the cream and continue stirring over the heat until most of the liquid has been absorbed, about 1 minute. Turn off the **SAUTÉ** function, remove the *hot* insert from the pot and set the lid askew over the insert. Set aside for 5 minutes to allow the pasta to absorb most of the remaining liquid. Stir well before serving.

Beyond

- You must halve the recipe for a 3-litre cooker.
- Stir up to 75g grated mozzarella or finely grated Parmigiano-Reggiano into the noodles with the cream.
- For a sweeter finish, reduce the stock to 500ml and add 200ml dry white wine.

Creamy Mushroom Pasta Casserole

4 to 6 servings

Remember school? Remember how bad school dinners could be? Here's how it could have been better. We use more liquid here than in some other pasta casseroles, then thicken the sauce at the end to give it a classic cream-sauce texture. It's best warm right out of the pot. Plates, optional.

1.

Press	Setting	Time	Press
SAUTÉ	MEDIUM, NORMAL or CUSTOM 150°C	10 minutes	START

2. Melt the butter in a **5.5- or 7.5-litre cooker**. Add the mushrooms and cook, stirring often, until they give off some liquid and start to soften, about 5 minutes.

3. Stir in the evaporated milk, stock, sage, thyme, salt and pepper until uniform. Turn off the **SAUTÉ** function. Stir in the pasta. Not every piece of pasta can be submerged; however, they should all be coated. Lock the lid onto the pot.

4.

Set the machine	Level	The valve must be	Time	Press
PRESSURE COOK	MAX	——	3 minutes with the KEEP WARM setting off	START
PRESSURE COOK or MANUAL	HIGH	Closed	4 minutes with the KEEP WARM setting off	START

5. Use the **quick-release method** to bring the pot's pressure back to normal. Unlatch the lid and open the pot.

6.

Press	Setting	Time	Press
SAUTÉ	MEDIUM, NORMAL or CUSTOM 150°C	5 minutes	START

7. Whisk the cream and cornflour into a small bowl until the cornflour dissolves. Stir this slurry into the pot. Cook, stirring constantly, until the sauce thickens considerably, 1 or 2 minutes. Turn off the **SAUTÉ** function; remove the *hot* insert from the cooker to stop the cooking. Stir several more times, then serve.

55g butter

450g white button mushrooms, thinly sliced

700ml regular or low-fat evaporated milk

700ml vegetable or chicken stock

1 teaspoon dried sage

½ teaspoon dried thyme

¼ teaspoon table salt

¼ teaspoon ground black pepper

350g dried egg pasta

60ml double cream

1 tablespoon cornflour

Beyond

- You must halve the recipe for a 3-litre cooker.

- For a fuller meal, stir up to 350g chopped skinless rotisserie chicken meat into the pot with the cream.

- Or stir in up to 155g chopped ham and up to 120g chopped broccoli florets.

2 tablespoons fat
  Choose from olive oil, almond oil, vegetable oil, corn oil, rapeseed oil, safflower oil, butter, rendered bacon fat, lard or schmaltz.

1 medium onion, chopped (160g prechopped)

1 or 2 medium sweet or mild peppers, stemmed, cored and cut into strips
  Choose from 1 red, yellow, orange or green pepper; or 2 large Cubanelle peppers, or 2 large Anaheim chillies.

450g lean mince
  Choose from beef, pork, veal, lamb, goat or turkey – or a 50/50 combo.

Up to 2 medium garlic cloves, peeled and finely chopped (1 teaspoon prechopped)

1½ tablespoons dried herb or seasoning blend
  Choose from Cajun, French, Italian, Mediterranean, herbes de Provence or other blends.

½ teaspoon table salt

Two 400g tins chopped tomatoes

700ml liquid
  Choose from vegetable or chicken stock, or a 50/50 combo of stock of any sort with either dry white wine or pale amber beer.

100g quick-cooking vegetables
  Choose one or a combination of trimmed and chopped green beans, chopped broccoli florets, chopped cauliflower florets, thinly sliced carrots, thinly sliced celery, and/or thawed frozen artichoke heart quarters.

225g dried pasta
  Choose from ziti, penne, penne rigate, rigatoni, fusilli, tortiglioni or radiatori.

One 175g tin tomato purée

115g finely grated cheese
  Choose from Cheddar, Swiss, semi-firm Gouda or Gruyère.

Road Map: Meat, Vegetable and Pasta Casserole

4 servings

Here's another chance to make a signature recipe of your own in the Instant Pot! As we indicated in the book's introduction, we recommend using reduced-sodium or even salt-free ingredients (like the tinned tomatoes and tomato purée here) because the pot tends to foreground salty flavours over earthy ones. (You can always add more salt at the table.)

The casserole isn't gooey until the cheese gets put on top at the end. If you have kids who like their casseroles with extra cheese (or if you're a kid at heart), *stir* the cheese into the casserole before you set the lid askew over the pot.

1.

Press	Setting	Time	Press
SAUTÉ	MEDIUM, NORMAL or CUSTOM 150°C	10 minutes	START

2. Warm or melt the fat in a **5.5- or 7.5-litre cooker**. Add the onion and pepper. Cook, stirring often, until the onion softens, about 4 minutes. Crumble in the mince and cook, stirring often to break up any clumps, until it loses its raw, pink colour, about 2 minutes.

3. Stir in the garlic, dried herb blend and salt until aromatic, just a few seconds. Then stir in the tomatoes and liquid, scraping up *every speck of browned stuff* on the pot's bottom. Turn off the **SAUTÉ** function and stir in the quick-cooking vegetables and pasta. Stir well until the mixture is uniform. Lock the lid onto the pot.

4.

Set the machine	Level	The valve must be	Time	Press
PRESSURE COOK	MAX	——	5 minutes with the KEEP WARM setting off	START
PRESSURE COOK or MANUAL	HIGH	Closed	7 minutes with the KEEP WARM setting off	START

5. Use the **quick-release method** to bring the pot's pressure back to normal. Unlatch the lid and open the pot.

6.

Press	Setting	Time	Press
SAUTÉ	MEDIUM, NORMAL or CUSTOM 150°C	5 minutes	START

7. Stir the tomato purée into the dish until dissolved. Continue stirring until thickened, about 2 minutes.

8. Sprinkle the cheese evenly over the top of the casserole. Remove the *hot* insert from the machine and set the lid askew on top of the insert for 5 minutes to begin to melt the cheese. Serve by the big spoonful.

Beyond

- You must halve the recipe for a 3-litre cooker.

- We don't recommend using chicken mince in this recipe, unless you use it in a 50/50 combo with beef or pork mince.

- Skip the cheese on top of the casserole and serve big spoonfuls of the casserole over mounds of regular or low-fat ricotta in the serving bowls.

2 tablespoons olive oil

550g lean beef mince

One 680g jar plain marinara (tomato) sauce

700ml chicken stock

350g dried spaghetti

Easy Spaghetti and Meat Sauce

4 servings

If you keep dried spaghetti and jars of plain marinara sauce to hand, you can have a fast lunch or dinner any day of the week. The dried pasta must be broken in half so they can sit in the sauce.

Here's the general rule for sauced pastas under pressure. The pasta doesn't necessarily need to be submerged, but it should be stirred so that it's well coated before you lock the lid onto the pot.

1.

Press	Setting	Time	Press
SAUTÉ	MEDIUM, NORMAL or CUSTOM 150°C	10 minutes	START

2. Warm the oil in a **5.5- or 7.5-litre cooker** for a minute or two. Crumble in the beef mince, stirring fairly often to break up any clumps, until well browned, about 4 minutes.

3. Stir in the marinara sauce and stock. Turn off the **SAUTÉ** function. Break the spaghetti in half and stir them into the sauce in the pot. Lock the lid onto the pot.

4.

Set the machine	Level	The valve must be	Time	Press
PRESSURE COOK	MAX	—	5 minutes with the KEEP WARM setting off	START
PRESSURE COOK or MANUAL	HIGH	Closed	6 minutes with the KEEP WARM setting off	START

5. Use the **quick-release method** to bring the pot's pressure back to normal. Unlatch the lid and open the pot. Stir well before serving.

Beyond

- For a 3-litre cooker, cut all of the ingredients in half. Also break the spaghetti into smaller bits so they'll fit.

- For more assertive flavours, feel free to substitute lean pork mince, mild Italian sausage meat (no casings) or even lamb mince for the beef. Or you could use a 50/50 combo of beef and pork mince.

Macaroni Cheese Chilli

6 servings

There may be no more quintessentially kid-friendly food than a combination of a tomato-based chilli and macaroni cheese. (For a variation on this theme, see Cincinnati Chilli on page 120.) Make sure that you scrape every bit of browned stuff off the bottom of the pot when the stock goes in. Otherwise, the pasta can stick and burn.

1.

Press	Setting	Time	Press
SAUTÉ	MEDIUM, NORMAL or CUSTOM 150°C	10 minutes	START

2. Warm the oil in a **5.5- or 7.5-litre cooker** for a minute or two. Add the onion and cook, stirring often, until it begins to soften, about 2 minutes. Add the chillies and garlic. Continue cooking, stirring once in a while, until the liquid has mostly evaporated, about 2 minutes.

3. Crumble in the beef mince. Cook, stirring often to break up any clumps, until the meat loses its raw, pink colour, about 2 minutes. Stir in the chilli powder, cumin and salt until fragrant, just a couple of seconds.

4. Stir in the stock and scrape up *every speck of browned stuff* on the bottom of the pot. Turn off the **SAUTÉ** function. Stir in the tomatoes, beans and ziti until the pasta is coated. Lock the lid onto the pot.

5.

Set the machine	Level	The valve must be	Time	Press
PRESSURE COOK	MAX	—	5 minutes with the KEEP WARM setting off	START
PRESSURE COOK or MANUAL	HIGH	Closed	7 minutes with the KEEP WARM setting off	START

6. Use the **quick-release method** to bring the pot's pressure back to normal. Unlatch the lid and open the pot. Stir in the cheese. Set the lid askew over the pot for 5 minutes to melt the cheese and mellow the flavours. Stir again before serving.

2 tablespoons olive oil

1 medium onion, chopped (160g prechopped)

Two 125g tins mild or hot chopped green chillies

1 medium garlic clove, peeled and finely chopped (1 teaspoon prechopped)

680g lean beef mince

25g standard chilli powder

2 teaspoons ground cumin

½ teaspoon table salt

500ml beef or chicken stock

Two 400g tins chopped tomatoes

One 400g tin kidney or pinto beans, drained and rinsed

225g dried ziti

125g grated Cheddar

Beyond

- You must halve the recipe for a 3-litre cooker.

- For a silkier finish, substitute 30g butter for the olive oil.

- For a hotter macaroni cheese chilli, use pure chipotle chilli powder (or a mixture of chipotle and standard chilli powder). If using pure chipotle chilli powder, increase the ground cumin to 1 tablespoon and add 2 teaspoons dried oregano.

- Or skip those substitutions and use standard chilli powder and switch to grated Cheddar flavoured with pepper.

2 tablespoons olive oil

900g lean beef mince

1 teaspoon onion powder

1 teaspoon dried oregano

½ teaspoon garlic powder

¼ teaspoon table salt

¼ teaspoon ground
black pepper

70g ketchup

60g pickle relish

2 tablespoons Dijon mustard

175g dried large elbow
macaroni or radiatore pasta

350ml chicken stock

250g grated Cheddar

Cheeseburger Casserole

6 servings

This one is actually a layered casserole with all the flavours of a cheeseburger (if you count the pasta as the bun). You can skip either the ketchup or mustard (why would you?), but the pickle relish adds essential moisture. Make the layers as even as possible, using a palette knife to spread the various ingredients across the open surface of the casserole.

1.

Press	Setting	Time	Press
SAUTÉ	MEDIUM, NORMAL or CUSTOM 150°C	10 minutes	START

2. Warm the oil in a **5.5-litre cooker** for a couple of minutes. Crumble in the beef mince and cook, stirring often to break up any clumps, until well browned, about 5 minutes. Stir in the onion powder, oregano, garlic powder, salt and pepper until aromatic, just a few seconds. Turn off the **SAUTÉ** function.

3. Use a large spoon to transfer two-thirds of the mixture from the pot to a nearby bowl. Now build the casserole. Spread out the remaining meat mixture in an even layer in the pot. Spread 2 tablespoons ketchup, 2 tablespoons relish and 1 tablespoon mustard over the meat mixture. Top with half the dried pasta. Add half of the remaining meat mixture in an even layer. Repeat with the rest of the ketchup, relish and mustard, then the rest of the pasta. Spread the rest of the meat mixture in an even layer over the top, then pour the stock evenly over the casserole. Top with an even layer of cheese. Lock the lid onto the pot.

4.

Set the machine	Level	The valve must be	Time	Press
PRESSURE COOK	MAX	—	5 minutes with the KEEP WARM setting off	START
PRESSURE COOK or MANUAL	HIGH	Closed	7 minutes with the KEEP WARM setting off	START

5. Use the **quick-release method** to bring the pot's pressure back to normal. Unlatch the lid and open the pot. Remove the *hot* insert from the machine and set the lid askew over the insert for 5–10 minutes to allow the casserole to set up.

Beyond

- You must halve the recipe for a 3-litre cooker.

- For a 7.5-litre cooker, you must increase all the ingredients by 50 per cent. You can then build all-round thicker layers in the pot, or simply add an extra layer.

- For a vegetarian casserole, use 680g textured soya protein (a beef-mince substitute) and 500ml vegetable stock.

- For a barbecue cheeseburger casserole, use a grated Tex-Mex cheese blend and barbecue sauce instead of the ketchup and mustard.

Easy Cheesy Meatballs and Ziti

4 servings

Consider this recipe a fast, Instant Pot version of spaghetti and meatballs. There's no need to soak the breadcrumbs in water or milk. Because of the way the pressure works, those breadcrumbs will soften to make the meatballs incredibly tender. The meatballs should also be fairly compact so they'll hold together. And make them small, no more than 5cm in diameter, so they'll cook in the time stated.

1. Mix the beef mince, breadcrumbs and cheese in a large bowl until uniform. Form into sixteen equal balls.

2. Mix the marinara sauce, stock and wine in a **5.5-litre cooker**. Stir in the ziti; nestle the meatballs in one layer into the sauce. Lock the lid onto the pot.

3.

Set the machine	Level	The valve must be	Time	Press
PRESSURE COOK	MAX	—	5 minutes with the KEEP WARM setting off	START
PRESSURE COOK or MANUAL	HIGH	Closed	7 minutes with the KEEP WARM setting off	START

4. Use the **quick-release method** to bring the pot's pressure back to normal. Unlatch the lid and open the pot. Stir gently before serving.

450g lean beef mince

25g Italian-seasoned dried breadcrumbs

25g finely grated Parmigiano-Reggiano

One 680g jar plain marinara (tomato) sauce

250ml beef or chicken stock

125ml white wine, such as Chardonnay

225g dried ziti

Beyond

- You must halve the recipe for a 3-litre cooker.

- For a 7.5-litre cooker, you must increase all the ingredients by 50 per cent.

- For a creamier dish, use 125ml chicken stock and 125ml evaporated milk.

- For a more refined dish, use the Cherry Tomato and Herb Pasta Sauce (page 136) in place of the bottled marinara sauce.

2 tablespoons vegetable, corn or rapeseed oil

1 large onion, chopped (240g prechopped)

1 medium green pepper, stemmed, cored and sliced into thin strips

550g lean beef mince

500ml beef or chicken stock

300ml barbecue sauce

225g dried rigatoni

Barbecue Beef and Pasta Casserole

4 servings

What if you swopped the marinara sauce for barbecue sauce in a pasta dish? Ta da! Customise this casserole by using whatever barbecue sauce you prefer. We tried it with both sweet and vinegary sauces. Both were good but we preferred the latter because the pressure cooker already highlights all sorts of sweet flavours (here the onion and beef mince). The only sauces that didn't work were exceptionally chunky ones that didn't provide enough liquid for the requisite steam.

1.

Press	Setting	Time	Press
SAUTÉ	MEDIUM, NORMAL or CUSTOM 150°C	10 minutes	START

2. Warm the oil in a **5.5-litre cooker** for a minute or two. Add the onion and pepper; cook, stirring often, until the onion begins to soften, about 4 minutes. Crumble in the beef mince and cook, stirring frequently to break up any clumps, until lightly browned, about 4 minutes.

3. Pour in the stock and scrape up *every speck of browned stuff* on the pot's bottom. Turn off the **SAUTÉ** function. Stir in the barbecue sauce and pasta. Lock the lid onto the pot.

4.

Set the machine	Level	The valve must be	Time	Press
PRESSURE COOK	MAX	—	5 minutes with the KEEP WARM setting off	START
PRESSURE COOK or MANUAL	HIGH	Closed	7 minutes with the KEEP WARM setting off	START

5. Use the **quick-release method** to bring the pot's pressure back to normal. Unlatch the lid and open the pot. Stir well before serving.

Beyond

- You must halve the recipe for a 3-litre cooker.

- For a 7.5-litre cooker, you must use 435ml barbecue sauce and increase the remaining ingredients by 50 per cent.

- Add cheese! Once you've opened the lid, stir up to 125g grated Cheddar into the casserole. Set the lid askew and set aside for 5 minutes, until the cheese has melted.

Mediterranean Minced Beef and Pasta Casserole

4 servings

Lemon, cinnamon and dill – if you haven't tried this Greek mélange, you don't know how delicious it is: aromatic and sweet, almost irresistible. This sort of pasta casserole is traditionally made with orzo, the little rice-shaped pasta. Unfortunately, orzo is so small that the 'grains' fall to the pot's bottom and burn. But this tasty one-pot meal comes out just as well with sturdier ziti. *Opa!*

1.

Press	Setting	Time	Press
SAUTÉ	MEDIUM, NORMAL or CUSTOM 150°C	10 minutes	START

2. Warm the oil in a **5.5- or 7.5-litre cooker** for a minute or two. Add the onion and cook, stirring often, until it softens, about 2 minutes. If using, add the anchovies and stir for 1 minute until the bits begin to melt. Stir in the lemon zest, garlic and pepper until fragrant, a few seconds.

3. Crumble in the beef mince and cook, stirring often to break up any clumps, until the meat loses its raw, pink colour, about 3 minutes. Stir in the wine, tomatoes, dill and cinnamon. Scrape up *every speck of browned stuff* on the pot's bottom. Turn off the **SAUTÉ** function. Stir in the pasta and stock until uniform. Lock the lid onto the pot.

4.

Set the machine	Level	The valve must be	Time	Press
PRESSURE COOK	MAX	—	5 minutes with the KEEP WARM setting off	START
PRESSURE COOK or MANUAL	HIGH	Closed	7 minutes with the KEEP WARM setting off	START

5. Use the **quick-release method** to bring the pot's pressure back to normal. Unlatch the lid and open the pot. Stir well before serving.

- 2 tablespoons olive oil
- 1 small onion, chopped (80g prechopped)
- 2 jarred anchovy fillets, finely chopped (optional)
- 2 teaspoons finely grated lemon zest
- 2 medium garlic cloves, peeled and finely chopped (2 teaspoons prechopped)
- ½ teaspoon ground black pepper
- 450g lean beef mince
- 250ml dry white wine, such as Chardonnay
- 2 medium plum or Roma tomatoes, chopped
- 10g fresh dill fronds, chopped
- ½ teaspoon ground cinnamon
- 225g dried ziti
- 350ml beef or chicken stock

Beyond

- You must halve the recipe for a 3-litre cooker.
- If you omit the anchovy fillets, you should also add 1 teaspoon table salt with the ground black pepper.
- For a more herbaceous dish, add up to 1 tablespoon finely chopped fresh oregano leaves with the dill.
- For a little heat, add up to ½ teaspoon crushed chilli flakes with the cinnamon.
- Feel free to substitute lamb mince for the beef mince.
- And be sure to crumble feta over the servings.

2 tablespoons vegetable,
corn or rapeseed oil

1 small red onion, halved
and sliced into thin
half-moons

1 tablespoon finely chopped
peeled fresh root ginger

450g beef mince

One 400g tin
chopped tomatoes

100g almond butter

2 tablespoons honey

2 teaspoons mild paprika

1 teaspoon ground cinnamon

1 teaspoon ground cloves

1 teaspoon ground coriander

1 teaspoon ground cumin

1 teaspoon table salt

½ teaspoon cayenne

550ml chicken stock

225g dried farfalle

Beef and Farfalle in Spicy Tomato-Almond Sauce

4 *servings*

This pasta casserole has the flavours of a Moroccan tagine: almonds, ginger and a heavy dose of dried spices. It's aromatic, decidedly right for a cold evening. It's even got a long-simmered flavour thanks to the almond butter, which adds a complexity similar to that gained through the long process of reducing a sauce on the hob.

If you're fortunate enough to live near a large gourmet supermarket or a Middle Eastern market, substitute 1 tablespoon ras al hanout for the cinnamon, cloves, ground coriander and cumin. *Ras el hanout* means something like 'top shelf' and is a blend of Middle Eastern spices, each blend proprietary to its maker (although any you find would do here).

1.

Press	Setting	Time	Press
SAUTÉ	MEDIUM, NORMAL or CUSTOM 150°C	10 minutes	START

2. Warm the oil in a **5.5- or 7.5-litre cooker** for a minute or two. Add the onion and ginger; cook, stirring often, until the onion begins to soften, about 3 minutes. Crumble in the beef mince; continue cooking, stirring frequently to break up any clumps, until the meat loses its raw, pink colour, about 3 minutes.

3. Stir in the tomatoes and almond butter until the almond butter dissolves in the sauce, all the while scraping up *every speck of browned stuff* on the pot's bottom. Stir in the honey, paprika, cinnamon, cloves, coriander, cumin, salt and cayenne until uniform. Turn off the **SAUTÉ** function; stir in the stock and pasta. Lock the lid onto the pot.

4.

Set the machine	Level	The valve must be	Time	Press
PRESSURE COOK	MAX	—	5 minutes with the KEEP WARM setting off	START
PRESSURE COOK or MANUAL	HIGH	Closed	7 minutes with the KEEP WARM setting off	START

5. Use the **quick-release method** to bring the pot's pressure back to normal. Unlatch the lid and open the pot. Stir well before serving.

Beyond

- You must halve the recipe for a 3-litre cooker.
- For a little heat, use tinned chopped tomatoes with chillies.
- For a (somewhat) more authentically Middle Eastern dish, substitute lamb mince for the beef mince and add 1 preserved lemon, deseeded and chopped, with the chopped tomatoes.
- Garnish with plain Greek yoghurt.
- For a more savoury dish, reduce the honey to 1 tablespoon and use 300ml dry white wine and 250ml stock.

Dan Dan Noodles

4 servings

Hot, spicy and satisfying, this streamlined version of the classic Sichuan dish will take the chill off any evening. It's traditionally made with fresh noodles, but by cooking dried spaghetti right in the sauce, the flavours meld into some cross between a pasta casserole and a Chinese classic. Have lots of beer to hand!

1.

Press	Setting	Time	Press
SAUTÉ	MEDIUM, NORMAL or CUSTOM 150°C	10 minutes	START

2. Heat the oil in a **5.5- or 7.5-litre cooker** for a minute or two. Crumble in the pork and cook, stirring often and breaking up any clumps, until grey but not browned, about 4 minutes. Stir in the spring onions, sambal oelek or hot sauce, garlic and ginger. Cook until aromatic, just a few seconds.

3. Add the tahini, soy sauce, vinegar, honey, sherry (or its substitutes) and Worcestershire sauce. Stir well until the tahini is uniform in the mixture, then stir in the stock. Turn off the **SAUTÉ** function, add the spaghetti and submerge the noodles in the sauce without their touching the bottom of the insert. Lock the lid onto the pot.

4.

Set the machine	Level	The valve must be	Time	Press
PRESSURE COOK	MAX	—	4 minutes with the KEEP WARM setting off	START
PRESSURE COOK or MANUAL	HIGH	Closed	6 minutes with the KEEP WARM setting off	START

5. Use the **quick-release method** to bring the pot's pressure back to normal. Unlatch the lid and open the cooker. Stir well before serving.

---

2 tablespoons peanut oil (or vegetable, corn or rapeseed oil)

450g lean pork mince

6 medium spring onions, trimmed and thinly sliced

Up to 2 tablespoons sambal oelek or a hot red pepper sauce such as Sriracha

3 medium garlic cloves, peeled and finely chopped (1 tablespoon prechopped)

1 tablespoon finely chopped peeled fresh root ginger

65g tahini

60ml soy sauce

3 tablespoons balsamic vinegar

2 tablespoons honey

2 tablespoons dry sherry, dry vermouth, or water

1 tablespoon Worcestershire sauce

500ml chicken stock

225g dried spaghetti, broken in half

Beyond

- You must halve the recipe for a 3-litre cooker.

- To make the flavour more authentic and less like sesame noodles, substitute sunflower seed butter for the tahini. Or skip the fancy stuff and use natural-style creamy peanut butter.

- To be more authentic, you can also substitute 60ml Chinese black vinegar for the balsamic vinegar and Worcestershire sauce.

- And substitute Shaoxing (a Chinese rice wine) for the sherry, vermouth or water.

- Finally, use roasted Chinese chillies in oil, particularly Laoganma Spicy Chili Crisp Sauce, instead of the sambal oelek or hot sauce.

30g flaked almonds

15g butter

1 small onion, chopped
(80g prechopped)

450g unseasoned chicken
breast cut for stir-fry,
any flavouring packets
discarded; or 450g boneless
skinless chicken breast, cut
into 1cm strips

1¼ teaspoons dried sage

1 teaspoon dried thyme

½ teaspoon dried oregano

¼ teaspoon grated nutmeg

¼ teaspoon table salt

600ml chicken stock

225g dried ziti

160ml regular or low-fat
evaporated milk

80g sun-dried tomatoes,
sliced into very thin strips

125ml double cream

1½ tablespoons plain flour

50g finely grated
Parmigiano-Reggiano

Creamy Chicken and Ziti Casserole with Cheese

4 servings

This pasta casserole is just about the fanciest recipe in this chapter. The dish requires a thickened sauce, sliced sun-dried tomatoes, sliced almonds…a whole fandango of kitchen prep. It's not fast, but it sure is tasty, a great family meal.

1. Spread the flaked almonds in a medium-sized dry frying pan set over a medium-low heat. Cook until lightly toasted, about 2 minutes, stirring often. Or toast the nuts in the pot – use the **SAUTÉ** function on **LOW** or **LESS**. Pour the almonds into a small bowl and set aside.

2.

Press	Setting	Time	Press
SAUTÉ	MEDIUM, NORMAL or CUSTOM 150°C	10 minutes	START

3. Melt the butter in a **5.5- or 7.5-litre cooker**. Add the onion and cook, stirring often, until softened, about 3 minutes. Add the chicken, sage, thyme, oregano, nutmeg and salt. Stir over the heat just until the chicken loses its raw colour, about 2 minutes.

4. Stir in the stock, ziti, evaporated milk and sun-dried tomatoes until uniform. Turn off the **SAUTÉ** function. Lock the lid onto the pot.

5.

Set the machine	Level	The valve must be	Time	Press
PRESSURE COOK	MAX	——	5 minutes with the KEEP WARM setting off	START
PRESSURE COOK or MANUAL	HIGH	Closed	7 minutes with the KEEP WARM setting off	START

6. Use the **quick-release method** to bring the pot's pressure back to normal. Unlatch the lid and open the pot. Whisk the cream and flour in a small bowl until the flour dissolves.

7.

Press	Setting	Time	Press
SAUTÉ	MEDIUM, NORMAL or CUSTOM 150°C	5 minutes	START

8. Stir until the sauce comes to a simmer. Whisk the cream mixture one time to make sure the flour is thoroughly combined. Stir this slurry into the pot and continue cooking, stirring almost constantly, until thickened, about 2 minutes. Turn off the **SAUTÉ** function and remove the *hot* insert from the pot. Stir in the cheese and set the lid askew over the insert for a couple of minutes to blend the flavours. Sprinkle the toasted almonds over individual servings.

Beyond

- You must halve the recipe for a 3-litre cooker.
- For a more authentic flavour, substitute pine nuts for the flaked almonds.
- For fewer ingredients, omit the sage, thyme, oregano and nutmeg. Instead, use 2 teaspoons salt-free dried poultry seasoning blend.

55g butter

1 medium onion, chopped (160g prechopped)

450g unseasoned chicken breast cut for stir-fry, any flavouring packets discarded; or 450g boneless skinless chicken breast, cut into 1cm strips

700ml chicken stock

3 tablespoons mild paprika

½ teaspoon caraway seeds

¼ teaspoon grated nutmeg

¼ teaspoon table salt

¼ teaspoon ground black pepper

175g dried egg pasta

125ml regular or low-fat soured cream

Chicken Noodle Paprikash

4 servings

This dish is hardly an authentic Hungarian version of paprikash but an interpretation à la American roadside diners: a rich, buttery stew over pasta, here morphed further into a one-pot casserole.

Don't blanch at the amount of butter. It provides the bulk of the sauce's flavour. And do not heat the soured cream once it is added or it will break and turn the sauce into a watery mess. If you plan on making some and saving it back for another meal, omit the soured cream from that portion and reheat it later before adding the soured cream.

1.

Press	Setting	Time	Press
SAUTÉ	MEDIUM, NORMAL or CUSTOM 150°C	10 minutes	START

2. Melt the butter in a **5.5- or 7.5-litre cooker.** Add the onion and cook, stirring often, until softened, about 3 minutes. Stir in the chicken strips and cook until they lose their pink colour, about 2 minutes.

3. Stir in the stock, paprika, caraway seeds, nutmeg, salt and pepper until aromatic, about 1 minute. Turn off the **SAUTÉ** function. Stir in the pasta and lock the lid onto the pot.

4.

Set the machine	Level	The valve must be	Time	Press
PRESSURE COOK	MAX	——	3 minutes with the KEEP WARM setting off	START
PRESSURE COOK or MANUAL	HIGH	Closed	4 minutes with the KEEP WARM setting off	START

5. Use the **quick-release method** to bring the pot's pressure back to normal. Unlatch the lid and open the pot. Stir in the soured cream until smooth just before serving.

Beyond

- You must halve the recipe for a 3-litre cooker.
- For an added punch of flavour, add up to 2 teaspoons finely chopped garlic with the chicken.
- Use a combination of mild and hot Hungarian paprika – or *all* hot Hungarian paprika (if you're brave).

Chicken Enchilada Casserole

4 servings

Given that this recipe is amongst the pasta casseroles, you already know it's not a true enchilada casserole. There are no corn tortillas. Instead, we created a good facsimile of this American favourite with ready-made enchilada sauce and lots of chicken and vegetables, all turned into a pasta sauce for ziti. There's a wide range of heat quotients amongst prepared enchilada sauces. Make sure you get one that fits your needs.

1. Mix the enchilada sauce, chicken, stock, beans, pepper, corn, onion, smoked paprika and cumin in a **5.5- or 7.5-litre cooker**. Stir in the ziti until coated. Lock the lid onto the pot.

2.

Set the machine	Level	The valve must be	Time	Press
PRESSURE COOK	MAX	—	5 minutes with the KEEP WARM setting off	START
PRESSURE COOK or MANUAL	HIGH	Closed	7 minutes with the KEEP WARM setting off	START

3. Use the **quick-release method** to bring the pot's pressure back to normal. Unlatch the lid and open the pot.

4.

Press	Setting	Time	Press
SAUTÉ	MEDIUM, NORMAL or CUSTOM 150°C	5 minutes	START

5. Bring the sauce to a simmer, stirring constantly. Add the cornmeal and continue cooking, stirring constantly, until thickened about 1 minute. Turn off the **SAUTÉ** function and remove the *hot* insert from the pot. Set the lid askew over the insert for 5 minutes to blend the flavours and continue to thicken the sauce. Stir well before serving.

Two 400g tins red enchilada sauce

450g boneless skinless chicken breast, diced into 1cm pieces

500ml chicken stock

One 400g tin kidney or pinto beans, drained and rinsed

1 large green pepper, stemmed, cored and cut into thin strips

200g fresh or frozen corn kernels (if frozen, do not thaw)

1 small onion, chopped (80g prechopped)

1 teaspoon mild smoked paprika

1 teaspoon ground cumin

225g dried ziti

2 tablespoons yellow cornmeal

Beyond

- You must halve the recipe for a 3-litre cooker.
- To add cheese, wait until the sauce has thickened with the cornmeal, then sprinkle up to 115g grated mozzarella evenly over the top of the casserole. As directed, set the pot's lid askew on top and set aside for 5 minutes to melt the cheese. But don't stir the stew at the end. Instead, dish up the cheese with the casserole below by the big spoonful.
- Garnish the servings with pickled jalapeño rings and/or sliced avocado.

500ml chicken stock

250ml regular or low-fat
evaporated milk

115g white button
mushrooms, thinly sliced

2 medium celery stalks,
thinly sliced

30g butter

1 teaspoon onion powder

1 teaspoon mustard powder

¼ teaspoon table salt

340g dried egg pasta

250ml double cream

Two 175g tins tuna,
preferably yellow fin tuna
packed in oil, drained

225g grated Swiss cheese

Tuna Pasta Casserole

6 servings

By cooking pasta in a mixture of stock and milk, we increase its
silkiness, rendering this Instant Pot version of the classic casserole
even more astounding.

    We leave the tuna out until *after* cooking, so the dish doesn't
become too fishy. There won't be a crunchy top, but we have a
suggestion for how to make one in the *Beyond* section.

1. Mix the stock, evaporated milk, mushrooms, celery, butter,
onion powder, mustard powder and salt in a **5.5- or 7.5-litre
cooker**. Stir in the pasta until well coated. Lock the lid onto
the pot.

2.

Set the machine	Level	The valve must be	Time	Press
PRESSURE COOK	MAX	——	3 minutes with the KEEP WARM setting off	START
PRESSURE COOK or MANUAL	HIGH	Closed	4 minutes with the KEEP WARM setting off	START

3. Use the **quick-release method** to bring the pot's pressure
back to normal. Unlatch the lid and open the pot. Stir in the
cream.

4.

Press	Setting	Time	Press
SAUTÉ	MEDIUM, NORMAL or CUSTOM 150°C	5 minutes	START

5. Cook, stirring often, until the sauce is bubbling fairly well,
about 1 minute. Turn off the **SAUTÉ** function and remove the
hot insert from the pot. Gently stir in the tuna and cheese. Set
the lid askew over the insert for a couple of minutes to melt
the cheese.

Beyond

- You must halve the recipe for
  a 3-litre cooker.

- For a richer dish, look for
  tinned or jarred *Italian* tuna
  packed in olive oil. Drain off
  the oil before stirring the
  chunks into the casserole.

- For a fresher flavour, add
  up to 1 tablespoon finely
  chopped fresh herbs with
  the tuna. Tarragon, thyme,
  oregano or parsley work best.

- For more kick, add up to
  ½ teaspoon garlic powder
  with the onion powder.

- Want a crunchy topping?
  Crush crisps over the top of
  each serving. (Omit the salt
  from the recipe.)

- Substitute two 175g tins
  salmon (drained), preferably
  wild Alaskan pink salmon, for
  the tuna for Salmon Noodle
  Casserole.

Seafood Newburg Casserole

6 servings

Here's a multi-cooker version of a dish fashionable in the Mad Men '50s and '60s. We've turned it into a more hearty family dinner, suitable for a weeknight when you still want to pull out all the stops.

The prawns are fairly small in order to cook in the same time as the scallops. If you can only find king prawns, peel and devein them, then chop them into pieces about as big as the scallop quarters.

600ml chicken stock

125ml dry sherry

30g butter

1 tablespoon fresh finely chopped tarragon leaves

½ teaspoon mild paprika

¼ teaspoon table salt

340g dried egg pasta

180ml double cream

1 large egg yolk

225g scallops, quartered

225g shell-on prawns, peeled, deveined and cut in half lengthways

1.

Press	Setting	Time	Press
SAUTÉ	MEDIUM, NORMAL or CUSTOM 150°C	5 minutes	START

2. Mix the stock, sherry, butter, tarragon, paprika and salt in a **5.5- or 7.5-litre cooker.** Cook until the butter melts, stirring occasionally, about 3 minutes. Turn off the **SAUTÉ** function and stir in the pasta until coated. Lock the lid onto the pot.

3.

Set the machine	Level	The valve must be	Time	Press
PRESSURE COOK	MAX	——	3 minutes with the KEEP WARM setting off	START
PRESSURE COOK or MANUAL	HIGH	Closed	4 minutes with the KEEP WARM setting off	START

4. Use the **quick-release method** to bring the pot's pressure back to normal. Unlatch the lid and open the pot.

5.

Press	Setting	Time	Press
SAUTÉ	LOW or LESS	5 minutes	START

6. Whisk the cream and egg yolk in a small bowl. Whisk about 250ml of the hot mixture from the pot into this cream mixture, then stir this new mixture back into the pot along with the scallops and prawns.

7. Cook, stirring constantly, just until the prawns are firm, not more than 2 minutes. Immediately turn off the **SAUTÉ** function, remove the hot insert from the pot to stop the cooking and continue stirring until any bubbling stops and the pasta are well coated.

Beyond

- You must halve the recipe for a 3-litre cooker.

- Stir 225g crab meat, picked over for shells and cartilage, into the casserole with the other seafood.

- If you don't want to use sherry, substitute an equivalent amount of bottled clam juice, available in some supermarkets.

- For a little heat, add up to 1 teaspoon crushed chilli flakes with the tarragon.

- Garnish the servings with finely chopped chives or the green parts of a spring onion.

SUPER EASY / FEWER THAN 10 INGREDIENTS /
QUICK RELEASE, THEN MODIFIED NATURAL RELEASE /
CAN BE GLUTEN-FREE

680g jar plain marinara
(tomato) sauce

60ml red or sweet vermouth

450g boneless pork loin,
cut into 1cm cubes

One 400g bag frozen gnocchi
(do not thaw)

155g frozen peas
(do not thaw)

Gnocchi Casserole with Pork and Peas

4 servings

Frozen gnocchi are an incredibly easy pasta(-like) addition to this casserole, but there are two tricks to success. First, cut the pork into small cubes, each a little smaller than the gnocchi, so they'll cook efficiently and at the same time, with none turning to mush.

Second, watch the pot during the second cooking. The moment the float valve comes up in the lid to lock the lid onto the pot, turn the machine off. In essence, the gnocchi don't cook under full pressure. They cook *just until* the lid locks into place. That second cooking should only be done at HIGH, not at MAX.

1. Mix the marinara sauce, vermouth and pork in a 5.5- or 7.5-litre cooker. Lock the lid onto the pot.

2.

Set the machine	Level	The valve must be	Time	Press
PRESSURE COOK	MAX	——	7 minutes with the KEEP WARM setting off	START
PRESSURE COOK or MANUAL	HIGH	Closed	10 minutes with the KEEP WARM setting off	START

3. Use the **quick-release method** to bring the machine's pressure back to normal. Unlatch the lid and open the pot. Stir in the gnocchi and peas.

4.

Press	Setting	The valve must be	Time	Press
PRESSURE COOK or MANUAL	HIGH	Closed	1 minute with the KEEP WARM setting off	START

5. *The moment* the float valve (or pin) pops up to lock the lid and the machine stops putting out steam, turn it off and let its pressure **return to normal naturally** for 1 minute. Then use the **quick-release method** to get rid of the residual pressure in the pot. Unlatch the lid and open the cooker. Stir well before serving.

Beyond

- You must halve the recipe for a 3-litre cooker.
- To avoid the alcohol, substitute no-added- sugar cranberry juice for the vermouth.
- For added heat, stir up to 1 teaspoon crushed chilli flakes into the pot with the marinara sauce.
- Sprinkle up to 100g finely grated Parmigiano-Reggiano over the top of the casserole in the pot.
- Substitute 450g boneless skinless chicken thighs, cut into 1cm pieces, for the pork.

Pesto Gnocchi Casserole with Cheese

4 servings

Here's an easy dump-and-stir casserole, ready in minutes, the sort of miracle we all want from a multi-cooker. Look for a decent pesto, not an oily mess. See the *Beyond* for a homemade version.

As in the previous recipe, stop the cooking the moment the pressure valve or pin rises to lock onto the pot. In other words, don't step away from the cooker and don't even let it come all the way up to pressure. Such vigilance seems a small price to pay for a rich casserole, a quick meal on its own or a great thing to serve alongside steaks or chops.

1. Mix the gnocchi, ham, stock, evaporated milk, pimientos and pesto in a **3- or 5.5-litre cooker**. Lock the lid onto the pot.

2.

Set the machine	Level	The valve must be	Time	Press
PRESSURE COOK or MANUAL	HIGH	Closed	1 minute with the KEEP WARM setting off	START

3. *The moment* the float valve rises to lock the lid onto the pot and the machine stops putting out steam, turn it off and let its pressure **return to normal naturally** for 1 minute. Then use the **quick-release method** to get rid of the pot's residual pressure. Unlatch the lid and open the cooker. Stir the cheese and cream into the casserole. Set the lid askew over the pot for 5 minutes to melt the cheese.

One 400g bag frozen gnocchi (do not thaw)

155g diced smoked ham

250ml chicken stock

125ml evaporated milk

One 115g jar diced pimientos, drained

3 tablespoons ready-made pesto

115g grated Swiss cheese

60ml double cream

Beyond

- For a 7.5-litre cooker, you must increase all the ingredients by 50 per cent.

- For a fast homemade pesto, put 60g basil leaves, 80ml olive oil, 35g finely grated Parmigiano-Reggiano, 40g nuts (walnut, almonds or pine nuts), 1 or 2 peeled medium garlic cloves and ½ teaspoon salt in a food processor. Cover and process until smooth, adding water a little at a time if you feel the sauce is too thick. Store any extra pesto with a thin coating of olive oil over the top in a sealed container in the fridge for up to 4 days.

- Use another white cheese in place of the Swiss, such as mozzarella, provolone, pecorino or Cheddar (mild, not mature).

One 680g jar pizza sauce

450g sweet Italian pork or turkey sausages, cut into 1cm pieces

350g frozen pepper strips (do not thaw)

One 140g package sliced pepperoni

125ml chicken or vegetable stock

115g mozzarella, diced

225g fresh pizza dough

25g finely grated Parmigiano-Reggiano

Pizza Casserole

4 servings

Here's the best way to make a pizza in a multi-cooker. The dish is actually something like a pasta casserole, given that the pizza dough is rolled into balls, then floated like dumplings in a sauce that tastes just like the one on a sausage and pepperoni pizza.

As to the cooking technique, it's a bit unusual. First, the sauce and other pizza ingredients are put under pressure. Then the 'dumplings' (made with pizza dough) are added and finished with the SLOW COOK function. Your model may not go as low as 25 minutes on that setting, in which case you'll need to set it with the minimum amount of time possible and also set a more traditional timer for the proper time.

1. Mix the pizza sauce, sausage, pepper strips, pepperoni and stock in a **5.5- or 7.5-litre cooker**. Lock the lid onto the pot.

2.

Set the machine	Level	The valve must be	Time	Press
PRESSURE COOK	MAX	——	5 minutes with the KEEP WARM setting off	START
PRESSURE COOK or MANUAL	HIGH	Closed	6 minutes with the KEEP WARM setting off	START

3. Use the **quick-release method** to bring the pot's pressure back to normal. Unlatch the lid and open the cooker. Stir the mixture inside, then scatter the mozzarella cubes over the top.

4. Form the pizza dough into 8 balls, each about the size of a ping-pong ball. Nestle these about one-quarter of the way into the sauce. Sprinkle the grated Parmigiano-Reggiano over the balls and the sauce.

5.

Set the machine	Level	The valve must be	Time	Press
SLOW COOK	HIGH	Opened	25 minutes with the KEEP WARM setting off	START

6. Turn off the machine when done, open the pot and serve without stirring.

Beyond

- You must halve the recipe for a 3-litre cooker.

- For a more savoury casserole, substitute plain marinara sauce for the pizza sauce.

- Add other pizza toppings you like with the pepperoni: 90g thinly sliced white or brown button mushrooms, 30g sliced pitted black olives, 40g chopped red onion and/or 2 or 3 chopped anchovy fillets.

- Rather than sprinkling the Parmigiano-Reggiano over the casserole, knead it into the pizza dough before making the eight balls.

Giant Couscous with Aubergine and Peppers

4 servings

Giant couscous is something like pasta: little dried balls of semolina or wheat flour, also called 'Israeli couscous', 'pearl couscous' and 'ptitim' (in Israel). The pasta has been toasted, so giant couscous has a bolder flavour, similar to barley. Giant couscous stands up to big flavours in a casserole like this one, which is something like a thick Mediterranean stew, or maybe a giant couscous version of pasta puttanesca.

1.

Press	Setting	Time	Press
SAUTÉ	MEDIUM, NORMAL or CUSTOM 150°C	10 minutes	START

2. Warm the oil in a **5.5- or 7.5-litre cooker** for a minute or two. Add the shallot, capers, garlic and crushed chilli flakes. Cook, stirring frequently, until the shallot softens, about 2 minutes. Stir in the aubergine and peppers. Continue cooking, stirring often, until the aubergine begins to soften, about 4 minutes.

3. Stir in the stock. Scrape up *every speck of browned stuff* on the pot's bottom. Turn off the **SAUTÉ** function. Stir in the tomatoes and couscous. Tuck the rosemary stalk into the mixture. Lock the lid onto the pot.

4.

Set the machine	Level	The valve must be	Time	Press
PRESSURE COOK	MAX	—	7 minutes with the KEEP WARM setting off	START
PRESSURE COOK or MANUAL	HIGH	Closed	10 minutes with the KEEP WARM setting off	START

5. Use the **quick-release method** to bring the pot's pressure back to normal. Unlatch the lid and open the cooker. Find and discard the rosemary stalk. Stir well, then set the lid askew over the pot for 5–10 minutes so that the casserole continues to set up just before serving.

---

2 tablespoons olive oil

1 medium shallot, finely chopped

1 tablespoon drained and rinsed capers, finely chopped

3 medium garlic cloves, peeled and finely chopped (1 tablespoon prechopped)

½ teaspoon crushed chilli flakes

One 450g aubergine, diced (no need to peel)

2 medium green peppers, stemmed, cored and chopped (350g prechopped)

600ml vegetable stock

One 400g tin chopped tomatoes

210g giant couscous

1 rosemary stalk, about 10cm in length

Beyond

- You must halve the recipe for a 3-litre cooker.
- Add 1 jarred anchovy fillet, finely chopped, with the shallot and other ingredients. (The dish, of course, will no longer be vegan.)
- Add up to 3 fresh oregano sprigs with the rosemary stalk.
- Grate lots of Parmigiano-Reggiano over each serving. (Again, no longer vegan.)

2 tablespoons olive oil

1 large onion, chopped (340g prechopped)

1 medium green pepper, stemmed, cored and chopped (175g prechopped)

2 medium celery stalks, thinly sliced

400g smoked sausage, preferably Cajun andouille, cut into 1cm slices

600ml chicken stock

One 400g tin chopped tomatoes

210g giant couscous

1 teaspoon dried thyme

1 teaspoon dried sage

½ teaspoon cayenne

½ teaspoon table salt

Cajun-Inspired Sausage and Giant Couscous Casserole

4 servings

This one-pot supper is stocked with big flavours, the better to pair with those little, toasted pasta balls (aka giant couscous). If the dish is too soupy for your taste, boil it down in the pot for a couple minutes after pressure-cooking, using the SAUTÉ setting at MEDIUM, NORMAL or CUSTOM 150°C.

However, don't make it too dry. The giant couscous will continue to absorb moisture as it sits. In fact, you'll need to thin out leftovers with a little extra broth when reheating.

1.

Press	Setting	Time	Press
SAUTÉ	MEDIUM, NORMAL or CUSTOM 150°C	5 minutes	START

2. Warm the oil in a **5.5- or 7.5-litre cooker** for a minute or two. Add the onion, pepper and celery. Cook, stirring often, until the onion begins to soften, about 5 minutes. Add the sausage and cook, stirring fairly often, until all the sausage is warmed through and its oil has begun to loosen, about 3 minutes.

3. Stir in the stock and scrape up *every speck of browned stuff* on the pot's bottom. Turn off the **SAUTÉ** function. Stir in the tomatoes, couscous, thyme, sage, cayenne and salt. Lock the lid onto the pot.

4.

Set the machine	Level	The valve must be	Time	Press
PRESSURE COOK	MAX	—	7 minutes with the KEEP WARM setting off	START
PRESSURE COOK or MANUAL	HIGH	Closed	10 minutes with the KEEP WARM setting off	START

5. Use the **quick-release method** to bring the pot's pressure back to normal. Unlatch the lid and open the cooker. Set the lid askew over the cooker for 5 minutes to let the casserole set up. Stir well before serving.

Beyond

- You must halve the recipe for a 3-litre cooker.

- Feel free to use smoked kielbasa or smoked bratwurst, although the dish won't have the characteristic Cajun flavour.

- The casserole may not be spicy enough for some tastes. Pass Tabasco sauce or other hot chilli sauce at the table.

Thai-Inspired Chicken and Rice Noodles

4 servings

We've tried to recreate a sort of streamlined version of a rice noodle Thai stir-fry, but one that is less sweet than most versions, more true sweet-and-sour, even packed with savoury flavours.

High-quality fish sauce is the key. You can find it in the Asian aisle of almost every supermarket. Don't worry about its odour. It mellows beautifully as it cooks.

And here's one more thing. Sambal oelek is a hot, thick, red chilli sauce, once from South East Asia but now found in almost every supermarket. However, you can substitute any thick red chilli sauce or paste.

1.

Press	Setting	Time	Press
SAUTÉ	MEDIUM, NORMAL or CUSTOM 150°C	10 minutes	START

2. Warm the oil in a **5.5- or 7.5-litre cooker** for a minute or two. Add the peppers and shallots. Cook, stirring often, until the shallot softens, about 4 minutes. Add the chicken and garlic. Cook, stirring frequently, until the chicken loses its raw, pink colour, about 3 minutes.

3. Stir in the stock, turn off the **SAUTÉ** function and scrape up *every speck of browned stuff* on the pot's bottom. Stir in the lime juice, fish sauce, brown sugar, sambal oelek and tomato purée until the brown sugar and tomato purée dissolve and the mixture is uniform in colour. Stir in the rice noodles, basil and peanuts. Lock the lid onto the pot.

4.

Set the machine	Level	The valve must be	Time	Press
PRESSURE COOK	MAX	—	3 minutes with the KEEP WARM setting off	START
PRESSURE COOK or MANUAL	HIGH	Closed	4 minutes with the KEEP WARM setting off	START

5. Use the **quick-release method** to bring the pot's pressure back to normal. Unlatch the lid and open the cooker. Stir well and serve with lime wedges to squeeze over each portion.

1 tablespoon peanut oil (or vegetable, corn or rapeseed oil)

2 medium peppers, stemmed, cored and sliced into thin strips

4 medium shallots, halved and thinly sliced lengthways

900g unseasoned chicken breast cut for stir-fry, any flavouring packets discarded; or 900g boneless skinless chicken breast, cut into 1cm strips

3 medium garlic cloves, peeled and finely chopped (1 tablespoon prechopped)

300ml chicken stock

60ml fresh lime juice

60ml fish sauce (nam pla)

45g packed light brown sugar

2 tablespoons sambal oelek

1 tablespoon tomato purée

225g dried rice stick noodles or rice noodles for pad Thai

15g fresh basil leaves, roughly chopped

40g chopped unsalted peanuts

Lime wedges for garnishing

Beyond

- You must halve the recipe for a 3-litre cooker.
- For a more authentic taste, substitute palm sugar or even coconut sugar for the brown sugar.

550g lean turkey mince

30g snipped chives or the green parts of spring onions

3 tablespoons yellow cornmeal

1 large egg white

1 teaspoon dried thyme

½ teaspoon table salt

½ teaspoon ground black pepper

2 medium shallots, chopped

700ml chicken stock

30g butter, cut into small bits

2 tablespoons finely chopped fresh sage leaves

60ml light, slightly sweet white wine, such as Pinot Grigio

200g dried rice stick noodles or rice noodles for pad Thai

60ml double cream

Turkey Meatballs and Rice Noodles in Cream Sauce

4 servings

This straightforward meatball dish requires two different techniques under pressure. First, you'll partially cook the meatballs in the sauce. Then you'll add the noodles and bring the pot not even to HIGH pressure, but *just until* the lid locks in place with the float valve or pin. Stopping the cooking at this moment ensures three things: 1) that the rice noodles don't stick, 2) that we don't have to make a soupy sauce to protect them and 3) that the meatballs are done without being dry.

1. Stir the turkey, chives or spring onions, cornmeal, egg white, thyme, salt and pepper in a large bowl until uniform. Form into 16 moderately small, compact balls, each from about 2 rounded tablespoons of the mixture. Place these in a **5.5- or 7.5-litre cooker.**

2. Scatter the shallots over the meatballs. Pour in the stock, then add the butter, sage and wine. Lock the lid onto the pot.

3.

Set the machine	Level	The valve must be	Time	Press
PRESSURE COOK	MAX	—	2 minutes with the KEEP WARM setting off	START
PRESSURE COOK or MANUAL	HIGH	Closed	3 minutes with the KEEP WARM setting off	START

4. Use the **quick-release method** to bring the pot's pressure back to normal. Unlatch the lid and open the cooker. Use a slotted spoon to transfer the meatballs to a large bowl.

5. Break up the rice noodles to fit in the pot. Stir them into the liquid mixture. Set the meatballs back on top. Lock the lid back onto the pot.

6.

Set the machine	Level	The valve must be	Time	Press
PRESSURE COOK or MANUAL	HIGH	Closed	1 minute with the KEEP WARM setting off	START

7. *The moment* the float valve (or pin) comes up to lock the lid in place and the machine stops putting out steam, turn it off and let its pressure **return to normal naturally** for 4 minutes. Then use the **quick-release method** to release any residual pressure in the pot. Unlatch the lid and open the pot again.

8.

Press	Setting	Time	Press
SAUTÉ	MEDIUM, NORMAL or CUSTOM 150°C	5 minutes	START

9. Stir in the cream. Bring the sauce to a low simmer, stirring gently, for less than 1 minute. Turn off the **SAUTÉ** function and remove the *hot* insert from the pot. Continue stirring gently until the bubbling stops and the sauce coats the noodles.

Beyond

- You must halve the recipe for a 3-litre cooker.
- For a more sophisticated dish, add up to 2 tablespoons of any number of chopped, fresh, green, leafy herbs to the sauce with the cream – think rosemary, oregano, marjoram or tarragon.
- For more kick, add up to 2 teaspoons finely chopped garlic with the shallots.
- For a warm, comforting flavour, add up to ½ teaspoon grated nutmeg to the meatball mixture.

700ml vegetable stock

90ml soy sauce

3 tablespoons rice vinegar

2 tablespoons finely chopped peeled fresh root ginger

1 tablespoon hoisin sauce

2 medium garlic cloves, peeled and finely chopped (2 teaspoons prechopped)

225g dried rice vermicelli

680g bagged frozen vegetables for stir-fry (do not thaw), any flavouring packets discarded

Vegetable Lo Mein with Rice Vermicelli

6 servings

It's hard to imagine an easier meal than this Instant Pot version of the take-away classic. Just mix the sauce in the cooker, then layer the noodles and frozen vegetables as directed in and onto the sauce. The machine doesn't really even come up to high pressure. When the float valve or pin rises to lock the lid onto the pot, turn it off and set it aside. Don't leave the pot unattended while it's coming to pressure. Pay attention to the cues in the instructions below.

1. Mix the stock, soy sauce, rice vinegar, ginger, hoisin sauce and garlic in a **5.5- or 7.5-litre cooker**. Break the rice vermicelli to fit the pot and add them to the sauce. Pour the vegetables in an even layer over the top of everything. Lock the lid onto the pot.

2.

Press	Setting	The valve must be	Time	Press
PRESSURE COOK or MANUAL	HIGH	Closed	1 minute with the KEEP WARM setting off	START

3. *The moment* the float valve (or pin) comes up to lock the lid in place and the machine stops putting out steam, turn it off and let its pressure **return to normal naturally** for 2 minutes. Then use the **quick-release method** to get rid of the residual pressure in the pot. Unlatch the lid and open the pot. Stir well before serving.

Beyond

- The dish will not work well in a 3-litre cooker as not enough of the rice vermicelli will make it into the sauce.

- Hoisin sauce is a sweet, pasty condiment, often made from soya beans or sweet potatoes. There are versions of gluten-free hoisin sauce on the market but the quality varies. If you want to make your own, combine 60ml gluten-free soy sauce, 2 tablespoons creamy natural-style peanut butter, 2 tablespoons treacle, 1 tablespoon toasted sesame oil, 2 teaspoons rice vinegar, 1 teaspoon finely chopped garlic, 1 teaspoon Sriracha, ¼ teaspoon mustard powder and ¼ teaspoon ground cloves in a small saucepan. Bring to a simmer over a medium-low heat, stirring very often. Then reduce the heat and cook, stirring very often, almost constantly, until thickened, about 4 minutes. Store in a sealed, glass jar in the fridge for up to 2 weeks.

Vegetable Stroganoff with Pasta

4 servings

Since this simple casserole contains so many vegetables, it's more like a full meal than some of the recipes in this chapter. (And check the suggestions amongst those in the *Beyond* section to add even more.)

Because all those vegetables give off moisture as they cook, the sauce may be a little soupy when you open the pot. It's impossible to say exactly how much moisture any given vegetable will give off. That's why we boil down the sauce before adding the soured cream. But check the consistency when you open the pot. You may not need to do that extra step.

1.

Press	Setting	Time	Press
SAUTÉ	MEDIUM, NORMAL or CUSTOM 150°C	10 minutes	START

2. Melt the butter in a **5.5- or 7.5-litre cooker.** Add the onion and cook, stirring often, until softened, about 3 minutes. Add the mushrooms, courgette and garlic; cook, stirring often, until the mushrooms begin to soften, about 3 minutes.

3. Stir in the mustard, thyme, salt and pepper until aromatic. Stir in the stock and scrape *every speck of brown stuff* on the bottom of the pot. Turn off the **SAUTÉ** function and stir in the pasta. All should be well coated but not all will be submerged. Lock the lid onto the pot.

4.

Set the machine	Level	The valve must be	Time	Press
PRESSURE COOK	MAX	—	3 minutes with the KEEP WARM setting off	START
PRESSURE COOK or MANUAL	HIGH	Closed	4 minutes with the KEEP WARM setting off	START

5. Use the **quick-release method** to bring the pot's pressure back to normal. Unlatch the lid and open the pot.

6.

Press	Setting	Time	Press
SAUTÉ	MEDIUM, NORMAL or CUSTOM 150°C	5 minutes	START

7. Bring the sauce to a simmer, stirring all the while. Stir until most of the liquid has evaporated, about 1 minute. Turn off the **SAUTÉ** function. Remove the *hot* insert from the pot and stir in the soured cream until uniform just before serving.

30g butter

1 small onion, chopped (80g prechopped)

225g chestnut mushrooms, thinly sliced

1 medium courgette, grated and squeezed for moisture

1 medium garlic clove, peeled and finely chopped (1 teaspoon prechopped)

1½ teaspoons Dijon mustard

1½ teaspoons dried thyme

¼ teaspoon table salt

¼ teaspoon ground black pepper

500ml vegetable stock

175g dried egg pasta

125ml regular or low-fat soured cream

Beyond

- Unfortunately, this recipe does not work well in a 3-litre cooker without major alterations.

- Feel free to substitute 1 chopped large shallot for the onion.

- For even more hearty vegetable goodness, add up to 80g grated carrot or up to 125g chopped cauliflower florets with the courgette.

- Garnish servings with fresh thyme leaves, finely grated lemon zest and/or more ground black pepper.

1 tablespoon olive oil

450g lean beef mince

2 medium garlic cloves, peeled and finely chopped (2 teaspoons prechopped)

2 teaspoons dried oregano

1 teaspoon fennel seeds

1 teaspoon dried thyme

½ teaspoon crushed chilli flakes

½ teaspoon table salt

Two 400g tins chopped tomatoes

500ml beef or chicken stock

225g dried lasagne sheets, broken into 5cm pieces to fit into the cooker

225g grated mozzarella

No-Layer Lasagne Casserole

2–4 servings

Before we get to the moulded lasagnes and spaghetti pies, we thought we'd offer a lasagne-like casserole with broken-up lasagne sheets that's made right in the pot (that is, rather than layered in a springform tin and steamed under pressure). Serve it by the big spoonful, rather than in neat squares. Brown the beef mince deeply so that it offers a complex flavour in this otherwise simple casserole.

1.

Press	Setting	Time	Press
SAUTÉ	MEDIUM, NORMAL or CUSTOM 150°C	10 minutes	START

2. Warm the oil in a **5.5- or 7.5-litre cooker** for a minute or two. Crumble in the beef mince and cook, stirring occasionally to break up the clumps, until lightly browned, about 6 minutes.

3. Stir in the garlic, oregano, fennel seeds, thyme, crushed chilli flakes and salt until aromatic, a few seconds. Pour in the tomatoes and stock; scrape up *every speck of browned stuff* on the pot's bottom. Turn off the **SAUTÉ** function. Stir in the broken lasagne sheets and lock the lid onto the pot.

4.

Set the machine	Level	The valve must be	Time	Press
PRESSURE COOK	MAX	—	5 minutes with the KEEP WARM setting off	START
PRESSURE COOK or MANUAL	HIGH	Closed	7 minutes with the KEEP WARM setting off	START

5. Use the **quick-release method** to return the machine's pressure to normal. Unlatch the lid and open the pot. Sprinkle the mozzarella over the casserole, then stir gently. Set the lid askew over the top of the pot for 5 minutes to melt the cheese and blend the flavours.

Beyond

- You must halve the recipe for a 3-litre cooker.

- Feel free to use a 50/50 combo of pork mince and beef mince.

- For added complexity, use a 50/50 combo of red wine and stock.

- Rather than adding the mozzarella to the pot, serve the stew over large dollops of ricotta in the bowls. For more zest, mix a little finely grated lemon zest into the ricotta before using.

Easy Lasagne Pie

4 *servings*

Here's the simplest of our layered lasagnes, made with purchased marinara and no-boil pasta in an 18cm round springform tin. Yes, the casserole takes time to build, cook and set up, particularly because a natural release works best to let the pasta continue to cook without being bombarded by the pressure.

   Of course, packaged lasagne sheets won't fit in this relatively small springform tin, so they must be broken to fit. Don't worry about making solid layers of the pasta. Since these are no-boil lasagne sheets, they will expand as they cook. And notice that this recipe is only to be cooked on HIGH (not on MAX, if your model offers that setting).

1. Generously coat the inside of an 18cm round springform tin with olive oil. Set a heat- and pressure-safe trivet in a 5.5- or 7.5-litre cooker. Add the water. Prepare an aluminium foil sling (see page 20).

2. Mix the ricotta, egg and nutmeg in a medium bowl until uniform.

3. Spread 60ml of the marinara sauce in the springform tin. Break one lasagne sheet to make a layer over the sauce, then dollop an even layer of ¼ of the ricotta mixture in tiny bits, followed by a sprinkled, even layer of ¼ of the mozzarella. Repeat to make three more layers. After each layer, press the pasta down slightly to help spread out the ricotta below. Complete the top with the last lasagne sheet, the remainder of the marinara sauce, and the Parmigiano-Reggiano in an even layer. Cover the springform tin tightly with aluminium foil. Use the sling to lower the tin onto the trivet in the pot; fold down the ends of the sling so they fit inside the pot. Lock the lid onto the cooker.

4.

Set the machine	Level	The valve must be	Time	Press
PRESSURE COOK or MANUAL	HIGH	Closed	20 minutes with the KEEP WARM setting off	START

5. Once the machine has finished cooking at pressure, turn it off and let the pressure in the pot **return to normal naturally**, about 20 minutes. Unlatch the lid and open the pot. Use the sling to lift the springform tin out of the pot. Uncover the tin and set aside for 10–15 minutes so the lasagne sets up. Run a small knife around the interior edges to loosen the lasagne from the pan, then unlatch the springform tin, remove the outer ring and cut the lasagne into quarters to serve.

Olive oil or olive oil spray for the baking dish

500ml water

250g regular ricotta

1 large egg

½ teaspoon grated nutmeg

435ml ready-made plain marinara (tomato) sauce

5 no-boil dried lasagne sheets

150g grated mozzarella

25g finely grated Parmigiano-Reggiano

Beyond

- Because of the size of the springform tin, none of these lasagnes will work in a 3-litre cooker.

- Although the casserole doesn't come to the top of the springform tin (and so doesn't touch the foil), you can add a layer of baking parchment before the foil, if you're worried about it touching acidic ingredients.

- Add basil or oregano leaves between some of the layers of the casserole.

- Add up to 1 teaspoon finely grated lemon zest to the ricotta mixture.

- Add up to 1 teaspoon crushed chilli flakes with the grated Parmigiano-Reggiano.

1 tablespoon olive oil, plus extra for the tin

225g bulk sweet Italian sausage meat (or sausages, with any casings removed)

40g baby kale leaves

500ml plain marinara (tomato) sauce

500ml water

6 dried no-boil lasagne sheets

350g grated mozzarella

Lasagne with Sausage and Kale

4 servings

This lasagne is a bit more like the classic standard (if made in an Instant Pot). However, we left out the ricotta and used only meat sauce and mozzarella, sort of like a pizza crossed with a lasagne, for more cheesy goodness in every bite. Don't stint on giving the lasagne time to set up as the pasta needs to absorb more of the sauce as the lasagne rests.

1.

Press	Setting	Time	Press
SAUTÉ	MEDIUM, NORMAL or CUSTOM 150°C	10 minutes	START

2. Warm the oil in a **5.5- or 7.5-litre cooker** for a minute or two. Crumble in the sausage and cook, stirring often to break up the clumps, until the meat loses its raw, red colour, about 3 minutes. Add the kale and continue cooking, stirring once in a while, until the leaves have wilted, about 3 minutes.

3. Turn off the **SAUTÉ** function. Pour in the marinara sauce and mix well, then transfer every drop of contents of the *hot* insert to a large bowl. Clean the insert and return it to the pot.

4. Set a heat- and pressure-safe trivet inside the pot, then add the water. Generously oil the inside of an 18cm round springform tin. Make an aluminium foil sling (see page 20).

5. Break up one lasagne sheet and use it cover the bottom of the prepared tin as well as you can. Top with even layers of the meat sauce and the mozzarella. Repeat five more times. Cover the springform tin tightly with foil. Use the sling to lower the tin onto the trivet in the pot. Fold down the ends of the sling and lock the lid onto the cooker.

6.

Set the machine	Level	The valve must be	Time	Press
PRESSURE COOK or MANUAL	HIGH	Closed	20 minutes with the KEEP WARM setting off	START

7. Once the machine has stopped cooking, turn it off and let the pressure **return to normal naturally**, about 20 minutes. Unlatch the lid and open the pot. Use the sling to lift the springform tin out of the pot. Uncover and set aside for 15 minutes so the lasagne can set up. Run a small knife around the inside of the springform tin to loosen the lasagne, then unlatch the pan, remove the outer ring, and cut the lasagne into quarters to serve.

Beyond

- For a more complex lasagne, use the Cherry Tomato and Herb Pasta Sauce (page 136).

- Feel free to substitute baby rocket for the baby kale.

- Go ahead and substitute fontina for the mozzarella.

Four-Cheese Spaghetti Pie

4 servings

Consider this a casserole version of an incredible four-cheese macaroni cheese. Unfortunately, you must cook the spaghetti in advance. Make it a day or two earlier, storing it in a sealed plastic bag in the fridge until you're ready.

    For this casserole (unlike the lasagnes that have come before), you can use the MAX setting, if available on your model, because the spaghetti has already been cooked (and isn't as delicate as the no-boil lasagne sheets). The spaghetti and cheese mixture makes quite a lot. Work to pack it into the tin as tightly as possible, pressing down against it with a rubber spatula to create an even layer of spaghetti pie.

1. Set a heat- and pressure-safe trivet inside a **5.5- or 7.5-litre cooker;** pour in the water. Generously butter the inside of an 18cm round springform tin. Make an aluminium foil sling (see page 20).

2. Whisk the egg, oregano, nutmeg and pepper in a large bowl until creamy. Add the cooked spaghetti and toss well to coat. Add the provolone, Swiss cheese and mozzarella; toss well until uniform. Pack this mixture tightly into the prepared pan. Top with the grated Parmigiano-Reggiano. Cover the tin tightly with foil. Use the sling to lower the tin onto the trivet in the pot. Fold down the ends of the sling and lock the lid onto the pot.

3.

Set the machine	Level	The valve must be	Time	Press
PRESSURE COOK	MAX	——	12 minutes with the KEEP WARM setting off	START
PRESSURE COOK or MANUAL	HIGH	Closed	15 minutes with the KEEP WARM setting off	START

4. When the machine has finished cooking, turn it off and let its pressure **return to normal naturally**, about 20 minutes. Unlatch the lid and open the pot. Use the sling to transfer the tin to a wire cooling rack. Uncover the tin and set aside for 10 minutes for the pie to set up. Run a small knife around the interior of the tin to loosen the spaghetti pie from the sides, then unlatch the pan, remove the outer ring and cut the spaghetti pie into quarters to serve.

500ml water

Butter for greasing the tin

1 large egg

1 teaspoon dried oregano

¼ teaspoon grated nutmeg

½ teaspoon ground black pepper

225g dried spaghetti, cooked, drained, rinsed and cooled to room temperature

115g grated provolone

115g grated Swiss cheese

115g grated mozzarella

2 tablespoons finely grated Parmigiano-Reggiano

Beyond

- As with the lasagnes, these spaghetti pies don't work in a 3-litre cooker because of the size of the springform tin.

- Go ahead and substitute grated fontina for the provolone, or grated Gruyère for the Swiss cheese.

- For a little heat, add up to ½ teaspoon crushed chilli flakes with the oregano.

500ml water

Butter for greasing the tin

2 large eggs

1½ teaspoons dried dill

½ teaspoon grated nutmeg

½ teaspoon table salt

½ teaspoon ground
black pepper

280g frozen chopped spinach,
thawed and squeezed dry
by the handful

250ml whole or low-fat milk

125ml whole-milk ricotta

40g pine nuts

225g dried spaghetti, cooked,
drained, rinsed and cooled
to room temperature

Spinach and Ricotta Spaghetti Pie

4 servings

This casserole is a cross between a frittata, a creamy pasta dish and a spaghetti pie. Consider it a rich treat for a cold evening. It needs a salad on the side. Dress mixed greens and sliced sugar snap peas with 1 part balsamic vinegar and 3 parts olive oil mixed with finely grated orange zest.

1. Set a heat- and pressure-safe trivet in a **5.5- or 7.5-litre cooker**, then pour in the water. Generously butter the inside of an 18cm round springform tin. Prepare an aluminium foil sling (see page 20).

2. Whisk the eggs, dill, nutmeg, salt and pepper in a large bowl until creamy. Stir in the spinach, milk, ricotta and pine nuts until uniform. Add the spaghetti and toss until well coated. Pack this mixture tightly into the prepared tin, cover the tin tightly with aluminium foil, then use the sling to lower the tin onto the trivet in the pot. Fold down the ends of the sling and lock the lid onto the pot.

3.

Set the machine	Level	The valve must be	Time	Press
PRESSURE COOK	MAX	——	15 minutes with the KEEP WARM setting off	START
PRESSURE COOK or MANUAL	HIGH	Closed	20 minutes with the KEEP WARM setting off	START

4. When the machine has finished cooking, turn it off and let the pressure **return to normal naturally**, about 20 minutes. Unlatch the lid and open the pot. Use the sling to transfer the springform tin to a wire cooling rack. Uncover the tin and set aside for 10 minutes for the pie to set up. Run a small knife around the interior of the tin to loosen the spaghetti pie from the sides, then unlatch the tin, remove the outer ring and cut the spaghetti pie into quarters to serve.

Beyond

- For a hint of sweetness, substitute sultanas for the pine nuts.
- Try adding 1 teaspoon fennel seeds with the dill and nutmeg.
- Substitute soft goat's cheese for the ricotta for a more intense flavour.
- Top the casserole with up to 50g finely grated Parmigiano-Reggiano before sealing with foil and cooking.

Spaghetti Carbonara Pie

4 servings

This one is something like a spaghetti quiche: a mixture of eggs and bacon in a casserole with lots of pasta. We almost put the recipe in the breakfast chapter for a weekend brunch. (And maybe that's how you'll want to serve it.) In any event, cool the bacon before adding it, so it doesn't begin to cook the eggs.

1. Set a heat- and pressure-safe trivet in a **5.5- or 7.5-litre cooker**, then pour in the water. Generously butter the inside of an 18cm round springform tin. Prepare an aluminium foil sling (see page 20).

2.

Press	Setting	Time	Press
SAUTÉ	MEDIUM, NORMAL or CUSTOM 150°C	10 minutes	START

3. Fry the bacon in the pot, stirring often, until crisp, about 6 minutes. Use a slotted spoon to transfer the bacon to a large bowl and leave to cool for 10 minutes. Meanwhile, clean and dry the relatively hot insert before returning it to the machine.

4. Stir the eggs, cream, cheese, thyme, onion powder and salt into the bowl with the bacon until uniform. Add the spaghetti and toss well until well coated. Pack this mixture into the prepared tin. Cover with aluminium foil. Then use the prepared sling to lower the tin onto the trivet in the cooker. Fold down the ends of the sling and lock the lid onto the pot.

5.

Set the machine	Level	The valve must be	Time	Press
PRESSURE COOK	MAX	—	15 minutes with the KEEP WARM setting off	START
PRESSURE COOK or MANUAL	HIGH	Closed	20 minutes with the KEEP WARM setting off	START

6. When the machine has finished cooking, turn it off and let the pressure **return to normal naturally**, about 20 minutes. Unlatch the lid and open the pot. Use the sling to transfer the tin to a wire cooling rack. Uncover the tin and set aside for 10 minutes for the pie to set up. Run a small knife around the interior of the tin to loosen the spaghetti pie from the sides, then unlatch the tin, remove the outer ring and cut the pie into quarters to serve.

500ml water

Butter for greasing the tin

175g streaky bacon, chopped

2 large eggs, well whisked in a small bowl

250ml double cream

100g Parmigiano-Reggiano, finely grated

1 teaspoon dried thyme

½ teaspoon onion powder

¼ teaspoon table salt

225g dried spaghetti, cooked, drained, rinsed, and cooled to room temperature

Beyond

- Feel free to substitute turkey bacon for the pork bacon.
- Try adding up to 15g finely ground dried porcini mushrooms to the egg mixture. (Grind them in a spice grinder.)
- Sprinkle the top of the casserole with up to 1 teaspoon coarsely ground black pepper before covering with foil and cooking.

5

All Things Pulled

Like a lot of people, we first got into pressure cooking because of the promise of pulled pork that didn't require manning a smoker all day. We even suspect that being able to make pulled pork in a fraction of the usual time is what has instigated the barbecue circuit's current obsession with burnt ends, the crunchy bits you can't get from a multi-cooker. Maybe the craze is coincidental, or maybe those pit masters are intimidated by a countertop cooker that locks moisture into the meat and produces some of the juiciest pork shoulder, chicken thighs and even pulled vegetables we can imagine.

That said, recipes for all things pulled require some accommodations for what the pot can (and cannot) do. First, there must be enough liquid to create the necessary steam to bring on the pressure. As a result, some sauces are wet and need to be boiled down.

Must you do so? No, you can live well in a wetter pulled-pork world. You can even use kitchen tongs to pull some the meat from the pot and mop it with some of the thinner sauce left behind (although that sauce will have less pronounced flavours). Or you can just leave the shredded meat in the pot for a while. It will continue to absorb more sauce as it sits. But no doubt about it, boiling down the sauce for a few minutes at the end brings the dish closer to perfection, which may or may not be worth it on any given Saturday afternoon.

All these recipes except one end with a natural release. Such news may not be the best for busy people. A natural release can add 30 minutes, 40 minutes, even an hour to the total cooking time. But using a quick release just means we have to include 20, 30, maybe 40 minutes additional time under pressure anyway. More important, a quick

release renders the meat too soft, even squishy, and makes for a wetter sauce. It doesn't allow the meat (or vegetables) to slowly reabsorb some of the liquid. We decided that since we were saving ourselves 10 hours at the smoker, we could allow for this slower release method.

Most of these recipes require condiments of some sort, such as mustard, ketchup, mayonnaise or chutney. Also be prepared with various fixings like buns, lettuce, tomato, pico de gallo, salsa or even ready-made coleslaw. Whatever's pulled is always a thing of beauty but it can look awfully lonely on the plate. It demands a party. Give it one.

FAQs

1. How do you pull the meat with two forks?
Although barbecue mavens insist on using meat forks, you can 'get 'er done' with sturdy flatware forks. (Cheap, flimsy ones can bend.) Stab the meat with one fork, then press the tines of the other fork into the meat 2.5–8cm away (depending on how thick the cut is). Pull that second fork away from the first, thereby beginning to shred the

meat into its fibres. Once you've got the hunk of meat into smaller bits, you can begin to pull those apart with the two forks, usually right in the pot.

There's some debate about how 'pulled' a pulled main course is. In our team, one of us likes them pulled until they're loose, meaty threads. The other (ahem, the Texan) leaves the meat in slightly larger hunks for (as he says) more 'chew on the bun'. Some people even like their pulled meat to be a knife-and-fork affair, leaving chunks of beef or pork that have to be further cut apart at the table. Then again, these people are probably serving the stuff in bowls and not on a bun.

2. Why do we sometimes remove that *hot* insert from the pot?

Some sauces have added sugar or are replete with natural sugars. The machine will continue to keep the stainless steel insert hot as it sits inside, especially on the bottom where the heating element lies. Think of the multi-cooker as an electric hob with burners that stay hot even after they're turned off. Removing the insert helps guarantee that any sugars will not burn against the insert's bottom.

The method for removing that *hot* insert is another matter entirely. For the first few times you do this, put kids and pets out of the kitchen. We suggest using silicone baking gloves to grab hold of its edges. If you don't have these, we find that a thick, clean, doubled-up tea towel in each hand works better than hot pads, which can either be too thin or don't bend enough to grasp the edge firmly. The insert can also tilt as it's lifted out. It can, even momentarily, come to rest against your forearm. A larger towel protects more of your skin. Trust us. We know.

3. What if the meat's not tender enough to pull?

Unfortunately, every cow or pig is not like every other cow or pig; no two cuts will ever get done at the exact same time. If we were manning a smoker or watching an oven, all we'd have to do is open the door and prod the meat to see if it's tender. But the Instant Pot has a locked-on lid. We can't check on how things are doing inside. Sometimes, that means waiting a long time for the pressure to come back to normal naturally, only to find that the brisket, pork loin or chicken thighs are not tender enough to shred. If this happens, lock the lid back onto the cooker and bring the machine back to **MAX** for 5 minutes or **HIGH** for 6 minutes. Follow the same release pattern as the recipe indicates, open the pot, and try again.

Sorry about that. From our New England test kitchen, there's little we can do about the vagaries of modern meat. That said, the pressure does even matters out, more so than an oven would. We once roasted three seemingly identical briskets for a magazine article and found that one took 4 hours, the second, 4½ hours, and the last, 5½ hours. We never had such time swings in testing the cuts for this chapter. On a couple of occasions, a cut needed a few extra minutes under pressure. At that point, there's nothing to be done except to give the meat its due.

All-American Pulled Pork

8 servings

Here's our standard recipe for pulled pork. We use smoked paprika to give the meat that characteristic 'smoker' flavour, rather than a bottled barbecue sauce that can end up too sweet. Even without burnt ends, the flavour will be intense and sweet.

Removing any big fatty blobs from the pork will mean that the sauce is not too greasy.

1. Pour the apple juice into a **5.5- or 7.5-litre cooker.** Mix the smoked paprika, brown sugar, chilli powder, mustard powder, onion powder, garlic powder, salt and pepper in a small bowl. Pat and rub this mixture all over the pork. Set the meat in the cooker and lock the lid onto the pot.

2.

Set the machine	Level	The valve must be	Time	Press
PRESSURE COOK	MAX	——	1 hour with the KEEP WARM setting off	START
MEAT/STEW, PRESSURE COOK or MANUAL	HIGH	Closed	1 hour 20 minutes with the KEEP WARM setting off	START
SLOW COOK	HIGH	Opened	5 hours with the KEEP WARM setting off (or on for no more than 4 hours)	START

3. If you've used a pressure setting, once the machine has finished cooking, turn it off and allow its pressure to **return to normal naturally,** about 30 minutes.

4. Unlatch the lid and open the pot. Use a meat fork and a large, slotted spoon or a large spatula to transfer the pork to a nearby chopping board (or transfer hunks of the pork, should the thing come apart). Use a large spoon to skim any excess surface fat from the sauce.

5.

Press	Setting	Time	Press
SAUTÉ	MEDIUM, NORMAL or CUSTOM 150°C	10 minutes	START

6. Bring the sauce to the boil, stirring a few times. Cook until the sauce has reduced to about half its volume, stirring occasionally, about 7 minutes. Meanwhile, shred the meat with two forks. When the sauce has reduced to the right consistency, turn off the **SAUTÉ** function and stir the meat into the sauce in the pot. Set aside for 5 minutes with the lid on top but askew to blend the flavours and let the meat further absorb the sauce.

350ml unsweetened cloudy apple juice

2 tablespoons mild smoked paprika

2 tablespoons dark brown sugar

1 tablespoon standard chilli powder

1 teaspoon mustard powder

1 teaspoon onion powder

1 teaspoon garlic powder

1 teaspoon table salt

½ teaspoon ground black pepper

1.3kg boneless pork shoulder, cut in half and any large chunks of fat removed

Beyond

- For a 3-litre cooker, you must use 700g pork, 250ml unsweetened cloudy apple juice and half of the dried spices for the rub.

- We prefer this pulled pork in slider buns, topped with lots of coleslaw.

- We also like it next to scrambled eggs for a weekend brunch.

- For a discussion of standard chilli powder (vs pure), see page 112.

- The best sauce for this pork is Alabama white sauce (see the *Beyond* by the Brisket and Butternut Squash Chilli recipe on page 123).

350ml jarred pickle brine

1 teaspoon dried dill

1 teaspoon ground coriander

1 teaspoon mustard powder

1 teaspoon table salt

½ teaspoon crushed chilli flakes

1.3kg boneless pork shoulder, cut in half and any large chunks of fat removed

Pickled Pulled Pork

8 servings

If you're a fan of pulled pork that is more savoury than sweet, don't throw out the pickle brine when you finish a jar of pickles. That brine is a ready-made marinade, even the base for a sauce, that adds a vinegary and herbaceous hit underneath the braised flavours. Use any sort of pickle brine you like: dill pickles, hot dills, super-vinegary pickles, you name it. And if you really do like sweet dishes, by all means use the brine from a jar of sweet-and-sour pickles. Honestly, we've even made this recipe with a 50/50 combo of brines from a jar of sweet-and-sour pickles and a jar of pickled jalapeño rings.

By the way, if you're not ready to make this pulled pork the moment you finish a jar of pickles, seal the jar and freeze the brine in it for up to 4 months.

1. Pour the brine into a **5.5- or 7.5-litre cooker**. Mix the dill, coriander, mustard powder, salt and chilli flakes in a small bowl. Spread this mixture evenly over the pork. Set the pork in the pot and lock on the lid.

2.

Set the machine	Level	The valve must be	Time	Press
PRESSURE COOK	MAX	——	1 hour with the KEEP WARM setting off	START
MEAT/STEW, PRESSURE COOK or MANUAL	HIGH	Closed	1 hour 20 minutes with the KEEP WARM setting off	START
SLOW COOK	HIGH	Opened	5 hours with the KEEP WARM setting off (or on for more than 4 hours)	START

3. If you've used a pressure setting, once the machine has finished cooking, turn it off and let the pressure **return to normal naturally,** about 30 minutes.

4. Unlatch the lid and open the pot. Use a meat fork and a large slotted spoon to transfer the pork (or hunks of it) to a chopping board. Use a large spoon to skim any excess surface fat from the sauce.

5. Shred the meat with two forks; stir these shreds back into the pot. There will be too much liquid in the pot for decent pulled pork. But since this liquid is intensely flavourful and will continue to 'marinate' the meat, keep the shredded meat in the liquid and use kitchen tongs to remove servings one at a time.

Beyond

- For a 3-litre cooker, you must halve all the ingredients but leave the 700g piece of pork shoulder whole.

- While buns are traditional, this pulled pork is also delicious on toasted rye bread with deli mustard.

- If you want a smoky flavour, add up to 1 tablespoon mild smoked paprika to the spice rub.

Cherry Chipotle Pulled Pork

8 servings

This pulled pork can be made with either a pork shoulder or
a picnic ham (which is technically a portion of the larger pork
shoulder). In either case, we call for a bone-in cut, mostly because
the flavour of the bone (and its attendant cartilage) will bring more
savoury flavour to the sauce, which is sweet and smoky, thanks to the
combination of the cherry jam and chillies in adobo sauce. True,
those chillies are fiery. But the pressure cooker will tame most of the
heat. However, use only one (or even half a chilli), if you're concerned.
Or if you love spicy food, use two chillies and don't deseed them.

1. Whisk the stock, jam, chipotles, paprika, Worcestershire sauce,
cumin, cloves and mustard powder in a **5.5- or 7.5-litre cooker.**
Add the pork and turn the piece in the sauce to coat all sides.
Lock the lid onto the pot.

2.

Set the machine	Level	The valve must be	Time	Press
PRESSURE COOK	MAX	—	1 hour 10 minutes with the KEEP WARM setting off	START
MEAT/STEW, PRESSURE COOK or MANUAL	HIGH	Closed	1½ hours with the KEEP WARM setting off	START
SLOW COOK	HIGH	Opened	5½ hours with the KEEP WARM setting off (or on for no more than 4 hours)	START

3. If you've used a pressure setting, when the machine has
finished cooking, turn it off and let the pressure **return to
normal naturally,** about 30 minutes.

4. Unlatch the lid and open the pot. Use a meat fork and a large,
slotted spoon to transfer the pork (or maybe pieces of it) to a
nearby chopping board. Cut out and discard the bone. Then
use a large spoon to skim the excess surface fat from the sauce
in the pot.

5.

Press	Setting	Time	Press
SAUTÉ	MEDIUM, NORMAL or CUSTOM 150°C	15 minutes	START

6. Bring the sauce to a simmer, stirring occasionally. Cook
until thickened like barbecue sauce, stirring more and more
frequently to prevent scorching, 5–10 minutes. Meanwhile,
shred the meat with two forks. Once the sauce has reduced
to the right consistency, stir the meat back into it, turn off the
SAUTÉ function and serve warm.

350ml beef or chicken stock

160g cherry jam

Up to 2 tinned chipotle
chillies in adobo sauce,
stemmed, deseeded (if
desired) and chopped

3 tablespoons mild paprika

2 tablespoons
Worcestershire sauce

1 teaspoon ground cumin

½ teaspoon ground cloves

½ teaspoon mustard powder

One 1.6kg bone-in pork
shoulder, any skin and
large chunks of fat removed

Beyond

- Because of the size of the
  pork (even halved), all the
  recipes with bone-in cuts for
  pulled pork cannot easily be
  made in a 3-litre cooker.

- If you boil down the sauce
  until it just coats the meat,
  this is the best pulled pork for
  quesadillas, served with lots
  of grated Cheddar.

- For a hotter version, add up
  to 1 tablespoon adobo sauce
  from the chipotle chilli can
  with the stock, then pass
  extra hot red pepper sauce,
  like Tabasco, at the table.

350ml water

115g chopped dried pineapple

1 small red onion, chopped

One 125g tin mild or hot green chillies

1 tablespoon treacle

Up to 1 teaspoon hot red pepper sauce, such as Tabasco

1 teaspoon dried thyme

1 teaspoon ground ginger

1 teaspoon ground allspice

½ teaspoon ground turmeric

½ teaspoon celery salt

½ teaspoon grated nutmeg

½ teaspoon table salt

One 1.6kg bone-in pork shoulder, any skin and large blobs of fat removed

Caribbean-Style Pulled Pork

8 servings

No, it's not just the pineapple in the mix that gives this pulled pork an island feel. It's actually the combination of thyme, ginger and allspice, with treacle as the sweetener. Those are the real secrets, though there's only a little treacle so the sauce isn't too sweet. We also don't care for the flavour of pineapple jam in this style of pulled pork, a common ingredient in recipes like this one. Instead, we opt for dried pineapple. The results highlight the natural sweetness of pork shoulder.

1. Stir the water, dried pineapple, onion, tinned chillies, treacle, pepper sauce, thyme, ginger, allspice, turmeric, celery salt, nutmeg and salt in a **5.5- or 7.5-litre cooker.** Add the pork and turn to coat on all sides. Lock the lid onto the pot.

2.

Set the machine	Level	The valve must be	Time	Press
PRESSURE COOK	MAX	——	1 hour 10 minutes with the KEEP WARM setting off	START
MEAT/ STEW, PRESSURE COOK or MANUAL	HIGH	Closed	1 hour 30 minutes with the KEEP WARM setting off	START
SLOW COOK	HIGH	Opened	5½ hours with the KEEP WARM setting off (or on for no more than 4 hours)	START

3. If you've used a pressure setting, when the machine has finished cooking, turn it off and let its pressure **return to normal naturally,** about 30 minutes.

4. Unlatch the lid and open the pot. Use a meat fork and a large slotted spoon to transfer the pork (or pieces of it) to a nearby chopping board. Use a large spoon to skim any excess surface fat from the sauce.

5.

Press	Setting	Time	Press
SAUTÉ	MEDIUM, NORMAL or CUSTOM 150°C	15 minutes	START

6. Bring the sauce in the pot to a simmer, stirring occasionally. Simmer until reduced to about 125ml, stirring more and more frequently as it cooks, 7–10 minutes. Meanwhile, shred the meat with two forks, discarding any additional blobs of fat. Stir the shredded meat into the sauce, turn off the **SAUTÉ** setting and serve warm.

Beyond

- Again, it's almost impossible to find smaller, bone-in cuts that work in a 3-litre cooker.

- For a simpler version, substitute 2 tablespoons bottled dry jerk seasoning blend for the hot red pepper sauce and spices. Check the bottling to see if it has any salt. If so, omit the salt in the recipe as well.

- Rather than serving this pulled pork in buns, try it in pitta pockets garnished with purchased pico de gallo, soured cream and fresh coriander leaves.

Cuban-Style Pulled Pork

8 servings

This pulled pork is a whimsical, piggy riff on Ropa Vieja (for a more authentic version, see page 214), a dish that is often made with the juice of sour oranges. However, many brands of orange marmalade are made with sour oranges (read the labels), making the flavour combination easily within reach for anyone near a supermarket. Use only fresh lime juice. It has to be tart enough to stand up to the sugar in the marmalade. Some bottlings have dulled flavours.

1. Whisk the stock, marmalade, lime juice, garlic, chilli, oregano, cumin and salt in a **5.5- or 7.5-litre cooker**. Add the pork and turn to coat on all sides. Lock the lid onto the pot.

2.

Set the machine	Level	The valve must be	Time	Press
PRESSURE COOK	MAX	——	1 hour 10 minutes with the KEEP WARM setting off	START
MEAT/STEW, PRESSURE COOK or MANUAL	HIGH	Closed	1 hour 30 minutes with the KEEP WARM setting off	START
SLOW COOK	HIGH	Opened	5½ hours with the KEEP WARM setting off (or on for no more than 4 hours)	START

3. If you've used a pressure setting, when the machine has finished cooking, turn it off and let its pressure **return to normal naturally**, about 30 minutes.

4. Unlatch the lid and open the pot. Use a meat fork and a large slotted spoon to transfer the pork (or pieces of it) to a nearby chopping board. Remove and discard the bone. Use a large spoon to skim any excess surface fat from the sauce.

5.

Press	Setting	Time	Press
SAUTÉ	MEDIUM, NORMAL or CUSTOM 150°C	15 minutes	START

6. Bring the sauce in the pot to a simmer, stirring occasionally. Simmer until reduced to a fairly thick sauce, about like a bottled barbecue sauce, stirring more and more frequently as it cooks, 5–10 minutes (depending on how much moisture the pork has given off). Meanwhile, shred the meat with two forks, discarding any additional blobs of fat. When the sauce has reached the right consistency, stir the shredded meat into the sauce, turn off the **SAUTÉ** setting and serve warm.

250ml beef or chicken stock

315g orange marmalade, preferably made from sour oranges

60ml fresh lime juice

6 medium garlic cloves, peeled and thinly sliced

1 small or medium fresh jalapeño chilli, stemmed and sliced into thin rings

2 tablespoons packed fresh oregano leaves

1 tablespoon ground cumin

1 teaspoon table salt

One 1.6kg bone-in pork shoulder, any skin and large blobs of fat removed

Beyond

- Again, it's almost impossible to find smaller, bone-in cuts that work in a 3-litre cooker.

- Serve this pulled pork over Black Turtle Beans and Rice (see page 403).

- For a condiment, make a Cuban version of chimichurri. Pulse 160ml olive oil, 10g fresh flat-leaf parsley leaves, 3 tablespoons fresh lime juice, 2 tablespoons red wine vinegar, 1 diced small red onion, up to 8 slivered and peeled medium garlic cloves, 2 teaspoons dried oregano and 1 tablespoon table salt in a food processor until it forms a chunky sauce. Store in a covered container in the fridge for up to 2 weeks. To prevent browning, pour a slim coating of olive oil over the sauce before refrigerating. Scrape this hardened oil off the top before serving.

1 tablespoon grated lime zest

2 teaspoons ground dried ginger

2 teaspoons ground cumin

2 teaspoons ground black pepper

1.3kg boneless pork shoulder, cut in half and any large bits of fat removed

2 large leeks (about 175g each), white and pale green parts only, halved lengthways, washed well and thinly sliced

180ml beef or chicken stock

90g creamy natural-style peanut butter

90ml soy sauce, preferably reduced-sodium

80g light brown sugar

90ml rice vinegar

2 large garlic cloves, peeled

Pulled Pork in Peanut Sauce

8 servings

This pulled pork has a vaguely South East Asian feel, thanks mostly to the combination of peanut butter, vinegar and soy sauce. It's actually more savoury than you might think, even with the brown sugar. The peanut butter gives the sauce a natural thickness, so it doesn't need to be boiled down. And the shreds of pork will continue to absorb sauce as they sit in it, so any extra sauce will mostly be gone by the time you get to seconds.

1. Mix the lime zest, ginger, cumin and pepper in a small bowl. Pat and rub this mixture all over the pork.

2. Stir the leeks, stock, peanut butter, soy sauce, brown sugar and rice vinegar in a **5.5- or 7.5-litre cooker** until the peanut butter and brown sugar have dissolved. Add the coated pork. Drop the garlic cloves into the sauce. Lock the lid onto the pot.

3.

Set the machine	Level	The valve must be	Time	Press
PRESSURE COOK	MAX	—	1 hour with the KEEP WARM setting off	START
MEAT/ STEW, PRESSURE COOK or MANUAL	HIGH	Closed	1 hour 20 minutes with the KEEP WARM setting off	START
SLOW COOK	HIGH	Opened	5 hours with the KEEP WARM setting off (or on for no more than 4 hours)	START

4. If you've used a pressure setting, once the machine has finished cooking, turn it off and let its pressure **return to normal naturally**, about 30 minutes.

5. Unlatch the lid and open the pot. Use a slotted spoon to transfer the pork pieces to a nearby chopping board. Use a large spoon to skim any excess surface fat from the sauce in the pot.

6. Shred the meat with two forks and stir these shreds back into the sauce. Set the lid askew over the pot and set aside for 5 minutes to blend the flavours and let the meat continue to absorb the sauce.

Beyond

- For a 3-litre cooker, you must halve all the ingredients but leave the 650g piece of pork shoulder whole.

- Serve this pulled pork in flour tortillas (like soft tacos with an Asian flair) with sambal oelek, finely chopped spring onions and/or chopped, unsalted peanuts as condiments.

Mexican Salsa Verde Pulled Pork

8 servings

This one's probably the easiest of all the pulled pork recipes, given that it uses ready-made salsa verde. It's also both probably the spiciest, given that it includes the brine from a jar of pickled jalapeños and the chillies themselves. All that heat is a nice contrast to the fresh, tart taste of jarred salsa verde. The sauce isn't boiled down since the salsa verde and brine are fairly salty. Reducing it will only turn it more so. If the overall dish is too wet, use kitchen tongs to pull the meat out of the sauce for serving.

1. Mix the salsa verde, liquid from the jalapeño rings, and jalapeños in a **5.5- or 7.5-litre cooker**. Add the pork and turn to coat on all sides. Lock the lid onto the pot.

2.

Set the machine	Level	The valve must be	Time	Press
PRESSURE COOK	MAX	—	1 hour 10 minutes with the KEEP WARM setting off	START
MEAT/ STEW, PRESSURE COOK or MANUAL	HIGH	Closed	1 hour 30 minutes with the KEEP WARM setting off	START
SLOW COOK	HIGH	Opened	5½ hours with the KEEP WARM setting off (or on for no more than 4 hours)	START

3. If you've used a pressure setting, once the machine has finished cooking, turn it off and let its pressure **return to normal naturally,** about 30 minutes.

4. Unlatch the lid and open the pot. Use a meat fork and a slotted spoon to transfer the pork pieces to a nearby chopping board. Remove and discard the bone. Use a large spoon to skim any excess surface fat from the sauce in the pot. Shred the meat with two forks. Add these shreds to the pot along with the coriander leaves. Stir well before serving warm.

500ml mild ready-made Mexican salsa verde

60ml liquid from a jar of pickled jalapeño rings

2 tablespoons pickled jalapeño rings

One 1.6kg bone-in pork shoulder, any skin and large bits of fat removed

10g fresh coriander leaves, chopped

Beyond

- Because of the size of the bone in even a smaller pork shoulder, this recipe will not work in a 3-litre cooker.

- If you want pulled pork for an enchilada casserole, here's your best bet.

- To go all out, make your own Mexican salsa verde: Mix 225g husked and chopped tomatillos, 180ml water, 40g chopped onion, 1 chopped and stemmed small jalapeño chilli, 1 tablespoon packed fresh oregano leaves, 1 tablespoon packed fresh coriander leaves, 1 teaspoon finely chopped garlic and ½ teaspoon ground cumin in a 5.5- or 7.5-litrepot set on the SAUTÉ function at MEDIUM, NORMAL OR CUSTOM 150°C – or in a medium saucepan set over a medium heat. Bring to a simmer, then reduce the SAUTÉ level in the pot to LOW or LESS or reduce the heat on the hob to low. Simmer slowly, stirring often, until the tomatillos are soft, about 10 minutes. Leave to cool for 10 minutes, then blend in a covered blender until smooth. Store any remaining sauce in a sealed container in the fridge for up to 1 week.

2 tablespoons vegetable, corn or rapeseed oil

One 1.3kg piece boneless beef chuck, cut into two chunks and any large bits of fat removed

½ teaspoon table salt

½ teaspoon ground black pepper

250ml water

250ml ketchup

60ml apple cider vinegar

2 tablespoons Dijon mustard

2 tablespoons Worcestershire sauce

2 tablespoons mild paprika

2 teaspoons celery seeds

1 teaspoon garlic powder

1 teaspoon onion powder

All-American Pulled Beef

8 servings

Here's a standard version of pulled beef, best for sandwiches on hamburger buns, or maybe loaded into jacket potatoes and topped with grated Cheddar.

Brown the meat. Don't get impatient. You can even get some fairly well-done ends of the chuck, sort of like 'burnt ends'. These will remain chewy (if not crunchy) even after the meat has undergone its cooking and been pulled. Even more importantly, all that browning will step up the savoury flavours of the dish, rendering this pulled beef far more than just a combo of meat and barbecue sauce.

1.

Press	Setting	Time	Press
SAUTÉ	MEDIUM, NORMAL or CUSTOM 150°C	20 minutes	START

2. Warm the oil in a **5.5- or 7.5-litre cooker** for a minute or two. Meanwhile, season the beef with the salt and pepper. Set one piece of chuck in the pot and brown well, turning once or twice, about 7 minutes. Transfer this piece of beef to a bowl and brown the second piece just as well before transferring it to the bowl.

3. Pour the water into the pot and scrape up the browned bits on the pot's bottom. Turn off the **SAUTÉ** function and stir in the ketchup, vinegar, mustard, Worcestershire sauce, paprika, celery seed, garlic powder and onion powder. Return both pieces of meat and any juices in the bowl to the pot; turn the meat on all sides to coat it in the sauce. Lock the lid onto the pot.

4.

Set the machine	Level	The valve must be	Time	Press
PRESSURE COOK	MAX	——	1 hour with the KEEP WARM setting off	START
MEAT/ STEW, PRESSURE COOK or MANUAL	HIGH	Closed	1 hour 20 minutes with the KEEP WARM setting off	START
SLOW COOK	HIGH	Opened	5 hours with the KEEP WARM setting off (or on for no more than 3 hours)	START

Beyond

- For a 3-litre cooker, you must halve all the ingredients. Keep the 650g piece of meat intact.

- The best condiment for this version of pulled beef is coleslaw, right on the sandwich with the meat in the bun. To make a super easy coleslaw, stir a 450g bag of slaw mix with 250ml bottled Ranch dressing.

5. If you've used a pressure setting, once the machine has finished cooking, turn it off and let its pressure **return to normal naturally,** about 30 minutes.

6. Unlatch the lid and open the pot. Use a meat fork and a large slotted spoon to transfer the pieces of meat to a nearby chopping board. Use a large spoon to skim any excess surface fat from the sauce in the pot.

7.

Press	Setting	Time	Press
SAUTÉ	MEDIUM, NORMAL or CUSTOM 150°C	15 minutes	START

8. Bring the sauce to a simmer, stirring often. Simmer until thickened, about like a loose wet barbecue sauce, stirring almost all the while, 5–10 minutes. Meanwhile, shred the beef into bits with two forks. Once the sauce has reached the desired consistency, stir the meat into it and cook for 1 minute, stirring often, until well coated. Turn off the **SAUTÉ** function and remove the *hot* insert from the pot. Set the lid askew over the insert and set aside for 5 minutes to blend the flavours and let the meat absorb more sauce.

1 tablespoon vegetable, corn or rapeseed oil

One 1.2kg piece boneless beef chuck, cut into two chunks and any large bits of fat removed

½ teaspoon table salt

½ teaspoon ground black pepper

125ml amber beer, preferably a pilsner or a pale ale (a gluten-free beer, if necessary)

180ml beef stock

120g ready-made white horseradish

2 tablespoons Worcestershire sauce

1 teaspoon ground ginger

½ teaspoon ground turmeric

2 medium garlic cloves, peeled and finely chopped (2 teaspoons prechopped)

2 bay leaves

Pulled Pot Roast

6 servings

We often make pot roast in the oven by slathering the beef with ready-made horseradish. The horseradish mellows into a sweet and savoury mix that then flavours the sauce. We brought that recipe idea into pulled beef to create what feels to us like a pot roast turned into all-American sandwich filling.

1.

Press	Setting	Time	Press
SAUTÉ	MEDIUM, NORMAL or CUSTOM 150°C	20 minutes	START

2. Warm the oil in a **5.5- or 7.5-litre pot** for a minute or two. Meanwhile, season the beef with the salt and pepper. Add one piece to the pot and brown it *well*, turning once or twice, about 7 minutes. Transfer to a bowl and add the second piece of beef. Brown this one just as well on both sides before transferring it to the bowl.

3. Pour the beer into the pot. Scrape up the browned stuff on the pot's bottom, then turn off the **SAUTÉ** function. Stir in the stock, horseradish, Worcestershire sauce, ginger, turmeric, garlic and bay leaves. Nestle the pieces of beef into this sauce, turning them to coat them on all sides. Lock the lid onto the pot.

4.

Set the machine	Level	The valve must be	Time	Press
PRESSURE COOK	MAX	—	55 minutes with the KEEP WARM setting off	START
MEAT/ STEW, PRESSURE COOK or MANUAL	HIGH	Closed	1 hour 10 minutes with the KEEP WARM setting off	START
SLOW COOK	HIGH	Opened	5 hours with the KEEP WARM setting off (or on for no more than 3 hours)	START

5. If you've used the pressure setting, once the machine has finished cooking, turn it off and let its pressure **return to normal naturally,** about 30 minutes.

6. Unlatch the lid and open the pot. Use a meat fork and a large, slotted spoon to transfer the pieces of meat to a nearby chopping board. Use a large spoon to skim any excess surface fat off the sauce. Also find and discard the garlic cloves and the bay leaves.

7.

Press	Setting	Time	Press
SAUTÉ	MEDIUM, NORMAL or CUSTOM 150°C	15 minutes	START

8. Bring the sauce to a simmer, stirring often. Simmer until thickened like a loose, wet barbecue sauce, stirring almost all the while, 5–10 minutes. Meanwhile, shred the meat with two forks.

9. When the sauce has reached the right consistency, stir the meat into it and cook, stirring often, until well coated and most of the liquid has been absorbed, about 1 minute. Turn off the **SAUTÉ** function and remove the *hot* insert from the pot. Set the lid askew over the insert and set aside for 5 minutes to blend the flavours and let the meat absorb more sauce.

Beyond

- For a 3-litre cooker, you must use a 700g piece of boneless beef chuck (keep it intact) and halve the remaining ingredients.

- For a sweeter sauce, add up to 2 tablespoons light brown sugar with the sauce ingredients.

- To use fresh horseradish, omit the prepared horseradish. Instead, grate 2 tablespoons peeled fresh horseradish into the sauce ingredients and add 1 tablespoon white wine vinegar.

- Serve this pulled beef on rolls with horseradish cream sauce. To make your own, whisk 120ml regular or low-fat soured cream, 120ml regular or low-fat mayonnaise, 60g jarred prepared white horseradish, 1 teaspoon white balsamic vinegar and ½ teaspoon ground black pepper in a medium bowl until smooth.

One 400g tin chopped tomatoes

125ml bold red wine, such as Zinfandel or Syrah

2 tablespoons balsamic vinegar

80g frozen baby onions (do not thaw)

8 baby carrots

8 pitted prunes

6 large pitted green olives, sliced

1 tablespoon fresh thyme leaves

2 medium garlic cloves, peeled and finely chopped (2 teaspoons prechopped)

½ teaspoon table salt

½ teaspoon ground black pepper

One 1.3kg piece beef brisket, trimmed and cut in half widthways

Pulled Brisket

8 servings

This recipe is a not-quite-French-inspired braise turned into pulled beef. It's also not-quite-Jewish tzimmes turned into Midwestern American comfort food. And it's also like all of them combined. (Somehow.)

The brisket needs a long time under pressure so that you can shred it, rather than just slice it. That said, it might not even be done with the timing stated. Brisket can be notoriously fussy, becoming tender at various times because of a range of factors well beyond just the size of the meat. If you find you can't shred the meat easily, put the hunk back in the sauce, bring it back to HIGH pressure, and cook for another 10 minutes, followed again by a natural release.

1. Mix the tomatoes, wine and vinegar in a **5.5- or 7.5-litre cooker.** Stir in the baby onions, carrots, prunes, olives, thyme, garlic, salt and pepper. Nestle the meat into the sauce, then turn the cut over to coat both sides. Lock the lid onto the pot.

2.

Set the machine	Level	The valve must be	Time	Press
PRESSURE COOK	MAX	—	1 hour 10 minutes with the KEEP WARM setting off	START
MEAT/ STEW, PRESSURE COOK or MANUAL	HIGH	Closed	1 hour 30 minutes with the KEEP WARM setting off	START
SLOW COOK	HIGH	Opened	6 hours with the KEEP WARM setting off (or on no more than 4 hours)	START

3. If you've used the pressure setting, when the machine has finished cooking, turn it off and let its pressure **return to normal naturally,** about 30 minutes.

4. Unlatch the lid and open the cooker. Use a meat fork and a big slotted spoon to transfer the brisket (whole or in pieces) to a chopping board. Use a large spoon to skim excess surface fat from the sauce in the pot.

5.

Press	Setting	Time	Press
SAUTÉ	MEDIUM, NORMAL or CUSTOM 150°C	15 minutes	START

6. Bring the sauce to a simmer, stirring once in a while. Simmer, stirring a few times, until the sauce looks like a loose, wet barbecue sauce, 5–10 minutes. Meanwhile, shred the brisket using two forks, or perhaps a knife to cut thick slices that can then be shredded with a fork.

7. Once the sauce has reached the right consistency, stir the shredded brisket into it and cook, stirring often, until coated, about 1 minute. Turn off the **SAUTÉ** function and remove the *hot* insert from the pot. Set the lid askew over the insert and set aside for 5 minutes to blend the flavours and let the meat continue to absorb the sauce.

Beyond

• You must halve the recipe for a 3-litre cooker.

• While you can serve this pulled brisket on rolls with pickle relish or pickled jalapeño rings, it's also great over No-Drain Potato Mash (page 424).

• To omit the wine, substitute beef stock and add 2 teaspoons dark brown sugar.

• For a sweeter sauce, substitute 30g raisins for the prunes.

• For a more complex flavour, substitute pomegranate molasses for the balsamic vinegar.

15g butter

One 1.3kg piece beef brisket, trimmed and cut in half widthways

1 large onion, thinly sliced and separated into rings

250ml very strong coffee

1 tablespoon treacle

60ml beef stock

One 10cm cinnamon stick

One 5cm strip orange zest

1 teaspoon dried thyme

½ teaspoon ground allspice

½ teaspoon table salt

1 teaspoon ground black pepper

Pulled Brisket with Coffee

8 servings

Braising in coffee is a terrific thing. The acidic notes mellow into an undertone of dark, earthy flavours. Here, we include coffee in a highly spiced sauce, the better to pair with the bolder flavours of brisket.

Use strong coffee, perhaps double the strength you would drink. Even espresso would be welcome (if still more assertive). And use a vegetable peeler to remove a long strip of orange zest. We use a zest strip because one strip is easy to find and remove. Zillions of little threads of orange zest end up an irritation.

1.

Press	Setting	Time	Press
SAUTÉ	MEDIUM, NORMAL or CUSTOM 150°C	15 minutes	START

2. Melt the butter in a **5.5- or 7.5-litre cooker,** then add one piece of brisket and brown it *very* well on both sides, turning once or twice, about 5 minutes. Transfer to a bowl and brown the other piece of meat just as well on both sides before transferring it to the bowl.

3. Pour the coffee and treacle into the pot. As it comes to a simmer, scrape up any browned bits in the pot. Turn off the **SAUTÉ** function. Pour in the stock, then stir in the cinnamon stick, orange zest, thyme, allspice, salt and black pepper. Return the meat to the cooker, turning them in the sauce to coat on all sides. Lock the lid onto the pot.

4.

Set the machine	Level	The valve must be	Time	Press
PRESSURE COOK	MAX	—	1 hour 10 minutes with the KEEP WARM setting off	START
MEAT/ STEW, PRESSURE COOK or MANUAL	HIGH	Closed	1 hour 30 minutes with the KEEP WARM setting off	START
SLOW COOK	HIGH	Opened	6 hours with the KEEP WARM setting off (or on for no more than 4 hours)	START

5. If you've used the pressure setting, when the machine has finished cooking, turn it off and let its pressure **return to normal naturally,** about 30 minutes.

6. Unlatch the lid and open the cooker. Use a meat fork and a big slotted spoon to transfer the brisket (whole or in pieces) to a nearby chopping board. Use a large spoon to skim any excess surface fat from the sauce in the pot. Also fish out and discard the orange zest strip and cinnamon stick.

7.

Press	Setting	Time	Press
SAUTÉ	MEDIUM, NORMAL or CUSTOM 150°C	10 minutes	START

8. Bring the sauce to a simmer, stirring once in a while. Simmer, stirring occasionally, until it is a thin wet gravy, 5–6 minutes. Meanwhile, shred the brisket using two forks, or perhaps use a knife to cut thick slices that can then be shredded with a fork.

9. When the sauce has reached the desired consistency, stir the shredded brisket into it and cook, stirring often, until coated in the sauce, about 1 minute. Turn off the **SAUTÉ** function and remove the insert from the pot. Set the lid askew over the insert and set aside for 5 minutes to blend the flavours and let the meat continue to absorb the sauce.

Beyond

- For a 3-litre cooker, use the full amount of butter and broth but halve the remaining ingredients.

- To make this a little easier, stop off at a coffee shop, buy a couple of shots of espresso, then use them with the rest of the volume of more standard drip coffee.

- For a sweeter flavour, substitute a dark beer, preferably a porter or a stout, for the beef stock.

- While this pulled beef is tasty in buns with mustard and even crisp-fried streaky bacon rashers, it's also good over cooked root vegetables mashed with butter, particularly mashed turnips and/or celeriac.

- Or boil some cauliflower rice, add a little butter and turn it into mashed cauliflower to serve as a bed for the pulled beef.

2 small onions, halved and thinly sliced into half-moons

2 large garlic cloves, peeled

250ml plain cola (do not use a diet soda)

60ml Worcestershire sauce

2 tablespoons apple cider vinegar

2 tablespoons ketchup-like chilli sauce

1 tablespoon mild paprika

1 teaspoon mustard powder

1 teaspoon table salt

½ teaspoon ground cloves

One 1.3kg piece boneless beef chuck, cut into two chunks and any large bits of fat removed

Cola Pulled Beef

6 servings

Although cola would seem to make this version of pulled beef super sweet, it's actually more of a sweet-and-sour mix, thanks to the vinegar and chilli sauce. There's no browning here. We found that the more complex flavours gained from browning actually muddied the flavours of the sauce.

1. Mix the onion, garlic, cola, Worcestershire sauce, vinegar, chilli sauce, paprika, mustard powder, salt and cloves in a **5.5- or 7.5-litre cooker**. Set the pieces of beef into this sauce, then turn to coat on all sides. Lock the lid onto the pot.

2.

Set the machine	Level	The valve must be	Time	Press
PRESSURE COOK	MAX	—	1 hour with the KEEP WARM setting off	START
MEAT/ STEW, PRESSURE COOK or MANUAL	HIGH	Closed	1 hour 20 minutes with the KEEP WARM setting off	START
SLOW COOK	HIGH	Opened	5 hours with the KEEP WARM setting off (or on for no more than 3 hours)	START

3. If you've used the pressure setting, once the machine has finished cooking, turn it off and let its pressure **return to normal naturally**, about 30 minutes.

4. Unlatch the lid and open the pot. Use a meat fork and a large slotted spoon to transfer the pieces of meat to a nearby chopping board. Use a large spoon to skim any excess surface fat off the sauce in the pot. Also find and discard the garlic cloves.

5.

Press	Setting	Time	Press
SAUTÉ	MEDIUM, NORMAL or CUSTOM 150°C	15 minutes	START

6. Bring the sauce to a simmer, stirring often. Simmer until thickened like a wet, loose barbecue sauce, stirring almost all the while, 5–10 minutes. Meanwhile, shred the beef with two forks. Once the sauce has reached the right consistency, stir the shredded meat into it and cook, stirring often, until well coated and most of the liquid has been absorbed, about 1 minute. Turn off the **SAUTÉ** function, remove the *hot* insert from the pot, set the lid askew over the insert and set aside for 5 minutes to blend the flavours and let the meat absorb more sauce.

Beyond

• For a 3-litre cooker, you must halve all the ingredients. Keep the 650g piece of meat intact.

• Consider condiments like pickle relish or dill pickle slices.

• Or serve the pulled beef in hot-dog buns with sliced dill pickles running along one side of the bun.

• For a hotter version, reduce the Worcestershire sauce to 2 tablespoons and add up to 2 tablespoons liquid from a jar of pickled jalapeño rings with the other sauce ingredients.

Barbacoa

8 servings

Barbacoa is a Caribbean dish usually made of spiced shredded beef cooked over an open fire. Making barbacoa in an Instant Pot will never let you get crispy bits of shredded meat, but see the *Beyond* for an idea. This highly seasoned version makes the best taco meat in the book.

1. Stir the lime juice, paprika, cumin, oregano, onion powder, salt and black pepper in a small bowl to make a paste. Rub this paste all over both sides of each piece of beef.

2.

Press	Setting	Time	Press
SAUTÉ	MEDIUM, NORMAL or CUSTOM 150°C	10 minutes	START

3. Warm the oil in a **5.5- or 7.5-litre cooker**. Add one piece of the beef and brown *lightly* on both sides, turning once, about 3 minutes. Transfer to a bowl and brown the other piece the same way before transferring it to the bowl.

4. Pour the stock into the pot, scrape up any browned bits on the pot's bottom, and turn off the **SAUTÉ** function. Stir in the tomato, garlic, chipotle, vinegar and honey. Return the meat and any juices in the bowl to the pot; turn the pieces of beef in the sauce to coat them. Lock the lid onto the pot.

5.

Set the machine	Level	The valve must be	Time	Press
PRESSURE COOK	MAX	—	1 hour with the KEEP WARM setting off	START
MEAT/STEW, PRESSURE COOK or MANUAL	HIGH	Closed	1 hour 20 minutes with the KEEP WARM setting off	START
SLOW COOK	HIGH	Opened	5 hours with the KEEP WARM setting off (or on for no more than 4 hours)	START

6. If you've used a pressure setting, when the machine has finished cooking, turn it off and let its pressure **return to normal naturally,** about 30 minutes.

7. Unlatch the lid and open the pot. Use a meat fork and a big slotted spoon to transfer the beef to a chopping board. Use a large spoon to skim any excess surface fat from the sauce in the pot. Shred the meat with two forks, then stir it back into the sauce in the pot. Set the lid askew over the pot for 10 minutes to blend the flavours and allow the meat to continue to absorb the sauce.

1½ tablespoons fresh lime juice

1½ tablespoons mild paprika

1½ teaspoons ground cumin

1½ teaspoons dried oregano

1 teaspoon onion powder

1½ teaspoons table salt

½ teaspoon ground black pepper

One 1.3kg piece boneless beef chuck, cut into two chunks and any large bits of fat removed

2 tablespoons olive oil

300ml beef stock

1 large tomato, chopped

Up to 6 medium garlic cloves, peeled and finely chopped (2 tablespoons prechopped)

Up to 1 tinned chipotle chilli in adobo sauce, stemmed, deseeded (if desired) and chopped

80ml red wine vinegar

3 tablespoons honey

Beyond

- For a 3-litre cooker, you must halve all the ingredients. Leave the 650g piece of chuck in one piece.

- For a more traditional flavour (if not necessarily gluten-free), substitute a dark beer, preferably a brown ale, for the stock.

- If you miss the crisp bits, spread the sauced, shredded meat on a large lipped baking tin, then pour and scrape any remaining sauce over the meat. Grill 10–15cm from the heating element until a bit crunchy without burning, 1–3 minutes.

- Serve in tortillas topped with sliced avocado, pickled onions, pickled jalapeño rings, grated cheese and/or coriander leaves.

500ml light but dry red wine, such as Pinot Noir

900g beef flank steak, such as bavette, cut into 3 pieces

3 fresh thyme sprigs

2 bay leaves

60ml olive oil

1 medium red onion, halved and sliced into thin half-moons

2 medium peppers, stemmed, cored and cut into thin strips

2 medium garlic cloves, peeled and finely chopped (2 teaspoons prechopped)

2 teaspoons dried oregano

1 teaspoon ground cumin

250ml tinned chopped tomatoes with lots of their juice

60ml beef or chicken stock

2 tablespoons red wine vinegar

Pulled Flank Steak with Red Peppers

6 servings

Without a doubt, this pulled dish is the fanciest in the book, more dinner party than weeknight supper. The flank steak is cut into pieces so that the shreds are smaller, more discreet – a better match for the vegetables, which make a sweet-and-sour mix. It's great alongside mashed or scalloped potatoes or in homemade popovers. Consider garnishing the servings with lots of fresh herbs, particularly oregano and thyme.

One important note: the cooking is a two-step process, first the meat on its own, then the meat in the sauce. During the second cooking, only use the HIGH pressure setting, not MAX (if available on your machine).

1. Pour the wine into a **5.5- or 7.5-litre cooker**. Add the flank steak pieces and turn to coat. Tuck the thyme sprigs and bay leaves round the meat. Lock the lid onto the pot.

2.

Set the machine	Level	The valve must be	Time	Press
PRESSURE COOK	MAX	——	35 minutes with the KEEP WARM setting off	START
MEAT/STEW, PRESSURE COOK or MANUAL	HIGH	Closed	45 minutes with the KEEP WARM setting off	START

3. When the machine has finished cooking, turn it off and let its pressure **return to normal naturally,** about 20 minutes. Unlatch and open the lid. Use a meat fork and a large slotted spoon to transfer the pieces of flank steak to a chopping board. Shred the meat with two forks and set aside. Discard all the liquid and aromatics in the pot. Clean and dry the insert and return it to the cooker.

4.

Press	Setting	Time	Press
SAUTÉ	MEDIUM, NORMAL or CUSTOM 150°C	10 minutes	START

5. Warm the oil in the pot for a minute or two, then add the onion and peppers. Cook, stirring often, until the onion begins to soften, about 4 minutes. Add the garlic, oregano and cumin; stir until aromatic, just a few seconds.

6. Turn off the **SAUTÉ** function and stir in the chopped tomatoes, stock and vinegar. Stir the shredded meat and any juices on the chopping board into the pot. Continue stirring until uniform, then lock the lid onto the pot.

7.

Set the machine	Level	The valve must be	Time	Press
MEAT/STEW, PRESSURE COOK or MANUAL	HIGH	Closed	0 minutes with the KEEP WARM setting off	START

8. When the machine has hit high pressure and finished cooking, turn it off and let the pressure **return to normal naturally,** about 5 minutes. Unlatch the lid and open the pot. Stir well before serving.

Beyond

- You must halve the recipe for a 3-litre cooker.
- Consider this a pulled beef version of ragù, to be served with cooked fettuccini.
- Or keep the meat in the sauce, then use kitchen tongs to pick up some and drain it before putting it in an Italian bread roll with sliced provolone and sliced peperoncini.

125g drained jarred pickled onions

90g pitted green olives, thinly sliced

180ml beef stock

60ml dry sherry or unsweetened apple juice

30g raisins

2 tablespoons tomato purée

2 teaspoons dried oregano

2 teaspoons dried sage

½ teaspoon table salt

½ teaspoon ground black pepper

900g beef flank steak, such as bavette

7g chopped parsley leaves

Ropa Vieja

6 servings

This legendary Cuban dish (the name of which means 'old clothes' because the beef is shredded into 'rags') is a boldly flavoured concoction, often served atop rice and beans. There are undoubtedly as many versions of it as there are Cuban grandmothers. Ours has been streamlined a bit, the better to make it a weeknight standard. By using purchased pickled onions, raisins and olives, we can get very close to the flavour of the long-simmered original.

1. Mix the pickled onions, olives, stock, sherry, raisins, tomato purée, oregano, sage, salt and pepper in a **5.5-litre cooker**. Nestle the steak into this sauce, turning it to coat both sides. Lock the lid onto the pot.

2.

Set the machine	Level	The valve must be	Time	Press
PRESSURE COOK	MAX	—	40 minutes with the KEEP WARM setting off	START
MEAT/ STEW, PRESSURE COOK or MANUAL	HIGH	Closed	55 minutes with the KEEP WARM setting off	START
SLOW COOK	HIGH	Opened	4½ hours with the KEEP WARM setting off (or on for no more than 2 hours)	START

3. If you've used a pressure setting, when the machine finishes cooking, turn it off and let its pressure **return to normal naturally**, about 25 minutes.

4. Unlatch the lid and open the pot. Use two forks to shred the meat right in the pot. Stir in the parsley, then set the lid askew over the pot and set aside for 10 minutes to blend the flavours and allow the meat to continue to absorb the sauce.

Beyond

• For a 7.5-litre cooker, you must increase the stock to 350ml and use the remaining ingredients as stated. The sauce will then need to be boiled down. Remove the meat from the pot and shred it on a chopping board as you cook the sauce on the SAUTÉ function at MEDIUM, NORMAL or CUSTOM 150°C until reduced to a wet barbecue sauce, stirring occasionally. Stir the shredded meat and parsley into the sauce, then set aside as directed.

• For a 3-litre cooker, you must use the full amount of stock (180ml) and halve the remaining ingredients. The sauce will also need to be reduced.

• Serve this pulled beef over Black Turtle Beans and Rice (page 403).

All-American Pulled Lamb

8 servings

Years ago, we were researching a book all about ham and went on an expedition across Kentucky, looking for country ham producers. We got sidetracked at the Moonlite Bar-B-Q Inn in Owensboro and obsessed about their pulled mutton. Mutton may be too gamey for most people. With leg of lamb, we can turn out a pretty good imitation of this long-smoked barbecue.

1. Mix the brown sugar, smoked paprika, cumin, mustard powder, onion powder, black pepper and garlic powder in a large bowl. Pat the spice mixture over all sides of the lamb.

2. Stir the stock, vinegar and soy sauce in a **5.5- or 7.5-litre cooker.** Set the meat into this sauce (do not turn over to coat). Lock the lid onto the pot.

3.

Set the machine	Level	The valve must be	Time	Press
PRESSURE COOK	MAX	——	1 hour 5 minutes with the KEEP WARM setting off	START
MEAT/STEW, PRESSURE COOK or MANUAL	HIGH	Closed	1 hour 20 minutes with the KEEP WARM setting off	START
SLOW COOK	HIGH	Opened	4½ hours with the KEEP WARM setting off (or on for no more than 3 hours)	START

4. If using a pressure setting, when the machine has finished cooking, turn it off and let its pressure **return to normal naturally,** about 30 minutes.

5. Use a meat fork and a big, slotted spoon to transfer the meat (whole or in pieces) to a chopping board. Shred the meat with two forks. Then use a large spoon to skim any excess surface fat from the sauce.

6.

Press	Setting	Time	Press
SAUTÉ	MEDIUM, NORMAL or CUSTOM 150°C	10 minutes	START

7. Bring the sauce to a full simmer, stirring occasionally. Cook, stirring more and more frequently, until the sauce has reduced to half its volume, 5–8 minutes. Stir the shredded meat into the sauce and cook, stirring to make sure the meat is thoroughly coated, for 1 minute. Turn off the **SAUTÉ** function and remove the *hot* insert from the cooker. Set the lid askew over the insert and set aside for 5–10 minutes.

1 tablespoon dark brown sugar

2 teaspoons mild smoked paprika

1½ teaspoons ground cumin

1 teaspoon mustard powder

1 teaspoon onion powder

1 teaspoon ground black pepper

½ teaspoon garlic powder

One 1.3kg boneless leg of lamb, the meat opened up, cut in half, and any large chunks of fat removed

250ml beef stock

60ml apple cider vinegar

2 tablespoons soy sauce

Beyond

- For a 3-litre cooker, you must use 180ml stock and halve the remaining ingredients. Keep the 650g boneless leg of lamb in one piece.

- This rub and braising technique will also work well for a 1.3kg piece beef brisket, cut in half. In that case, let the meat go under pressure at MAX for 1 hour 20 minutes or at HIGH for 1 hour 45 minutes, either followed by a natural release.

- Serve with mayonnaise on toasted hamburger buns along with a slice of tomato and thinly sliced red onion.

500ml pomegranate juice

1 medium lemon, scrubbed to remove any waxy coating, then quartered, deseeded and finely chopped

4 medium garlic cloves, peeled and finely chopped (4 teaspoons prechopped)

1 tablespoon dried oregano

2 teaspoons ground cinnamon

2 teaspoons dried dill

1 teaspoon table salt

One 1.3kg piece bone-in lamb shoulder

1 large red onion, thinly sliced and broken into rings

2 tablespoons honey

Pulled Lamb Shoulder with Pomegranate and Cinnamon

8 servings

If you're a fan of bright flavours, this might be the pulled dish for you. The pomegranate juice retains much of its sour pop (aided, of course, by the chopped lemon). To really ramp things up, there's the incredible combination of cinnamon and dill, a savoury and warming mix that works well with the relatively fatty cut of lamb.

1. Pour the pomegranate juice into a **5.5- or 7.5-litre cooker**. Mix the lemon, garlic, oregano, cinnamon, dill and salt in a small bowl. Pat and rub this mixture evenly over the lamb shoulder. Set the meat in the cooker, scatter the onion all round and onto the meat and lock the lid onto the pot.

2.

Set the machine	Level	The valve must be	Time	Press
PRESSURE COOK	MAX	——	1 hour 10 minutes with the KEEP WARM setting off	START
MEAT/STEW, PRESSURE COOK or MANUAL	HIGH	Closed	1½ hours with the KEEP WARM setting off	START
SLOW COOK	HIGH	Opened	5 hours with the KEEP WARM setting off (or on for more than 3 hours)	START

3. If you've used a pressure setting, when the machine finishes cooking, turn it off and let its pressure **return to normal naturally,** *about 30 minutes.*

4. Unlatch the lid and open the cooker. Use a meat fork and a large slotted spoon to transfer the meat to a chopping board. Shred the meat with two forks, discarding the bone as well as any additional bits of cartilage or fat. Then use a large spoon to skim any excess surface fat from the sauce in the pot.

5.

Press	Setting	Time	Press
SAUTÉ	MEDIUM, NORMAL or CUSTOM 150°C	15 minutes	START

6. Bring the sauce to a simmer, stirring occasionally. Stir in the honey and cook, stirring more and more frequently, until reduced to about half its volume, 5–10 minutes. Stir the meat into the sauce and cook, stirring to coat every thread of meat, for 1 minute. Turn off the **SAUTÉ** function and remove the insert from the cooker. Set the lid askew over the insert for 5–10 minutes to blend the flavours and allow the meat to absorb the sauce.

Beyond

- This bone-in cut will not work well in a 3-litre cooker.

- Serve with orzo pasta and top with finely chopped fresh mint and flat-leaf parsley.

- Or serve in pitta pockets with chopped lettuce and tahini sauce. To make enough sauce for 8 servings, whisk together 90g tahini, 90ml plain full-fat yoghurt and 60ml fresh lemon juice in a small bowl. Whisk in water, a little at a time, until the mixture is the consistency of creamy salad dressing. Whisk in a pinch of salt and lots of ground black pepper.

All-American Pulled Chicken

6 servings

Root beer in pulled chicken? Stick with us. It makes for a combination of herbal and sweet flavours that bring a subtle complexity to the sauce. Okay, so maybe the recipe isn't 'all-American'. Maybe we named it so in the hope it will become the standard, made with chicken breasts for a faster, less fatty *and* more meaty pulled chicken.

1. Pour the root beer into a **5.5-litre cooker**. Add the chicken and stir well. Scatter the onions over the top, then dollop or sprinkle the barbecue sauce, Worcestershire sauce, black pepper and garlic powder over everything. Lock the lid onto the pot.

2.

Set the machine	Level	The valve must be	Time	Press
PRESSURE COOK	MAX	———	18 minutes with the KEEP WARM setting off	START
MEAT/STEW, PRESSURE COOK or MANUAL	HIGH	Closed	25 minutes with the KEEP WARM setting off	START
SLOW COOK	HIGH	Opened	2 hours with the KEEP WARM setting off (or on for no more than 1 hour)	START

3. If you've used a pressure setting, when the machine has finished cooking, turn it off and let its pressure **return to normal naturally,** about 20 minutes.

4. Unlatch the lid and open the pot. Use two forks to shred the chicken in the pot. Stir well, then set the lid askew over the top for 5 minutes to allow the meat to continue to absorb the sauce.

180ml root beer
(do not use diet)

1.2kg boneless skinless
chicken breasts, preferably
two or three giant breasts

2 small red onions, thinly
sliced and broken into rings

90ml barbecue sauce of any
sort, just not a chunky
or creamy sauce

2 tablespoons
Worcestershire sauce

1 teaspoon ground
black pepper

½ teaspoon garlic powder

Beyond

- For a 3-litre cooker, you must use 125ml root beer and halve the remaining ingredients.

- For a 7.5-litre cooker, you must increase *all* the ingredients by 50 per cent.

- For a spicier pulled chicken, omit the Worcestershire sauce and use 2 tablespoons of a hot red pepper sauce like Tabasco or even the brine from a jar of pickled jalapeño rings.

- Serve with vinegary condiments like dill pickle relish, Dijon mustard or spicy (not sweet) relish.

125ml chicken stock

125ml regular coconut milk

2 medium shallots, thinly sliced and separated into rings

4 medium garlic cloves, peeled and slivered

2 tablespoons thinly sliced thin lemongrass (peeled if necessary)

2 tablespoons hot red pepper sauce, preferably Sriracha

2 tablespoons light brown sugar

½ teaspoon ground turmeric

½ teaspoon table salt

1.2kg boneless skinless chicken breasts, preferably two or three giant breasts

Thai-Inspired Pulled Chicken Breasts

6 servings

This recipe is a flight of fancy: an American pulled chicken combined with a Thai braise. Make sure you stir the solid fat into the coconut milk in the tin to make the dish as rich as possible.

Lemongrass can be woody, even fibrous, especially the stuff that shows up in supermarkets. Trim off any husk-like, desiccated outer rings and only use the tender inner parts of the white and pale green parts of the stalk.

1. Mix the stock, coconut milk, shallots, garlic, lemongrass, pepper sauce, brown sugar, turmeric and salt in a **5.5-litre cooker** until the brown sugar dissolves. Set the chicken breasts into this sauce, turning the pieces to coat them on all sides. Lock the lid onto the pot.

2.

Set the machine	Level	The valve must be	Time	Press
PRESSURE COOK	MAX	—	18 minutes with the KEEP WARM setting off	START
MEAT/STEW, PRESSURE COOK or MANUAL	HIGH	Closed	25 minutes with the KEEP WARM setting off	START
SLOW COOK	HIGH	Opened	2 hours with the KEEP WARM setting off	START

3. If you've used a pressure setting, when the machine has finished cooking, turn it off and let the pressure **return to normal naturally**, about 15 minutes.

4. Unlatch the lid and open the pot. Use two forks to shred the chicken right in the pot. Stir well, then set the lid askew over the pot and set aside for 5–10 minutes to blend the flavours and allow the meat to absorb some of the sauce.

Beyond

- For a 3-litre cooker, you must use 125ml stock and halve the remaining ingredients.
- For a 7.5-litre cooker, you must increase *all* the ingredients by 50 per cent.
- Serve over long-grain white rice and top the servings with fresh coriander leaves, finely chopped red onion and fresh bean sprouts.
- For a hotter dish, add up to 2 small serrano chillies, stemmed and thinly sliced, with the other sauce ingredients.
- For a less aromatic but sweeter dish, substitute 2 tablespoons finely chopped peeled fresh root ginger for the lemongrass.

Tikka-Style Pulled Chicken Thighs

6 servings

Chicken tikka is an East Indian dish, but surely not ever a pulled dish! Oh, but yes. We've taken the iconic flavours and revamped them to create a savoury riff on an American classic: creamy, filling, with lots of warming spices. (Look elsewhere for Chicken Tikka Masala: page 242.) For the richest taste, use full-fat Greek yoghurt, rather than fat-free.

1. Mix the tomatoes, stock, onion, ginger, smoked paprika, cinnamon, coriander, turmeric and salt in a **5.5-litre cooker.** Add the chicken thighs and toss well to coat. Lock the lid onto the pot.

2.

Set the machine	Level	The valve must be	Time	Press
PRESSURE COOK	MAX	——	14 minutes with the KEEP WARM setting off	START
MEAT/STEW, PRESSURE COOK or MANUAL	HIGH	Closed	20 minutes with the KEEP WARM setting off	START
SLOW COOK	HIGH	Opened	2 hours with the KEEP WARM setting off (or on for no more than 2 hours)	START

3. If you've used a pressure setting, when the machine has finished cooking, turn it off and let its pressure **return to normal naturally,** about 15 minutes.

4. Unlatch the lid and open the pot. Shred the meat with two forks in the pot. Add the yoghurt and coriander, then stir well until uniform.

One 400g tin chopped tomatoes

125ml chicken stock

1 small red onion, chopped

2 tablespoons finely chopped peeled fresh root ginger

2 tablespoons mild smoked paprika

1 teaspoon ground cinnamon

1 teaspoon ground coriander

1 teaspoon ground turmeric

1 teaspoon table salt

900g boneless skinless chicken thighs

60g Greek yoghurt

7g fresh coriander leaves

Beyond

- For a 3-litre cooker, you must use 125ml stock and halve the remaining ingredients.
- For a 7.5-litre cooker, you must increase *all* the ingredients by 50 per cent.
- Serve over long-grain brown rice, a nutty contrast to the complex flavours.
- Or serve in pitta pockets with a little finely chopped red onion and a hearty dollop of chutney.
- For more heat, add up to 2 serrano chillies, stemmed and thinly sliced, with the onion.

180ml chicken stock

60ml balsamic vinegar

80g strawberry jam
(do not use sugar-free)

1 tablespoon Dijon mustard

1 tablespoon ground black
pepper, preferably coarsely
ground

1 teaspoon table salt

1.2kg boneless skinless
chicken thighs

1 large rosemary sprig

Balsamic-Black Pepper Pulled Chicken

6 servings

Since chicken thighs have a lot of meaty flavour, we felt free to use a lot of black pepper for a super spicy bump. It's worth it to grind your own pepper for the freshest taste. The surprise here may well be the strawberry jam, a sweet contrast to the vinegar and pepper, a balance of flavours.

1. Mix the stock, vinegar, jam, mustard, black pepper and salt in a **5.5-litre cooker** until the jam dissolves. Add the chicken thighs and toss well to coat. Tuck the rosemary sprig into the mix and lock the lid onto the pot.

2.

Set the machine	Level	The valve must be	Time	Press
PRESSURE COOK	MAX	——	14 minutes with the KEEP WARM setting off	START
MEAT/STEW, PRESSURE COOK or MANUAL	HIGH	Closed	20 minutes with the KEEP WARM setting off	START
SLOW COOK	HIGH	Opened	2 hours with the KEEP WARM setting off (or on for no more than 2 hours)	START

3. If you've used a pressure setting, when the machine has finished cooking, turn it off and let its pressure **return to normal naturally,** about 20 minutes.

4. Unlatch the lid and open the pot. Fish out and discard the rosemary sprig. Shred the meat with two forks in the pot, then stir well to coat with sauce. Set the lid askew over the pot for 5–10 minutes to allow the chicken to continue absorbing the sauce.

Beyond

- For a 3-litre cooker, you must use 125ml stock and halve the remaining ingredients.

- For a 7.5-litre cooker, you must increase all the ingredients by 50 per cent.

- Serve in radicchio cups with soured cream. Or serve over an undressed chopped salad of cucumber, celery, chicory and red onion.

Thanksgiving-Inspired Pulled Turkey

8 servings

The sun doesn't rise and set on pork, beef and chicken when it comes to pulled dishes. You can even cook turkey tenderloins until they can be pulled into what can only be described as a one-pot version of a Thanksgiving meal, made with cranberry sauce, sage and thyme. The grated sweet potato adds lots of sweetness *and* thickens the sauce as the pieces melt into it.

Although turkey tenderloins work best because they shred into a 'pulled' consistency, a chunk of boneless skinless turkey breast will do fine even if it's not so easy to shred. Cut it into three even pieces to match the approximate size and shape of turkey tenderloins.

1. Mix the stock, cranberry sauce, sage, thyme and salt in a **5.5-litre cooker**. Stir in the grated sweet potato, then set the turkey into this sauce, turning it to coat. Lock the lid onto the pot.

2.

Set the machine	Level	The valve must be	Time	Press
PRESSURE COOK	MAX	—	18 minutes with the KEEP WARM setting off	START
MEAT/ STEW, PRESSURE COOK or MANUAL	HIGH	Closed	25 minutes with the KEEP WARM setting off	START

3. When the machine has finished cooking, turn it off and let its pressure **return to normal naturally**, about 20 minutes. Unlatch the lid and open the pot. Shred the meat with two forks in the pot, then stir well until coated with sauce. Set the lid askew over the pot for 5–10 minutes to blend the flavours and allow the turkey to continue to absorb the sauce.

180ml chicken stock

140g whole berry cranberry sauce

2 tablespoons packed fresh sage leaves, finely chopped

2 teaspoons fresh thyme leaves

1 teaspoon table salt

1 small sweet potato (about 225g), peeled and grated through the large holes of a box grater

1.2kg boneless skinless turkey tenderloins (that is, the long strip of white meat hidden under the turkey breast)

Beyond

- For a 3-litre cooker, you must use 125ml stock and halve the remaining ingredients.

- For a 7.5-litre cooker, you must increase *all* the ingredients by 50 per cent.

- Unfortunately, this recipe doesn't work well on the slow cooker setting. The turkey dries out too quickly.

- For the full Thanksgiving treatment, buy corn (polenta) muffins, split them in half, then toast them cut-side down on a baking tin in a 200°C oven until crisp at the edges. Serve the pulled turkey over them in bowls.

1 tablespoon lemon pepper seasoning blend

1.2kg boneless turkey tenderloins, or boneless skinless turkey breast cut into 3 pieces

160ml chicken stock

80g ginger jam

2 tablespoons fresh lemon juice

2 tablespoons red wine vinegar

2 tablespoons packed fresh oregano leaves, finely chopped

½ teaspoon crushed chilli flakes

Lemon and Ginger Pulled Turkey

6 servings

These are amongst the brightest flavours in this chapter: a sweet and tart mix that's much more suited to a spring day than a winter one. In all truth, this recipe is our pressure-cooker homage to the ever-popular New York restaurant Rao's lemon chicken. It would even be great for lunch on slices of toasted, wholewheat bread, sort of like pulled turkey salad. Check the label of your lemon pepper seasoning blend. If it doesn't contain salt, add up to 1½ teaspoons salt with the sauce ingredients.

1. Pat and massage the lemon pepper seasoning into the turkey tenderloins or pieces. Mix the stock, jam, lemon juice, vinegar, oregano and crushed chilli flakes in a **5.5-litre cooker** until the jam dissolves into the sauce. Set the turkey into this sauce (without turning the meat over). Lock the lid onto the pot.

2.

Set the machine	Level	The valve must be	Time	Press
PRESSURE COOK	MAX	—	18 minutes with the KEEP WARM setting off	START
MEAT/ STEW, PRESSURE COOK or MANUAL	HIGH	Closed	25 minutes with the KEEP WARM setting off	START

3. When the machine has finished cooking, turn it off and let its pressure **return to normal naturally,** about 20 minutes. Unlatch the lid and open the pot. Shred the meat with two forks in the pot, then stir to coat with sauce. Set the lid askew over the pot for 5–10 minutes to blend the flavours and allow the meat to continue to absorb the sauce.

Beyond

- For a 3-litre cooker, you must use 125ml stock and halve the remaining ingredients.

- For a 7.5-litre cooker, you must increase *all* the ingredients by 50 per cent.

- Garnish with more fresh oregano leaves and finely grated lemon zest.

- Substitute lemon marmalade for the ginger jam for all-lemon pulled turkey.

All-American Pulled Vegetables

6 servings

By cooking lentils and then puréeing them, we can add a creamy texture that's often missing from pulled vegetables (and highly prized in the more meaty versions of pulled fare). We include lots of grated (rather than chopped or diced) vegetables for a smooth 'pulled' finish.

The sauce is quite smoky, thanks to a heavy hit of smoked paprika. However, there's just a touch of heat, since the pressure cooker will destroy much of it from the Rotel tomatoes. If you'd like a hotter dish, pass extra hot red pepper sauce at the table.

1. Mix the water and lentils in a **5.5-litre cooker**. Lock the lid onto the pot.

2.

Set the machine	Level	The valve must be	Time	Press
PRESSURE COOK	MAX	—	12 minutes with the KEEP WARM setting off	START
MEAT/STEW, PRESSURE COOK or MANUAL	HIGH	Closed	15 minutes with the KEEP WARM setting off	START

3. Use the **quick-release method** to bring the pot's pressure back to normal. Unlatch the lid and open the pot. Drain the contents of the *hot* insert through a fine-mesh sieve and set in the sink. Cool a few minutes, then put the lentils in a food processor and process until smooth, stopping the machine and scraping down the inside at least once.

4. Do not clean the insert; set it back in the machine. Stir the sweet potato, green cabbage, red cabbage, carrots, Rotel tomatoes, onion, apple juice, Worcestershire sauce, mustard, brown sugar, smoked paprika and chilli powder into the pot. Lock the lid back on the cooker.

5.

Set the machine	Level	The valve must be	Time	Press
PRESSURE COOK	MAX	—	4 minutes with the KEEP WARM setting off	START
MEAT/STEW, PRESSURE COOK or MANUAL	HIGH	Closed	5 minutes with the KEEP WARM setting off	START

6. Use the **quick-release method** to bring the pot's pressure back to normal. Unlatch the lid and open the pot. Scrape the lentil purée into the pot; stir well until uniform. Set the lid askew over the pot for 5–10 minutes to blend the flavours and allow the vegetables to continue to absorb the liquid.

600ml water

170g Puy lentils

280g grated sweet potato

150g shredded green cabbage leaves

150g shredded red cabbage leaves

240g grated carrots

One 280g tin Rotel tomatoes

1 small red onion, halved and thinly sliced into half-moons

180ml unsweetened apple juice

2 tablespoons Worcestershire sauce

2 tablespoons Dijon mustard

2 tablespoons dark brown sugar

2 tablespoons mild smoked paprika

1 tablespoon standard chilli powder

Beyond

- For a 3-litre cooker, you must use 125ml apple juice and halve the remaining ingredients. For a 7.5-litre cooker, you must increase the apple juice to 250ml and use the stated amounts of the remaining ingredients.

- It's hard to predict exactly how much moisture all the vegetables will give off because various heads of cabbage will have varying water content. If you find the mix too soupy, don't boil it down. Instead, use a slotted spoon to serve up the pulled vegetables, letting some of the liquid drain back into the pot.

6

All Things Curried

Welcome to the biggest flavours in this book. Some of these recipes are not for the faint-hearted. From a road map for tagine-style suppers to an aromatic, irresistible chana dal, these dishes bring out the best of what the Instant Pot can do: preserve internal moisture in just about everything; mellow the flavours of dried spices; and save you time (and money) with tasty cuts and root vegetables.

Since curry is such a wide designation, you'll even find soups and noodle dishes here, recipes you might have expected in other chapters. For more about the specifics of curry and curry powder, see the FAQs below. But before the recipes, it's important to point out that most curry calls for cooked rice. So we should bend the discussion that way first.

Simply put, rice is not just rice. Even long-grain white rice is not just long-grain white rice. Some varietals have a delicate fragrance, a tantalising blend of sweet and herbaceous flavours; others offer nothing more than a dull, flat, starchy ho-hum. It's tempting to say that you get what you pay for, but that's not always the case. Unfortunately, a taste test amongst brands is the only sure way to know. But for a shot at the best, look for plump grains, white or brown, either beautifully polished to a pearly lustre or evenly brown across the batch.

Because of its intact germ and bran, brown rice can go off relatively quickly; it will last maybe 4 months or a little longer if stored in a dark, cool pantry or up to a year in a sealed container in the freezer. Uncooked rice should not smell musty or off.

Rice grains come in various lengths. For our recipes, we've gone with the standard three: short (almost never used in this book); medium (used a bit more often, if not much in this chapter); and long (the most common type throughout this chapter and the book as a whole). When it comes

to long-grain rice, we prefer white or brown basmati, simply because these are less floral than jasmine rice.

Medium-grain rice, most often found as the varietal Arborio, has a stickier consistency. And short-grain rice, sometimes called 'sushi rice', can be quite gummy. Either medium- or short-grain rice works well as a base for the soupy curries in this chapter, particularly those based on recipes from Thailand and South East Asia.

If you want to cook rice in the Instant Pot, be careful. The *Rice* function is calibrated differently amongst the models. Some will *not* automatically accommodate for brown rice; you must set the cook time manually. Read your pot's instruction manual. It (or the included recipe booklet) offers specific instructions on how to make plain rice in your model.

FAQs

1. What is curry powder?
Curry is the English version of a Tamil word that means 'sauce'. *Curry powder* is the blend of spices that flavour said sauce, which has either been rendered from the natural juices of meats and vegetables or created from ingredients like stock or coconut milk.

When most Americans think of curry powder, they think of a golden, dried-spice blend. Where applicable, we call for it. Sometimes, in the

Beyond section of a recipe, we even offer a specific blend you can concoct if you want to go all out. But with the advent of gourmet supermarkets and the growing interest in world foods, gone are the days when 'curry powder' meant just one thing. It and all other sorts of curry powders are now available in an almost overwhelming range of quality and flavour amongst proprietary blends. Some taste of nothing but acrid, low-grade turmeric; others offer an array of dried spices (and therefore a more complex flavour). In higher-end spice stores, you can even sample the offerings. If you search around at speciality spice merchants or Indian markets (even online), you'll be astounded at what's available.

2. Since curry powder is a spice blend, can I make my own?

Of course! Beyond any special blends we recommend in the recipes themselves, here's how to make a basic batch. Start with 1 tablespoon each of *at least* three, if not all four, of these spices: ground coriander, ground cumin, ground turmeric and/or ground ginger. Add 1 teaspoon table salt and *up to* 1 teaspoon ground cayenne. Then add *at least* two but preferably three or four of the following: 1 teaspoon ground cinnamon, 1 teaspoon dried thyme, 1 teaspoon dried sage, ½ teaspoon grated nutmeg, ½ teaspoon ground fenugreek, ¼ teaspoon ground mace and/or ¼ teaspoon ground cloves. You'll be the envy of your neighbourhood.

3. Is there salt in commercial curry powder?

Sometimes, but not always. Check the label if you have health concerns or don't like a salty dish. If salt appears in the ingredients list, and particularly if it's near the top, consider omitting any additional salt in the recipe and passing extra at the table.

4. Can I use other dried curry blends instead of the standard curry powder?

By all means! There are hot curry powders as well as speciality, regional blends, not only from India, but also from South Africa and the Caribbean. In truth, there are probably as many curry powders used in Indian and South East Asian cooking as there are people in those regions standing at a hob right now. Don't get hung up on authenticity. Experiment, check out other bottlings, see what you like and keep your experience in the kitchen fresh and exciting.

5. What is garam masala?

First off, it's a Hindi or Punjabi term that means 'hot spice blend'. The 'hot' doesn't refer to its being spicy but to the way the spices are said to raise the body's internal temperature. In the same way, we might say 'warming spices' for blends with, say, cinnamon and nutmeg.

As with curry powder, there's a wide range of quality and flavour amongst garam masalas on the market. You can also create your own. Over the years, we've come up with some blends that match various proteins. We're giving you house secrets here. Use them wisely. Each will make about 2 tablespoons of garam masala.

- For lamb and beef, mix together 2 teaspoons ground coriander, 1 teaspoon ground cinnamon, 1 teaspoon ground cumin, 1 teaspoon ground turmeric, ½ teaspoon ground cardamom, ¼ teaspoon ground cloves and up to ¼ teaspoon ground cayenne.
- For pork, chicken, veal or tofu, mix together 2 teaspoons ground coriander, 1 teaspoon ground cumin, 1 teaspoon mild paprika, 1 teaspoon fennel seeds, ½ teaspoon ground cinnamon, ¼ teaspoon ground allspice and up to ¼ teaspoon ground cayenne.

- For fish and shellfish, mix together 2 teaspoons ground coriander, 1 teaspoon ground turmeric, 1 teaspoon mild paprika, ½ teaspoon ground fenugreek, ½ teaspoon ground ginger, ½ teaspoon mustard powder, ¼ teaspoon grated nutmeg and up to ¼ teaspoon saffron threads.

6. What's a curry paste?

It's a wet blend of dried spices, fresh chillies, fresh aromatics and oil or ghee. The basics are red, yellow and green curry pastes, available in small jars, tins or plastic tubs in the Asian or East Indian aisle of almost all supermarkets. Once opened, the packages can be covered and stored in the refrigerator for at least 4 months, maybe longer.

Red curry paste has a complex, bright flavour and is usually the hottest, although it can have plenty of sweet notes. Yellow curry paste is usually milder and more herbaceous than red (and sometimes milder than green). Green curry paste has sour notes and a fresh flavour, often from lemongrass. Some green curry pastes are absurdly hot since they're made from what seems like a ton of pulverised fresh green chillies.

But there are more blends than those three that you can use in these recipes. Massaman curry paste is heavy with warming spices (like cinnamon, cloves and nutmeg) and is generally the mildest of the pastes. Penang curry paste is a fiery red mix, heavy with lemongrass and makrut lime leaves, guaranteed to knock your tongue for a loop. Sour vegetable curry paste is just what it sounds like: a sour, musty mélange missing coconut (which is in many of the others) but made with fermented shrimp paste (and therefore stinky, although it mellows over the heat).

No matter which of these you use, read the labels. If the first ingredient listed is chillies or cayenne, you've got a banging-hot version in your hand. If you're worried, use half the stated amount of curry paste the first time you make a dish. But remember. You can't add more curry paste as a garnish. It'll be too pungent, too 'raw'. Instead, use a hot red pepper sauce like Sriracha for heat at the table.

7. What's ghee?

It's clarified butter, in other words, butter with the milk solids removed. Whenever you melt butter, you've surely noticed those white blotchy bits at the bottom of the liquid fat. Take those out and essentially you've got ghee.

To make your own, cut up 115g of butter in a shallow bowl (a soup plate works best) and microwave on high in 10-second increments until melted, then leave to cool for 15–20 minutes at room temperature to let the milk solids settle to the bottom. Skim the clear, oily fat off the top, leaving the solids (and inevitably some of the oil) behind. Store the clarified butter (the ghee) in a covered small glass jar in the fridge for a month or two. It will solidify again but you can scrape out what you need. Discard the solids and the small amount of oil with them, or save them for a few days in the fridge to add with the thickener to custards (particularly ice cream custards) for extra richness.

And here's one final note. Watch out if you buy ghee. Some brands are quite literally nothing more than butter-flavoured shortening. Others are the real deal: clarified butter.

8. What's chana dal?

Basically, these are split and processed chickpeas. (They are *not* yellow lentils, nor actually lentils of any sort.) The chickpeas (aka garbanzo beans) are of a specific variety that are then dried and cut into pieces about the size of corn kernels. They cook quickly with a grainy texture and an earthy flavour. You cannot substitute other sorts of lentils or 'dal' (split pulses or legumes) for chana dal. Look for it in the aisle near the whole grains.

1 tablespoon vegetable,
corn or rapeseed oil

1 fresh serrano chilli,
stemmed, halved
lengthways, deseeded
and chopped

1 teaspoon cumin seeds

1 teaspoon garam masala

1 teaspoon ground coriander

1 teaspoon ground turmeric

Up to ½ teaspoon ground
cayenne

½ teaspoon granulated white
sugar

½ teaspoon table salt

2 medium plum or Roma
tomatoes, chopped

300ml water

340g baby spinach

450g extra-firm tofu,
cut into 2.5cm cubes

Vegan Saag Paneer

4 *servings*

Technically, this is 'palak paneer', that is, a *spinach* braise with a spicy
sauce, although the dish is frequently called 'saag paneer', despite
its lack of 'saag', a mustard green.

Paneer has a fairly high melting point (for cheese anyway) and
stays in chunks when it's folded into the sauce. We've crafted a vegan
dish by subbing extra-firm tofu for the cheese. Serve the stew over
cooked white basmati rice.

1.

Press	Setting	Time	Press
SAUTÉ	MEDIUM, NORMAL or CUSTOM 150°C	10 minutes	START

2. Heat the oil in a **5.5- or 7.5-litre cooker** for a minute or two.
Add the chilli and cumin seeds. Cook, stirring all the while, just
to toast the cumin seeds, about 1 minute. Stir in the garam
masala, coriander, turmeric, cayenne, sugar and salt until
fragrant, just a few seconds.

3. Stir in the tomatoes and cook, stirring occasionally, until they
begin to break down, about 2 minutes. Stir in the water and
scrape up any browned bits on the pot's bottom. Turn off the
SAUTÉ function, then stir in the spinach, pressing the leaves
down into the liquid. Lock the lid onto the pot.

4.

Set the machine	Level	The valve must be	Time	Press
PRESSURE COOK	MAX	—	6 minutes with the KEEP WARM setting off	START
PRESSURE COOK or MANUAL	HIGH	Closed	8 minutes with the KEEP WARM setting off	START

5. Use the **quick-release method** to bring the pot's pressure
back to normal. Unlatch the lid and open the cooker. Gently
stir in the tofu.

6.

Press	Setting	Time	Press
SAUTÉ	MEDIUM, NORMAL or CUSTOM 150°C	10 minutes	START

7. Cook, stirring occasionally but gently to keep the tofu intact,
until the liquid has boiled down to a loose, wet sauce, about
5 minutes. Turn off the **SAUTÉ** function and set the lid askew
over the pot for 5 minutes to blend the flavours. Stir gently
again before serving.

Beyond

- You must halve the recipe for
a 3-litre cooker.

- Pure tofu is gluten-free.
However, there are cross-
contamination issues with
some brands. Buy certified
gluten-free tofu if this is
a concern.

- If you can find paneer,
complete the recipe until
you need to add the tofu.
Omit the tofu, then continue
on with step 6, boiling down
the sauce as directed. After
you turn off the SAUTÉ
function, gently stir in 450g
paneer, cut into 5cm chunks.
Set aside with the lid askew
for 5 minutes to blend the
flavours and warm the cheese.

Perfect Chana Dal

4 servings

Chana dal is something like a savoury porridge, spicy and earthy. It is the single most important side dish you can make to go along with just about every East Indian-inspired curry in this chapter. It won't go with the dishes with noodles or any made from a wet curry paste, but it is exactly right with, say, Better Butter Chicken (page 235) or Savoury-Sweet Beef and Tomato Curry (page 244). Serve it either alongside cooked rice in the bowls with the curry as the other third of the bowl or spoon it right on top of the curry. We even just top chana dal with a poached egg and call it a day.

700ml vegetable stock

35g chana dal (see page 227)

1 tablespoon vegetable, corn or rapeseed oil

1 teaspoon ground turmeric

1 teaspoon table salt

½ teaspoon ground cardamom

½ teaspoon ground cumin

½ teaspoon ground black pepper

1. Mix all the ingredients in a **3-, 5.5- or 7.5-litre cooker**. Lock the lid onto the pot.

2.

Set the machine	Level	The valve must be	Time	Press
PRESSURE COOK	MAX	——	7 minutes with the KEEP WARM setting off	START
PRESSURE COOK or MANUAL	HIGH	Closed	10 minutes with the KEEP WARM setting off	START

3. When the machine has finished cooking, turn it off and let its pressure **return to normal naturally**, about 25 minutes. Unlatch the lid and open the cooker. Stir well, then set the lid askew over the pot. Set aside for 5 minutes so that the mixture continues to thicken. Serve warm.

Beyond

- This recipe can (but doesn't have to) be doubled in a 5.5- or 7.5-litre cooker.

- For an easy soup, add 700ml vegetable (or chicken) stock after cooking and purée the soup right in the pot with a hand blender.

- If you're not vegan, substitute butter or ghee for the oil. And stir up to 60ml double cream into the mixture *after* cooking. Set aside with the lid over the pot for 5 minutes to take the raw taste off the cream.

QUICK RELEASE / VEGAN /
CAN BE GLUTEN-FREE / FREEZES WELL

30g butter

1 medium onion, chopped
(160g prechopped)

1 tablespoon finely chopped
peeled fresh root ginger

1 tablespoon curry powder

1 tablespoon light brown
sugar

1 litre vegetable stock

900g frozen butternut squash
cubes (do not thaw)

Up to 2 tablespoons hot red
pepper sauce, preferably
Sriracha

¼ teaspoon table salt

250ml regular or low-fat
coconut milk

Spicy Curried Butternut Squash Soup

4–6 servings

This is a creamy (if cream-free) soup that uses frozen butternut squash cubes to make a tasty, light main course (or a starter). The coconut milk adds an intense richness, a better foil to the heat.

We call for a lot of hot sauce in this recipe. If you're worried, make the soup the first time with only 1 tablespoon (or even less) of hot red pepper sauce. You can always add more before puréeing the soup.

If you have to purée the soup in batches in a blender, remove the centre knob in the lid and cover the opening with a clean tea towel to prevent a pressure build-up and a subsequent explosion of soup all over the walls.

1.

Press	Setting	Time	Press
SAUTÉ	MEDIUM, NORMAL or CUSTOM 150°C	10 minutes	START

2. Melt the butter in a **5.5- or 7.5-litre cooker**. Add the onion and cook, stirring often, until softened, about 4 minutes. Add the ginger and stir until aromatic, just a few seconds. Stir in the curry powder and brown sugar until the brown sugar melts.

3. Pour in the stock and scrape up any browned bits on the pot's bottom. Turn off the **SAUTÉ** function, then stir in the butternut squash, hot sauce and salt. Lock the lid onto the pot.

4.

Set the machine	Level	The valve must be	Time	Press
PRESSURE COOK	MAX	————	7 minutes with the KEEP WARM setting off	START
SOUP/ BROTH, PRESSURE COOK or MANUAL	HIGH	Closed	10 minutes with the KEEP WARM setting off	START

5. Use the **quick-release method** to bring the pot's pressure back to normal. Unlatch the lid and open the pot. Add the coconut milk, then use a hand blender to purée the soup in the pot. Or purée the soup in batches in a blender. Serve warm.

Beyond

- You must halve the recipe for a 3-litre cooker.
- For a more substantial meal, set a mound of lump crabmeat in the centre of each bowl.
- Or hang cooked king prawns off the rim of the bowl (or pile them on a plate nearby) to dip in the soup as you eat it.
- Or serve over cooked white rice and top with bean sprouts.

Empty-the-Root-Cellar Curry

6 servings

Okay, we don't have a root cellar. But here's a vegetarian curry – or even, vegan, if you use a vegan yoghurt – that may be just the thing in the late autumn when root vegetables are the only thing left fresh at the farmers' markets.

This curry has no added sweetener, letting the high-starch roots handle the job. You might be surprised how savoury the dish is. Just make sure all the vegetables are chopped to the right size so they cook in the time stated. If you buy some of the roots prechopped (and why not?), you may need to cut the pieces down even smaller to match the requirements here.

1. Mix the parsnips, beetroot, potatoes, carrots, onion, stock, almonds, ginger, curry powder and salt in a **5.5- or 7.5-litre cooker**. Stir well, then lock the lid onto the pot.

2.

Set the machine	Level	The valve must be	Time	Press
PRESSURE COOK	MAX	——	7 minutes with the KEEP WARM setting off	START
PRESSURE COOK or MANUAL	HIGH	Closed	10 minutes with the KEEP WARM setting off	START

3. Use the **quick-release method** to bring the pot's pressure back to normal. Unlatch the lid and open the cooker. Stir well before serving in bowls with dollops of yoghurt as a garnish.

450g medium parsnips, peeled and cut into 2.5cm sections

450g yellow beetroot, peeled and cut into 2.5cm cubes

450g large potatoes, such as Desiree or Charlotte (2 or 3 potatoes), quartered

340g carrots, peeled and cut into 2.5cm sections

1 medium onion, chopped (160g prechopped)

500ml vegetable stock

80g whole roasted unsalted almonds

3 tablespoons finely chopped peeled fresh root ginger

2 tablespoons yellow curry powder

½ teaspoon table salt

Plain regular or low-fat yoghurt for garnishing

Beyond

- You must halve the recipe for a 3-litre cooker.

- Make your own curry blend. Instead of the ready-made curry powder, mix together 1½ teaspoons ground cinnamon, 1½ teaspoons ground cumin, 1½ teaspoon ground coriander, 1 teaspoon ground turmeric and up to ½ teaspoon ground cayenne. Or use 2 tablespoons of a signature blend you can make, using the instructions on page 226.

- Dollop chutney as well as yoghurt on each serving. Don't just think mango chutney. Try a cranberry one with these roots.

2 tablespoons vegetable, corn or rapeseed oil

1 medium red onion, halved and sliced into thin half-moons

1 fresh small serrano chilli, stemmed, halved, deseeded and thinly sliced

2 medium garlic cloves, peeled and finely chopped (2 teaspoons prechopped)

1 tablespoon finely chopped peeled fresh root ginger

1 tablespoon garam masala

1 teaspoon ground cumin

1 teaspoon mild smoked paprika

½ teaspoon table salt

350ml vegetable stock

Two 400g tins chickpeas, drained and rinsed

450g potatoes, such as Desiree or Charlotte, cut into 2.5cm cubes

125ml regular or low-fat coconut milk

60g baby spinach leaves

1 tablespoon fresh lemon juice

Beyond

- You must halve the recipe for a 3-litre cooker.
- Make your own garam masala: use 1 teaspoon ground coriander, ½ teaspoon ground cardamom, ½ teaspoon ground cinnamon, ¼ teaspoon ground cloves, ¼ teaspoon mustard powder and a bay leaf. Remove the bay leaf before serving.
- Heat about 1cm of vegetable oil in a small saucepan over a medium-high heat until the oil shimmers. Add curry leaves and fry, turning once, until crisp, about 1 minute. Lay these leaves over each serving.

Smoky Chickpea and Potato Curry

4 *servings*

Chickpeas and potatoes are two of the most common ingredients in East Indian cooking. We use them together in this simple, dairy-free curry, substituting coconut milk for the more traditional yoghurt. By softening the vegetables and aromatics first, we can get natural sugars into the stew without adding any other sweetener. The stew is so delicious, it may well turn you into a vegan (or at least help you see that eating vegan once in a while is a tasty thing).

1.

Press	Setting	Time	Press
SAUTÉ	MEDIUM, NORMAL or CUSTOM 150°C	10 minutes	START

2. Warm the oil in a **5.5- or 7.5-litre cooker** for a minute or two. Add the onion and cook, stirring often, until softened, about 4 minutes. Add the chilli, garlic and ginger. Continue cooking, stirring almost constantly, for 1 minute.

3. Stir in the garam masala, cumin, smoked paprika and salt until fragrant, just a few seconds. Pour in the stock and scrape up any browned bits on the pot's bottom. Turn off the **SAUTÉ** function. Stir in the chickpeas, potatoes and coconut milk until uniform. Lock the lid onto the pot.

4.

Set the machine	Level	The valve must be	Time	Press
PRESSURE COOK	MAX	—	5 minutes with the KEEP WARM setting off	START
PRESSURE COOK or MANUAL	HIGH	Closed	7 minutes with the KEEP WARM setting off	START

5. Use the **quick-release method** to bring the pot's pressure back to normal. Unlatch the lid and open the pot. Stir in the baby spinach and lemon juice. Set the lid askew over the pot; set aside for 5 minutes to wilt the spinach and blend the flavours. Stir again before serving.

Three-Lentil Dal Makhani

6 servings

This one's a creamy lentil curry, often made with black lentils and kidney beans. Unfortunately, black lentils are tough to track down outside of speciality markets. Easier to find, red kidney beans do indeed break down and thicken the curry, giving it a characteristic texture. But dried kidney beans make the recipe overly complicated (soaking, pre-cooking separately, etc). And tinned kidney beans end up too squishy under pressure for this long. To solve all those problems, we use a mixture of lentils to revamp this dish, even red lentils (sometimes called 'pink lentils'), which dissolve under pressure and thicken the dish while giving it an earthy flavour. Although this is a vegetarian main course, feel free to serve it alongside almost anything from the grill. Pork loin would be welcome. Beef ribs, too.

1.

Press	Setting	Time	Press
SAUTÉ	MEDIUM, NORMAL or CUSTOM 150°C	5 minutes	START

2. Melt the butter or ghee in a 3-, 5.5- or 7.5-litre cooker. Add the garlic, ginger, garam masala, cumin, turmeric, salt, cayenne, cinnamon stick, cardamom pods and bay leaves. Stir until fragrant, about 1 minute. Add the tomato and cook, stirring often, until it just begins to break down, 1–2 minutes.

3. Turn off the **SAUTÉ** function. Stir in the red lentils, brown lentils and chana dal until coated in the spices. Stir in the water and lock the lid onto the pot.

4.

Set the machine	Level	The valve must be	Time	Press
PRESSURE COOK	MAX	—	16 minutes with the KEEP WARM setting off	START
MEAT/ STEW, PRESSURE COOK or MANUAL	HIGH	Closed	20 minutes with the KEEP WARM setting off	START

5. Use the **quick-release method** to bring the pot's pressure back to normal. Unlatch the lid and open the cooker. Remove and discard the cinnamon stick, cardamom pods and bay leaves. Stir in the cream until uniform, then set the lid askew over the pot for 5 minutes to blend the flavours. Stir again before serving.

30g butter or 2 tablespoons ghee

6 medium garlic cloves, peeled and finely chopped (2 tablespoons prechopped)

2 tablespoons finely chopped peeled fresh root ginger

1 tablespoon garam masala

1 teaspoon ground cumin

1 teaspoon ground turmeric

½ teaspoon table salt

Up to ½ teaspoon ground cayenne

One 10cm cinnamon stick

4 green or white cardamom pods

2 bay leaves

200g chopped tomatoes

125g red lentils

95g brown lentils

20g chana dal (see page 27)

1 litre water

125ml double cream

Beyond

- If you want to have the 'full bean' experience (and a less thick curry), substitute dried black-eye beans for the red lentils.

- Serve the curry with packaged na'an or other flatbreads.

1.3kg boneless skinless meat, cut into 5cm cubes

Choose from chicken thighs, beef rump, leg of lamb, or fresh (not cured or smoked) ham.

2 tablespoons curry powder

Choose from yellow, red, speciality blends, even tandoori or an Asian curry powder or make your own (see page 226).

3 tablespoons oil

Choose from vegetable, corn, rapeseed, safflower, peanut, grapeseed, avocado, coconut or olive oil.

250g chopped aromatics

Choose one or two from onions (of any sort), shallots, spring onions, fennel, celery and/or leeks (white and pale green parts only, well washed).

2 tablespoons finely chopped peeled fresh root ginger

2 medium garlic cloves, peeled and finely chopped (2 teaspoons prechopped)

60g chopped dried fruit

Choose from raisins, sultanas, currants, pitted prunes, dried pineapple, pitted dried nectarines, pitted dried peaches or stemmed dried figs.

80g unsalted shelled nuts

Choose from pistachios, walnuts, pecans or almonds.

250ml liquid

Choose a stock of any sort; or a 50/50 combo of stock and a dry white wine, such as Chardonnay.

½ teaspoon table salt

Beyond

- You must halve the recipe for a 3-litre cooker.
- For a 7.5-litre cooker, you must use 435ml liquid and increase the remaining ingredients by 50 per cent.

Road Map: Tagine-Style Curry

6 servings

A tagine is a North African curry, often a combination of meat, dried fruit, nuts and aromatics, traditionally made in a shallow pot with a conical lid. Here's a streamlined recipe that lets you create your own version in an Instant Pot. Leaner cuts of meat work better, so we don't recommend lamb, pork shoulder or beef chuck, any of which produce an oily, thick sauce.

Serve the spiced stew over fluffed couscous, long-grain white rice, giant couscous or plain mashed potatoes.

1. Toss the meat and curry powder in a large bowl until the pieces are evenly and thoroughly coated in the spices.

2.

Press	Setting	Time	Press
SAUTÉ	MEDIUM, NORMAL or CUSTOM 150°C	15 minutes	START

3. Warm the oil in a **5.5-litre cooker** for a minute or two, then add the aromatics. Cook, stirring often, until softened, 3–4 minutes. Add the ginger and garlic; cook, stirring often, until aromatic, less than 1 minute.

4. Add the meat, scraping every last speck of dried spices into the pot. Cook, stirring occasionally, until the meat loses its raw, pink colour and browns lightly, about 5 minutes. Turn off the **SAUTÉ** function. Stir in the dried fruit and nuts, then the liquid and salt, just until everything is well combined. Lock the lid onto the pot.

5.

Set the machine	Level	The valve must be	Time	Press
PRESSURE COOK	MAX	——	35 minutes with the KEEP WARM setting off	START
MEAT/STEW, PRESSURE COOK or MANUAL	HIGH	Closed	45 minutes with the KEEP WARM setting off	START
SLOW COOK	HIGH	Opened	3 hours with the KEEP WARM setting off (or on for no more than 2 hours)	START

6. If you've used a pressure setting, when the machine has finished cooking, turn it off and let the pressure **return to normal naturally**, about 30 minutes.

7. Unlatch the lid and open the cooker. Stir well before serving.

Better Butter Chicken

6 servings

Here's our version of an internet craze: a buttery, tomato-laced, cream-rich sauce enrobing meaty pieces of chicken. Unfortunately, many recipes use cut-up bits of boneless, skinless chicken breast, which become tough shards, or chicken thighs, which leave the sauce greasy. We use bone-in skin-off chicken breasts to give the sauce a more savoury, bony flavour, with some collagen melted into it to enrich every bite.

　　To remove the skin from a chicken breast, grab the skin on the narrow, pointy end with a piece of kitchen paper and pull the skin back and off the meat. Remove any large blobs of fat on the meat. Then cut each breast in half widthways so there's about the same amount of meat in each portion.

1.

Press	Setting	Time	Press
SAUTÉ	MEDIUM, NORMAL or CUSTOM 150°C	5 minutes	START

2. Mix the tomatoes, stock or wine, butter, onion, curry powder, ginger and salt in a **5.5-litre cooker**. Cook, stirring occasionally, until the butter melts, about 2 minutes. Turn off the SAUTÉ function, add the chicken and toss well in the sauce to coat. Lock the lid onto the pot.

3.

Set the machine	Level	The valve must be	Time	Press
PRESSURE COOK	MAX	——	12 minutes with the KEEP WARM setting off	START
MEAT/STEW, PRESSURE COOK or MANUAL	HIGH	Closed	15 minutes with the KEEP WARM setting off	START

4. Use the **quick-release method** to bring the pot's pressure back to normal. Unlatch the lid and open the pot. Use kitchen tongs to transfer the chicken breasts to a serving platter or individual serving bowls.

5.

Press	Setting	Time	Press
SAUTÉ	MEDIUM, NORMAL or CUSTOM 150°C	5 minutes	START

6. Bring the sauce to a simmer, stirring quite frequently. Stir in the cream and cook the sauce at a low simmer, stirring quite often, until slightly thickened, about 2 minutes. Turn off the SAUTÉ function and spoon the sauce over the chicken breasts.

One 400g tin chopped tomatoes

125ml chicken stock or dry white wine

55g butter, cut into bits

1 small onion, chopped (80g prechopped)

2 tablespoons yellow curry powder

1 tablespoon finely chopped peeled fresh root ginger

¼ teaspoon table salt

Three 450g bone-in skinless chicken breasts, cut in half widthways

125ml double cream

Beyond

- You must halve the recipe for a 3-litre cooker.

- For a 7.5-litre cooker, you must increase all the ingredients by 50 per cent.

- The curry's buttery enough to serve over mashed potatoes (page 424).

- Or serve it on top of split-open baked sweet potatoes.

- Or serve it over riced cauliflower. There's no need to cook the cauliflower. The warm sauce will do the job for you if you serve it immediately and set the bowls aside for a minute or two.

- Garnish servings with finely chopped fresh coriander and/ or chives. And sprinkle unsalted shelled chopped pistachios over them, too.

1.2kg large boneless skinless chicken thighs, halved

2 tablespoons red wine vinegar

1½ tablespoons vindaloo curry dried spice blend

2 teaspoons dark brown sugar

½ teaspoon ground cinnamon

2 tablespoons vegetable oil

2 medium onions, halved and sliced into thin half-moons

1½ tablespoons finely chopped fresh root ginger

250ml chicken stock

550g potatoes, such as Desiree or Charlotte, cut into 4cm pieces

Plain Greek yoghurt and mango chutney for garnishing

Chicken Vindaloo

4 servings

Vindaloo means 'wine and potatoes', but it has come to mean 'fiery hot'. Actually, there's no wine in our version. It's a bit strange, we admit, but we wanted to skew the dish more savoury, given that the pot highlights sweet flavours. Note that there's no need for rice. With the potatoes, this is a one-pot meal.

The recipe may seem to use a lot of vindaloo spice. You'll be amazed at how it mellows. If you're in doubt, or if you have children at the table, use at most 1 tablespoon and pass some bottled hot red chilli sauce at the table to spice up some of the servings.

1. Mix the chicken, vinegar, spice blend, brown sugar and cinnamon in a large bowl until evenly coated. Set aside at room temperature for up to 20 minutes. (Or cover and set in the fridge for up to 10 hours.)

2.

Press	Setting	Time	Press
SAUTÉ	MEDIUM, NORMAL or CUSTOM 150°C	10 minutes	START

3. Warm the oil in a **5.5-litre cooker** for a minute or two. Add the onions and cook, stirring often, until softened, about 5 minutes. Add the ginger and continue cooking, stirring often, until fragrant, about 1 minute.

4. Add the meat and every drop of its marinade and spices. Stir to mix amongst the onions. Turn off the **SAUTÉ** function, then pour in the stock and stir well. Lock the lid onto the pot.

5.

Set the machine	Level	The valve must be	Time	Press
PRESSURE COOK	MAX	—	5 minutes with the KEEP WARM setting off	START
MEAT/ STEW, PRESSURE COOK or MANUAL	HIGH	Closed	8 minutes with the KEEP WARM setting off	START

6. Use the **quick-release method** to bring the pot's pressure back to normal. Unlatch the lid and open the cooker. Stir in the potatoes. Lock the lid back onto the pot.

7.

Set the machine	Level	The valve must be	Time	Press
PRESSURE COOK	MAX	—	8 minutes with the KEEP WARM setting off	START
MEAT/STEW, PRESSURE COOK or MANUAL	HIGH	Closed	10 minutes with the KEEP WARM setting off	START

8. Use the **quick-release method** to bring the pot's pressure back to normal. Unlatch the lid and uncover the cooker. Stir well, then serve with dollops of yoghurt and a spoonful of chutney or two over each bowlful.

Beyond

- For a 3-litre cooker, you must use 125ml stock and halve the remaining ingredients.

- For a 7.5-litre cooker, you must increase *all* the ingredients by 50 per cent.

- If the curry is too soupy for your taste after the second cooking, bring the stew to a high simmer using the SAUTÉ function on its MEDIUM, NORMAL or CUSTOM 150°C setting. Cook, stirring almost constantly, to reduce the sauce a bit, 2–3 minutes.

- Substitute butter or even ghee (clarified butter) for the vegetable oil.

- Omit the dried spice blend and make your own vindaloo powder. Increase the ground cinnamon to 1 teaspoon, and add the following spices to the bowl with the meat and vinegar: 1 teaspoon ground turmeric, 1 teaspoon hot paprika or ground red chillies, 1 teaspoon ground coriander, ½ teaspoon ground cumin, ½ teaspoon ground cloves, ½ teaspoon mustard powder and ½ teaspoon table salt.

450g plain boneless skinless chicken breast cut for stir-fry; or boneless skinless chicken breasts cut into 1cm strips

1 litre chicken stock

350ml regular or low-fat coconut milk

1 medium yellow pepper, stemmed, cored and chopped (175g prechopped)

One 225g tin sliced bamboo shoots, drained

115g shiitake mushroom caps, sliced

1 tablespoon finely chopped peeled fresh root ginger

1 tablespoon curry powder

1 tablespoon white granulated sugar

1 tablespoon fresh lime juice

1 tablespoon hot red pepper sauce, such as Sriracha (optional)

Curried Chicken Soup

6 servings

There's no faster chicken soup in this book, particularly if you buy boneless skinless chicken breasts already prepped for stir-frying (that is, cut into long, thin strips). Make sure those strips are not marinated and discard any seasoning packets that come with them. And stir the coconut milk in the tin with a fork before using to mix the coconut solids into the liquid.

1. Mix all the ingredients in a **5.5- or 7.5-litre cooker**. Lock the lid onto the pot.

2.

Set the machine	Level	The valve must be	Time	Press
PRESSURE COOK	MAX	—	5 minutes with the KEEP WARM setting off	START
SOUP/ BROTH, PRESSURE COOK or MANUAL	HIGH	Closed	7 minutes with the KEEP WARM setting off	START
SLOW COOK	HIGH	Opened	3 hours with the KEEP WARM setting off (or on for 1 hour)	START

3. If using the pressure-cooking setting, when the machine has finished cooking, use the **quick-release method** to return its pressure to normal.

4. Unlatch the lid and open the pot. Stir well before serving.

Beyond

- You must halve the recipe for a 3-litre cooker.

- For more flavour, add up to 1 tablespoon coriander seeds and/or 1 tablespoon yellow mustard seeds with the other ingredients.

- Put a handful of fresh bean sprouts in each bowl, ladle the soup on top and garnish with fresh coriander leaves as well as lime wedges to squeeze over each portion.

- For a bigger meal, serve the soup over cooked white or brown rice vermicelli.

Garlic Lovers' Chicken Curry

6 servings

If you're a fan of garlic, you know why you're here. But if you're a fan of sweeter curries, you've also come to the right place. There are so many onions (and then wine, plus sultanas) that the curry's overall finish is a good balance between those sweet flavours and the heady aroma from all that garlic.

This curry cooks for a shorter amount of time but with a natural release. We changed the pressure-release method because of the amount of (natural) sugar in the recipe. There's now less chance of sputtering. Plus, the immediate, rapid boil of a quick release would turn the sultanas to mush.

1. Mash the vinegar, garlic, ginger, coriander, cumin, cayenne, mustard powder, salt and cloves into a paste in a small bowl. Set aside.

2.

Press	Setting	Time	Press
SAUTÉ	MEDIUM, NORMAL or CUSTOM 150°C	15 minutes	START

3. Melt the butter in a **5.5-litre cooker.** Add the onions and cook, stirring often, until softened, about 10 minutes. Stir in the garlic paste and the sultanas; cook, stirring all the while, until fragrant, about 1 minute.

4. Add the chicken and stir well to coat in the spices and liquid. Pour in the stock and scrape up any browned bits on the pot's bottom. Turn off the **SAUTÉ** function and stir in the wine. Lock the lid onto the pot.

5.

Set the machine	Level	The valve must be	Time	Press
PRESSURE COOK	MAX	—	7 minutes with the KEEP WARM setting off	START
MEAT/ STEW, PRESSURE COOK or MANUAL	HIGH	Closed	10 minutes with the KEEP WARM setting off	START

6. When the machine has finished cooking, turn it off and let its pressure **return to normal naturally,** about 20 minutes. Unlatch the lid and open the cooker. Stir well before serving.

1 tablespoon white vinegar

6 medium garlic cloves, peeled and finely chopped (2 tablespoons prechopped)

1 tablespoon finely chopped peeled fresh root ginger

½ teaspoon ground coriander

½ teaspoon ground cumin

½ teaspoon ground cayenne

½ teaspoon mustard powder

½ teaspoon table salt

¼ teaspoon ground cloves

55g butter

3 medium onions, chopped (480g prechopped)

30g sultanas

1.2kg large boneless skinless chicken thighs (6–8 thighs), cut in half and trimmed of any large hunks of fat

250ml chicken stock

60ml sweet white wine, such as a Riesling, or unsweetened apple juice

Beyond

- For a 3-litre cooker, you must use 200ml stock and halve the remaining ingredients.

- For a 7.5-litre cooker, you must increase all the ingredients by 50 per cent except use 300ml stock.

- This curry needs cooked rice, particularly long-grain brown rice.

- Also serve this curry with lots of buttered, grilled bread (or maybe na'an).

60ml apple cider vinegar

2 teaspoons ground coriander

2 teaspoons ground cumin

1 teaspoon ground cardamom

1 teaspoon ground cinnamon

1 teaspoon table salt

1 teaspoon ground
black pepper

½ teaspoon ground cloves

1.3kg bone-in skinless
chicken thighs (about 8),
any large chunks of fat
removed

2 tablespoons vegetable,
corn or rapeseed oil

2 teaspoons fennel seeds

1 medium onion, chopped
(160g prechopped)

1 tablespoon finely chopped
peeled fresh root ginger

1 medium garlic clove,
peeled and finely chopped
(1 teaspoon prechopped)

180ml chicken stock

45g flaked almonds

60g tomato passata

1 tablespoon dark
brown sugar

12 dried apricots, halved

Chicken Sali Boti

6–8 servings

Sali boti (or sometimes *salli boti*) is a curry from Parsi ethnic groups who practise Zoroastrianism and have settled mostly in the western parts of modern-day India. We prefer the *jardaloo* (apricot) version for the way the dried fruit adds a tart pop against the spices.

The dish is commonly made with lamb (or even mutton), although there are vegetarian renditions. We felt that chicken thighs worked better in the Instant Pot because lamb ended up a little too strongly flavoured against the delicate spice blend. (Braising the meat in the oven would give the lamb a chance to mellow more than it does in the multi-cooker.)

There's no doubt that this one's got a lot of dried spices. It's also dramatic, even dinner-party worthy. You can't substitute a standard curry powder blend and get this very warming, aromatic mix. Stock up on spices and plan on making sali boti often.

1. Stir the vinegar, coriander, cumin, cardamom, cinnamon, salt, pepper and cloves in a large bowl to make a paste. Add the chicken thighs and toss well until thoroughly coated in the spice mixture. Set aside at room temperature for 15 minutes.

2.

Press	Setting	Time	Press
SAUTÉ	MEDIUM, NORMAL or CUSTOM 150°C	15 minutes	START

3. Warm the oil in a **5.5-litre cooker** for a minute or two. Add the fennel seeds and stir until toasted, about 1 minute. Add the onion, ginger and garlic. Cook, stirring often, just until the onion turns fragrant, about 2 minutes.

4. Add the chicken thighs and every last bit of spice from the bowl. Stir well, then cook, turning and rearranging occasionally, until lightly browned, about 10 minutes.

5. Pour in the stock and scrape up the browned bits on the pot's bottom. Turn off the **SAUTÉ** function. Stir in the almonds, tomato passata, brown sugar and apricots until the brown sugar dissolves. Lock the lid onto the pot.

6.

Set the machine	Level	The valve must be	Time	Press
PRESSURE COOK	MAX	—	15 minutes with the KEEP WARM setting off	START
MEAT/STEW, PRESSURE COOK or MANUAL	HIGH	Closed	18 minutes with the KEEP WARM setting off	START

7. When the machine has finished cooking, turn it off and let its pressure **return to normal naturally,** about 20 minutes. Unlatch the lid and open the pot. Stir well before serving.

Beyond

- For a 3-litre cooker, you must use 125ml stock and halve the remaining ingredients.

- For a 7.5-litre cooker, you must use 300ml stock and the stated amounts of the remaining ingredients. Or just double the recipe in a 7.5-litre cooker.

- If you can't find bone-in chicken thighs without skin, remove the slippery skin from the meat by gripping one loose end with a piece of kitchen paper and pulling the skin across and off the cut.

- Some versions of sali boti are made with potatoes, and this dish would indeed work well over mashed potatoes, particularly those mixed with soured cream and butter.

- For a more authentic flavour, substitute grated palm sugar for the brown sugar.

- For a sweeter dish, substitute 4 chopped dried pears for the dried apricots.

15g butter or 1 tablespoon ghee

1 small onion, chopped (80g prechopped)

3 medium garlic cloves, peeled and finely chopped (1 tablespoon prechopped)

1 tablespoon finely chopped peeled fresh root ginger

1 tablespoon garam masala

2 teaspoons white granulated sugar

1 teaspoon ground turmeric

1 teaspoon ground cumin

Up to 1 teaspoon ground cayenne

½ teaspoon table salt

1.2kg boneless skinless chicken breasts, cut into 5cm chunks

250ml low-fat coconut milk

125ml chicken stock

2 tablespoons tomato purée

60ml double cream

Chicken Tikka Masala

6 servings

Here's a take-away classic, morphed into a simple braise. Tikka masala is usually made with yoghurt. But because yoghurt can break under pressure, we use coconut milk for richness when cooking, then cream to finish the dish. That said, we had better success with low-fat coconut milk, which is not as heavy as full-fat.

1.

Press	Setting	Time	Press
SAUTÉ	MEDIUM, NORMAL or CUSTOM 150°C	10 minutes	START

2. Melt the butter or ghee in a **5.5- or 7.5-litre cooker**. Add the onion, garlic and ginger. Cook, stirring often, until the onion softens, about 3 minutes. Stir in the garam masala, sugar, turmeric, cumin, cayenne and salt until aromatic, just a few seconds.

3. Add the chicken and toss until the meat is well and evenly coated in the spices and aromatics. Pour in the coconut milk and stock. Add the tomato purée and stir until uniform. Turn off the **SAUTÉ** function and lock the lid onto the pot.

4.

Set the machine	Level	The valve must be	Time	Press
PRESSURE COOK	MAX	—	5 minutes with the KEEP WARM setting off	START
MEAT/STEW, PRESSURE COOK OR MANUAL	HIGH	Closed	7 minutes with the KEEP WARM setting off	START

5. Use the **quick-release method** to bring the pot's pressure back to normal. Unlatch the lid and open the cooker. Stir in the cream until uniform, then set the lid askew over the pot and set aside for 5 minutes to blend the flavours. Stir again before serving.

Beyond

- You must halve the recipe for a 3-litre cooker.
- Garnish the servings with toasted unsweetened coconut.
- Try using homemade garam masala (see page 226 for a blend that works with chicken).
- Although the pairing is not traditional, the curry is good with peas. Add 155g fresh shelled or frozen peas (do not thaw) with the onion. If you use peas, omit the sugar.

Curried Chicken Couscous Casserole

4–6 servings

Hardly a standard couscous dish, this one's a one-pot supper – sort of like curried fried rice (that is, with couscous standing in for the rice). There may be a little liquid in the pot, even after it's been set aside for 10 minutes at the end. Scoop portions off the top and keep stirring the remainder after each serving. That extra liquid will continue to be absorbed into the couscous as the dish sits.

1.

Press	Setting	Time	Press
SAUTÉ	MEDIUM, NORMAL or CUSTOM 150°C	10 minutes	START

2. Melt the butter or ghee in a **5.5- or 7.5-litre cooker.** Add the onion and cook, stirring often, until softened, about 4 minutes. Add the chicken and cook, stirring frequently, just until it loses its raw, pink colour, about 2 minutes.

3. Stir in the curry powder, cinnamon, cumin, salt and cloves to coat the chicken. Pour in the stock and scrape up any browned bits on the pot's bottom. Turn off the **SAUTÉ** function, then stir in the raisins and pistachios. Lock the lid onto the pot.

4.

Set the machine	Level	The valve must be	Time	Press
PRESSURE COOK	MAX	——	5 minutes with the KEEP WARM setting off	START
PRESSURE COOK or MANUAL	HIGH	Closed	7 minutes with the KEEP WARM setting off	START

5. Use the **quick-release method** to bring the pot's pressure back to normal. Unlatch the lid and open the pot. Stir in the couscous until uniform. Remove the insert from the pot and set the lid askew over the insert for 10 minutes so that the couscous can absorb the liquid and get tender. Stir again before serving.

30g butter or 2 tablespoons ghee

1 medium onion, chopped (160g prechopped)

675g boneless skinless chicken breasts, cut into 2.5cm chunks

2 teaspoons curry powder

½ teaspoon ground cinnamon

½ teaspoon ground cumin

½ teaspoon table salt

¼ teaspoon ground cloves

1 litre chicken stock

60g raisins

35g shelled unsalted pistachios

500g quick-cooking (or instant) couscous

Beyond

- You must halve the recipe for a 3-litre cooker.
- Try substituting chopped, pitted dates (preferably Medjool) for the raisins.
- Use a red curry powder blend for a hotter dish.
- Even with the curry powder, pass extra hot sauce, particularly sambal oelek.
- Top the servings with chopped, stemmed chard or spinach that's been sautéed with a little butter or ghee (and perhaps a splash of stock to stop the thinner bits of the greens sticking to the hot surface of the frying pan).

2 tablespoons vegetable,
corn or rapeseed oil

2 large onions, thinly sliced,
the rings separated

2 tablespoons yellow
curry powder

2 medium garlic cloves,
peeled and finely chopped
(2 teaspoons prechopped)

2 large tomatoes, chopped

90g desiccated coconut

1.2kg beef rump, trimmed
and cut into 5cm pieces

250ml beef or chicken stock

3 tablespoons mango chutney

One 10cm cinnamon stick

1 bay leaf

Savoury-Sweet Beef and Tomato Curry

6 servings

Fresh tomatoes are a bit of an unusual ingredient in a curry. Unsweetened coconut is, too (although plenty of curries use coconut milk). But both the tomatoes and the coconut add a natural sweetness that blends nicely with beef, aromatic vegetables and spices.

1.

Press	Setting	Time	Press
SAUTÉ	MEDIUM, NORMAL or CUSTOM 150°C	10 minutes	START

2. Warm the oil in a **5.5- or 7.5-litre cooker** for a minute or two. Add the onions and cook, stirring often, just until they begin to soften, about 5 minutes. Stir in the curry powder and garlic until fragrant, just a few seconds.

3. Add the tomatoes and coconut. Cook, stirring occasionally, until the tomatoes begin to break down, about 4 minutes. Turn off the **SAUTÉ** function. Stir in the beef, stock, chutney, cinnamon stick and bay leaf until the chutney melts. Lock the lid onto the pot.

4.

Set the machine	Level	The valve must be	Time	Press
PRESSURE COOK	MAX	——	30 minutes with the KEEP WARM setting off	START
MEAT/STEW, PRESSURE COOK or MANUAL	HIGH	Closed	40 minutes with the KEEP WARM setting off	START

5. When the machine has finished cooking, turn it off and let its pressure **return to normal naturally**, about 30 minutes. Unlatch the lid and open the cooker. Remove and discard the cinnamon stick and bay leaf. Stir well before serving.

Beyond
- You must halve the recipe for a 3-litre cooker.
- This curry is so heavily spiced, it would go well over Brown Rice and Lentils (page 404), Barley Pilaf (page 406) or Buckwheat Pilaf (page 407).

Choose-Your-Colour Beef and Potato Curry

6 servings

The standard paste we would use in a recipe like this one is massaman curry paste, especially because of the potatoes, common in this style of dish. But don't stand on ceremony. There are plenty of aromatics in the dish's mix, so any curry paste will work, a blend of flavours to match your taste. This one's not quite a road map recipe. But it can become a signature recipe when you find the curry paste you prefer. (Notice that the second cooking is only at HIGH pressure, even in a Max machine.)

1.

Press	Setting	Time	Press
SAUTÉ	MEDIUM, NORMAL or CUSTOM 150°C	5 minutes	START

2. Warm the oil in a **5.5- or 7.5-litre cooker** for a minute or two. Add the curry paste and stir until toasty, about 1 minute. Add the beef, cinnamon stick, cardamom pods and cloves. Stir until the beef is well coated in the curry paste.

3. Turn off the **SAUTÉ** function. Stir in the coconut milk and brown sugar until the brown sugar dissolves. Lock the lid onto the pot.

4.

Set the machine	Level	The valve must be	Time	Press
PRESSURE COOK	MAX	——	30 minutes with the KEEP WARM setting off	START
MEAT/STEW, PRESSURE COOK OR MANUAL	HIGH	Closed	40 minutes with the KEEP WARM setting off	START

5. When the machine has finished cooking, turn it off and let its pressure **return to normal naturally**, about 25 minutes. Unlatch the lid and open the cooker. Stir in the potatoes. Lock the lid back onto the pot.

6.

Set the machine	Level	The valve must be	Time	Press
MEAT/STEW, PRESSURE COOK, or MANUAL	HIGH	Closed	5 minutes with the KEEP WARM setting off	START

7. Use the **quick-release method** to bring the pot's pressure back to normal. Unlatch the lid and open the cooker. Remove and discard the cinnamon stick, cardamom pods and whole cloves. Stir again to serve.

1 tablespoon vegetable, corn or rapeseed oil

2 tablespoons wet red, yellow, green, massaman or Penang curry paste

1.3kg beef rump, cut into 5cm pieces

One 10cm cinnamon stick

6 cardamom pods

10 whole cloves

250ml regular or low-fat coconut milk

125ml beef or chicken stock

2 tablespoons dark brown sugar

675g baby potatoes, each no larger than a ping-pong ball, halved

Beyond

- You must halve the recipe for a 3-litre cooker.
- To make a massaman curry paste, stem and deseed 2 dried red chillies, then pour boiling water over them in a large bowl. Leave to soak for 10 minutes. Drain, reserving the soaking liquid. Place the chillies in a blender. Add 1 medium shallot, quartered, 4 large, peeled garlic cloves, 1 thinly sliced lemongrass stalk (white part only), one 2.5cm piece of fresh root ginger, peeled and quartered, 1 teaspoon ground cinnamon, 1 teaspoon ground cardamom, 1 teaspoon salt, ½ teaspoon ground cloves, ½ teaspoon grated nutmeg and 6 fresh coriander sprigs (including the stems). Cover and blend until smooth, adding a little soaking liquid to get a smooth paste. For a more authentic flavour, omit the salt and add 1 teaspoon shrimp paste. Store, covered, in a small container in the fridge for up to 1 week or freeze for up to 3 months.

2 teaspoons ground coriander

2 teaspoons ground ginger

1 teaspoon ground cinnamon

½ teaspoon ground cloves

½ teaspoon ground cumin

½ teaspoon ground turmeric

Up to ½ teaspoon ground cayenne

½ teaspoon table salt

1.2kg piece beef rump, cut into 5cm pieces

2 tablespoons vegetable, corn or rapeseed oil

1 medium onion, chopped (160g prechopped)

500ml beef or chicken stock

60ml dry, light white wine, such as Pinot Grigio

90g dried wheat berries, preferably spring white wheat berries

60g small pitted green olives

1 tablespoon honey

East-West Beef Curry with Wheat Berries

4 to 6 servings

We've fused the aromas of a curry – even created a unique spice blend – with a more Western flavour profile that includes wine and olives, giving a sort of Mediterranean undertow to the dish. We did all this because the curry is stocked with wheat berries. It's a decidedly different take on the standard curry, sort of a global bowlful, best on a cold night.

1. Stir the coriander, ginger, cinnamon, cloves, cumin, turmeric, cayenne and salt in a large bowl. Add the beef and toss until the pieces are evenly coated in the spices.

2.

Press	Setting	Time	Press
SAUTÉ	MEDIUM, NORMAL or CUSTOM 150°C	20 minutes	START

3. Warm the oil in a **5.5-litre cooker** for a minute or two. Add the onion and cook, stirring often, until softened, about 4 minutes. Add the meat and every last speck of dried spice from the bowl. Cook, stirring occasionally, until lightly browned, about 10 minutes.

4. Pour in the stock and scrape up *every speck of browned stuff* on the pot's bottom. Turn off the **SAUTÉ** function. Stir in the wine, wheat berries, olives and honey until the honey dissolves. Lock the lid onto the pot.

5.

Set the machine	Level	The valve must be	Time	Press
PRESSURE COOK	MAX	—	35 minutes with the KEEP WARM setting off	START
MEAT/STEW, PRESSURE COOK or MANUAL	HIGH	Closed	45 minutes with the KEEP WARM setting off	START

6. When the machine has finished cooking, turn it off and let its pressure **return to normal naturally,** about 35 minutes. Unlatch the lid and open the cooker. Stir well before serving.

Beyond

- You must halve the recipe for a 3-litre cooker.

- For a 7.5-litre cooker, you must increase the stock to 600ml but use the remaining ingredients as stated.

- Substitute dried Kamut berries for a more buttery flavour in the curry.

- Or substitute dried rye berries for an earthier yet more herbal flavour on top of the spices.

- To skip the wine, decrease the stock to 435ml and add 60ml unsweetened apple juice.

Pork Shoulder Curry

4 servings

It seems almost sacrilegious to make curry with pork, yet we couldn't resist the hearty flavours of one made with pork shoulder. This one bends a little more South East Asian in its flavours with the rice vinegar and soy sauce, a sour curry with earthy notes from the turmeric.

1 teaspoon ground turmeric

½ teaspoon ground cinnamon

½ teaspoon ground black pepper

¼ teaspoon ground cloves

1.2kg piece boneless skinless pork shoulder, trimmed of any large hunks of fat, the meat cut into 5cm pieces

2 tablespoons vegetable, corn or rapeseed oil

2 medium shallots, peeled and quartered

1 tablespoon finely chopped peeled fresh root ginger

3 medium garlic cloves, peeled and finely chopped (1 tablespoon prechopped)

60ml unseasoned rice vinegar

2 tablespoons soy sauce

250ml chicken stock

40g chopped kale leaves

1. Stir the turmeric, cinnamon, pepper and cloves in a large bowl until uniform. Add the pork chunks and toss well until they are all coated evenly in the spice mixture.

2.

Press	Setting	Time	Press
SAUTÉ	MEDIUM, NORMAL or CUSTOM 150°C	10 minutes	START

3. Warm the oil in a **5.5-litre cooker** for a minute or two. Add the shallots, ginger and garlic. Cook, stirring quite often, until the shallot starts to soften, 2–3 minutes. Add the meat and every last speck of spice in the bowl. Cook, stirring and rearranging once in a while, until all the meat has lost its raw, pink colour, about 3 minutes.

4. Pour in the vinegar and soy sauce; scrape up any browned bits on the pot's bottom. Turn off the **SAUTÉ** function, pour in the stock and stir well. Lock the lid onto the pot.

5.

Set the machine	Level	The valve must be	Time	Press
PRESSURE COOK	MAX	—	25 minutes with the KEEP WARM setting off	START
MEAT/STEW, PRESSURE COOK or MANUAL	HIGH	Closed	35 minutes with the KEEP WARM setting off	START

6. When the machine has finished cooking, turn it off and let its pressure **return to normal naturally**, about 30 minutes. Unlatch the lid and open the cooker. Stir in the kale. Lock the lid back onto the pot.

7.

Set the machine	Level	The valve must be	Time	Press
MEAT/STEW, PRESSURE COOK, OR MANUAL	HIGH	Closed	5 minutes with the KEEP WARM setting off	START

8. Use the **quick-release method** to bring the pot's pressure back to normal. Unlatch the lid and open the cooker. Stir well before serving.

Beyond

- You must halve the recipe for a 3-litre cooker.

- For a 7.5-litre cooker, you must increase the stock to 320ml and use the remaining ingredients as stated.

- Skip long-grain white rice and serve over cornmeal grits.

- Take things to another level with fresh turmeric. Omit the ground and add 1 tablespoon fresh finely chopped peeled turmeric with the ginger.

- For a more traditional flavour, substitute boneless lamb shoulder, cut into 5cm pieces, for the pork.

40g butter

3 medium onions, roughly chopped

2 medium garlic cloves, peeled and finely chopped (2 teaspoons prechopped)

2 teaspoons finely chopped peeled fresh root ginger

675g boneless centre-cut pork loin chops, cut into 4cm cubes

1½ tablespoons yellow curry powder

1 tablespoon garam masala

500ml chicken stock

450g carrots, peeled and cut into 5cm pieces

1 tablespoon tomato purée

2 tablespoons soy sauce

1 tablespoon cornflour or potato starch

The Pork Curry That Every Japanese Mum Makes

4 servings

If you watch as much Japanese TV as we do (you don't?), you know there's a certain pork curry that's a home staple, one of those childhood meals that becomes comfort food for adults. It seems as if every kid who has a bad day ends up eating this stuff! So here's our version, simplified for the Instant Pot and tweaked for the Western supermarket.

Most Japanese pork curries use a boxed 'curry roux', but we can build those flavours by starting with butter, then ending with tomato purée and soy sauce. Most Japanese versions also use quick-cooking shredded pork; but we feel that the centre-cut pork chops give the dish more heartiness, and are easily cubed.

1.

Press	Setting	Time	Press
SAUTÉ	MEDIUM, NORMAL or CUSTOM 150°C	10 minutes	START

2. Melt the butter in a **5.5- or 7.5-litre cooker**. Add the onions and cook, stirring often, until they begin to soften, about 5 minutes. Add the garlic and ginger; cook, stirring all the while, until fragrant, just a few seconds.

3. Add the meat and toss well until coated in the butter and aromatics. Stir in the curry powder and garam masala; keep stirring until the meat is evenly coated. Turn off the **SAUTÉ** function and pour in the stock. Stir in the carrots until uniform, then lock the lid onto the pot.

4.

Set the machine	Level	The valve must be	Time	Press
PRESSURE COOK	MAX	——	12 minutes with the KEEP WARM setting off	START
MEAT/STEW, PRESSURE COOK or MANUAL	HIGH	Closed	15 minutes with the KEEP WARM setting off	START

5. Use the **quick-release method** to bring the pot's pressure back to normal. Unlatch the lid and open the cooker. Stir in the tomato purée until uniform.

6.

Press	Setting	Time	Press
SAUTÉ	MEDIUM, NORMAL or CUSTOM 150°C	5 minutes	START

7. As the sauce comes to a bubble in the pot, whisk the soy sauce and cornflour or potato starch in a small bowl until smooth. Once the sauce is at a good simmer, stir this slurry into it and cook until thickened, no more than 1 minute. Turn off the **SAUTÉ** function and remove the *hot* insert from the pot. Set the lid askew on top of the insert and set aside for 5 minutes to blend the flavours.

Beyond

- You must halve the recipe for a 3-litre cooker.

- Always serve this curry alongside white rice, preferably a medium-grain rice.

- Search for Japanese pickled vegetables, like daikon or carrots, to serve as a garnish.

- For a more authentic flavour, omit the curry powder and garam masala and use 2½ tablespoons of a ready-made Asian curry powder, such as S & B Oriental Curry Powder, Asian Boy Curry Powder, or Golden Smell Curry Powder.

2 tablespoons peanut oil

3 medium red onions,
halved and sliced into
thin half-moons

2 tablespoons finely chopped
peeled fresh root ginger

1 teaspoon coriander seeds

1 teaspoon fennel seeds

1 teaspoon whole cloves

One 5cm cinnamon stick

½ teaspoon table salt

½ teaspoon ground
black pepper

1.3kg boned leg of lamb,
trimmed of any big pieces
of fat, the meat cut into
4cm pieces

180ml chicken stock

2 tablespoons red
wine vinegar

1 tablespoon tomato purée

Lamb Curry 101

6 servings

Here's our basic lamb curry, an aromatic mix with lots of seeds and spices to bump up the flavours and pair them with the lamb. We use leg of lamb because it's less fatty than lamb shoulder. It also cooks a little more quickly than shoulder meat, without a tendency to break into squishy bits under pressure. By the way, the cloves are edible after cooking under pressure (but may be irritating to those not expecting them).

1.

Press	Setting	Time	Press
SAUTÉ	MEDIUM, NORMAL or CUSTOM 150°C	10 minutes	START

2. Warm the oil in a **5.5-litre cooker** for a minute or two. Add the onions and cook, stirring often, until softened, about 5 minutes. Stir in the ginger and cook until aromatic, just a few seconds. Add the coriander, fennel, cloves, cinnamon stick, salt and pepper. Stir well for a few seconds until the spices are evenly distributed in the onions.

3. Add the meat and stir over the heat until the pieces are evenly coated in the onion and spice mixture. Turn off the **SAUTÉ** function, then stir in the stock, vinegar and tomato purée until uniform. Lock the lid onto the pot.

4.

Set the machine	Level	The valve must be	Time	Press
PRESSURE COOK	MAX	—	35 minutes with the KEEP WARM setting off	START
MEAT/ STEW, PRESSURE COOK or MANUAL	HIGH	Closed	45 minutes with the KEEP WARM setting off	START
SLOW COOK	HIGH	Opened	4 hours with the KEEP WARM setting off (or on for no more than 3 hours)	START

5. If you've used a pressure setting, when the machine has finished cooking, turn it off and let its pressure **return to normal naturally,** about 30 minutes. Unlatch the lid and open the cooker. Stir well; discard the cinnamon stick and the whole cloves before serving.

Beyond

- For a 3-litre cooker, you must use 125ml stock and halve the remaining ingredients.

- For a 7.5-litre cooker, you must increase *all* the ingredients by 50 per cent.

- If you like, substitute 30g butter or ghee for the oil.

- For a beef curry, use 1.3kg rump, cut into 4cm pieces.

- Serve over long-grain white rice that's been tossed with butter and a little soy sauce.

Pub-Style Korma

6 servings

The type of korma served in pubs in the UK is not an authentic korma, but it has become a classic British comfort food, often made with nuts for richness as well as lots of coconut milk. We've adapted the traditional technique by creating a nut-and-spice mixture in a blender, then using this wet 'sauce' in the Instant Pot as a vehicle for chunks of lamb.

1. Put the cashews, shallot, chilli, garlic, ginger, garam masala, fennel seeds, coriander, cumin, turmeric and salt in a large blender. Pour in the stock and coconut milk. Cover and blend until smooth, stopping the machine at least once to scrape down the inside.

2. Pour and scrape every drop of the spice mixture into a 5.5- or 7.5-litre cooker. Add the lamb and stir until all the pieces are coated in the spice mixture. Lock the lid onto the pot.

3.

Set the machine	Level	The valve must be	Time	Press
PRESSURE COOK	MAX	——	35 minutes with the KEEP WARM setting off	START
MEAT/STEW, PRESSURE COOK or MANUAL	HIGH	Closed	45 minutes with the KEEP WARM setting off	START
SLOW COOK	HIGH	Opened	4 hours with the KEEP WARM setting off (or on for no more than 3 hours)	START

4. If you've used a pressure setting, when the machine has finished cooking, turn it off and let its pressure **return to normal naturally,** about 30 minutes.

5. Unlatch the lid and open the cooker.

6.

Press	Setting	Time	Press
SAUTÉ	MEDIUM, NORMAL OR CUSTOM 150°C	5 minutes	START

7. Bring the sauce to a simmer, stirring frequently. Stir in the tomato purée until smooth. Continue cooking, stirring often, until thickened a bit, about like a wet gravy, 2–4 minutes. Turn off the **SAUTÉ** function, remove the *hot* insert from the machine and set the lid askew over the insert for 5 minutes to blend the flavours. Stir well before serving.

50g roasted unsalted cashews

1 large shallot, peeled and quartered

1 medium serrano chilli, stemmed, halved lengthways and deseeded (if desired)

5 medium garlic cloves, peeled

1½ tablespoons finely chopped peeled fresh root ginger

1 tablespoon garam masala

1½ teaspoons fennel seeds

1½ teaspoons ground coriander

1½ teaspoons ground cumin

1½ teaspoons ground turmeric

1 teaspoon table salt

350ml chicken stock

180ml regular coconut milk or coconut cream

1.3kg boned leg of lamb, trimmed of any large chunks of fat, the meat cut into 4cm pieces

3 tablespoons tomato purée

Beyond

- You must halve the recipe for a 3-litre cooker.

- Although long-grain white rice is the traditional accompaniment, we prefer this curry over large cubes of toasted bread.

- Or even over chips, the way it would be served in some pubs.

2 tablespoons vegetable, corn or rapeseed oil

3 medium leeks (about 125g each), white and pale green parts only, halved lengthways, well washed, and thinly sliced

1 tablespoon finely chopped peeled fresh root ginger

1½ teaspoons ground coriander

1½ teaspoons mild paprika

1½ teaspoons ground turmeric

1 teaspoon ground cinnamon

Up to ½ teaspoon ground cayenne

½ teaspoon table salt

1.3kg boned leg of lamb, any large chunks of fat removed, the meat cut into 4cm pieces

250ml chicken stock

125ml buttermilk

2 tablespoons orange marmalade

South-African-Style Lamb Curry

6 servings

Curry is global fare. Here's a version from South Africa that uses buttermilk for a tangy richness. The buttermilk can break under pressure, so we stir it in at the end, then simmer it a little to mellow the flavours and thicken the sauce (with help from orange marmalade, which brings everything into balance).

1.

Press	Setting	Time	Press
SAUTÉ	MEDIUM, NORMAL or CUSTOM 150°C	5 minutes	START

2. Warm the oil in a **5.5- or 7.5-litre cooker** for a minute or two. Add the leeks and root ginger; cook, stirring often, until softened, about 3 minutes. Stir in the coriander, paprika, turmeric, cinnamon, cayenne and salt until fragrant, just a few seconds.

3. Add the lamb and toss until the meat is thoroughly coated in the spices and aromatics. Pour in the stock and stir well. Turn off the **SAUTÉ** function and lock the lid onto the pot.

4.

Set the machine	Level	The valve must be	Time	Press
PRESSURE COOK	MAX	—	35 minutes with the KEEP WARM setting off	START
MEAT/STEW, PRESSURE COOK or MANUAL	HIGH	Closed	45 minutes with the KEEP WARM setting off	START
SLOW COOK	HIGH	Opened	4 hours with the KEEP WARM setting off (or on for no more than 3 hours)	START

5. If you've used a pressure setting, when the machine has finished cooking, turn it off and let its pressure **return to normal naturally**, about 30 minutes.

6. Unlatch the lid and open the cooker.

7.

Press	Setting	Time	Press
SAUTÉ	MEDIUM, NORMAL or CUSTOM 150°C	5 minutes	START

8. Stir in the buttermilk and marmalade as the sauce comes to a simmer. Continue cooking, stirring almost constantly, until a little thickened and reduced, about 2 minutes. Turn off the **SAUTÉ** function and set the lid askew over the pot for 5 minutes to blend the flavours. Stir again before serving.

Beyond

- You must halve the recipe for a 3-litre cooker.

- Not all marmalades are created equal. Some are just jelly; others have large bits of orange in the mixture. Some are 'sweet marmalades', probably too sweet for the lamb. The best would be a marmalade made from bitter oranges, by a brand such as Dundee.

- Or substitute lemon or even lime marmalade for a more bitter pop.

Road Map: Thai Seafood Curry

4–6 servings

Thai curry is a spicy hotchpotch, made with coconut milk and lots of fresh vegetables, best served over *short-grain* white rice or white or brown rice noodles. There's one warning, however. The fish or shellfish will get done at varying times, a little difficult to note exactly in a road map recipe. If you see that the fish bits are done but the prawns aren't quite pink yet, turn off the SAUTÉ function and set the lid askew over the pot for a couple of minutes so that the prawns (in this case) cook in the residual heat. As a general rule, avoid oily fish (like salmon or trout) or thin, white-fleshed fish fillets (like sole or tilapia).

1.

Press	Setting	Time	Press
SAUTÉ	MEDIUM, NORMAL Or CUSTOM 150°C	10 minutes	START

2. Warm the oil in a **5.5- or 7.5-litre cooker** for a minute or two. Add the allium aromatics and cook, stirring often, until softened, 2–4 minutes. Add the root ginger and cook until aromatic, just a few seconds.

3. Stir in the wet curry paste until everything is well coated; then add the tomatoes, coconut milk, lime juice, brown sugar and fish sauce. Stir until the brown sugar has dissolved, then turn off the **SAUTÉ** function and lock the lid onto the pot.

4.

Set the machine	Level	The valve must be	Time	Press
PRESSURE COOK	MAX	—	5 minutes with the KEEP WARM setting off	START
MEAT/STEW, PRESSURE COOK or MANUAL	HIGH	Closed	7 minutes with the KEEP WARM setting off	START

5. Use the **quick-release method** to bring the pot's pressure back to normal. Unlatch the lid and open the pot.

6.

Press	Setting	Time	Press
SAUTÉ	MEDIUM, NORMAL or CUSTOM 150°C	5 minutes	START

7. Bring the sauce to a full simmer. Stir in the fish or shellfish and the quick-cooking vegetables. Continue cooking, stirring gently, until the shellfish or fish is cooked through, 3–5 minutes. Turn off the **SAUTÉ** function, remove the *hot* insert from the machine, and serve warm.

2 tablespoons oil
Choose from peanut oil, coconut oil or any neutral-flavoured oil you like: vegetable, corn, safflower, rapeseed, avocado or grapeseed.

250g chopped allium aromatics
Choose from one or two onions (of any sort), spring onions, leeks (white and pale green parts only, well washed) and/or shallots.

Up to 15g finely chopped peeled fresh ginger

Up to 2 tablespoons wet curry paste
Choose from red, green or yellow Thai curry paste, or even massaman or Penang curry paste.

One 400g tin chopped tomatoes

250ml regular or low-fat coconut milk

1½ tablespoons fresh lime juice

1½ tablespoons light brown sugar

1½ tablespoons fish sauce (nam pla)

675g fish or shellfish
Choose from peeled and deveined medium prawns, scallops, swordfish fillets cut into 5cm cubes, monkfish fillets cut into 5cm pieces, cod fillets cut into 5cm pieces, hake fillets cut into 5cm pieces or halibut fillets cut into 2.5cm pieces.

450g chopped quick-cooking vegetables
Choose one or two from trimmed green or runner beans, courgettes, yellow summer squash, stemmed and deseeded peppers, cored Chinese cabbage, Chinese water spinach, cauliflower or broccoli florets, and sugar snap peas.

Beyond

- You must halve the recipe for a 3-litre cooker.

- For a hotter curry, add 2–5 small, hot, red or green chillies (like bird's-eye), stemmed and split.

2 tablespoons vegetable, corn
or rapeseed oil

1 medium red onion, chopped

2 medium garlic cloves,
peeled and finely chopped
(2 teaspoons prechopped)

2 tablespoons finely chopped
peeled fresh root ginger

1 tablespoon yellow
curry powder

2 teaspoons mild
smoked paprika

½ teaspoon table salt

Two 400g tins chopped
tomatoes with chillies

450g frozen sliced okra
(do not thaw)

125ml water

675g skinless cod fillets,
cut into 10–12 pieces

Curried Cod with Tomatoes and Okra

6 servings

Okra is such a common ingredient in curries that we felt we needed to include it in at least one recipe. Where we live in rural New England, we can only find fresh okra at an East Indian grocery store over an hour away. However, we can always find frozen okra at our local supermarket, and the frozen works better in the Instant Pot anyway (less slime, a better texture). We advocate for a much hotter curry here and get the burn by using tinned chopped tomatoes with chillies. But you can use regular chopped tomatoes and pass bottled hot sauce at the table.

1.

Press	Setting	Time	Press
SAUTÉ	MEDIUM, NORMAL or CUSTOM 150°C	10 minutes	START

2. Warm the oil in a **5.5- or 7.5-litre cooker** for a minute or two. Add the onion and cook, stirring often, until softened, about 5 minutes. Add the garlic and ginger; cook until aromatic, stirring all the while, maybe half a minute. Stir in the curry powder, smoked paprika and salt until fragrant, just a few seconds.

3. Pour in the tomatoes and scrape up any browned bits on the pot's bottom. Turn off the **SAUTÉ** function and stir in the okra and water. Lock the lid onto the pot.

4.

Set the machine	Level	The valve must be	Time	Press
PRESSURE COOK	MAX	—	4 minutes with the KEEP WARM setting off	START
PRESSURE COOK or MANUAL	HIGH	Closed	5 minutes with the KEEP WARM setting off	START

5. Use the **quick-release method** to bring the pot's pressure back to normal. Unlatch the lid and open the cooker. Nestle the cod pieces into the sauce. Set the lid askew over the pot.

6.

Press	Setting	Time	Press
SAUTÉ	LOW or LESS	10 minutes	START

7. Simmer the cod in the sauce until cooked through, about 10 minutes. Turn off the **SAUTÉ** function and remove the *hot* insert from the pot to stop the cooking. Serve warm.

Beyond

- You must halve the recipe for a 3-litre cooker.
- This curry needs rice in the bowls, preferably *brown* basmati for an earthier finish.
- For a sweeter finish to the curry, add 1 chopped medium carrot with the onion.
- Substitute swordfish fillets for the cod – or thinner, white-fleshed, skinless fillets like sea bass, but cook thin fillets for only 2–3 minutes in the sauce.

Curried Prawns with Rice Vermicelli

6 servings

Here's a simple, speedy curry made with rice noodles right in the pot. Remember that the world does not revolve around curry powder. You could substitute other curry powders, even garam masala, a warming blend of dried spices without any heat (see page 226). Red curry powders can be quite hot, thanks to an abundance of cayenne. Check the labels to make sure you end up with one that suits your taste. Note that the dish can only be cooked on HIGH, even in a Max machine.

1. Mix the stock, soy sauce, rice vinegar, curry powder and sambal oelek in a **5.5- or 7.5-litre cooker**. Break the vermicelli to fit in the pot and set them in the sauce. Lay the prawns over the noodles and sauce, then pour the frozen mixed vegetables in an even layer on top. Lock the lid onto the pot.

2.

Set the machine	Level	The valve must be	Time	Press
PRESSURE COOK or MANUAL	HIGH	Closed	0 minutes with the KEEP WARM setting off	START

3. *The moment* the float valve (or pin) pops up to lock the lid onto the pot and the machine stops putting out steam, turn off the machine and let the pressure **return to normal naturally** for 3 minutes. Then use the **quick-release method** to release any residual pressure in the pot. Unlatch the lid and open the pot. Stir well before serving.

700ml chicken stock

90ml soy sauce

2 tablespoons rice vinegar

1 tablespoon yellow curry powder

Up to 1 tablespoon sambal oelek

225g dried rice vermicelli

340g small shell-on prawns, peeled and deveined

450g mixed frozen vegetables for stir-fry, any seasoning packets discarded (do not thaw)

Beyond

- This recipe does not work well in a 3-litre cooker because the noodles have to be broken into too many, very small pieces.

- If you can't find small prawns, use peeled and deveined king prawns but cut each one lengthways in half.

- If you don't want to use (or buy) sambal oelek, use your favourite hot sauce.

7

All Things Steamed and Cooked *with the* Sous Vide Method

Without a doubt, this chapter is the most 'gourmet', the most cheffy. Technically, lots of dishes in a pressure cooker are steamed. But this chapter isn't about steaming a head of cauliflower (see page 428). Or making perfect whole grains (page 395). It's about using the pot's naturally steamy environment (and the attendant pressure) to make some pretty impressive meals, such as a a giant crabcake in a Bundt tin, a family-friendly meatloaf and some of the best-ever fried–yes, fried–chicken. This chapter is mostly not about 'dinner in minutes'. It's about upping your Instant Pot game, although a pot of steamed clams is awfully quick and tasty (see page 275).

This chapter also holds the recipes for the sous vide technique (French, *soo-veed*, 'under'–or in–'a vacuum'). Basically, sous vide involves cooking food in an anaerobic environment at a low temperature to tenderise the interstitial cartilage without compromising any internal texture or losing any moisture.

Okay, wow, a lot–so let's break that down. An anaerobic environment is one without air, or more specifically, without oxygen (thus, the 'vide' or vacuum in the terminology). We want to remove the air so that, ahem, bad bugs have nothing to live on as the meat or fish cooks below the temperature 'kill point' for bacteria. So we seal the food in bags, as you'll see.

The low cooking temperature–way lower than what an oven can handle, even lower than the boiling point of water–is somewhere around 51°C. Maintaining that temperature in the pot, we then immerse the food in the warm water. And since the food is in a bag, it can't be waterlogged. We go to all this trouble so that the food is the most tender imaginable–and 1) we can get steaks that are rare edge to edge without a dried-out exterior, 2) we can actually eat super-tender but also rare short ribs that can be crunched up on the grill for just a minute or two, 3) we can set eggs to a ridiculously jammy centre, and 4) we can keep fish fillets moist and flavourful.

The Max machine allows you to turn the Instant Pot into a sous vide device without any other gadget. (Most sous vide cooking is done with an immersion circulator attached to a big pot of water.) The notion that the pot can make this jump to a cheffy level is pretty revolutionary in and of itself, even if cooking short ribs or a brisket by the sous vide method isn't right for a run-of-the-mill weeknight.

Because of the size and shape of the pot, the sous vide recipes don't make large quantities. There has to be enough room for the warm water's convection currents to circulate around the food. In the end, use these sous vide recipes as a way to introduce yourself to the technique. If you like what happens, try another recipe, then another, and soon you'll buy an immersion circulator, have a big pot of water with a dozen short ribs on the countertop for a dinner party and step off on the road to cheffy bliss.

Before you go, we need to address one or two safety concerns. Sous vide works because there is *no* air inside the bag that holds the food. Some online sous vide mavens are pretty lazy when it comes to this point. 'Oh, just get the air out as good as you can,' they say.

No, do it better. Get *all* the air out of the bag. Those so-called experts are trying to sell website clicks. They're not concerned about your safety.

We'll get to the specifics below in the FAQs, then the recipes themselves. And although sous vide is an Instant Pot game-changer, more than half of the recipes in this chapter can be used in any Instant Pot model. These recipes ask you to steam food as the first step in a culinary process that results in maximum rewards: not plain old broccoli florets or carrot spears but State Fair Turkey Legs (page 265) and some astonishing Brisket Skewers (page 266).

So head off to some of the most inventive dishes in the book. They'll help you use the pot to take your cooking to the next level.

FAQs

1. Okay, fine. But I still just want to open the pot and eat dinner. What's the deal?
In this chapter, head to the Down-Home Meatloaf (page 270), the Prawn Boil (page 278) and the Crabcake (page 276). Unlatch the lid and voilà! But after those and a few more, hie thee to other chapters. Some of this chapter's remaining recipes are more complicated. Without even mentioning the sous vide recipes, many of the steamed ones ask you to do something with the food once it's out of the pot: fry the chicken, crisp the steaks, grill the brisket skewers. Most of us got into pressure cooking because we wanted to get out of the kitchen quickly. Most of the recipes in this

book are set up so we can. They're just not the bulk of this chapter.

2. Can I make the sous vide recipes in a machine other than the Max?
No. Only the Max has the capabilities to maintain the low temperature for safe and proper cooking. If you have another model of Instant Pot, you can, of course, make any of these sous vide recipes with a more traditional sous vide immersion circulator set up either on the side of the pot you have (preferably a **7.5-litre cooker**) or in a larger casserole. But the trouble may not be worth it. Yes, some cooks have been using older models of the Instant Pot to make a sort of ad hoc sous vide machine. Such experiments are ill-advised. The recipes in this chapter are for smaller portions because of the narrowness of the Instant Pot's insert and the way convection currents have to move around the sealed bags.

3. Why do you give the thickness of the meat in the sous vide recipes?
Because in this specialised technique, the thickness is as important as the weight. In fact, the timings are *based* on the thickness. A 2.5cm steak that is 10cm long will cook via the sous vide method at the same rate as a 2.5cm steak that's 20 or even 25cm long. It's all about how the heat comes through the surface plane of the cut to permeate the core. Since sous vide is a professional chef's favourite trick, one would expect precision to be part of the game.

4. What's the water bath method for removing air in the bags?

First off, the best tool for removing air from the bags is a vacuum sealer. Unfortunately, it's an expensive gadget. More importantly, it pulls any liquids (along with the air) out of the bag. Some sealers have a so-called 'moist setting'. We find that even this function pulls most of the liquid out. (We tried and tried to make it work.) Sometimes, it's best to lean to the water bath method.

Put the food and any marinade in a zip-sealed plastic bag of the size we recommend. Fill a large bowl or pot with water. You can use water already in the Instant Pot insert for the sous vide process, so long as the machine has not yet been turned on and the water's still cool. With the bag open, grasp the two corners at the ends of the sealing strip and *slowly* lower the filled bag into the water. (Note the operative, italicised word in that sentence.) The surrounding water will push the air out of the bag as it's submerged. When the water level is right at the sealing strip, zip the bag closed and pull it out of the water.

5. If I'm putting something under sous vide for days, can I just leave the pot alone?

No. Please refer to the Max machine's instruction manual. You must open the lid occasionally and check the water level. It may have dropped. You may need to add more water. And you can't just add cold water or you'll throw the cooking time off and may induce food safety problems. You'll need to heat water on the hob to about the temperature of the water in the cooker (use an instant-read meat thermometer to be sure). Then add that warm water to the pot and lock the lid on top again.

2 tablespoons flavourful solid or liquid fat

Choose from room-temperature butter, room-temperature rendered bacon fat, room-temperature schmaltz, olive oil, avocado oil, walnut oil, pecan oil, hazelnut oil or peanut oil.

2 tablespoons dried herb or a dried herb blend

Choose several to make the full amount from dried basil, chives, marjoram, parsley, rosemary, oregano, sage, savory, tarragon or thyme – or choose a single spice blend such as Cajun, Italian, Greek, curry powder, herbes de Provence, za'atar or another favourite.

1 teaspoon sea salt flakes

One 1.6–1.8kg whole chicken, any giblets or neck removed

500ml chicken stock or water

Beyond

- Add up to 1 tablespoon liquid smoke to the water for a pseudo-smoked chicken.

- If you've used ready-made stock (and not liquid smoke), the liquid after cooking in the pot has become rich and highly seasoned. Strain it and freeze it to use in place of or along with ready-made stock in another recipe.

- The chicken will no doubt taste better if it's browned before cooking. To do so, set the SAUTÉ function to LOW or LESS. Add 1 tablespoon vegetable, corn, rapeseed or olive oil to the pot, set the bird in it and brown it on all sides, keeping it on one side until you can easily release it from the hot surface to turn it to another, 15–20 minutes in total. Transfer the browned chicken to a chopping board and leave to cool for 10 minutes. Make the seasoning paste, rub it on the bird and continue with the recipe in step 2.

Road Map: Rotisserie-Style Chicken

4–6 servings

Why would you put a whole chicken in a multi-cooker when you can buy a rotisserie chicken at the grocery store? First, because you can catch sales on whole chickens and squirrel them away in the freezer to make this simple meal more economical. (But be forewarned: A frozen 1.8kg bird will take 36–48 hours to thaw in the fridge.) Second (and more importantly), because the steam environment of the cooker makes a much juicier bird than those endlessly turning racks at the supermarket.

The easiest way to carve a chicken is with poultry shears. A good pair costs about twenty pounds. Once the chicken has cooled for 10 minutes, pull the thigh and leg away from the body, then cut right in the centre of the joints. For the breast, you can snip it off whole, about like using scissors to cut a ball out of fabric; then snip the meat into chunks right on the chopping board.

1. Use a fork to mash or mix the solid or liquid fat, dried herb(s) and salt in a small bowl until uniform. Rub this mixture all over the exterior of the chicken.

2. Pour the stock or water into a **5.5- or 7.5-litre cooker**. Set a heat- and pressure-safe trivet inside the pot. Set the bird breast-side up on the trivet. Lock the lid onto the pot.

3.

Set the machine	Level	The valve must be	Time	Press
PRESSURE COOK	MAX	—	30 minutes with the KEEP WARM setting off	START
STEAM, PRESSURE COOK or MANUAL	HIGH	Closed	36 minutes with the KEEP WARM setting off	START

4. When the machine has finished cooking, turn it off and let its pressure **return to normal naturally**, about 1 hour. Unlatch the lid and open the cooker. Leave the chicken to cool in the pot for a few minutes, then use large kitchen tongs and a large palette knife to transfer the bird to a nearby chopping board. Take care: the juices inside the bird will be hot. Put children and pets out of the room. Leave to cool for another 5–10 minutes, then carve the bird as desired.

Road Map: Chicken Wings

4–6 servings

Here's how to turn chicken wings into a sure hit at your next gathering. Steam the wings in your Instant Pot to make them tender, then grill them to crisp the skin. Pair the spice blend in the pot with the coating mixture under the grill: barbecue rub with barbecue sauce or curry powder with chutney. Think how the flavours will play out, especially after the wings have turned into tasty, crunchy bits on the baking tin.

1. Place the chicken wing pieces, the dried spice blend and the salt (if using) in a large bowl. Toss well until the chicken pieces are evenly and thoroughly coated in the spice blend.

2. Pour the liquid into a **5.5-litre cooker**. Set a heat- and pressure-safe collapsible steaming basket in the pot. Pile all the coated wings onto the basket. Lock the lid onto the cooker.

3.

Set the machine	Level	The valve must be	Time	Press
MAX	—	PRESSURE COOK	4 minutes with the KEEP WARM setting off	START
HIGH	Closed	STEAM, PRESSURE COOK or MANUAL	5 minutes with the KEEP WARM setting off	START

4. When the machine has finished cooking, turn it off and let the pressure **return to normal naturally** for 10 minutes. Then use the **quick-release method** to get rid of any residual pressure in the pot. Unlatch the lid and open the cooker.

5. Use kitchen tongs or a large spoon to transfer the *hot* chicken wings to a large bowl. Add the coating mixture and toss well.

6. Position the rack 10–15cm from the grill heat source and preheat the grill for a few minutes. Spread the coated wings into a single layer on a large, lipped baking tin. Grill until crisp and irresistible, turning once, about 5 minutes.

1.5kg chicken wings, cut into their three parts, any flappers removed and discarded

3 tablespoons dried spice blend
> **Choose** from Cajun, Chinese, French, Italian, curry powder, herbes de Provence, five-spice powder (see page 88) or a favourite barbecue rub.

Up to 1 teaspoon table salt (optional)

250ml liquid
> **Choose** from water, beer, white wine, stock or unsweetened cloudy apple juice.

250ml coating mixture
> **Choose** from barbecue sauce, chutney, French dressing, honey mustard, Ranch dressing, stir-fry sauce, Thai chilli sauce or a 50/50 combo of a hot red pepper sauce like Sriracha and ketchup.

Beyond

- For a 3-litre cooker, you must use 180ml of the liquid but halve the amount of the remaining ingredients.

- For a 7.5-litre cooker, you must use 350ml of the liquid but otherwise keep the stated amount of the other ingredients. Or you can increase everything by 50 per cent in a 7.5-litre cooker.

- For a dipping sauce, mix a hot red pepper sauce like Sriracha with lime zest, melted butter and finely chopped fresh mint or coriander.

- Or mix apricot preserve with Dijon mustard and a little Worcestershire sauce.

1½ teaspoons mild paprika

1½ teaspoons sea salt flakes

1 teaspoon onion powder

½ teaspoon dried sage

½ teaspoon dried thyme

½ teaspoon ground
black pepper

¼ teaspoon garlic powder

350ml water

Six 225–300g bone-in skin-on
chicken thighs

Peanut oil, vegetable oil or
solid vegetable shortening,
for frying

Fried Chicken

6 servings

No, we're not frying in the pot. And we're not pressure-frying chicken. The pot's not built for such measures. Instead, we're using the pressure in the pot to tenderise the chicken and infuse the flavours into the meat, rendering out a little of the fat to make the thighs even crisper when they eventually hit the hot oil.

After cooking under pressure, we can't fry them in the pot with the SAUTÉ function on HIGH or MORE. First, we can only fit two at a time, slowing down the process. But more importantly, since we suggest pan-frying the chicken, rather than deep-frying it, the high-sided pot catches and keeps steam inside the insert, rendering the exposed skin above the oil too gummy.

1. Mix the paprika, salt, onion powder, sage, thyme, pepper and garlic powder on a large plate until uniform. Pat the chicken thighs dry with kitchen paper and roll the chicken in this mixture to coat the pieces evenly and thoroughly.

2. Pour the water into a **5.5- or 7.5-litre cooker**. Set a heat- and pressure-safe trivet in the pot. Stack the thighs on the trivet. Lock the lid onto the cooker.

3.

Set the machine	Level	The valve must be	Time	Press
PRESSURE COOK	MAX	—	10 minutes with the KEEP WARM setting off	START
STEAM, PRESSURE COOK or MANUAL	HIGH	Closed	15 minutes with the KEEP WARM setting off	START

4. Use the **quick-release method** to bring the pot's pressure back to normal. Unlatch the lid and open the cooker. Line a large lipped baking sheet with kitchen paper. Use kitchen tongs to transfer the *hot* thighs to a large, lipped baking sheet. Leave to dry for at least 20 minutes or up to 1 hour.

5. Set a 30cm frying pan over a medium heat. Pour in enough oil to come about 1cm up the sides – or melt enough shortening in the skillet to come to the same depth. Continue heating until the fat shimmers.

6. Slip three of the thighs skin-side down into the oil. Fry until golden and crisp, about 10 minutes. Turn and continue frying until golden and cooked through, about another 10 minutes. Transfer the thighs to a wire cooling rack and salt as desired. Add enough oil or shortening to get the depth back to 1cm if necessary and wait a moment or two make sure the oil is again hot. Fry the remainder of the thighs in the same way. Serve warm.

Beyond

- You must halve the recipe for a 3-litre cooker.

- Pressure-cook the chicken ahead of time. Once the thighs have dried on the baking sheet for 20 minutes, transfer them to a bowl, cover and refrigerate for up to 1 day. Bring the thighs to room temperature before frying them.

- For crunchier skin, put about 120g plain flour in a large paper bag, add the cooked thighs, seal and shake to coat them. Transfer them out one by one to the hot frying pan, knocking off the excess flour before they get into the oil. Fry as directed.

- For a Korean-inspired dish, toss the cooked and fried thighs with up to 125ml sweet Thai chilli sauce before serving.

Chinese-Take-Away Lacquered Chicken Legs

4–6 servings

Sticky, sweet, salty and tender, these chicken legs make great picnic snacks in the summer. They're equally good as part of a buffet. But no matter the season, you'll need plenty of napkins. Use only reduced-sodium soy sauce so the basting liquid doesn't become too salty.

250ml reduced-sodium soy sauce

60ml rice vinegar

12 skin-on chicken legs

60g white granulated sugar

1. Pour the soy sauce and vinegar into a **5.5-litre cooker**. Set a heat- and pressure-safe collapsible steaming basket in the pot. Pile the chicken legs into the basket. Lock the lid onto the cooker.

2.

Set the machine	Level	The valve must be	Time	Press
PRESSURE COOK	MAX	—	10 minutes with the KEEP WARM setting off	START
STEAM, PRESSURE COOK or MANUAL	HIGH	Closed	12 minutes with the KEEP WARM setting off	START

3. Use the **quick-release method** to bring the pot's pressure back to normal. Unlatch the lid and open the cooker. Use kitchen tongs to transfer the chicken legs to a large, lipped baking sheet. Remove the steaming basket from the pot. Stir the sugar into the liquids in the pot.

4. Position the rack 10cm from the grill; preheat the grill for a minute or two. Baste the legs with the sauce in the pot, then grill them until coated and crunchy, about 2 minutes, turning a couple of times and basting each time with more of the pot liquid. Serve warm.

Beyond

- You must halve the recipe for a 3-litre cooker.

- For a 7.5-litre cooker, you must increase all the ingredients by 50 per cent – or simply increase the soy sauce and vinegar by 50 per cent.

- For more flavour, put a 10cm cinnamon stick, up to 6 green or white cardamom pods and/ or 1 star anise pod in the pot with the soy sauce and vinegar.

- Before serving, sprinkle sesame seeds all over the chicken legs.

30g butter, softened to room temperature

1 teaspoon mild paprika

1 teaspoon sea salt flakes

½ teaspoon dried sage

½ teaspoon onion powder

½ teaspoon ground black pepper

¼ teaspoon garlic powder

One 2–2.25kg bone-in, skin-on turkey breast

500ml chicken stock or water

Steam-Roasted Turkey Breast

6–8 servings

A turkey breast is our go-to make-ahead for weekend guests. We keep one in the fridge for sandwiches or for slices at breakfast for those who want a little more protein beyond granola. Some turkey breasts have a flat 'bottom' so the breast meat sits nicely up top of the bones. Others have flapping bits of the ribs still attached (that can cause the meat to tip this way and that). Remove any extraneous bits with poultry shears so the breast will sit flat in the cooker.

There's no way to crisp the skin in an Instant Pot. If you're making the turkey ahead, it may not matter, given that the bird will be cold. But see the *Beyond* for one way to get the job done.

1. Use a fork to mash the butter, paprika, salt, sage, onion powder, pepper and garlic powder into a paste in a small bowl. Smear this mixture all over the skin of the turkey breast.

2. Pour the stock or water into a **5.5- or 7.5-litre cooker.** Set a heat- and pressure-safe trivet in the pot. Set the turkey breast skin-side up on the trivet. Lock the lid onto the pot.

3.

Set the machine	Level	The valve must be	Time	Press
PRESSURE COOK	MAX	—	18 minutes with the KEEP WARM setting off	START
STEAM, PRESSURE COOK or MANUAL	HIGH	Closed	25 minutes with the KEEP WARM setting off	START

4. When the machine has finished cooking, turn it off and let its pressure **return to normal naturally**, about 45 minutes. Unlatch the lid and open the cooker. Use large kitchen tongs and a large palette knife to transfer the *hot* turkey breast to a nearby chopping board. Cool for 5 minutes, then carve into slices 5mm–1cm thick.

Beyond

- Because of the size of the turkey breast, this recipe won't work in a 3-litre cooker.

- For brown, crunchy skin, position the rack in the centre of the oven and heat the oven to 230°C as the turkey cooks in the machine. When done, transfer the turkey breast skin-side up to a small roasting tin. Roast in the oven until the skin has browned, about 10 minutes.

State Fair Turkey Legs

4 servings

These turkey legs will fit the bill whenever the weather's warm and the day's gorgeous. In fact, if you want to make a barbecue or cookout more sophisticated, consider a tray of these legs for the under-twelve set. There will undoubtedly be an adult who's hankering to play Henry VIII.

1. Mix the chilli powder, smoked paprika, onion powder, salt and pepper in a small bowl until uniform. Smear some oil all over each turkey leg, then coat them evenly in the spice mixture.

2. Pour the water into a **5.5- or 7.5-litre cooker**. Set a heat- and pressure-safe trivet in the pot. Pile the legs onto the trivet. Lock the lid onto the pot.

3.

Set the machine	Level	The valve must be	Time	Press
PRESSURE COOK	MAX	—	32 minutes with the KEEP WARM setting off	START
STEAM, PRESSURE COOK or MANUAL	HIGH	Closed	40 minutes with the KEEP WARM setting off	START

4. When the machine has finished cooking, turn it off and let its pressure **return to normal naturally** for 10 minutes. Then use the **quick-release method** to get rid of any residual pressure in the pot. Unlatch the lid and open the cooker. Use kitchen tongs to transfer the turkey legs to a large, lipped baking tin.

5. Position the rack 15cm from the grill. Preheat the grill for 1–2 minutes. Meanwhile, whisk the honey, vinegar and 1–2 teaspoons of the cooking water from the pot in a small bowl to make a sauce with the consistency of thick barbecue sauce.

6. Brush some of this honey mixture over the turkey legs, then grill to brown and crisp, about 2 minutes, turning a couple of times and basting with more of the mopping sauce. Cool for 5 minutes before serving.

1 tablespoon standard chilli powder

1 teaspoon mild smoked paprika

1 teaspoon onion powder

1 teaspoon table salt

1 teaspoon ground black pepper

2 tablespoons vegetable, corn or rapeseed oil

Four 350g skin-on turkey legs

500ml water

90g honey

1 tablespoon apple cider vinegar

Beyond

- Turkey legs are too long to fit well in a 3-litre cooker.
- To make these turkey legs on the SLOW COOK setting, only add 125ml water to the pot and do not use the trivet. Set the legs in the pot, latch on the lid, keep the pressure valve open (as necessary) and press the SLOW COOK function on HIGH. Cook for 4 hours with the KEEP WARM setting off or on for 2 hours. Grill as directed in steps 5 and 6.

900g piece brisket, cut into 4cm cubes

1 tablespoon mild smoked paprika

1 teaspoon onion powder

½ teaspoon garlic powder

½ teaspoon table salt

Twelve to sixteen 10cm bamboo or metal skewers

250ml water

One 100ml bottle liquid smoke

Brisket Skewers

4–6 servings

Here's something we can *only* do in a multi-cooker: tenderise brisket enough that it can be served as skewered cubes on kebabs. We use liquid smoke to give the brisket a smokehouse flavour, then crisp the skewers in a grill rack or on the grill until they're an unbelievable combination of fatty brisket and tender beefiness.

Use short skewers. You may need to break standard bamboo skewers in half (watch out for splinters). But there's not much else to do. Maybe provide a dip for the skewers? How about barbecue sauce, ketchup, honey mustard or even a creamy soured cream and horseradish sauce? Oh, and beer. Not in the cooker. You'll need a cold beer in your hand.

1. Toss the brisket cubes, smoked paprika, onion powder, garlic powder and salt in a large bowl until the meat is evenly and thoroughly coated. Thread two cubes onto each of the skewers.

2. Pour the water and liquid smoke into a **5.5-litre cooker**. Set a heat- and pressure-safe trivet in the pot. Pile the skewers onto the trivet. Lock the lid onto the pot.

3.

Set the machine	Level	The valve must be	Time	Press
PRESSURE COOK	MAX	—	42 minutes with the KEEP WARM setting off	START
STEAM, PRESSURE COOK or MANUAL	HIGH	Closed	50 minutes with the KEEP WARM setting off	START

4. When the machine has finished cooking, turn it off and let its pressure **return to normal naturally**, about 20 minutes. Unlatch the lid and open the pot.

5. Heat a large cast-iron grill pan over medium-high heat until smoking or brush the grill grates and prepare the grill for high heat cooking directly over the heat source. Grill the skewers (in batches in the grill pan) until crisp and browned, about 2 minutes, turning occasionally.

Beyond

- For a 3-litre cooker, use 250ml water but halve the remaining ingredients.

- For a 7.5-litre cooker, you must use 500ml water and increase the remaining ingredients by 50 per cent, or simply increase the water to 500ml (while keeping the stated amounts of the other ingredients).

- Serve the skewers with Mexican salsa verde, regular salsa or even barbecue sauce for dipping.

- Make these skewers ahead of time. Cook them through step 4, then leave to cool for a few minutes with the pot open. Use kitchen tongs to remove the trivet underneath them, then store the skewers (and meat) right in the steaming medium. Leave to cool for 20 minutes, then remove the insert from the machine, cover the insert with clingfilm and store it in the fridge for up to 24 hours. Grill the skewers an extra minute or so to warm them up.

SUPER EASY / FEWER THAN 10 INGREDIENTS / NATURAL RELEASE, THEN MODIFIED NATURAL RELEASE / CAN BE GLUTEN-FREE / FREEZES WELL

ALL THINGS STEAMED AND COOKED WITH THE SOUS VIDE METHOD **267**

Smoky Corned Beef

6–8 servings

In essence, this recipe uses ready-made corned beef and the Instant Pot to make pastrami. It calls for a lot of corned beef. You may need to stack two 680g packs of corned beef on top of each other.

    For a real treat, you then cook potatoes right in the smoky liquid in the pot. Of course, you needn't bother. You can skip steps 5 through 7 and simply slice the corned beef for sandwiches on rye bread topped with deli mustard and maybe ready-made coleslaw.

1. Mix the dried mustard, coriander and pepper in a small bowl. Dry the corned beef with kitchen paper, then pat this spice rub all over the meat.

2. Pour the water in a **5.5- or 7.5-litre cooker**; stir in the liquid smoke. Put a heat- and pressure-safe trivet in the pot, then set the coated corned beef on top. Lock the lid onto the pot.

3.

Set the machine	Level	The valve must be	Time	Press
PRESSURE COOK	MAX	——	1 hour 10 minutes with the KEEP WARM setting off	START
MEAT/STEW, PRESSURE COOK or MANUAL	HIGH	Closed	1 hour 30 minutes with the KEEP WARM setting off	START

4. When the machine has finished cooking, turn it off and let its pressure **return to normal naturally**, about 40 minutes. Unlatch the lid and open the pot. Transfer the corned beef to a nearby chopping board. Tent with foil to keep warm.

5. Remove the trivet from the pot. Stir the potatoes into the liquid inside. Lock the lid back onto the pot.

6.

Set the machine	Level	The valve must be	Time	Press
PRESSURE COOK	MAX	——	7 minutes with the KEEP WARM setting off	START
STEAM, PRESSURE COOK or MANUAL	HIGH	Closed	10 minutes with the KEEP WARM setting off	START

7. When the machine has finished cooking, turn it off and let its pressure **return to normal naturally** for 5 minutes. Then use the **quick-release method** to get rid of any residual pressure in the pot. Unlatch the lid and open the cooker. Drain the potatoes from the *hot* insert into a colander set in the sink. Slice the corned beef against the grain into 1cm strips and serve with the potatoes.

1 teaspoon mustard powder

1 teaspoon ground coriander

1 teaspoon ground black pepper

One 1.3–1.6kg corned beef, any spice packets removed and discarded, the meat well rinsed

500ml water

Two 100ml bottles liquid smoke

900g small red- or yellow-skinned potatoes, each about the size of a ping-pong ball, scrubbed of any surface dirt

Beyond

- For a 3-litre cooker, halve all the ingredients. However, the 680g corned beef may not fit. Slice it into two equal sections and stack these on each other on the rack.

- For the best Reuben sandwich, carve the warm pastrami against the grain into slices 1cm in thickness. Set these on toasted rye bread with lots of sauerkraut and Russian dressing (see page 425). Notice what's missing? Cheese. Every single kosher deli cannot be wrong.

1 tablespoon mild
smoked paprika

2 teaspoons dried oregano

2 teaspoons dried thyme

1 teaspoon mustard powder

1 teaspoon onion powder

½ teaspoon table salt

½ teaspoon ground
black pepper

1.6kg boneless beef short ribs

350ml water

2 tablespoons vegetable,
corn or rapeseed oil

1 tablespoon white
granulated sugar

1 tablespoon apple
cider vinegar

Crisped and Mopped Beef Short Ribs

6 servings

Sure, the best thing about the Instant Pot is being able to open the lid after cooking and look at dinner. But here, we use the pot to steam short ribs that have been coated in a fit-for-the-smoker rub. Those short ribs are put back into the pot later and made crisp over the heat. All in all, there's some effort required but a big dividend: crunchy short ribs that are meltingly tender, with a rich, sweet glaze.

1. Mix the smoked paprika, oregano, thyme, mustard, onion powder, salt and pepper in a large bowl. Add the short ribs and toss well, until they are evenly and thoroughly coated. (There should be no dried spice mixture left in the bowl.)

2. Pour the water into a **5.5- or 7.5-litre cooker.** Set a heat- and pressure-safe collapsible steaming basket in the pot. Pile the coated short ribs into the basket, then lock the lid onto the pot.

3.

Set the machine	Level	The valve must be	Time	Press
PRESSURE COOK	MAX	—	35 minutes with the KEEP WARM setting off	START
STEAM, PRESSURE COOK or MANUAL	HIGH	Closed	45 minutes with the KEEP WARM setting off	START

4. When the machine has finished cooking, turn it off and let
its pressure **return to normal naturally**, about 20 minutes. Unlatch
the lid and open the cooker. Use kitchen tongs to transfer the
short ribs to a nearby bowl. Pour any liquid in the cooker into
a second bowl, then clean and dry the machine's insert before
returning it to the pot.

5.

Press	Setting	Time	Press
SAUTÉ	MEDIUM, NORMAL or CUSTOM 150°C	30 minutes	START

6. Warm the oil in the pot for a minute or two. Add about
one-third of short ribs and cook, turning occasionally, until
crisped on all sides, about 6 minutes. Transfer these to a serving
platter and brown the remaining two batches in the same way.

7. Once all the meat is on the platter, pour the reserved liquid
into the pot and bring it to a full simmer. Stir in the sugar and
vinegar. Continue cooking, stirring often, until this liquid has
reduced to a thick glaze, about 6 minutes. Turn off the **SAUTÉ**
function, then smear and spread this glaze over the short ribs
before serving.

Beyond

- For a 3-litre cooker, you must use 250ml water but halve the remaining ingredients.
- Serve these with Baked Beans (page 444).
- Or serve them set over Creamy Black-Eye Beans (page 438).

700g lean beef mince

One 225g baking potato, peeled and grated through the large holes of a box grater

15g plain panko breadcrumbs

1 large egg

2 tablespoons Worcestershire sauce

2 tablespoons ketchup

1 teaspoon dried oregano

1 teaspoon dried thyme

1 teaspoon onion powder

½ teaspoon garlic powder

1 teaspoon table salt

½ teaspoon ground black pepper

Olive oil spray

350ml water

Down-Home Meatloaf

6 servings

A Bundt tin makes a meatloaf in a snap in the Instant Pot. But you'll need one more piece of equipment, which is an instant-read meat thermometer. Taking the internal temperature of the loaf after cooking guarantees that the dish is safe to eat. Of course, some people like a crunchy top to an oven-roasted meatloaf. We've got a solution to that in the *Beyond* section. If you're looking for a braised meatloaf, see page 367.

1. Mix the beef mince, potato, breadcrumbs, egg, Worcestershire sauce, ketchup, oregano, thyme, onion powder, garlic powder, salt and pepper in a large bowl until uniform.

2. Generously coat the inside of an 18cm Bundt tin with olive oil spray. Pack the beef-mince mixture into this tin, creating an even, smooth layer. Cover with aluminium foil; poke a fairly large hole in the centre of the foil where the hole exists in the centre post of the Bundt tin.

3. Pour the water into a 3-, 5.5- or 7.5-litre cooker. Set a heat- and pressure-safe trivet inside the pot. Set the covered Bundt tin on the trivet. Lock the lid onto the cooker, taking care that the lid seals to the pot without any foil sticking out around the rim.

4.

Set the machine	Level	The valve must be	Time	Press
PRESSURE COOK	MAX	——	22 minutes with the KEEP WARM setting off	START
STEAM, PRESSURE COOK or MANUAL	HIGH	Closed	30 minutes with the KEEP WARM setting off	START

5. When the machine has finished cooking, turn it off and let its pressure **return to normal naturally**, about 20 minutes. Unlatch the lid and open the cooker. Poke an instant-read meat thermometer through the foil and into the centre of the loaf without touching metal in at least two places to make sure the meatloaf's temperature is 72°C. If it is not, latch the lid onto the cooker with the pressure valve closed and cook for another 5 minutes at HIGH, followed by the **quick-release method**. Unlatch the lid, open the cooker and take the meatloaf's internal temperature again.

6. Once done, use the handle of a wooden spoon leveraged into the centre hole of the Bundt tin (also wear oven gloves) to transfer the *hot* Bundt tin to a wire rack. Leave to cool for a few minutes, just until you can handle the tin. Using oven gloves, tilt the Bundt tin slightly over the bin to pour off any juices around the meatloaf. Set a platter over the tin, invert the whole thing (watch out for more hot juices!), and remove the tin. Leave to cool for a few more minutes before slicing.

Beyond

- To glaze the meatloaf, whisk 2 tablespoons Worcestershire sauce, 2 tablespoons ketchup and 1 tablespoon balsamic, sherry or red wine vinegar in a small bowl until smooth. Invert the cooled meatloaf onto a large roasting tin, then smear this mixture over the top and sides of the meatloaf. Grill about 15cm from the heated element until bubbling and set, about 1 minute.

Olive oil spray

1½ teaspoons ground black pepper

700g lean pork mince

35g dehydrated potato flakes

1 large egg

2 tablespoons Dijon mustard

2 tablespoons Worcestershire sauce

2 teaspoons dried dill

1 teaspoon caraway seeds

½ teaspoon celery seeds

350ml water

Pork Meatloaf

4–6 servings

This meatloaf is a little smaller than the last one because it's missing all the grated potato. We make up for it with dehydrated potato flakes (aka instant mashed potatoes). These catch and hold on to any released moisture, increasing in volume like little potato sponges, all to make sure the meatloaf is tender when cooked through. Beyond a fine main course, this pork loaf is great when sliced into thin bits and served on cocktail sticks for a snack with cocktails. Slices also make a great sandwich on toasted multigrain bread with lots of deli mustard and sliced, ripe tomato.

1. Generously coat the inside of an 18cm Bundt tin with olive oil spray. Sprinkle the pepper all over the interior of the tin, tilting the tin to coat it evenly.

2. Mix the pork mince, potato flakes, egg, mustard, Worcestershire sauce, dill, caraway seeds and celery seeds in a large bowl until uniform. Pack this mixture into the prepared tin, taking care not to knock the ground black pepper off the sides but getting the mixture into an even layer in the tin. Cover tightly with aluminium foil.

3. Pour the water into a **3-, 5.5- or 7.5-litre cooker**. Set a heat- and pressure-safe trivet in the pot. Transfer the filled Bundt tin to the trivet. Lock the lid onto the cooker, taking care that the lid seals properly without any foil sticking out of the rim.

4.

Set the machine	Level	The valve must be	Time	Press
PRESSURE COOK	MAX	—	18 minutes with the KEEP WARM setting off	START
STEAM, PRESSURE COOK or MANUAL	HIGH	Closed	25 minutes with the KEEP WARM setting off	START

Beyond

- For a savoury and sour kick, add 120g squeezed sauerkraut to the meat mixture before cooking.

- Or add 70g finely diced gherkins.

5. When the machine has finished cooking, turn it off and let its pressure **return to normal naturally**, about 20 minutes. Unlatch the lid and open the cooker. Poke an instant-read meat thermometer through the foil and into the centre of the loaf without touching metal in at least two places to make sure the meatloaf's temperature is 72°C. If it is not, cover the Bundt tin again, then latch the lid onto the cooker with the pressure valve closed and cook for another 5 minutes at HIGH, followed by the **quick-release method**. Unlatch the lid, open the cooker and take the loaf's internal temperature again.

6. Transfer the Bundt tin to a wire cooling rack. Uncover and leave to cool for a few minutes. Pick up the filled Bundt tin with oven gloves and tilt it slightly over the bin to pour off any hot juices around the interior perimeter of the tin. Set a serving platter over the tin, invert the whole thing, and remove the *hot* Bundt tin. Leave to cool for a few more minutes before slicing and serving.

450g lean beef mince

One 225g tin whole or sliced
water chestnuts, drained
and chopped

1 large egg white

2 tablespoons dry sherry,
dry vermouth or dry
white wine

1 tablespoon finely chopped
peeled fresh root ginger

60ml plus 1 tablespoon rice
vinegar

1 teaspoon five-spice powder
(see page 88)

½ teaspoon ground
black pepper

220g uncooked short-grain
white rice

250ml water

60ml soy sauce

60ml Worcestershire sauce

Chinese-Take-Away Porcupine Meatballs

2–4 servings

If you've never ordered these as a takeaway, now's the time to try these tasty little covered in sticky rice at home. You can use medium-grain or even long-grain white rice to coat the balls, although chewy, short-grain sushi rice gives a decidedly chewy 'coating' to the meatballs. The dipping sauce is fairly traditional, although you could omit it and use Chinese duck sauce or even just Sriracha thinned out with a little stock or sherry.

1. Mix the beef, chestnuts, egg white, sherry, vermouth or wine, ginger, 1 tablespoon vinegar, the five-spice powder and pepper in a medium bowl until uniform. Form this mixture into 18 balls, each about the size of a golf ball, made from about 2 tablespoons of the mixture.

2. Pour the rice onto a large plate, platter or chopping board. Roll the balls in the rice, getting the grains to adhere evenly all over each ball.

3. Pour the water into a **5.5-litre cooker**. Set a heat- and pressure-safe collapsible steaming basket in the pot, opened out as much as you can. Pile the balls into the basket and lock the lid onto the pot.

4.

Set the machine	Level	The valve must be	Time	Press
PRESSURE COOK	MAX	——	8 minutes with the KEEP WARM setting off	START
STEAM, PRESSURE COOK or MANUAL	HIGH	Closed	10 minutes with the KEEP WARM setting off	START

5. While the meatballs cook, whisk the soy sauce, Worcestershire sauce and the remaining 60ml rice vinegar in a small serving bowl. Set aside.

6. When the machine has finished cooking, turn it off and let its pressure **return to normal naturally** for 10 minutes. Then use the **quick-release method** to get rid of any residual pressure in the pot. Unlatch the lid and open the cooker. Lift the *hot* steamer basket out of the cooker or gently transfer the balls one by one to a serving platter with kitchen tongs. Serve with the dipping sauce on the side.

Beyond

- You must halve the recipe for a 3-litre cooker.

- For a 7.5-litre cooker, you must use 350ml water but keep the remaining ingredients the same (there's no way to get a double recipe of 36 balls into a vegetable steamer).

- For more authentic flavour, substitute Shaoxing (a Chinese rice wine) for the sherry and ground white pepper for the black pepper.

- And use a 15cm bamboo steaming basket, rather than a metal vegetable steamer.

Road Map: Steamed Clams

4 servings

There may be no better dinner to have while bingeing whatever's streaming tonight. Make a pot, remove the insert, carry it to the coffee table, set it on several hot pads, break out some bowls, grab a roll of kitchen paper for the drips and have a crunchy baguette on hand to mop up the sauce.

The exterior of clam shells can be sandy, even if you don't feel the sand with your fingers. Scrub the shells well with a plastic brush or even a brand-new sponge that has a scouring side.

Sometimes, clams don't open after cooking – or sometimes they are a tad older and their shells' hinges are strong. If you find that over half aren't opened when you unlatch the pot's lid, put it back in place with the pressure valve open and bring the sauce to a simmer with the SAUTÉ function on MEDIUM, NORMAL or CUSTOM 150°C. Cook for 1–2 minutes. They should all open. Discard any that do not because they could be locked closed with 'sea muck', which you do not want in the sauce.

1. Mix the liquid, fat, acid, herbs and garlic in a **5.5-litre cooker.** Stir in the clams. Lock the lid onto the pot.

2.

Set the machine	Level	The valve must be	Time	Press
PRESSURE COOK	MAX	—	2 minutes with the KEEP WARM setting off	START
STEAM, PRESSURE COOK or MANUAL	HIGH	Closed	4 minutes with the KEEP WARM setting off	START

3. When the machine has finished cooking, turn it off and let its pressure **return to normal naturally**, about 15 minutes. Unlatch the lid and open the cooker. Spoon the clams into bowls. (Discard any that do not open.) Ladle lots of the sauce from the pot over them in the bowls.

250ml liquid

> **Choose one or two** from wine of any sort, beer of any sort, stock of any sort, sherry, vermouth and/or unsweetened apple juice.

2 tablespoons liquid or solid fat

> **Choose** from butter, rendered bacon fat, coconut oil or lard – or olive, vegetable, corn, rapeseed, safflower or any nut oil.

2 tablespoons acid

> **Choose** from vinegar of any sort, lemon juice or lime juice.

2 tablespoons finely chopped fresh herb leaves

> **Choose one or preferably two** from basil, coriander, marjoram, parsley, oregano, sage, savory, tarragon and/or thyme.

Up to 3 medium garlic cloves, peeled and finely chopped (1 tablespoon prechopped)

1.3kg small clams, scrubbed

Beyond

- For a 3-litre cooker, you must use 180ml liquid and halve the remaining ingredients.

- For a 7.5-litre cooker, you must increase all the ingredients by 50 per cent.

- For heat in the mixture, add up to 1 medium fresh jalapeño, stemmed and sliced into thin rings; or up to 5 dried chillies de árbol or small dried Asian red chillies.

2 tablespoons olive oil, plus extra for greasing the tin

2 medium celery stalks, thinly sliced

1 small onion, chopped (80g prechopped)

1 small yellow pepper, stemmed, cored and chopped (90g prechopped)

350ml water

1 teaspoon mild paprika

60g plain panko breadcrumbs

120ml regular or low-fat mayonnaise

1 large egg white

2 tablespoons Dijon mustard

1 tablespoon dried sage

1 teaspoon ground black pepper

½ teaspoon dried thyme

Several dashes hot red pepper sauce, such as Tabasco (optional)

450g white crabmeat, picked over for shells and cartilage

Crabcake

6 servings

For us, this was the most surprising recipe after months of testing: a single Bundt tin crabcake, maybe a loaf cake, not fried crisp but steamed and light. No, it's not authentic, but it's a tasty meal with a salad on the side.

Don't use expensive giant or jumbo lump crabmeat. But also don't use the cheaper claw meat, which can be quite fishy. Instead, use standard lump, back fin or 'special' crabmeat.

1.

Press	Setting	Time	Press
SAUTÉ	MEDIUM, NORMAL or CUSTOM 150°C	5 minutes	START

2. Warm the oil in a 3-, 5.5- or 7.5-litre cooker for a minute or two. Add the celery, onion and pepper. Cook, stirring occasionally, until the onion softens, about 3 minutes. Scrape this mixture into a large bowl and set aside to cool to room temperature, about 20 minutes. Meanwhile, clean and dry the insert; return it to the pot.

3. Pour the water into the insert. Set a heat- and pressure-safe trivet in the pot. Generously oil the inside of an 18cm Bundt tin. Sprinkle the paprika evenly around the interior of the tin, giving it a light coating.

4. Stir the breadcrumbs, mayonnaise, egg white, mustard, sage, pepper, thyme and hot red pepper sauce (if using) into the onion mixture until uniform. Gently stir in the crabmeat, then pack this mixture into the prepared tin.

5. Cover the tin tightly with foil, then use a knife to poke a large hole in the centre of the foil where the centre hole of the Bundt tin is. Transfer the tin to the trivet in the cooker. Lock the lid onto the pot, making sure the lid seals tight without any foil sticking out around the rim.

6.

Set the machine	Level	The valve must be	Time	Press
PRESSURE COOK	MAX	——	15 minutes with the KEEP WARM setting off	START
STEAM, PRESSURE COOK or MANUAL	HIGH	Closed	20 minutes with the KEEP WARM setting off	START

7. When the machine has finished cooking, turn it off and let its pressure **return to normal naturally**, about 20 minutes. Unlatch the lid and open the cooker. Transfer the *hot* Bundt tin to a wire cooling rack. Leave to cool for 15 minutes, then set a plate over the tin, invert the whole thing and remove the tin. Leave to cool for another 5 minutes or so before slicing into wedges to serve.

Beyond

- The crabcake isn't crunchy. To make it crunchy, leave the unmoulded cake to cool to room temperature, about 1 hour. Slice it into thick wedges, then fry these in butter in a nonstick frying pan set over a medium heat, turning once, until browned on both sides, 3–4 minutes in all.

**900g shell-on small prawns,
deveined**

**700g small red-skinned
potatoes, each slightly
smaller than a ping-pong
ball, halved**

2 tablespoons olive oil

**Up to 2 tablespoons fish
seasoning, such as Old Bay**

500ml water

250ml red chilli sauce

**2 tablespoons fresh
lemon juice**

**1 tablespoon prepared jarred
white horseradish**

**1 tablespoon finely chopped
fresh dill fronds**

**Several dashes hot red
pepper sauce, such as
Tabasco**

Prawn Boil

4 servings

Well, okay, this isn't technically a prawn boil as they'd prepare it
along the East Coast of the USA. But our rendition's close enough
for a great meal! Keeping the shells on the prawns means they can
withstand a bit more of the pressure and the shells add more briny
flavour to the potatoes.

To devein prawns without peeling them, make a slit along the
convex curve (the side of the shell opposite the legs). Use the tip of
a paring knife to nick up and remove the dark, squishy 'vein' that
runs just under the meat. Or buy shell-on deveined prawns,
probably in the freezer section at the supermarket. Yes, it's messy
at the table to remove the shells but the flavour is worth it!

1. Mix the prawns, potatoes, olive oil and seasoning blend
in a large bowl until the prawns and potatoes are evenly and
thoroughly coated.

2. Pour the water into a **5.5- or 7.5-litre cooker.** Set a heat- and
pressure-safe collapsible steaming basket in the pot. Open it out
as much you can. Pile the prawns and potatoes into the basket.
Lock the lid onto the pot.

3.

Set the machine	Level	The valve must be	Time	Press
PRESSURE COOK	MAX	—	7 minutes with the KEEP WARM setting off	START
STEAM, PRESSURE COOK or MANUAL	HIGH	Closed	10 minutes with the KEEP WARM setting off	START

4. Meanwhile, make the cocktail sauce. Whisk the chilli sauce,
lemon juice, horseradish, dill and hot red pepper sauce in a small
serving bowl. Set aside.

5. Use the **quick-release method** to bring the pot's pressure back
to normal. Unlatch the lid and open the pot. Lift the *hot* steamer
out of the pot and pour the prawns and potatoes onto a serving
plate. Serve with the cocktail sauce on the side.

Beyond

- You must halve the recipe for
a 3-litre cooker.
- Skip the cocktail sauce and
make a quick tartar sauce.
Mix together 250ml regular
or low-fat mayonnaise,
1½ tablespoons dill pickle
relish, 1 tablespoon finely
chopped green part of a
spring onion, 1 tablespoon
fresh lemon juice and
½ teaspoon table salt in
a small bowl.

Perfect in-the-Shell Sous Vide Eggs

1–6 servings

Water as needed

1–6 large eggs, at room temperature

We already have a recipe for in-the-shell eggs (page 34). Why a second one? Because this one uses the sous vide function of the Max machine to produce absolutely perfect eggs every time. Although the recipe in the breakfast chapter is certainly faster, this one can keep the eggs at the right temperature for your taste for up to 1 hour. Any weekend when you have guests, set up the cooker and head back to the shower. By the time everyone's downstairs, the eggs will be waiting and perfect – and silkier, smoother than you can believe.

1. Set a heat-safe trivet inside a Max Instant Pot. Fill the insert two-thirds or to the **Max Fill** line with water.

2. Set the machine to its SOUS VIDE function. Set the timer for 2 hours. Set the temperature based on the following criteria:

- 63°C for soft-boiled eggs with barely set whites and loose, runny yolks

- 65°C for soft-boiled eggs with whites that hold their shape and yolks that are soft at the centre

- 68°C for soft-boiled eggs with definitely set whites and yolks with a jammy, caramel-like consistency, such as the eggs often placed in Ramen Broth (page 104)

- 72°C for hard-boiled eggs with firm whites and still-moist yolks

- 74°C for hard-boiled eggs with firm whites and drier yolks, better for chopping in egg salad

3. Lock the lid onto the pot. Press the START button.

4. When the machine reaches the appropriate temperature, uncover the pot and lower the eggs onto the trivet. (A slotted spoon works best.) Latch the lid back onto the pot (the valve will be open by default) and cook for 1 hour. The eggs will be ready at this point. However, they can be held at the set temperature for 1 additional hour.

Beyond

- For the best egg salad, mix 4–6 peeled and chopped hard-boiled eggs with 60–90ml regular or low-fat mayonnaise, up to 35g finely chopped celery, 1 tablespoon white wine vinegar, up to 2 teaspoons yellow mustard, 1 teaspoon white granulated sugar, 1 teaspoon table salt and ½ teaspoon onion powder.

Water as needed

Two 300–340g boneless
sirloin steaks, each
2.5cm thick

2 tablespoons olive oil

1 teaspoon sea salt flakes

½ teaspoon ground
black pepper

12 fresh chives,
cut in half widthways

2 medium garlic cloves,
peeled and thinly sliced

Sous Vide Sirloin Steaks with Chives and Garlic

2 servings

When you cook sirloin steaks with the sous vide technique, you end up with rare steaks all the way to the edge, a solid block of red (or pink) tender meat that is incredibly juicy and perfect every time. Many so-called experts put the steaks in the water bath for 1½, maybe 2 hours. This may result in a faster dinner but not a better one. After 2 hours, the cartilage has not softened; the interstitial fat has not begun to melt. In our minds, such culinary silliness is only a souped-up version of bringing a steak to room temperature before grilling it. What's the point? If we're going to the trouble to put sirloin steaks through the sous vide process, we want them at maximum perfection. Thus, these go for 10 hours. After that, they are unbelievably tender and juicy, the best medium-rare steak you'll ever have.

1. Fill a Max Instant Pot two-thirds or to the **Max Fill** line with water. Set the machine's heat-safe trivet in the pot's bottom. Latch the lid onto the pot.

2. Set the machine to its SOUS VIDE function. Set the timer for 10 hours. Set the temperature for 54°C. Press the START button.

3. As the water heats, rub the steaks with the oil; season them with salt and pepper. Set each steak in a small vacuum-sealer bag; add half the chives and half the garlic. Seal the bags on the regular setting of the vacuum sealer. If you don't have a vacuum-sealer, set each steak in a 1-litre zip-closed plastic bag, add the chives and garlic, and seal using the water method (see page 259).

4. When the water is at the right temperature, unlatch the pot's lid and open the cooker. Use kitchen tongs to lower each bag with its steak into the cooker; use the handles of the trivet to hold them down onto it. The bags must not touch; they must have enough room between them that convection currents can circulate between them, as well as between the bags and the insert's sides. Latch the lid onto the cooker again. Cook for 10 hours, paying careful attention to the water level in the pot (page 259).

5. When the steaks are ready, keep them in the water bath and set a cast-iron frying pan over a medium-high heat until smoking. Or, prepare the BBQ for high-heat cooking (about 260°C). Unlatch the lid and open the cooker. Use kitchen tongs to get the bags out of the cooker. Open them and remove the steaks. Discard the chives and garlic, as well as the plastic bags.

6. Blot the steaks dry, then set them in the frying pan or directly on the grill. Cook for 1–2 minutes, turning once, for a good crust. Serve immediately.

Beyond

- For the best steak sauce, whisk 90ml ketchup, 2 teaspoons soy sauce, 2 teaspoons Worcestershire sauce, ½ teaspoon onion powder, ¼ teaspoon red wine vinegar, ¼ teaspoon garlic powder and several dashes of hot red pepper sauce, like Tabasco.

Sous Vide Steak Teriyaki

2 servings

Once again, we ask the pertinent question for sous vide. What is the point of going to all the trouble if you're not going to do it long enough make a big difference? By letting a sirloin steak cook at a very low temperature in a soy and mirin mixture, the sweet flavours fuse against the outside of the steak, later producing a fantastic crust in a hot pan or on a hot grill. Soya and mirin, of course, are not a traditional teriyaki mixture. They're simpler. Mirin is a sweetened cooking rice wine. Look for it near the soy sauce in almost every supermarket.

1. Fill a Max Instant Pot two-thirds or to the **Max Fill** line with water. Set the machine's heat-safe trivet in the pot's bottom. Latch the lid onto the pot.

2. Set the machine to its SOUS VIDE function. Set the timer for 10 hours. Set the temperature for 54°C. Press the START button.

3. Put the steak, soy sauce and mirin in a 1-litre zip-closed freezer bag. Use the water method to remove the air from the bag (see page 259). Seal the bag shut.

4. When the water is at the right temperature, unlatch the pot's lid and open the cooker. Use kitchen tongs to lower the bag with the steak onto the trivet, using the trivet's handles to keep it in place without pressing down. Latch the lid onto the cooker again. Cook for 10 hours, paying careful attention to the water level in the pot (page 259).

5. When the steak is ready, keep it in the water bath and set a cast-iron frying pan over a medium-high heat until smoking or prepare the BBQ for high-heat cooking (about 260°C).

6. Unlatch the pot's lid and open the cooker. Use kitchen tongs to get the bag out of the cooker. Open it and remove the steak. Discard the bag and marinade.

7. Blot the meat dry and set it in the frying pan or on the grill directly over the heat source. Cook for 2 minutes, turning once, for a good crust. Serve at once, slicing it into strips 5mm in thickness against the grain (see page 87).

Water as needed

One 450–700g, 2.5cm-thick boneless piece of sirloin steak

2 tablespoons soy sauce

2 tablespoons mirin

Beyond

- Garnish the steak with sesame seeds before slicing.

- Serve it with a simple sunomono salad. Slice a seedless cucumber into very thin discs. Mix these with 1 teaspoon table salt and set aside for 10 minutes. Squeeze them dry by the handfuls over the sink. (Don't be scared of squashing them but also don't reduce them to pulp.) Place them in a serving bowl and dress them with 3 tablespoons rice vinegar, 2 teaspoons white granulated sugar and 1 teaspoon soy sauce. Toss well before serving.

Water as needed

1 tablespoon dark brown sugar

1 teaspoon mild smoked paprika

½ teaspoon dried thyme

½ teaspoon onion powder

½ teaspoon sea salt flakes

¼ teaspoon garlic powder

Two 300–350g boneless beef short ribs, 4cm in thickness

Sous Vide Southwestern Beef Short Ribs

2 servings

This recipe is the real deal, the whole reason you want to master the sous vide process. By cooking beef short ribs at such a low temperature for so long, the meat becomes impossibly tender yet still medium-rare. You'll end up with something like a cross between brisket and a sirloin steak, kind of like a medium-rare, super-tender pot roast. It makes no sense. It's a miracle. It's sous vide.

1. Fill a Max Instant Pot two-thirds or to the **Max Fill** line with water. Set the machine's heat-safe trivet in the pot's bottom. Latch the lid onto the pot.

2. Set the machine to its SOUS VIDE function. Set the timer for 48 hours. Set the temperature for 54°C. Press the START button.

3. Mix the brown sugar, paprika, thyme, onion powder, salt and garlic powder on a plate until uniform. Roll the short ribs in this mixture to coat them on all sides. Put each of the short ribs in a small vacuum-sealer bag. Seal the bags on the regular setting of the vacuum sealer. If you don't have a vacuum-sealer, set each coated short rib in a 1-litre zip-closed plastic bag and seal using the water method (see page 259).

4. When the water is at the right temperature, unlatch the pot's lid and open the cooker. Use kitchen tongs to lower each bag with its rib onto the trivet; use the handles of the trivet to hold them down. The bags must not touch; they must have enough room between them that convection currents can circulate between them, as well as between the bags and the insert's sides. Latch the lid onto the cooker again. Cook for 48 hours, keeping watch on the water level in the pot (see page 259).

5. When the ribs are ready, keep them in the water bath and set a cast-iron frying pan over a medium-high heat until smoking, or prepare a BBQ for high-heat cooking (about 260°C).

6. Unlatch the lid and open the cooker. Use kitchen tongs to get the bags out of the cooker. Open them and remove the short ribs. Discard the bags.

7. Blot the short ribs dry and set them in the frying pan or on the BBQ grill. Cook for 1 minute per larger side and ½ minute for short sides (the perimeter) to get a good crust. Serve immediately.

Beyond

- You can double this recipe but it will take double the time. Prepare two short ribs as directed, then drop them (still in their bags) into a big bowl of iced water. When cold, store the still-sealed bags in the refrigerator for 2 days while you make 2 more short ribs.

- Serve these as a starter at a dinner party. Slice the short ribs against the grain into strips 1cm in thickness, then either serve on cocktail sticks, or set them in a pool of salsa, Mexican salsa verde, pico de gallo or Butternut Squash Mash (page 432).

- Skip our barbecue rub and use any dried herb blend or rub you like, even a bottled, dry, barbecue rub.

Sous Vide Smokehouse Brisket

4–6 servings

We offer two ways to get a brisket done under sous vide. Either cook it for 72 hours at 60°C for an astonishingly rare but tender brisket that cuts like a steak but tastes like the work of a good smokehouse. Or cook it for 48 hours at 68°C for a more traditional texture, falling apart and very soft, the way a braised brisket can get (see page 352). Once cooked and cooled, the brisket can be sealed in clingfilm and frozen for up to 2 months. Thaw in the fridge for 48 hours, then let it come to room temperature before crisping as suggested.

1. Fill a Max Instant Pot to the **Max Fill** line with water. Set the machine's heat-safe trivet in the pot's bottom. Latch the lid onto the pot.

2. Set the machine to its SOUS VIDE function. Set the timer for either 48 hours at 68°C or 72 hours at 60°C. Press the START button.

3. Put the brisket in a 4-litre-sized zip-closed plastic freezer bag. Add the liquid smoke and Worcestershire sauce. Seal the bag and rub the liquids all over the meat through the plastic. Open the bag and use the water method (see page 259) to remove all the air from the bag before sealing it tight.

4. When the water is at the right temperature, unlatch the pot's lid and open the cooker. Use kitchen tongs to lower the bag into the cooker; use the handles of the trivet to hold it down with pressing on it. Latch the lid onto the cooker again. Cook for 48 or 72 hours, paying careful attention to the water level in the cooker (see page 259).

5. When the brisket is ready, keep it in the water bath and set a cast-iron frying pan over a medium-high heat until smoking or prepare a BBQ for high-heat cooking (about 260°C).

6. Unlatch the lid and open the cooker. Use kitchen tongs to get the bag out of the cooker. Open it and remove the brisket. Discard the bag and any liquid inside.

7. Blot the brisket dry and set it in the frying pan or on the BBQ. Cook for 3–4 minutes, turning once for a good crust. Slice against the grain and serve at once.

Water as needed

One 700g piece lean beef brisket with an even thickness

2 tablespoons liquid smoke

2 tablespoons Worcestershire sauce

Beyond

- Without grilling or searing it, slice the brisket against the grain for sandwiches. Make the best with toasted rye bread, plenty of deli mustard, iceberg lettuce leaves and maybe sliced dill pickles.

Water as needed

Two 225g, 2.5cm-thick
boneless skinless
chicken breasts

125g ready-made pesto
(or homemade,
see page 177)

Sous Vide Pesto Chicken Breasts

2 servings

These chicken breasts are infused with the flavours of pesto. More importantly, after sous vide, they're ridiculously juicy. They're ready right out of the pot, but you can crisp them on the outside with a little olive oil in a hot grill pan. The meat will be white but tinged pink. However, because of the long time at that temperature, it is safe. If you have concerns, use only organic free-range chicken. And skip this recipe for anyone who has a compromised immune system. For a fuller explanation of how sous vide cooking is safe, visit the sous vide section on the USDA website, or refer to the UK Food Standards Agency website.

1. Fill a Max Instant Pot two-thirds or to the **Max Fill** line with water. Set the machine's heat-safe trivet in the pot's bottom. Latch the lid onto the pot.

2. Set the machine to its SOUS VIDE function. Set the timer for 3 hours. Set the temperature for 65°C. Press the START button.

3. Put 1 chicken breast and half the pesto in each of two 1-litre zip-closed plastic freezer bags. Seal the bag and massage the pesto against the meat through the plastic. Open the bag and use the water method (see page 259) to remove all the air from the bag. Seal closed.

4. When the water is at the right temperature, unlatch the pot's lid and open the cooker. Use kitchen tongs to lower each bag with its chicken breast onto the trivet; use the trivet's handles to hold the bags down without pressing against them. The bags must not touch; they must have enough room between them that convection currents can circulate between them, as well as between the bags and the insert's sides. Latch the lid onto the cooker again. Cook for 3 hours.

5. When the cooking is finished, unlatch the lid and open the cooker. Use kitchen tongs to remove the bags from the water. Open them and remove the chicken breasts, keeping as much pesto on them as possible. Discard the bags. Slice the chicken breasts into 5mm thick strips to serve.

Beyond

- Set these atop a composed salad made with chopped lettuce, cucumbers, celery and tomatoes, dressing with olive oil, balsamic vinegar and seasoned with salt, pepper and dried oregano.

- Or make chicken salad. Cut the chicken slices into bite-sized bits, then mix them with mayonnaise, soured cream, sliced celery, sliced radishes and finely chopped onion and maybe chopped walnuts, seedless green grapes and/or chopped, marinated artichoke hearts.

Sous Vide Salmon Fillets

2 servings

Why would anyone go to the trouble of cooking fish with the sous vide method? Simply because the results are so sublime: soft, mellow salmon, about like confit. As in other recipes, you can't use a vacuum sealer to remove the air here as it would suck the olive oil right out of the bag.

1. Fill a Max Instant Pot two-thirds or to the **Max Fill** line with water. Set the machine's heat- and pressure-safe trivet in the pot's bottom. Latch the lid onto the pot.

2. Set the machine to its SOUS VIDE function. Set the timer for 3 hours. Set the temperature for 54°C. Press the START button.

3. Put one salmon fillet, 2 tablespoons olive oil and 2 dill fronds in each of two 1-litre zip-closed plastic freezer bags. Gently rub the oil into the fish through the plastic. Use the water method (see page 259) to get rid of any excess air in the bag. Seal closed.

4. When the water is at the right temperature, unlatch the pot's lid and open the cooker. Use kitchen tongs to lower each bag with its fillet onto the trivet; use the trivet's handles to hold the bags down without pressing them down. The bags must not touch; they must have enough room between them that convection currents can circulate between them, as well as between the bags and the insert's sides. Latch the lid onto the cooker again. Cook for 3 hours.

5. When the fish is ready, unlatch the lid and open the cooker. Use kitchen tongs to remove the bags from the water. Open the bags and remove the salmon fillets. Discard the bags, dill and any liquid in the bags. Serve at once with a little more olive oil and some sea salt flakes sprinkled over each fillet.

Water as needed

Two 175–225g skin-on salmon fillets

60ml olive oil, plus more for garnishing

4 fresh dill fronds

Sea salt flakes for garnishing

Beyond

- For a light summer meal, serve these on a bed of lettuce leaves. Top with thinly sliced red onion and some thinly sliced cucumber. Then mix some mayonnaise with a little Sriracha or harissa and dollop it on top of each serving.

- Chill the salmon fillets and serve them cold with a homemade horseradish sauce made by whisking together 60g ready-made horseradish sauce, 2 tablespoons soured cream, 1 tablespoon mayonnaise, 2 teaspoons fresh lemon juice, ¼ teaspoon table salt and several dashes hot red pepper sauce like Tabasco.

Water as needed

Four 115–140g raw frozen
lobsters tails in their shells,
thawed

60g butter

4 large tarragon
or thyme sprigs

Sea salt flakes and ground
black pepper for garnishing

Sous Vide Buttery Lobster Tails

2–4 servings

Lobster tails can be notoriously rubbery, overcooked seconds after they're perfectly cooked. By using the sous vide method, we can poach them in butter with herbs and end up with pure luxury each time. The best lobster tails for this technique are small. Whether they make two servings or four servings with lots of sides is up to you. We can suggest Corn on the Cob (page 429) and Three-Bean Salad (page 445).

1. Fill a Max Instant Pot two-thirds or to the **Max Fill** line with water. Set the machine's heat-safe trivet in the pot's bottom. Latch the lid onto the pot.

2. Set the machine to its SOUS VIDE function. Set the timer for 3 hours. Set the temperature for 54°C. Press the START button.

3. Remove the lobster tails from their shells with sturdy kitchen scissors. Cut the pale white underside from the thicker end towards the fanned tail. Peel open the shell on either side, loosen the meat from the shell and pull the meat out.

4. Put two tails in a small vacuum-sealer bag; add 30g butter and 2 herb sprigs. Repeat with a second bag. Seal the bags on the regular setting of the vacuum sealer. If you don't have a vacuum-sealer, set two tails in a 1-litre zip-closed plastic bag; add half the butter and herbs. Prepare a second bag in the same way and seal them both using the water method (see page 259).

5. When the water is at the right temperature, unlatch the pot's lid and open the cooker. Use kitchen tongs to lower each bag with its lobster tails onto the trivet; use the trivet's handles to hold the bags down without pressing on them. The bags must not touch; they must have enough room between them that convection currents can circulate between them, as well as between the bags and the insert's sides. Latch the lid onto the cooker again. Cook for 3 hours.

6. When the machine is finished cooking, unlatch the lid and open the cooker. Use kitchen tongs to take the bags out of the cooker. Split them open and use kitchen tongs to pull out the tails. Discard the bags, any liquid in them and the herbs. Garnish the tails with salt and pepper to taste before serving.

Beyond

- The best lobster rolls start with hot-dog buns. Slather the insides with mayonnaise, set a lobster tail in each (or maybe two in one bun!), and garnish with snipped chives.

- Or brush the cut sides of the buns with melted butter and toast them cut-side down on a griddle, in a grill pan or under a preheated grill until lightly browned, 1–2 minutes. Chop the poached tails into bite-sized pieces (none too small), then mix them with 125ml regular or low-fat mayonnaise, 1 thinly sliced medium celery stalk and 1 tablespoon fresh lemon juice. Pile this mixture into the warm hot-dog buns and serve straight away.

8

Shorter Braises and Stews

(Fewer than Twenty Minutes Under Pressure)

This chapter may well be where you found yourself as you first flipped through the book. There's a lot of comfort food here, no doubt. And the recipes are done quickly, although you'll notice from the title that the time signature only refers to the time under pressure, not any prepping you might do, nor any time the pot might have to come back to normal pressure naturally (rather than with a quick release). We're not trying to pull any funny stuff with that 'Twenty Minutes' in the header. We're just trying to give you a heads-up about where to find some of the shorter braises and stews.

As you'd expect, there's a lot of chicken and beef mince in this chapter, even some pork chops. As you might *not* expect, there are fish and shellfish dishes. Cooking seafood in the pot requires careful timing, but we can also use this countertop appliance to build a flavourful sauce that the fish or shellfish then gets poached in.

There are just four road maps in this chapter: seared chicken breasts, beef mince stew, braised pork chops and mussels. Many quick-cooking cuts require a little finesse to keep them from drying out and getting tough. We'll explain more in the headnotes, including why boneless skinless chicken breasts, while doable, are not doable except with specific considerations. (Check out the pulled recipes that use boneless skinless chicken breasts, starting on page 291.) The same goes for boneless centre-cut pork loin chops.

What you won't find are classic quick-cooking proteins like filet mignons, turkey scaloppini or tilapia. Things that cook in a frying pan or on the grill in a minute or two are simply not Instant-Pot-worthy. For one thing, by the time the pot heats up and cooks under pressure, you could already be eating dinner with a more traditional preparation. And for another, the diminished fat and cartilage content of some of these items makes them a tough sell (or just tough) in the pot's über-hot environment.

And here's one important warning before you get to the recipes. Pay attention to the differences amongst *bone-in, boneless, skin-on* or *skinless*. These recipes have been developed and written to address specific problems associated with each.

Beyond those concerns, this chapter is probably the most diverse in the book. Some recipes include cooking tricks, some are unexpected concoctions and some are just the sort of thing an average night requires.

FAQs

1. What's the difference between a stew and a braise?
Definitions like these are endlessly debated among cookery book writers. By and large, a braise has less liquid than a stew. There's an old rule, advocated by the hoary dons, that the liquid in a braise must come no more than halfway up a piece of protein and that, by contrast, the liquid for a stew must swamp it. Maybe. In the end, many of these recipes fall on the line between a stew and a braise. Call them well-stocked stews. Or high-moisture braises. We've just tried to create the best flavour pairings we could, given the amount of liquid needed to make steam in the pot.

2. What happened to my favourite recipe for [insert main course title here]?
It's probably elsewhere, like in the chapters on all things pulled, all things curried and all things steamed, as well as among the pasta casseroles and pasta sauces. There are main-course casseroles in the grain chapter, too. (Try that chicken and rice some time, page 412.) In some ways, this chapter was designed to catch the things that didn't fall in those chapters, such as meatballs, mole, golumpkis and much more.

Road Map: Perfect Seared Chicken Breasts

4 servings

Here's the problem. Despite the pot's high-moisture environment, boneless, skinless chicken breasts dry out and turn to shards in a multi-cooker. So, here's our solution. Brown them first, then set them on a rack (or the machine's trivet) to keep them off the insert's superheated bottom when they undergo all that pressure. After cooking, a modified quick release lets them then sit in the steam a bit, so they can plump as they reabsorb some of their natural liquids.

Notice that these boneless skinless breasts are a bit larger than those sold in bulk bags at the supermarket. Notice, too, that you should brown the meat thoroughly. The chicken needs good colour for the best flavour.

1.

Press	Setting	Time	Press
SAUTÉ	MEDIUM, NORMAL or CUSTOM 150°C	15 minutes	START

2. Melt the fat or warm the oil in a **5.5- or 7.5-litre cooker**. Season the chicken breasts with the dried herbs or seasoning blend and salt (if using). Set 2 breasts in the pot and brown *well*, turning once, about 6 minutes. Transfer these to a nearby plate and brown the other two breasts in the same way before getting them onto the plate.

3. Turn off the **SAUTÉ** function. Set a heat- and pressure-safe trivet in the pot. Pour in the liquid. Set the chicken breasts on the trivet, overlapping thick ends over thin ends as necessary. Lock the lid onto the pot.

4.

Set the machine	Level	The valve must be	Time	Press
PRESSURE COOK	MAX	—	6 minutes with the KEEP WARM setting off	START
MEAT/STEW, PRESSURE COOK or MANUAL	HIGH	Closed	8 minutes with the KEEP WARM setting off	START

5. Use the **quick-release method** to bring the pot's pressure back to normal – but *do not open the cooker*. Set it aside for 3 minutes with the valve open but the cooker off. Unlatch the lid and open the pot. Serve at once.

2 tablespoons solid or liquid fat

> **Choose** from butter, lard, rendered bacon fat, schmaltz or an oil of almost any sort: olive, avocado, vegetable, corn, rapeseed, safflower, grapeseed, walnut, almond or pecan – or a 50/50 combo of a solid fat and a liquid fat.

Four 300–340g boneless skinless chicken breasts

2 tablespoons dried herbs or a seasoning blend

> **Choose at least two** or many to make up the total amount from any dried herb like thyme, oregano or parsley; ground cinnamon, ground dried ginger or ground dried turmeric; a curry powder of any sort, herbes de Provence or any dried spice seasoning blend from Cajun to Italian, French to Greek.

½ teaspoon table salt (optional)

350ml liquid

> **Choose** from water, stock of any sort, beer, wine of any sort, dry vermouth, dry sherry, unsweetened cloudy apple juice, unsweetened pear nectar or a 50/50 combo of water or stock and wine.

Beyond

- You must halve the recipe for a 3-litre cooker.

- After cooking, garnish the breasts with lots of ground black pepper.

- You'll get even better results if you brine the breasts. Buy chicken breasts that have not been injected with 'a solution that may contain…' (read the label). Whisk 2 tablespoons sea salt flakes into 2 litres cool water until dissolved, then submerge the breasts in the brine for at least 20 minutes but no more than 40. Discard the brine, pat the breasts dry, then proceed with the recipe.

500ml chicken stock

1 small onion, peeled and halved

1 medium carrot, cut into 5cm pieces

5g fresh parsley leaves

1 teaspoon table salt

1 teaspoon ground black pepper

Four 225–340g boneless skinless chicken breasts

½ teaspoon mild paprika

½ teaspoon dried thyme

½ teaspoon garlic powder

½ teaspoon onion powder

Perfect Poached Chicken Breasts

4 servings

Here's another way to stop boneless skinless chicken breasts becoming chicken splinters. Poach them in an aromatic broth, *then* coat them with a spice mixture while they're warm, so the spices adhere and the flavours have a chance to meld with the natural juices. As in the previous road map recipe, this one requires larger boneless skinless chicken breasts, not the small ones typically sold in bags of individually packaged breasts.

1. Stir the stock, onion, carrot, parsley, ½ teaspoon salt and ½ teaspoon pepper in a **3, 5.5- or 7.5-litre pot**. Set the chicken breasts in this sauce, then lock the lid onto the pot.

2.

Set the machine	Level	The valve must be	Time	Press
PRESSURE COOK	MAX	——	7 minutes with the KEEP WARM setting off	START
MEAT/STEW, PRESSURE COOK or MANUAL	HIGH	Closed	10 minutes with the KEEP WARM setting off	START

3. Meanwhile, mix the paprika, thyme, garlic powder, onion powder, the remaining ½ teaspoon salt and the remaining ½ teaspoon ground black pepper in a small bowl until uniform.

4. Use the **quick-release method** to return the pot's pressure to normal. Unlatch the lid and open the cooker. Use kitchen tongs to transfer the chicken breasts to a chopping board; use a fork to pick off any extraneous bits like random parsley leaves. Sprinkle the paprika blend over the hot breasts on all sides and set aside for 5–10 minutes. Serve whole or slice at will – or store the chicken breasts, lightly covered on a plate, in the fridge for up to 3 days.

Beyond

- The highly flavoured stock remaining in the pot after cooking is culinary gold. Strain it, then save it in the fridge or freezer to add to soups, stews or braises.

- Like more garlic flavour? Add 2 large peeled garlic cloves to the pot with the onion.

- For the best chicken salad, chop two of the cooled chicken breasts and stir them in a bowl with 125ml mayonnaise, 60g thinly sliced celery, 60ml soured cream, 1 tablespoon yellow mustard, and up to 40g finely chopped red onion.

Spicy Apricot Chicken Breasts

6 servings

A final way to keep boneless skinless chicken breasts moist and tender in the Instant Pot is to submerge them in a rich, thick, sugar-laced sauce that can protect them during the pressure siege.

Please note that, unlike the previous two recipes, the chicken breasts here are smaller. They can cook more quickly with this technique and thus preserve a better texture.

30g butter

6 medium spring onions, trimmed and thinly sliced

180ml chicken stock

100g apricot jam

2 tablespoons white wine vinegar

1 teaspoon mustard powder

Up to ½ teaspoon ground cayenne

¼ teaspoon table salt

Six 175–225g boneless skinless chicken breasts

1.

Press	Setting	Time	Press
SAUTÉ	MEDIUM, NORMAL or CUSTOM 150°C	5 minutes	START

2. Melt the butter in a **5.5-litre cooker**. Add the spring onions and cook, stirring often, until softened, about 2 minutes. Stir in the stock, jam, vinegar, mustard, cayenne and salt until the jam melts. Turn off the **SAUTÉ** function; nestle the chicken breasts into the sauce. Lock the lid onto the pot.

3.

Set the machine	Level	The valve must be	Time	Press
PRESSURE COOK	MAX	——	9 minutes with the KEEP WARM setting off	START
MEAT/STEW, PRESSURE COOK or MANUAL	HIGH	Closed	12 minutes with the KEEP WARM setting off	START

4. Use the **quick-release method** to bring the pot's pressure back to normal. Unlatch the lid and open the pot. Serve the chicken breasts with the sauce ladled on them.

Beyond

- For a 3-litre cooker, you must use 125ml stock and halve the remaining ingredients.

- For a 7.5-litre cooker, you must increase the stock to 350ml and the remaining ingredients by at least 50 per cent. (You can also double the remaining ingredients.)

- Serve the breasts and their sauce over brown rice or brown or white rice stick noodles.

- Bulk up the meal by adding up to 2 thinly sliced medium celery stalks and/or 4 thinly sliced large radishes with the spring onions.

- Enrich the sauce by removing the cooked chicken breasts and stirring up to an additional 30g butter into it before serving.

- The sauce may be too thin for your taste. Thicken it (or even turn it into a glaze) by using the SAUTÉ function set at MEDIUM, NORMAL or CUSTOM 150°C, stirring quite often, for 3–6 minutes.

2 tablespoons olive oil

115g lean pork mince

70g skinned hazelnuts, chopped

1 teaspoon ground cinnamon

1 teaspoon ground ginger

½ teaspoon table salt

1.2kg boneless skinless chicken breasts, cut into strips 1cm in thickness

250ml chicken stock

1 tablespoon honey

Up to ½ teaspoon crushed chilli flakes

Up to ¼ teaspoon saffron

1 tablespoon fresh lemon juice

Portuguese-Inspired Chicken Braise with Hazelnuts

6 servings

This recipe's a sweet-and-savoury mix, reminiscent of stews served in Portugal (although we've adapted the ingredients for the American supermarket). The dish includes a classic Portuguese combo, pork mince and hazelnuts, plus a little saffron for an earthy flavour.

Unfortunately, chicken already cut for stir-frying won't work in this recipe because the strips are too thin (and will overcook). Instead, you'll need to slice the breasts into long strips 1cm in thickness. To do so, set them on a chopping board so an axis line drawn from the narrowed end across the length of the breast lies parallel to you. Slice the meat on the diagonal to get the widest strips, particularly from the middle.

1.

Press	Setting	Time	Press
SAUTÉ	MEDIUM, NORMAL or CUSTOM 150°C	10 minutes	START

2. Warm the oil in a **5.5-litre cooker** for a minute or two. Crumble in the pork mince and cook, stirring often to break up any clumps, until lightly browned, about 4 minutes. Add the hazelnuts, cinnamon, ginger and salt, stirring until fragrant, for about 30 seconds.

3. Add the chicken and stir well until evenly coated. Stir in the stock, turn off the **SAUTÉ** function, and scrape up any browned bits on the pot's bottom. Stir in the honey, crushed chilli flakes and saffron. Lock the lid onto the pot.

4.

Set the machine	Level	The valve must be	Time	Press
PRESSURE COOK	MAX	——	3 minutes with the KEEP WARM setting off	START
MEAT/STEW, PRESSURE COOK or MANUAL	HIGH	Closed	5 minutes with the KEEP WARM setting off	START

5. Use the **quick-release method** to bring the pot's pressure back to normal. Unlatch the lid and open the cooker. Stir in the lemon juice before serving.

Beyond

- You must halve the recipe for a 3-litre cooker.

- For a 7.5-litre cooker, you must increase all the ingredients by 50 per cent.

- For a briny take, more reminiscent of authentic Portuguese cooking, add up to 2 finely chopped jarred anchovy fillets with the hazelnuts. Or add one 185g can chopped clams, drained, with the honey and other spices.

- Increase the braise's flavour by toasting the hazelnuts in a dry frying pan or in the Instant Pot with the SAUTÉ function on LOW or LESS until lightly browned in spots, stirring often, about 3 minutes. Leave the nuts to cool, then chop.

Bone-in Chicken Breasts with Mushrooms

4 servings

Even *bone-in* chicken breasts need protection from the pressure, although they do have the natural defence of more fat and cartilage around the bones, especially when the skin is left on the meat. Although this recipe is not a road map, you can customise it by using various dried herb blends. Or mix together two or three dried herbs to make your own blend, such as oregano, rosemary and thyme, or thyme, sage and allspice. If you use a ready-made blend, consider using a salt-free one. Or if there's salt in the mix, omit it from the seasoning for the chicken.

1.

Press	Setting	Time	Press
SAUTÉ	MEDIUM, NORMAL or CUSTOM 150°C	20 minutes	START

2. Melt the butter in a **5.5-litre cooker**. Season the chicken breasts with the salt (if using) and pepper, then add two of them skin-side down to the pot. Brown *well* without turning, about 5 minutes. Transfer the breasts to a nearby bowl and brown the other two in the same way before transferring them to the bowl.

3. Add the onion and cook, stirring occasionally, until softened, about 4 minutes. Add the mushrooms and cook, stirring more often, until they give off their internal liquid and it reduces to a glaze, about 5 minutes.

4. Stir in the spice blend until aromatic, just a few seconds. Pour in the stock, turn off the **SAUTÉ** function and scrape up any browned bits on the pot's bottom. Nestle the breasts skin-side up in the sauce, overlapping them to fit. Lock the lid onto the cooker.

5.

Set the machine	Level	The valve must be	Time	Press
PRESSURE COOK	MAX	—	10 minutes with the KEEP WARM setting off	START
MEAT/STEW, PRESSURE COOK or MANUAL	HIGH	Closed	14 minutes with the KEEP WARM setting off	START

6. Use the **quick-release method** to bring the pot's pressure back to normal. Unlatch the lid and open the cooker. Use kitchen tongs to transfer the breasts to serving bowls. Spoon the sauce and vegetables over them.

30g butter

Four 340g bone-in skin-on chicken breasts, any rib bits or large hunks of fat removed

½ teaspoon table salt (optional)

½ teaspoon ground black pepper

1 large onion, chopped (240g prechopped)

225g thinly sliced white button mushrooms

1 tablespoon dried spice blend, such as herbes de Provence, an Italian blend or a Cajun blend

250ml chicken stock

Beyond

- For a 3-litre cooker, you must use 160ml and halve the remaining ingredients.

- For a 7.5-litre cooker, you must increase all the ingredients by 50 per cent.

- Go nuts and substitute more exotic, fresh mushrooms for the white button mushrooms, such as porcini, hen of the woods or shiitake caps, for example. Remember that mushrooms grow in, um, 'dirt' and should be washed. Don't use portobello caps or they'll turn the sauce a depressing brown-grey.

- The sauce may be too thin for your taste. (We actually liked this one fairly soupy when we were testing it.) Thicken the sauce after removing the chicken by boiling it on the SAUTÉ function at HIGH or MORE until about half its volume, stirring often, about 3 minutes.

- For a richer dish, add up to 125ml double cream to the sauce before you boil it down.

2 tablespoons olive oil

Four 300–340g bone-in
skin-on chicken breasts

1 medium onion, chopped
(160g prechopped)

3 medium peppers, one red,
one yellow and one green,
each stemmed, cored and
cut into thin strips

3 medium garlic cloves,
peeled and finely chopped
(1 tablespoon prechopped)

1 tablespoon packed fresh
rosemary leaves, finely
chopped

1 tablespoon packed fresh
oregano leaves, finely
chopped

1 to 2 jarred anchovy fillets,
finely chopped

¼ teaspoon table salt

2 tablespoons balsamic
vinegar

300ml chicken stock

Beyond

- You must halve the recipe for
a 3-litre cooker.

- As in other braises, the sauce
may be a tad thin for your
taste. Once the chicken
breasts have been removed,
reduce it by using the SAUTÉ
function on MEDIUM,
NORMAL or CUSTOM 150°C,
stirring often, 3–5 minutes.

- This dish needs garlic bread.
Split a loaf of Italian bread
or a French baguette in half
lengthways. Brush the cut sides
with olive oil, then sprinkle
them with finely chopped
garlic. Sprinkle finely grated
Parmigiano-Reggiano over
the cut sides, then place
under the grill cut side-up
10–15cm from the heat source
until golden, 1–2 minutes.

Sicilian-Style Braised Bone-in Chicken Breasts

4 servings

This supper is packed with Mediterranean flavours. Make sure the chicken breasts are well browned, otherwise the skin will be squishy after braising. The anchovies add a bit of umami flavour to the sauce. No one will know they're there. They'll just remark on how savoury the dish is.

1.

Press	Setting	Time	Press
SAUTÉ	MEDIUM, NORMAL or CUSTOM 150°C	15 minutes	START

2. Warm the oil for a minute or two in a **5.5- or 7.5-litre cooker**. Add two of the chicken breasts skin-side down and brown *well* without turning, about 5 minutes. Transfer the breasts to a bowl and brown the other two in the same way before transferring them to the bowl.

3. Add the onion and all the pepper strips. Cook, stirring occasionally, until softened, about 4 minutes. Stir in the garlic, rosemary, oregano, anchovies and salt until aromatic, just a few seconds.

4. Pour in the vinegar and scrape up any browned bits on the pot's bottom. Turn off the **SAUTÉ** function. Pour in the stock and stir well. Nestle the chicken breasts skin-side up in the sauce and drizzle in any juice from their bowl. Lock the lid onto the pot.

5.

Set the machine	Level	The valve must be	Time	Press
PRESSURE COOK	MAX	—	13 minutes with the KEEP WARM setting off	START
MEAT/STEW, PRESSURE COOK or MANUAL	HIGH	Closed	16 minutes with the KEEP WARM setting off	START

6. Use the **quick-release method** to bring the pot's pressure back to normal. Unlatch the lid and open the pot. Transfer the chicken breasts to serving plates or a serving platter. Spoon some of the sauce over them before serving.

Chicken Bulgogi

4 servings

Bulgogi is a traditional Korean dish that starts as a braise (as here) but ends up as a fry-up (see the Beyond). It's absurdly aromatic, although we've simplified it a bit for the Western supermarket (again, see the Beyond to take it to another level).

   This dish is a sweet and spicy mixture that should be served alongside cooked long-grain white rice and lots of kimchi.

1. Mix the onion, garlic, stock, apple juice, soy sauce, sesame oil, brown sugar, ginger and chilli paste in a **3- or 5.5-litre cooker** until the brown sugar dissolves. Stir the chicken into the sauce and lock the lid onto the pot.

2.

Set the machine	Level	The valve must be	Time	Press
PRESSURE COOK	MAX	—	10 minutes with the KEEP WARM setting off	START
MEAT/STEW, PRESSURE COOK or MANUAL	HIGH	Closed	12 minutes with the KEEP WARM setting off	START

3. Use the **quick-release method** to bring the pot's pressure back to normal. Unlatch the lid and open the pot. Spoon the chicken and sauce into bowls and top with the spring onions and sesame seeds.

1 medium onion, halved and sliced into thin half-moons

3 medium garlic cloves, peeled and finely chopped (1 tablespoon prechopped)

180ml chicken stock

60ml unsweetened cloudy apple juice

3 tablespoons soy sauce

2 teaspoons toasted sesame oil

2 tablespoons light brown sugar

1 tablespoon finely chopped peeled fresh root ginger

1 tablespoon red chilli paste, such as sambal oelek, or ssamjang

800g boneless skinless chicken thighs (6–8 thighs), any hunks of fat removed, the meat halved

Up to 4 medium spring onions, trimmed and thinly sliced

2 teaspoons white sesame seeds

Beyond

- For a 7.5-litre cooker, you must increase all the ingredients by 50 per cent.
- For a more traditional preparation, use kitchen tongs to remove the pieces of cooked chicken from the sauce. Use the SAUTÉ function on MEDIUM, NORMAL or CUSTOM 150°C to boil the sauce almost to a glaze, stirring quite often, 6–8 minutes. Meanwhile, set a large, well-seasoned cast-iron frying pan over a medium-high heat until smoking. When the sauce is done, turn off the SAUTÉ function and remove the hot insert from the pot. Crisp the chicken pieces in the very hot pan in batches, turning once, until charred in places, about 3 minutes per batch. Toss these with the glaze-sauce and serve with the spring onions and sesame seeds as a garnish.

115g smoked streaky bacon rashers, chopped

Four 300–340g bone-in skinless chicken thighs

1 medium onion, chopped (160g prechopped)

1 medium green pepper, stemmed, cored and chopped (175g prechopped)

1 medium red pepper, stemmed, cored and chopped (175g prechopped)

1 teaspoon Dijon mustard

½ teaspoon dried thyme

½ teaspoon caraway seeds

½ teaspoon celery seeds

½ teaspoon table salt

½ teaspoon ground black pepper

125ml dry white wine, such as Chardonnay

125ml chicken stock

3 medium sweet potatoes (about 900g), peeled and quartered lengthways into wedges

Southern-Style Braised Bone-in Chicken Thighs

4 servings

Sweet potatoes, bacon, chicken – it doesn't get much more down-home than this recipe. Because of the long time the thighs cook, they must be skinless for this braise. (The skin would otherwise become too rubbery.) To remove the skin, grasp one 'corner' at a thigh's smaller end with kitchen paper, then pull the skin off the meat, holding onto the skin with the kitchen paper. (The skin can easily slip out of a bare hand.)

1.

Press	Setting	Time	Press
SAUTÉ	MEDIUM, NORMAL or CUSTOM 150°C	25 minutes	START

2. Cook the bacon in a **5.5-litre cooker** until crisp, stirring occasionally, about 4 minutes. Use a slotted spoon to transfer the bacon pieces to a nearby bowl. Add two of the thighs and brown *well* on both sides, turning a couple of times, about 6 minutes. Transfer these thighs to a bowl, add the other two and brown them in the same way before transferring them to that bowl.

3. Add the onion and both peppers. Cook, stirring occasionally, until softened, about 4 minutes. Stir in the mustard, thyme, caraway seeds, celery seeds, salt and pepper until aromatic, just a few seconds. Pour in the wine and scrape up any browned bits on the pot's bottom.

4. Turn off the **SAUTÉ** function. Pour in the stock and stir well. Return the chicken thighs and any juices in their bowl to the pot. Scatter the sweet potatoes pieces on top of everything. Lock the lid onto the cooker.

5.

Set the machine	Level	The valve must be	Time	Press
PRESSURE COOK	MAX	—	13 minutes with the KEEP WARM setting off	START
MEAT/STEW, PRESSURE COOK or MANUAL	HIGH	Closed	16 minutes with the KEEP WARM setting off	START
SLOW COOK	HIGH	Opened	4 hours with the KEEP WARM setting off (or on for no more than 2 hours)	START

6. If you've used a pressure setting, when the pot has finished cooking, use the **quick-release method** to bring its pressure back to normal.

7. Unlatch the lid and open the cooker. Use kitchen tongs to transfer the thighs and sweet potato pieces to serving plates or a serving platter. Use a large spoon to skim any excess surface fat from the sauce.

8.

Press	Setting	Time	Press
SAUTÉ	HIGH or MORE	10 minutes	START

9. Bring the sauce to the boil and cook, stirring quite often, until reduced to about half its volume, 2–4 minutes. Turn off the **SAUTÉ** function. Spoon the sauce over the chicken and sweet potatoes before serving.

Beyond

- You must halve the recipe for a 3-litre cooker.
- For a 7.5-litre cooker, you must increase all the ingredients by 50 per cent.
- Serve garnished with corn relish.
- Although we suggest boiling down the sauce, you can skip that step, but the dish should then be served in bowls.
- For a cleaner flavour (without the smoky taste), substitute diced pancetta for the bacon.

2 tablespoons olive oil

Six 300–340g bone-in skin-on chicken thighs

1 teaspoon table salt

½ teaspoon ground black pepper

1 large red onion, chopped (240g prechopped)

2 tablespoons finely chopped peeled fresh root ginger

155g unsalted almonds, chopped

7g fresh coriander leaves

1 tablespoon mild paprika

1 teaspoon ground coriander

300ml chicken stock

Braised Chicken with Ginger and Almonds

6 servings

This braise is truly comforting, particularly for someone under the weather. The flavour profile is somewhat Middle Eastern, although the coriander adds a grassy base to the sauce and the root ginger gives it a peppery hit. Okay, it's hard to categorise the flavours, other than to say that they'd be welcome over No-Drain Potato Mash (page 424), cooked and drained giant couscous or medium-grain white or brown Arborio rice.

1.

Press	Setting	Time	Press
SAUTÉ	MEDIUM, NORMAL or CUSTOM 150°C	15 minutes	START

2. Warm the oil for 1 or 2 minutes in a **5.5- or 7.5-litre cooker**. Season the chicken pieces with the salt and pepper, then add about half of them skin-side down to the pot and brown *well* without turning, about 4 minutes. Transfer these pieces to a nearby bowl and continue browning the remainder before transferring them to the bowl.

3. Add the onion and cook, stirring occasionally, until softened, about 4 minutes. Stir in the ginger and cook, stirring often, for 1 minute. Stir in the almonds, coriander leaves, paprika and ground coriander until fragrant, just a few seconds.

4. Pour in the stock, turn off the **SAUTÉ** function and scrape up any browned bits on the pot's bottom. Return the chicken pieces to the pot, overlapping them so that they mostly fit in the sauce. Pour any juices in their bowl over them, then lock the lid onto the cooker.

5.

Set the machine	Level	The valve must be	Time	Press
PRESSURE COOK	MAX	——	13 minutes with the KEEP WARM setting off	START
MEAT/STEW, PRESSURE COOK or MANUAL	HIGH	Closed	16 minutes with the KEEP WARM setting off	START
SLOW COOK	HIGH	Opened	4 hours with the KEEP WARM setting off (or on for no more than 2 hours)	START

6. If you've used a pressure setting, when the machine has finished cooking, use the **quick-release method** to bring the pot's pressure back to normal.

7. Unlatch the lid and open the cooker. Transfer the chicken to individual bowls or a large serving bowl. Use a large spoon to skim any excess surface fat from the sauce. Serve the chicken with lots of the sauce ladled around it.

Beyond

- You must halve the recipe for a 3-litre cooker.

- Dollop the servings with plain Greek yoghurt, garnish with a little finely chopped red onion as desired, and offer pitta bread alongside.

- For a more aromatic dish, substitute mild smoked paprika for the regular mild paprika.

- For an even more aromatic dish, toast whole almonds in a dry frying pan set over a low heat or in the pot with the SAUTÉ function on LOW or LESS until lightly browned and very aromatic, about 4 minutes. Cool before chopping the almonds into smaller pieces.

55g butter, 30g melted
and cooled

1 small onion, chopped
(80g prechopped)

2 medium celery stalks,
thinly sliced

700g chicken breast mince

1 teaspoon dried sage

1 teaspoon dried thyme

½ teaspoon ground
black pepper

¼ teaspoon celery seeds
(optional)

500ml chicken stock

115g frozen peas
(do not thaw)

2 tablespoons
Worcestershire sauce

1 tablespoon Dijon mustard

120g plain flour

2 teaspoons baking powder

½ teaspoon table salt

125ml regular buttermilk

½ teaspoon mild paprika

Chicken Stew with Buttermilk Dumplings

4 servings

Rather than using cut-up chicken, which would need to be browned, cooked and taken off the bone, we simplified this recipe dramatically with chicken mince, which can dry out a bit under pressure. To compensate, we've upped the stock to ensure the stew is moist, even a little soupy, although it will continue to reduce a bit as the dumplings cook at the end.

The second time the lid goes on the pot is for the SLOW COOK setting. If your cooker can only be set for 30 minutes at the lowest, or even 1 hour, you'll need to set a more run-of-the-mill timer for 20 minutes and stop the machine's cooking at that point.

1.

Press	Setting	Time	Press
SAUTÉ	MEDIUM, NORMAL or CUSTOM 150°C	10 MINUTES	START

2. Melt the 55g butter in a **5.5- or 7.5-litre cooker**. Add the onion and celery. Cook, stirring occasionally, until the onion softens, about 3 minutes. Crumble in the chicken mince and continue cooking, stirring occasionally to break up any clumps, until the meat loses its raw, pink colour, about 3 minutes.

3. Stir in the sage, thyme, black pepper and celery seeds (if using) until aromatic, just a few seconds. Turn off the **SAUTÉ** function and stir in the stock, peas, Worcestershire sauce and mustard until uniform. Lock the lid onto the pot.

4.

Set the machine	Level	The valve must be	Time	Press
PRESSURE COOK	MAX	—	3 minutes with the KEEP WARM setting off	START
MEAT/STEW, PRESSURE COOK or MANUAL	HIGH	Closed	5 minutes with the KEEP WARM setting off	START

5. As the stew cooks, whisk the flour, baking powder and salt in a large bowl. Stir in the buttermilk and the 2 tablespoons of melted and cooled butter until a wet dough forms.

6. When the stew has finished cooking, use the **quick-release method** to bring the pot's pressure back to normal. Unlatch the lid and open the cooker. Drop the dough in 6 even blobs across its surface. Sprinkle them with the paprika. Latch the lid onto the pot.

7.

Set the machine	Level	The valve must be	Time	Press
SLOW COOK	HIGH	Opened	20 minutes with the KEEP WARM setting off	START

8. Turn off the **SLOW COOK** function, unlatch the lid and open the pot. Set aside to cool for a few minutes, then serve by the big spoonful in bowls.

Beyond

- You must halve the recipe for a 3-litre cooker.

- If you have a 7.5-litre pot and want to make 6 servings, you can increase all the ingredients by 50 per cent.

- For plain dumplings, omit these and use the dumplings given with the beef stew on page 345.

- Omit the dumplings entirely and use pizza dough. Buy 225g of fresh dough (not tinned but fresh, usually in the chilled section, or buy it from a pizza shop). Divide the dough into 6 balls, drop them into the stew, sprinkle them with paprika and cook the SLOW COOK function, covered and with the pressure valve open, until done, about 20 minutes.

- Or skip dumplings of any sort and simply serve the stew over Buttery Pasta (page 155).

2 tablespoons olive oil

Six 300–340g bone-in skin-on chicken thighs

130g frozen baby onions (do not thaw)

2 medium garlic cloves, peeled and finely chopped (2 teaspoons prechopped)

½ teaspoon crushed chilli flakes

Two 400g tins chopped tomatoes

85g pitted black olives

125ml dry red wine, such as Cabernet Sauvignon, or chicken stock

2 teaspoons dried basil

2 teaspoons dried oregano

Chicken Cacciatore

6 servings

Cacciatore is a simple braise, a 'hunter's stew' (or really, a 'hunter's wife's stew', given how the name works out in its Italian dialect). We nixed any game meats (a traditional ingredient) and used *bone-in, skin-on* chicken thighs to enrich the sauce considerably. For the best success, use oil- or brine-cured black olives, which are much better tasting than tinned olives.

1.

Press	Setting	Time	Press
SAUTÉ	MEDIUM, NORMAL or CUSTOM 150°C	20 minutes	START

2. Warm the oil in a 5.5- or 7.5-litre cooker for 1–2 minutes. Add three of the chicken thighs skin-side down and brown *well* without turning, about 5 minutes. Transfer these to a nearby bowl and brown the remainder of the chicken thighs in the same way before transferring them to the bowl.

3. Add the baby onions; cook, stirring occasionally, until lightly browned in spots, about 4 minutes. Stir in the garlic and crushed chilli flakes until aromatic, just a few seconds. Pour in the tomatoes and scrape up any browned bits on the pot's bottom.

4. Turn off the **SAUTÉ** function. Stir in the olives, wine or stock, basil and oregano. Nestle the thighs skin-side up in the pot, overlapping them to fit in the sauce. Pour any juices in their bowl over them and lock the lid onto the pot.

5.

Set the machine	Level	The valve must be	Time	Press
PRESSURE COOK	MAX	——	13 minutes with the KEEP WARM setting off	START
MEAT/STEW, PRESSURE COOK or MANUAL	HIGH	Closed	16 minutes with the KEEP WARM setting off	START

6. Use the **quick-release method** to bring the pot's pressure back to normal. Unlatch the lid and open the cooker. Use a large slotted spoon to transfer the thighs to a large serving bowl or individual bowls; also scoop out and sprinkle the onions and olives over the chicken.

7.

Press	Setting	Time	Press
SAUTÉ	MEDIUM, NORMAL or CUSTOM 150°C	10 minutes	START

8. Bring the sauce to a full simmer; then cook, stirring often, until reduced to a wet pasta sauce rather than a soupy sauce, about 5 minutes. Turn off the **SAUTÉ** function and pour the sauce over the chicken.

Beyond

- You must halve the recipe for a 3-litre cooker.

- Before browning the chicken, add up to 115g diced pancetta to the pot and fry until crisp, stirring often, about 6 minutes. Use a slotted spoon to transfer to a bowl before browning the chicken as directed.

- Add up to 90g chopped, trimmed fennel and/or 65g chopped carrots with the baby onions.

- Serve the braise over Polenta (page 443).

16 dried chillies, preferably
a blend of New Mexico red
chillies and ancho chillies,
stemmed and deseeded

4 large garlic cloves, peeled

700ml chicken stock

30g flaked almonds

30g raisins

½ teaspoon cumin seeds

½ teaspoon ground cloves

1.3kg chicken mini-fillets

Chicken Mole Rojo

6 servings

Mole rojo ('red sauce' in Spanish, *MOH-lay ROH-hoh*), is a classic red chilli sauce with as many variations as there are cooks in Oaxaca. Most pressure cooker versions call for the chicken to be shredded into the sauce after cooking because the meat inevitably gets overcooked and ends up none too appealing. Our version asks you to make a sauce first, purée it and then quickly cook chicken mini-fillets in it for much more flavour and a better texture in the meat. Call it 'spicy bliss'.

Note that the recipe only uses HIGH pressure (not MAX) on the first cooking, so that the chillies and raisins don't get too mushy before you add the chicken mini-fillets. For more information about selecting, buying and using dried chillies, see page 111.

1. Stir the chillies, garlic, stock, almonds, raisins, cumin and cloves in a **5.5- or 7.5-litre cooker.** Lock the lid onto the pot.

2.

Set the machine	Level	The valve must be	Time	Press
PRESSURE COOK or MANUAL	HIGH	Closed	4 minutes with the KEEP WARM setting off	START

3. Use the **quick-release method** to bring the pot's pressure back to normal. Unlatch the lid and open the cooker. Use a hand blender to purée the ingredients in the pot. Or purée the contents of the pot in a covered blender with the lid's centre knob removed and a clean tea towel placed over the opening. Pour the sauce back into the pot.

4. Add the chicken mini-fillets and stir until they are evenly and thoroughly coated in the sauce. Lock the lid back onto the pot.

5.

Set the machine	Level	The valve must be	Time	Press
PRESSURE COOK	MAX	—	4 minutes with the KEEP WARM setting off	START
MEAT/STEW, PRESSURE COOK or MANUAL	HIGH	Closed	6 minutes with the KEEP WARM setting off	START

6. When the machine has finished cooking, turn it off and let its pressure **return to normal naturally**, about 15 minutes. Unlatch the lid and open the cooker. Use kitchen tongs to remove the chicken from the sauce to serve.

Beyond

- You must halve the recipe for a 3-litre cooker.

- Serve the meat in corn or flour tortillas filled with sliced avocado, sliced radishes, thinly sliced spring onions, fresh coriander leaves, regular or low-fat soured cream, grated Gouda cheese and/or purchased pico de gallo.

- For a smoky flavour, substitute dried chipotles for up to two of the chillies.

- Substitute 1.3kg pork tenderloin, cut into 5cm pieces, for the chicken.

- Or substitute 1.3kg turkey breast cutlets, each cut into 3 pieces.

- Or skip the tortillas and serve the chicken and the sauce over Black Turtle Beans and Rice (page 403).

Chicken Mole Verde

6 servings

As its name indicates, mole verde is a green sauce, made with *fresh* tomatillos and *fresh* chillies. We've calmed down the fire in this version, although you can bump it up by keeping the seeds in the jalapeño (or even adding another one for good measure). The flavours here are tart and bright, better as a summertime braise than winter comfort food.

1. Mix the stock, tomatillos, coriander, pepitas, jalapeño, garlic, cumin and salt in a **5.5-litre cooker**. Nestle the chicken pieces into the sauce, overlapping them as necessary. Lock the lid onto the cooker.

2.

Set the machine	Level	The valve must be	Time	Press
PRESSURE COOK	MAX	—	13 minutes with the KEEP WARM setting off	START
MEAT/STEW, PRESSURE COOK or MANUAL	HIGH	Closed	16 minutes with the KEEP WARM setting off	START
SLOW COOK	HIGH	Opened	4 hours with the KEEP WARM setting off (or on for no more than 2 hours)	START

3. If you've used a pressure setting, when the machine has finished cooking, turn it off and lets its pressure **return to normal naturally,** about 25 minutes.

4. Unlatch and open the lid. Use kitchen tongs to transfer the chicken pieces to a chopping board. Use a hand blender right in the pot to purée the ingredients into a sauce. Or purée the contents of the pot in a covered blender with the centre knob removed from the lid and a clean tea towel placed over the opening. Pour the sauce back into the pot.

5.

Press	Setting	Time	Press
SAUTÉ	MEDIUM, NORMAL or CUSTOM 150°C	15 minutes	START

6. Bring the sauce to a simmer then cook, stirring quite often, until reduced to the consistency of double cream, 8–10 minutes. Return the chicken pieces to the pot, stir well and cook for 1 minute. Turn off the **SAUTÉ** function, remove the *hot* insert from the pot and set the lid askew over the insert for 5 minutes to blend the flavours.

250ml chicken stock

225g fresh tomatillos, husked and chopped

15g fresh coriander leaves, chopped

30g pepitas (green pumpkin seeds)

1 medium fresh jalapeño chilli, stemmed, halved lengthways, deseeded (if desired) and thinly sliced

2 medium garlic cloves, peeled and finely chopped (2 teaspoons prechopped)

1 teaspoon ground cumin

1 teaspoon table salt

Six 300–340g skin-off, bone-in chicken thighs (see page 241 for instructions for removing the skin)

Beyond

- You must halve the recipe for a 3-litre cooker.

- For a 7.5-litre cooker, you must increase the stock to 350ml, but otherwise use the ingredient list as stated. The sauce will need another 3–4 minutes to boil down at the end.

- Once the chicken is returned to the reduced sauce and cooks for 1 minute, pour the contents of the insert into a 23 x 33cm grill-safe baking dish. Cover with 225g grated Cheddar and grill 10–15cm from the heat source until the cheese melts, about 1 minute.

2 tablespoons vegetable, corn or rapeseed oil

Six 300–340g bone-in skin-on chicken thighs

1 large onion, chopped (240g prechopped)

160ml chicken stock

60ml apple cider vinegar

60ml soy sauce

2 tablespoons white granulated sugar

2 tablespoons sauce from a tin of chipotle chillies in adobo sauce (optional)

6 medium garlic cloves, peeled and finely chopped (2 tablespoons prechopped)

2 teaspoons mild paprika

2 teaspoons ground black pepper

2 bay leaves

Beyond

- You must halve the recipe for a 3-litre cooker.

- For a more traditional, thicker sauce, use kitchen tongs to transfer the cooked thighs to a chopping board. Strain the sauce through a fine-mesh sieve like a *chinois* (or a colander lined with a double thickness of muslin), then discard the solids and return the sauce to the pot. Use the SAUTÉ function on MEDIUM, NORMAL or CUSTOM 150°C to bring the sauce to the boil. Then simmer, stirring quite often, until the sauce has reduced to two-thirds of its volume, about 5 minutes. Pour this sauce over the chicken before serving.

- Substitute six 300–340g centre-cut boneless pork loin chops for the chicken thighs. They'll brown much more quickly than the chicken skin.

- In true Filipino style, serve the meat and sauce over chips, even frozen oven chips you've baked up.

Chicken Adobo

6 servings

Adobo is a traditional Filipino sauce, familiar from those tins of chipotles packed in adobo sauce (which get a lot of play in this book). Adobo sauce is a sweet and vinegary concoction. Rather than using the tinned version, this recipe lets you create your own. Yes, for a little more body we suggest adding a little sauce from the tin of chipotles in adobo to fill out our simplified sauce. (Maybe you've got some of the tinned stuff saved back in the fridge after making another recipe in this book?) That tinned sauce will add some extra spices we don't call for. But in truth, if you don't add it, the pot's sauce will be a little brighter in its flavours. If you want to make the sauce spicier, stem and chop one of the chipotles from that tin and add it to the sauce with the other ingredients.

   The pot's sauce will be a tad soupy. In recipe-testing, we liked this wetter sauce on long-grain, white rice.

1.

Press	Setting	Time	Press
SAUTÉ	MEDIUM, NORMAL or CUSTOM 150°C	20 minutes	START

2. Warm the oil in a **5.5- or 7.5-litre cooker** for a minute or two. Add half the chicken thighs skin-side down and brown well without turning, about 5 minutes. Transfer the thighs to a nearby bowl and brown the remaining thighs in the same way before transferring to the bowl.

3. Add the onion and cook, stirring often, until softened, about 5 minutes. Pour in the stock and scrape up any browned bits on the pot's bottom. Turn off the **SAUTÉ** function and stir in the vinegar, soy sauce, sugar, adobo sauce (if using), garlic, paprika, pepper and bay leaves.

4. Return the thighs skin-side up to the pot, overlapping them to fit in the sauce. Add any juice from their bowl and lock the lid onto the cooker.

5.

Set the machine	Level	The valve must be	Time	Press
PRESSURE COOK	MAX	——	13 minutes with the KEEP WARM setting off	START
MEAT/STEW, PRESSURE COOK or MANUAL	HIGH	Closed	16 minutes with the KEEP WARM setting off	START

6. When the machine has finished cooking, turn it off and let its pressure **return to normal naturally**, about 20 minutes. Unlatch the lid and open the pot. Serve the chicken and sauce in bowls.

Turkey Mince Stew

6 servings

A turkey mince mixture is dropped into this stew in small bits (don't get OCD on their size, just small) so that they end up mimicking little bites of turkey burger in the tomato-laced stew. The croutons even stand in for the buns. You can buy boxed croutons or look for better ones in the bakery section of most supermarkets. Or make your own (page 345).

1. Mix the turkey, egg white, mustard, sage, salt and pepper in a medium bowl until uniform. Set aside.

2.

Press	Setting	Time	Press
SAUTÉ	MEDIUM, NORMAL or CUSTOM 150°C	10 minutes	START

3. Melt the butter in a **5.5- or 7.5-litre cooker.** Add the onion and carrots. Cook, stirring often, until the onion softens, about 3 minutes. Add the mushrooms and cook, stirring more often, until they release their internal moisture and it thickens into a sauce, about 5 minutes. Stir in the garlic, thyme and celery seeds until aromatic, just a few seconds.

4. Pour in the stock, scrape the browned bits off the pot's bottom and turn off the **SAUTÉ** function. Stir in the tomatoes and tomato purée. Drop the ground turkey mixture in heaping teaspoonfuls into the stew. Stir very gently to keep them breaking up, then lock the lid onto the pot.

5.

Set the machine	Level	The valve must be	Time	Press
PRESSURE COOK	MAX	—	8 minutes with the KEEP WARM setting off	START
MEAT/STEW, PRESSURE COOK or MANUAL	HIGH	Closed	10 minutes with the KEEP WARM setting off	START

6. Use the **quick-release method** to bring the pot's pressure back to normal. Unlatch the lid and open the pot. Stir gently. Serve in bowls with the croutons sprinkled on top.

700g lean turkey mince

1 large egg white

2 tablespoons Dijon mustard

2 teaspoons dried sage

½ teaspoon table salt

½ teaspoon ground black pepper

45g butter

1 medium onion, chopped (160g prechopped)

125g thinly sliced carrots

225g thinly sliced white button mushrooms

2 medium garlic cloves, peeled and finely chopped (2 teaspoons prechopped)

1 teaspoon dried thyme

½ teaspoon celery seeds

1 litre chicken stock

One 400g tin chopped tomatoes

1 tablespoon tomato purée

60g ready-made plain croutons

Beyond

- You must halve the recipe for a 3-litre cooker.

- To add greens (and more heft), stir 60g washed, stemmed and chopped spinach leaves into the stew after opening it in step 5. Use the SAUTÉ function at MEDIUM, NORMAL or CUSTOM 150°C to simmer the sauce until the spinach wilts, about 2 minutes.

- Sprinkle the servings with grated Gouda.

1 large jarred roasted
red pepper

6 sun-dried tomatoes packed
in oil

60ml dry but light red wine,
such as Pinot Noir

1 tablespoon mild paprika

½ teaspoon ground cinnamon

½ teaspoon table salt

¼ teaspoon crushed
chilli flakes

15g butter

450g lean turkey mince

One 400g tin black-eye beans,
drained and rinsed

One 400g tin chopped
tomatoes

125ml chicken stock

2 tablespoons loosely packed
fresh dill fronds,
finely chopped

Turkey Mince Stew with Black-Eye Beans

4 *servings*

As a base for this simple stew, you'll first make a tasty condiment for the braising medium with a jarred roasted red pepper, a concoction that's also a thickener as the stew cooks. Although final dish is a little saucy, we didn't feel the need to boil it down.

We recommend using only turkey breast mince or white meat turkey mince (with no skin or cartilage in the mixture) for a pressure or slow cooker. Any extra fat will have no place to go except into the sauce.

1. Put the roasted pepper, sun-dried tomatoes, wine, paprika, cinnamon, salt and crushed chilli flakes in a food processor. Cover and pulse to create a coarse but thin sauce, stopping the machine at least once to scrape down the inside.

2.

Press	Setting	Time	Press
SAUTÉ	MEDIUM, NORMAL or CUSTOM 150°C	10 minutes	START

3. Melt the butter in a **3- or 5.5-litre cooker**. Crumble in the turkey mince and cook, stirring often to break up any clumps, until lightly browned, about 4 minutes. Scrape every bit of the red pepper paste into the cooker and cook, stirring all the while, for 1 minute.

4. Turn off the **SAUTÉ** function. Stir in the black-eye beans, tomatoes, stock and dill until uniform. Lock the lid onto the pot.

5.

Set the machine	Level	The valve must be	Time	Press
PRESSURE COOK	MAX	——	3 minutes with the KEEP WARM setting off	START
MEAT/STEW, PRESSURE COOK or MANUAL	HIGH	Closed	5 minutes with the KEEP WARM setting off	START

6. Use the **quick-release method** to bring the pot's pressure back to normal. Unlatch the lid and open the cooker. Stir well before serving.

Beyond

- For a 7.5-litre cooker, you must increase all the ingredients by 50 per cent.

- To omit the wine, use chicken stock in its place but add 1–2 tablespoons unsweetened cloudy apple juice with the stock in step 4.

- Add greens for a bigger meal. After cooking, stir 35g chopped stemmed chard into a 3-litre cooker, 70g chopped stemmed chard into a 5.5-litre cooker, or 100g chopped stemmed chard into a 7.5-litre cooker. Set the lid over the pot and set aside for 5 minutes to wilt the greens.

Turkey Meatballs in a Lemony Sauce

4–6 servings

This braise is a Greek diner version of meatballs, served in a rich, lemony sauce thickened with eggs, maybe like a meatball version of avgolemono. (Check out our recipe for that soup on page 73.)

Whisk constantly and efficiently after the egg mixture goes into the pot. The sauce should never come back to a simmer or the eggs can scramble. Keep your wits about you.

1. Mix the turkey, parsley, couscous, 1 egg, garlic, vinegar, onion powder, dill, oregano, salt and pepper in a large bowl until uniform. Form this mixture into 16 balls.

2. Pour the stock into a **5.5- or 7.5-litre cooker**. Put the meatballs in the pot in as even a layer (or two) as possible. Lock the lid onto the pot.

3.

Set the machine	Level	The valve must be	Time	Press
PRESSURE COOK	MAX	——	2 minutes with the KEEP WARM setting off	START
MEAT/STEW, PRESSURE COOK or MANUAL	HIGH	Closed	5 minutes with the KEEP WARM setting off	START

4. Use the **quick-release method** to bring the pot's pressure back to normal. Unlatch the lid and open the cooker. Use a slotted spoon to transfer the meatballs to a large bowl. (They're fragile, so take care.)

5.

Press	Setting	Time	Press
SAUTÉ	LOW or LESS	5 minutes	START

6. Bring the sauce in the cooker to a simmer. Meanwhile, whisk the lemon juice and cornflour in a medium bowl until smooth. Whisk the remaining 3 eggs into this lemon juice mixture, then whisk about 250ml of the sauce from the cooker into this mixture. Whisk this combined mixture into the sauce in the pot, whisking just until thickened, *not* returned to the boil. Immediately turn off the **SAUTÉ** function and remove the *hot* insert from the pot. Whisk a few more times, then return the meatballs to the sauce, tossing gently to coat them. Serve hot.

700g lean turkey mince

10g fresh parsley leaves, finely chopped

100g instant couscous

4 large eggs

2 medium garlic cloves, peeled and finely chopped (2 teaspoons prechopped)

3 tablespoons white wine vinegar

1 teaspoon onion powder

1 teaspoon dried dill

1 teaspoon dried oregano

1 teaspoon table salt

½ teaspoon ground black pepper

700ml chicken stock

60ml fresh lemon juice

1½ tablespoons cornflour

Beyond

- You must halve the recipe for a 3-litre cooker.

- To pair this with a classic Greek diner salad, start with chopped iceberg lettuce, then add chopped cucumbers, sliced pitted black olives and thinly sliced red onion. Add olive oil and red wine vinegar in a 4:1 oil to vinegar ratio. Season the salad with dried oregano, table salt and ground black pepper. Toss well and crumble feta over the top of each serving.

2 tablespoons olive oil

Two poussin, giblets and necks removed, each halved lengthways

1 large leek (about 175g), white and pale green parts only, halved lengthways, well washed and thinly sliced

350ml chicken stock

1 small lemon, scrubbed to remove any waxy coating, then halved and sliced into thin half-moons, any pips removed

1 tablespoon honey

1 tablespoon picked fresh thyme leaves

1 teaspoon salt-free lemon pepper seasoning

1 teaspoon table salt

Poached Poussin in a Lemon-Thyme Sauce

4 servings

Although roasting poussin gives them a crisp skin, the birds can also be poached. Here, little bits of lemon will soften under pressure, a great match to the meat. Although we suggest removing the necks and giblets, you can certainly add the necks to the pot, even if you don't intend to eat them, mostly to give the sauce a more assertive 'poultry' flavour. In fact, you can even chop up the hearts and gizzards, if available, and add them to the pot. (Do not use the liver.)

1.

Press	Setting	Time	Press
SAUTÉ	MEDIUM, NORMAL or CUSTOM 150°C	15 minutes	START

2. Warm the oil in a **5.5- or 7.5-litre cooker** for a minute or two. Add the two halves of one bird skin-side down and brown *well* without turning, about 5 minutes. Transfer the halves to a bowl and brown the remaining halves in the same way before transferring them to that bowl.

3. Add the leek and cook, stirring often, until softened, about 3 minutes. Stir in the stock and scrape up any browned bits on the pot's bottom. Turn off the **SAUTÉ** function and mix in the lemon slices, honey, thyme, lemon pepper seasoning and salt. Nestle the birds skin-side up in the sauce, overlapping them to fit. Pour any juices from their bowl over them, then lock the lid onto the cooker.

4.

Set the machine	Level	The valve must be	Time	Press
PRESSURE COOK	MAX	—	12 minutes with the KEEP WARM setting off	START
MEAT/STEW, PRESSURE COOK or MANUAL	HIGH	Closed	15 minutes with the KEEP WARM setting off	START

5. Use the **quick-release method** to bring the pot's pressure back to normal. Unlatch the lid and open the pot. Serve the poussin halves in bowls with the pot's sauce over them.

Beyond

- You must halve the recipe for a 3-litre cooker.

- For a more classic sauce, remove the cooked poussin from the pot. Scoop out all the lemon pieces, too, reserving them as a garnish. Bring the remaining sauce in the pot to a simmer using the SAUTÉ function at MEDIUM, NORMAL or CUSTOM 150°C. Cook, stirring often, until somewhat reduced, about 3 minutes. Turn off the SAUTÉ function and whisk in up to 55g butter. Spoon this sauce over the birds, then top with some of the lemon bits.

- For a little heat, add up to ½ teaspoon crushed chilli flakes with the thyme.

Stuffed Peppers

4 servings

This old-school main course is much easier in the cooker. But because of the way the pressure works, it's better to cook the filling for the peppers in advance. When we tested the peppers with a raw-meat filling, it was too 'pudding-like', even mousse-y. And because the Italian seasoning blend and jarred marinara sauce may have added salt, we suggest adding the salt only if you like really salty food.

1.

Press	Setting	Time	Press
SAUTÉ	MEDIUM, NORMAL or CUSTOM 150°C	10 minutes	START

2. Warm the oil in a **5.5-litre cooker** for a minute or two. Crumble in the beef mince and cook, stirring occasionally, partly to break up any clumps, until browned, about 5 minutes. Stir in half of the cheese, the beans, rice, Italian seasoning blend and salt (if using). Stir well, then turn off the **SAUTÉ** function and scrape this mixture from the *hot* insert into a large bowl. Return the insert to the cooker. (There's no need to clean it.)

3. Remove the 'tops' of the peppers by cutting off the stem and about 1cm of the pepper below it. Use a large spoon (preferably a serrated grapefruit spoon) to remove the core, seeds and any white membranes from inside the peppers. Stuff them with the beef mixture.

4. Pour the marinara sauce and water into the cooker. Stand the peppers up in the sauce, leaning against one another and the sides of the cooker. Divide the remaining cheese amongst the tops of the stuffed peppers.

5.

Set the machine	Level	The valve must be	Time	Press
PRESSURE COOK	MAX	—	10 minutes with the KEEP WARM setting off	START
MEAT/STEW, PRESSURE COOK or MANUAL	HIGH	Closed	12 minutes with the KEEP WARM setting off	START

6. When the machine has finished cooking, turn it off and let its pressure **return to normal naturally** for 10 minutes. Then use the **quick-release method** to get rid of any residual pressure in the pot. Unlatch the lid and open the cooker. Use a large spoon and a palette knife to transfer the peppers to serving bowls. Spoon lots of the sauce around them.

1 tablespoon olive oil

450g lean beef mince

115g grated semi-firm mozzarella

130g tinned red kidney beans, drained

50g long-grain white rice

1 tablespoon dried Italian seasoning blend

½ teaspoon table salt (optional)

4 large peppers (green, yellow, orange or red)

One 680g jar classic marinara (tomato) sauce

125ml water

Beyond

- You must halve the recipe for a 3-litre cooker.

- For a 7.5-litre cooker, you must increase all the ingredients by 50 per cent (in other words, make 6 stuffed peppers).

- Feel free to substitute lean turkey mince for the beef mince.

- To make a Tex-Mex version, substitute black turtle beans for the kidney beans, 115g shredded Mexican blend of cheeses for the mozzarella, 1 tablespoon chilli powder for the dried Italian seasoning blend and 680g plain bottled salsa for the marinara sauce.

**1 tablespoon solid
or liquid fat**

Choose from vegetable, corn, rapeseed, safflower, grapeseed, olive, avocado or any nut oil; or butter, coconut oil, lard, schmaltz, duck, goose or rendered bacon fat.

1700g lean beef mince

250ml stock

Choose any sort.

2 tablespoons tomato purée

750–900g chopped quick-cooking vegetables

Choose at least two from cored and deseeded peppers of any sort, broccoli florets, carrots, cauliflower florets, celery, corn kernels (if frozen, do not thaw), frozen edamame (do not thaw), frozen sliced okra (do not thaw), onions of any sort, peas (if frozen, do not thaw), trimmed green beans and/or courgettes.

2 tablespoons vinegar

Choose from apple cider (with or without the mother), red wine, white wine, balsamic or white balsamic (but not a flavoured vinegar).

Up to 1½ tablespoons dried herbs and/or spices

Choose at least two from ground cinnamon, ground coriander, caraway seeds, celery seeds, fennel seeds, basil, oregano, parsley, rosemary, sage, savory and/or thyme (remembering that dried spices are more powerful than dried herbs), or a purchased spice blend such as herbes de Provence, a dried Italian blend or other blends.

1 tablespoon soy sauce

1 teaspoon ground black pepper

Up to 1 teaspoon crushed chilli flakes (optional)

115–225g grated semi-firm cheese

Choose from mild or mature Cheddar, Gouda, Swiss, or a ready-made grated cheese blend (without any added spices).

Road Map: Beef Mince Stew

6 servings

This beef mince stew with cheese may well be one of the most classic expressions of comfort food. Don't tell the kids, but we've snuck in lots of vegetables. We've used soy sauce, too, perhaps a bit of a surprise, in a bid to bump up the umami flavours often lost under pressure.

This same stew will actually work with any minced meat, such as turkey, chicken, pork or veal. Just use a lean mince to stop the stew becoming too fatty.

1.

Press	Setting	Time	Press
SAUTÉ	MEDIUM, NORMAL or CUSTOM 150°C	5 minutes	START

2. Warm the oil or melt the fat in a **5.5-litre cooker**. Crumble in the beef mince and cook, stirring often, partly to break up any clumps, until the meat loses its raw, pink colour, 2–3 minutes. Pour in the stock and add the tomato purée. Stir until the purée has dissolved.

3. Turn off the **SAUTÉ** function. Add the quick-cooking vegetables, vinegar, dried herb and/or spice blend, soy sauce, black pepper and crushed chilli flakes (if using). Stir until uniform, then lock the lid onto the pot.

4.

Set the machine	Level	The valve must be	Time	Press
PRESSURE COOK	MAX	——	5 minutes with the KEEP WARM setting off	START
MEAT/STEW, PRESSURE COOK or MANUAL	HIGH	Closed	7 minutes with the KEEP WARM setting off	START

5. Use the **quick-release method** to bring the pot's pressure back to normal. Unlatch the lid and open the cooker. Stir in the cheese, then set the lid askew over the pot for 5 minutes to melt the cheese and blend the flavours. Stir again before serving.

Beyond

- You must halve the recipe for a 3-litre cooker.

- For a 7.5-litre cooker, you must increase all the ingredients by 50 per cent.

- If you'd rather not add the cheese, don't. Serve this simpler stew over long-grain white or brown rice or over cooked and drained wheat berries (see page 395) instead.

- Omit the semi-firm cheese and freeze 115g cream cheese or fresh mozzarella for 30 minutes, then dice into small cubes and let it return to room temperature. Stir into the hot stew after cooking.

- Omit the stirred-in cheese and serve the stew over small mounds of ricotta.

- If you're looking for a beef mince and pasta casserole, see page 167.

2 tablespoons vegetable, corn or rapeseed oil

1 medium onion, chopped (160g prechopped)

700g lean beef mince

125g thinly sliced carrots

225g fresh green beans, trimmed and cut into 2.5cm pieces

2 medium garlic cloves, peeled and finely chopped (2 teaspoons prechopped)

1 tablespoon Worcestershire sauce

1 tablespoon yellow mustard

1 tablespoon tomato purée

2 teaspoons dried thyme

1 teaspoon table salt

½ teaspoon ground black pepper

500ml beef or chicken stock

135g plain flour

1 teaspoon baking powder

1 teaspoon bicarbonate of soda

1 teaspoon white granulated sugar

125ml regular or low-fat milk

30g butter, melted and cooled

Beef Mince and Vegetable Stew with Dumplings

4–6 servings

Tender dumplings can be a bit of a problem in the cooker, mostly because of the brilliant way it keeps moisture inside. But by stirring together a slightly wetter dough *and* making smaller dumplings than perhaps normal, we can indeed steam dumplings over the stew as it simmers after cooking under pressure.

That said, the pot's interior environment is, well, humid. The dumplings will never become light and fluffy. They'll remain dense and slippery, if still a nice match to the stew underneath. If the timing of your machine cannot be set as low as 20 minutes on the SLOW COOK function, set it as low as it can, then set another timer for the dumplings.

1.

Press	Setting	Time	Press
SAUTÉ	MEDIUM, NORMAL or CUSTOM 150°C	10 minutes	START

2. Warm the oil in a **5.5- or 7.5-litre cooker** for a minute or two. Add the onion and cook, stirring occasionally, until softened, about 4 minutes. Crumble in the beef mince and cook, stirring often, partly to break up any clumps, until the meat loses its raw, pink colour, about 2 minutes.

3. Stir in the carrots and green beans until uniform; then add the garlic, Worcestershire sauce, mustard, tomato purée, thyme, ½ teaspoon salt and the pepper. Stir until aromatic, just a few seconds. Pour in the stock and stir well to scrape up any browned bits on the pot's bottom. Turn off the **SAUTÉ** function and lock the lid onto the pot.

4.

Set the machine	Level	The valve must be	Time	Press
PRESSURE COOK	MAX	—	5 minutes with the KEEP WARM setting off	START
MEAT/STEW, PRESSURE COOK or MANUAL	HIGH	Closed	7 minutes with the KEEP WARM setting off	START

5. As the stew cooks, whisk the flour, baking powder, bicarbonate of soda, sugar and the remaining ½ teaspoon salt in a medium bowl until uniform. Stir in the milk and melted butter to form a wet dough, sort of like a thick batter.

6. When the machine has finished cooking, use the **quick-release method** to bring the pot's pressure back to normal. Unlatch the lid and open the cooker. Stir the stew, then drop the dough/batter by six or seven blobs over the top. Latch the lid back onto the pot.

7.

Set the machine	Level	The valve must be	Time	Press
SLOW COOK	HIGH	Opened	20 minutes with the KEEP WARM setting off	START

8. Switch off the **SLOW COOK** function. Unlatch the lid and open the pot. Leave to cool for a few minutes and then serve by the big spoonful without stirring.

Beyond

- You must halve the recipe for a 3-litre cooker.
- You can increase all the ingredients in a 7.5-litre cooker.
- Add up to 2 tablespoons finely chopped fresh parsley, oregano or thyme to the dumpling dough/batter as you add the milk and butter.
- Or add up to 55g grated Cheddar or Swiss cheese with the milk and butter.
- For a richer stew, omit the oil and cook the onion in 30g butter.
- Omit this dumpling dough and use the one given for buttermilk dumplings on page 302.

Two 400g tins chopped tomatoes

500ml beef or chicken stock

1 medium green or red pepper, stemmed, cored and chopped (175g prechopped)

1 small onion, chopped (80g prechopped)

125g thinly sliced carrots

2 teaspoons dried basil or oregano

1 teaspoon dried thyme

½ teaspoon table salt

¼ teaspoon grated nutmeg

450g lean beef mince

450g bulk sweet or mild Italian sausage meat (no casings)

1 large egg

50g Italian-seasoned dried breadcrumbs

60ml regular or low-fat milk

Braised Italian Meatballs

6 servings

For these tasty meatballs poached in a light tomato sauce, we use Italian sausage and seasoned breadcrumbs so we don't have to empty a spice pantry to get the right flavours. You could even serve the meatballs on split Italian bread rolls with shredded mozzarella cheese and some of the sauce from the pot.

For more classic flair, skip the dried herbs and add 1 tablespoon each of finely chopped fresh basil and oregano, as well as 2 teaspoons fresh thyme leaves.

1. Stir the tomatoes, stock, pepper, onion, carrot, basil or oregano, thyme, salt and nutmeg in a **5.5- or 7.5-litre cooker.**

2. Mix the beef mince, sausage meat, egg, breadcrumbs and milk in a large bowl until uniform. With clean, dry hands, form the mixture into 12 evenly sized balls. Gently immerse these meatballs into the tomato mixture in the cooker. Lock the lid onto the pot.

3.

Set the machine	Level	The valve must be	Time	Press
PRESSURE COOK	MAX	—	10 minutes with the KEEP WARM setting off	START
MEAT/STEW, PRESSURE COOK or MANUAL	HIGH	Closed	12 minutes with the KEEP WARM setting off	START

4. When the machine has finished cooking, turn it off and let its pressure **return to normal naturally**, about 25 minutes. Unlatch the lid and open the pot. Serve the meatballs in bowls with lots of the sauce.

Beyond

- You must halve the recipe for a 3-litre cooker.

- The sauce is thin. If desired, transfer the meatballs to a serving platter, then stir 60g tomato purée into the sauce and use the SAUTÉ function at MEDIUM, NORMAL or CUSTOM 150°C to reduce and thicken the sauce, stirring often, 2–3 minutes.

- For more flavour, brown the meatballs before cooking them in the pot on a large baking tin in a 180°C oven for 10 minutes, turning occasionally. (They are fragile so handle them gently.)

- Grate lots of Parmigiano-Reggiano over the servings, and/or drizzle with balsamic vinegar.

Meatballs with Red Cabbage, Tomato and Dill

4 servings

If you're looking for something beyond the ordinary, try this meatball stew, made with a combination of cabbage, dill and cinnamon. Some supermarkets sell red cabbage shredded into long, thin strips. If yours doesn't, split a medium head in half, remove the tough core and set the cabbage head cut-side down on a chopping board. Make cuts every 5mm across the head, then separate the shreds. Cut long shreds in half, if not thirds.

As a technique note, the previous recipe had a natural release; this one, a quick release. There, we wanted a deeply 'braised' flavour, letting the meatballs absorb some of the sauce as the pressure returned to normal. Here, we use a quick release to stop the cabbage getting too soft.

700g lean beef mince

1 large egg

50g long-grain white rice

½ teaspoon dried oregano

½ teaspoon garlic powder

½ teaspoon onion powder

½ teaspoon table salt

½ teaspoon ground black pepper

2 tablespoons olive oil

1 medium onion, chopped (160g prechopped)

280g cored and shredded red cabbage

125ml dry but fruit-forward red wine, such as Zinfandel

One 400g tin chopped tomatoes

125ml beef or chicken stock

12g fresh dill fronds, finely chopped

1 teaspoon ground cinnamon

1. Mix the beef mince, egg, rice, oregano, garlic powder, onion powder, salt and pepper in a large bowl until uniform. With clean and dry hands, form this mixture into 12 evenly sized balls. Set them aside.

2.

Press	Setting	Time	Press
SAUTÉ	MEDIUM, NORMAL or CUSTOM 150°C	10 minutes	START

3. Warm the oil in a **5.5- or 7.5-litre cooker** for a minute or two. Add the onion and cook, stirring occasionally, until softened, about 4 minutes. Add the cabbage and cook, stirring more often, until it begins to wilt, about 3 minutes. Pour in the wine and scrape up any browned bits on the pot's bottom.

4. Turn off the **SAUTÉ** function. Stir in the tomatoes, stock, dill and cinnamon; scrape up any browned bits on the pot's bottom. Nestle the meatballs into this sauce. Lock the lid onto the pot.

5.

Set the machine	Level	The valve must be	Time	Press
PRESSURE COOK	MAX	—	10 minutes with the KEEP WARM setting off	START
MEAT/STEW, PRESSURE COOK or MANUAL	HIGH	Closed	12 minutes with the KEEP WARM setting off	START

6. Use the **quick-release method** to bring the pot's pressure back to normal. Unlatch the lid and open the cooker. Stir gently before serving.

Beyond

- You must halve the recipe for a 3-litre cooker.
- For a brighter flavour, stir up to 2 tablespoons red wine vinegar or balsamic vinegar into the stew after cooking.
- Garnish the servings with soured cream.
- Serve with crunchy pretzels instead of bread. Or serve the meatballs and vegetables with a little sauce on pretzel rolls. (They'll be messy. Keep any white linens away from the table.)

2 tablespoons olive oil

1 small onion, chopped
(80g prechopped)

130g chopped carrots

1 medium celery stalk, thinly
sliced

1 medium garlic clove,
peeled and finely chopped
(1 teaspoon prechopped)

1 teaspoon dried thyme

700g lean beef mince

155g fresh or frozen peas
(if frozen, do not thaw)

300ml beef or chicken stock

1½ tablespoons tomato purée

1 tablespoon Worcestershire
sauce

700g potatoes,such as King
Edward, peeled and grated
through the large holes of
a box grater

1 teaspoon table salt

½ teaspoon onion powder

½ teaspoon ground black
pepper

1 teaspoon mild paprika

Mock Shepherd's Pie

4–6 servings

Why 'mock'? It's because we put seasoned, grated potatoes over
this beef mince stew to mimic mashed potatoes. The potatoes
won't be fluffy and creamy, but they'll have a better texture
(mashed potatoes under pressure can get gummy). And the
potatoes' starch will thicken the stew below, turning this retro
casserole into a one-pot meal.

1.

Press	Setting	Time	Press
SAUTÉ	MEDIUM, NORMAL or CUSTOM 150°C	10 minutes	START

2. Warm the oil in a **5.5-litre cooker** for a minute or two. Add the
onion, carrots and celery. Cook, stirring occasionally, until the
onion softens, about 3 minutes. Stir in the garlic and thyme until
aromatic, for just a few seconds.

3. Crumble in the beef mince and cook, stirring more often,
partly to break up any clumps, until the meat loses its raw, red
colour, about 3 minutes. Turn off the **SAUTÉ** function and stir in
the peas, stock, tomato purée and Worcestershire sauce until the
purée dissolves, scraping up any browned bits on the pot's
bottom.

4. Toss the grated potatoes, salt, onion powder and pepper in a
large bowl until uniform. Scatter this mixture evenly over the top
of the beef mixture. Sprinkle the paprika evenly over the top.
Lock the lid onto the pot.

5.

Set the machine	Level	The valve must be	Time	Press
PRESSURE COOK	MAX	—	7 minutes with the KEEP WARM setting off	START
MEAT/ STEW, PRESSURE COOK or MANUAL	HIGH	Closed	10 minutes with the KEEP WARM setting off	START

6. When the machine has finished cooking, turn it off and let its
pressure **return to normal naturally** for 10 minutes. Then use the
quick-release method to get rid of any remaining pressure in the
pot. Unlatch the lid and open the cooker. Serve by scooping up
the potatoes and stew by big spoonfuls and into bowls.

Beyond

- You must halve the recipe
  for a 3-litre cooker.
- For a 7.5-litre cooker, you
  must increase all the
  ingredients by 50 per cent.
- Try seasoning the potatoes
  by omitting the onion powder
  and pepper and using up to
  2 teaspoons of a dried spice
  blend. Or omit the onion
  powder and mix 1 medium
  spring onion, trimmed and
  finely chopped, with the
  potatoes.
- For a richer dish, dot up to
  30g butter over the potatoes
  before the dish is cooked
  under pressure.

Pork Chops and Potatoes with Mexican Salsa Verde

4 servings

The surprising combination of butter and salsa verde (sometimes called 'tomatillo salsa') gives this dish a range of sour and sweet flavours, a great way to make a simple braise more sophisticated. Salsa verde can be salty, so there's no added salt in the recipe.

1. Mix the salsa verde and stock in a **5.5-litre cooker**. Nestle the pork chops into the mixture, overlapping them to fit. Make a layer with the potato wedges skin-side down on top, then pour the melted butter over them. Sprinkle the potatoes with the paprika and pepper. Lock the lid onto the cooker.

2.

Set the machine	Level	The valve must be	Time	Press
PRESSURE COOK	MAX	—	8 minutes with the KEEP WARM setting off	START
MEAT/STEW, PRESSURE COOK or MANUAL	HIGH	Closed	10 minutes with the KEEP WARM setting off	START

3. When the machine has finished cooking, turn it off and let its pressure **return to normal naturally** for 5 minutes. Then use the **quick-release method** to get rid of any residual pressure in the pot. Unlatch the lid and open the cooker. Serve the potatoes and pork chops with the sauce ladled around them.

250ml jarred Mexican salsa verde

90ml chicken stock

Four 4cm-thick, boneless, centre-cut pork loin chops

Four 175g waxy potatoes, such as Desiree, quartered

55g butter, melted

½ teaspoon mild paprika

½ teaspoon ground black pepper

Beyond

- For a 3-litre cooker, you must use 125ml stock but halve the remaining ingredients.

- For a 7.5-litre cooker, you must increase the stock to 180ml but use the stated amount f the remaining ingredients. Or you can increase all the ingredients by 50 per cent in a 7.5-litre cooker.

- Feel free to substitute four 225–300g boneless skinless chicken thighs (the giant ones) for the pork chops.

2 tablespoons solid or liquid fat

Choose from butter, lard, schmaltz, duck fat, or goose fat; or vegetable, corn, rapeseed, safflower, olive, avocado or any nut oil – or choose a 50/50 combo of a solid and a liquid fat.

Four 300–340g bone-in pork loin chops

½ teaspoon table salt

½ teaspoon ground black pepper

350g chopped quick-cooking vegetables

Choose at least two from carrots, celery, frozen artichoke heart quarters (do not thaw), leeks (white and pale green parts only, well washed), brown or white button mushrooms, onions (of any sort), shallots, shelled edamame (if frozen, do not thaw), peas (if frozen, do not thaw), stemmed and cored pepper, trimmed spring onions, trimmed fennel, yellow summer squash and/or courgettes.

2 tablespoons finely chopped fresh herbs

Choose one or two from marjoram, parsley, oregano, rosemary, sage, savory and/or thyme.

Up to 1 teaspoon dried spices (optional)

Choose one or two from cardamom pods (seeds only), grated nutmeg, ground allspice, ground cardamom, ground coriander, ground cinnamon, ground fenugreek and/or ground mace.

350ml liquid

Choose a stock of any sort, or a combination of stock and white wine, dry vermouth or dry sherry, most likely in a ratio of 250ml stock and 125ml wine, or perhaps in a ratio of 300ml stock and 60ml wine for a more savoury dish.

Road Map: Braised Pork Chops

4 servings

Although boneless centre-cut pork loin chops need extra care in the pot to stay juicy, those with the bone attached have some natural protection, as well as more fat and cartilage. All of this guarantees a better meal. Pay careful attention here to the size of the chops. These are substantial cuts. (The thin ones cook in just a few minutes on the hob anyway.)

1.

Press	Setting	Time	Press
SAUTÉ	MEDIUM, NORMAL or CUSTOM 150°C	20 minutes	START

2. Melt the fat or warm the oil in a **5.5- or 7.5-litre cooker**. Season the pork chops with salt and pepper, then put two in the cooker. Brown well on both sides, turning a couple of times, about 6 minutes. Transfer the chops to a nearby bowl and brown the other two in the same way before transferring them to the bowl.

3. Add the chopped vegetables and cook, stirring often, until a little softened, about 3 minutes. Stir in the herbs and spices (if using) until aromatic, just a few seconds. Pour in the liquid and scrape up any browned bits on the pot's bottom.

4. Turn off the **SAUTÉ** function and nestle the pork chops into the sauce, overlapping them as necessary. Pour any juice from their bowl on top and lock the lid onto the cooker.

5.

Set the machine	Level	The valve must be	Time	Press
PRESSURE COOK	MAX	——	9 minutes with the KEEP WARM setting off	START
MEAT/STEW, PRESSURE COOK or MANUAL	HIGH	Closed	12 minutes with the KEEP WARM setting off	START

6. Use the **quick-release method** to return the pot's pressure to normal. Unlatch the lid and open the pot. Transfer the pork chops to serving plates or bowls; ladle the sauce on top.

Beyond

- You must halve the recipe for a 3-litre cooker.

- For a 7.5-litre cooker, you can increase the ingredients by 50 per cent.

- To add a hint of sweetness, use some chopped, cored and peeled apple as part of the quick-cooking mix. Or use peeled and deseeded butternut or winter squash, diced into 5mm pieces.

- If the sauce is too thin for your taste, remove the cooked pork chops and use a slotted spoon to remove the vegetables, too. Bring the sauce to a simmer using the SAUTÉ function at MEDIUM, NORMAL or CUSTOM 150°C. Cook for 1 minute, then stir in a slurry of 1 tablespoon cornflour or potato starch whisked with 1 tablespoon water. Stir until thickened, then turn off the SAUTÉ function and remove the hot insert from the pot to stop the cooking.

2 teaspoons mild smoked
paprika

1 teaspoon ground black
pepper

½ teaspoon table salt

4 boneless pork loin chops,
each 4cm in thickness

2 tablespoons olive oil

115g smoked streaky bacon,
chopped

1 small red onion, chopped
(80g prechopped)

2 medium garlic cloves,
peeled and finely chopped
(2 teaspoons prechopped)

1 tinned chipotle chilli in
adobo sauce, stemmed,
deseeded (if desired)
and chopped

1 tablespoon adobo sauce
from the tin

1 teaspoon dried oregano

125ml chicken stock

180ml porter, preferably
a smoky porter

12 baby carrots or 2 medium
carrots, cut into 1cm
sections

Smoky Pork Chops and Carrots

4 servings

To keep *boneless* centre-cut pork chops juicy, they must be on the thick side: 4cm, in fact. We also increase the fats and sugars in the sauce so that it will coat and protect the meat. Consider these the guidelines for success with almost any boneless pork chop recipe in the pot.

If you can't find boneless pork chops this thick, buy a boneless pork loin and cut it into chops yourself. The streaky bacon adds bits of chewy smokiness to the sauce.

1. Mix the smoked paprika, pepper and salt in a small bowl. Pat the pork chops dry with kitchen paper, then pat and rub this spice mixture onto both sides of the meat. Set aside.

2.

Press	Setting	Time	Press
SAUTÉ	MEDIUM, NORMAL or CUSTOM 150°C	15 minutes	START

3. Warm the oil in a **5.5-litre cooker** for a minute or two. Set two pork chops in the cooker and brown lightly on both sides, turning a couple of times, about 4 minutes. Transfer them to a nearby bowl and brown the other two pork chops in the same way before transferring them to the bowl.

4. Add the bacon and onion. Cook, stirring often, until the bacon browns a bit and the onion softens, about 4 minutes. Stir in the garlic, chipotle, adobo sauce and oregano until aromatic, about 30 seconds. Pour in the stock and scrape up any browned bits on the pot's bottom.

5. Turn off the **SAUTÉ** function. Stir in the porter, then nestle the pork chops into the sauce, overlapping them as necessary. Pour any juice from their bowl on top, scatter the carrots around the cooker and lock the lid onto the pot.

6.

Set the machine	Level	The valve must be	Time	Press
PRESSURE COOK	MAX	——	8 minutes with the KEEP WARM setting off	START
MEAT/STEW, PRESSURE COOK or MANUAL	HIGH	Closed	10 minutes with the KEEP WARM setting off	START

7. When the machine has finished cooking, turn it off and let its pressure **return to normal naturally** for 5 minutes. Then use the **quick-release method** to get rid of any residual pressure in the pot. Unlatch the lid and open the cooker. Use kitchen tongs to transfer the chops to serving plates and spoon the carrots, onions, bacon and sauce around them.

Beyond

- You must halve the recipe for a 3-litre cooker.

- For a 7.5-litre cooker, you must increase all the ingredients by 50 per cent.

- Substitute additional stock for the porter but increase the smoked paprika to 1 tablespoon and add up to 2 teaspoons dark brown sugar with the garlic.

- For a built-in side, pile up to 70–140g shredded, cored green cabbage over the carrots and pork chops before locking the lid onto the cooker. (Do not pack ingredients above the Max Fill line.)

1 tablespoon olive oil

Four boneless pork loin chops, each 4 cm in thickness

½ teaspoon table salt

½ teaspoon ground black pepper

65g frozen baby onions (do not thaw)

1 medium garlic clove, peeled and finely chopped (1 teaspoon prechopped)

One 400g tin chopped tomatoes with green chillies

180ml chicken stock

70g dried black-eye beans

2 teaspoons mild paprika

1 teaspoon dried thyme

½ teaspoon grated nutmeg

300g frozen sliced okra (do not thaw)

1 tablespoon white wine vinegar

Pork Chops with Black-Eye Beans and Okra

4 servings

This down-home braise is Southern comfort food, made a little spicy by the tinned tomatoes with chillies. If desired, tame it by using regular tinned chopped tomatoes (preferably fire-roasted for more flavour). Or up the heat by also adding up to 1 teaspoon hot red pepper sauce, such as Tabasco or Sriracha, with the dried spices.

1.

Press	Setting	Time	Press
SAUTÉ	MEDIUM, NORMAL or CUSTOM 150°C	10 minutes	START

2. Warm the oil in a **5.5-litre cooker** for a minute or two. Season the pork chops with the salt and pepper, then lightly brown two in the cooker, turning occasionally, about 3 minutes. Transfer them to a nearby bowl and brown the remaining two in the same way before transferring them to the bowl.

3. Add the baby onions and cook, stirring occasionally, until lightly browned in a few places, about 3 minutes. Add the garlic and cook, stirring all the while, until aromatic, about 20 seconds. Stir in the tomatoes and stock; scrape up any browned bits on the pot's bottom.

4. Turn off the **SAUTÉ** function and stir in the black-eye beans, paprika, thyme and nutmeg until uniform. Lock the lid onto the cooker.

5.

Set the machine	Level	The valve must be	Time	Press
PRESSURE COOK	MAX	—	10 minutes with the KEEP WARM setting off	START
MEAT/STEW, PRESSURE COOK or MANUAL	HIGH	Closed	12 minutes with the KEEP WARM setting off	START

6. Use the **quick-release method** to bring the pot's pressure back to normal. Unlatch the lid and open the cooker. Nestle the pork chops into the hot sauce. Pour any juice from their bowl over them and scatter the okra on top. Lock the lid back onto the pot.

7.

Set the machine	Level	The valve must be	Time	Press
PRESSURE COOK	MAX	——	10 minutes with the KEEP WARM setting off	START
MEAT/STEW, PRESSURE COOK or MANUAL	HIGH	Closed	12 minutes with the KEEP WARM setting off	START

8. Once again, use the **quick-release method** to bring the pot's pressure back to normal. Unlatch the lid and open the cooker. Transfer the pork chops to serving plates or bowls. Stir the vinegar into the sauce with the okra, then ladle this mixture over the pork chops.

Beyond

- You must halve the recipe for a 3-litre cooker.

- For a 7.5-litre cooker, you must increase all the ingredients by 50 per cent.

- Frozen okra works best because it won't be as slimy. Even if you buy fresh, it's best to cut it into 2.5cm chunks and freeze it for this recipe.

700g lean pork mince

65g long-grain white rice,
such as white basmati

1 large egg

½ teaspoon onion powder

½ teaspoon grated nutmeg

½ teaspoon table salt

½ teaspoon ground black
pepper

1 large savoy cabbage

55g thick-cut bacon, chopped

1 small onion, chopped
(80g prechopped)

130g chopped carrots

1 medium celery stalk, thinly
sliced

30g raisins

500ml chicken stock

60g tomato purée

1 tablespoon red wine
vinegar

1 teaspoon caraway seeds

Golumpkis

6 servings

A recipe for Polish stuffed cabbage rolls may seem an odd one
in a chapter of *short* braises. But the pot does make the cooking
go much faster than an hours-long simmer. Save this one for
a winter night.

As an aside, if you've got our book *The Kitchen Shortcut Bible*,
you already know that you can freeze the cabbage leaves and skip
the step of blanching them for the rolls.

1. Mix the pork mince, rice, egg, onion powder, nutmeg, salt
and pepper in a large bowl until uniform. Set aside. Remove
12 leaves from the cabbage head. Reserve the remaining leaves
for another purpose (and even freeze the core for a future batch
of Vegetable Stock, page 101).

2.

Press	Setting	Time	Press
SAUTÉ	HIGH or MORE	20 minutes	START

3. Fill a **5.5- or 7.5-litre cooker** about halfway with water and
bring the water to the boil. Meanwhile, set up a large bowl
of iced water on your work surface. Submerge two or three
cabbage leaves in the boiling water and blanch for 2 minutes,
then transfer to the iced water. Continue cooking more cabbage
leaves as directed, adding more ice to the water in the bowl
to keep it cold.

4. Once all the leaves have been blanched, turn off the **SAUTÉ**
function and drain the *hot* insert from the cooker. Return the
insert to the machine.

5. Drain the cabbage leaves into a large colander set in the sink.
Cut a V-shaped notch out of the stem end of each leaf to remove
any of the tough, pale white core.

6. Place one cabbage leaf on your work surface with the
V-shaped notch towards you. Set about 60g of the minced pork
filling in the middle of the leaf. Fold the two sides over the filling,
then roll the leaf closed, starting at the V side. Set aside,
seam-side down, and make 11 more rolls.

7.

Press	Setting	Time	Press
SAUTÉ	MEDIUM, NORMAL or CUSTOM 150°C	5 minutes	START

8. Add the bacon to the cooker and sauté, stirring often, until lightly browned. Add the onion, carrots, celery and raisins. Continue cooking, stirring often, until the onion softens, about 3 minutes. Use a slotted spoon to transfer about two-thirds of the mixture in the cooker to a nearby bowl. Turn off the **SAUTÉ** function.

9. Whisk the stock, tomato purée, vinegar and caraway seeds in a medium bowl until the tomato purée dissolves. Pour 125ml of this mixture into the cooker.

10. Layer about half the stuffed leaves seam-side down in the cooker. Top with half of the reserved bacon mixture. Make a second layer of rolls seam side-down and top with the remaining bacon mixture. Pour the remainder of the tomato purée mixture over the rolls.

11.

Set the machine	Level	The valve must be	Time	Press
PRESSURE COOK	MAX	——	13 minutes with the KEEP WARM setting off	START
MEAT/STEW, PRESSURE COOK or MANUAL	HIGH	Closed	18 minutes with the KEEP WARM setting off	START
SLOW COOK	HIGH	Opened	3 hours with the KEEP WARM setting off (or on for no more than 2 hours)	START

12. If you've used a pressure setting, turn the machine off when it has finished cooking and let its pressure **return to normal naturally,** about 30 minutes.

13. Unlatch the lid and open the cooker. Use a large spoon to transfer the stuffed rolls and the sauce to serving bowls.

Beyond

- **You must halve the recipe for a 3-litre cooker.**
- **Feel free to substitute turkey mince for the pork mince.**
- **For a fresher taste, add up to 200g freshly chopped tomatoes with the onions and other vegetables in the sauce and/or add up to 1 tablespoon fresh lemon juice and/or 1 teaspoon finely chopped lemon zest to the stock mixture.**
- **For a less sweet dish, omit the raisins as well as the salt from the filling. Add 1 tablespoon soy sauce to the tomato purée mixture.**

1.2kg smoked boneless ham, cut into 2.5cm pieces, any coatings or rubs removed

700g small white 'boiling' potatoes (do not use russets or baking potatoes), cut into 2.5cm pieces

125ml chicken stock

125ml fresh orange juice

130g chopped carrots

1–2 medium fresh jalapeño chillies, stemmed, halved lengthways, deseeded (if desired) and thinly sliced

2 tablespoons orange marmalade

1 tablespoon apple cider vinegar

½ teaspoon ground cinnamon

½ teaspoon ground ginger

Up to ½ teaspoon ground cloves

Spicy Ham and Spud Stew

6 servings

Flavourful, porky and luxurious, smoked ham is a great stewing meat for the Instant Pot. Here, it creates a dish that's like a glazed ham in stew form. Look for a whole smoked ham at the deli counter, or use smoked ham slices (sometimes called 'ham steaks'). Make sure there are no added flavourings to the meat. Slice off any rubs or marinade that may lay along its outer surface.

1. Stir all the ingredients in a **5.5-litre cooker** until the marmalade dissolves. Lock the lid onto the pot.

2.

Set the machine	Level	The valve must be	Time	Press
PRESSURE COOK	MAX	——	6 minutes with the KEEP WARM setting off	START
MEAT/STEW, PRESSURE COOK or MANUAL	HIGH	Closed	8 minutes with the KEEP WARM setting off	START
SLOW COOK	HIGH	Opened	3 hours with the KEEP WARM setting off (or on for no more than 2 hours)	START

3. If you've used a pressure setting, use the **quick-release method** to bring the pot's pressure back to normal.

4. Unlatch the lid and open the cooker. Stir well before serving.

Beyond

- You must halve the recipe for a 3-litre cooker.

- For a 7.5-litre cooker, you must increase all the ingredients by 50 per cent.

- The ham is salty, so there's no added salt. For a saltier dish, add up to 1 tablespoon soy sauce with the vinegar.

- For a more aromatic stew, substitute ginger marmalade for the orange marmalade.

- For a less sweet stew, omit the orange marmalade and increase the stock to 180ml.

- If you don't want a spicy stew, omit the jalapeños, reduce the marmalade to 1 tablespoon, reduce the orange juice to 60ml and increase the stock to 180ml.

Savoury Ham and Sweet Potato Stew

6 *servings*

If sweet potato hash were turned into a tomato-based stew, you'd have this dish. Even consider it a weekend breakfast if you bake a quick bread to go alongside.

1.

Press	Setting	Time	Press
SAUTÉ	MEDIUM, NORMAL or CUSTOM 150°C	5 minutes	START

2. Warm the oil in a **5.5-litre cooker** for a minute or two. Add the onion and peppers. Cook, stirring occasionally, until the onion softens, about 4 minutes. Turn off the **SAUTÉ** function.

3. Stir in all the remaining ingredients. Lock the lid onto the cooker.

4.

Set the machine	Level	The valve must be	Time	Press
PRESSURE COOK	MAX	—	6 minutes with the KEEP WARM setting off	START
MEAT/STEW, PRESSURE COOK or MANUAL	HIGH	Closed	8 minutes with the KEEP WARM setting off	START
SLOW COOK	HIGH	Opened	3 hours with the KEEP WARM setting off (or on for no more than 2 hours)	START

5. If you've used a pressure setting, use the **quick-release method** to bring the pot's pressure back to normal.

6. Unlatch the lid and open the cooker. Stir gently (to protect the sweet potatoes) before serving.

1 tablespoon vegetable, corn or rapeseed oil

1 medium onion, chopped (160g prechopped)

2 medium green peppers, stemmed, cored and chopped (350g prechopped)

1.2kg boneless smoked ham, cut into 2.5cm pieces, any coatings or rubs removed

2 large sweet potatoes (about 340g each), peeled and cut into 2.5cm pieces

250g tinned chopped tomatoes with plenty of their juice

125ml chicken stock

1 tablespoon Worcestershire sauce

1 tablespoon soy sauce

1 tablespoon jarred white horseradish

½ teaspoon ground cinnamon

½ teaspoon celery seeds

¼ teaspoon ground cloves

Up to ¼ teaspoon ground cayenne

Beyond

- You must halve the recipe for a 3-litre cooker.

- For a 7.5-litre cooker, you must increase all the ingredients by 50 per cent.

- For a sweeter stew, omit the soy sauce, increase the Worcestershire sauce to 2 tablespoons and add 1 tablespoon light brown sugar with the ham and other ingredients in step 3.

Two 400g tins chopped tomatoes

55g dark brown sugar

2–3 tablespoons apple cider vinegar

2 tablespoons Worcestershire sauce

1 tablespoon mild smoked paprika

1 tablespoon mustard powder

2 teaspoons ground cumin

½ teaspoon ground cloves

½ teaspoon garlic powder

½ teaspoon onion powder

½ teaspoon ground black pepper

¼ teaspoon table salt

1.2kg mild or hot Italian sausages, cut into 2.5cm pieces

2 tablespoons tomato purée

Barbecue Sausage Bites

6–8 servings

This easy sausage braise could become a standard on your buffet. It could also become an easy lunch or dinner any time you want a rich, sweet barbecue sauce to coat sausages. Yes, we're asking you to make your own barbecue sauce, rather than dumping in a bottle of the stuff. The flavours will be more balanced, more present, better all round.

1. Stir the tomatoes, brown sugar, vinegar, Worcestershire sauce, smoked paprika, mustard powder, cumin, cloves, garlic powder, onion powder, black pepper and salt in a **5.5-litre cooker** until the brown sugar dissolves. Add the sausage pieces and stir until evenly coated. Lock the lid onto the cooker.

2.

Set the machine	Level	The valve must be	Time	Press
PRESSURE COOK	MAX	—	5 minutes with the KEEP WARM setting off	START
MEAT/STEW, PRESSURE COOK or MANUAL	HIGH	Closed	7 minutes with the KEEP WARM setting off	START

3. Use the **quick-release method** to bring the pot's pressure back to normal. Unlatch the lid and open the cooker. Stir in the tomato purée.

4.

Press	Setting	Time	Press
SAUTÉ	MEDIUM, NORMAL or CUSTOM 150°C	5 minutes	START

5. Bring the dish to a simmer and cook, stirring often, until the sauce has thickened somewhat, about 3 minutes. Turn off the **SAUTÉ** function and serve as a stew in bowls or remove the insert and serve with cocktail sticks (for picking the sausage pieces out of the sauce).

Beyond

- You must halve the recipe for a 3-litre cooker.

- For a 7.5-litre cooker, you must increase all the ingredients by 50 per cent.

- To make a larger meal, add a 450g bag of frozen mixed vegetables, thawed, with the tomato purée in step 3, and serve over cooked ziti.

Sausage, Greens and Butternut Squash Stew

4–6 servings

Not much could be easier than this stew, especially if you buy bagged, chopped spring greens and pre-cubed butternut squash (which you'll probably need to cut into smaller pieces). The flavours skew a little more Italian than Southern USA, a surprising twist on a bowl of such comfort.

1.

Press	Setting	Time	Press
SAUTÉ	MEDIUM, NORMAL or CUSTOM 150°C	10 minutes	START

2. Warm the oil in a **5.5- or 7.5-litre cooker** for a minute or two. Add the sausage pieces and brown well, turning occasionally, about 6 minutes. Add the spring greens and cook, stirring occasionally, until wilted, about 2 minutes.

3. Add the butternut squash, sage, fennel seeds, crushed chilli flakes and nutmeg. Stir for 1 minute, then pour in the stock Scrape up any browned bits on the pot's bottom and turn off the **SAUTÉ** function. Stir in the vinegar and lock the lid onto the pot.

4.

Set the machine	Level	The valve must be	Time	Press
PRESSURE COOK	MAX	—	5 minutes with the KEEP WARM setting off	START
MEAT/STEW, PRESSURE COOK or MANUAL	HIGH	Closed	7 minutes with the KEEP WARM setting off	START

5. Use the **quick-release method** to bring the pot's pressure back to normal. Unlatch the lid and open the cooker. Stir well, then sprinkle the cheese over the top. Set the lid askew over the cooker for 5 minutes to melt the cheese. Stir again before serving.

1 tablespoon olive oil

700g mild or sweet Italian sausages, cut into 5cm pieces

1.2kg spring greens, washed, stemmed and chopped

1 small butternut squash, peeled, deseeded and cut into 2.5cm cubes

1 teaspoon dried sage

½ teaspoon fennel seeds

¼ teaspoon crushed chilli flakes

¼ teaspoon grated nutmeg

600ml chicken stock

1½ tablespoons white wine vinegar

55g finely grated Parmigiano-Reggiano

Beyond

- Since spring greens are so bulky, this recipe does not work well in a 3-litre cooker.

- Substitute Cajun andouille, smoked kielbasa, bratwurst, chicken and apple sausage or even chorizo sausage for the Italian sausage.

- For a less assertive flavour, substitute stemmed and chopped kale for the spring greens. (Avoid chard and spinach, which can get too squishy.)

- For a sweeter dish, substitute 2 medium sweet potatoes, peeled and cut into 2.5cm cubes, for the butternut squash.

350ml water

900g small clams, scrubbed for sand

30g butter

2 tablespoons olive oil

1 medium onion, chopped (160g prechopped)

1 small fennel bulb (175g), trimmed and chopped

2 medium celery stalks, thinly sliced

65g chopped carrots

1 small green pepper, stemmed, cored and chopped (90g prechopped)

3 medium garlic cloves, peeled and finely chopped (1 tablespoon prechopped)

Two 400g tins crushed tomatoes

500ml chicken stock

10g fresh parsley leaves, finely chopped

2 tablespoons tomato purée

1 tablespoon Worcestershire sauce

1 teaspoon dried oregano

1 teaspoon dried thyme

½ teaspoon ground black pepper

225g thick-fleshed, skinless white fish fillets, cut into 2.5cm pieces

225g shell-on prawns, peeled and deveined

225g small scallops, halved

Crushed chilli flakes for garnishing (optional)

Cioppino-Style Seafood Stew

6 servings

Cioppino is a fast dish, but you may not know it was first made with ketchup, which we forgo in a pressure cooker in favour of crushed tomatoes and tomato purée for a better sauce in very little time. We can also cook the clams under pressure, thereby creating a flavourful clam broth for the stew ahead.

Be aware that the water from the clams can be sandy and must be strained. If you don't have a *chinois* (see page 48) or muslin to line a colander, you can filter the liquid into a bowl through a coffee filter set in a small strainer. (Pour slowly so none of the liquid slops over the edge of the filter and into the bowl below.) Or just set the clam cooking liquid aside for 15 minutes to let the sand sink to the bottom of the bowl. Use only the top of the clam cooking liquid, avoiding the sand below and adding enough water to make 350ml total volume.

1. Pour the water into a **5.5- or 7.5-litre cooker**. Add the clams and lock the lid onto the pot.

2.

Set the machine	Level	The valve must be	Time	Press
PRESSURE COOK	MAX	——	2 minutes with the KEEP WARM setting off	START
PRESSURE COOK or MANUAL	HIGH	Closed	3 minutes with the KEEP WARM setting off	START

3. Use the **quick-release method** to bring the pot's pressure back to normal. Unlatch the lid and open the cooker. Use a slotted spoon to transfer the clams to a large bowl. Discard any clams that do not open.

4. Strain the liquid in the *hot* insert through a fine-mesh sieve like a *chinois* (or a colander lined with a double layer of muslin) into a bowl. Rinse out the insert and return it to the machine.

5.

Press	Setting	Time	Press
SAUTÉ	MEDIUM, NORMAL or CUSTOM 150°C	10 minutes	START

6. Melt the butter in the oil, then add the onion, fennel, celery, carrots, pepper and garlic. Cook, stirring often, until the onion softens and the vegetables are fragrant, about 6 minutes.

7. Stir in the tomatoes, stock and the reserved, strained clam cooking water. Scrape up any browned bits on the pot's bottom and turn off the **SAUTÉ** function. Stir in the parsley, tomato purée, Worcestershire sauce, oregano, thyme and pepper until the tomato purée dissolves. Lock the lid onto the pot.

8.

Set the machine	Level	The valve must be	Time	Press
PRESSURE COOK	MAX	—	5 minutes with the KEEP WARM setting off	START
PRESSURE COOK or MANUAL	HIGH	Closed	7 minutes with the KEEP WARM setting off	START

9. Use the **quick-release method** to bring the pot's pressure back to normal. Unlatch the lid and open the cooker. Stir well.

10.

Press	Setting	Time	Press
SAUTÉ	MEDIUM, NORMAL or CUSTOM 150°C	5 minutes	START

11. Add the fish, prawns and scallops. Stir gently, then cook, stirring very carefully and only occasionally, until the prawns are pink and firm, about 4 minutes. Turn off the **SAUTÉ** function and gently stir the reserved clams into the sauce. Set the lid askew over the pot and set aside for 5 minutes to warm the clams and blend the flavours. Serve in big bowls with crushed chilli flakes on the side, if desired, for sprinkling over each helping.

Beyond

- You must halve the recipe for a 3-litre cooker.

- Because clams are salty and also because we use Worcestershire sauce for its umami qualities, there's no added salt in this dish. Pass more at the table.

- For a fish-only version of this stew, ask the fishmonger for about 225g of fish tails, fins, heads and bones. Cook these as you would the clams, then strain them out (and any particulate matter). Discard all that, keeping the cooking liquid to use in the stew. After the stew has been released from pressure the second time, omit the shellfish and add 700g thick-fleshed, skinned, white fish fillets and cook as directed in step 10.

1.25 litres vegetable stock

250ml dry white wine, such as Chardonnay

1 small lemon, scrubbed to remove any waxy coating, then thinly sliced and pips removed

4–5 fresh dill fronds

1 teaspoon black peppercorns

1 bay leaf

One 900g skin-on salmon fillet

125ml regular or low-fat mayonnaise

125ml regular or low-fat soured cream

2 tablespoons fresh lemon juice

2 tablespoons finely chopped dill fronds

2 tablespoons jarred ready-made horseradish sauce

1 tablespoon finely snipped chives or finely chopped spring onions (green part only)

½ teaspoon ground black pepper

Beyond

- Because of the size of smaller salmon fillets, this recipe will not work well in a 3-litre cooker.

- If you don't want to use wine, use 1.4 litres vegetable stock, but also add 1 teaspoon white granulated sugar to the sauce mixture.

- Serve portions of the salmon on lettuce leaves with sliced radishes, chopped tomato and/or sprouts, all topped with the horseradish sauce.

- Make an easy salmon salad for sandwiches by chopping the poached salmon and mixing it right into the horseradish sauce.

Poached Salmon with Horseradish Sauce

6 servings

Cold poached salmon may be summer's best meal, a make-ahead that's ready for lunch in outside in the garden whenever the time's right. Notice that the salmon poaches here at LOW pressure to preserve the meat and stop it overcooking.

Look for a salmon fillet without a thick fat end and a thin, belly flap end. (Have the fishmonger cut an even piece from the middle of the fillet.) Also, make sure the pin bones have been removed. Run your fingers lightly over the fillet – careful! – to feel for them. Use cleaned tweezers to pull them out of the fish. Or ask that fishmonger to do the deed for you. If the salmon has been previously frozen, make sure the meat is not splitting and cracking but is intact and solid. Finally, fattier salmon (such as Atlantic) poaches better than leaner salmon (such as sockeye).

1. Mix the stock, wine, lemon, dill, peppercorns and bay leaf in a **5.5- or 7.5-litre cooker**. Set the salmon skin-side down in the stock mixture. Lock the lid onto the pot.

2.

Set the machine	Level	The valve must be	Time	Press
PRESSURE COOK or MANUAL	LOW	Closed	4 minutes with the KEEP WARM setting off	START

3. Use the **quick-release method** to bring the pot's pressure back to normal. Unlatch the lid and open the cooker. Remove the *hot* insert from the cooker and set aside at room temperature for 10 minutes, then set the insert (with the salmon inside) on a towel on a shelf in the refrigerator and leave to cool for 1 hour.

4. Meanwhile, whisk the mayonnaise, soured cream, lemon juice, dill, horseradish, chives or spring onions and pepper in a small bowl until smooth. Cover and refrigerate until you're ready to serve.

5. After an hour, transfer the salmon from the insert to a platter. Discard the liquid and solids in the insert. Slice the fish and serve at once. Or, cover and refrigerate for up to 2 days, offering the horseradish sauce on the side.

Halibut Poached in Red Wine with Roasted Peppers

4 servings

We're not using pressure to cook these halibut fillets. We're using it to create a deeply flavoured sauce. It may seem odd to cook fish in red wine, but it's actually a culinary practice that dates back to the Renaissance. The wine offers a bold flavour that's great with halibut, a fish with a more meat-like texture to stand up to all that surrounds it.

1. Mix the wine, red pepper, chickpeas, olives, garlic, oregano, cinnamon stick and saffron (if using) in a 5.5- or 7.5-litre cooker. Lock the lid onto the pot.

2.

Set the machine	Level	The valve must be	Time	Press
PRESSURE COOK	MAX	—	5 minutes with the KEEP WARM setting off	START
PRESSURE COOK or MANUAL	HIGH	Closed	7 minutes with the KEEP WARM setting off	START

3. Use the **quick-release method** to bring the pot's pressure back to normal. Unlatch the lid and open the cooker. Remove and discard the cinnamon stick. Stir well.

4.

Press	Setting	Time	Press
SAUTÉ	MEDIUM, NORMAL OR CUSTOM 150°C	10 minutes	START

5. Bring the sauce to a simmer, stirring occasionally. Slip the fillets into the sauce and set the cover askew over the pot. Cook until the fish is opaque throughout, 4–6 minutes. Turn off the **SAUTÉ** function and remove the *hot* insert from the pot to stop the cooking. Serve the fillets in bowls with lots of sauce around them.

350ml full-bodied, fruit-forward red wine, such as Syrah

1 jarred roasted red pepper, chopped

120g drained tinned chickpeas, rinsed

30g pitted black olives

2 medium garlic cloves, peeled and finely chopped (2 teaspoons prechopped)

2 teaspoons fresh oregano leaves, finely chopped

One 5cm cinnamon stick

⅛ teaspoon saffron threads (optional)

Four 175–225g skinless halibut fillets

Beyond

- You must halve the recipe for a 3-litre cooker.

- For a richer sauce, transfer the cooked halibut fillets to serving bowls, then whisk up to 45g butter into the sauce as it continues to simmer.

- For a more aromatic sauce, add up to 2 teaspoons finely grated orange zest to the red wine mixture before it cooks under pressure.

- Serve this stew over garlic bread croutons. Buy a loaf of ready-to-bake garlic bread. Cut the loaf into cubes and spread out on a baking tin in a 180°C oven. Stir and turn them occasionally until crunchy, 10–12 minutes.

700ml chicken stock or Fish
Stock (see page 105)

250ml beer, preferably an
amber ale

110g butter, cut into chunks

90g tomato purée

Up to 6 medium garlic cloves,
peeled and finely chopped
(2 tablespoons prechopped)

2 teaspoons dried thyme

1 teaspoon dried oregano

1 teaspoon fennel seeds

Up to 1 teaspoon crushed
chilli flakes

½ teaspoon table salt

½ teaspoon celery seeds
(optional)

1.3kg shell-on king prawns,
peeled and deveined

Crunchy bread, for serving

Spicy Buttery Prawns

6–8 servings

Once again, we use the pressure cooker to build a sweet, buttery and even tongue-spanking sauce, then gently poach the prawns in it to keep them as tender as possible. The bread is not optional! You'll want it to mop up every drop.

1. Stir the stock, beer, butter, tomato purée, garlic, thyme, oregano, fennel seeds, crushed chilli flakes, salt and celery seeds (if using) in a **5.5- or 7.5-litre cooker**. Lock the lid onto the pot.

2.

Set the machine	Level	The valve must be	Time	Press
PRESSURE COOK	MAX	—	5 minutes with the KEEP WARM setting off	START
MEAT/STEW, PRESSURE COOK or MANUAL	HIGH	Closed	7 minutes with the KEEP WARM setting off	START

3. Use the **quick-release method** to bring the pot's pressure back to normal. Unlatch the lid and open the pot.

4.

Press	Setting	Time	Press
SAUTÉ	MEDIUM, NORMAL or CUSTOM 150°C	5 minutes	START

5. Stir the sauce as it comes to a simmer. Add the prawns, stir well and set the lid askew over the pot. Cook until the prawns are pink and firm, about 2 minutes. Turn off the **SAUTÉ** function and remove the hot insert from the machine to stop the cooking. Pour the contents of the insert into a large serving bowl and serve with the crunchy bread to mop up the sauce.

Beyond

- You must halve the recipe for a 3-litre cooker.
- For a 7.5-litre cooker, you can (but don't have to) increase all the ingredients by 50 per cent (for up to about 10 servings).
- For more flavour, use deveined medium-sized prawns still in their shells. You'll need to provide plenty of napkins for the peel-and-eat fest.

Prawn Stew with White Beans and Spinach

4 servings

Surprisingly elegant, this Italian-inspired stew is a great supper for weekend guests. Don't use baby spinach but make sure you wash the larger spinach leaves to get rid of any sandy grit.

1.

Press	Setting	Time	Press
SAUTÉ	MEDIUM, NORMAL OR CUSTOM 150°C	5 minutes	START

2. Warm the oil in a **5.5- or 7.5-litre cooker** for a minute or two. Add the onion and cook, stirring occasionally, until softened, about 4 minutes. Stir in the garlic, rosemary and crushed chilli flakes (if using) until aromatic, just a few seconds.

3. Pour in the stock and scrape up any browned bits on the pot's bottom. Turn off the **SAUTÉ** function, add the beans and stir well. Lock the lid onto the cooker.

4.

Set the machine	Level	The valve must be	Time	Press
PRESSURE COOK	MAX	—	3 minutes with the KEEP WARM setting off	START
PRESSURE COOK or MANUAL	HIGH	Closed	4 minutes with the KEEP WARM setting off	START

5. Use the **quick-release method** to bring the pot's pressure back to normal. Unlatch the lid and open the cooker.

6.

Press	Setting	Time	Press
SAUTÉ	MEDIUM, NORMAL OR CUSTOM 150°C	5 minutes	START

7. Bring the sauce to a simmer, stirring occasionally. Add the prawns and spinach. Stir well, then set the lid askew over the pot and cook for 1 minute. Turn off the **SAUTÉ** function and stir in the lemon juice, salt and pepper. Set the lid askew again over the pot and set aside for 3 minutes to blend the flavours and further cook the prawns. Serve hot in bowls.

2 tablespoons olive oil

1 medium onion, chopped (160g prechopped)

3 medium garlic cloves, peeled and finely chopped (1 tablespoon prechopped)

1 tablespoon loosely packed fresh rosemary leaves, finely chopped

Up to ½ teaspoon crushed chilli flakes (optional)

700ml chicken stock

One 400g tin white beans, drained and rinsed

450g shell-on prawns, peeled and deveined

120g chopped and stemmed spinach leaves

Up to 2 tablespoons fresh lemon juice

½ teaspoon table salt

½ teaspoon ground black pepper

Beyond

- You must halve the recipe for a 3-litre cooker.

- Using even 150ml of Fish Stock (page 105), and thus only 550ml chicken stock, will dramatically improve the flavour of the sauce.

- To give this dish a Spanish flair, substitute one 400g tin chickpeas, drained and rinsed, for the white beans. Add 1 teaspoon mild smoked paprika and ¼ teaspoon saffron with the rosemary.

**2 tablespoons solid fat
or liquid fat**

> **Choose one or two** from less assertive flavours like butter or schmaltz; or vegetable, corn, rapeseed, safflower, olive, avocado and/or grapeseed oil.

**115g sausage
or cured meat, chopped**

> **Choose** from sausages of any sort (cut into 1cm pieces), bacon (of any sort except flavoured), pancetta, chorizo or prosciutto.

80g chopped (and trimmed if necessary) allium aromatics

> **Choose** from onion (of any sort), shallots, spring onions or leeks (white and pale green parts only, well washed).

Up to 1 tablespoon finely chopped garlic or up to 1 tablespoon finely chopped peeled fresh root ginger (optional)

250ml liquid

> **Choose** either stock of any sort or a dry but light white wine such as Pinot Grigio or a combo of both, either 50/50 or perhaps 75 stock/25 wine.

350g chopped (and stemmed and cored or trimmed as necessary) quick-cooking vegetables

> **Choose one or two** from peppers, celery, fresh tomatoes of any sort, frozen artichoke heart quarters (do not thaw), peas (if frozen, do not thaw), sugar snap peas, yellow summer squash and/or courgettes.

2 tablespoons finely chopped fresh herbs

> **Choose one or two** from basil, coriander, marjoram, parsley, oregano, rosemary, sage, savory and/or thyme.

900g mussels, scrubbed for exterior sand and debearded if necessary

Road Map: A Pot of Mussels

2 servings

There may be no better weeknight supper! By cooking mussels for just a minute or two under pressure, we make sure they flavour the broth but stay tender and juicy. Don't forget a bowl to hold all the shells.

1.

Press	Setting	Time	Press
SAUTÉ	MEDIUM, NORMAL or CUSTOM 150°C	10 minutes	START

2. Melt the fat or warm the oil in a **5.5- or 7.5-litre cooker.** Add the sausage or cured meat and cook, stirring often, until well browned, 4–6 minutes. Add the allium and cook, stirring occasionally, until the onion has softened, about 3 minutes. Stir in the garlic or ginger (if using) until aromatic, just a few seconds.

3. Pour in the liquid and scrape up any browned bits on the pot's bottom. Turn off the **SAUTÉ** function and stir in the quick-cooking vegetables and the herbs. Stir in the mussels, then lock the lid onto the pot.

4.

Set the machine	Level	The valve must be	Time	Press
PRESSURE COOK	MAX	——	1 minute with the KEEP WARM setting off	START
PRESSURE COOK or MANUAL	HIGH	Closed	2 minutes with the KEEP WARM setting off	START

5. Use the **quick-release method** to bring the pot's pressure back to normal. Unlatch the lid and open the cooker. Discard any mussels that have not opened. Pour the contents of the *hot* insert into a large bowl to serve.

Beyond

- For a 3-litre cooker, use 180ml liquid but halve the remaining ingredients.

- If when you open the cooker in step 5, more than one-quarter of the mussels have not opened, they were larger than expected and have not cooked long enough. Lock the lid back onto the cooker and cook on HIGH only for 1 minute, followed by the quick-release method.

- You'll want bread for mopping up this mussel broth.

9

Longer Braises and Stews

(*More than Twenty Minutes* **Under Pressure**)

Back in the day, recipes like the ones in this chapter were the real reason our grandmothers bought their rather scary pressure cookers: to make cheap cuts of meat in much less time than those cuts would take on the hob or in the oven.

Times have changed. First off, those cuts aren't cheap anymore. Have you seen the price of brisket lately? Or short ribs? The kids have caught on that chuck, pork neck end and lamb shoulder offer some pretty fine eating. Supply, demand: you know the story. As a result, those cuts deserve more than a bag of baby carrots. They need to be dressed up to justify the cost. You probably want to make an entire celebration out of a joint of beef that cost you £30.

Start with one of the road maps in this chapter: beef stew, pot roast, brisket or pork stew (which could be morphed into a lamb stew). These non-standard recipes will offer the best success for creating a satisfying meal, one customised to your taste. They'll also help you get the hang of the slightly larger set of complications that a once-inexpensive cut of meat requires.

Speaking of those flavours, we've felt free to bump them up in this chapter. Since many of these recipes require time and effort, we wanted to make them more sophisticated (or at least a little beyond the norm). How about Pork Belly Mapo Dofu (page 378)? It's absurdly delicious, since pork belly is so luxurious and the pot cooks it so quickly. In that recipe (and in others, too), we also offer ways to make the dish more legit, using some ingredients that might not be in your pantry. With one exception as you'll see, the recipes still retain our go-to rule: we only used ingredients we could find in our rural grocery store. But what lies in the *Beyond* section might require a little internet shopping.

So enjoy the time it takes to make what your grandmother would have considered a cheap cut of meat. Just as she did, you, too, can make it in a fraction of the time.

FAQs

1. What does it mean when it says to 'slice the meat against the grain'?

Meat – or to be accurate *and* gross, muscle tissue – is fibrous. To do its job, it has to bend, flex and twist. For poultry and most pork, the matter of its grain is moot. The meat has been butchered in such a way that the fibres already run against the cuts, so carving a pork loin, for example, into individual round slices is no problem. But beef (along with veal and buffalo) is not typically butchered to make slicing and carving an easy task. (At least not here in the USA. Other countries butcher red meat more in keeping with its grain.).

To get long slices that don't fall apart or turn to stringy bits, slice cuts like sirloin or brisket 'against the grain'. Once cooked, run your fingers across the meat's surface. Notice which way the fibres run. Now carve 90 degrees from the direction of those fibres, cutting across them (that is, 'against' them).

2. What's with all the frozen baby onions?

Have you ever tried to peel fresh ones? Maddening! They're worse than garlic: zillions of bits of papery hull. Frozen baby onions are already peeled. Ta-da! But more importantly, they hold up better under pressure, especially if they're still frozen when they hit the pot. As they brown, their exteriors contract with moisture loss, the interiors are still a little chilled, and the onions remain (basically) intact once the pressure hits. Sure, a few come apart. But they offer a great way to get texture and tooth into a long-braised dish.

2 tablespoons fat
Choose from butter, lard, schmaltz, rendered bacon fat, goose fat, duck fat, olive oil, vegetable oil, corn oil, rapeseed oil, safflower oil, peanut oil, grapeseed oil, avocado oil, sesame oil or any nut oil – or a 50/50 combo of a solid fat and a liquid fat.

175g cured and/or smoked meat, chopped
Choose from bacon (of any sort but not flavoured), pancetta, prosciutto or chorizo.

1.2kg stewing steak, cubed

160g chopped (and trimmed if necessary) allium aromatics
Choose from onions (of any sort), shallots or leeks (white and pale green part only, well washed).

180g sliced mushrooms (optional)
Choose any variety (but no shiitake mushroom stems).

60g dried fruit (optional)
Choose from raisins, currants, pitted and chopped prunes, chopped apricots or stemmed and chopped figs.

1 tablespoon stemmed, finely chopped fresh herbs
Choose one or a combination from basil, chives, marjoram, parsley, oregano, rosemary, sage, savory, tarragon and/or thyme.

1½ teaspoons dried spices
Choose one or two from caraway seeds, fennel seeds, ground allspice, ground cinnamon, ground coriander, ground cumin, mild regular and/or smoked paprika.

Up to 3 medium garlic cloves, peeled and finely chopped (1 tablespoon prechopped)

1 tablespoon flavour enhancer
Choose from vinegar or any sort, Dijon mustard, fresh lemon juice, Worcestershire sauce, hoisin sauce (see page 184), soy sauce, pesto, pomegranate molasses, tomato purée, barbecue sauce or a vinegary dill pickle relish.

350ml liquid
Choose from beef or chicken stock, beer or a 50/50 combo of stock with either red wine, white wine, dry sherry or dry vermouth.

Road Map: Beef Stew

6–8 servings

We hope this recipe becomes the basis of one of your weeknight standards. There's quite a bit of variety here, including the choice between mushrooms and dried fruit. Mushrooms, of course, will give the stew an earthier edge. (If you really want to develop umami in the stew, use mushrooms *and* soy sauce, and perhaps consider omitting the fresh herbs.) Dried fruit will yield a sweeter stew. You can even use both mushrooms and dried fruit for a very complex mixture of flavours.

As to the herb and spice choices, good combinations are thyme, cinnamon and allspice; parsley, tarragon and regular paprika; and oregano, thyme, fennel seeds and smoked paprika.

1.

Press	Setting	Time	Press
SAUTÉ	MEDIUM, NORMAL or CUSTOM 150°C	25 minutes	START

2. Melt the fat or warm the oil in a **5.5- or 7.5-litre cooker**. Add the smoked and/or cured meat. Cook, stirring occasionally, until well browned or even crisp, 3–5 minutes. Use a slotted spoon to transfer the meat to a nearby bowl.

3. Add the stewing steak and cook, stirring occasionally and rearranging the pieces, until *well* browned, about 10 minutes. Add the allium aromatic(s) and continue cooking, stirring more often, until it begins to soften, 2–3 minutes. If desired, stir in the mushrooms and/or dried fruit until well combined.

4. Stir in the fresh herbs, dried spices and garlic until aromatic, just a few seconds, then stir in the flavour enhancer. Turn off the **SAUTÉ** function, pour in the liquid and scrape up the browned bits on the pot's bottom. Lock the lid onto the pot.

450g waxy potatoes, such as
Desiree or Charlotte, cut into
2.5cm pieces

450g medium carrots, cut into
2.5cm pieces

**Sea salt flakes for garnishing
(optional)**

5.

Set the machine	Level	The valve must be	Time	Press
PRESSURE COOK	MAX	——	40 minutes with the KEEP WARM setting off	START
MEAT/STEW, PRESSURE COOK or MANUAL	HIGH	Closed	50 minutes with the KEEP WARM setting off	START
SLOW COOK	HIGH	Opened	4 hours with the KEEP WARM setting off (or on for no more than 3 hours)	START

6. If you've used a pressure setting, when the machine finishes cooking, turn it off and let its pressure **return to normal** naturally, about 30 minutes.

7. Unlatch the lid and open the cooker. Stir in the potatoes and carrots. Lock the lid onto the pot.

8.

Set the machine	Level	The valve must be	Time	Press
PRESSURE COOK	MAX	——	5 minutes with the KEEP WARM setting off	START
MEAT/STEW, PRESSURE COOK or MANUAL	HIGH	Closed	7 minutes with the KEEP WARM setting off	START

9. Use the **quick-release method** to bring the pot's pressure back to normal. Unlatch the lid and open the cooker. Stir well. Because there's no way to figure out the amount of salt in your particular version, garnish servings with salt as desired.

Beyond

- You must halve the recipe for a 3-litre cooker.

- For a simpler stew, omit the potatoes and carrots (that is, skip steps 7, 8 and 9). We then recommend thickening the stew. First, increase the meat's cooking time to 45 minutes for MAX or 57 minutes on HIGH in step 5. (The time for slow-cooking the stew will not change.) Then whisk 2 tablespoons water and 1½ tablespoons cornflour in a small bowl until smooth. Once you've opened the pot, use the SAUTÉ setting on MEDIUM, NORMAL Or CUSTOM 150°C to bring the sauce to a simmer. Stir in the cornflour slurry and cook, stirring often until thickened, 1–2 minutes. Immediately turn off the SAUTÉ function and remove the hot insert from the pot to stop the cooking.

- If the stew is too wet for your taste with the potatoes and carrots, we don't advise using a slurry to thicken it. Instead, boil it down with the SAUTÉ setting on HIGH or MORE, stirring often, 1–3 minutes.

- Our favourite way to serve beef stew, even with potatoes in the mix, is over big, crunchy croutons. Buy a baguette, cut it into slices 2.5cm in thickness and toast these on a large baking tin in a 190°C oven, turning occasionally, until brown and crisp.

2 tablespoons fat
Choose from either a solid fat like butter, rendered bacon fat, lard, schmaltz, goose fat or duck fat; or a tasty liquid fat like olive oil, sesame oil, walnut oil, pecan oil or pumpkin seed oil – or a 50/50 combo of solid and liquid fat.

1.6kg piece boneless beef chuck

½ teaspoon table salt (optional)

½ teaspoon ground black pepper

240g chopped (and trimmed if necessary) allium aromatics
Choose from onions (of any sort), shallots or leeks (white and pale green parts only, well washed).

2 medium garlic cloves, peeled and finely chopped (2 teaspoons prechopped)

2 large sprigs of fresh herbs
Choose from basil, marjoram, oregano, parsley, rosemary, sage, tarragon or thyme.

Up to 1½ teaspoons dried spice
Choose one or two from ground allspice, ground coriander, ground cumin, mild paprika, mild smoked paprika, fennel seeds, caraway seeds and/or mustard seeds.

350ml liquid
Choose from stock of any sort; or a 50/50 combo of stock and wine of any sort, beer, dry sherry or dry vermouth; or a two-thirds/ one-third combo of stock and gin, whisky and/or bourbon.

2 tablespoons flavour enhancer
Choose from tomato purée, barbecue sauce, Dijon mustard, chutney, ready-made horseradish, pesto, tapenade, chilli sauce, Thai sweet chilli sauce, tamarind paste or hoisin sauce (see page 184).

700g peeled roots or tubers, chopped into 5cm pieces
Choose one or a selection from waxy potatoes, red-skinned potatoes, sweet potatoes, parsnips, carrots, turnips, swede, celeriac and/or yellow beetroot.

2 tablespoons water

1½ tablespoons cornflour

Road Map: Pot Roast

6–8 servings

The road map given here for beef chuck will let you customise the preparation to suit your taste and enable you to experiment with the dish for years to come. But think about whether you want to salt the meat before you do so, as the flavour enhancer you use may be loaded with salt.

Any cut of beef chuck will work but flatter cuts may come apart after being under pressure for so long. For better aesthetics, consider tying the meat. Wrap butchers' string around its perimeter and tie securely but not tightly, holding the meat in place without scrunching it up. Snip this string off before carving. If you don't mind a soupier sauce, ignore steps 9 and 10. In all honesty, we often decide whether we want to thicken the sauce once we open the pot and remove the meat in step 8.

1.

Press	Setting	Time	Press
SAUTÉ	MEDIUM, NORMAL or CUSTOM 150°C	20 minutes	START

2. Melt the fat or warm the oil in a **5.5- or 7.5-litre cooker**. Season the meat with the salt (if using) and pepper. Set it in the cooker and brown *well* on both sides, turning once or twice, 8–10 minutes. Transfer to a nearby chopping board.

3. Add the allium aromatics and cook, stirring often, until softened, 2–5 minutes. Stir in the garlic until aromatic, just a few seconds; then add the fresh herb sprigs and the dried spice(s).

4. Stir well, turn off the **SAUTÉ** function, pour in the liquid, and scrape up the browned bits on the pot's bottom. Stir in the flavour enhancer until smooth and nestle the beef into the sauce. Pour any juices on the chopping board into the pot and lock the lid onto the cooker.

5.

Set the machine	Level	The valve must be	Time	Press
PRESSURE COOK	MAX	—	40 minutes with the KEEP WARM setting off	START
MEAT/ STEW, PRESSURE COOK or MANUAL	HIGH	Closed	55 minutes with the KEEP WARM setting off	START

6. Use the **quick-release method** to bring the pot's pressure back to normal. Unlatch the lid and open the cooker. Scatter the roots or tubers around the meat. Lock the lid back onto the pot.

7.

Set the machine	Level	The valve must be	Time	Press
PRESSURE COOK	MAX	———	20 minutes with the KEEP WARM setting off	START
MEAT/ STEW, PRESSURE COOK or MANUAL	HIGH	Closed	28 minutes with the KEEP WARM setting off	START

8. When the machine has finished cooking, turn it off and let its pressure **return to normal naturally**, about 30 minutes. Unlatch the lid and open the cooker. Use a wide spatula and a large cooking spoon (for balance) to transfer the meat to a nearby chopping board (the cut may fall into large chunks, especially if it wasn't tied). Use a large spoon to skim any excess surface fat from the sauce in the pot.

9.

Press	Setting	Time	Press
SAUTÉ	MEDIUM, NORMAL or CUSTOM 150°C	15 minutes	START

10. As the sauce and vegetables come to a simmer, whisk the water and cornflour in a small bowl until smooth. Once the sauce is bubbling, stir this slurry into the pot. Continue cooking, stirring constantly, until thickened, 1–2 minutes. Turn off the SAUTÉ function and remove the *hot* insert from the pot to stop the cooking. Slice the meat into chunks and serve in bowls with lots of the sauce and vegetables.

Beyond

- You must halve the recipe for a 3-litre cooker.
- To use the SLOW COOK setting, complete the recipe through step 4. Scatter the roots and/or tubers on top of and around the beef. With the pressure valve open, lock the lid onto the pot and cook on HIGH for 6 hours (then leave on the KEEP WARM setting for up to 2 hours). When done, complete the second half of step 8, as well as steps 9 and 10 as written.

15g butter

1 tablespoon olive oil

1.3–1.6kg piece boneless
beef chuck

2 medium onions, halved and
sliced into thin half-moons

2 medium garlic cloves,
peeled and finely chopped
(2 teaspoons prechopped)

1 tablespoon fresh
thyme leaves

1 teaspoon fennel seeds

¼ teaspoon grated nutmeg

¼ teaspoon crushed
chilli flakes

200g chopped fresh tomatoes

30g pitted black olives

30g raisins

300ml beef or chicken stock

2 tablespoons tomato purée

Braised Chuck with Raisins and Olives

6 servings

If you're not in the mood to figure out your own road map for a pot roast, try this recipe with its sweet-and-savoury sauce, a nice match to the naturally sweet flavours in the beef. There's no salt in the sauce as the olives add plenty. If you miss the salt (or want a more savoury dish), drizzle the servings with soy sauce.

1.

Press	Setting	Time	Press
SAUTÉ	MEDIUM, NORMAL or CUSTOM 150°C	20 minutes	START

2. Melt the butter and the oil in a **5.5- or 7.5-litre cooker**. Add the beef and brown *well* on all sides, even around the perimeter, turning occasionally but not too often, about 10 minutes. Use a wide spatula and a big cooking spoon to transfer the meat to a nearby chopping board.

3. Add the onions and cook, stirring often, until they begin to soften, about 4 minutes. Stir in the garlic, thyme, fennel seeds, nutmeg and crushed chilli flakes until fragrant, just a few seconds. Add the chopped tomato, olives and raisins.

4. Stir well, turn off the **SAUTÉ** function, pour in the stock and scrape up any browned bits on the pot's bottom. Whisk the tomato purée into the sauce. Return the beef and any juices on the chopping board to the pot. Lock the lid onto the cooker.

5.

Set the machine	Level	The valve must be	Time	Press
PRESSURE COOK	MAX	——	1 hour with the KEEP WARM setting off	START
MEAT/STEW, PRESSURE COOK or MANUAL	HIGH	Closed	1 hour 20 minutes with the KEEP WARM setting off	START
SLOW COOK	HIGH	Opened	5 hours with the KEEP WARM setting off (or on for no more than 3 hours)	START

6. If you've used a pressure setting, when the machine has finished cooking, turn it off and let its pressure **return to normal naturally,** about 30 minutes.

7. Unlatch the lid and open the cooker. Use that same large spatula and a big spoon to transfer the meat to a chopping board (it may fall into chunks). Leave to cool for a couple of minutes. Meanwhile, use a large spoon to skim the excess surface fat off the sauce in the pot. Chunk the meat into pieces or carve into slices 1cm in thickness, then serve in bowls with lots of the sauce.

Beyond

- You must halve the recipe for a 3-litre cooker.

- Look for better quality olives at the deli counter at your supermarket.

- Serve this braise in split-open jacket potatoes, or even on top of cooked wheat berries (see page 395).

- Although the thyme/fennel/ nutmeg combo is particularly pleasing with the olives, try adding tarragon/caraway seeds/ground allspice in equal measures to the original set of spices instead.

2 tablespoons vegetable,
corn or rapeseed oil

1.3–1.6kg piece boneless
beef chuck

½ teaspoon ground
black pepper

6 medium spring onions,
trimmed and thinly sliced

3 medium garlic cloves,
peeled and finely chopped
(1 tablespoon prechopped)

Up to 2 small fresh jalapeño
chillies, stemmed, halved
lengthways, deseeded
and thinly sliced

1 tablespoon packed fresh
oregano leaves

½ teaspoon ground allspice

¼ teaspoon grated nutmeg

1 bay leaf

250ml plain cola
(do not use diet)

180ml beef or chicken stock

60ml dark rum

1 tablespoon soy sauce

Cuba-Libre-Braised Chuck

6 servings

Cuba Libre is that classic cruise-ship cocktail: a rum and Coke.
However, in pressure cooking, standard gold or white rum doesn't
have enough oomph to stand up to the pressure and the
complicated sauce. Use only dark rum, a sweet and sticky
concoction that turns pot roast into something special.

1.

Press	Setting	Time	Press
SAUTÉ	MEDIUM, NORMAL or CUSTOM 150°C	15 minutes	START

2. Warm the oil in a **5.5- or 7.5-litre cooker** for a minute or two.
Season the beef with the pepper, set it in the cooker, then brown
well on all sides, even the perimeter, turning occasionally, about
10 minutes. Transfer to a nearby chopping board.

3. Add the spring onions, garlic, jalapeño(s), oregano, allspice,
nutmeg and bay leaf. Stir well until aromatic, just a few seconds.
Pour in the cola and scrape up any browned bits on the pot's
bottom. Turn off the **SAUTÉ** function.

4. Stir in the stock, rum and soy sauce. Return the beef and any
juices on the chopping board to the cooker. Lock the lid onto
the pot.

5.

Set the machine	Level	The valve must be	Time	Press
PRESSURE COOK	MAX	——	1 hour with the KEEP WARM setting off	START
MEAT/ STEW, PRESSURE COOK or MANUAL	HIGH	Closed	1 hour 20 minutes with the KEEP WARM setting off	START
SLOW COOK	HIGH	Opened	5 hours with the KEEP WARM setting off (or on for no more than 3 hours)	START

6. If you've used a pressure setting, when the machine has finished cooking, turn it off and let its pressure **return to normal naturally**, about 30 minutes.

7. Unlatch the lid and open the cooker. Use a large metal spatula and a big cooking spoon to transfer the meat to a clean chopping board. Leave to cool for 5–10 minutes. Meanwhile, fish out and discard the bay leaf. Use a large spoon to skim any excess surface fat from the sauce. Chunk the meat into pieces or carve into slices 1cm in thickness, then serve in bowls with lots of the sauce.

Beyond

- You must halve the recipe for a 3-litre cooker.
- Add up to 115g chopped streaky bacon. Crisp it in the oil, then use a slotted spoon to transfer the bacon to a nearby bowl before browning the beef.
- Rather than potatoes, serve this over Black Turtle Beans and Rice (page 403).

**2 tablespoons solid
or liquid fat**

    Choose from butter, lard, rendered bacon fat, goose fat, duck fat, olive oil, avocado oil, sesame oil, vegetable oil, corn oil, rapeseed oil, peanut oil, grapeseed oil or any nut oil – or a 50/50 combo of solid and liquid fat.

1.3kg rolled beef brisket, any surface fat trimmed to 5mm thick

½ teaspoon table salt (optional)

½ teaspoon ground black pepper

320g chopped (and trimmed if necessary) allium aromatics

    Choose one or two from onions (of any sort), spring onions, shallots, leeks (white and pale green parts only, well washed) and/or frozen baby onions (do not thaw).

4 medium garlic cloves, peeled

1 tablespoon dried herbs and/or spices

    Choose at least two from basil, chervil, fennel seeds, marjoram, oregano, rosemary, sage, savory, thyme, ground allspice, ground cinnamon, ground coriander, ground cumin, mild paprika and/or mild smoked paprika; or choose a dried herb blend, such as herbes de Provence, an Italian blend, a Cajun blend or others (keeping in mind that dried spices are usually more potent than dried herbs).

125ml liquid enhancer

    Choose from red wine, white wine, dry vermouth, dry sherry, brandy, bourbon or beer (particularly a dark beer).

180ml stock (any sort)

Up to 60ml flavour booster

    Choose one from mustard of any sort, ketchup, chutney of any sort, barbecue sauce of any sort, soy sauce, orange marmalade, hoisin sauce (page 184) or oyster sauce.

Road Map: Braised Brisket

6–8 servings

This recipe calls for a leaner piece without a cap of fatty meat at one end. Choose a brisket with a fairly even thickness. A 1.3kg rolled brisket might not fit in a **5.5-litre cooker**, depending on its overall shape. It's fine to cut one in half widthways and stack the pieces on each other (you'll probably have to brown them in two steps). And it's fine to mush a single piece of brisket against the sides of the pot *a bit* (but not a lot) because the meat will shrink as it cooks.

    As you make up your own version of this recipe, keep the flavours fairly simple. Work with a ready-made spice blend if you're unsure how to blend spices. Over the long cooking, the meat will become quite soft, almost velvety. It won't be much good for slicing for sandwiches, but the leftovers will make a fine, tasty, chopped beef sandwich the next day.

1.

Press	Setting	Time	Press
SAUTÉ	MEDIUM, NORMAL or CUSTOM 150°C	20 minutes	START

2. Melt the fat on its own or in some oil, or warm the oil for a minute or two in a **5.5- or 7.5-litre cooker**. Season the brisket with the salt (if using) and pepper, then set it in the pot and brown *well* on both sides, turning only once or twice, about 10 minutes. Transfer to a nearby chopping board.

3. Add the allium aromatics and cook, stirring often, until they begin to soften, 2–4 minutes. Add the garlic cloves and the dried spices, stir well, then pour in the liquid enhancer. Scrape up any browned bits on the pot's bottom as it comes to a simmer.

4. Turn off the **SAUTÉ** function, then stir in the liquid and some of the flavour booster. Taste for salt and add more flavour booster, if desired. Return the brisket and any juices on the chopping board to the pot, nestling the meat into the sauce. Lock the lid onto the pot.

5.

Set the machine	Level	The valve must be	Time	Press
PRESSURE COOK	MAX	—	1 hour with the KEEP WARM setting off	START
MEAT/ STEW, PRESSURE COOK or MANUAL	HIGH	Closed	1 hour 20 minutes with the KEEP WARM setting off	START

6. When the machine has finished cooking, turn it off and let its pressure **return to normal naturally,** about 30 minutes.

7. Unlatch the lid and open the cooker. Transfer the brisket to a clean chopping board. Leave to cool for 5–10 minutes. Meanwhile, use a large spoon to skim any excess surface fat from the sauce in the pot. Slice the brisket into strips 1cm in thickness against the grain. Serve lapped with the sauce from the pot.

Beyond

- You must halve the recipe for a 3-litre cooker.

- For a traditional Jewish brisket, substitute 250g chopped tomatoes for the liquid enhancer and the flavour booster. Increase the stock to 250ml. If desired, add up to 30g raisins with the garlic and dried spices.

- For a thicker sauce, use a hand blender after you've removed the brisket to purée the allium aromatics.

- Or after transferring the brisket to a chopping board, boil down the sauce using the SAUTÉ function at its HIGH or MORE setting, stirring often, until reduced to about half its volume, 4–6 minutes.

- Or transfer the brisket to a chopping board, then bring the sauce to a simmer using the SAUTÉ function at its MEDIUM, NORMAL or CUSTOM 150°C setting. Whisk 2 tablespoons water and 1 tablespoon cornflour in a small bowl until smooth, then scrape every drop of this slurry into the sauce. Cook, stirring all the while, until thickened, 1–2 minutes. Immediately turn off the SAUTÉ function and remove the insert from the pot to stop the cooking.

35g butter, 20g of it at room temperature

2 thin rashers of streaky bacon, chopped

1.6kg boneless beef short ribs

1 small red onion, chopped (80g prechopped)

450g thinly sliced chestnut mushrooms

250ml dry red wine, such as Cabernet Sauvignon

125ml beef or chicken stock

2 teaspoons dried thyme

1 teaspoon dried sage

½ teaspoon table salt

½ teaspoon ground black pepper

2 bay leaves

1½ tablespoons plain flour

Bistro-Style Braised Short Ribs with Mushrooms

6 servings

Although cooking beef short ribs in the Instant Pot cuts down on the time they need to braise, we haven't shaved any time off any of the other steps in this fairly traditional recipe, even using a classic *beurre manié* (French, *burh mahn-YAY*, a butter and flour mixture) to thicken the sauce into silky richness. The meat will be so tender that you'll barely need knives at the table, so the short ribs are best served in bowls.

1.

Press	Setting	Time	Press
SAUTÉ	MEDIUM, NORMAL or CUSTOM 150°C	35 minutes	START

2. Melt 15g of the butter in a **5.5- or 7.5-litre cooker**. Add the bacon and fry until crisp, stirring occasionally, about 4 minutes. Use a slotted spoon to transfer the bacon to a nearby large bowl.

3. Add half the short ribs and brown them *well* on all sides, turning occasionally, about 10 minutes. Transfer these to that bowl and add the remaining short ribs, browning them in just the same way. Transfer these to the bowl, too.

4. Add the onion and cook, stirring often, until softened, about 3 minutes. Add the mushrooms and continue cooking, stirring occasionally, until they give off their internal moisture and that liquid evaporates to a glaze in the pot, about 5 minutes.

5. Pour in the wine and scrape up the browned bits on the pot's bottom. Turn off the **SAUTÉ** function and stir in the stock, thyme, sage, salt, pepper and bay leaves. Return the short ribs, bacon and any juices in that bowl to the pot. Stir well, then lock the lid onto the cooker.

6.

Set the machine	Level	The valve must be	Time	Press
PRESSURE COOK	MAX	—	1 hour 10 minutes with the KEEP WARM setting off	START
MEAT/STEW, PRESSURE COOK or MANUAL	HIGH	Closed	1 hour 30 minutes with the KEEP WARM setting off	START
SLOW COOK	HIGH	Opened	4 hours with the KEEP WARM setting off (or on for no more than 3 hours)	START

Beyond

- You must halve the recipe for a 3-litre cooker.
- For a sweet finish in the sauce, add up to 2 medium carrots, chopped (130g prechopped), with the onion.
- Or add up to 2 teaspoons finely chopped garlic with the dried herbs.
- Serve this stew alongside (or even over) crunchy roast potatoes.

7. If you've used a pressure setting, when the machine has finished cooking, turn it off and let its pressure **return to normal naturally**, about 30 minutes.

8. Unlatch the lid and open the cooker. Find and discard the bay leaves. Use kitchen tongs and a slotted spoon to transfer the short ribs, bacon and any vegetables to a serving platter. Tent with aluminium foil to keep warm. Use a large spoon to skim any excess surface fat from the sauce in the pot.

9.

Press	Setting	Time	Press
SAUTÉ	MEDIUM, NORMAL or CUSTOM 150°C	5 minutes	START

10. As the sauce comes to a simmer, use a fork to make a smooth paste out of the flour and the room-temperature 20g butter in a small bowl. As the sauce simmers, whisk this flour mixture into the pot a little at a time, whisking until it's all been added and the sauce has thickened, 1–2 minutes. Turn off the **SAUTÉ** function and pour the sauce in the *hot* insert over the meat and vegetables on the platter.

700g boneless beef chuck, tied around its perimeter with butchers' string

700g bone-in beef short ribs

1 medium onion, peeled and halved

1 medium head of garlic, any loose papery bits removed, then halved

6 large thyme sprigs

1 tablespoon black peppercorns

1 teaspoon table salt, plus more as needed

1 bay leaf

Water as needed

2 medium leeks, white and pale green parts only, halved lengthways and well washed

4 medium carrots, peeled and halved widthways

4 medium parsnips, peeled and halved widthways

4 medium waxy potatoes, quartered

Streamlined Pot au Feu

4–6 servings

Pot au feu (French, *paw-toh-FUH*, 'pot on the fire') may well be the definition of homesickness for many a French national living abroad. It's also the definition of an all-day dish – or was until now. In essence, it's boiled meat, rather plain (although we add interest with vegetables like parsnips). It's quite brothy, like a rich soup with meat and vegetables. Our process takes two steps: first, to build the broth, then to cook the meat in that broth with other vegetables until everything's meltingly tender, just about ready for a spoon.

1. Put the beef chuck, short ribs, onion, garlic, thyme, peppercorns, 1 teaspoon salt and the bay leaf in a **5.5- or 7.5-litre cooker**, arranging the meat in fairly compact layers. Add enough water to just cover everything without going above the **Max Fill** line. Lock the lid onto the pot.

2.

Set the machine	Level	The valve must be	Time	Press
PRESSURE COOK	MAX	—	40 minutes with the KEEP WARM setting off	START
MEAT/STEW, PRESSURE COOK or MANUAL	HIGH	Closed	55 minutes with the KEEP WARM setting off	START

3. When the machine has finished cooking, turn it off and let its pressure **return to normal naturally**, about 45 minutes. Unlatch the lid and open the cooker. Use kitchen tongs and a large metal spatula to transfer the meat to a nearby chopping board.

4. Strain the liquid in the cooker through a fine-mesh sieve like a *chinois* (or a colander lined with a double thickness of muslin) into a large bowl below. Discard all the solids; pour the strained broth into the cooker. Return the meat and any juices as well.

5. Add the leeks, carrots, parsnips and potatoes, submerging them as much as possible in the liquid. (If for any reason the broth, meat and vegetables come above the **Max Fill** line, ladle out enough broth so that the liquid level falls below that marker.) Lock the lid back onto the cooker.

6.

Set the machine	Level	The valve must be	Time	Press
PRESSURE COOK	MAX	—	7 minutes with the KEEP WARM setting off	START
MEAT/ STEW, PRESSURE COOK or MANUAL	HIGH	Closed	10 minutes with the KEEP WARM setting off	START

7. Use the **quick-release method** to return the pot's pressure to normal. Unlatch the lid and open the cooker. Dish the meat, vegetables and broth into large serving bowls. Season with more salt, as needed.

Beyond

- You must halve the recipe for a 3-litre cooker.
- Garnish the meat in each serving with a little Dijon mustard and serve with a crunchy baguette on the side.
- For an old-world version, omit the potatoes and use 4 medium turnips, peeled and quartered.
- Some traditional cooks add a little wine to sweeten the broth. Add up to 125ml light red wine, such as Pinot Noir, with the vegetables in step 5.

30g butter

1 large onion, chopped
(240g prechopped)

260g chopped carrots

1.2kg beef rump, cut into
2.5cm pieces

2 tablespoons packed sage
leaves, finely chopped

1 tablespoon picked
thyme leaves

½ teaspoon table salt

½ teaspoon ground
black pepper

600ml beef or chicken stock

240g dried black-eye beans

Beef Rump Braised with Black-Eye Beans

6 servings

Beef rump is highly flavourful, with little bits of cartilage and fat held in the meat. Those inner bits melt under pressure, offering you quick one-pot comfort food. For a recipe such as this, sirloin steak cubes, for example, would simply overcook and dry out.

And quickly glance over the dried black-eye beans, just to make sure there are no little hulls, stones or extraneous bits amongst them.

1.

Press	Setting	Time	Press
SAUTÉ	LOW or LESS	20 minutes	START

2. Warm the butter in a **5.5- or 7.5-litre cooker** for a minute or two. Add the onion and carrot. Cook, stirring often, until the onion is exceptionally soft, even a little browned, about 15 minutes. Add the beef and continue cooking, stirring occasionally, until it loses its pink, raw colour, about 3 minutes.

3. Stir in the sage, thyme, salt and pepper until aromatic, just a few seconds. Pour in the stock and scrape up any browned bits on the pot's bottom. Turn off the **SAUTÉ** function and stir in the black-eye beans. Lock the lid onto the cooker.

4.

Set the machine	Level	The valve must be	Time	Press
PRESSURE COOK	MAX	—	20 minutes with the KEEP WARM setting off	START
MEAT/STEW, PRESSURE COOK or MANUAL	HIGH	Closed	30 minutes with the KEEP WARM setting off	START

5. Use the **quick-release method** to bring the pot's pressure back to normal. Unlatch the lid and open the cooker. Stir well before serving.

Beyond

- You must halve the recipe for a 3-litre cooker.
- Try these flavour variations. Add 1 large tomato, chopped, with the black-eye beans.
- And/or add up to 1 tablespoon finely chopped garlic with the fresh herbs.
- And/or add up to 2 teaspoons finely grated orange zest.
- And/or add up to ½ teaspoon crushed chilli flakes.

Tea-Braised Topside of Beef

6–8 servings

A smoky tea is an amazing braising medium, especially under pressure. It becomes irresistibly sweet, turning the broth for this down-home, Chinese braise into a spiced sensation. You needn't add the Sichuan peppercorns, although they're readily available these days at large supermarkets. We'll confess that their use here breaks our oath about using ingredients only from our rural supermarket. (For more information, see the headnote to Pork Belly Mapo Dofu on page 378.)

1. Bring the water to the boil in a medium saucepan set over a high heat. Remove the pan from the heat and stir in the loose tea or add the tea bags. Cover and set aside until very dark, about 10 minutes. Strain the tea into a medium bowl or remove and discard the bags.

2.

Press	Setting	Time	Press
SAUTÉ	MEDIUM, NORMAL Or CUSTOM 150°C	15 minutes	START

3. Warm the oil in a **5.5- or 7.5-litre cooker** for a minute or two. Add the beef and brown it *well* on all sides, turning occasionally, about 10 minutes. Transfer the meat to a nearby chopping board. Pour the tea into the pot and stir to get up all the browned bits on the pot's bottom.

4. Turn off the **SAUTÉ** function; stir in the ginger, Sichuan peppercorns (if using) and salt. Return the beef to the pot. Add the leeks and chilli, making sure these are mostly in the broth. Lock the lid onto the pot.

5.

Set the machine	Level	The valve must be	Time	Press
PRESSURE COOK	MAX	—	55 minutes with the KEEP WARM setting off	START
MEAT/STEW, PRESSURE COOK or MANUAL	HIGH	Closed	1 hour 15 minutes with the KEEP WARM setting off	START
SLOW COOK	HIGH	Opened	5 hours with the KEEP WARM setting off (or on for no more than 4 hours)	START

6. If you've used a pressure setting, when the machine has finished cooking, turn it off and let its pressure **return to normal naturally,** about 30 minutes.

7. Unlatch the lid and open the pot. Transfer the beef to a chopping board and leave to cool for 5 minutes. Carve into slices 1cm thick and serve in bowls with lots of the broth from the pot.

500ml water

25g loose Lapsang Souchong tea or 6 Lapsang Souchong tea bags, any labels removed

2 tablespoons vegetable, corn or rapeseed oil

1.3kg piece beef topside

1 teaspoon ground ginger

1 teaspoon Sichuan peppercorns (optional)

½ teaspoon table salt

1 medium leek, white and pale green part only, halved lengthways, washed well and thinly sliced

1 small fresh serrano chilli, stemmed, halved lengthways, deseeded (if desired) and thinly sliced

Beyond

- You must halve the recipe for a 3-litre cooker.

- Make the tea in the Instant Pot. Set the SAUTÉ function on HIGH or MORE and bring the water to a simmer. Add the loose tea leaves or tea bags and turn off the SAUTÉ function. Cover and steep as directed, then either strain the liquid into another bowl to remove the loose tea or remove and discard the tea bags and pour the liquid into a nearby bowl.

- Stir a little hot red chilli sauce like sambal oelek into individual servings.

- Use other sorts of smoky tea, particularly Pu'er (sometimes spelled 'pu-erh'), a tea that's been allowed to ferment until rich and whisky-like.

- Don't discard any extra broth after serving dinner. Store it in the fridge. The next day, heat it up and mix it with cooked and drained rice noodles, a little sliced spring onion and plenty of fresh bean sprouts.

2 tablespoons peanut or
toasted sesame oil

900g–1.2kg beef skirt steak
(also called thin flank,
hanger steak or onglet),
cut in half widthways

10 medium spring onions,
trimmed and cut into
5cm pieces

225g shiitake mushrooms,
the stems discarded and
the caps thinly sliced

2 medium garlic cloves,
peeled and finely chopped
(2 teaspoons prechopped)

2 tablespoons finely chopped
peeled fresh root ginger

350ml beef or chicken stock

2 tablespoons soy sauce

2 tablespoons dark
brown sugar

3 medium carrots, cut into
2.5cm chunks

Teriyaki-Style Braised Skirt Steak

6 servings

This recipe's a braise-y cross between teriyaki and negimaki, those rolls of beef around spring onions in a sweet sauce that are served as starters in some Japanese restaurants. We deconstructed all those flavours into a rich broth for the steak. It will be too large for the pot, so cut it in half and overlap these pieces without setting one directly on top of the other.

1.

Press	Setting	Time	Press
SAUTÉ	MEDIUM, NORMAL or CUSTOM 150°C	25 minutes	START

2. Warm 1 tablespoon oil in a **5.5- or 75.-litre cooker** for one or two minutes. Add one piece of skirt steak and brown it on both sides, turning occasionally, about 8 minutes. Transfer the steak to a nearby chopping board, add the remaining 1 tablespoon oil, and brown the second piece of skirt steak in the same way before getting it to the chopping board.

3. Add the spring onions, mushrooms, garlic and ginger to the pot. Cook, stirring often, until the mushrooms begin to soften, about 2 minutes. Pour in the stock and scrape up any browned bits on the pot's bottom.

4. Turn off the **SAUTÉ** function, then stir in the soy sauce and brown sugar until dissolved. Return the meat and any juices to the pot. Put the carrots on top and lock the lid onto the cooker.

5.

Set the machine	Level	The valve must be	Time	Press
PRESSURE COOK	MAX	—	50 minutes with the KEEP WARM setting off	START
MEAT/STEW, PRESSURE COOK or MANUAL	HIGH	Closed	1 hour 5 minutes with the KEEP WARM setting off	START
SLOW COOK	HIGH	Opened	5 hours with the KEEP WARM setting off (or on for no more than 3 hours)	START

6. If you've used a pressure setting, when the machine has finished cooking, turn it off and let its pressure **return to normal naturally,** about 35 minutes.

7. Unlatch the lid and open the pot. Transfer the meat to a clean chopping board. Carve the meat against the grain into slices 1cm in thickness and serve in bowls with the sauce and carrots.

Beyond

- For a 3-litre cooker, you must use 250ml stock and halve the remaining ingredients.

- To thicken the sauce, transfer the carrots to the chopping board with the meat. Use the SAUTÉ function at MEDIUM, NORMAL or CUSTOM 150°C to bring the sauce to a simmer. Whisk 2 tablespoons water and 1 tablespoon cornflour in a small bowl until smooth, then whisk this mixture into the sauce. Cook, whisking constantly, until thickened, 1–2 minutes. Turn off the SAUTÉ function and remove the hot insert from the pot to stop the cooking. Spoon the sauce over the slices.

- Serve the slices and broth over cooked and drained rice noodles of any sort, or even vermicelli.

1.6–1.8kg piece beef silverside

1 medium onion, peeled
  and halved

2 medium carrots,
  halved widthways

2 medium celery stalks,
  halved widthways

One 15cm rosemary sprig

6 large fresh sage leaves

2 teaspoons sea salt flakes

1 teaspoon ground
  black pepper

2 bay leaves

250ml plus 1 tablespoon
  white wine vinegar

Water as needed

80g fresh breadcrumbs

80g fresh parsley leaves
  and stems

Up to 4 jarred anchovy fillets

Up to 3 medium garlic cloves,
  peeled and finely chopped
  (1 tablespoon prechopped)

2 teaspoons drained and
  rinsed capers

Up to 120ml olive oil

Streamlined Bollito Misto

8 servings

Bollito misto, like Pot au Feu (page 356), is a boiled meat dish, although this one is Italian rather than French. We've streamlined it by using only silverside (rather than a big range of meat cuts, so ours is not really a bollito *misto*, more like a bollito *uno*).

Don't eat the vegetables after cooking. In culinary terms, they're 'spent', meaning that they've added all their flavour to the savoury broth served with the meat. But the broth and the meat will be pure bliss, savoury and satisfying.

1. Set the beef in a **5.5- or 7.5-litre cooker**. Place the onion, carrots, celery, rosemary, sage, salt, pepper and bay leaves around the beef. Drizzle 1 tablespoon vinegar over everything, then add enough water to a depth of about three-quarters of the way up the meat. (The liquid level must not go above the **Max Fill** line. Set the meat in the pot so that it's as flat as possible.) Lock the lid onto the pot.

2.

Set the machine	Level	The valve must be	Time	Press
PRESSURE COOK	MAX	—	1 hour with the KEEP WARM setting off	START
MEAT/ STEW, PRESSURE COOK or MANUAL	HIGH	Closed	1 hour 30 minutes with the KEEP WARM setting off	START
SLOW COOK	HIGH	Opened	5½ hours with the KEEP WARM setting off (or on for no more than 4 hours)	START

3. Meanwhile, mix the breadcrumbs and the remaining 250ml vinegar in a large bowl and set aside for 20 minutes.

4. If you've used a pressure setting, when the machine has finished cooking, turn it off and let its pressure **return to normal naturally**, about 40 minutes.

5. Unlatch the lid and open the cooker. Use a large metal spatula and a big cooking spoon to transfer the beef to a nearby chopping board. Use a slotted spoon to find and discard everything else in the pot. Tent the meat with aluminium foil while you make the salsa verde.

6. Squeeze the breadcrumbs dry by handfuls over the sink, then add them to a food processor. Add the parsley, anchovies, garlic, capers and 60ml olive oil. Cover and pulse to create a coarse sauce, stopping the machine to scrape down the inside occasionally and adding more olive oil through the feed tube to get a sauce-like consistency (but no more than 60ml additional olive oil).

7. Carve the beef into slices 1cm in thickness and serve with lots of the salsa verde on top. The leftover sauce can stay in a covered container in the fridge for up to 3 days, so long as you smooth it out in a container and pour a thin layer of olive oil on top of it to prevent oxidation (aka browning).

Beyond

- You must halve the recipe for a 3-litre cooker.

- Make a full meal by offering traditional antipasto ingredients on the side, such as jarred roasted red peppers, marinated artichoke hearts, olives or even small mozzarella balls.

- Or serve this dish with Better Syracuse Potatoes (page 425).

15g butter

1 tablespoon vegetable,
corn or rapeseed oil

1.2kg piece beef silverside

½ teaspoon table salt

½ teaspoon ground
black pepper

1 large onion, chopped
(240g prechopped)

260g chopped carrots

2 medium garlic cloves,
peeled and finely chopped
(2 teaspoons prechopped)

125ml dry but fruit-forward
red wine, such as Zinfandel

125ml beef stock

125ml red wine vinegar

1 teaspoon granulated sugar

½ teaspoon caraway seeds

½ teaspoon ground allspice

4 bay leaves

1 tablespoon tomato purée

Sauerbraten-Style Pot Roast

4–6 servings

Taking advantage of the way pressure can (sort of) marinate meat *as* it cooks, here's a way to prepare a tasty replica of more traditional sauerbraten just about any weekend evening. Silverside gives the dish some richness without becoming too oily (as, say, chuck would). Use good-quality, very flavourful red wine, the sort you're apt to finish off the evening you make this meal.

1.

Press	Setting	Time	Press
SAUTÉ	MEDIUM, NORMAL or CUSTOM 150°C	20 minutes	START

2. Melt the butter in the oil in a **5.5- or 7.5-litre cooker**. Season the beef with the salt and pepper, get it in the pot and brown it *well*, turning a couple of times, about 10 minutes. Transfer the beef to a nearby chopping board.

3. Add the onion and carrots. Cook, stirring often, until the onion just begins to soften, about 2 minutes. Add the garlic and stir until aromatic, just a few seconds. Pour in the wine and scrape up any browned bits on the pot's bottom.

4. Turn off the **SAUTÉ** function. Stir in the stock, vinegar, sugar, caraway seeds, allspice and bay leaves. Return the meat and any juices to the pot, nestling the meat into the sauce. Lock the lid onto the pot.

5.

Set the machine	Level	The valve must be	Time	Press
PRESSURE COOK	MAX	——	55 minutes with the KEEP WARM setting off	START
MEAT/STEW, PRESSURE COOK or MANUAL	HIGH	Closed	1 hour 15 minutes with the KEEP WARM setting off	START
SLOW COOK	HIGH	Opened	5 hours with the KEEP WARM setting off (or on for no more than 4 hours)	START

Beyond

- You must halve the recipe for a 3-litre cooker.
- This version is not very sweet. Increase the sugar to 1 tablespoon, if desired.
- Serve the meat and sauce over Buttery Pasta (page 155).

6. If you've used a pressure setting, when the machine has finished cooking, turn it off and let its pressure **return to normal naturally**, about 40 minutes.

7. Unlatch the lid and open the cooker. Using a large metal spatula and a big cooking spoon, transfer the meat to a clean chopping board. Find and discard the bay leaves.

8.

Press	Setting	Time	Press
SAUTÉ	MEDIUM, NORMAL or CUSTOM 150°C	5 minutes	START

9. When the sauce comes to a simmer, stir in the tomato purée and cook, stirring often, until the sauce has thickened slightly, 2–3 minutes. Turn off the **SAUTÉ** function, then remove the *hot* insert from the machine to stop the cooking. Carve the meat against the grain into slices 1cm in thickness. Serve in bowls with lots of the sauce.

2 tablespoons olive oil

6 bone-in pieces beef shin, 1–2cm in thickness, each about 350g

115g frozen baby onions (no need to thaw)

175g thinly sliced chestnut mushrooms

250ml dark beer, preferably brown ale

180ml beef or chicken stock

2 tablespoons Worcestershire sauce

1 tablespoon Dijon mustard

1 teaspoon caraway seeds

1 teaspoon dried thyme

Beer-Braised Beef Shin

6 servings

Shin is a fantastic cut of beef, being like osso buco but more savoury, less soft. It makes a hearty meal for chilly weather. The shins are big so they won't all be submerged in the cooking liquids. Overlap them as necessary.

And one note: we also tested this recipe with grass-fed-and-finished beef. They needed an extra 5 minutes under pressure at either pressure level (but no additional time on the SLOW COOK function).

1.

Press	Setting	Time	Press
SAUTÉ	MEDIUM, NORMAL Or CUSTOM 150°C	30 minutes	START

2. Warm the oil in a **5.5- or 7.5-litre cooker** for a minute or two. Add two or three of the shins and brown well, turning a few times, about 10 minutes. Transfer these to a nearby bowl and soldier on, browning the remaining pieces without crowding them before getting them into the bowl.

3. Add the baby onions and mushrooms to the pot. Cook, stirring often, until the mushrooms begin to soften, about 3 minutes. Pour in the beer and scrape up the browned bits on the pot's bottom.

4. Turn off the **SAUTÉ** function. Stir in the stock, Worcestershire sauce, mustard, caraway seeds and thyme. Return the beef shin and any juices to the pot, nestling them into the sauce as well as you can. Lock the lid onto the pot.

5.

Set the machine	Level	The valve must be	Time	Press
PRESSURE COOK	MAX	——	40 minutes with the KEEP WARM setting off	START
MEAT/STEW, PRESSURE COOK or MANUAL	HIGH	Closed	50 minutes with the KEEP WARM setting off	START
SLOW COOK	HIGH	Opened	5 hours with the KEEP WARM setting off (or on for no more than 4 hours)	START

6. If you've used a pressure setting, when the machine has finished cooking, turn it off and let its pressure **return to normal naturally,** about 30 minutes.

7. Unlatch the lid and open the pot. Serve the shins in bowls with lots of the sauce around them.

Beyond

- You must halve the recipe for a 3-litre cooker.
- Have toast to hand so that you can cut it on the diagonal and use the tip to dig the marrow out of the bones before spreading it on the toast.
- Serve the shins, vegetables and broth over cooked and drained orzo.

Italian-Style Braised Meatloaf

4–6 servings

Braising a meatloaf gives it a smooth, luxurious texture. The breadcrumbs do not have to be soaked because they take on so much liquid and soften so well under pressure. If the breadcrumbs you buy have salt in the mixture, reduce the Worcestershire sauce to 1½ teaspoons. (And for a more traditional – albeit made in a Bundt tin – meatloaf, see page 270.)

The only way to get this behemoth of a loaf out of the pot after cooking is with a wide, flexible palette knife. If you're worried, cut the loaf in half in the pot, then transfer the two halves to a chopping board.

1. Mix the tomatoes, onion, pepper, garlic, stock, vinegar, basil, oregano, nutmeg, crushed chilli flakes and salt in a **5.5-litre cooker.**

2. Stir the beef mince, breadcrumbs, egg, Worcestershire sauce, garlic powder and pepper in a large bowl until uniform. (The egg must be thoroughly mixed in.) Using clean, dry hands, form this mixture into an 18cm meatloaf, about like a rugby ball cut in half from point to point, then the ends rounded to form a more compact loaf. Set this loaf into the sauce in the cooker; spoon some of the sauce over the loaf. Lock the lid onto the pot.

3.

Set the machine	Level	The valve must be	Time	Press
PRESSURE COOK	MAX	—	18 minutes with the KEEP WARM setting off	START
MEAT/STEW, PRESSURE COOK or MANUAL	HIGH	Closed	25 minutes with the KEEP WARM setting off	START

4. When the machine has finished cooking, turn it off and let its pressure **return to normal naturally**, about 25 minutes. Unlatch the lid and open the cooker. Transfer the meatloaf to a chopping board. Leave to cool for a few minutes, then slice and serve with the sauce from the pot.

One 400g tin chopped tomatoes

1 small onion, chopped (80g prechopped)

1 small green pepper, stemmed, cored and chopped (90g prechopped)

1 medium garlic clove, peeled and finely chopped (1 teaspoon prechopped)

125ml beef or chicken stock

1 tablespoon balsamic vinegar

2 teaspoons dried basil

2 teaspoons dried oregano

½ teaspoon grated nutmeg

½ teaspoon crushed chilli flakes

½ teaspoon table salt

900g lean beef mince

50g Italian-seasoned dried breadcrumbs

1 large egg

1 tablespoon Worcestershire sauce

½ teaspoon garlic powder

½ teaspoon ground black pepper

Beyond

- For a 3-litre cooker, you must use 125ml stock (as stated in the recipe) but halve the remaining ingredients.

- For a 7.5-litre cooker, you must increase all the ingredients by 50 per cent.

- If the sauce is too wet for your taste, bring it to a simmer with the SAUTÉ setting on MEDIUM, NORMAL or CUSTOM 150°C. Whisk in 2 tablespoons tomato purée, then continue cooking, whisking occasionally, until thickened, 2–4 minutes.

2 tablespoons fat

> **Choose** from either a solid fat like butter, lard or rendered bacon fat, or a tasty liquid fat like olive oil, sesame oil, walnut oil, pecan oil or pumpkin seed oil – or a 50/50 combo of solid and liquid fat.

1.8kg bone-in pork shoulder, cut into 2.5cm pieces

½ teaspoon table salt

½ teaspoon ground black pepper

2 medium garlic cloves, peeled and finely chopped (2 teaspoons prechopped)

1 tablespoon dried spices

> **Choose a selection** from whole cloves, coriander seeds, cumin seeds, fennel seeds, mild smoked paprika, mild paprika, dried oregano, dried thyme and/or dried sage – or a bottled blend such as an Italian or Cajun blend, even herbes de Provence (but probably not any sort of curry powder).

One 5cm cinnamon stick (optional)

500ml liquid

> **Choose** stock of any sort or a 50/50 combo of stock and beer or white wine.

60ml flavour enhancer

> **Choose** from soy sauce, mustard of any type, chutney, marmalade, pesto, tapenade or barbecue sauce.

2 tablespoons acid

> **Choose** from vinegar of any sort (except white distilled vinegar), lemon juice, lime juice, orange juice or grapefruit juice.

Road Map: Pork Stew

6–8 servings

This road map recipe results in a simple stew, without onions, other allium aromatics or even root vegetables. The point is to make truly porcine fare, letting the flavours of the meat shine. It works best with 2.5cm pieces of bone-in pork *shoulder*, which has a mixture of fat, meat and bone that makes for a satisfying stew.

1.

Press	Setting	Time	Press
SAUTÉ	MEDIUM, NORMAL or CUSTOM 150°C	20 minutes	START

2. Warm the oil or melt the fat in a **5.5- or 7.5-litre cooker**. Season the pork with the salt and pepper. Then add about half the meat to the cooker and brown *well*, turning and rearranging occasionally, about 7 minutes. Use kitchen tongs or a slotted spoon to transfer the pork pieces to a nearby bowl and brown the remainder of the pork in the same way before transferring to the bowl.

3. Add the garlic, spices and cinnamon stick (if using) to the pot. Stir until aromatic, just a few seconds. Pour in the liquid and scrape up any browned bits on the pot's bottom. Turn off the **SAUTÉ** function, then stir in the flavour enhancer and the acid. Return the pork and any juices to the pot, stir well and lock the lid onto the cooker.

4.

Set the machine	Level	The valve must be	Time	Press
PRESSURE COOK	MAX	——	24 minutes with the KEEP WARM setting off	START
MEAT/ STEW, PRESSURE COOK or MANUAL	HIGH	Closed	30 minutes with the KEEP WARM setting off	START
SLOW COOK	HIGH	Opened	4 hours with the KEEP WARM setting off (or on for no more than 2 hours)	START

5. If you've used a pressure setting, when the machine has finished cooking, turn it off and let its pressure **return to normal naturally,** about 20 minutes.

6. Unlatch the lid and open the pot. Use a slotted spoon to transfer the pieces of pork to a large bowl. Discard the cinnamon stick, if you've used it. Use a large spoon to skim any excess surface fat from the sauce. Stir the pork back into the sauce and serve in bowls.

Beyond

- You must halve the recipe for a 3-litre cooker.
- The sauce is wet, like a stew. Boil it down, if desired. Remove the pork from the pot as directed. Turn the SAUTÉ function on HIGH or MORE. Cook, stirring almost constantly, as the sauce boils, reducing it to about half its original volume, about 5 minutes. Turn off the SAUTÉ function and stir well before serving.
- Serve this dish over cooked medium-grain white rice, cooked and drained orzo, Butternut Squash Mash (page 432), White Bean Purée (page 451) or Polenta (page 443).
- Use this same road map to make an easy lamb stew by substituting 1.8kg bone-in lamb shoulder chops, cut into 2.5cm pieces, for the pork.

One 400g tin chopped
tomatoes with chillies

125g natural-style smooth
or crunchy peanut butter

180ml chicken stock

1 tablespoon packed fresh
oregano leaves, finely
chopped

½ teaspoon grated nutmeg

Up to ½ teaspoon ground
cayenne

½ teaspoon table salt

2 tablespoons peanut oil

1.3kg boneless skinless pork
shoulder, halved

1 large red onion, halved
and sliced into very thin
half-moons

2 medium garlic cloves,
peeled and finely chopped
(2 teaspoons prechopped)

1 tablespoon finely chopped
peeled fresh root ginger

90ml light but dry white
wine, such as Sauvignon
Blanc

2 bay leaves

2 tablespoons fresh lime juice

Pork Shoulder and Peanut Butter Stew

6 servings

This stew has a West African flavour profile, although it's made with pork shoulder, which is not exactly traditional in the area. The pork gives the stew a rich flavour that is a great match to both the heat from the chillies and the smooth, creamy texture the peanut butter gives to the sauce. Similar stews are made with ground peanuts, but peanut butter gives the stew a 'reduced' flavour, as if it's been simmering for hours (provided, however, that you use a natural-style variety, without extra fat or sugar).

1. Whisk the tomatoes, peanut butter, stock, oregano, nutmeg, cayenne and salt in a large bowl until the peanut butter dissolves. Set aside.

2.

Press	Setting	Time	Press
SAUTÉ	MEDIUM, NORMAL, or CUSTOM 150°C	15 minutes	START

3. Warm the oil in a 5.5-litre cooker for a minute or two. Add half the pork shoulder and brown *lightly* on all sides, turning occasionally, about 4 minutes. Transfer to a bowl and brown the other half in the same way before transferring it to a bowl.

4. Add the onion and cook, stirring often, until softened, about 4 minutes. Stir in the garlic and ginger until aromatic, just a few seconds. Pour in the wine, add the bay leaves and scrape up any browned bits on the pot's bottom.

5. Turn off the **SAUTÉ** function. Pour in the tomato mixture. Return the pork and any juices to the pot, then lock the lid onto the cooker.

6.

Set the machine	Level	The valve must be	Time	Press
PRESSURE COOK	MAX	——	40 minutes with the KEEP WARM setting off	START
MEAT/STEW, PRESSURE COOK or MANUAL	HIGH	Closed	50 minutes with the KEEP WARM setting off	START
SLOW COOK	HIGH	Opened	5 hours with the KEEP WARM setting off (or on for no more than 3 hours)	START

7. If you've used a pressure setting, when the machine has finished cooking, turn it off and let its pressure **return to normal naturally,** about 30 minutes.

8. Unlatch the lid and open the pot. Transfer the pork to a chopping board; find and discard the bay leaves. Use a large spoon to skim any excess surface fat from the sauce in the pot. Stir the lime juice into the sauce. Carve the pork into slices 1cm in thickness (or just small chunks) and serve with the sauce ladled on top.

Beyond

- You must halve the recipe for a 3-litre cooker.
- For a 7.5-litre cooker, you must increase all the ingredients by 50 per cent.
- For more vegetables in the stew, add up to 2 chopped medium carrots, 6 waxy potatoes, 140g each, halved, 225g frozen sliced okra (do not thaw) and/or 1 large, stemmed, cored and roughly chopped red pepper with the tomato mixture.
- Serve with flatbread such as lavash, lefse, even large flour tortillas.

1 tablespoon vegetable,
corn or rapeseed oil;
or peanut oil

175g streaky bacon
rashers, diced

1 large leek (about 175g),
white and pale green parts
only, halved lengthways,
well washed and thinly
sliced

2 tablespoons finely chopped
peeled fresh root ginger

1.2kg boneless pork loin, cut
into 5cm cubes

Two 225g tins whole water
chestnuts, drained

300ml beef or chicken stock

125ml reduced-sodium
soy sauce

One 10cm cinnamon stick

1 star anise pod

2 tablespoons water

1 tablespoon cornflour

Chinese-Take-Away Pork Loin and Bacon Stew

4–6 servings

This easy version of a classic American-Chinese stew is given a decidedly comfort-food twist with the addition of streaky bacon. Use only reduced-sodium soy sauce to avoid an overly salty dish. The water chestnuts will keep a lot of their crunch, even under pressure.

1.

Press	Setting	Time	Press
SAUTÉ	MEDIUM, NORMAL or CUSTOM 150°C	10 minutes	START

2. Warm the oil in a **5.5- or 7.5-litre cooker** for a minute or two. Add the diced bacon and cook, stirring occasionally, until well browned, about 4 minutes. Add the leek and ginger; continue cooking, stirring more often, until the leek has softened, about 2 minutes.

3. Add the pork and toss well to combine. Turn off the **SAUTÉ** function; stir in the water chestnuts, stock, soy sauce, cinnamon stick and star anise pod. Lock the lid onto the cooker.

4.

Set the machine	Level	The valve must be	Time	Press
PRESSURE COOK	MAX	——	16 minutes with the KEEP WARM setting off	START
MEAT/STEW, PRESSURE COOK or MANUAL	HIGH	Closed	20 minutes with the KEEP WARM setting off	START
SLOW COOK	HIGH	Opened	3 hours with the KEEP WARM setting off (or on for no more than 2 hours)	START

5. If you've used a pressure setting, when the machine has finished cooking, turn it off and let its pressure **return to normal naturally,** about 20 minutes.

6. Unlatch the lid and open the cooker. Find and discard the cinnamon stick and star anise pod.

7.

Press	Setting	Time	Press
SAUTÉ	MEDIUM, NORMAL or CUSTOM 150°C	5 minutes	START

8. Bring the sauce to a low simmer. Meanwhile, whisk the water and cornflour in a small bowl until smooth. Whisk this slurry into the stew, then cook, stirring all the while, until thickened, 1–2 minutes. Turn off the **SAUTÉ** function and remove the *hot* insert from the machine to stop the cooking. Set the lid askew over the insert for 5 minutes to blend the flavours. Stir again before serving.

Beyond

- You must halve the recipe for a 3-litre cooker.
- You can increase all the ingredients by 50 per cent in a 7.5-litre cooker.
- Serve the stew over long-grain white rice and/or wilted spinach. Or, better yet, steamed and crisp-tender Chinese water spinach.
- Drizzle the servings with toasted sesame oil and maybe Sriracha.

2 tablespoons olive oil

6 bone-in pork ribs
(900g–1.2kg total weight)

1 medium red onion, chopped
(160g prechopped)

250ml unsweetened cloudy
apple juice

65g chopped dried apples

125ml chicken stock

1 tablespoon Dijon mustard

2 teaspoons dark
brown sugar

1 teaspoon dried sage

1 teaspoon dried thyme

½ teaspoon table salt

Cider-Braised Country-Style Pork Ribs

6 servings

It's hard to make a successful pork chop braise in a pressure cooker without using thick bone-in pork chops (for a road map to do just that, see page 321). As an easier alternative, look for bone-in pork ribs. They'll help create a fine pork braise with little fuss. Note that this dish, while lip-smackingly fatty and rich, is not a full meal. It needs Brown Rice and Lentils (page 404) or maybe Buckwheat Pilaf (page 407) on the side.

1.

Press	Setting	Time	Press
SAUTÉ	MEDIUM, NORMAL or CUSTOM 150°C	20 minutes	START

2. Warm the oil in a **5.5- or 7.5-litre cooker** for a minute or two. Add half the pork ribs and brown *well* on all sides, turning occasionally, about 8 minutes. Transfer the meat to a nearby bowl and brown the remaining ribs in the same way before getting them into that bowl.

3. Add the onion and cook, stirring often, until softened, about 3 minutes. Pour in the apple juice, turn off the **SAUTÉ** function and scrape up any browned bits on the pot's bottom. Stir in the dried apples, stock, mustard, brown sugar, sage, thyme and salt. Nestle the ribs into the sauce; add any juice from their bowl. Lock the lid onto the pot.

4.

Set the machine	Level	The valve must be	Time	Press
PRESSURE COOK	MAX	—	28 minutes with the KEEP WARM setting off	START
MEAT/STEW, PRESSURE COOK or MANUAL	HIGH	Closed	35 minutes with the KEEP WARM setting off	START
SLOW COOK	HIGH	Opened	4 hours with the KEEP WARM setting off (or on for no more than 2 hours)	START

5. If you've used a pressure setting, when the machine has finished cooking, turn it off and let its pressure **return to normal naturally**, about 25 minutes.

6. Unlatch the lid and open the pot. Use kitchen tongs to transfer the ribs to a serving platter. Use a large spoon to skim any excess surface fat from the sauce.

7.

Press	Setting	Time	Press
SAUTÉ	HIGH or MORE	10 minutes	START

8. Bring the sauce in the pot to the boil. Cook, stirring often, until reduced to half its original volume, about 5 minutes. Turn off the **SAUTÉ** function. Serve the ribs with lots of the sauce drizzled over them and more on the side for dipping.

Beyond

- Because of the length of the ribs, this recipe will not work well in a 3-litre cooker.

- For a more savoury dish, reduce the apple juice to 125ml and increase the chicken stock to 250ml.

- For a sweeter, more aromatic dish, add up to 2 chopped, medium carrots and up to 1 tablespoon finely chopped root ginger with the onion.

- Feel free to use parsley or dill instead of the sage.

350ml chicken stock

160g lime marmalade

15g fresh basil leaves, chopped

6 medium garlic cloves, peeled and finely chopped (2 tablespoons prechopped)

2 teaspoons ground cumin

1 teaspoon table salt

1.3kg boneless skinless pork shoulder, any large hunks of fat removed, the meat cut into 5cm pieces

At least 2 tablespoons vegetable, corn or rapeseed oil; lard; or rendered bacon fat

Kick-Butt Carnitas

6 servings

There are a million different sauces and glazes for carnitas, a Mexican staple. After a trip eating our way through Texas last year, we became enamoured of the combination of lime and basil, a sort of nouveau Southwestern tweak on the classic. The lime marmalade will not only provide the essentially sour pop but offer some sugar, which will be crucial in the next step of frying the pieces of cooked pork to render them irresistibly crunchy.

1. Whisk the stock, marmalade, basil, garlic, cumin and salt in a **5.5- or 7.5-litre cooker** until the marmalade dissolves. Add the pork pieces and stir until uniform. Lock the lid onto the pot.

2.

Set the machine	Level	The valve must be	Time	Press
PRESSURE COOK	MAX	——	30 minutes with the KEEP WARM setting off	START
MEAT/ STEW, PRESSURE COOK or MANUAL	HIGH	Closed	40 minutes with the KEEP WARM setting off	START

3. When the machine has finished cooking, turn it off and let its pressure **return to normal naturally**, about 20 minutes. Unlatch the lid and open the cooker. Use kitchen tongs to transfer the pieces of pork to a large chopping board. Use a large spoon to skim any excess surface fat from the sauce in the pot.

4.

Press	Setting	Time	Press
SAUTÉ	HIGH or MORE	10 minutes	START

5. Bring the sauce to a boil and cook, stirring very often, until reduced to the consistency of a barbecue sauce, 6–7 minutes. Turn off the **SAUTÉ** function and pour the sauce into a small, heat-safe serving bowl.

6. Heat the oil or melt the fat in a large frying pan set over a medium heat. Add about one-third of the pork pieces (maybe more, but no crowding!) and cook, turning occasionally, until brown and crisp, about 5 minutes. Transfer to a serving platter and continue browning more of the pork. When done, ladle the thickened sauce over the pieces to serve.

Beyond

- You must halve the recipe for a 3-litre cooker.
- You can fry the pork right in the Instant Pot, using the SAUTÉ function on HIGH or MORE. Because the surface area of the pot is smaller than that of a frying pan, you'll need to work with a greater number of batches.
- For a more savoury dish, reduce the lime marmalade to 100g and add 1 tablespoon soy sauce.
- For a sweeter dish, substitute orange marmalade for the lime.
- Serve with lots of corn or flour tortillas, soured cream and ready-made pico de gallo.

Pork Belly Braised in Ginger Beer

6 servings

Pork belly is fatty luxuriance and so is best either smoked or finished with a sweet flavour profile (as here, with ginger beer). To compensate for the sweetness of that liquid, we bumped up the aromatics with orange zest, star anise and cinnamon.

1.

Press	Setting	Time	Press
SAUTÉ	HIGH or MORE	25 minutes	START

2. Warm the oil in a **5.5- or 7.5-litre cooker** for a minute or two. Add half the pork belly pieces and brown *well* on all sides, turning occasionally, about 10 minutes. Transfer these to a nearby bowl and brown the remaining pieces the same way before transferring them to the bowl.

3. Pour the ginger beer into the cooker and scrape up any browned bits on the pot's bottom. Turn off the **SAUTÉ** function, then stir in the soy sauce, orange juice, spring onions, orange zest, garlic, ginger, cinnamon and star anise pods. Return the pork belly pieces and any juices to the cooker. Lock the lid onto the pot.

4.

Set the machine	Level	The valve must be	Time	Press
PRESSURE COOK	MAX	————	25 minutes with the KEEP WARM setting off	START
MEAT/STEW, PRESSURE COOK or MANUAL	HIGH	Closed	35 minutes with the KEEP WARM setting off	START

5. Use the **quick-release method** to bring the pot's pressure back to normal. Unlatch the lid and open the cooker. Transfer the pork belly to a serving platter or serving bowls. Find and discard the star anise pods. Use a large spoon to skim the excess surface fat from the sauce. Chunk up the meat, then spoon the sauce and spring onions over it in bowls.

---

1 tablespoon vegetable, corn, or rapeseed oil

1kg piece skinless pork belly, cut into 6 pieces

One 350ml bottle ginger beer

90ml soy sauce, preferably reduced-sodium

90ml fresh orange juice

4 medium spring onions, trimmed and cut into 2.5cm pieces

2 tablespoons grated orange zest

1 medium garlic clove, peeled and finely chopped (1 teaspoon prechopped)

2 tablespoons finely chopped peeled fresh root ginger

½ teaspoon ground cinnamon

2 star anise pods

Beyond

- You must halve the recipe for a 3-litre cooker.

- For a thicker sauce, skim it of fat, then reduce it using the SAUTÉ function at MEDIUM, NORMAL or CUSTOM 150°C, stirring quite often, until thickened, 7–8 minutes.

- Serve the broth, pork belly and spring onions over cooked and drained udon noodles.

- For a heartier dish, open the pot in step 5 after cooking, then lay 80g stemmed and chopped kale on top of the pork and sauce. Lock the lid back onto the pot and cook at MAX for 2 minutes or at HIGH for 3 minutes, followed by a quick release. You won't be able to skim the sauce because of the greens, which will have become coated in the pork fat.

1 tablespoon toasted
    sesame oil

450g skinless pork belly,
    cut into 1cm pieces

4 medium spring onions,
    trimmed and thinly sliced

1 tablespoon finely chopped
    peeled fresh root ginger

1 teaspoon Sichuan
    peppercorns

2 tablespoons chilli paste,
    such as sambal oelek

1 teaspoon white
    granulated sugar

250ml chicken stock

1 tablespoon soy sauce

1 tablespoon balsamic
    vinegar

1 tablespoon
    Worcestershire sauce

450g extra-firm silken tofu,
    drained and cut into
    1cm cubes

1 tablespoon cornflour

1 tablespoon water

Pork Belly Mapo Dofu

4–6 servings

Mapo dofu (literally, 'old pock-marked grandmother's tofu') is a traditional Sichuan braise that can be notoriously hot, though more authentic versions are balanced and aromatic. The dish is usually made with a little pork mince or maybe beef mince. We couldn't resist replacing those with pork belly since the Instant Pot cooks it so quickly.

Our version has some tweaks to fit most modern supermarkets with the exception of the Sichuan peppercorns, the one ingredient for which we broke our local-supermarket-only rule. These are not peppercorns at all but rather the dried hulls from seeds of a citrus plant. They are highly prized for their spicy *and* numbing quality, an absolutely essential flavour for this dish. Look for Sichuan peppercorns at Asian supermarkets and from an almost endless array of online sellers. For a more authentic version of the sauce, see the *Beyond* attached to this recipe.

1.

Press	Setting	Time	Press
SAUTÉ	MEDIUM, NORMAL or CUSTOM 150°C	10 minutes	START

2. Warm the oil in a 3- or 5.5-litre cooker for a minute or two. Add the pork belly and cook, stirring often, until the pieces are lightly browned at the edges, about 4 minutes. Stir in the spring onions, root ginger and peppercorns until aromatic, about 1 minute.

3. Add the chilli paste and sugar. Leave to cook until bubbling and sizzling with the meat, about 1 minute. Stir in the stock and scrape up any browned bits on the pot's bottom. Turn off the SAUTÉ function and stir in the soy sauce, balsamic vinegar and Worcestershire sauce. Lock the lid onto the pot.

4.

Set the machine	Level	The valve must be	Time	Press
PRESSURE COOK	MAX	—	10 minutes with the KEEP WARM setting off	START
MEAT/STEW, PRESSURE COOK or MANUAL	HIGH	Closed	12 minutes with the KEEP WARM setting off	START

5. When the machine has finished cooking, turn it off and let its pressure **return to normal naturally**, about 20 minutes. Unlatch the lid and open the cooker.

6.

Press	Setting	Time	Press
SAUTÉ	MEDIUM, NORMAL or CUSTOM 150°C	5 minutes	START

7. Stir the dish as it comes to a simmer. Add the tofu and cook, stirring gently once or twice, for 1 minute. Meanwhile, whisk the cornflour and water in a small bowl or teacup until smooth, then gently stir this slurry into the simmering sauce. Cook, stirring gently a few times, until thickened, less than 1 minute. Turn off the **SAUTÉ** function and remove the *hot* insert from the machine. Set the lid askew over the insert and set aside for 5 minutes to blend the flavours.

Beyond

- For a 7.5-litre cooker, you must increase all the ingredients by 50 per cent.

- For a more authentic flavour, make these three substitutions: 1) dobanjiang paste (a fermented bean and chilli paste from Asian markets) for the chilli paste; 2) 2 tablespoons Chinese black vinegar for the balsamic vinegar and Worcestershire sauce; and 3) drizzle (or bathe) the servings with red chilli oil.

- Although it's almost always served over long-grain white rice, we prefer our nouveau version over medium-grain white rice, such as Arborio or Valencia.

30g butter

1 medium shallot,
finely chopped

1 medium garlic clove, peeled
and finely chopped
(1 teaspoon prechopped)

115g bulk sweet Italian
sausage meat (or buy
Italian sausages and
remove the casings)

30g raisins, chopped

80g fresh breadcrumbs

1 teaspoon finely grated
lemon zest (optional)

½ teaspoon fennel seeds

1.2kg boneless skinless
turkey breast, butterflied
flat and opened up

½ teaspoon table salt

½ teaspoon ground
black pepper

350ml chicken stock

2 fresh oregano sprigs

1½ tablespoons water

1 tablespoon cornflour

Braised Stuffed Turkey Breast

4–6 servings

This recipe's a fair amount of work, but you'll end up with a dish worthy of a festive table. The turkey breast is butterflied, then stuffed with meat and breadcrumbs before being rolled, tied and braised.

The easiest way to butterfly a boneless skinless turkey breast is to have the butcher do it for you. Just ask! To DIY it, set the breast on a chopping board so that the smoother side that had the skin is facing down. Holding the blade of a large chef's knife parallel to the chopping board, cut into the thinner side of the meat as if you were cutting into the pages of an open book from the side, working the knife through the meat until about 2.5cm remains at the fatter side. Open the breast up like said book, that 2.5cm section now like a book's spine.

1.

Press	Setting	Time	Press
SAUTÉ	MEDIUM, NORMAL or CUSTOM 150°C	10 minutes	START

2. Melt 15g butter in a **5.5- or 7.5-litre cooker**. Add the shallot and garlic; cook, stirring often, until softened, 2 minutes. Crumble in the sausage meat. Cook, stirring to break it up, until well browned, about 4 minutes.

3. Turn off the **SAUTÉ** function and scrape the contents of the pot's insert into a large bowl. Leave to cool for 5 minutes; then stir in the raisins, breadcrumbs, lemon zest (if using) and fennel seeds. Leave to cool for 10 minutes.

4. Lay the turkey breast split-side up on a large chopping board. Spread the breadcrumb mixture in an even layer over the meat. Roll the meat up from the long edge to form a compact spiralled 'log', then tie this log in three places with butchers' string to keep it closed. Season the outside of the log with the salt and pepper.

5.

Press	Setting	Time	Press
SAUTÉ	MEDIUM, NORMAL or CUSTOM 150°C	10 minutes	START

6. Melt the remaining 15g butter in the cooker. Add the stuffed turkey breast (bending it to fit if need be) and brown *lightly* on all sides, turning occasionally, about 5 minutes. Turn off the SAUTÉ function, then pour in the stock. Tuck the oregano sprigs round the meat and lock the lid onto the cooker.

7.

Set the machine	Level	The valve must be	Time	Press
PRESSURE COOK	MAX	—	25 minutes with the KEEP WARM setting off	START
MEAT/ STEW, PRESSURE COOK or MANUAL	HIGH	Closed	35 minutes with the KEEP WARM setting off	START

8. When the machine has finished cooking, turn it off and let its pressure **return to normal naturally**, about 25 minutes. Unlatch the lid and open the cooker. Find and discard the oregano sprigs. Use a metal spatula and a spoon (for balance) to transfer the turkey roll to a nearby chopping board.

9.

Press	Setting	Time	Press
SAUTÉ	MEDIUM, NORMAL or CUSTOM 150°C	5 minutes	START

10. As the sauce comes to a simmer, whisk the water and cornflour in a small bowl until smooth. Whisk this slurry into the sauce and continue cooking, whisking constantly, until thickened somewhat, 1–2 minutes. Immediately turn off the SAUTÉ function and remove the insert from the pot to stop the cooking. Carve the stuffed turkey breast into slices 2.5cm in thickness and serve with the sauce ladled on top.

Beyond

- Because of the size of this roll, the recipe will not work well in a 3-litre cooker.
- Serve with Perfect Sweet Potatoes (page 427) and Spicy Spring Greens (page 437).
- Instead of using sweet Italian sausage meat, try spicy chorizo sausage meat, and use cumin seeds in place of the fennel seeds.

250ml bold red wine, such as Cabernet Franc

180ml chicken stock

2 tablespoons hoisin sauce (see page 184)

2 tablespoons honey

2 tablespoons soy sauce

4 medium spring onions, trimmed and thinly sliced

2 medium garlic cloves, peeled and finely chopped (2 teaspoons prechopped)

1 tablespoon finely chopped peeled fresh root ginger

½ teaspoon five-spice powder (see page 88)

2 tablespoons peanut oil

4 turkey legs, each about 340g

Turkey Legs Braised in Red Wine with Asian Spices

4 servings

Turkey legs are often better braised than roasted, although we also turn them into state-fair-worthy drumsticks on page 265. Braised, more of the meat at the tendons gets tender and the tasty bits around them get softer. Here, we braise them in red wine with a few aromatics for a new twist on an old favourite.

Unfortunately, only certain turkey legs can fit in an Instant Pot. They can be no longer than 18cm end to end. Sad to say, the only way to be sure is to take a tape measure to the shop. People will think you're mad but you won't be caught without a dinner plan that evening.

1. Whisk the wine, stock, hoisin sauce, honey and soy sauce in a medium bowl until smooth. Stir in the spring onions, garlic, ginger and five-spice powder. Set aside.

2.

Press	Setting	Time	Press
SAUTÉ	MEDIUM, NORMAL or CUSTOM 150°C	15 minutes	START

3. Warm the oil in a **5.5- or 7.5-litre cooker**. Add two turkey legs and brown *well*, turning occasionally, about 6 minutes. Transfer to a nearby bowl and brown the other two turkey legs in the same way before getting them into that bowl.

4. Pour in the wine mixture and scrape up any browned bits on the pot's bottom. Turn off the **SAUTÉ** function. Put the turkey legs back in the pot, stacking and arranging them so that they are each in some of the sauce. Lock the lid onto the pot.

5.

Set the machine	Level	The valve must be	Time	Press
PRESSURE COOK	MAX	—	21 minutes with the KEEP WARM setting off	START
MEAT/STEW, PRESSURE COOK or MANUAL	HIGH	Closed	30 minutes with the KEEP WARM setting off	START
SLOW COOK	HIGH	Opened	4 hours with the KEEP WARM setting off (or on for no more than 2 hours)	START

6. If you've used a pressure setting, when the machine has finished cooking, turn it off and let its pressure **return to normal naturally,** about 20 minutes.

7. Unlatch the lid and open the cooker. Transfer the turkey legs to a serving platter; tent with aluminium foil to keep warm.

8.

Press	Setting	Time	Press
SAUTÉ	MEDIUM, NORMAL or CUSTOM 150°C	5 minutes	START

9. Bring the sauce in the cooker to the boil, stirring occasionally. Cook, stirring more frequently especially as it boils down, until reduced to one-third of its original volume, about 6 minutes. Turn off the **SAUTÉ** function. Spoon and pour this sauce over the turkey legs before serving.

Beyond

- Because of their size, turkey legs will not fit in a 3-litre cooker.
- If you want crisp skin on the legs, preheat the grill to high. Put the cooked legs on a large baking tin and set it 10–15cm from the hot grill element, turning occasionally, until crisp and dark brown, about 6 minutes.

70g butter, at room
temperature

Two 700g skin-on, bone-in
turkey thighs

½ teaspoon table salt

½ teaspoon ground
black pepper

1 large onion, chopped
(240g prechopped)

3 medium celery stalks,
thinly sliced

1 teaspoon dried sage

½ teaspoon dried thyme

350ml chicken stock

175g jarred peeled
whole chestnuts

40g dried cranberries

3 tablespoons plain flour

Braised Turkey Thighs with Cranberries and Chestnuts

4 servings

Turkey thighs are terrific for cooking under pressure (or slow cooking) but their skin is a problem. You *must* brown it well. Leave the skin against the hot surface in the pot until the natural sugars caramelise and the whole thing can be popped off the bottom without tearing. You'll probably be able to fit both thighs in a **7.5-litre cooker;** you may have to work in batches in a **5.5-litre cooker**. Afterwards, carve turkey thighs by slicing the meat off the bones in long strips. (The bones offer tremendous gnawing possibilities.)

1.

Press	Setting	Time	Press
SAUTÉ	MEDIUM, NORMAL or CUSTOM 150°C	20 minutes	START

2. Melt 30g butter in a **5.5- or 7.5-litre cooker.** Season the turkey thighs with the salt and pepper, then add them skin-side down to the pot, working in batches if necessary to avoid crowding. Brown *well* without turning, until the skin easily releases from the pot's surface, 4–5 minutes. Turn and continue browning until golden, about 3 minutes. Transfer them to a nearby bowl.

3. Add the onion and celery; cook, stirring often, until the onion begins to soften, about 4 minutes. Stir in the sage and thyme until fragrant, just a few seconds. Pour in the stock and scrape up the browned bits on the pot's bottom.

4. Turn off the **SAUTÉ** function, then stir in the chestnuts and dried cranberries. Nestle the thighs skin-side up into the sauce and add any juices from their bowl. Lock the lid onto the pot.

5.

Set the machine	Level	The valve must be	Time	Press
PRESSURE COOK	MAX	——	25 minutes with the KEEP WARM setting off	START
MEAT/ STEW, PRESSURE COOK or MANUAL	HIGH	Closed	32 minutes with the KEEP WARM setting off	START
SLOW COOK	HIGH	Opened	4 hours with the KEEP WARM setting off (or on for no more than 2 hours)	START

6. Meanwhile, use a fork to mash the flour into the remaining 40g butter to make a paste in a small bowl.

7. If you've used a pressure setting, when the machine is finished cooking, use the **quick-release method** to bring its pressure back to normal.

8. Unlatch the lid and open the pot. Transfer the turkey thighs to a serving platter. Use a slotted spoon to get the vegetables and dried fruit onto the platter with the thighs.

9.

Press	Setting	Time	Press
SAUTÉ	MEDIUM, NORMAL Or CUSTOM 150°C	5 minutes	START

10. Bring the sauce to a simmer, whisking often. Whisk in the butter paste a little at a time, incorporating it into the sauce before adding the next. Once all the paste has been added, continue whisking over the heat until the sauce has thickened, about 1 minute. Turn off the **SAUTÉ** function and remove the *hot* insert from the pot to stop the cooking. Ladle the sauce over the turkey thighs when serving.

Beyond

- You must halve the recipe for a 3-litre cooker.
- Many dried cranberries have been sweetened. For a more savoury dish, look out for those without the additives, at health-food stores or online.

30g butter

Two 700g skin-on, bone-in
turkey thighs

¼ teaspoon table salt

¼ teaspoon ground
black pepper

65g frozen baby onions
(do not thaw)

450g white button
mushrooms, thinly sliced

60ml brandy

160ml chicken stock

2 teaspoons dried tarragon
or thyme

1 teaspoon Dijon mustard

60ml double cream

Braised Turkey Thighs with Mushrooms and Cream

4 servings

These turkey thighs are cooked for less time than those in the previous recipe. Here, we want them to have a more 'roasted' texture to go with the cream sauce, rather than the falling-off-the-bone dark-meat texture that went better with the last braise's sauce.

1.

Press	Setting	Time	Press
SAUTÉ	MEDIUM, NORMAL, or CUSTOM 150°C	25 minutes	START

2. Melt the butter in a **5.5-litre cooker**. Season the turkey thighs with the salt and pepper, then add them skin-side down to the cooker, working in batches if necessary. Brown *well* without turning, until the skin easily releases from the pot's surface, 4–5 minutes. Turn and continue browning until golden, about 3 minutes. Transfer them to a nearby bowl.

3. Add the baby onions and cook, stirring occasionally, until lightly browned in places, about 4 minutes. Add the mushrooms and continue cooking until they give off their internal liquid and it reduces to a glaze, about 5 minutes.

4. Pour in the brandy and scrape up any browned bits on the pot's bottom. Turn off the **SAUTÉ** function and stir in stock, tarragon and mustard. Nestle the thighs into the sauce and pour any of their juice in the bowl over them. Lock the lid onto the pot.

5.

Set the machine	Level	The valve must be	Time	Press
PRESSURE COOK	MAX	——	16 minutes with the KEEP WARM setting off	START
MEAT/ STEW, PRESSURE COOK or MANUAL	HIGH	Closed	20 minutes with the KEEP WARM setting off	START

6. When the machine is finished cooking, turn it off and let its pressure **return to normal naturally**, about 15 minutes. Unlatch the lid and open the cooker. Transfer the thighs to a chopping board.

7.

Press	Setting	Time	Press
SAUTÉ	MEDIUM, NORMAL or CUSTOM 150°C	5 minutes	START

8. Bring the sauce to a simmer, stirring occasionally. Stir in the cream and continue cooking for 2 minutes, to reduce the sauce a little and thoroughly incorporate the flavours of the cream. Turn off the **SAUTÉ** function and remove the insert from the pot to stop the cooking. Ladle the sauce over the turkey thighs when serving.

Beyond

- For a 3-litre cooker, you must use 125ml stock and halve the remaining ingredients.

- For a 7.5-litre cooker, you must increase all the ingredients by 50 per cent.

- Go ahead and use more exotic mushrooms, like porcini, hen of the wood or shiitake caps. But avoid chestnut mushrooms or portobello caps. Both will turn the sauce a dark brown.

- Rather than mashed potatoes, try this dish over Yellow Rice Pilaf (page 400).

LONGER BRAISES AND STEWS

2 tablespoons olive oil

1.3–1.8kg boned leg of lamb

1 teaspoon table salt

½ teaspoon ground black pepper

250ml dry but light red wine, such as Pinot Noir

125ml chicken stock

1 medium onion, peeled and halved

4 whole cloves

3 medium Roma or plum tomatoes, chopped

2 large carrots, cut into 5cm sections

6 large garlic cloves, peeled

2 teaspoon dried thyme

Spoon Lamb

6–8 servings

This is the fastest way to make *gigot à sept heures* (French, *gee-GOH-ah-set-uhr*, 'seven-hour leg of lamb'). The meat becomes so tender, you don't need a knife.

Or if the supermarket sells only butterflied, boneless leg of lamb (mostly for the grill), roll it into a compact log and tie it in several places with butchers' string.

1.

Press	Setting	Time	Press
SAUTÉ	MEDIUM, NORMAL or CUSTOM 150°C	15 minutes	START

2. Warm the oil in a 5.5- or 7.5-litre cooker for a minute or two. Season the lamb with the salt and pepper, then set it in the pot and brown well on all sides, even the ends, turning occasionally, about 12 minutes. Transfer the leg of lamb to a nearby bowl.

3. Pour in the wine and stock, then scrape up any browned bits on the pot's bottom. Turn off the **SAUTÉ** function. Stud the onion pieces with the whole cloves; add these to the pot along with the tomatoes, carrots, garlic and thyme. Return the lamb to the cooker and lock the lid onto the pot.

4.

Set the machine	Level	The valve must be	Time	Press
PRESSURE COOK	MAX	——	1 hour 10 minutes with the KEEP WARM setting off	START
MEAT/ STEW, PRESSURE COOK or MANUAL	HIGH	Closed	1 hour 30 minutes with the KEEP WARM Setting off	START
SLOW COOK	HIGH	Opened	5 hours with the KEEP WARM setting off (or on for no more than 2 hours)	START

Beyond

- You must halve the recipe for a 3-litre cooker.
- For an aromatic kick, substitute gin for the red wine. Also add 4 juniper berries and 4 allspice berries when you add the onions.

5. If you've used a pressure setting, when the machine has finished cooking, turn it off and let its pressure **return to normal naturally,** about 25 minutes.

6. Unlatch and open the lid. Transfer the leg of lamb to a clean chopping board.

7. Fish out and discard the onions, carrots and the cloves that have slipped off the onions. Use a hand blender right in the cooker to blend the remaining ingredients in the pot into a sauce. Or, pour the contents of the insert into a blender, cover, remove the centre knob of the lid, cover the hole with a clean tea towel and blend until smooth. To serve, carve the meat into 2.5cm slices and/or chunks, then serve them with the sauce ladled on top.

2 tablespoons olive oil

1.2kg boned leg of lamb, any chunks of fat removed and the meat cut into 4cm pieces

1 large onion, chopped (240g prechopped)

2 medium garlic cloves, peeled and finely chopped (2 teaspoons prechopped)

250ml dry white wine, such as Chardonnay

125ml chicken stock

1 medium butternut squash, peeled, deseeded and cubed

75g sultanas

1 tablespoon apple cider vinegar

½ teaspoon table salt

½ teaspoon ground black pepper

1 large rosemary sprig

2 large thyme sprigs

2 bay leaves

Lamb and Butternut Squash Stew

6 servings

Although this is a *fast/slow* stew, the overall texture will differ depending on which function you've used, which is often the case with fairly fatty cuts of meat. Under pressure, the lamb and the butternut squash will retain some of their natural chew; with the SLOW COOK mode, the meat and vegetables will become very tender, almost velvety. No matter which method you use, the easiest way to make this stew is to buy prechopped butternut squash. If you do, cut each piece into 4cm pieces.

1.

Press	Setting	Time	Press
SAUTÉ	MEDIUM, NORMAL or CUSTOM 150°C	25 minutes	START

2. Warm the oil in a **5.5- or 7.5-litre cooker**. Add half the lamb pieces and brown well, turning occasionally, about 8 minutes. Transfer the lamb to a nearby bowl and brown the remaining lamb pieces in the same way before getting them into that bowl.

3. Add the onion and cook, stirring often, until softened, about 4 minutes. Stir in the garlic until aromatic, just a few seconds. Pour in the wine and scrape up any browned bits on the pot's bottom.

4. Turn off the **SAUTÉ** function and stir in the stock, butternut squash, sultanas, vinegar, salt, pepper, rosemary, thyme and bay leaves. Return the lamb pieces and any juices in their bowl to the cooker. Stir well, then lock the lid onto the pot.

5.

Set the machine	Level	The valve must be	Time	Press
PRESSURE COOK	MAX	—	21 minutes with the KEEP WARM setting off	START
MEAT/STEW, PRESSURE COOK or MANUAL	HIGH	Closed	30 minutes with the KEEP WARM setting off	START
SLOW COOK	HIGH	Opened	3½ hours with the KEEP WARM setting off (or on for no more than 3 hours)	START

6. If you've used a pressure setting, when the machine has finished cooking, use the quick-release method to **return the pressure to normal naturally**, about 25 minutes.

7. Unlatch the lid and open the cooker. Find and discard the herb sprigs and the bay leaves. Stir well before serving.

Beyond

- You must halve the recipe for a 3-litre cooker.

- To omit the wine, use 125ml unsweetened cloudy apple juice and increase the stock to 250ml.

- For heat, add up to 4 dried small red chillies, preferably chillies de árbol. Remove these before serving.

- Brighten the flavours with a little lemon juice just before serving.

- For a more savoury stew, omit the salt, reduce the sultanas to 3 tablespoons and add 2 tablespoons soy sauce.

Buttery Lamb Stew with Wheat Berries and Pecans

6 servings

This big bowl of stew with whole grains is best on a day when you're in from an autumnal garden cleanup or a winter run on the slopes. Lamb shoulder chops require a long time to get tender, so there's a built-in time lag that can be used to cook the wheat berries, too. In this recipe (unlike all others in this book), we soak the wheat berries to ensure they're done at the same time as the lamb.

1. Soak the wheat berries in a big bowl of water for at least 8 hours or up to 12 hours. Drain in a fine-mesh sieve set in the sink.

2.

Press	Setting	Time	Press
SAUTÉ	MEDIUM, NORMAL Or CUSTOM 150°C	25 minutes	START

3. Melt 30g butter in a **5.5- or 7.5-litre cooker**. Add about half the lamb pieces and brown well, turning and rearranging occasionally, about 8 minutes. Transfer these to a nearby bowl, add the remaining 30g butter, and brown the remainder of the lamb in the same way before transferring the pieces to the bowl.

4. Add the onion and cook, stirring occasionally, until softened, about 4 minutes. Pour in the stock and scrape up any browned bits on the pot's bottom. Turn off the **SAUTÉ** function, then stir in the soaked wheat berries, as well as the pecans, sage, crushed chilli flakes and salt. Return the lamb pieces and any of the juices in their bowl to the cooker. Stir well and lock the lid onto the pot.

5.

Set the machine	Level	The valve must be	Time	Press
PRESSURE COOK	MAX	—	30 minutes with the KEEP WARM setting off	START
MEAT/ STEW, PRESSURE COOK or MANUAL	HIGH	Closed	40 minutes with the KEEP WARM setting off	START

6. When the machine is finished cooking, turn it off and let its pressure **return to normal naturally**, about 25 minutes. Unlatch the lid and open the cooker. Stir well before serving.

85g dried wheat berries, preferably soft white wheat berries

60g butter

1.2kg boneless lamb shoulder, any chunks of fat removed, the meat cut into 5cm pieces

1 large onion, chopped (240g prechopped)

600ml chicken stock

60g chopped pecans

2 teaspoons dried sage

½ teaspoon crushed chilli flakes

½ teaspoon table salt

Beyond

- You must halve the recipe for a 3-litre cooker.
- To enrich the sauce, add up to 125ml double cream after cooking. Set the SAUTÉ function on MEDIUM, NORMAL or CUSTOM 150°C and bring to a simmer for 1 minute, stirring often, to cook out the cream's raw taste and blend the flavours.

10

Rice and Grains
(Mains and Sides)

This chapter has a split personality. A little over half of its recipes are for grain side dishes: a range of pilafs (rice to quinoa) as well as a road map for risotto and even a hearty combination of beans and lentils that goes alongside anything from the grill. The remainder of the recipes are grain-based main courses, from a good ole chicken-and-rice casserole to aromatic biryani and even paella.

But don't miss the first recipe for perfect wheat berries. We're whole grain fanatics. We almost always keep cooked wheat berries in the fridge

to toss into soups, add to salads or bulk up smoothies. We'd like to convince you to do the same.

And now for an inevitable warning. Grains, whole or not, can be funky. Yes, a multi-cooker prepares them quickly and efficiently. But grains don't move off a grocery store's shelf quickly. They can go off. If you open the package and the grains have an acrid smell, take them back for a refund.

Even so, there's also the question of the grains' internal moisture content. Individual grains contain varying amounts, which means they get tender at different times.

Because of these variables, consider the timings here as educated guesses, more so than those in any other chapter of this book. Yes, we tested the recipes several times. Often, we wrote timings that were an average of the results. For example, 7 minutes for one batch, 9 for another and 8 for a third. So, 8 minutes appears in this book.

If you open the pot and find the grains are still a tad too *al dente*, lock the lid back on, open the pressure valve and set the machine aside for a few minutes. If the grains are too hard to soften this way, check to make sure there's still enough liquid in the pot (you'll need about 180ml in a **3-litre**, 300ml in a **5.5-litre** or 435ml in a **7.5-litre**), lock the lid back on and bring it to HIGH pressure (not MAX) for 1 or 2 minutes, followed by the **quick-release method**. At this point, the valve may sputter. Have a clean tea towel to hand to lay over it.

Frankly, such culinary fiddling around seems a small price to pay for a pilaf in minutes or a comforting rice casserole in a few more.

FAQs

1. How do I store all these grains?

Whole grains aren't really whole. For the most part, they include three parts of the grain: the germ, the bran and the endosperm. In almost all cases (except for corn), the hulls are missing because they are indigestible. Refined grains like white rice or pearl barley, by contrast, are missing the germ and bran. Refined grains withstand longer storage (up to 8 months in some cases) in a sealed container in a cool, dry cupboard because they are missing all the natural oils in the germ and bran, the very things that get smelly. We keep all whole grains (like wheat berries and brown rice) in labelled, sealed, plastic containers in a dark pantry for a couple of months, or in the freezer for up to 1 year.

2. Why do grain dishes sometimes turn out soupy?

There's only one way to make the pot work: boiling liquid → steam → pressure. You must increase the liquid in the pot more than you might in a saucepan on the hob to make sure 1) you get the pressure needed, and 2) you have enough liquid that the grains (or lentils or beans) can dance in the water as they cook without ending up burnt on the pot's bottom.

All this means you may have to boil a dish down after cooking to keep it from being too soupy. Of course, you can skip the whole process and serve the grains with a slotted spoon or even in bowls.

3. What's with all the white *basmati* rice?

We feel it's the best variety for a pressure cooker. Standard, packaged, long-grain rice (that is, the store brand) can turn hideously gummy as the kernels break down. Basmati hold up better. True, basmati is more expensive but we find the payoff worth it.

Perfect Wheat Berries

Makes about 750g cooked grains

In this recipe, we don't provide a chart of cooking times because of the way different models of the Instant Pot work. But no matter which you own, the recipe is a time-saver because the raw grains cook more quickly under pressure. They also don't need to be soaked overnight, the way they would if we were cooking them on the hob.

Toss cooked and drained wheat berries in a green salad, use them to bulk up tuna or chicken salad, add them to chickpeas to make a thicker hummus in a food processor or toss them into chillies or stews for the last 5 minutes of cooking. You can use them instead of cooked rice for a new take on fried 'rice' in a wok, add a few to a smoothie to make it richer or even enjoy them as a healthier cold breakfast cereal with milk, some blackberries and a little sugar.

1. Stir the water, wheat berries and fat in a **3-, 5.5- or 7.5-litre cooker**. Lock the lid onto the pot with the pressure valve closed.

2. For **Lux, Duo, Smart** or **Ultra** models, press the **MULTIGRAIN** button for **HIGH** pressure. Set the time for 30 minutes and press **START** if necessary. The machine will automatically soak the grains in a 45-minute warm-water bath, then cook them at **HIGH** pressure for 30 minutes. When the machine has finished cooking, turn it off and let its pressure **return to normal naturally,** about 30 minutes.

For a **Max** machine, turn on the **SAUTÉ** function to **HIGH** and heat the contents until it is quite steamy but not boiling. Switch the **SAUTÉ** function off, latch the lid onto the pot and set aside for 45 minutes. Then set the machine to cook at **MAX** for 25 minutes. Press **START**. When the machine has finished cooking, turn it off and let its pressure **return to normal naturally,** about 25 minutes.

3. Unlatch the lid and open the cooker. Drain the wheat berries from the *hot* insert into a fine-mesh sieve such as a *chinois* or through a colander lined with a double thickness of kitchen paper. Leave to cool for 5 minutes, then refresh the grains with cool water to stop any residual cooking. Shake the sieve or colander a few times to get rid of excess moisture. Use the cooked wheat berries at once or store them in a sealed container in the fridge for up to 3 days or in the freezer for up to 2 months.

1 litre water

170g raw, soft, white (or spring) wheat berries

1 tablespoon vegetable, corn, rapeseed or olive oil; or butter

Beyond

- For a more buttery flavour, substitute Kamut berries, an organic strain of khorasan wheat.

- For raw hard red (or winter) wheat berries, rye berries, hull-less barley or raw oat groats (not pinhead, coarse oatmeal or rolled oats of any sort but whole oat groats), use the first technique for cooking at HIGH in older models for 40 minutes, followed by a natural release; or use the second technique for warming the water, then cooking at MAX for 35 minutes, followed by a natural release.

**2 tablespoons solid
or liquid fat**

Choose from butter, lard,
schmaltz, coconut oil, goose fat
or duck fat; or olive, vegetable,
corn, rapeseed, safflower,
grapeseed, avocado or any nut
oil – or a 50/50 combo of a solid
fat and a liquid fat.

**160g chopped (and trimmed
if necessary) allium aromatics**

Choose from onions (of any sort),
shallots, leeks (white and pale
green parts only, well washed)
or spring onions.

**330g medium-grain white
rice, preferably white Arborio
rice**

**125ml flavour-enhancing
liquid**

Choose from white wine (of any
sort), dry vermouth, dry sherry,
strongly brewed tea, a pale-
coloured beer such as an IPA
or a Pilsner, unsweetened apple
juice or mushroom stock.

**2 tablespoons finely chopped
fresh herb leaves**

Choose one or several from basil,
chives, marjoram, oregano,
parsley, rosemary, sage, savory,
tarragon and/or thyme.

**Up to 3 medium garlic cloves,
peeled and finely chopped
(1 tablespoon prechopped)**

**Up to .05g saffron threads
(optional)**

1 litre stock

Use any sort – chicken, beef,
vegetable, turkey or fish – or
(better) use a homemade stock,
even in as little as a 25/75 ratio
with ready-made stock.

Road Map: Risotto

4–6 servings

This road map leads you to a simple risotto. You can but don't need
to add vegetables. If you make plain risotto to serve with a steak off
the grill, you'll get about six servings out of the pot. But this road
map can also create a full dinner. If you make a risotto stocked with
vegetables, plan on four servings for a main course.

Use only white medium-grain rice. Arborio is the standard,
although you can use bomba, Valencia, and even more generic
varieties. This technique won't work with brown Arborio, nor with
short- or long-grain rice of any sort.

The risotto may be a tad soupy when you open the pot,
depending on the moisture content of the uncooked rice grains
and the natural moisture packed into the vegetables. Solve this
soupiness in two ways. After you add the cheese in step 5, set the
pot aside with the lid askew for several minutes, even up to 10. The
rice will continue to absorb moisture. Or *before* you add any cheese,
use the **SAUTÉ** function on **LOW** or **LESS** to gently simmer the
risotto, stirring almost constantly, until most of the liquid has been
absorbed, maybe 2 or 3 minutes.

1.

Press	Setting	Time	Press
SAUTÉ	MEDIUM, NORMAL or CUSTOM 150°C	10 minutes	START

2. Melt the fat or heat the oil in a 3-, 5.5- or 7.5-litre cooker for
a minute or two. Add the allium aromatics and cook, stirring
often, until softened, 3–5 minutes. Stir in the rice and cook until
it is coated in the fat and the tips of the grains have begun
to turn translucent, about 1 minute.

3. Stir in the flavour-enhancing liquid and scrape up any browned bits on the pot's bottom. Stir in the herbs, garlic, and saffron (if using) until aromatic, just a few seconds. Turn off the **SAUTÉ** function, pour in the stock, scrape up any browned bits on the pot's bottom, and stir in the quick-cooking vegetables (if using). Lock the lid onto the cooker.

4.

Set the machine	Level	The valve must be	Time	Press
PRESSURE COOK	MAX	—	7 minutes with the KEEP WARM setting off	START
PRESSURE COOK or MANUAL	HIGH	Closed	9 minutes with the KEEP WARM setting off	START

5. Use the **quick-release method** to bring the pot's pressure back to normal. Unlatch the lid and open the cooker. Add the cheese and stir well. Set the lid askew over the pot for about 2 minutes to melt the cheese. Stir again and season with salt and pepper as desired.

Up to 300g prepped quick-cooking vegetables (optional)

Choose one or two from cored and chopped chicory; diced carrots; frozen butternut squash cubes (do not thaw); frozen edamame beans (do not thaw); frozen mixed vegetables of any sort without any spice or flavourings added (do not thaw); jarred peeled chestnuts; diced peeled carrots or parsnips; diced, deseeded and peeled fresh butternut squash or other winter squash; peas (fresh or frozen); washed and stemmed chard, kale or other leafy greens; thinly sliced shiitake mushroom caps; thinly sliced white button mushrooms or chestnut mushrooms; and/or thinly sliced fresh porcini mushrooms.

60–125g grated semi-firm or firm cheese

Choose from Asiago, Cheddar, Edam, Havarti, Gorgonzola, Gouda, mozzarella, Parmigiano-Reggiano, pecorino, Swiss or Gouda.

Table salt and ground black pepper for garnishing

Beyond

- For a variation in flavour and texture, substitute up to 125g of a soft cheese like chèvre or ricotta (or even 125g crème fraîche) for the semi-firm or firm cheese. Stir well to melt.

- For heat, add up to 1 teaspoon crushed chilli flakes with the fresh herbs.

45ml olive oil

Up to 3 medium garlic cloves,
peeled and finely chopped
(1 tablespoon prechopped)

Up to .05g saffron threads
(optional)

400g long-grain white rice,
such as white basmati

1 litre vegetable stock

90g chopped raisins

40g flaked almonds

1 teaspoon table salt

½ teaspoon ground allspice

½ teaspoon ground
black pepper

White Rice Pilaf

6 servings

This straightforward rice side dish goes with almost anything
roasted or grilled, such as a platter of olive-oil-slathered and
lemon-zest-sprinkled, grilled chicory, fennel slices, quartered
cauliflower heads and/or courgette spears. There's plenty of stock
to cook the rice so the grains stay tender and have enough room
to move in the pot without sticking to the bottom. Most of that
liquid should get absorbed when you set the pot aside in the last
step, steaming the rice to perfection.

1.

Press	Setting	Time	Press
SAUTÉ	MEDIUM, NORMAL or CUSTOM 150°C	10 minutes	START

2. Heat the oil in a **3-, 5.5- or 7.5-litre cooker** for a minute or two.
Add the garlic and saffron (if using) and cook, stirring often,
until aromatic, about 20 seconds. Stir in the rice and get the
grains coated in the oil and spices.

3. Turn off the **SAUTÉ** function. Stir in the stock, raisins, almonds,
salt, allspice and pepper. Lock the lid onto the pot.

4.

Set the machine	Level	The valve must be	Time	Press
PRESSURE COOK	MAX	—	7 minutes with the KEEP WARM setting off	START
PRESSURE COOK or MANUAL	HIGH	Closed	9 minutes with the KEEP WARM setting off	START

5. Use the **quick-release method** to bring the pot's pressure back
to normal – but *do not open the cooker*. Set aside with the lid
latched and the valve open for 10 minutes. Unlatch the lid and
open the pot. Stir well before serving.

Beyond

- If the pilaf is too soupy, set
the SAUTÉ function on LOW
or LESS function and cook,
uncovered, for a few minutes,
stirring quite often to make
sure the rice doesn't stick.

- Feel free to swop the almonds
for pine nuts, chopped
walnuts or chopped pecans.

- For a less sweet pilaf, instead
of the raisins, use 2 thinly
sliced, medium celery stalks.

Brown Rice Pilaf

6 servings

Brown rice pilaf is not often a successful dish. The grains get hard on the outside before they're tender on the inside, then half of them start to break apart and become like a porridge before the rest are done. But the high-steam environment inside a multi-cooker makes all the grains plump and chewy. It also puts this healthy side dish within reach almost any weekday. In fact, with a poached egg on top of each serving, this pilaf can easily become a main course.

30g butter

1 medium red onion, chopped (160g prechopped)

125g chopped pecans

1 teaspoon dried thyme

1 teaspoon dried sage

¼ teaspoon table salt

¼ teaspoon ground black pepper

400g brown long-grain rice, such as brown basmati

1 litre vegetable stock

30g dried cranberries, chopped

1.

Press	Setting	Time	Press
SAUTÉ	MEDIUM, NORMAL or CUSTOM 150°C	5 minutes	START

2. Melt the butter in a **3-, 5.5- or 7.5-litre cooker**. Add the onion and cook, stirring occasionally, until softened, about 3 minutes. Add the pecans, thyme, sage, salt and pepper. Stir until aromatic, just a few seconds. Add the rice and cook, stirring often, until coated in the herbs and fat.

3. Pour in the stock and scrape up *every speck of browned stuff* on the pot's bottom. Turn off the **SAUTÉ** function and stir in the cranberries. Lock the lid onto the cooker.

4.

Set the machine	Level	The valve must be	Time	Press
PRESSURE COOK	MAX	—	22 minutes with the KEEP WARM setting off	START
PRESSURE COOK or MANUAL	HIGH	Closed	28 minutes with the KEEP WARM setting off	START

5. Use the **quick-release method** to bring the pot's pressure back to normal – but *do not open the pot*. Set it aside with the lid latched but the pressure valve open for 10 minutes. Unlatch the lid and open the cooker. Stir well before serving.

Beyond

- You can use this recipe as a road map for a brown rice pilaf. Swop the butter for just about any fat. The same goes for the pecans and dried cranberries, substituting other nuts or dried fruits (chopped as necessary) to create your own signature version.

1 tablespoon very warm
water from the kettle

½ teaspoon saffron threads

3 tablespoons olive oil

1 large onion, chopped (240g
prechopped)

Up to 1 teaspoon
ground turmeric

½ teaspoon ground ginger

½ teaspoon table salt

¼ teaspoon crushed chilli
flakes

300g long-grain white rice,
preferably jasmine

700ml vegetable stock

Yellow Rice Pilaf

6 servings

Here's a recipe for a true 'yellow' rice pilaf, almost always made
with saffron and turmeric. This pilaf is the best bed for skewers
or kebabs.

1. Pour the water over the saffron threads in a small bowl or
a teacup. Set aside as you continue with the recipe.

2.

Press	Setting	Time	Press
SAUTÉ	MEDIUM, NORMAL or CUSTOM 150°C	10 minutes	START

3. Heat the oil in a 3-, 5.5- or 7.5-litre cooker for a minute or two.
Add the onion and cook, stirring often, until softened, about
5 minutes. Stir in the turmeric, ginger, salt and crushed chilli
flakes until fragrant, just a few seconds.

4. Add the rice and cook, stirring all the while, until the grains
are evenly coated in the oil and spices. Turn off the **SAUTÉ**
function, pour in the stock and scrape up *every speck of browned
stuff* on the pot's bottom. Stir in the saffron and its soaking
water. Lock the lid onto the cooker.

5.

Set the machine	Level	The valve must be	Time	Press
PRESSURE COOK	MAX	—	10 minutes with the KEEP WARM setting off	START
PRESSURE COOK or MANUAL	HIGH	Closed	12 minutes with the KEEP WARM setting off	START

6. Use the **quick-release method** to bring the pot's pressure back
to normal – but *do not open the cooker.* Set it aside with the lid
still latched and the pressure valve open for 10 minutes. Unlatch
the lid and open the pot. Stir well before serving.

Beyond

- Try adding any number of
  other things to the pot before
  you lock the lid on. Consider
  10g baby kale leaves; 80g
  peas (thawed if frozen); 30g
  drained and chopped jarred
  pimientos; or 40g sliced,
  pitted green olives.

- For a little crunch, add up
  to 40g shelled, unsalted
  pistachios with the spices.
  Or finely chop those pistachios
  and sprinkle them over each
  serving.

- For a richer (if not vegetarian)
  version, substitute chicken
  stock for the vegetable stock.

Herbed Green Rice

6 servings

No, we don't mean rice that ends up green because it has been soaked in the juice squeezed from chlorophyll-rich young bamboo. We mean a highly herbed rice side dish, a great idea with a spring meal. The fresh herbs can get squishy after so long under pressure. Make sure they are very finely chopped so they almost melt into the mixture.

1.

Press	Setting	Time	Press
SAUTÉ	MEDIUM, NORMAL or CUSTOM 150°C	5 minutes	START

2. Melt the butter in a 3-, 5.5- or 7.5-litre cooker. Add the leek and cook, stirring constantly, until softened, about 2 minutes. Stir in the chillies and garlic until fragrant, about 1 minute. Pour in the rice and stir until the grains are evenly and thoroughly coated in the butter and aromatics.

3. Turn off the **SAUTÉ** function and stir in the stock, parsley, coriander, oregano and salt. Lock the lid onto the pot.

4.

Set the machine	Level	The valve must be	Time	Press
PRESSURE COOK	MAX	—	10 minutes with the KEEP WARM setting off	START
PRESSURE COOK or MANUAL	HIGH	Closed	12 minutes with the KEEP WARM setting off	START

5. Use the **quick-release method** to bring the pot's pressure back to normal – but *do not open the cooker*. Set it aside with the lid still latched and the pressure valve open for 10 minutes. Unlatch the lid, open the cooker and stir well before serving.

30g butter

1 large leek (about 175g), white and pale green parts only, halved lengthways, well washed and thinly sliced

One 125g tin chopped mild or hot green chillies

2 medium garlic cloves, peeled and finely chopped (2 teaspoons prechopped)

300g long-grain white rice, preferably jasmine

700ml vegetable stock

20g fresh parsley leaves, finely chopped

10g fresh coriander leaves, finely chopped

2 tablespoons loosely packed fresh oregano leaves, finely chopped

½ teaspoon table salt

Beyond

- You might like to swop the green herbs for other favourites. The parsley is integral to the dish, but try rounding it out with sage and savory or oregano and thyme or just tarragon. In total (with the parsley), you're looking for a little less than 35g fresh herbs.

200g small dried red beans

2 tablespoons vegetable, corn or rapeseed oil

1 medium onion, chopped (160g prechopped)

1 medium pepper, stemmed, cored and chopped (175g prechopped)

3 medium celery stalks, thinly sliced

3 medium garlic cloves, peeled and finely chopped (1 tablespoon prechopped)

300g long-grain white rice, preferably basmati

1 teaspoon dried thyme

1 teaspoon dried sage

½ teaspoon celery seeds

Up to ½ teaspoon ground cayenne

½ teaspoon table salt

2 bay leaves

950ml vegetable or chicken stock

Red Beans and Rice

4–6 servings

This recipe yields a Louisiana version of the classic grain/legume side dish. (See the next recipe for our take on the Cuban version.) There are many variations for this dish among Cajun cooks, some with myriad spices and additions; others, little more than the grain and the legume together. Ours is about midway between the fussy and the simple. Consider it a go-to starchy side dish to put underneath any spicy stew or braise.

1. Soak the beans in a large bowl of water for 8 hours or up to 12 hours. Drain them in a colander set in the sink.

2.

Press	Setting	Time	Press
SAUTÉ	MEDIUM, NORMAL OR CUSTOM 150°C	10 minutes	START

3. Warm the oil in a **5.5- or 7.5-litre cooker** for a minute or two. Add the onion, pepper and celery. Cook, stirring occasionally, until the onion softens, about 4 minutes. Add the garlic and cook, stirring more frequently, for 1 minute. Add the rice, thyme, sage, celery seeds, cayenne, salt and bay leaves. Stir until the grains are evenly and thoroughly coated in the fat and mixed into the vegetables.

4. Pour in the stock and scrape up *every speck of browned stuff* on the pot's bottom. Turn off the **SAUTÉ** function. Stir in the beans and lock the lid onto the pot.

5.

Set the machine	Level	The valve must be	Time	Press
PRESSURE COOK	MAX	—	10 minutes with the KEEP WARM setting off	START
PRESSURE COOK or MANUAL	HIGH	Closed	12 minutes with the KEEP WARM setting off	START

6. Use the **quick-release method** to bring the pot's pressure back to normal – but *do not open the cooker*. Set it aside with the lid latched and the pressure valve open for 10 minutes. Unlatch the lid and open the cooker. Find and discard the bay leaves. Stir well before serving.

Beyond

- You must halve the recipe for a 3-litre cooker.

- For a meatier (and by some accounts, more classic) version, cook up to 115g loose sausage meat in the oil. Transfer the meat to a bowl, then continue on with the recipe. Add the meat back in with the drained beans.

Black Turtle Beans and Rice

4–6 servings

Here's a Cuban version of the classic grain/legume side dish (see the previous recipe for our simplified take on the Louisiana version). This one goes really well under our Picadillo-Style Ragù (page 143). It is also the gold standard for taco night and alongside a grilled Southwest-style rubbed pork loin.

1. Soak the beans in a large bowl of water for 8 hours or up to 12 hours. Drain them in a colander set in the sink.

2. Pour the beans into a 5.5- or 7.5-litre cooker. Add the remaining ingredients and stir well. Lock the lid onto the cooker.

3.

Set the machine	Level	The valve must be	Time	Press
PRESSURE COOK	MAX	—	10 minutes with the KEEP WARM setting off	START
PRESSURE COOK or MANUAL	HIGH	Closed	12 minutes with the KEEP WARM setting off	START

4. Use the **quick-release method** to bring the pot's pressure back to normal – but *do not open the cooker.* Set it aside with the lid latched and the pressure valve open for 10 minutes. Unlatch the lid and open the cooker. Stir well before serving.

260g dried black turtle beans

950ml vegetable or chicken stock

300g long-grain white rice, preferably basmati

15g coriander leaves, finely chopped

One 125g tin chopped mild or hot green chillies

1½ teaspoons dried oregano

½ teaspoon ground cumin

½ teaspoon table salt

½ teaspoon ground black pepper

Beyond

- You must halve the recipe for a 3-litre cooker.

- For heat, add up to 1 medium fresh jalapeño, stemmed, halved lengthways, deseeded (if desired) and thinly sliced.

- For more zip, add up to 2 teaspoons grated orange zest; up to a 115g jar of chopped pimientos, drained and rinsed; and/or up to 1 teaspoon mild smoked paprika.

60ml olive oil

6 medium garlic cloves,
peeled and finely chopped
(2 tablespoons prechopped)

½ teaspoon crushed
chilli flakes

125ml vermouth,
either dry (white)
or sweet (red)

400g long-grain brown rice

110g Puy lentils

1 teaspoon table salt

1 litre vegetable
or chicken stock

Brown Rice and Lentils

6 servings

This easy side dish is highly spiced because the oil steeps with
the aromatics before you assemble the dish. Although it's great
alongside a roast of just about any sort, it also makes the base for
a great breakfast. Serve it up on plates, then top each serving
with a fried egg (or two) and hot sauce, like Sriracha.

1. Before turning on the heat, pour the oil into a 3-, 5.5-
or 7.5-litre cooker. Add the garlic and crushed chilli flakes.

2.

Press	Setting	Time	Press
SAUTÉ	LOW or LESS	5 minutes	START

3. Heat the oil slowly until the garlic is golden at the edges,
stirring often, 3–4 minutes. Stir in the vermouth and scrape
up any browned bits on the pot's bottom.

4. Pour in the rice, lentils and salt. Stir until the rice grains are
evenly and thoroughly coated in the fat and aromatics. Turn
off the **SAUTÉ** function and stir in the stock. Lock the lid onto
the pot.

5.

Set the machine	Level	The valve must be	Time	Press
PRESSURE COOK	MAX	—	23 minutes with the KEEP WARM setting off	START
PRESSURE COOK or MANUAL	HIGH	Closed	30 minutes with the KEEP WARM setting off	START

6. When the machine has finished cooking, turn it off and let its
pressure **return to normal naturally**, about 20 minutes. Unlatch
the lid and open the cooker. Stir well before serving.

Beyond

- For more punch, finely chop
  1 tinned anchovy fillet. Add
  it with the garlic and crushed
  chilli flakes but leave out the
  salt.

- To avoid using alcohol,
  substitute 60ml unsweetened
  apple juice and an additional
  65ml vegetable stock for the
  red vermouth or use all stock.

- If you've used a 5.5- or 7.5-litre
  cooker, try stirring up to 90g
  packed baby rocket or baby
  kale and 1 tablespoon balsamic
  vinegar into the finished dish.
  Set the lid askew over the
  pot for 2–3 minutes to wilt
  the greens.

Wild Rice Pilaf

6 servings

Wild rice is not rice. It's a grass grain, once found almost exclusively in the upper Midwest and the southern portions of Ontario, in Canada. Today, there are many varietals on the market: some brown, some black, many grown in California. This recipe was designed for *black* wild rice, the sort that splits when cooked to reveal a creamy, white core.

There's something of a reversal in this technique as the wild rice is cooked under pressure and then the other ingredients are added to the pot. We found that keeping the apple and spring onions out from under the pressure gave them a better texture to match the wild rice.

1. Pour the wild rice in a **3-, 5.5- or 7.5-litre cooker**, add 15g of the butter, and fill the cooker with water until the wild rice is submerged by 5cm. Lock the lid onto the pot.

2.

Set the machine	Level	The valve must be	Time	Press
PRESSURE COOK	MAX	—	28 minutes with the KEEP WARM setting off	START
PRESSURE COOK or MANUAL	HIGH	Closed	40 minutes with the KEEP WARM setting off	START

3. Use the **quick-release method** to bring the pot's pressure back to normal. Unlatch the lid and open the pot. Drain the wild rice from the hot insert into a fine-mesh sieve such as a *chinois* or through a colander lined with a single layer of muslin. Rinse out the insert and return it to the machine.

4.

Press	Setting	Time	Press
SAUTÉ	MEDIUM, NORMAL or CUSTOM 150°C	10 minutes	START

5. Melt the remaining 30g butter in the pot, then add the walnuts, apple, spring onions and celery. Cook, stirring occasionally, until the spring onions soften, about 3 minutes. Stir in the cooked and drained wild rice, then add the sage and salt. Cook, stirring all the while, to blend the flavours, about 1 minute. Turn off the **SAUTÉ** function and remove the *hot* insert from the pot to stop the cooking. Serve warm.

200g black wild rice

45g butter

Water as needed

60g chopped walnuts

1 firm, sour, green apple, such as Granny Smith, cored and diced (no need to peel)

2 medium spring onions, trimmed and thinly sliced

1 medium celery stalk, thinly sliced

1 tablespoon packed fresh sage leaves, finely chopped

½ teaspoon table salt

Beyond

- For a sweeter finish, substitute 1 firm ripe pear, cored and chopped, for the apple.
- Feel free to substitute pecans or even skinned hazelnuts for the walnuts.

2 tablespoons vegetable,
corn or rapeseed oil;
or 30g butter

2 medium shallots, peeled
and chopped

2 medium garlic cloves,
peeled and finely chopped
(2 teaspoons prechopped)

330g pearl barley

600ml vegetable
or chicken stock

1 medium carrot, grated
through the large holes
of a box grater

2 tablespoons packed fresh
dill fronds, finely chopped

Up to 1 tablespoon fresh
lemon juice

1 teaspoon finely grated
lemon zest

½ teaspoon table salt

½ teaspoon ground
black pepper

Barley Pilaf

6 servings

Pearl barley has a mild, sweet flavour that pairs well with lemon
and dill. This one's a filling side dish, a welcome addition to a festive
table alongside roast beef or turkey.

1.

Press	Setting	Time	Press
SAUTÉ	MEDIUM, NORMAL OR CUSTOM 150°C	10 minutes	START

2. Heat the oil for a minute or two (or melt the butter) in
a 5.5- or 7.5-litre cooker. Add the shallots and cook, stirring
occasionally, until softened, about 3 minutes. Add the garlic
and cook until fragrant, just a few seconds. Stir in the barley
until it is evenly and thoroughly coated in the fat.

3. Pour in the stock, turn off the **SAUTÉ** function and scrape
up *every speck of browned stuff* on the pot's bottom. Stir in the
carrot, dill, lemon juice, lemon zest, salt and pepper. Lock the
lid onto the pot.

4.

Set the machine	Level	The valve must be	Time	Press
PRESSURE COOK	MAX	—	18 minutes with the KEEP WARM setting off	START
PRESSURE COOK or MANUAL	HIGH	Closed	25 minutes with the KEEP WARM setting off	START

5. When the machine has finished cooking, turn it off and let its
pressure **return to normal naturally**, about 20 minutes. Unlatch
the lid and open the cooker. Stir well before serving.

Beyond

- You must halve the recipe for
a 3-litre cooker.
- Garnish servings with
crumbled feta or soft goat's
cheese. Or even crumbled
blue cheese.
- This pilaf is also good as a bed
for sausages off the grill,
particularly smoked
bratwurst or kielbasa.

Buckwheat Pilaf

6 servings

Buckwheat may not sound gluten-free ('wheat', after all); but it is *not* a cereal grain. It's the seed from a grass cultivar not even distantly related to wheat. It cooks up sticky and thick, with a subtle texture of oats but with a more herbaceous flavour. Do not use kasha, the name for *toasted* buckwheat groats. The flavour will be far too strong, even bitter. Plain buckwheat groats go off quickly at room temperature. Store them in a sealed container in the freezer for up to 6 months.

1.

Press	Setting	Time	Press
SAUTÉ	MEDIUM, NORMAL or CUSTOM 150°C	10 minutes	START

2. Warm the oil for a minute or two (or melt the butter) in a 5.5- or 7.5-litre cooker. Add the onion and celery; cook, stirring occasionally, until the onion has softened, about 3 minutes. Add the pecans, cranberries, sage and thyme; stir well until fragrant, about 30 seconds.

3. Pour in the stock, turn off the **SAUTÉ** function and scrape up *every speck of browned stuff* on the pot's bottom. Stir in the buckwheat and salt. Lock the lid onto the cooker.

4.

Set the machine	Level	The valve must be	Time	Press
PRESSURE COOK	MAX	—	3 minutes with the KEEP WARM setting off	START
PRESSURE COOK or MANUAL	HIGH	Closed	5 minutes with the KEEP WARM setting off	START

5. Use the **quick-release method** to bring the pot's pressure back to normal – but *do not open the pot*. Set it aside with the lid latched and the pressure valve open for 7 minutes. Unlatch the lid and open the cooker. Stir well before serving.

1 tablespoon vegetable, corn, or rapeseed oil; or 15g butter

1 small onion, chopped (80g prechopped)

2 medium celery stalks, thinly sliced

60g chopped pecans

60g dried cranberries

2 tablespoons packed fresh sage leaves, finely chopped

1 tablespoon stemmed fresh thyme leaves

1 litre vegetable or chicken stock

340g raw buckwheat groats

½ teaspoon table salt

Beyond

- You must halve the recipe for a 3-litre cooker.

- Because of varying amounts of moisture in uncooked groats, the pilaf may be a little soupy. If so, use the SAUTÉ function on MEDIUM, NORMAL or CUSTOM 150°C to boil away the excess liquid, stirring almost constantly, 2–3 minutes. Be careful: the groats can quickly fuse to the pot's bottom. Turn off the SAUTÉ function and remove the hot insert from the pot immediately to stop the cooking. Continue to stir a few times to stop the buckwheat sticking.

30g butter

1 medium onion, chopped
(160g prechopped)

2 medium garlic cloves,
peeled and finely chopped
(2 teaspoons prechopped)

½ teaspoon cumin seeds

½ teaspoon ground ginger

200g red or white quinoa,
thoroughly rinsed in
a fine-mesh sieve or a
colander lined with muslin

500ml vegetable stock

450g cauliflower florets,
roughly chopped

One 400g tin chopped
tomatoes

¼ teaspoon table salt

Quinoa and Cauliflower Pilaf

4–6 servings

There has been a debate recently about whether quinoa has a protein similar enough to gluten to knock it out of the diets of those with coeliac disease or gluten sensitivities. Extensive tests published in *The American Journal of Gastroenterology* discovered that those with gluten intolerances can actually improve their overall digestive health by including quinoa in their diet. So make this tasty pilaf side dish for weekend or festive gatherings when you know someone at the table can't enjoy the bread or the stuffing in the turkey. Or just make it for yourself. It's a tasty, earthy side dish that glitzes up the simplest meal.

1.

Press	Setting	Time	Press
SAUTÉ	MEDIUM, NORMAL or CUSTOM 150°C	10 minutes	START

2. Melt the butter in a **5.5- or 7.5-litre cooker**. Add the onion and cook, stirring occasionally, until softened, about 4 minutes. Add the garlic, cumin seeds and ginger; stir until aromatic, just a few seconds. Pour in the quinoa and stir until the grains are evenly distributed through the other ingredients.

3. Pour in the stock, turn off the **SAUTÉ** function and scrape up *every speck of browned stuff* on the pot's bottom. Stir in the cauliflower, tomatoes and salt. Lock the lid onto the cooker.

4.

Set the machine	Level	The valve must be	Time	Press
PRESSURE COOK	MAX	——	4 minutes with the KEEP WARM setting off	START
PRESSURE COOK or MANUAL	HIGH	Closed	5 minutes with the KEEP WARM setting off	START

5. Use the **quick-release method** to bring the pot's pressure back to normal. Unlatch the lid and open the cooker.

6.

Press	Setting	Time	Press
SAUTÉ	MEDIUM, NORMAL or CUSTOM 150°C	5 minutes	START

7. Cook, stirring often, until the liquid has boiled down to a sauce, about 3 minutes. Turn off the **SAUTÉ** function and remove the *hot* insert from the machine to stop the cooking. Set the lid askew over the top of the insert and set aside for 5 minutes so the grains continue to absorb the liquid and the flavours meld.

Beyond

- You must halve the recipe for a 3-litre cooker.

- If you skip steps 6 and 7, the dish will be soupier, better for small bowls than served right alongside the main course on a plate.

- Turn this into a quinoa and tomato soup by increasing the stock to 1.5 litres in a 5.5- or 7.5-litre cooker.

2 tablespoons vegetable,
corn or rapeseed oil;
or 30g butter

1 medium onion, chopped
(160g prechopped)

250g red or white quinoa,
rinsed in a fine-mesh sieve
or a colander lined with
muslin

40g buckwheat groats (do not
use kasha–aka toasted
buckwheat groats)

60ml dry white wine, such
as Chardonnay

900ml vegetable or chicken
stock

One 400g tin chopped
tomatoes

1 teaspoon dried thyme

¼ teaspoon grated nutmeg

¼ teaspoon table salt

50g finely grated Parmigiano-
Reggiano (optional)

Quinoa and Buckwheat Risotto

6 servings

In this tweaked take on risotto, there's no rice. Instead, the buckwheat lends the dish the creamy texture of the Italian classic. It's faux risotto, a bit healthier than the original and a great match for Bollito Misto (page 362) or Perfect Seared Chicken Breasts (page 291).

1.

Press	Setting	Time	Press
SAUTÉ	MEDIUM, NORMAL or CUSTOM 150°C	10 minutes	START

2. Warm the oil for a minute or two (or melt the butter) in a **5.5- or 7.5-litre cooker**. Add the onion and cook, stirring occasionally, until softened, about 3 minutes. Stir in the quinoa and buckwheat groats until coated in the fat.

3. Pour in the wine and scrape up *every speck of browned stuff* on the pot's bottom. Turn off the **SAUTÉ** function. Stir in the stock, tomatoes, thyme, nutmeg and salt. Lock the lid onto the cooker.

4.

Set the machine	Level	The valve must be	Time	Press
PRESSURE COOK	MAX	—	6 minutes with the KEEP WARM setting off	START
PRESSURE COOK or MANUAL	HIGH	Closed	8 minutes with the KEEP WARM setting off	START

5. Use the **quick-release method** to bring the pot's pressure back to normal. Unlatch the lid and open the cooker. Stir in the cheese (if using). Set the lid askew over the pot for 5 minutes to blend the flavours. Stir again before serving.

Beyond

- You must halve the recipe for a 3-litre cooker.
- To bulk up this side dish, add up to 260g chopped carrots, peeled sweet potatoes or chopped seeded peeled winter or butternut squash.
- Or stir in up to 40g baby kale with the cheese in step 5.

Beef, Barley and Mushroom Casserole

6 servings

Here's the first of our grain main courses, a favourite soup turned into a savoury, sloppy-joe-style casserole. Sloppy joe fillings can be sweet, but this preparation is quite savoury and even 'dry', in keeping with its casserole consistency, rather than the filling for a messy sandwich (which you can find on page 131). This main course can be even more savoury if you use grass-fed beef. Because of the way a pressure cooker works, the barley picks up lots of the beefy flavour. And since we opted for beef mince rather than a cubes, the casserole is relatively easy to prepare.

1.

Press	Setting	Time	Press
SAUTÉ	MEDIUM, NORMAL or CUSTOM 150°C	15 minutes	START

2. Melt the butter in a **3-, 5.5- or 7.5-litre cooker**. Add the onion and cook, stirring occasionally, until softened, about 3 minutes. Add the mushrooms and continue cooking, stirring more frequently, until they give off their internal moisture and it evaporates to a glaze, about 5 minutes. Stir in the garlic until aromatic, just a few seconds.

3. Crumble in the beef mince and cook, stirring occasionally to break up any clumps, until the meat loses its raw, pink colour, about 2 minutes. Stir in the barley, tomato, sage, nutmeg, salt and pepper until the barley is evenly distributed throughout the mixture.

4. Pour in the stock, turn off the **SAUTÉ** function and scrape up any browned bits on the pot's bottom. Lock the lid onto the cooker.

5.

Set the machine	Level	The valve must be	Time	Press
PRESSURE COOK	MAX	—	18 minutes with the KEEP WARM setting off	START
PRESSURE COOK or MANUAL	HIGH	Closed	25 minutes with the KEEP WARM setting off	START

6. When the machine has finished cooking, turn it off and let its pressure **return to normal naturally**, about 25 minutes. Unlatch the lid and open the pot. Stir well, then set the lid askew over the pot and set aside for 5 minutes to blend the flavours.

30g butter

1 medium onion, chopped (160g prechopped)

225g thinly sliced chestnut mushrooms

2 medium garlic cloves, peeled and finely chopped (2 teaspoons prechopped)

350g lean beef mince

220g pearl barley

200g tomatoes, chopped

1 tablespoon packed fresh sage leaves, chopped

Up to ½ teaspoon grated nutmeg

½ teaspoon table salt

½ teaspoon ground black pepper

420ml beef or chicken stock

Beyond

- Substitute turkey or pork mince for the beef mince or use a 50/50 combo of different kinds of mince. (However, chicken mince is not successful in this casserole.)

- Make this vegetarian by using 350g unseasoned soya (or other plant-based) protein crumbles instead of beef mince, and 425ml vegetable stock rather than beef or chicken.

15g butter

350g smoked pork sausage,
such as kielbasa, cut into
2.5cm pieces

1 medium onion, chopped
(160g prechopped)

700g boneless skinless
chicken thighs, any large
bits of fat removed, the
meat cut into 2.5cm pieces

200g long-grain white rice,
preferably basmati

155g peas (if frozen, no need
to thaw)

1½ teaspoons mild paprika

½ teaspoon dried sage

½ teaspoon dried thyme

¼ teaspoon table salt

500ml chicken stock

Chicken and Rice Casserole

4–6 servings

This is really a chicken, *sausage* and rice casserole. The addition
of a little porky goodness turns the family favourite into something
special even on a Wednesday night. It's like a cross between arroz
con pollo and the well-known American stand-by.

1.

Press	Setting	Time	Press
SAUTÉ	MEDIUM, NORMAL or CUSTOM 150°C	15 minutes	START

2. Warm the butter in a **5.5-litre cooker** for a minute or two.
Add the sausage and cook, stirring occasionally, until it begins
to brown at the edges, about 4 minutes. Add the onion and
cook, stirring occasionally, until softened, about 3 minutes.
Add the chicken and stir just until it loses its raw, pink colour,
about 2 minutes.

3. Stir in the rice, peas, paprika, sage, thyme and salt until
uniform. Stir in the stock, turn off the **SAUTÉ** function and
scrape *every speck of browned stuff* off the pot's bottom.
Lock the lid onto the cooker.

4.

Set the machine	Level	The valve must be	Time	Press
PRESSURE COOK	MAX	—	10 minutes with the KEEP WARM setting off	START
PRESSURE COOK or MANUAL	HIGH	Closed	12 minutes with the KEEP WARM setting off	START

5. Use the **quick-release function** to bring the pot's pressure
back to normal – but *do not open the cooker*. Set it aside with the
lid latched and the pressure valve open for 10 minutes. Unlatch
the lid, open the pot and stir well before serving.

Beyond

- You must halve the recipe for a 3-litre cooker.

- For a 7.5-litre cooker, you must increase all the ingredients by 50 per cent.

- If you want to omit the sausage and return to a more standard rendition, use 900g of boneless skinless chicken thighs.

- For a bit more heft, add 1 stemmed, cored and chopped medium pepper (of any colour) with the onion.

- Also try adding up to 225g thinly sliced white or chestnut mushrooms with the onions. Cook, stirring occasionally, until the mushrooms give off their liquid and it reduces to a glaze, about 6 minutes.

- For more kick, substitute mild or hot smoked paprika for the regular paprika.

Orange Beef 'Fried Rice' Casserole

4 servings

We can't make fried rice well in a multi-cooker. But we can make main-course rice casseroles that use the flavours of classic Chinese take-away dishes, morphing them into a cross between more traditional fried rice and a casserole. The beef needs longer to cook, so brown rice is a better alternative here (rather than having to cook the dish in two steps, beef for a while, then rice added later).

1.

Press	Setting	Time	Press
SAUTÉ	MEDIUM, NORMAL or CUSTOM 150°C	10 minutes	START

2. Warm the oil in a **3- or 5.5-litre cooker** for a minute or two. Add the spring onions, ginger and zest. Cook, stirring often, just until the spring onions begin to soften, about 1 minute. Add the beef and cook, stirring occasionally, until it loses its raw, red colour, about 2 minutes. Add the rice and stir well until the grains are uniformly distributed throughout.

3. Pour in the stock, turn off the **SAUTÉ** function, and scrape up *every speck of browned stuff* on the pot's bottom. Stir in the soy sauce, orange juice, hoisin sauce and vinegar until uniform. Lock the lid onto the cooker.

4.

Set the machine	Level	The valve must be	Time	Press
PRESSURE COOK	MAX	——	17 minutes with the KEEP WARM setting off	START
PRESSURE COOK or MANUAL	HIGH	Closed	20 minutes with the KEEP WARM setting off	START

5. Use the **quick-release method** to bring the pot's pressure back to normal – but *do not open the cooker.* Set it aside with the lid latched and the pressure valve open for 10 minutes. Unlatch the lid, open the pot and stir well before serving.

- 2 tablespoons vegetable, corn or rapeseed oil
- 6 medium spring onions, trimmed and thinly sliced
- 2 tablespoons finely chopped peeled fresh root ginger
- 2 tablespoons grated orange zest
- 450g beef flank steak, such as bavette, cut in half lengthways, then cut against the grain into strips 5mm in thickness
- 200g long-grain brown rice
- 300ml beef stock
- 60ml soy sauce
- 60ml fresh orange juice
- 2 tablespoons hoisin sauce (see page 184)
- 1 tablespoon apple cider vinegar

Beyond

- For a 7.5-litre cooker, you must increase all the ingredients by 50 per cent.
- For a more vegetable-heavy dish, add up to 80g edamame (do not thaw if frozen) with the rice and/or up to 60g frozen broccoli florets (do not thaw) with the stock.
- Go ahead and substitute an equivalent amount of boneless skinless chicken thighs, cut into strips 5mm in thickness, for the beef.
- Garnish with snipped chives or the green parts of a finely chopped spring onion.

2 tablespoons vegetable,
corn or rapeseed oil

1 medium onion, chopped
(160g prechopped)

15g finely chopped peeled
fresh root ginger

450g lean pork mince

2 medium garlic cloves,
peeled and finely chopped
(2 teaspoons prechopped)

500ml chicken stock

250g long-grain white rice,
preferably basmati

60ml soy sauce

60ml rice vinegar

½ teaspoon five-spice powder
(see page 88)

Pork Mince and Ginger 'Fried Rice' Casserole

4 servings

This recipe has a traditional flavour profile for fried rice except that it uses *a lot* of ginger. Feel free to cut down on the copious amount, although we feel all that ginger gives the dish an irresistible, aromatic flair. Because we used pork mince, definitely a quick-cooker, we chose white rice instead of longer-cooking brown rice.

1.

Press	Setting	Time	Press
SAUTÉ	MEDIUM, NORMAL or CUSTOM 150°C	10 minutes	START

2. Warm the oil in a **3- or 5.5-litre cooker** for a minute or two. Add the onion and ginger. Cook, stirring often, until the onion begins to soften, about 4 minutes. Crumble in the pork mince and cook, stirring occasionally to break up any clumps, until it loses its raw, pink colour, about 4 minutes. Stir in the garlic until aromatic, just a few seconds.

3. Pour in the stock, turn off the **SAUTÉ** function and scrape up *every speck of browned stuff* on the pot's bottom. Add the rice, soy sauce, vinegar and five-spice powder. Stir well until the grains are evenly distributed, then lock the lid onto the pot.

4.

Set the machine	Level	The valve must be	Time	Press
PRESSURE COOK	MAX	—	7 minutes with the KEEP WARM setting off	START
PRESSURE COOK or MANUAL	HIGH	Closed	9 minutes with the KEEP WARM setting off	START

5. Use the **quick-release method** to bring the pot's pressure back to normal – but *do not open the cooker*. Set it aside with the lid latched and the pressure valve open for 10 minutes. Unlatch the lid, open the pot and stir well before serving.

Beyond

- For a 7.5-litre cooker, you must increase all the ingredients by 50 per cent.

- For a fresher flavour, substitute 6 medium spring onions, trimmed and thinly sliced, for the onion.

- For heat, add up to 1 tablespoon red chilli paste, such as sambal oelek or Sriracha, with the stock.

Chicken Biryani Casserole

4–6 servings

Although biryani is usually a layered rice dish, we've turned it into a one-pot casserole. The spice mixture for biryani can be complex, so we simplified it to just garam masala and fresh root ginger, mostly in the interest of getting dinner on the table quickly. (To make your own garam masala, see page 226.) Because of the way the rice continues to absorb moisture in the dish, this one's not very successful as leftovers the next day.

1. Mix the water and saffron in a small bowl or teacup. Set aside.

2. Whisk the yoghurt, garlic, ginger, garam masala, lemon juice, turmeric, cayenne and salt in a large bowl until uniform. Add the chicken and toss well to coat evenly and thoroughly. Set aside.

3.

Press	Setting	Time	Press
SAUTÉ	MEDIUM, NORMAL or CUSTOM 150°C	15 minutes	START

4. Melt 30g butter (or 30ml ghee) in a **5.5- or 7.5-litre cooker**. Add the onions and cook, stirring often, until golden, about 10 minutes. Use a slotted spoon to transfer half the onions to a bowl.

5. Add the remaining butter (or ghee), then the chicken and every bit of its marinade as well as the bay leaves. Cook, stirring almost constantly, for 2 minutes. Pour in the stock, turn off the **SAUTÉ** function and scrape up *every speck of browned stuff* on the pot's bottom. Sprinkle the rice over the top of the dish. Stir gently just so the grains are submerged (they need not be thoroughly and evenly incorporated). Lock the lid onto the cooker.

6.

Set the machine	Level	The valve must be	Time	Press
PRESSURE COOK	MAX	—	7 minutes with the KEEP WARM setting off	START
PRESSURE COOK or MANUAL	HIGH	Closed	9 minutes with the KEEP WARM setting off	START

7. Use the **quick-release method** to bring the pot's pressure back to normal – but *do not open the cooker*. Set it aside with the lid latched and the pressure valve open for 10 minutes.

8. Stir the water and saffron threads into the reserved onions and spread this mixture over the top of the casserole in the cooker without stirring it. Set the lid askew over the pot for 5 minutes to heat the onions and blend the flavours. Serve big spoonfuls, discarding the bay leaves as you find them.

1 tablespoon warm water from the kettle

Up to 1 teaspoon saffron threads

185g plain regular or low-fat yoghurt (do not use fat-free or Greek yoghurt)

3 medium garlic cloves, peeled and finely chopped (1 tablespoon prechopped)

1 tablespoon finely chopped peeled fresh root ginger

1 tablespoon garam masala

1 tablespoon fresh lemon juice

½ teaspoon ground turmeric

Up to ½ teaspoon ground cayenne

½ teaspoon table salt

1.2kg boneless skinless chicken thighs, any large bits of fat removed, the meat quartered

60g butter or 60ml ghee (see page 227)

2 large onions, halved and cut into thin half-moons

2 bay leaves

700ml chicken stock

300g long-grain white basmati rice

Beyond

- You must halve the recipe for a 3-litre cooker.
- Garnish individual servings with lots of finely chopped fresh coriander and mint leaves.
- Go ahead and add up to 155g peas (thawed if frozen) with the rice before the second cooking.

2 tablespoons vegetable, corn or rapeseed oil

2 medium onions, halved and sliced into thin half-moons

2 teaspoons coriander seeds

1 teaspoon cumin seeds

1 teaspoon table salt

½ teaspoon ground turmeric

½ teaspoon ground black pepper

8 green or white cardamom pods, lightly crushed

8 whole cloves

One 10cm cinnamon stick

1 bay leaf

300g long-grain brown rice

900g boned leg of lamb, any large bits of fat removed, the meat cut into 2.5cm pieces

600ml beef or chicken stock

Lamb Biryani Casserole

6 servings

This recipe uses long-grain *brown* rice to make a biryani-style casserole, with sweet flavours to match the earthy whole grain and lots of spices for big pops of flavour. Those spices are whole and will soften under pressure. You might not find many spice bits because of the way the pressure acts on them. But warn anyone who won't appreciate a sudden mouthful to pick out any whole spices found on their plate.

1.

Press	Setting	Time	Press
SAUTÉ	MEDIUM, NORMAL or CUSTOM 150°C	15 minutes	START

2. Warm the oil in a **5.5- or 7.5-litre cooker** for a minute or two. Add the onions and cook, stirring occasionally, until golden yellow, about 8 minutes. Stir in the coriander seeds, cumin seeds, salt, turmeric, pepper, cardamom pods, cloves, cinnamon stick and bay leaf until aromatic, about 20 seconds. Stir in the rice until the grains are evenly distributed throughout the mix.

3. Stir in the lamb until it's evenly coated in the spices and rice. Pour in the stock, turn off the **SAUTÉ** function and scrape up *every speck of browned stuff* on the pot's bottom. Stir well and lock the lid onto the cooker.

4.

Set the machine	Level	The valve must be	Time	Press
PRESSURE COOK	MAX	—	17 minutes with the KEEP WARM setting off	START
PRESSURE COOK or MANUAL	HIGH	Closed	20 minutes with the KEEP WARM setting off	START

5. When the machine has finished cooking, turn it off and let its pressure **return to normal naturally**, about 25 minutes. Unlatch the lid and open the cooker. Find and discard the cinnamon stick and bay leaf. Stir well before serving.

Beyond

- You must halve the recipe for a 3-litre cooker.
- Garnish the servings with chutney of any sort, as well as toasted flaked almonds.
- Or drizzle the servings with crème fraîche and top them with chopped fresh parsley, coriander and/or mint leaves.
- Serve with Perfect Chana Dal (page 229).

Spicy Vegetable Biryani Casserole

4 servings

Flavourful and comforting, this casserole can get very hot if you use the full amount of jalapeño (even though the pressure cooker tames the capsaicin in the chilli). Even with the heat, for us this casserole is the most comforting of any in the book. It goes best with beer, like a pale ale or IPA.

1.

Press	Setting	Time	Press
SAUTÉ	MEDIUM, NORMAL or CUSTOM 150°C	10 minutes	START

2. Warm the oil in a **5.5- or 7.5-litre cooker** for a minute or two. Add the coriander seeds, cumin seeds, cardamom pods, cloves and bay leaves. Stir until very aromatic, about 1 minute. Add the onion and jalapeño. Cook, stirring often, until the onion begins to soften, about 3 minutes. Stir in the garlic, ginger, garam masala and smoked paprika until aromatic, just a few seconds.

3. Stir in the rice, pepper, okra, cauliflower and peas until the rice grains are evenly distributed throughout the mixture. Pour in the stock, turn off the **SAUTÉ** function and scrape up *every speck of browned stuff* on the pot's bottom. Lock the lid onto the cooker.

4.

Set the machine	Level	The valve must be	Time	Press
PRESSURE COOK	MAX	—	7 minutes with the KEEP WARM setting off	START
PRESSURE COOK or MANUAL	HIGH	Closed	9 minutes with the KEEP WARM setting off	START

5. Use the **quick-release method** to bring the pot's pressure back to normal – but *do not open the cooker*. Set it aside with the lid latched and the pressure valve open for 10 minutes. Unlatch the lid and open the cooker. Find and discard the bay leaves. Stir well and serve generous spoonfuls.

2 tablespoons vegetable, corn or rapeseed oil

1 teaspoon coriander seeds

1 teaspoon cumin seeds

4 green or white cardamom pods, lightly crushed

8 whole cloves

2 bay leaves

1 large red onion, chopped (240g prechopped)

Up to 2 medium fresh jalapeño chillies, stemmed, halved lengthways, deseeded (if desired) and thinly sliced

1 medium garlic clove, peeled and finely chopped (1 teaspoon prechopped)

1 teaspoon finely chopped peeled fresh root ginger

1 teaspoon garam masala (see page 226)

1 teaspoon mild smoked paprika

300g long-grain white rice, preferably basmati

1 large red pepper, stemmed, cored and chopped (260g prechopped)

120g frozen sliced okra (do not thaw)

125g chopped fresh cauliflower florets (do not use frozen)

80g frozen peas (do not thaw)

700ml vegetable stock

Beyond

- You must halve the recipe for a 3-litre cooker.
- Garnish the servings with roasted cashews and chopped fresh coriander leaves.
- And/or top them with vegan yoghurt (or plain Greek yoghurt, if you don't mind the dairy).

225g mussels, scrubbed and debearded

6 small clams, scrubbed

6 king prawns (deveined but shell-on)

350ml water

2 tablespoons olive oil

1 medium onion, chopped (160g prechopped)

1 medium green pepper, stemmed, cored and chopped (175g prechopped)

350g mild or hot Italian sausages, cut into 2.5cm pieces

450g boneless skinless chicken thighs, any large hunks of fat removed, the meat cut into 2.5cm pieces

2 teaspoons mild smoked paprika

2 teaspoons dried oregano

½ teaspoon fennel seeds

¼ teaspoon saffron threads

¼ teaspoon table salt

One 400g tin chopped tomatoes

435ml chicken stock

275g medium-grain white rice, such as Arborio, bomba or Valencia

Yes, Paella

6 servings

It's hard to believe that paella can come from an Instant Pot. True, you won't get a crunchy bottom, the way paella turns out in a giant pan over an open fire. Even so, this recipe's a fine imitation, fit for weekend guests.

Steaming the shellfish first makes a great stock. If you've got some muslin, triple-line a colander and drain the shellfish into this contraption in step 3, catching the stock in a bowl below. It should now be free of sand. Then in step 6, use 125ml of this shellfish stock as a replacement for 125ml of the chicken stock (and, therefore, also use 300ml chicken stock) for a way tastier paella. Save any extra shellfish stock in a small, sealed container in the freezer for up to 1 year to add to other seafood soups or stews.

1. Put the mussels, clams and prawns in a **5.5- or 7.5-litre cooker.**
Add the water and lock the lid onto the pot.

2.

Set the machine	Level	The valve must be	Time	Press
PRESSURE COOK	MAX	——	2 minutes with the KEEP WARM setting off	START
PRESSURE COOK or MANUAL	HIGH	Closed	4 minutes with the KEEP WARM setting off	START

3. When the machine has finished cooking, turn it off and let its pressure **return to normal naturally**, about 10 minutes. Unlatch the lid and open the cooker. Drain the contents of the *hot* insert into a colander set in the sink. Wipe out the insert and return it to the machine.

4.

Press	Setting	Time	Press
SAUTÉ	MEDIUM, NORMAL or CUSTOM 150°C	10 minutes	START

5. Warm the oil in the cooker for a minute or two, then add the onion and pepper. Cook, stirring occasionally, until the onion softens, about 4 minutes. Add the sausage and chicken; cook, stirring more often, just until the chicken loses its raw, pink colour, about 2 minutes. Stir in the smoked paprika, oregano, fennel seeds, saffron and salt until aromatic, just a few seconds.

6. Pour in the tomatoes, turn off the **SAUTÉ** function and scrape up *every speck of browned stuff* on the pot's bottom. Stir in the stock and rice until the rice is evenly mixed throughout. Lock the lid onto the pot.

7.

Set the machine	Level	The valve must be	Time	Press
PRESSURE COOK	MAX	——	9 minutes with the KEEP WARM setting off	START
PRESSURE COOK or MANUAL	HIGH	Closed	12 minutes with the KEEP WARM setting off	START

8. Use the **quick-release method** to bring the pot's pressure back to normal. Unlatch the lid and open the cooker. Stir the rice mixture in the cooker, then pile the seafood on top. Cover the cooker without engaging the pressure valve. Set aside for 10 minutes to continue steaming the rice and warm the seafood. Serve in bowls by the big spoonful.

Beyond

- You must halve the recipe for a 3-litre cooker.
- For a 7.5-litre cooker, you can (but don't have to) increase all the ingredients by 50 per cent.
- For an even heartier meal, cube up to 225g skinless thin white-fleshed fish fillets (such as tilapia or flounder) into 2.5cm pieces, then gently stir into the rice in step 8 before piling the shellfish on top and steaming the dish for 10 minutes.
- Add up to 155g peas (thawed if frozen) with the stock and rice.
- For heat, add up to 2 teaspoons crushed chilli flakes with the saffron and other spices.

11
More Sides

Maybe this chapter's title should be Faster Sides. Or Better Sides? As you'll see, we solved the perennial problems of mushy carrots and overcooked green beans by altering standard pressure-cooker methods with a bit of cookery school know-how.

What's more, there's no point in trying to cook some greens like Swiss chard in an Instant Pot, unless it's part of a well-stocked soup. Chard is done in minutes on the hob. Meanwhile, the multi-cooker is still coming up to pressure. We love leafy greens but add them late in the cooking process of most dishes to retain as much of their vibrancy and flavour as possible.

Or maybe the chapter should have been More Sides That Could Become Main Courses. Many of these side dishes can be vegetarian or vegan main courses on their own. And many more can become a main course with a small tweak: add a poached egg on top of the Warm White Bean Salad (page 446); pile the Buttery Mushrooms with Cheese (page 442) into jacket potatoes; or serve the Loaded Bundt Cornbread (page 431) alongside a chopped salad.

These days, side dishes are often afterthoughts. They're assembled, rather than cooked – or just boxed up from a supermarket's buffet. We see a lot of people shopping at the salad bar with a package of raw chicken breasts in their trolley.

That's fair enough, because life moves fast. But that's why you've got an Instant Pot. Consider having a second, smaller cooker just to make sides to go along with the main course; most of these recipes work well in a **3-litre cooker**. Those Creamy Black-Eye Beans (page 438) would be welcome with Fried Chicken (page 262) or Brisket Skewers (page 266). And Baked Beans (page 444) are great all summer long, especially ones made right, the real way, with dried beans and lots of aromatic spices. What could be better?

FAQs

1. What's a potato masher?

Your grandmother knew. It's a hand-held old-school gadget, either a wire zigzag on a metal handle or a flat circle (or oval) with slats across its surface. You work it (the way you might suspect) by pressing down into cooked potatoes so that they 'mash' through or against the metal. You have to work it through the spuds (or other ingredients) many times. The more you do, the creamier the mash.

When it comes to mashed potatoes, we prefer a potato masher to an electric mixer. We've never been a fan of those ultra-creamy, French-bistro potatoes, the kind with just enough potato in the batch to hold the cream and butter in suspension. We prefer hearty mashed potatoes, even a little chunky, with the skins still on the spuds.

2. My raw potatoes are turning green. What do I do?

Cut out those green bits! In fact, cut them out deeply, maybe one-quarter of the potato. The potato has been exposed to light for too long. (It did grow underground, after all.) It's started to produce chlorophyll (which isn't bad for you) and so has also started to produce solanine (which is bad and can cause an upset stomach). Make sure you pick spuds at the shop without green bits. Once these start, they're not going away. We rarely buy potatoes in bags. We pick them out one by one.

By the way, did you know the fridge is no good for potatoes? The cooler temperatures cause the potato's natural starches to begin to convert into sugars, making the tuber sweeter, less earthy and less flavourful. It's best to store potatoes in a cool, dark place, a spot somewhere around 10°C. That's hard to find at home. Maybe a basement cupboard? Failing that, buy them and use them promptly. The shop often has a cool room where it can store spuds properly until they're ready to move to the produce shelf and then to your home.

3. How do I store all these leafy greens?

Many of these side dishes use greens in some way. For cabbage heads, do not wash them when you get them home. Instead, wrap them tightly in clingfilm and store them in the coolest part of the fridge for up to a week. For most other leafy greens, again do not wash them. Wrap slightly damp kitchen paper around the bunch, then seal it in clingfilm and store it in the coolest part of the fridge for up to 4 days.

Kale is the exception. You still don't wash the leaves, but you should chop them into smaller bits if desired and store them in a sealed but perforated plastic bag in the coolest part of the refrigerator for just a day or two.

Jacket Potatoes

4–6 servings

350ml water

**4–6 medium baking potatoes
(225g each)**

All the best toppings for jacket potatoes? Got those? Then go ahead and make this classic side dish as fancy as you want it. We even keep an already-baked potato or two in the fridge at all times so we can cut one into wedges and dip them in ketchup for an afternoon snack.

Make sure the potatoes are equal in size so they cook at the same rate. They are also super-heated when they come out of the pot. Keep them away from kids until they've cooled a bit.

1. Pour the water into a **5.5- or 7.5-litre cooker**. Set a heat- and pressure-safe trivet in the pot. Prick the potatoes in several places with a fork. Set them on the trivet either stacked flat or standing upright. Lock the lid onto the pot.

2.

Set the machine	Level	The valve must be	Time	Press
PRESSURE COOK	MAX	——	10 minutes with the KEEP WARM setting off	START
PRESSURE COOK or MANUAL	HIGH	Closed	12 minutes with the KEEP WARM setting off	START

3. When the machine has finished cooking, turn it off and let the pressure **return to normal naturally** for 10 minutes. Then use the **quick-release method** to get rid of any residual pressure in the pot. Unlatch the lid and open the cooker. Use large kitchen tongs to transfer the potatoes to a serving platter or serving plates. Leave to cool for several minutes before serving.

Beyond

- You must halve the recipe for a 3-litre cooker.

- If you like a crisp skin on a jacket potato, position the rack on the middle shelf of the oven and heat it to 220°C as the pot cooks. When the potatoes are done, transfer them to a baking tin and roast until the skin dries out and becomes crunchy, 10–15 minutes.

1.2kg waxy potatoes, such as
Desiree or Charlotte, cut
into halves or quarters, so
each piece is about the size
of a small apricot

300ml vegetable
or chicken stock

45g butter

½ teaspoon table salt

90ml double cream,
single cream or whole milk

60ml regular or low-fat
soured cream

1 tablespoon Dijon mustard

Ground black pepper
for garnishing

No-Drain Potato Mash

4–6 servings

By cooking cut-up potatoes in stock, we can create a rich version
of mashed potatoes without ever draining the insert. The leached
starch is invaluable for thickening the stock (a bit) and making the
mashed potatoes creamy. If you don't have a potato masher, dump
the contents of the insert into a large bowl and use an electric
mixer at medium-low speed to make the mashed potatoes. (If
possible, use only the paddle attachment.) However, they will be
a little looser than those mashed directly in the pot.

1. Stir the potatoes, stock, butter and salt in a 5.5- or 7.5-litre
cooker. Lock the lid onto the pot.

2.

Set the machine	Level	The valve must be	Time	Press
PRESSURE COOK	MAX	——	7 minutes with the KEEP WARM setting off	START
PRESSURE COOK or MANUAL	HIGH	Closed	10 minutes with the KEEP WARM setting off	START

3. When the machine has finished cooking, turn it off and let its
pressure **return to normal naturally**, about 20 minutes. Unlatch
the lid and open the cooker. Add the cream, soured cream and
mustard. Use a potato masher right in the pot to mash the
potatoes to your liking, chunky or smooth. Grind black pepper
over individual servings, if desired.

Beyond

- You must halve the recipe for a 3-litre cooker.

- We like a coarser texture in mashed potatoes. If you like ultra-smooth mashed potatoes, peel the potatoes before cooking.

- For hot mashed potatoes, turn the SAUTÉ function on LOW or LESS after opening the pot, then add the ingredients in step 3 and mash over this low heat. Turn off the SAUTÉ function when the potatoes are right and remove the insert from the machine.

- Feel free to omit the cream, mustard and soured cream. Add 60g additional butter to the pot after you open it.

Better Syracuse Potatoes

6 servings

Syracuse potatoes are sometimes called 'salt potatoes' because they're cooked in brine under pressure. They're delicious, but we've improved the recipe with the addition of vinegar, which complements the natural sweetness of the spuds and makes them absurdly addictive.

This dish is only cooked on HIGH, even in the Max machine. The higher MAX pressure would split the potatoes.

Also, this recipe will not work if you use larger potatoes and halve them, or if you peel the potatoes or poke them in any way. The skin protects the delicate, creamy white richness underneath.

1. Mix the water, salt and vinegar in a **5.5- or 7.5-litre cooker** until the salt dissolves. Add the potatoes and stir well. Lock the lid onto the cooker.

2.

Set the machine	Level	The valve must be	Time	Press
PRESSURE COOK or MANUAL	HIGH	Closed	2 minutes with the KEEP WARM setting off	START

3. When the machine has finished cooking, turn it off and let its pressure **return to normal naturally** for 15 minutes. Then use the **quick-release method** to get rid of any residual pressure in the pot. Unlatch the lid and open the cooker. Drain the potatoes in a large colander set in the sink. Serve warm.

1.5 litres water

225g sea salt flakes

250ml distilled white vinegar

1.3kg small red-skinned potatoes, each 2.5–4cm in diameter

Beyond

- You must halve the recipe for a 3-litre cooker.

- Pour the cooked potatoes onto a large baking tin and leave to cool to room temperature. The salt will form a crust on each spud. Serve on toothpicks with cold cocktails.

- Or pile the hot potatoes in a bowl and pour a little melted butter over them, add lots of ground black pepper, and toss well.

- Or serve potatoes tossed with a quick Russian dressing. Whisk 250g regular or low-fat mayonnaise, 60ml bottled red chilli sauce and 2 tablespoons dill pickle relish in a medium bowl. Add some or all of this to the potatoes and toss well. (Save any remaining dressing in a covered bowl in the fridge for up to 3 days.)

1.3kg russet or baking potatoes, peeled and cut into 2.5cm pieces

500ml water

60ml apple cider vinegar

3 large eggs

250ml regular or low-fat mayonnaise

3 medium celery stalks, thinly sliced

Up to 1 small red onion, chopped (up to 80g prechopped)

Up to 12g fresh dill fronds, chopped

2 tablespoons white balsamic vinegar

1 tablespoon Dijon mustard

1 tablespoon Worcestershire sauce

Up to 1½ teaspoons table salt

½ teaspoon ground black pepper

Up to ½ teaspoon garlic powder

Potato Salad

8 servings

Here's a great idea. Cook potatoes and eggs together in the Instant Pot, then add them to a creamy, spicy dressing for an (almost) instant salad. Waxy red-skinned potatoes proved too dry here while yellow potatoes broke down too much. Russets or other baking potatoes, although not traditional in recipes for the hob, have the right amount of starch to hold together yet become creamy and delicate in the salad.

1. Put the potatoes into a **5.5- or 7.5-litre cooker.** Pour in the water and apple cider vinegar. Set the eggs in their shells on top of the potatoes. Lock the lid onto the cooker.

2.

Set the machine	Level	The valve must be	Time	Press
PRESSURE COOK or MANUAL	LOW	Closed	10 minutes with the KEEP WARM setting off	START

3. As the potatoes and eggs cook, whisk the mayonnaise, celery, onion, dill, vinegar, mustard, Worcestershire sauce, salt, pepper and garlic powder in a large bowl. Set aside.

4. When the machine has finished cooking, use the **quick-release method** to bring the pot's pressure back to normal. Unlatch the lid and open the cooker. Transfer the eggs to a chopping board. Drain the potatoes in a colander set in the sink. Add them hot to the dressing and toss well. Peel the still-warm hard-boiled eggs, chop them, add them to the potato mixture and stir gently. Serve warm or cover and refrigerate for up to 1 day.

Beyond

- You must halve the recipe for a 3-litre cooker. (Use 1 or 2 eggs.)

- Feel free to omit the Dijon and add 1 tablespoon ready-made horseradish sauce to the dressing.

- Add crunch with 120g sliced radishes, 100g diced cucumber or 125g thinly sliced carrots.

- The dressing is not sweet, but you can add up to 1 tablespoon white granulated sugar, if desired.

Perfect Sweet Potatoes

Makes 1–6 sweet potatoes

Pressure cooking sweet potatoes makes them smoother, silkier and creamier than roasting them in an oven. Oddly enough, they're also less sweet and more savoury, since the sugars are not condensed and concentrated as in the oven. This makes them a better side to beef and chicken stews that already have a sweet edge. Make sure the sweet potatoes are the same size for even cooking.

1. Pour the water into a **5.5- or 7.5-litre cooker.** Set a heat- and pressure-safe trivet inside the pot. Pile the potatoes onto the trivet. Lock the lid onto the pot.

2.

Set the machine	Level	The valve must be	Time	Press
PRESSURE COOK	MAX	—	15 minutes with the KEEP WARM setting off	START
PRESSURE COOK or MANUAL	HIGH	Closed	20 minutes with the KEEP WARM setting off	START

3. When the machine has finished cooking, turn it off and let its pressure **return to normal naturally**, about 20 minutes. Unlatch the lid and open the cooker. Use large kitchen tongs to transfer the sweet potatoes to a serving platter or serving plates. Leave to cool for a few minutes before serving.

350ml water

1–6 small sweet potatoes (175g each and 13–15cm long)

Beyond

- Because of the sweet potatoes' size and shape, this recipe will not work well in a 3-litre cooker.

- For sweet potato mash, leave the sweet potatoes to cool for 5 minutes. Peel them and put them in a large bowl. Then add up to 85g butter, cut into small pieces, as well as 1 teaspoon table salt. Use a potato masher to mash them right in the bowl until creamy.

- Go beyond butter, salt and pepper. Split cooked sweet potatoes open and top them with vanilla yoghurt, cranberry sauce or a chilli sauce.

- Seal a few cooled, cooked sweet potatoes in cling film and store them in the fridge for up to 4 days to add them by quarters to smoothies.

350ml water

1 teaspoon table salt

1 medium cauliflower,
450–700g, any green
leaves removed

Steamed Cauliflower

4–6 servings

This recipe yields a rather unadorned, steamed *head* of cauliflower.
What you do with it is up to you, but see the *Beyond* for several
ideas.

Did you know that green leaves on a head of cauliflower are
edible and provide a big punch of flavour to stocks of almost any
sort? Save them in a zip-sealed plastic bag in the freezer for up to
6 months until you're ready to make stock (see the recipes starting
on page 101).

1. Stir the water and salt in a 3-, 5.5- or 7.5-litre cooker until the
salt dissolves. Set a heat- and pressure-safe trivet in the pot.
Set the cauliflower stem side up on the trivet. Lock the lid onto
the pot.

2.

Set the machine	Level	The valve must be	Time	Press
PRESSURE COOK	MAX	—	4 minutes with the KEEP WARM setting off	START
PRESSURE COOK or MANUAL	HIGH	Closed	6 minutes with the KEEP WARM setting off	START

3. Use the **quick-release method** to bring the pot's pressure back
to normal. Unlatch the lid and open the pot. Use two large forks
(even large flatware forks) to stab the cauliflower on either side,
then lift it out of the cooker and onto a serving platter. Serve warm.

Beyond

- Leave the cauliflower to cool
for 5 minutes, then use two
forks to break it into florets.
Toss these with melted butter,
or with yoghurt and curry
powder. Or with the same
dressing used to make potato
salad (page 426).

- Leave the cauliflower to cool
for 20–30 minutes, then slice
it into 'steaks' 1cm in thickness.
Oil these and rub them with
your favourite spice blend.
Grill over high heat until
lightly browned, 1–2 minutes
a side.

- Or set the warm cauliflower
in a serving bowl and pour
a cheese sauce on top. Melt
30g butter in a medium
saucepan over a medium
heat. (Or in the cleaned and
dried insert with the SAUTÉ
function on MEDIUM,
NORMAL or CUSTOM 150°C.)
Whisk in 2 tablespoons plain
flour until smooth, then whisk
in 250ml whole or low-fat
milk in small amounts until
smooth. Once all the milk has
been added, cook until
slightly thickened, whisking
constantly, about 1 minute.
Whisk in 115g grated Cheddar
or Swiss cheese until smooth.
Remove from the heat, leave
to cool for a minute or two
and then pour over the
cauliflower.

Corn on the Cob

2–8 servings

350ml water

2–8 medium ears of corn, shucked

Steaming corn in the Instant Pot ensures that the kernels are tender and plump. Better yet, you don't have to be ready to serve the corn the moment it's done if you use the KEEP WARM setting.

The best way to shuck corn is to grab the individual green leaves and any silks around them, then pull these down and back towards the stem. Work your way around the ear, leaf section by leaf section. At the end, lightly moisten some kitchen paper and rub it along the ear to remove any errant silks.

1. Pour the water into a **5.5- or 7.5-litre cooker.** Set a heat- and pressure-safe trivet in the pot. Pile and stack the ears of corn on the trivet. Lock the lid onto the pot.

2.

Set the machine	Level	The valve must be	Time	Press
PRESSURE COOK	MAX	—	0 minutes with the KEEP WARM setting on for up to 30 minutes	START
PRESSURE COOK or MANUAL	HIGH	Closed	1 minute with the KEEP WARM setting on for up to 30 minutes	START

3. Use the **quick-release method** to bring the pot's pressure back to normal. If desired, set aside with the pressure valve open and the **KEEP WARM** setting on for up to 30 minutes. Unlatch the lid and open the cooker. Use kitchen tongs to transfer the corn ears to a serving platter or serving plates.

Beyond

- For a 3-litre cooker, you must break each ear in half to make them fit. At most, 3 halved ears will fit well in the pot. Use 250ml water.

- Serve steamed corn with a compound butter. Soften 110g butter at room temperature, about 30 minutes. Add up to 2 tablespoons finely chopped fresh herbs or 2 teaspoons dried herbs or 1 teaspoon garlic or onion powder. Add up to ½ teaspoon table salt. Mash the ingredients together to serve with the warm corn.

- Or forgo tradition and serve the corn with finely grated Parmigiano-Reggiano, finely grated lemon zest and ground black pepper.

900g frozen corn kernels, thawed

160ml whole milk

115g regular cream cheese

30g butter, melted and cooled to room temperature, plus more for greasing the baking dish

2 teaspoons white granulated sugar

½ teaspoon dried thyme

Up to 1 teaspoon crushed chilli flakes (optional)

½ teaspoon table salt

½ teaspoon ground black pepper

350ml water

Cream-Style Corn

6–8 servings

We loved cream-style corn when we were kids. Of course, growing up in the convenience-crazed seventies, we only knew about the tinned stuff. We've always wanted to make a 'cornier' version, less pasty and porridge-like. We've tried dozens of recipes in the pot. Most break (ick), a few curdle (ick, again), many are too oily (still ick) and the rest are just plain forgettable. So here's our take. It's a creamy, somewhat soupy side dish that should be served up in small bowls near the main plate.

1. Pour about one-quarter of the corn kernels into a blender. Add the milk, cream cheese, butter, sugar, thyme, crushed chilli flakes (if using), salt and pepper. Cover and blend until fairly smooth.

2. Generously butter the inside of a 2-litre, high-sided, round baking dish. Make an aluminium foil sling (see page 20) and set this dish in the centre of the sling. Pour the remaining three-quarters (or so) of the corn kernels into this dish. Add the purée from the blender and stir gently but well. Cover the baking dish with aluminium foil.

3. Pour the water into a **5.5- or 7.5-litre cooker**. Set a heat- and pressure-safe trivet in the cooker. Use the sling to pick up and transfer the baking dish to the trivet. Fold down the ends of the sling so they fit in the pot. Lock the lid onto the cooker.

4.

Set the machine	Level	The valve must be	Time	Press
PRESSURE COOK	MAX	——	15 minutes with the KEEP WARM setting off	START
PRESSURE COOK or MANUAL	HIGH	Closed	20 minutes with the KEEP WARM setting off	START

5. Use the **quick-release method** to bring the pot's pressure back to normal. Unlatch the lid and open the cooker. Use the sling to transfer the *hot* baking dish to a wire cooling rack. Uncover and leave to cool for a couple of minutes. Serve hot.

Beyond

- For a 3-litre cooker, you must use 250ml water, halve the remaining ingredients, and use a 1-litre, high-sided, round soufflé fish.

Loaded Bundt Cornbread

8 servings

This easy cornbread is a great addition to a barbecue. Packed with cheese, corn, even chillies, it's almost a meal. Our recipe is not very sweet but you can even halve the sugar, if desired. We find that less sugar means more of the other great flavours.

1. Whisk the cornmeal, flour, baking powder, sugar and salt in a medium bowl until uniform. Set aside.

2. Pour the water into a **5.5- or 7.5-litre cooker**. Set a heat- and pressure-safe trivet in the pot. Generously butter the inside of a 18cm Bundt tin. Make an aluminium foil sling (see page 20) and set the tin in the middle of the sling.

3. Whisk the eggs and buttermilk in a large bowl until smooth and creamy. Stir in the corn, mozzarella, butter and chillies. Pour in the cornmeal mixture and stir until the flour and cornmeal are moistened and uniform throughout the batter. Pour and scrape into the prepared tin.

4. Use the sling to pick up and transfer the tin to the trivet in the cooker. Lay a large piece of kitchen paper on top of the Bundt tin. Fold down the ends of the sling so they fit in the cooker without touching the kitchen paper. Lock the lid onto the cooker.

5.

Set the machine	Level	The valve must be	Time	Press
PRESSURE COOK	MAX	—	20 minutes with the KEEP WARM setting off	START
PRESSURE COOK or MANUAL	HIGH	Closed	25 minutes with the KEEP WARM setting off	START

6. When the machine has finished cooking, turn it off and let its pressure **return to normal naturally**, about 20 minutes. Unlatch the lid and open the cooker. Use the sling to transfer the Bundt tin to a wire cooling rack. Remove the kitchen paper and leave to cool for 5–10 minutes. To unmould, set a chopping board over the tin and turn both the (still warm) tin and chopping board upside-down. Jiggle the tin to loosen the cake, then remove the tin. If desired, reinvert the cake so it sits right-side up. Continue cooling for at least 10 minutes before slicing into wedges.

150g yellow cornmeal

90g plain flour

2 teaspoons baking powder

2 teaspoons white granulated sugar

½ teaspoon table salt

350ml water

2 large eggs, at room temperature

180ml regular buttermilk

150g frozen corn kernels, thawed

55g semi-firm mozzarella, grated

60g butter, melted and cooled to room temperature, plus more for greasing the tin

60g tinned hot or mild chopped green chillies

Beyond

- For a 3-litre cooker, use the ingredients as stated but do not set kitchen paper on top of the Bundt tin in the cooker. If you want a perfect edge, fill the tin only to within 1cm of the rim. (Discard the remaining batter.)

- For more pizzazz, cook up to 160g chopped onions and up to 175g chopped green pepper in some butter in a frying pan set over a medium heat (or in the pot on the SAUTÉ function at MEDIUM, NORMAL or CUSTOM 150°C) until quite soft, stirring often, about 5 minutes. Leave to cool to room temperature, then add to the batter with the cheese and chillies.

350ml water

900g butternut squash, peeled, halved, deseeded and cut into 10cm pieces

55g butter

2 tablespoons single or double cream

1 tablespoon packed fresh sage leaves, finely chopped

½ teaspoon table salt

½ teaspoon ground black pepper

Butternut Squash Mash

6 servings

The next time you have a savoury braise for dinner, ladle the meat, vegetables and sauce right on top of this creamy purée in bowls. You'll need a vegetable steamer insert for this recipe, not the more standard trivet we often use. Without a steamer, the butternut squash pieces will fall through the trivet and end up waterlogged. You can use purchased, cut-up butternut squash, but for proper cooking, the pieces must be 10cm long and 2.5–5cm thick.

1. Pour the water into a 3-, 5.5- or 7.5-litre cooker. Set a heat- and pressure-safe vegetable steamer inside the pot. Pile the butternut squash pieces into the steamer. Lock the lid onto the cooker.

2.

Set the machine	Level	The valve must be	Time	Press
PRESSURE COOK	MAX	——	5 minutes with the KEEP WARM setting off	START
PRESSURE COOK or MANUAL	HIGH	Closed	8 minutes with the KEEP WARM setting off	START

3. Use the **quick-release method** to bring the pot's pressure back to normal. Unlatch the lid and open the steamer. Pick up the *hot* vegetable steamer and take it out of the pot. Drain the liquid in the pot. Return all the butternut squash pieces to the pot.

4.

Press	Setting	Time	Press
SAUTÉ	LOW or LESS	5 minutes	START

5. Use a potato masher to begin mashing the squash. Add the butter, cream, sage, salt and pepper. Continue to mash the ingredients together until as smooth as you like, about 1 minute. Turn off the **SAUTÉ** function and remove the *hot* insert from the pot to stop the cooking. Serve warm.

Beyond

- For more warming flavours, omit the sage and add up to 1 teaspoon ground cinnamon, ½ teaspoon ground allspice and/or ½ teaspoon grated nutmeg to the mash instead.

Maple Glazed Carrots

6–8 servings

This easy side dish is great for festive winter meals or at a barbecue in the summer. Maple syrup gives the carrots a more complex flavour than brown sugar would. Do not use pancake syrup. Go for the real thing.

900g medium carrots, peeled and cut into 2.5cm pieces

500ml water

45g butter

2 tablespoons maple syrup

½ teaspoon table salt

1. Put the carrots and water in a **3-, 5.5- or 7.5-litre cooker**. Lock the lid onto the pot.

2.

Set the machine	Level	The valve must be	Time	Press
PRESSURE COOK	MAX	——	2 minutes with the KEEP WARM setting off	START
PRESSURE COOK or MANUAL	HIGH	Closed	3 minutes with the KEEP WARM setting off	START

3. Use the **quick-release method** to bring the pot's pressure back to normal. Unlatch the lid and open the cooker. Drain the carrots in the *hot* insert into a colander set in the sink.

4.

Press	Setting	Time	Press
SAUTÉ	MEDIUM, NORMAL or CUSTOM 150°C	5 minutes	START

5. Melt the butter in the cooker. Stir in the syrup and salt until bubbling. Add the carrots and continue cooking, stirring constantly, until the carrots are glazed, 2–3 minutes. Turn off the **SAUTÉ** function and remove the *hot* insert from the cooker to stop the cooking. Pour the carrots and any remaining glaze into a serving bowl and leave to cool for a couple of minutes before serving.

Beyond

- Try adding spices to the butter glaze: ½ teaspoon ground allspice, ½ teaspoon ground cardamom, ½ teaspoon ground cinnamon, ¼ teaspoon ground cloves or ¼ teaspoon grated nutmeg.
- Add heat to the butter glaze with several dashes of hot red pepper sauce.

250ml pomegranate juice

125ml plus 1 tablespoon water

55g light brown sugar

1 tinned chipotle chilli in adobo sauce, stemmed, deseeded (if desired) and finely chopped

1 tablespoon adobo sauce from the tin of chipotle chillies

¼ teaspoon table salt

900g cored and shredded red cabbage

3 large thyme sprigs

2 teaspoons cornflour

Spicy and Tangy Red Cabbage

6–8 servings

Cooked red cabbage should be a standard along with sausages or wieners from a grill pan, a griddle or the grill. Our version makes the usual a little more elegant with the zing of tinned chipotles in adobo sauce *and* the pop of pomegranate juice – a bright, almost citrusy flavour with the cabbage. If you use bagged shredded cabbage, make sure the pieces are not tiny threads but slightly larger bits for a better texture.

1. Stir the juice, 125ml water, brown sugar, chipotle chilli, adobo sauce and salt in a **5.5- or 7.5-litre cooker** until the sugar dissolves. Add the cabbage and thyme sprigs. Toss well until evenly and thoroughly coated. Lock the lid onto the pot.

2.

Set the machine	Level	The valve must be	Time	Press
PRESSURE COOK	MAX	——	10 minutes with the KEEP WARM setting off	START
PRESSURE COOK or MANUAL	HIGH	Closed	12 minutes with the KEEP WARM setting off	START

3. Use the **quick-release method** to bring the pot's pressure back to normal. Unlatch the lid and open the cooker.

4.

Press	Setting	Time	Press
SAUTÉ	MEDIUM, NORMAL or CUSTOM 150°C	5 minutes	START

5. Whisk the remaining 1 tablespoon water and the cornflour in a small bowl until smooth. Stir this slurry into the bubbling cabbage mixture. Continue cooking, stirring almost constantly, until the liquid in the pot thickens to a sauce, 1–2 minutes. Turn off the **SAUTÉ** function and remove the *hot* insert from the cooker to stop the cooking. Pour the cabbage and any sauce into a large serving bowl and leave to cool for a couple of minutes before serving.

Beyond

- You must halve the recipe for a 3-litre cooker.

- For a more vinegary sauce, stir up to 2 tablespoons red wine vinegar into the pomegranate juice mixture before adding the cabbage.

- Or use up to 3 tablespoons pickle brine from a jar of dill or kosher pickles.

- Or for a much hotter dish, add up to 3 tablespoons of the brine from a jar of pickled jalapeño rings.

Spiced Green Cabbage with Yoghurt

6–8 servings

This East-Indian-inspired side is loaded with all sorts of seeds that will soften and almost melt into the sauce. The flavourful mélange is great with curries and on top of jacket potatoes for an easy vegetarian meal.

1.

Press	Setting	Time	Press
SAUTÉ	MEDIUM, NORMAL or CUSTOM 150°C	10 minutes	START

2. Melt the butter in a **5.5-litre cooker**. Add the mustard seeds, coriander seeds, cumin seeds, turmeric and crushed chilli flakes. Cook, stirring constantly, until aromatic, less than 1 minute. Add the onion and cook, stirring occasionally, until softened, about 4 minutes.

3. Turn off the **SAUTÉ** function. Add the cabbage and stir well until evenly and thoroughly coated in the fat and spices. Pour in the stock and stir well. Lock the lid onto the cooker.

4.

Set the machine	Level	The valve must be	Time	Press
PRESSURE COOK	MAX	——	8 minutes with the KEEP WARM setting off	START
PRESSURE COOK or MANUAL	HIGH	Closed	10 minutes with the KEEP WARM setting off	START

5. Use the **quick-release method** to bring the pot's pressure back to normal. Unlatch the lid and open the cooker. Add the yoghurt and stir well until uniform. Pour into a large serving bowl and serve hot.

30g butter

2 teaspoons brown mustard seeds

1½ teaspoons coriander seeds

1½ teaspoons cumin seeds

½ teaspoon ground turmeric

Up to ½ teaspoon crushed chilli flakes

1 large onion, halved and sliced into thin half-moons

One 900g green cabbage, cored and shredded

250ml chicken or vegetable stock

185g plain full-fat, low-fat, or fat-free Greek yoghurt

Beyond

- For a 3-litre cooker, you must use 125ml stock and halve the remaining ingredients.

- For a 7.5-litre cooker, you must increase all the ingredients by 50 per cent.

- Top the serving dish or individual servings with toasted, unsweetened coconut.

350ml water

900g frozen cut leaf spinach,
thawed and squeezed dry
by the handful

250ml whole milk

180ml double cream

55g semi-firm mozzarella,
grated

30g butter, melted and cooled
to room temperature,
plus extra for greasing
the baking dish

30g regular cream cheese,
cut into tiny bits

½ teaspoon onion powder

¼ teaspoon garlic powder

Up to ¼ teaspoon grated
nutmeg

¼ teaspoon table salt

¼ teaspoon ground
black pepper

Creamed Spinach

6–8 servings

This steakhouse side dish is faster and easier than ever, so long as you use only frozen cut-leaf spinach (not chopped spinach). Cut-leaf spinach won't turn into a squishy mess in the pot. Our version is not soupy or pasty. Rather, it's spinach in a creamy sauce. It's also made in a 2-litre baking dish and should be served by the big spoonful. It needs a sirloin or a rib-eye steak. Fire up the barbecue.

1. Pour the water into a **5.5- or 7.5-litre cooker**. Set a heat- and pressure-safe trivet in the pot. Generously butter the inside of a 2-litre, high-sided, round baking dish. Make an aluminium foil sling (see page 20) and set the baking dish at the centre of the sling.

2. Mix the spinach, milk, cream, mozzarella, melted butter, cream cheese, onion powder, garlic powder, nutmeg, salt and pepper in a large bowl until uniform. Pile this mixture into the prepared baking dish and cover tightly with aluminium foil. Use the sling to pick up and transfer the baking dish to the trivet. Lock the lid onto the pot.

3.

Set the machine	Level	The valve must be	Time	Press
PRESSURE COOK	MAX	——	15 minutes with the KEEP WARM setting on for up to 30 minutes	START
PRESSURE COOK or MANUAL	HIGH	Closed	20 minutes with the KEEP WARM setting on for up to 30 minutes	START

4. Use the **quick-release method** to bring the pot's pressure back to normal. Unlatch the lid and open the cooker. Use the sling to transfer the *hot* baking dish to a wire cooling rack. Uncover and leave to cool for 5 minutes before serving.

Beyond

- For a 3-litre cooker, you must use 250ml water, halve the remaining ingredients, and use a 1-litre, high-sided, round soufflé dish.

- To add heat, increase the ground black pepper to up to 1 or even 2 teaspoons.

- For more flavour, add up to 4 medium spring onions, thinly sliced, with the other ingredients.

Spicy Spring Greens

6 servings

Long before kale became the 'it' green, Southerners knew about collard greens (called spring greens in the UK). They're a bit chewier, never spongy, with a pleasant, herbal flavour that's a little grassy and just a tad bitter – a good contrast to roasted meat. This version makes a spectacular addition to wraps with thinly sliced ham or turkey and cheese. If you use the spring greens this way, pull them out of any sauce with kitchen tongs so the wrap isn't too soupy.

1.

Press	Setting	Time	Press
SAUTÉ	MEDIUM, NORMAL or CUSTOM 150°C	10 minutes	START

2. Warm the oil in a **5.5-litre cooker** for a minute or two. Add the garlic and crushed chilli flakes; cook, stirring often, until fragrant, about 20 seconds. Add the tomato and cook, stirring occasionally, until it breaks down a bit, about 3 minutes. Stir in the stock and scrape up any browned bits on the pot's bottom.

3. Turn off the **SAUTÉ** function. Stir in the wine and salt. Add the spring greens and toss well until evenly and thoroughly coated in the sauce and spices. Lock the lid onto the pot.

4.

Set the machine	Level	The valve must be	Time	Press
PRESSURE COOK	MAX	——	4 minutes with the KEEP WARM setting off	START
PRESSURE COOK or MANUAL	HIGH	Closed	5 minutes with the KEEP WARM setting off	START

5. Use the **quick-release method** to bring the pot's pressure back to normal. Unlatch the lid and open the cooker. Stir well before serving.

2 tablespoons olive oil

3 medium garlic cloves, peeled and finely chopped (1 tablespoon prechopped)

Up to 1 teaspoon crushed chilli flakes

250g chopped tomatoes

125ml vegetable stock

125ml dry white wine, such as Chardonnay

½ teaspoon table salt

700g spring greens, stemmed and chopped

Beyond

- For a 3-litre cooker, you must use 170ml stock and halve the remaining ingredients.

- For a 7.5-litre cooker, you must increase the stock to 250ml and use the remaining ingredients as stated.

- To omit the wine, add the same amount of additional stock plus 1 tablespoon unsweetened apple juice.

- For a hotter, more sophisticated dish, omit the crushed chilli flakes and add up to 2 tablespoons purchased harissa with the garlic.

- For a curried take, leave out the crushed chilli flakes and add up to 1 tablespoon wet red curry paste along with the garlic.

60g butter

1 medium onion, chopped (160g prechopped)

1 medium red pepper, stemmed, cored and chopped (175 prechopped)

2 medium garlic cloves, peeled and finely chopped (2 teaspoons prechopped)

1 teaspoon dried thyme

1 teaspoon dried sage

1 teaspoon mild paprika

½ teaspoon table salt

¼ teaspoon celery seeds

¼ teaspoon grated nutmeg

700ml vegetable or chicken stock

240g dried black-eye beans

125ml double cream

Creamy Black-Eye Beans

6 servings

Black-eye beans have long been a harbinger for good luck on New Year's Day in some parts of the USA. But don't make this recipe a seasonal one. Consider it a fine 'starch side' all year long. It is more than just black-eye beans and vegetables but a creamy, rich side dish, best with roasted or grilled proteins. There is an extra step here that uses a purée of some of the beans and cream to make a thickener for the sauce.

1.

Press	Setting	Time	Press
SAUTÉ	MEDIUM, NORMAL or CUSTOM 150°C	5 minutes	START

2. Melt the butter in a **5.5- or 7.5-litre cooker**. Add the onion and pepper; cook, stirring occasionally, until the onion softens, about 3 minutes. Stir in the garlic, thyme, sage, paprika, salt, celery seeds and nutmeg until fragrant, just a few seconds.

3. Pour in the stock and scrape up any browned bits on the pot's bottom. Turn off the **SAUTÉ** function and stir in the black-eye beans. Lock the lid onto the cooker.

4.

Set the machine	Level	The valve must be	Time	Press
PRESSURE COOK	MAX	—	19 minutes with the KEEP WARM setting off	START
PRESSURE COOK or MANUAL	HIGH	Closed	23 minutes with the KEEP WARM setting off	START

5. Use the **quick-release method** to bring the pot's pressure back to normal. Unlatch the lid and open the cooker. Stir well, then transfer 500ml of the bean and liquid mixture in the pot to a blender. Add the cream, cover, remove the centre knob in the blender's lid, place a clean tea towel over the opening and blend until a smooth purée. Pour this mixture into the remaining black-eye beans. Stir well before serving.

Beyond

- You must halve the recipe for a 3-litre cooker.

- Rather than thickening the dish in step 5, omit the cream (and puréeing the beans). Instead, stir up to 65g baby kale into the pot, then set the lid askew over it and set it aside for 5 minutes to blend the flavours and wilt the greens.

- Or add the cream but skip the thickening step. Instead, stir up to 45g instant couscous into the pot after cooking. Again, set the lid over the pot and set it aside for 5 minutes to soften the couscous (which will absorb much of the cooking liquid).

Spaghetti Squash with Herbs and Butter

6 servings

It's fast and easy to steam a spaghetti squash in an Instant Pot. The flesh, once cooked, separates into tiny threads, like little bits of spaghetti (or more like bright yellow short spiralised butternut squash noodles). We've fancied-up this simple preparation a little with fresh herbs and lots of butter. The easiest way to remove the seeds from the squash halves before steaming is with a serrated grapefruit spoon.

1. Pour the water into a **5.5- or 7.5-litre cooker**. Put the spaghetti squash halves skin-side down in the pot – not both flat, of course, but maybe one flat and one angled up against it. Lock the lid onto the cooker.

2.

Set the machine	Level	The valve must be	Time	Press
PRESSURE COOK	MAX	—	8 minutes with the KEEP WARM setting off	START
PRESSURE COOK or MANUAL	HIGH	Closed	10 minutes with the KEEP WARM setting off	START

3. Use the **quick-release method** to bring the pot's pressure back to normal. Unlatch the lid and open the cooker. Use large kitchen tongs and a metal spatula to transfer the *hot* squash halves to a nearby chopping board. Leave to cool for 10 minutes. Discard the water in the insert. Use a fork to scrape the flesh into threads and into a large bowl.

4.

Press	Setting	Time	Press
SAUTÉ	MEDIUM, NORMAL or CUSTOM 150°C	5 minutes	START

5. Melt the butter in the cooker. Add the oregano, thyme, salt and pepper. Stir well, then add the squash threads. Cook, stirring almost constantly, until the squash has absorbed the butter and the herbs are evenly distributed, 1–2 minutes. Turn off the **SAUTÉ** function, pour the contents of the *hot* insert into a serving bowl and leave to cool for a minute or two before serving.

50ml water

One 1.3–1.6kg spaghetti squash, halved lengthways, the seeds scraped out

60g butter

1 tablespoon packed fresh oregano leaves, finely chopped

1 tablespoon stemmed fresh thyme leaves

½ teaspoon table salt

½ teaspoon ground black pepper

Beyond

- For a 3-litre cooker, look for a small, 550–700g spaghetti squash. Use 250ml water and halve the remaining ingredients.

- Use the cooked squash 'threads' as a substitute for pasta. Don't put them back in the pot with the butter and herbs. Rather, use them as a bed for Buttery Marinara Sauce (page 133) or Cherry Tomato and Herb Pasta Sauce (page 136).

- Use any fresh herbs you like, such as basil, marjoram, parsley, rosemary or savory, among others, in any proportions, whether all 2 tablespoons of one or a mix between two (or even three).

- For a more sophisticated flavour, substitute 3 tablespoons walnut or pecan oil for the butter.

2 tablespoons olive oil

700g cherry tomatoes, halved

2 medium garlic cloves,
peeled and finely chopped
(2 teaspoons prechopped)

½ teaspoon table salt

700g fresh green beans,
trimmed

15g fresh basil leaves, finely
chopped

2 tablespoons pine nuts

Warm Green Beans and Smashed Tomatoes

6 servings

Here's a side dish that's great alongside sandwiches in the winter when large round tomatoes aren't at their best. Believe it or not, there's enough liquid in the cherry tomatoes as they break down to create the necessary steam without any added stock but *only if you use cherry tomatoes.* Almost all other small tomatoes are not juicy enough for this technique. Because the green beans cook quickly (and are easily overcooked), only use LOW pressure for this dish.

1.

Press	Setting	Time	Press
SAUTÉ	MEDIUM, NORMAL or CUSTOM 150°C	5 minutes	START

2. Warm the oil in a **5.5-litre cooker** for a minute or two. Add the tomatoes, garlic and salt. Cook, stirring often, until the tomatoes begin to break down and give off their liquid, 2–3 minutes. Stir in the green beans and turn off the **SAUTÉ** function. Lock the lid onto the pot.

3.

Set the machine	Level	The valve must be	Time	Press
PRESSURE COOK or MANUAL	LOW	Closed	1 minute with the KEEP WARM setting off	START

4. Use the **quick-release method** to bring the pot's pressure back to normal. Unlatch the lid and open the cooker. Stir in the basil and pine nuts, then set aside with the lid askew over the pot to blend the flavours for 5 minutes.

Beyond

- For a 3-litre cooker, you must use 450g cherry tomatoes, halved, and halve the remaining ingredients.

- For a 7.5-litre cooker, you must use 900g cherry tomatoes, halved, and the remaining ingredients as stated.

- Try another finely chopped nut instead of the pine nuts, such as pecans, walnuts or even skinned hazelnuts.

Aubergine, Courgettes and Tomatoes

6 servings

This side dish is like a mock ratatouille, made faster with tinned tomatoes (and the pot's pressure, of course). There's enough liquid in the tomatoes and vegetables to make the requisite steam for a **5.5-litre cooker**. See the *Beyond* instructions to add more liquid for a **7.5-litre cooker**.

1. Stir all the ingredients in a **5.5-litre cooker**. Lock the lid onto the pot.

2.

Set the machine	Level	The valve must be	Time	Press
PRESSURE COOK	MAX	—	5 minutes with the KEEP WARM setting off	START
PRESSURE COOK or MANUAL	HIGH	Closed	7 minutes with the KEEP WARM setting off	START

3. Use the **quick-release method** to bring the pot's pressure back to normal. Unlatch the lid, open the cooker and stir well. Fish out and discard the bay leaf. Set the lid askew over the pot and set aside for 5 minutes to blend the flavours before serving in small bowls.

Two 400g tins chopped tomatoes with or without chillies

2 medium courgettes (about 450g), diced

1 medium aubergine (about 450g), stemmed and diced (no need to peel)

1 small onion, chopped (80g prechopped)

Up to 4 medium garlic cloves, peeled and finely chopped (4 teaspoons prechopped)

2 tablespoons olive oil

1 tablespoon fresh lemon juice

1 teaspoon dried oregano

1 teaspoon dried thyme

½ teaspoon table salt

½ teaspoon ground black pepper

1 bay leaf

Beyond

- You must halve the recipe for a 3-litre cooker.
- For a 7.5-litre cooker, you must add 125ml stock or water and use the remaining ingredients as stated.
- If the mixture is too soupy for your taste, use the SAUTÉ function at LOW or LESS after cooking to boil the mixture down for a minute or two, stirring almost constantly.

300ml boiling water

30g dried porcini mushrooms

30g butter

1 medium shallot,
peeled and chopped

700g thinly sliced white
or chestnut mushrooms

60ml dry vermouth, dry white
wine or vegetable stock

2 teaspoons picked fresh
thyme leaves

½ teaspoon table salt

½ teaspoon ground black
pepper

30g Parmigiano-Reggiano,
finely grated

5g fresh parsley leaves,
finely chopped

Buttery Mushrooms with Cheese

6 servings

This simple side dish belongs next to chicken or fish off the grill. Or use it as a condiment right on top of steaks or chops. Or spoon the mushrooms over jacket potatoes.

Unfortunately, mushrooms lose a little of their flavour pop in a multi-cooker. We solve that by including dried mushrooms. Although we call for porcini (because they're common in our supermarket), substitute any sort of dried mushroom you like, even a less expensive blend of dried mushrooms. Do not substitute large Chinese dried mushrooms.

1. Pour the boiling water over the dried mushrooms in a small bowl. Set aside at room temperature for 10 minutes.

2.

Press	Setting	Time	Press
SAUTÉ	MEDIUM, NORMAL or CUSTOM 150°C	10 minutes	START

3. Melt the butter in a 3-, 5.5- or 7.5-litre cooker. Add the shallot and cook, stirring occasionally, until softened, about 2 minutes. Add the mushrooms and cook, stirring, until they give off their internal moisture and it evaporates to a glaze, about 4 minutes.

4. Turn off the **SAUTÉ** function and pour in the vermouth. Scrape up any browned bits on the pot's bottom. Stir in the thyme, salt and pepper; pour in the soaked mushrooms and their soaking liquid. Stir well, then lock the lid onto the cooker.

5.

Set the machine	Level	The valve must be	Time	Press
PRESSURE COOK	MAX	—	6 minutes with the KEEP WARM setting off	START
PRESSURE COOK or MANUAL	HIGH	Closed	8 minutes with the KEEP WARM setting off	START

6. Use the **quick-release method** to bring the pot's pressure back to normal. Unlatch the lid and open the cooker. Stir well.

7.

Press	Setting	Time	Press
SAUTÉ	HIGH or MORE	10 minutes	START

8. Bring the mushroom mixture to a full simmer, stirring occasionally. Continue cooking until the liquid in the pot has reduced to a glaze, stirring more and more frequently as it does, 5–6 minutes. Turn off the **SAUTÉ** function; stir in the cheese and parsley. Set the lid askew over the pot to meld the flavours for a couple of minutes before serving.

Beyond

- For a sweeter dish (better alongside smoked foods), substitute red (or sweet) vermouth for the dry vermouth.

- For a creamier dish, almost a sauce, add up to 125ml double cream to the mix before you reduce it down in step 8. In this case, don't get rid of all the moisture in the pot but keep the final dish a little 'loose'.

Polenta

4–6 servings

This is a quick and easy way to make the classic Italian side dish in an Instant Pot. Serve this polenta as a bed for any ragù or thick pasta sauce found in this book. Don't use cornmeal or instant polenta. Instead, use coarse-ground yellow polenta, sometimes called 'polenta corn grits'.

1 litre water

60g butter

½ teaspoon table salt

150g regular polenta

30g finely grated Parmigiano-Reggiano

1.

Press	Setting	Time	Press
SAUTÉ	MEDIUM, NORMAL or CUSTOM 150°C	10 minutes	START

2. Put the water, butter and salt in a **3- or 5.5-litre cooker.** Cook, stirring occasionally, until the butter melts and the mixture starts to bubble, 3–4 minutes. Stir in the polenta and cook, stirring quite often, for 2 minutes. Turn off the **SAUTÉ** function and lock the lid onto the cooker.

3.

Set the machine	Level	The valve must be	Time	Press
PRESSURE COOK	MAX	—	6 minutes with the KEEP WARM setting off	START
PRESSURE COOK or MANUAL	HIGH	Closed	8 minutes with the KEEP WARM setting off	START

4. When the machine has finished cooking, turn it off and let its pressure **return to normal naturally**, about 20 minutes. Unlatch the lid and open the cooker. Stir in the cheese, then set the lid askew for a couple of minutes to melt the cheese and blend the flavours. Stir well before serving warm.

Beyond

- For a 7.5-litre cooker, you must increase all the ingredients by 50 per cent or even double them.

- For a richer polenta, warm up to 125ml double or single cream in a small saucepan on the hob over a medium-low heat until bubbles fizz around its perimeter. Stir this into the polenta along with the cheese. Set aside, partially covered, for 5 minutes.

- Substitute other cheeses for the Parmigiano-Reggiano, such as a similar amount of finely grated pecorino of any sort or a hard, aged goat's cheese. Or substitute 55g grated semi-firm cheese like Swiss, Gruyère or Emmental.

- For Southern-style comfort, leave out the cheese. Pour the cooked polenta into a buttered 23cm square baking dish and leave to cool to room temperature, then cover and refrigerate for up to 2 days. Turn out the solidified polenta cake onto a chopping board, cut into squares, and fry them in butter in a nonstick frying pan set over a medium heat until brown and crunchy, turning a couple of times. Serve this 'fried mush' with fried, scrambled or poached eggs.

450g dried pinto beans

225g streaky bacon rashers, diced

1 medium onion, chopped (160g prechopped)

600ml chicken or vegetable stock

80g tinned chopped tomatoes

60ml treacle

45g light brown sugar

2 tablespoons apple cider vinegar

2 teaspoons mustard powder

½ teaspoon ground cloves (optional)

½ teaspoon table salt

½ teaspoon ground black pepper

Baked Beans

8 servings

Baked beans are a summer treat. But who wants to heat up the kitchen in the middle of July? The pot's the answer! Better yet, plug it in on the deck or patio, never bringing any of that steam into the house. The cloves are optional but they do give the dish the ketchup-y quality some people like in baked beans.

1. Soak the beans in a large bowl of water for at least 8 hours or up to 12 hours. Drain in a colander set in the sink.

2.

Press	Setting	Time	Press
SAUTÉ	MEDIUM, NORMAL or CUSTOM 150°C	10 minutes	START

3. Add the bacon to a **5.5- or 7.5-litre cooker.** Cook, stirring often, until the pieces begin to get brown and crisp, about 4 minutes. Add the onion and cook, stirring occasionally, until the onion softens, about 3 minutes. Pour in the stock and scrape up *every speck of browned stuff* on the pot's bottom.

4. Turn off the **SAUTÉ** function. Stir in the drained beans, the tomatoes, treacle, brown sugar, vinegar, mustard, cloves (if using), salt and pepper. Lock the lid onto the pot.

5.

Set the machine	Level	The valve must be	Time	Press
PRESSURE COOK	MAX	——	10 minutes with the KEEP WARM setting off	START
PRESSURE COOK or MANUAL	HIGH	Closed	12 minutes with the KEEP WARM setting off	START

6. When the machine has finished cooking, turn it off and let its pressure **return to normal naturally,** about 30 minutes. Unlatch the lid and open the cooker. Stir well before serving.

Beyond

- You must halve the recipe for a 3-litre cooker.

- The beans will continue to set up as the mixture cools. If it's too soupy for your taste, stir 2–3 tablespoons tomato purée into the hot mixture and set aside for 5 minutes with the lid askew over the pot before serving.

- For less sweet but hotter baked beans, reduce the brown sugar to 2 tablespoons and add up to 2 tablespoons hot red pepper sauce, such as Sriracha or sambal oelek with the treacle. Also, omit the salt and add up to 2 teaspoons soy sauce.

Not-Your-Mother's Three-Bean Salad

6 servings

Why don't you just open a few tins of beans and make a salad? Because of the texture of those beans! If you've got the time, dried beans (and here, chickpeas) will produce a more luxurious salad, better alongside burgers and hot dogs. And with fresh green beans, too, the salad will seem like summer on the plate.

The dish is best while the beans are fresh from the pot, added warm to the dressing. That said, you can cover the salad and set it in the fridge for up to 2 days, although the spring onions and beans will leach moisture as they sit in the dressing, rendering the whole dish quite a bit soupier.

1. Soak the beans and chickpeas in a big bowl of water for at least 8 hours or up to 12 hours. Drain in a colander set in the sink.

2. Pour the beans into a **5.5- or 7.5-litre cooker**. Add enough water so that they're submerged by 5cm. Add 1 tablespoon olive oil and lock the lid onto the pot.

3.

Set the machine	Level	The valve must be	Time	Press
PRESSURE COOK	MAX	—	10 minutes with the KEEP WARM setting off	START
PRESSURE COOK or MANUAL	HIGH	Closed	12 minutes with the KEEP WARM setting off	START

4. Use the **quick-release method** to bring the pot's pressure back to normal. Unlatch the lid and open the cooker. Stir in the green beans. Set the lid askew over the pot and set aside for 2 minutes, then drain the contents of the *hot* insert into a large colander set in the sink. Rinse with cool water to stop the cooking. Drain well, shaking the colander to get rid of excess moisture.

5. Whisk the remaining 60ml oil and the vinegar in a large serving bowl until uniform. Stir in the spring onions, garlic, salt, oregano, cumin, smoked paprika and pepper. Add the contents of the colander and toss well.

250g dried red kidney beans

160g dried chickpeas

Water as needed

60ml plus 1 tablespoon olive oil

225g fresh green beans, trimmed and cut into 1cm pieces

3 tablespoons red wine vinegar

4 medium spring onions, trimmed and thinly sliced

1 medium garlic clove, peeled and finely chopped (1 teaspoon prechopped)

1 teaspoon table salt

½ teaspoon dried oregano

½ teaspoon ground cumin

½ teaspoon mild smoked paprika

½ teaspoon ground black pepper

Beyond

- You must halve the recipe for a 3-litre cooker.
- Substitute dried haricot, cannellini or pinto beans for either the kidney beans or the chickpeas.
- We offer up our favourite dressing for this salad. But you can skip it and use up to 60ml bottled Italian dressing instead.

300g dried cannellini
or haricot beans

Water as needed

60ml plus 1 tablespoon
olive oil

2 tablespoons white
wine vinegar

1 small red onion, chopped
(80g prechopped)

5g fresh parsley leaves,
finely chopped

2 medium garlic cloves,
peeled and finely chopped
(2 teaspoons prechopped)

2 teaspoons drained and
rinsed capers,
finely chopped

2 teaspoons fresh rosemary
leaves, finely chopped

½ teaspoon table salt

¼ teaspoon crushed
chilli flakes

Warm White Bean Salad

6 servings

This side dish has Italian flavours, so consider it a go-to accompaniment for prawns or scallops in just about any way you can prepare them. Or make a Tuscan T-bone by rubbing the meat with olive oil, a little finely chopped garlic, crunchy sea salt and ground black pepper, then grilling to rare or medium-rare. Serve this warm salad spooned on top of the steak.

1. Soak the beans in a big bowl of water for at least 8 hours or up to 12 hours. Drain in a colander set in the sink.

2. Pour the beans into a 5.5- or 7.5-litre cooker. Add enough water so they're submerged by 5cm. Add 1 tablespoon olive oil and lock the lid onto the cooker.

3.

Set the machine	Level	The valve must be	Time	Press
PRESSURE COOK	MAX	—	10 minutes with the KEEP WARM setting off	START
PRESSURE COOK or MANUAL	HIGH	Closed	12 minutes with the KEEP WARM setting off	START

4. As the beans cook, whisk the remaining 60ml olive oil and the vinegar in a large, heat-safe serving bowl until smooth. Stir in the onion, parsley, garlic, capers, rosemary, salt and crushed chilli flakes.

5. When the machine has finished cooking, use the **quick-release method** to bring the pot's pressure back to normal. Unlatch the lid and open the cooker. Drain the contents of the *hot* insert into a colander set in the sink. Shake the colander to make sure the beans dry well. Pour them into the bowl with the dressing and toss well. Serve warm.

Beyond

- You must halve the recipe for a 3-litre cooker.
- This salad is a good base for canned, Italian-style tuna, particularly the tuna packed in olive oil. Crumble it on top or toss it into the salad after you've mixed the beans into the dressing.

Butter Beans and Greens

6 servings

Here's a hearty side that could become a light main course or lunch, particularly on a chilly day. Or top each serving with a poached egg for an easy dinner. It's a bit soupy, so plan on serving it in bowls.

Escarole is a traditional Italian green, a compact if floppy head with moderately thick leaves and a sweet but pleasingly bitter flavour that mellows when cooked. The inner leaves can be quite sandy. Rinse them well and pat them dry with kitchen paper. If you can't find escarole, substitute stemmed spring greens or large, stemmed kale leaves.

1. Soak the butter beans in a large bowl of water for at least 8 hours or up to 12 hours. Drain in a colander set in the sink.

2.

Press	Setting	Time	Press
SAUTÉ	MEDIUM, NORMAL or CUSTOM 150°C	10 minutes	START

3. Warm the oil in a **5.5- or 7.5-litre cooker** for a minute or two. Add the onion and cook, stirring occasionally, until softened, about 3 minutes. Stir in the garlic, oregano and crushed chilli flakes until fragrant, just a few seconds. Stir in the tomatoes and scrape up any browned bits on the pot's bottom.

4. Turn off the **SAUTÉ** function and stir in the stock, wine, vinegar and salt. Add the escarole and drained butter beans. Stir well and lock the lid onto the cooker.

5.

Set the machine	Level	The valve must be	Time	Press
PRESSURE COOK	MAX	—	7 minutes with the KEEP WARM setting off	START
PRESSURE COOK or MANUAL	HIGH	Closed	9 minutes with the KEEP WARM setting off	START

6. When the machine has finished cooking, turn it off and let its pressure **return to normal naturally**, about 20 minutes. Unlatch the lid and open the cooker. Stir well before serving.

- 500g dried butter beans
- 2 tablespoons olive oil
- 1 medium onion, chopped (160g prechopped)
- 2 medium garlic cloves, peeled and finely chopped (2 teaspoons prechopped)
- 2 teaspoons finely chopped fresh oregano leaves
- Up to ½ teaspoon crushed chilli flakes
- One 400g tin chopped tomatoes
- 250ml vegetable stock
- 125ml fairly fruit-forward white wine, such as Pinot Grigio
- 2 tablespoons apple cider vinegar
- ½ teaspoon table salt
- 1 small head of escarole (about 225g), cored and chopped

Beyond

- You must halve the recipe for a 3-litre cooker.
- For more heft, stir up to 55g grated Parmigiano-Reggiano into the pot after cooking. Set the lid askew over the top and set aside for 5 minutes to melt the cheese.
- If you don't care about the dish being vegan, fry bacon rashers and crumble them over each serving.

30g butter or olive oil

130g frozen baby onions
(do not thaw)

2 medium garlic cloves,
peeled and finely chopped
(2 teaspoons prechopped)

500ml vegetable stock

2 tablespoons tomato purée

1 tablespoon picked fresh
thyme leaves

1 tablespoon packed fresh
sage leaves, finely chopped

½ teaspoon table salt

½ teaspoon ground
black pepper

2 bay leaves

Two 400g tins haricot or
cannellini beans, drained
and rinsed

450g celeriac, peeled
and chopped

450g medium parsnips,
peeled and cut into
2.5cm sections

White Beans and Roots

8 servings

If you don't want to fool around with soaking dried beans, try this
simple side (or a satisfying vegan main course) that uses tinned
beans for an earthy, slightly braise-y mix.

Celeriac is the root of a specific varietal of celery. It should be
firm (not soft and mushy in places) and have a herbaceous,
celery-like aroma. It can be hard to peel because it's gnarled and
'hairy' with little root filaments. We find that a vegetable peeler
works best to get most of the peel off, then a paring knife gets into
the crevices. Make sure the cubes are no larger than 2.5cm so it
cooks in the time stated.

1.

Press	Setting	Time	Press
SAUTÉ	MEDIUM, NORMAL or CUSTOM 150°C	10 minutes	START

2. Melt the butter in a **5.5- or 7.5-litre cooker.** Add the baby
onions and cook, stirring occasionally, until lightly browned
in places, about 4 minutes. Stir in the garlic until aromatic, just
a few seconds. Turn off the **SAUTÉ** function, add the stock and
scrape up any browned bits on the pot's bottom.

3. Stir in the tomato purée, thyme, sage, salt, pepper and bay
leaves until the tomato purée dissolves. Add the beans, celeriac
and parsnips. Stir well and lock the lid onto the cooker.

4.

Set the machine	Level	The valve must be	Time	Press
PRESSURE COOK	MAX	——	5 minutes with the KEEP WARM setting off	START
PRESSURE COOK or MANUAL	HIGH	Closed	8 minutes with the KEEP WARM setting off	START

5. Use the **quick-release method** to bring the pot's pressure back
to normal. Unlatch the lid and open the cooker. Stir well before
serving.

Beyond

- You must halve the recipe for
  a 3-litre cooker.

- For a main course (that's
  obviously not vegan), serve
  the mixture over a big spoonful
  of whole-milk ricotta.

Red Beans, Spinach and Sweet Potatoes

6–8 servings

Larger spinach leaves can turn squishy under pressure unless they are few in number and surrounded by lots of liquid. In this hearty side dish, we use baby spinach for a milder flavour *and* for a better texture since those small leaves never undergo pressure but are simply warmed in the sauce.

1.

Press	Setting	Time	Press
SAUTÉ	MEDIUM, NORMAL or CUSTOM 150°C	5 minutes	START

2. Warm the oil in a **5.5- or 7.5-litre cooker** for a minute or two. Add the onion and cook, stirring occasionally, until softened, about 3 minutes. Add the garlic, ginger, coriander, crushed chilli flakes and salt. Cook, stirring often, until aromatic, about 20 seconds.

3. Turn off the **SAUTÉ** function, add the stock and scrape up any browned bits on the pot's bottom. Stir in the tomatoes, sweet potatoes and beans. Lock the lid onto the cooker.

4.

Set the machine	Level	The valve must be	Time	Press
PRESSURE COOK	MAX	——	6 minutes with the KEEP WARM setting off	START
PRESSURE COOK or MANUAL	HIGH	Closed	8 minutes with the KEEP WARM setting off	START

5. Use the **quick-release method** to bring the pot's pressure back to normal. Unlatch the lid and open the cooker. Add the spinach and stir well. Set the lid askew over the pot and set aside for 5 minutes to wilt the spinach and blend the flavours. Stir well before serving.

2 tablespoons vegetable, corn or rapeseed oil

1 medium onion, chopped (160g prechopped)

3 medium garlic cloves, peeled and finely chopped (1 tablespoon prechopped)

1 tablespoon finely chopped peeled fresh root ginger

1 teaspoon ground coriander

Up to ½ teaspoon crushed chilli flakes

½ teaspoon table salt

250ml vegetable stock

One 400g tin chopped tomatoes

700g sweet potatoes, peeled and cut into 2.5cm cubes

One 400g tin kidney beans, drained and rinsed

60g baby spinach leaves

Beyond

- You must halve the recipe for a 3-litre cooker.

- To turn this side into a full meal, add up to 100g thinly sliced smoked sausage, such as smoked kielbasa or bratwurst, with the onions.

250ml water

2–4 garlic heads

About 1–2 tablespoons
olive oil

'Roasted' Garlic

Makes 2–4 garlic heads

No, you can't roast garlic in the pot. But you can make a pretty good approximation in a few minutes (versus an hour). True, the garlic will not 'reduce', meaning that internal moisture will not condense in the cloves, making them exceptionally sweet. And they will not brown. But they *will* have a more intense, garlicky punch, terrific to mix with butter and spread on bread, to drop into olive oil for a few days to flavour it, to add to stews and braises for a flavour kick or to mix into potato mash for a garlicky side.

1. Pour the water into a 3- or 5.5-litre cooker. Set a heat- and pressure-safe trivet in the pot.

2. Cut the top quarter off each garlic head (that is, the end towards the tip, away from the wider, flat root end), partly exposing the garlic cloves below. (Not every single clove need be exposed.)

3. Rub about ½ tablespoon olive oil into the cut part of the garlic head, getting the olive oil down among the cloves, particularly inside the papery skins. Set the garlic heads cut-side up on the trivet in the pot. Lock the lid onto the cooker.

4.

Set the machine	Level	The valve must be	Time	Press
PRESSURE COOK	MAX	—	5 minutes with the KEEP WARM setting off	START
PRESSURE COOK or MANUAL	HIGH	Closed	7 minutes with the KEEP WARM setting off	START

5. When the machine has finished cooking, turn it off and let its pressure **return to normal naturally**, about 20 minutes. Unlatch the lid and open the cooker. Use kitchen tongs to gently pick up and transfer the garlic heads to a large plate. Leave to cool for several minutes, then either squeeze the warm cloves out of their paper hulls or leave to cool to room temperature, about 1 hour, then seal the heads individually in clingfilm and refrigerate for up to 1 week.

Beyond

- For a 7.5-litre cooker, you must use 350ml water.
- To brown the garlic, drizzle the cooked heads with a little more olive oil, then set them cut-side up on a large baking tin. Place 10–15cm from the heating element and grill until lightly browned, 1–3 minutes.

White Bean Purée

6–8 servings

Is this a dip for celery sticks, baby carrots or cucumber spears before dinner? Is it a spread for wraps? Is it a substitute for mashed potatoes under a rich beef or chicken stew? Is it a sauce that goes on top of a steak or chop off the grill? Yes! Depending on how much olive oil you add, you can control the final consistency: dip, purée or sauce.

1. Soak the beans in a big bowl of water for at least 8 hours or up to 12 hours. Drain in a colander set in the sink.

2. Pour the beans into a 3-, 5.5- or 7.5-litre cooker. Add enough water so they're submerged by 5cm. Add 1 tablespoon olive oil and lock the lid onto the pot.

3.

Set the machine	Level	The valve must be	Time	Press
PRESSURE COOK	MAX	—	10 minutes with the KEEP WARM setting off	START
PRESSURE COOK or MANUAL	HIGH	Closed	12 minutes with the KEEP WARM setting off	START

4. Use the **quick-release method** to bring the pot's pressure back to normal. Unlatch the lid and open the cooker. Drain the contents of the *hot* insert into a colander set in the sink. Shake the colander to remove excess water, then pour the warm beans into a large food processor.

5. Add 2 tablespoons olive oil, the roasted pepper, almonds, garlic, vinegar, fennel seeds, salt and pepper. Cover and process until smooth, adding more olive oil through the feed tube in 1-tablespoon increments until the purée is smooth and creamy. Serve warm.

200g dried haricot or cannellini beans

Water as needed

At least 90ml olive oil

1 jarred roasted yellow pepper

60g flaked almonds

1 large garlic clove, peeled and finely chopped

1 tablespoon white wine vinegar

1 teaspoon fennel seeds

½ teaspoon table salt

½ teaspoon ground black pepper

Beyond

- If you're not going to serve the purée straight away, scrape it into a medium bowl and refrigerate, covered, for up to 3 days. Warm it up in the microwave on high in 15-second bursts, stirring after each and thinning with additional stock or water as needed.

12
Puddings and Desserts

We'll confess that when we first got into pressure cooking, we were more surprised about a chapter like this one than almost anything else. It just didn't seem right: steam + pressure = cake. Seriously?

Well, it *doesn't* make sense for some desserts. No, you'll never get the same crumb in a pressure-cooker cake that you can get in one from the oven. And no, you'll never get the chewy density of a New-York-style cheesecake out of an Instant Pot without some added chemical craziness that we don't care for.

You wouldn't ask a food processor to make a roast beef. You shouldn't ask an Instant Pot to make a three-layer birthday cake. But if you work within the parameters of what the machine can do, you can make wonderful desserts – and some of the best cheesecakes we know, even if they're not the NY deli standard.

In fact, the pot seems made for puddings. And for steamed cakes, those British classics that are due for a renaissance. It's also the only way we make Dulce de Leche these days (page 455).

More than any other chapter, these recipes are set in stone. Baking is chemistry and works because of certain, long-established ratios. There are no road maps in this chapter because the formulas are sacrosanct. Experiment only if you know what you're doing before you do it.

With this chapter, we come to the end of the book and bid you a sweet, happy farewell. Yes, cook more often. You bought a pot to do so. But slow down. Make dinner, even if it's a faster meal. The world needs time, in shorter supply than ice in the Arctic. In our lives, there are three ways to find that lost time: walks down New England country roads with our collies; hours spent binge-watching Scandinavian shows; and having dinner with friends and family. That last is hands down the best. We hope we've shared it with you.

FAQs

1. What's the best way to make a digestive biscuit crumb base in a springform tin?
By using your clean, dry fingers. Once you get the crumbs and the butter mixed together, dump them into the tin, just not right in its centre. Spread them out as you pour them in. Get your fingers into the tin to press and shape the mixture evenly across the bottom, then up the sides. Make a fairly compact and flat bottom, then begin to work that bottom towards the tin's seam and up the edges, starting at the centre and eventually pushing the crumb mixture up the sides (and working around and around the tin as you do so, of course). Once the crumb base is in place, check to make sure that it's not too thick at the seam (where the side meets the bottom). Push this excess back towards the centre or up the sides of the tin.

2. Why are the eggs at room temperature here?
Because just like you, egg proteins curl up when they're cold. By bringing them to room temperature, they stretch out. When they're elongated, they can create a better structure in the batter, catching the air and holding it in the mixture (along with the gluten in the flour). Lighter, more tender baked goods – even those made in a steamy pot – are better every time with room-temperature eggs. For advice on getting eggs to room temperature, see page 25.

3. Why does my cheesecake smell like curry?
There's a running debate among Instant Pot users about how much the sealing ring in the pot's lid translates the odours of former dishes into the one currently under pressure. For almost every recipe in this book, we barely noticed a difference: a curry followed by a beef stew, a chicken casserole followed by a pasta one. But one day we tested the Dulce de Leche (page 455) right after the Brisket Skewers (page 266) and ended up with a smoky, meatish dessert sauce. Put simply: *No, thanks.* So our best advice is to buy a couple of extra rings, especially for more delicate desserts like cheesecake and Butterscotch Pudding (page 458). There are even colour-coded rings available, if you're a supertaster. Just remember which ring is for which sort of dish.

Dulce de Leche

Makes 250ml

Normally, dulce de leche is an exercise in patience: stirring, stirring, stirring in a saucepan on the hob. But the Instant Pot makes it an (almost) everyday treat. It's a creamy, sweet sauce that can be made in about an hour, start to finish. The results are thick and honey-like, with the distinct taste of caramelised sugar.

350ml water plus 3 tablespoons warm water from the kettle

½ teaspoon bicarbonate of soda

One 400g tin full-fat sweetened condensed milk

1. Pour 350ml water into a **5.5- or 7.5-litre cooker.** Set a heat- and pressure-safe trivet in the pot. Whisk the 3 tablespoons warm water and the bicarbonate of soda in a 2-litre, high-sided, round soufflé dish. Whisk in the condensed milk until smooth. Set this bowl on the trivet and lock the lid onto the cooker.

2.

Set the machine	Level	The valve must be	Time	Press
PRESSURE COOK	MAX	——	30 minutes with the KEEP WARM setting off	START
PRESSURE COOK or MANUAL	HIGH	Closed	40 minutes with the KEEP WARM setting off	START

3. When the machine has finished cooking, turn it off and let its pressure **return to normal naturally**, about 15 minutes. Unlatch the lid and open the cooker. Whisk the dulce de leche until smooth or use a hand blender right in the insert to make the sauce super smooth. Pour the sauce into a small bowl and set it in the fridge for an hour or two. Cover and refrigerate for up to 5 days, microwaving small portions to loosen them up before serving.

Beyond

- Unfortunately, dulce de leche cannot be made in a soufflé dish smaller than the one required here, and therefore cannot be made in a 3-litre cooker. Even halved, the mixture roils too much to be contained in a 1-litre baking dish. The recipe also cannot be doubled in the standard 2-litre baking dish we call for.

- Serve dulce de leche drizzled over vanilla, butter pecan, chocolate or any nut ice cream. It's particularly delicious over cashew milk ice cream.

- Drizzle warm dulce de leche over blackberries and top with whipped cream.

- Or spread it on toast as a change from other nut-flavoured spreads.

- Or dip salty pretzel logs into the sauce as a great dessert.

4 large eggs

500ml whole milk

3 tablespoons white caster sugar

½ teaspoon vanilla extract

¼ teaspoon table salt

350ml water

Silky Vanilla Custard

4 servings

Custards from a multi-cooker come out a little firmer than those off of the hob, similar in texture to silken tofu (and definitely not dry, given the pot's moist environment). They also don't need to set up in the refrigerator but are ready to eat warm from the cooker.

Make sure the eggs are whisked fully into the custard base with no bits of the whites floating loose. The easiest way to get the egg mixture into the custard cups is to use a ladle, rather than trying to pour from the rim of a bowl (unless your mixing bowl has a pouring spout).

1. Whisk the eggs, milk, sugar, vanilla and salt in a large bowl until very smooth. Divide this mixture evenly among four heat- and pressure-safe 250ml ramekins. Cover each ramekin with a small piece of foil.

2. Pour the water into a **5.5- or 7.5-litre cooker**. Set a heat- and pressure-safe trivet in the cooker. Stack the ramekins in the cooker (probably three on the rack and then one balanced in the middle on the edges of the three below). Lock the lid onto the cooker.

3.

Set the machine	Level	The valve must be	Time	Press
PRESSURE COOK	MAX	—	3 minutes with the KEEP WARM setting off	START
PRESSURE COOK or MANUAL	HIGH	Closed	5 minutes with the KEEP WARM setting off	START

4. When the machine has finished cooking, turn it off and let its pressure **return to normal naturally**, about 15 minutes. Unlatch the lid and open the cooker. Transfer the *hot* covered ramekins to a wire rack, uncover and leave to cool for 15 minutes. Serve warm, or cover again and refrigerate for at least 2 hours or up to 4 days.

Beyond

- Because of the size of the ramekins, this recipe cannot be halved for a 3-litre cooker.

- You can (but don't have to) increase all the ingredients by 50 per cent and make six 250ml ramekins of pudding in a 7.5-litre cooker. Or you can cut the recipe by half (or even cut it to a quarter of its original and make just one custard) using 2 ramekins (or just 1) in a 5.5- or 7.5 litre cooker. However, you must keep the water the same (350ml).

- Sprinkle up to ½ teaspoon ground cinnamon and/or ½ teaspoon grated nutmeg onto each ramekin of custard base before baking.

- Try adding up to ½ teaspoon rum, almond or lemon extract with the vanilla extract.

Chocolate Pudding

4 servings

Our chocolate pudding is made with melted chocolate, not unsweetened cocoa powder. That chocolate gives the pudding a thick, super rich texture, like a cross between pudding and frosting. A little goes a long way, though whipping cream would be welcome to (ahem) lighten the dessert.

1. Place both types of chocolate in a large, heat-safe bowl. Set aside.

2. Pour the milk and cream into a microwave-safe bowl. Heat on high until steaming, 1–2 minutes. Pour the hot milk mixture over the chocolate and steep for 1 minute. Stir until creamy and melted. Leave to cool for 5 minutes, whisking occasionally.

3. Whisk in the egg yolks, vanilla and salt until smooth. Divide this mixture between four heat- and pressure-safe 250ml ramekins. Cover each tightly with aluminium foil. Pour the water into a **5.5- or 7.5-litre cooker**. Set a heat- and pressure-safe trivet in the pot, then stack the ramekins on the trivet, probably three on the bottom and one on top in the centre on their edges. Lock the lid onto the cooker.

4.

Set the machine	Level	The valve must be	Time	Press
PRESSURE COOK	MAX	—	10 minutes with the KEEP WARM setting off	START
PRESSURE COOK or MANUAL	HIGH	Closed	12 minutes with the KEEP WARM setting off	START

5. When the machine has finished cooking, turn it off and let its pressure **return to normal naturally**, about 20 minutes. Unlatch the lid and open the pot. Transfer the *hot* covered ramekins to a wire rack, uncover and leave to cool for 15 minutes. Serve warm or cover again and refrigerate for at least 2 hours until chilled or up to 4 days.

175g dark chocolate, chopped

15g unsweetened chocolate, chopped (half of a 30g square of standard baking chocolate, or about 1½ tablespoons chopped unsweetened chocolate)

250ml whole milk

125ml double cream

4 large egg yolks

Up to 2 teaspoons vanilla extract

¼ teaspoon salt

350ml water

Beyond

- Because of the size of the ramekins, this recipe cannot be halved for a 3-litre cooker.
- The best whipped cream is made with chilled utensils. Set the bowl and the beaters of a mixer (or a whisk, if you're old-school) in the refrigerator for at least 3 hours or up to 24 hours before making whipped cream. Our preferred ratio is 1 tablespoon icing sugar and ¼ teaspoon vanilla extract for every 170ml double cream. Pour the cream into the chilled bowl and beat at high speed with a stand mixer with the whip attachment or a hand-held electric mixer (or even with a whisk by hand) until somewhat thickened. Add the sugar and vanilla and continue beating on high until soft, light peaks can be formed off the ends of the turned-off whisk attachment or beaters (or the hand-held whisk).

45g butter

115g dark brown sugar

350ml whole milk

125ml double cream

6 large egg yolks

¼ teaspoon vanilla extract

⅛ teaspoon salt

350ml water

Butterscotch Pudding

4 servings

This pudding is like butterscotch *pot de crème*, made by turning butter and brown sugar into caramel, then creating a custard base to steam-cook in the ramekins. The results are wonderfully smooth. Don't be surprised if it really serves just two (since each of you will eat two).

1.

Press	Setting	Time	Press
SAUTÉ	MEDIUM, NORMAL or CUSTOM 150°C	10 minutes	START

2. Melt the butter in a **5.5- or 7.5-litre cooker**. Stir in the brown sugar until smooth and cook until constantly bubbling, about 3 minutes. Stir in the milk and cream until the sugar mixture melts again and becomes smooth. Turn off the **SAUTÉ** function and pour the mixture from the *hot* insert into a nearby large bowl. Cool for 15 minutes. Meanwhile, clean and dry the insert; return it to the machine.

3. Whisk the egg yolks, vanilla and salt into the milk mixture until smooth. Divide this mixture evenly among four heat- and pressure-safe 250ml ramekins. Cover each with aluminium foil.

4. Pour the water into the cooker and set a heat- and pressure-safe trivet in the machine. Stack the ramekins on the trivet, balancing a second layer on the edge of more than one ramekin below. Lock the lid onto the pot.

5.

Set the machine	Level	The valve must be	Time	Press
PRESSURE COOK	MAX	—	7 minutes with the KEEP WARM setting off	START
PRESSURE COOK or MANUAL	HIGH	Closed	10 minutes with the KEEP WARM setting off	START

6. When the machine has finished cooking, turn it off and let its pressure **return to normal naturally**, about 20 minutes. Unlatch the lid and open the cooker. Transfer the *hot* covered ramekins to a wire rack, uncover and leave to cool for 15 minutes. Serve warm or cover again and refrigerate for at least 2 hours or up to 4 days.

Beyond

- Because of the size of the ramekins, this recipe cannot be halved for a 3-litre cooker.

- In a 7.5-litre cooker, you can (but don't have to) increase all the ingredients by 50 per cent (if desired) and make six 250ml ramekins of pudding. Use 350ml water, as directed, in the cooker.

- If you've used oven-safe ramekins, you can put a meringue on these puddings (as long as they're still hot). To do so, beat 3 large egg whites and ⅛ teaspoon table salt in a medium bowl with an electric mixer (with a whisk attachment, if available) at medium speed until foamy, about 1 minute. Beat in 90g white caster sugar in a slow, steady stream until the sugar dissolves and you can form soft peaks off the end of a rubber spatula dipped into the mixture. Divide this mixture amongst the tops of the puddings, sealing it to the edges. Use the spatula to make peaks and valleys in the beaten egg-white mixture. Set the hot ramekins in a large baking tin and bake in a 190°C oven until lightly browned, 8–10 minutes. Leave to cool for at least 15 minutes before serving.

Tapioca Pudding

4–6 servings

We followed the advice of eight bazillion internet recipes and tried (and tried and tried) to make tapioca pudding right in the pot's insert. It burned every time, no matter what size tapioca pearls we used. The only sure path to success was to use a soufflé dish in the pot, then whisk an egg and an egg yolk into the pudding after cooking to make the whole thing rich and creamy.

For this recipe, you must use instant tapioca, the stuff your grandmother used to thicken pie fillings. It's found in the baking aisle near the bicarbonate of soda. You cannot use larger tapioca pearls, familiar from bubble teas. And for safety's sake, use only organic eggs (because they're not cooked but only heated in the rice mixture). If you are cooking for someone with immune system problems, search out in-the-shell pasteurised eggs.

700ml whole, low-fat or fat-free milk

125g white caster sugar

75g instant tapioca

1 teaspoon vanilla extract

¼ teaspoon table salt

350ml water

1 large egg, at room temperature

1 large egg yolk, at room temperature

1. Whisk the milk, sugar, tapioca, vanilla and salt in a 2-litre, high-sided, round, heat- and pressure-safe soufflé dish until the sugar dissolves. Do not cover.

2. Pour the water into a **5.5- or 7.5-litre cooker**. Set a heat- and pressure-safe trivet in the pot. Set the baking dish on the trivet and lock the lid onto the pot.

3.

Set the machine	Level	The valve must be	Time	Press
PRESSURE COOK	MAX	—	5 minutes with the KEEP WARM setting off	START
PRESSURE COOK or MANUAL	HIGH	Closed	7 minutes with the KEEP WARM setting off	START

4. When the machine has finished cooking, turn it off and let its pressure **return to normal naturally**, about 20 minutes. Unlatch the lid and open the cooker. Whisk the hot mixture in the baking dish until smooth, scraping up any clumped tapioca on the bottom.

5. Whisk the egg and egg yolk in a medium bowl until smooth. Whisk the hot tapioca custard in small portions into the eggs, then more and more of it, until all of the milk mixture is incorporated and smooth. Set in the refrigerator to chill for 2 hours, then serve or cover and store in the fridge for up to 4 days.

Beyond

- For a 3-litre cooker, you must use 250ml water in the cooker, halve all the remaining ingredients and use a 1-litre, high-sided, round soufflé dish.

- Stir dried fruit into the pudding after you've incorporated all the eggs. Try 20g dried blueberries, 60g dried cranberries, 70g dried currants or 60g raisins.

- Or stir up to 2 peeled and thinly sliced bananas into the pudding after the eggs have been incorporated.

15g butter

165g white Arborio rice

350ml whole or low-fat evaporated milk

125ml water

125g white granulated sugar

Up to 2 teaspoons vanilla extract

¼ teaspoon table salt

1 large egg, at room temperature

1 large egg yolk, at room temperature

90ml double cream

Rice Pudding

4–6 servings

Our rice pudding recipe is basically a sweetened modification of our risotto recipe – and the whole thing gets enriched with eggs and cream. As in the previous recipe for Tapioca Pudding, only use organic or even in-the-shell pasteurised eggs for safety's sake.

1.

Press	Setting	Time	Press
SAUTÉ	MEDIUM, NORMAL Or CUSTOM 150°C	5 minutes	START

2. Melt the butter in a **5.5-litre cooker**. Add the rice and cook, stirring constantly, until the tips of the grains turn translucent, about 1 minute. Stir in the evaporated milk, water, sugar, vanilla and salt until the sugar dissolves. Turn off the **SAUTÉ** function and lock the lid onto the pot.

3.

Set the machine	Level	The valve must be	Time	Press
PRESSURE COOK	MAX	——	7 minutes with the KEEP WARM setting off	START
PRESSURE COOK or MANUAL	HIGH	Closed	10 minutes with the KEEP WARM setting off	START

4. When the machine has finished cooking, turn it off and let its pressure **return to normal naturally**, about 15 minutes. Unlatch the lid and open the cooker. Stir the rice mixture a couple of times.

5. Whisk the egg, egg yolk and cream in a large bowl until smooth. Whisk about 250ml of the rice mixture into this egg mixture until smooth, then whisk this combined mixture back into the remaining rice mixture in the pot. Set aside for 5 minutes, then serve warm or spoon into a large, clean bowl and refrigerate until chilled, about 1 hour. Covered, the pudding can stay in the fridge for up to 2 days.

Beyond

- For a 3-litre cooker, you must halve all the ingredients.

- For a 7.5-litre cooker, you must increase all the ingredients by 50 per cent.

- Stir in up to 60g dried fruit after the combined egg-and-pudding mixture has cooled for 5 minutes. Choose raisins, currants or cranberries – or choose among any chopped dried fruit like pineapple, nectarines, pitted dates or stemmed figs.

- Once cooled, stir in up to 75g mini chocolate chips. Or go Italian and stir in up to 80g finely chopped glacé (or candied) cherries, candied orange rind or candied citron (any of that chopped fruitcake fruit).

Sweet Coconut Rice with Mango

6 servings

Here's a quick rendition of a dessert served in Thai restaurants. You'll need sweet glutinous rice, not sushi or other short-grain varietals of white rice. You should be able to find it in an Asian market or you can order it online – although we did luck out and find it at our rural supermarket on two occasions. It's sometimes called 'sweet rice'. But beware: some manufacturers label other short-grain white rices as 'sweet'. Just be sure it has the word 'glutinous' on the label. (By the way, there is no wheat gluten in glutinous rice.)

One 400g tin full-fat coconut milk or coconut cream

125g white granulated sugar

½ teaspoon vanilla extract

½ teaspoon table salt

850ml water

300g sweet, glutinous white rice

3 medium ripe mangos, peeled, deseeded and cut into bite-size chunks

1.

Press	Setting	Time	Press
SAUTÉ	MEDIUM, NORMAL Or CUSTOM 150°C	10 minutes	START

2. Mix the coconut milk, sugar, vanilla and salt in a **5.5- or 7.5-litre cooker**. Cook, stirring often, until bubbling, about 4 minutes. Turn off the **SAUTÉ** function, remove the *hot* insert from the machine and scrape every drop of the coconut mixture into a heat-safe, large bowl. Set aside.

3. Clean the insert and return it to the machine. Pour 350ml water into the pot, then set a heat- and pressure-safe trivet in the pot. Mix the rice and the remaining 500ml water in a 2-litre, high-sided, round soufflé dish. Set this dish on the trivet and lock the lid onto the pot.

4.

Set the machine	Level	The valve must be	Time	Press
PRESSURE COOK	MAX	——	12 minutes with the KEEP WARM setting off	START
PRESSURE COOK or MANUAL	HIGH	Closed	15 minutes with the KEEP WARM setting off	START

5. Use the **quick-release method** to bring the pot's pressure back to normal – *but do not open the pot*. Set aside for 10 minutes, then unlatch the lid and open the cooker. Remove the *hot* bowl from the trivet.

6. Stir all but 90ml of the coconut milk mixture into the cooked rice. Serve the rice warm in bowls with mango pieces all over the top and drizzle the portions with as much of the remaining coconut milk mixture as desired.

Beyond

- For a 3-litre cooker, you must use 250ml water in the cooker, halve the remaining ingredients and use a 1-litre, high-sided, round soufflé dish.

- This dessert is much easier with presliced mangos. They are often sold in spears, which you can chop into smaller pieces.

- Split a vanilla pod in half lengthways and add it with the sugar to the coconut milk mixture. Remove the vanilla pod halves before serving.

125g plus 90g white caster sugar

350ml plus 3 tablespoons water

3 large eggs

300ml double cream

180ml whole milk

2 teaspoons vanilla extract

⅛ teaspoon table salt

Burnt Sugar Flan

4 servings

These little custard cups steam with a burnt sugar sauce in the bottom of each. The sugar syrup is first poured into the cups, it hardens, then turns wet again as the custards cook and cool. How dark you cook that sugar syrup is a matter of culinary debate. If you like a sweet, mild flavour, cook it only until it is barely amber. Go darker for a more robust flavour. But remember that it will continue to cook (and darken) for a little while after the pot has been removed from the heat.

Why not just cook the syrup with the **SAUTÉ** function on HIGH in the pot? Because it's hard to judge exactly how dark the syrup has become inside the pot and because it's very difficult to pour from the insert.

1. Melt the 125g sugar and the 3 tablespoons water in a small saucepan set over a medium heat until amber or even a little darker, stirring occasionally until the sugar melts then undisturbed to your desired colour, 4–6 minutes. Pour the *hot* sugar syrup evenly into four heat- and pressure-safe 250ml ramekins, preferably Pyrex custard cups. Grasp the ramekins with oven gloves and tilt them a little to coat their sides a bit. Leave to cool at room temperature for 15 minutes.

2. Whisk the eggs, cream, milk, vanilla, salt and the remaining 90g sugar in a medium bowl until the sugar dissolves and the mixture is smooth. Divide this mixture evenly among the coated custard cups. Cover each tightly with aluminium foil.

3. Pour the 350ml water into a **5.5- or 7.5-litre cooker**. Set a heat- and pressure-safe trivet in the pot, then stack the filled ramekins on the trivet, probably three below and one balanced in the centre on their rims. Lock the lid onto the pot.

4.

Set the machine	Level	The valve must be	Time	Press
PRESSURE COOK	MAX	—	7 minutes with the KEEP WARM setting off	START
PRESSURE COOK or MANUAL	HIGH	Closed	9 minutes with the KEEP WARM setting off	START

5. When the machine has finished cooking, turn it off and let its pressure **return to normal naturally**, about 20 minutes. Unlatch the lid and open the cooker. Transfer the *hot* custard cups to a wire rack, uncover them and leave to cool for 10 minutes. Then set them in the fridge and leave to cool for 1 hour. Cover and continue cooling for at least 1 more hour or up to 3 days. To serve, turn one upside down onto a plate and jiggle it a bit to release.

Beyond

- Because of the size of the ramekins, this recipe won't work in a 3-litre cooker.
- Add up to ½ teaspoon orange extract with the vanilla.
- Or sprinkle up to ¼ teaspoon finely chopped culinary lavender on top of each custard before sealing and steaming.

Buttery Caramel Pears

4 servings

Strangely enough, this dessert returns to the butter-and-bicarbonate-of-soda technique we used when we poached vegetables to make a creamy (but cream-free) soup. In this recipe, you don't purée the mixture. This isn't soup, after all. Instead, the pears get poached in a sweet butter sauce that is thickened after cooking.

1.

Press	Setting	Time	Press
SAUTÉ	MEDIUM, NORMAL Or CUSTOM 150°C	5 minutes	START

2. Put the butter, brown sugar, cinnamon, nutmeg, bicarbonate of soda and salt in a **3- or 5.5-litre cooker** and stir until the butter has melted. Stir in the apple juice until smooth, then add the pears and stir well. Turn off the **SAUTÉ** function and lock the lid onto the pot.

3.

Set the machine	Level	The valve must be	Time	Press
PRESSURE COOK	MAX	——	3 minutes with the KEEP WARM setting off	START
PRESSURE COOK or MANUAL	HIGH	Closed	4 minutes with the KEEP WARM setting off	START

4. When the machine has finished cooking, turn it off and let its pressure **return to normal naturally**, about 15 minutes. Unlatch the lid and open the cooker.

5.

Press	Setting	Time	Press
SAUTÉ	MEDIUM, NORMAL Or CUSTOM 150°C	5 minutes	START

6. As the sauce comes to a simmer, whisk the cornflour and water in a small bowl until smooth. Stir this slurry into the pears and sauce. Stir constantly until thickened a bit, about 1 minute. Turn off the **SAUTÉ** function and remove the *hot* insert from the machine. Leave to cool for 5–10 minutes before serving.

115g butter, cut into 4 or 5 pieces

165g light brown sugar

1 teaspoon ground cinnamon

¼ teaspoon grated nutmeg

¼ teaspoon bicarbonate of soda

¼ teaspoon table salt

125ml unsweetened apple juice

4 large firm ripe pears, peeled, cored and each cut into 4–6 wedges

2 teaspoons cornflour

2 teaspoons water

Beyond

- For a 7.5-litre cooker, you must increase all the ingredients by 50 per cent.

- Split a vanilla pod lengthways and add it to the pot with the pears.

- Spoon the pears and syrup over a small mound of soft goat's cheese or fresh ricotta.

- Sprinkle coarsely crumbled digestive biscuits over each serving.

175g dried egg pasta

1.5 litres water, plus 350ml water

2 large eggs

90g white caster sugar

90ml regular or low-fat soured cream

90g regular or low-fat cream cheese

60ml regular or low-fat evaporated milk

30g butter, melted and cooled, plus extra butter as needed

½ teaspoon ground cinnamon

½ teaspoon vanilla extract

¼ teaspoon table salt

30g raisins

Noodle Kugel

6 servings

A New York deli favourite, noodle kugel (*KOO-guhl*, which means something like 'baked casserole') is often served with brisket. We think kugel's better as a dessert, falling somewhere between a rice pudding and a sweet custard with egg pasta. While you can use low-fat dairy, do not use fat-free, which has stabilisers that can break down under pressure. As with other savoury dishes that use egg pasta, the best gluten-free alternative for a pressure cooker is pasta made with a mixture of grains, preferably corn and rice.

1. Put the pasta into a **5.5- or 7.5-litre cooker** and pour in the 1.5 litres water. Lock the lid onto the pot.

2.

Set the machine	Level	The valve must be	Time	Press
PRESSURE COOK or MANUAL	HIGH	Closed	4 minutes with the KEEP WARM setting off	START

3. Use the **quick-release method** to bring the pot's pressure back to normal. Unlatch the lid and open the cooker. Drain the pasta out of the *hot* insert and into a colander set in the sink. Wipe out the insert and return it to the pot. Leave the pasta to cool for 10 minutes, tossing occasionally to stop them sticking.

4. Meanwhile, generously butter the inside of an 18cm round springform tin. Put the eggs, sugar, soured cream, cream cheese, evaporated milk, melted butter, cinnamon, vanilla and salt in a blender. Cover and blend until smooth, stopping the machine at least once to scrape down the inside.

5. Pour the egg mixture into a large bowl; stir in the pasta and raisins until uniform. Pour and scrape this mixture into the prepared springform tin, packing it down gently. Cover tightly with foil.

6. Pour the 350ml water into the cooker, then set a heat- and pressure-safe trivet inside the pot. Make an aluminium foil sling (see page 20) and set the covered springform tin on it. Using the sling, lower the tin onto the trivet; fold the ends of the sling down into the pot. Lock the lid onto the cooker.

7.

Set the machine	Level	The valve must be	Time	Press
PRESSURE COOK	MAX	——	15 minutes with the KEEP WARM setting off	START
PRESSURE COOK or MANUAL	HIGH	Closed	20 minutes with the KEEP WARM setting off	START

8. When the machine has finished cooking, turn it off and let its pressure **return to normal naturally**, about 20 minutes. Unlatch the lid and open the cooker. Use the foil sling to lift the *hot* springform tin out of the cooker. Set on a wire rack and leave to cool for 10 minutes. Unlatch the ring of the springform tin and remove it. Leave to cool another 5 minutes before slicing into wedges and serving warm. Or, leave to cool to room temperature, then wrap in clingfilm and store in the fridge for up to 3 days.

Beyond

- For a 3-litre cooker, you must halve the ingredients and use a 1-litre, high-sided, round soufflé dish (rather than a springform tin). Scoop out big spoonfuls, rather than cutting it into wedges.

- Drizzle servings with double cream and maple syrup.

- It may be unheard of among traditionalists, but you could try using dried blueberries, cherries or cranberries in place of the raisins.

- Or omit the raisins, go old-school and use 65g tinned fruit cocktail.

100g digestive biscuit crumbs

70g butter, melted and cooled, plus additional butter for greasing the tin

450g regular cream cheese

125g white caster sugar

2 large eggs

60ml regular soured cream

2 teaspoons finely grated lemon zest

1 tablespoon fresh lemon juice

½ teaspoon vanilla extract

¼ teaspoon table salt (optional)

1½ tablespoons plain flour

350ml water

Classic Cheesecake

6–8 servings

If social media is to be believed (does Facebook lie?), a cheesecake is one of the first things people make in their Instant Pots. We've seen a lot of techniques over the years – and written a lot of pressure-cooker cheesecake recipes, too – and we can tell you we heartily don't get why people tend to overcomplicate what can be a fairly simple process for a rich, mousse-like (*not* New-York-style) cheesecake.

First, don't cover the cheesecake. True, it can get a drop or two of moisture on top. You can blot these off with kitchen paper when you open the lid. A cover on the tin gets in the way as the batter rises. You end up with a top that's partly fused to the foil, often a mess.

Second, never use the quick-release method, which instantly brings any liquid left in the cheesecake to a near boil even after the cake has mostly set, resulting in bumps and cracks. Instead, use a natural release for a better texture, set and look.

Finally, cook the cheesecake only on HIGH pressure, not MAX, which is too aggressive for a successful cheesecake.

1. Generously butter the inside of an 18cm round springform tin. Mix the digestive biscuit crumbs and the melted butter in a medium bowl and pour into the prepared tin. Press this mixture evenly across the bottom and about halfway up the sides of the tin to make a base.

2. Put the cream cheese and sugar in a food processor, cover and process until smooth, about 1 minute. Add the eggs one at a time, processing each until smooth. Open the machine, scrape down the inside and add the soured cream. Cover and process until smooth.

3. Add the lemon zest, lemon juice, vanilla and salt (if using). Process again until smooth – and again, stop the machine and scrape down the inside. Add the flour and process for 1 minute. Pour this mixture into the prepared base in the tin (it will rise above the base on the sides). Do not cover the tin.

4. Pour the water into a **5.5- or 7.5-litre cooker.** Set a heat- and pressure-safe trivet in the cooker. Make an aluminium foil sling (see page 20), set the filled springform tin on it, and use it to lower the tin into the pot. Fold down the ends of the sling so that they do not touch the batter in the tin. Lock the lid onto the pot.

5.

Set the machine	Level	The valve must be	Time	Press
PRESSURE COOK or MANUAL	HIGH	Closed	25 minutes with the KEEP WARM setting off	START

6. When the machine has finished cooking, turn it off and let its pressure **return to normal naturally**, about 20 minutes. Unlatch the lid and open the cooker. Use the sling to transfer the *hot* springform tin to a wire rack. Leave to cool for 15 minutes, then refrigerate for 1 hour. Cover and continue refrigerating for at least 1 more hour or up to 2 days.

7. To serve, uncover and run a thin knife between the tin and the cake. Unlatch the sides of the tin and open it to remove the cake inside. If desired, use a long, thin knife to slice the cake off the bottom of the tin. Use a large palette knife or metal spatula to transfer the cheesecake to a serving platter.

Beyond

- Unfortunately, these ratios and this tin won't work in a 3-litre cooker.

- Top the slices with strawberry or raspberry jam, warmed for a few seconds on high in the microwave and then whisked until smooth.

- Or top with slightly warmed chocolate sauce.

- Or make a cherry sauce. Mix one 450g bag frozen sweet or sour cherries (do not thaw), 125g white granulated sugar and 125ml water in a medium saucepan. Bring to the boil over a medium heat, stirring often. Whisk 1 tablespoon lemon juice and 2 teaspoons cornflour in a small bowl until smooth, then stir this slurry into the bubbling cherry mixture. Cook, stirring constantly, until thickened, about 1 minute. Immediately remove from the heat and continue stirring until the bubbling stops. Leave to cool for at least 30 minutes at room temperature before serving with the cheesecake.

100g digestive biscuit crumbs

70g butter, melted and cooled, plus extra butter for greasing the tin

450g regular cream cheese

185g white caster sugar

2 large eggs, at room temperature

1 large egg yolk, at room temperature

60ml regular soured cream

340g dark chocolate, preferably 70% cocoa solids, melted and cooled

2 tablespoons unsweetened cocoa powder

350ml water

Chocolate-Soured Cream Cheesecake

6–8 servings

This cheesecake is thick and chewy, sort of like a cross between chocolate frosting and cheesecake. Even more than the classic cheesecake, this one needs to ripen in the fridge, if only to develop its sophisticated flavour.

For the best success, start with bittersweet chocolate (around 70% cocoa solids). Chop it and set it in a microwave-wave safe bowl. Microwave on high in 5-second bursts, stirring after each, until about two-thirds melted, then remove the bowl and continue stirring until smooth. Leave to cool to room temperature, 20–30 minutes.

1. Generously butter the inside of an 18cm round springform tin. Mix the digestive biscuit crumbs and melted butter in a medium bowl, then pour into the prepared tin. Press this mixture evenly across the bottom and about halfway up the sides of the tin to make a base.

2. Put the cream cheese and sugar in a food processor, cover and process until smooth, about 1 minute. Add the eggs one at a time, processing each until smooth. Then add the egg yolk and process until smooth. Open the machine, scrape down the inside and add the soured cream. Cover and again process until smooth.

3. Add the melted and cooled chocolate and the cocoa powder. Process again until smooth – and once again, stop the machine and scrape down the inside. Pour this mixture into the prepared biscuit-crumb base in the tin (it will rise above the base on the sides).

4. Pour the water into a **5.5- or 7.5-litre cooker.** Set a heat- and pressure-safe trivet in the cooker. Make an aluminium foil sling (see page 20), set the filled but uncovered springform tin on it, and use the sling to lower the tin into the pot. Fold down the ends of the sling so that they do not touch the cheesecake batter in the pan. Lock the lid onto the pot.

5.

Set the machine	Level	The valve must be	Time	Press
PRESSURE COOK or MANUAL	HIGH	Closed	25 minutes with the KEEP WARM setting off	START

6. When the machine has finished cooking, turn it off and let its pressure **return to normal naturally**, about 20 minutes. Unlatch the lid and open the cooker. Use the sling to transfer the *hot* springform tin to a wire rack. Leave to cool for 15 minutes, then refrigerate for 1 hour. Cover and then continue refrigerating for at least 1 more hour or up to 2 days.

7. To serve, uncover and run a thin knife between the tin and the cake. Unlatch the sides of the tin and open it to remove the cake inside. If desired, use a long, thin knife to slice the cake off the bottom of the tin and then use a large palette knife or metal spatula to transfer the cheesecake to a serving platter.

Beyond

- Unfortunately, these ratios and this tin won't work in a 3-litre cooker.
- Top the cheesecake with curls of chocolate, shaved off a bar of 70% chocolate using a cheese plane.
- Or top the cheesecake with a sprinkling of crunchy sea salt.

60g flaked almonds

65g digestive biscuit crumbs

125g plus 2 tablespoons white caster sugar

45g butter, melted and cooled, plus extra butter for greasing the tin

450g regular cream cheese

1 small very ripe banana

30g dehydrated, crisp, unsweetened, unsalted banana chips

2 large eggs

1 tablespoon plain flour

½ teaspoon almond extract

350ml water

Banana Cheesecake

6–8 servings

This cheesecake requires a very ripe banana: one with black spots on its skin, quite soft, beyond what you'd slice onto cereal. A banana with just a few brown spots won't do. We also add dehydrated banana chips (rather than artificial banana flavouring) to make the cheesecake a banana lover's paradise.

1. Generously butter the inside of an 18cm round springform tin. Mix the almonds, digestive biscuit crumbs, 2 tablespoons sugar. and the melted butter in a medium bowl until uniform; then pour into the prepared tin. Press this mixture evenly across the bottom and about halfway up the sides of the tin to make a base for the cheesecake.

2. Put the remaining 125g sugar, the cream cheese, banana and banana chips in a food processor, cover and process until smooth, about 1 minute. Add the eggs one at a time, processing each until smooth. Open the machine, scrape down the inside and add the flour and almond extract. Cover and process until smooth. Pour this mixture onto the prepared base in the tin (it will rise above the base on the sides). Do not cover the tin with foil.

3. Pour the water into a **5.5- or 7.5-litre cooker**. Set a heat- and pressure-safe trivet in the cooker. Make an aluminium foil sling (see page 20), set the filled springform tin on it and use it to lower the tin into the pot. Fold down the ends of the sling so that they do not touch the cheesecake batter in the tin. Lock the lid onto the pot.

4.

Set the machine	Level	The valve must be	Time	Press
PRESSURE COOK or MANUAL	HIGH	Closed	25 minutes with the KEEP WARM setting off	START

5. When the machine has finished cooking, turn it off and let its pressure **return to normal naturally,** about 20 minutes. Unlatch the lid and open the cooker. Use the sling to transfer the *hot* springform tin to a wire rack. Leave to cool for 15 minutes, then refrigerate for 1 hour. Cover and continue refrigerating for at least 1 more hour or up to 2 days.

6. To serve, uncover and run a thin knife between the tin and the cake. Unlatch the sides of the tin and open it to remove the cake inside. If desired, use a long, thin knife to slice the cake off the tin's base and use a large palette knife or metal spatula to transfer the cheesecake to a serving platter.

Beyond

- Unfortunately, these ratios and this tin won't work in a 3-litre cooker.

- To make a simple chocolate sauce, stir together 250ml water and 125g white granulated sugar in a small saucepan over a medium heat until the sugar dissolves. Whisk in 80g unsweetened cocoa powder, 2 teaspoons vanilla extract and ¼ teaspoon table salt. Continue whisking until slightly thickened, about 2 minutes. Remove from the heat and leave to cool for at least 15 minutes, whisking occasionally (the sauce will continue to thicken off the heat).

Eggnog Cheesecake

6–8 servings

Eggnog is sometimes made with brandy and sometimes with a mixture of brandy and whisky, so feel free to use 1½ tablespoons brandy and 1½ tablespoons whisky in this recipe. Or go all out with 1 tablespoon brandy, 1 tablespoon whisky and 1 tablespoon gold rum.

1. Generously butter the inside of an 18cm round springform tin. Mix the biscuit crumbs, melted butter and icing sugar in a medium bowl until uniform; then pour into the prepared tin. Press this mixture evenly across the bottom and about halfway up the sides of the tin.

2. Put the cream cheese and sugar in a food processor, cover and process until smooth, about 1 minute. Add the egg and process until smooth. Then add the egg yolks one at a time, processing each before adding the next.

3. Open the machine, scrape down the inside and add brandy and cream. Cover and process until smooth. Add the flour, nutmeg and salt (if using). Process again until smooth. Pour this mixture into the prepared base in the tin (it will rise above the base on the sides). Do not cover the tin with foil.

4. Pour the water into a **5.5- or 7.5-litre cooker.** Set a heat- and pressure-safe trivet in the cooker. Make an aluminium foil sling (see page 20), set the filled springform tin on it and use it to lower the tin into the pot. Fold down the ends of the sling so that they do not touch the cheesecake batter in the tin. Lock the lid onto the pot.

5.

Set the machine	Level	The valve must be	Time	Press
PRESSURE COOK or MANUAL	HIGH	Closed	25 minutes with the KEEP WARM setting off	START

6. When the machine has finished cooking, turn it off and let its pressure **return to normal naturally,** about 20 minutes. Unlatch the lid and open the cooker. Use the sling to transfer the *hot* springform tin to a wire rack. Leave to cool for 15 minutes, then refrigerate for 1 hour. Cover and continue refrigerating for at least 1 more hour or up to 2 days.

7. To serve, uncover and run a thin knife between the tin and the cake. Unlatch the sides of the tin and open it to remove the cake inside. If desired, use a thin knife to slice the cake off the bottom of the tin and a large palette knife or metal spatula to transfer the cheesecake to a platter.

150g vanilla wafer biscuit crumbs

55g butter, melted and cooled, plus extra butter for greasing the tin

2 tablespoons icing sugar

450g regular cream cheese

125g white caster sugar

1 large egg, at room temperature

3 large egg yolks, at room temperature

3 tablespoons brandy

3 tablespoons double cream

2 tablespoons plain flour

½ teaspoon grated nutmeg

¼ teaspoon salt (optional)

350ml water

Beyond

- Unfortunately, these ratios and this tin won't work in a 3-litre cooker.

- Sprinkle up to 20g finely chopped candied lemon peel over the crushed biscuit base before you pour the cheesecake batter into the tin.

- Crumble amaretti biscuits over each piece as a garnish.

350ml water

Nonstick baking spray

160g white caster sugar

1 large egg, at room temperature

1 large egg white, at room temperature

80g butter, melted and cooled to room temperature

60ml regular soured cream (do not use low-fat or fat-free)

60ml fresh lemon juice

1 teaspoon vanilla extract

½ teaspoon lemon extract

120g plain flour

½ teaspoon baking powder

½ teaspoon bicarbonate of soda

¼ teaspoon table salt

Lemon Sponge

8 servings

Here's a Bundt sponge, a springy, light cake that's great with fresh berries (particularly hulled sliced strawberries macerated with a little sugar and a touch of vanilla extract). As with most sponges, this one's better the day it's made since the cake continues to collapse and condense even after it has cooled. If you have leftovers, consider cutting them into wedges and frying the pieces in butter (in a nonstick frying pan set over a medium heat) until lightly browned on both cut sides.

1. Pour the water into a 3-, 5.5- or 7.5-litre cooker. Set a heat- and pressure-safe trivet in the pot. Generously spray the inside of an 18cm Bundt tin with baking spray, taking care to spray right into all the crevices. Make an aluminium foil sling (see page 20) and set the tin into the middle of the sling.

2. Put the sugar, egg, egg white, melted butter, soured cream, lemon juice and vanilla and lemon extracts in a food processor. Cover and process until smooth. Stop the machine and scrape down the inside. Add the flour, baking powder, bicarbonate of soda and salt. Cover and process until smooth.

3. Pour and scrape this mixture into the prepared tin. Use the sling to lower the tin onto the trivet in the cooker. Fold the ends of the sling down to fit inside without touching the batter. Lay a large piece of kitchen paper over the top of the Bundt tin. Lock the lid onto the cooker. (Take care in a **3-litre cooker** that the kitchen paper doesn't block the seal.)

4.

Set the machine	Level	The valve must be	Time	Press
PRESSURE COOK	MAX	——	18 minutes with the KEEP WARM setting off	START
PRESSURE COOK or MANUAL	HIGH	Closed	25 minutes with the KEEP WARM setting off	START

5. When the machine has finished cooking, turn it off and let its pressure **return to normal naturally**, about 20 minutes. Unlatch the lid and open the pot. Remove the kitchen paper. Use the sling to transfer the *hot* Bundt tin to a wire cooling rack. Cool for 5 minutes, then invert the tin onto a chopping board and release the cake. Slip it from the board to the cooling rack and leave to cool for at least another 15 minutes before cutting into wedges to serve.

Beyond

- For even more lemon flavour, add up to 2 teaspoons finely grated lemon zest to the processor with the vanilla and lemon extracts.

- Add up to 1 tablespoon poppy seeds or 2 teaspoons picked fresh thyme leaves after the batter has been made. Pulse the processor once or twice to combine them.

- For a lemon glaze, put 250g icing sugar in a medium bowl. Whisk in lemon juice in 1-teaspoon increments until the mixture forms a thick paste that holds its shape but runs off the whisk, like super thick honey. Drizzle the glaze over the cooled cake and serve at once, or set aside for 20 minutes for the glaze to set firm.

Chocolate Lava Cakes

4 servings

There was a point in the early 2000s when just about every celebrity chef claimed to have invented the molten cake, the lava cake or whatever they called it. Not one of them made the cake in a multi-cooker! Too bad, because the steam creates a super light cake surrounding a liquid chocolate centre. You can unmould these cakes on plates, although they can tear (and immediately run) if you haven't greased the ramekin well enough for the cake to pop loose. Run a palette knife around the inside perimeter, put a dessert plate over the ramekin, turn the whole operation upside down, and tap gently until the cake comes free. Or simply serve the warm cakes in their ramekins with spoons and plenty of whipped cream.

1. Put the butter and chocolate in a large, microwave-safe bowl. Microwave on high in 10-second bursts, stirring well after each, until a little over half of the butter has melted. Remove from the microwave and continue stirring until smooth.

2. Set the chocolate mixture aside and leave to cool to room temperature, stirring occasionally, about 20 minutes. Meanwhile, generously butter the inside of four heat- and pressure-safe 250ml ramekins.

3. Stir the icing sugar into the chocolate mixture until smooth. Stir in the eggs one at a time, making sure each is well incorporated before adding the next. Stir in the egg yolk until smooth, then the flour and salt, stirring again until smooth. Divide this mixture evenly amongst the prepared ramekins. Do not cover the ramekins.

4. Pour the water in a **5.5- or 7.5-litre cooker**. Set a trivet in the pot. Stack the ramekins on the trivet, placing three on the bottom layer and one on the top, balanced on the three below. Lock the lid onto the cooker.

5.

Set the machine	Level	The valve must be	Time	Press
PRESSURE COOK	MAX	—	8 minutes with the KEEP WARM setting off	START
PRESSURE COOK or MANUAL	HIGH	Closed	10 minutes with the KEEP WARM setting off	START

6. When the machine has finished cooking, turn it off and let its pressure **return to normal naturally**, about 20 minutes. Unlatch the lid and open the cooker. Transfer the *hot* ramekins to a wire rack and leave to cool for 15 minutes. Serve warm or cover and chill in the fridge for up to 1 day, serving them right in their ramekins.

115g butter, cut into small chunks, plus extra for greasing the ramekins

225g dark chocolate, preferably 70% cocoa solids, chopped

250g icing sugar

3 large eggs, at room temperature

1 large egg yolk, at room temperature

45g plain flour

¼ teaspoon table salt

350ml water

Beyond

- Because of the shape of the ramekins, this recipe will not work (even halved) in a 3-litre cooker.

- Add up to 2 teaspoons vanilla extract, ½ teaspoon almond extract or ¼ teaspoon orange extract with the eggs.

100g orange marmalade

115g cool butter, cut into chunks, plus extra for greasing the dish and the foil

60g white caster sugar

45g light brown sugar

2 large eggs, at room temperature

3 tablespoons Triple Sec or Grand Marnier

1 tablespoon vanilla extract

90g finely ground pecans

60g plain flour

¼ teaspoon table salt

350ml water

Orange Pecan Pudding Cake

6 servings

Here's the first of two recipes for 'pudding cake', a cross between a steamed pudding and a more traditional cake. They both have an exceptionally light texture, which unfortunately tends to turn a tad gummy if they're left too long before serving. We found a way to improve their longevity by increasing the flour, although doing so also made the cakes tough. So you'll need to serve them the day they're made. But since they're both so easy, you'll have no problem whipping them up.

This one's a bit of a marvel. It's a cake with a marmalade sauce that soaks into the crumb to make a sticky, caramel topping.

1. Generously butter the inside of a 2-litre, high-sided, round soufflé dish. Spread the marmalade over the bottom of this dish.

2. Using an electric hand mixer at medium speed in a large bowl, beat the butter and the white and brown sugars until creamy and light, about 5 minutes. Beat in the eggs one at a time, making sure the first is well incorporated before adding the second.

3. Scrape down the inside of the bowl. Beat in the Triple Sec or Grand Marnier and vanilla until smooth. At low speed, beat in the ground pecans, flour and salt just until incorporated. Pour this batter into the prepared baking dish and smooth the top. Butter one side of a piece of aluminium foil and use to cover the dish, buttered-side down. Tightly seal this foil over the baking dish.

4. Pour the water into a **5.5- or 7.5-litre cooker**. Set a heat- and pressure-safe trivet in the pot. Make a foil sling (see page 20), set the baking dish on it and use the sling to lower the dish onto the trivet. Fold down the ends of the sling and lock the lid onto the pot.

5.

Set the machine	Level	The valve must be	Time	Press
PRESSURE COOK	MAX	——	25 minutes with the KEEP WARM setting off	START
PRESSURE COOK or MANUAL	HIGH	Closed	35 minutes with the KEEP WARM setting off	START

6. When the machine has finished cooking, turn it off and let its pressure **return to normal naturally**, about 20 minutes. Unlatch the lid and open the cooker. Use the sling to transfer the *hot* baking dish to a wire rack. Uncover and leave to cool for 5 minutes. Run a palette knife around the inside perimeter of the dish to loosen the cake. Set a large platter or cake stand over the baking dish. Turn the whole operation upside down, then tap and jiggle the baking dish to make the cake come free. Serve warm or cool to room temperature, about 1 hour. The cake can stay uncovered at room temperature for about 3 hours.

Beyond

- For a 3-litre cooker, use 250ml water, halve the remaining ingredients, and use a 1-litre, high-sided, round baking dish.
- Skip the whipped cream and go for clotted cream on each serving.
- Or drizzle the pieces with Dulce de Leche (page 455).

100g chopped baking dates

½ teaspoon bicarbonate of soda

90ml boiling water

1 large egg, at room temperature

60ml whole or low-fat milk (do not use fat-free)

45g butter, melted and cooled, plus extra butter for greasing the ramekins and the foil

2 tablespoons bourbon, whisky or rum

80g plain flour

30g finely chopped walnuts

1 teaspoon baking powder

½ teaspoon ground ginger

½ teaspoon ground cinnamon

300g plus ½ teaspoon white granulated sugar

½ teaspoon table salt

500ml water

250ml double cream

1 teaspoon vanilla extract

Date Nut Pudding Cakes

4 servings

Dextrose-coated baking dates are found in the baking aisle of almost all large supermarkets. The dates are already sweet, but these individual pudding cakes aren't terribly so. Instead, they're a rather savoury date nut bread pudding with a sweet sauce poured on top. The cakes are so light and tender, they may break apart if they're not cooled before serving, which gives you time to make and cool the sauce. If you want to eat them very warm (a comforting dessert indeed!), don't bother turning them out. Keep them in their ramekins and serve with tablespoons, the caramel sauce on the side.

1. Mix the baking dates and bicarbonate of soda in a small bowl until uniform. Stir in the boiling water and leave to cool to room temperature, stirring occasionally, about 30 minutes. Meanwhile, generously butter the inside of four heat- and pressure-safe 250ml ramekins.

2. Whisk the egg, milk, melted butter and bourbon in a large bowl until smooth and uniform, about 2 minutes. Whisk in the flour, walnuts, baking powder, ginger, cinnamon, the ½ teaspoon sugar and ¼ teaspoon salt. Add the date mixture and stir well. Divide this batter amongst the four prepared ramekins.

3. Butter four small pieces of aluminium foil and use these, buttered-side down, to seal the ramekins. Pour 375ml of the water into a **5.5- or 7.5-litre cooker**. Set a heat- and pressure-safe trivet inside the pot. Stack the four filled ramekins on the trivet, using three for the first layer and balancing the remaining in the centre on the edges of the three below. Lock the lid onto the pot.

4.

Set the machine	Level	The valve must be	Time	Press
PRESSURE COOK	MAX	—	25 minutes with the KEEP WARM setting off	START
PRESSURE COOK or MANUAL	HIGH	Closed	35 minutes with the KEEP WARM setting off	START

5. Meanwhile, make the caramel sauce. Whisk the remaining 300g sugar, the remaining 125ml water and the remaining ¼ teaspoon salt in a medium saucepan set over a medium heat until the sugar melts. Continue cooking undisturbed until the mixture turns amber, 5–6 minutes. Reduce the heat as low as you can. Taking care because the mixture will roil, whisk in the cream and vanilla. Continue whisking until smooth. Remove the pan from the heat and leave to cool at room temperature in the pan for at least 30 minutes or up to 2 hours, whisking occasionally.

6. When the machine has finished cooking, turn it off and let its pressure **return to normal naturally**, about 20 minutes. Transfer the *hot* ramekins to a wire rack and remove the foil coverings. Leave to cool for 5 minutes, then invert the ramekins onto serving plates; gently tap and shake the ramekins to release the cakes inside. Spoon some of the warm caramel sauce over each.

Beyond

- Because of the size of the ramekins, this recipe cannot be made (or even halved) in a 3-litre cooker.
- If you don't want the alcohol in the cakes, substitute orange juice.

120g plain flour

1 teaspoon baking powder

1 teaspoon ground cinnamon

125g butter, plus extra
   for greasing the dish

60ml maple syrup

2 medium Bramley apples,
   peeled, cored
   and thinly sliced

350ml water

125g white caster sugar

2 large eggs, at room
   temperature

2 teaspoons vanilla extract

3 tablespoons whole milk

Apple Maple Upside-Down Cake

6 servings

Why go with the standard pineapple upside-down cake when you can make one with apples and maple syrup, an autumnal treat any time of year? Don't let this cake sit in its baking dish too long or it will begin to stick, not only to the caramel apple sauce on the bottom but also to the sides of the dish as the cake cools. This sweet dessert goes particularly well with a strong cup of coffee.

1. Whisk the flour, baking powder and cinnamon in a medium bowl. Set aside. Generously butter the inside of one 2-litre, high-sided, round soufflé dish.

2.

Press	Setting	Time	Press
SAUTÉ	MEDIUM, NORMAL or CUSTOM 150°C	10 minutes	START

3. Melt 30g of the butter in a **5.5- or 7.5-litre cooker**. Add the maple syrup and stir until warmed. Add the apples and cook, stirring often, until softened, about 5 minutes. Pour every drop of the mixture from the *hot* insert into the prepared baking dish; smooth the apple mixture into an even layer.

4. Clean and dry the insert, then return it to the machine. Pour the water into the cooker. Set a heat- and pressure-safe trivet inside.

5. Using an electric hand mixer at medium speed, beat the remaining butter and the sugar in a large bowl until smooth and creamy, about 4 minutes. Beat in the eggs one at a time, making sure the first is thoroughly incorporated before adding the second. Beat in the vanilla extract, then reduce the mixer's speed to low. Beat in the flour mixture just until incorporated. Add the milk and beat until uniform. Pour this batter over the apples in the prepared dish. Cover tightly with aluminium foil.

6. Make a foil sling (see page 20). Set the baking dish on the sling and lower it onto the trivet. Fold down the ends of the sling so they don't touch the batter, then lock the lid onto the pot.

7.

Set the machine	Level	The valve must be	Time	Press
PRESSURE COOK	MAX	——	25 minutes with the KEEP WARM setting off	START
PRESSURE COOK or MANUAL	HIGH	Closed	35 minutes with the KEEP WARM setting off	START

8. When the machine has finished cooking, turn it off and let its pressure **return to normal naturally**, about 20 minutes. Unlatch the lid and open the cooker. Use the sling to transfer the *hot* baking dish to a wire rack. Uncover and leave to cool for 5 minutes. Run a palette knife around the inner perimeter of the dish to loosen the cake. Set a large platter or cake stand over the baking dish. Turn the whole operation upside down, then tap and jiggle the dish to make the cake come free and let the apple 'sauce' pour over the cake. Leave to cool for 15 minutes, then serve warm.

Beyond

- For a 3-litre cooker, use 250ml water, halve the remaining ingredients and use a 1-litre, high-sided, round baking dish.

- Drizzle slices with warmed double cream.

- Substitute 2 medium pears, stemmed, cored and thinly sliced, for the apples.

- Stir up to 30g raisins into the cake batter after adding the milk.

Butter for greasing the dish and foil

350ml water

3 large eggs, separated and at room temperature

185g white caster sugar

250ml regular cultured buttermilk

1 tablespoon finely grated lime zest, preferably from key limes

80ml bottled or fresh key lime juice (from 3–4 key limes)

2 teaspoons vanilla extract

½ teaspoon table salt

45g plain flour

Key Lime Soufflé Cake

6 servings

The uniquely flavoured key lime is so called because it was first grown only in the Florida Keys, but you can use regular limes (see *Beyond*). This dessert is quite soft and can't be unmoulded, so serve it in bowls, with some whipped cream, if liked (see the *Beyond* section on page 457).

1. Generously butter the inside of a 2-litre, high-sided, round soufflé dish. Pour the water into a **5.5- or 7.5-litre cooker**. Set a heat- and pressure-safe trivet inside the pot.

2. Using an electric hand mixer at high speed, beat the egg whites in a medium bowl until they make soft peaks off the end of a spatula, about 3 minutes. Beat in 60g sugar in a slow, steady stream until the mixture is thick and forms silky peaks, about 2 minutes.

3. Clean and dry the beaters. In a large bowl, beat the egg yolks and remaining 125g sugar until thick and pale yellow, about 4 minutes. Scrape down the inside of the bowl, then beat in the buttermilk, lime zest, lime juice, vanilla and salt until smooth. Remove the beaters.

4. Use a rubber spatula to fold the flour into the egg yolk mixture until thoroughly moistened. Fold in the egg whites gently until incorporated but not completely dissolved. There should be white streaks in the batter.

5. Pour and scrape the batter into the prepared baking dish. Lightly butter a piece of aluminium foil and cover the cake loosely with it, buttered-side down. Make a foil sling (see page 20), set the baking dish in the centre of the sling and use the sling to lower the baking dish onto the trivet. Fold down the ends of the sling so they don't touch the batter, then lock the lid onto the pot.

Beyond

- For a 3-litre cooker, use 250ml water, two-thirds of the remaining ingredients and a 1-litre, high-sided, round baking dish.

- Skip the whipped cream and serve the pudding soufflé topped with sweetened soured cream. Whisk 30g icing sugar and 1 teaspoon vanilla extract into 250ml regular or low-fat soured cream until smooth.

- If you can get hold of bottled key lime juice, do use it. If you cannot get a key lime for the zest, use a standard lime but make sure the zest is finely grated. You can also use regular lime juice instead of key lime juice but add ½ tablespoon fresh lemon juice to 60ml lime juice.

6.

Set the machine	Level	The valve must be	Time	Press
PRESSURE COOK	MAX	——	15 minutes with the KEEP WARM setting off	START
PRESSURE COOK or MANUAL	HIGH	Closed	20 minutes with the KEEP WARM setting off	START

7. When the machine has finished cooking, turn it off and let its pressure **return to normal naturally**, about 20 minutes. Unlatch the lid and open the cooker. Use the sling to transfer the *hot* baking dish to a wire rack. Uncover and leave to cool for at least 10 minutes or up to 1 hour. Serve in bowls or on small plates.

Blueberry Bread Pudding

6 servings

There are two bread puddings in the breakfast chapter (starting on page 41) that you could also make for dessert. This version is sweeter than those, with a bright fresh taste, thanks to the blueberries. Use only fresh, not frozen. And check out the headnote to the Peanut Butter Bread Pudding recipe on page 41 for a discussion of the best sort of bread to use in an Instant Pot bread pudding. After that, just make a pot of coffee. Even in the evening, you'll want it with this sweet, berry-filled dessert.

1. Generously butter the inside of a 2-litre, high-sided, round soufflé dish. Pour the water into a **5.5- or 7.5-litre cooker.** Set a heat- and pressure-safe trivet in the cooker. Also, make a foil sling (see page 20) and set the buttered baking dish in the centre of this sling.

2. Whisk the eggs in a large bowl until uniform. Whisk in the milk, sugar, vanilla and salt until the sugar dissolves. Use a rubber spatula to stir the bread cubes into the egg mixture until evenly coated. Add the blueberries and fold very gently until evenly distributed.

3. Pour and pile this mixture into the prepared baking dish. Butter one side of a piece of aluminium foil and cover the baking dish tightly with it, buttered-side down. Use the sling to pick up and lower the baking dish onto the trivet. Lock the lid onto the pot.

4.

Set the machine	Level	The valve must be	Time	Press
PRESSURE COOK	MAX	—	20 minutes with the KEEP WARM setting off	START
PRESSURE COOK or MANUAL	HIGH	Closed	26 minutes with the KEEP WARM setting off	START

5. When the machine has finished cooking, turn it off and let its pressure **return to normal naturally,** about 20 minutes. Unlatch the lid and open the cooker. Use the sling to transfer the *hot* baking dish to a wire rack. Uncover and leave to cool for 10 minutes. Serve by large spoonfuls in bowls.

Butter for greasing the dish and foil

350ml water

4 large eggs, at room temperature

500ml whole or low-fat milk (do not use fat-free)

125g white caster sugar

1 teaspoon vanilla extract

¼ teaspoon table salt

225g white bread, cut into 2.5cm squares (do not remove the crusts)

155g fresh blueberries

Beyond

- For a 3-litre cooker, use 250ml water, halve the remaining ingredients and use a 1-litre, high-sided, round baking dish.

- Use raspberries or blackberries instead of blueberries.

- For a more exotic flavour, add up to ½ teaspoon ground cardamom to the milk mixture.

Acknowledgements

When we're writing a cookbook, it seems as if the whole thing's no more than two guys in a rural New England home, cooking, writing, arguing (lots) and eating (lots more). Then the manuscript goes to our publisher – and wow, it commands a lot of people!

Many thanks to the editor of our dreams, Mike Szczerban: conscientious, smart, honest about what he needs and absurdly faithful to our vision, too.

Thanks, too, to his assistant, Nicky Guerriero, for being so eagle-eyed and so quick to reply. Did we even hit send on that email?

Deri Reed, you are the best copyeditor, hands down, no questions, period. (Try to edit that sentence, will you?) Thanks, too, to Jeffrey Gantz for proofreading this book under a crazy deadline and to Amy Novick for indexing it.

We owe a big debt to Laura Palese for turning this beast into a beautiful book, better than we could have imagined. And to Julianna Lee and Kapo Ng for designing the cover, perfect for what we wanted to do.

At Little, Brown, we stand 'hats off' to our publisher, Reagan Arthur, and our deputy publisher, Craig Young, for taking on another Bible. Thanks, too, to Lauren Velasquez for marketing our tome; to Jules Horbachevsky and her assistant, Elora Weil, for working on its PR; and to Lisa Ferris, Mike Noon and Michael Gaudet for working magic to produce a five-hundred-pager in, oh, five weeks or so, right?

We truly couldn't have done this book without Robert Wang at Instant Pot who was so fast to answer our texts and emails, sometimes in the wee hours. And to Anna Di Meglio for working out the details and sending us a dozen (!) cookers.

And much gratitude to Lori Sobelson and Brenda Gibson at Bob's Red Mill for a ginormous box of rice, wheat berries and other grains. Beyond helpful. Even more delicious!

Closer to home, we couldn't have done the last seven (!!) books without Eric Medsker, a no-drama photographer extraordinaire (and a great friend). Many thanks, too, to Caroline Dorn, a prop stylist with some of the best eyes we've ever seen. Those photo shoots with the four of us! So many bottles of wine, so much food!

Finally, how can we ever thank our agent, Susan Ginsburg, at Writers House, or her assistant, Stacy Testa? Thirty books? In nineteen years? What's next?

Index

Bold type indicates road map recipes.